City of Kinston, North Carolina
Central Business District
1996

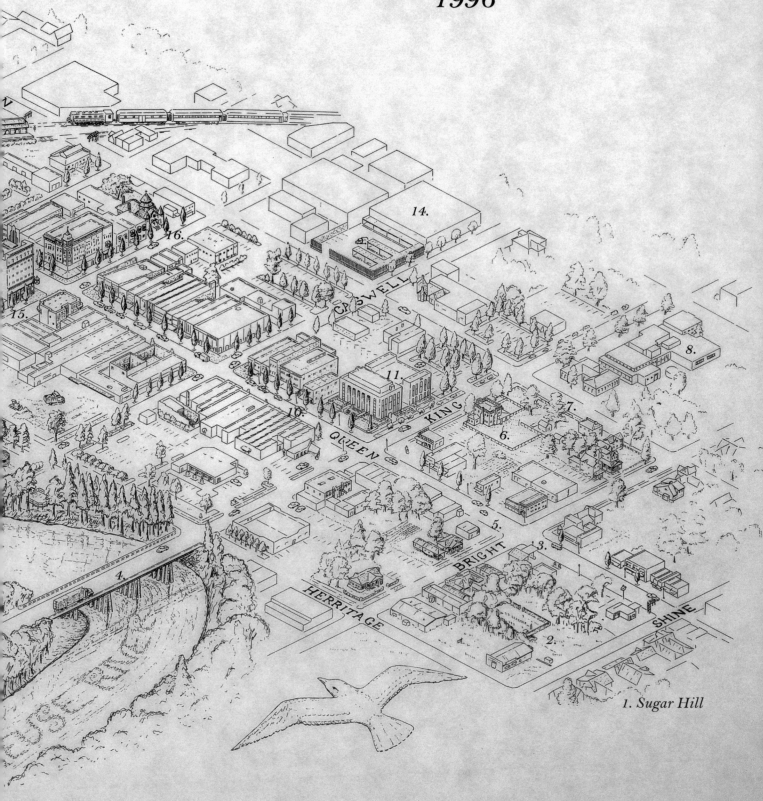

14.

CASWELL

16.

15.

11.

10.

QUEEN

KING

8.

7.

6.

5.

BRIGHT

3.

SHINE

4.

HERRITAGE

2.

1. Sugar Hill

Martin D. Peebles 1996

COASTAL PLAIN AND FANCY

THE HISTORIC ARCHITECTURE
OF
LENOIR COUNTY
AND
KINSTON, NORTH CAROLINA

Essay by
M. Ruth Little

Catalogue by
Robbie D. Jones, Penne Smith, Scott Power and M. Ruth Little

The City of Kinston and the Lenoir County Historical Association

1998

First Printing
1998

Printed in the United States of America
by
Jostens Printing & Publishing
Winston-Salem
North Carolina

Please address all correspondence & orders to:

The Lenoir County Historical Association Inc.
P.O. Box 1132
Kinston NC 28503

Table of Contents

Preface

There is an old African proverb which says that when an old person dies, a whole library burns down. This is especially true in Lenoir County, because the library (registry) of deeds, the records which trace land ownership, has already burned down, making the oral tradition, the stories told from one generation to another, even more precious. When an arson burned the second courthouse of Lenoir County on the early morning of October 21, 1878, the fire destroyed almost all of over one hundred and fifty years of records of the land area which had been, in succession, Craven, Johnston, Dobbs and finally Lenoir County. Some records were saved and moved to a temporary courthouse, but then in 1880 this building burned, destroying all remaining records except the grantee index of deeds. Thus buildings constructed before 1880 cannot be traced through the public record to determine ownership.

In 1954 Talmage C. Johnson and Charles R. Holloman published *The Story of Kinston and Lenoir County*, the first history of the city and county. In 1963 William S. Powell published *Annals of Progress: The Story of Lenoir County and Kinston, North Carolina*. Both books document the primary role of the county in the Revolutionary War, the Civil War, and during peacetime as well. Both books are appropriately named "the story," for gaps in the historical record are filled in with the oral tradition, recollections both published and passed along orally by families, some of whom have lived for over two hundred and fifty years rooted to Lenoir County soil.

Old families cannot prove whether or not their ancestors received the land in a grant from the King, because the old grants burned in the courthouse fires, but they can pass along stories of how big the plantation used to be, or of how their kinfolk outsmarted the Yankees during the Civil War, or of why the plantation house escaped burning by Union troops, or which ancestor planted the ancient live oak tree. My own mother, born and raised in Lenoir County in a family of storytellers, starts out her own stories with the words, "A tale they tell...."

In Lenoir County, if you look far enough back on the family tree, everyone is your cousin. The cousins have stories about nearly every old house. A tale they tell is that the Dunn-Wiggins House was Baptist preacher Lewis Whitfield's plantation named LaFayette. They tell that it served as a tavern and also as a Masonic lodge. They tell that the big upstairs bedroom was a ballroom. They tell that the big upstairs bedroom at Monticello, another Whitfield plantation, was a ballroom. They tell that Lewis Whitfield owned all the land between LaFayette and Monticello. They tell that the Carraway baby left on the Whitfields' doorstep, who grew up to marry the Whitfield daughter and to own Monticello, was named "Snoad" because it snowed that day.

They tell tales about the Ram Neuse, the ironclad vessel built here in the 1860s. Was the vessel a formidable weapon in the Confederate arsenal or a folly which never stood a chance of navigating the upper Neuse River to threaten Union armies? They tell tales about which house Governor Richard Caswell lived in, and which old house or old church was used as a Civil War hospital. They tell tales about sitting on the "piazza," that fancy Italian term for a porch which is embedded in everyday county language. They tell tales about the menfolk sitting out in the old detached kitchen cooking possum and collard greens over an open fire. No wonder so many kitchens were in separate buildings removed from the house. Eyebrows have been raised and tongues have wagged about the notorious red-light district known as "Sugar Hill," located in the original area of Kinston where the founding fathers built their town houses.

Historical and architectural mysteries abound in Lenoir County. What kind of housing did the slaves, who outnumbered whites for much of the antebellum period, live in? Why did the popular boarding school, the Lenoir Collegiate Institute, close up abruptly about 1860? Do the handful of nineteenth century log houses that still stand represent an important method of dwelling construction? What did Kinston, which has completely rebuilt itself since 1900, look like before the turn of the century? Of the tales they tell about ballrooms and such, how much truth is in them?

This book does not explain the mysteries, it acknowledges them. It tries to juxtapose the written records, and the "tales they tell," with the buildings in which the history took place. In the early 1900s Mrs. Lillie Archbell published her United Daughters of the Confederacy magazine for "our busy people who always have time to make history but never time for research." In the late 1900s we dedicate this book to the busy people of Lenoir County and Kinston in the hope that they will have time to enjoy the history of their buildings, in the hope that they will collect and publish more tales so that we can all enjoy and learn from them, and in the hope that the historic buildings that are still standing will be saved and cherished by succeeding generations.

The Historic Architecture of Lenoir County and Kinston culminates some thirty years of work by many, many people in Lenoir County and throughout North Carolina. Interested county citizens, with the technical assistance and encouragement of the North Carolina Division of Archives and History, have systematically supervised the recordation of the county's historic architecture, beginning in 1968-1969 with the original historic architecture survey of the county, one of the first such inventories conducted in North Carolina. This survey, coordinated by Isabelle Fletcher Perry and Beverly Lee Wooten and conducted by A. J. P. Edwards and Andrew Smith, documented many of the county's oldest structures, since demolished or greatly altered. Martha A. Dreyer with the assistance of Kenneth Hill, conducted the inventory of historic buildings in the city of Kinston in 1979-1980 and authored the report, "Kinston's Architecture 1762-1930." Allison Black prepared a series of National Register nominations, including four districts, for the city of Kinston in 1989.

In 1992 an anonymous donor with Lenoir County roots offered an unsolicited gift of $10,000 as a challenge grant to encourage a survey of historic buildings in the county. This generous gift plus other local funds enabled the county to obtain a matching grant from the N.C. Division of Archives and History. With this funding Robbie D. Jones conducted a comprehensive historic architecture survey of the county, as well as LaGrange and Pink Hill, in 1993-1994. The citizens committee, chaired by Millie Matthis, that provided oversight for the rural survey included James and Catherine Stewart, Reginald Stroud, George E. Loftin, Wilbur A. Tyndall, Billy and Marsha Brewer, Phil Crawford, Mrs. Hugh H. Hardy, Mallie B. Stocks, Emily Knott McCleary, Catherine Shedrick, Richie Green, Isabelle Fletcher Perry, Richard Johnson, Jacob West Jr., Robert A. Smith, Joyce G. Cherry, Lillian McNorris, Melvin Fordham, Helen Dail, Lynetta B. Fields, J. P. Walters, Lynn James, John and Nola Jennings, and Sandra Snapp. M. Ruth Little and Penne Smith updated the Kinston survey in 1994-1995. Staff members Scott Powers and Stan Little of the Eastern Office of the N. C. Division of Archives and History and Catherine W. Bishir of the State Historic Preservation Office of the Division of Archives and History provided patient coordination of the rural survey, the Kinston survey update, and of the manuscript preparation.

Authorship of the book is likewise a joint affair. M. Ruth Little wrote the essay. Penne Smith made an important contribution through her research on African Americans in Kinston, supplemented by many interviews. Her report on African Americans in Kinston is incorporated into the essay. The Kinston neighborhood overviews and building entries are the work of Penne Smith. The remaining catalogue entries are the work of Robbie D. Jones, Penne Smith, Scott Power and M. Ruth Little. The photographs in the book are the work of many different photographers, including Robbie D. Jones, Penne Smith, M. Ruth Little, Scott Power, Bob Clark, and Jim Shell. Robin Stancil drew the floor plans and site plans. Martin D. Peebles drew the amazing bird's eye view map of downtown Kinston for the book in 1996. Judy Johnson prepared the catalogue township maps; Jennifer Wisener prepared the Kinston catalogue maps. Catherine Bishir, Scott Power, and Jerry Cross of the N. C. Division of Archives and History provided invaluable review as the manuscript took shape. Kathleen B. Wyche of the N. C. Museum of History served as copy editor; Susan Trimble of the N. C. Division of Archives and History as indexer. Editorial assistant Michelle Kullen revised the catalogue after copy-editing and organized the photographs.

The book has been a goal of Lenoir County preservationists for many years. The Kinston Historic District Commission sheparded the Kinston inventories and National Register nominations, as well as serving as cosponsors of this book. Bob Clark, director of the City of Kinston Department of Planning and Community Development, provided leadership throughout the Kinston inventories. Staff member Colin Ingraham prepared the expanded Kinston Commercial District nomination in 1994, as well as assisted with grant writing and other fund raising. The Lenoir County Historical Association, under the leadership of James Stewart, cosponsored the book and provided fundraising and historical review. Other members who provided special assistance are Frank Brooks, Joyce Cherry, Jim Bailey, W. D. Moxley, Becky Peele, and Brad Guth. The editorial committee, composed of the following persons, reviewed the manuscript for historical accuracy: Isabelle Fletcher, Reginald Stroud, Wilbur A. Tyndall, James Stewart, and Emily Knott McCleary. Lorraine Allen, Sue Taylor Sutton, and Berkey Walters reviewed the LaGrange section of the catalogue. Others who provided review were J. Winton Odham, Jack Randle Sutton, Ray M. Hardy, Mrs. Hugh M. Hardy, and Florence Wood Adams. Sue Johnson Rouse and Renita Gaskins at Heritage Place, Lenoir Community College, made available their extensive collection of historical photographs, maps, and other archival material, and gave generously of their expertise and time. Dr. Rose Pully and Dr. Ed Cooper assisted with obtaining support from the medical community. Dr. Pully also contacted some foundations and obtained valuable mailing lists. Ed Adams helped make important contacts with manufacturers.

Contributors

This book was made possible by the financial assistance of the following contributors:

Major Contributors

Poole Foundation Inc
Board of commissioners of Lenoir County
North Carolina General Assembly
North Carolina Department of Cultural Resources
Kinston-Lenoir Co. Tourism Development Authority
City of Kinston
Town of LaGrange
Town of Pink Hill
Lenoir County Historical Association
Kinston Noon Rotary Club
Ely J. Perry, Jr.
Dan E. Perry
Warren S. Perry
Margaret Harvey

Laura C. Weyher Foundation
Frank & Sandra Brooks
Lenoir County Dental Association
Kinston Neuse Corporation
William & Dillon Rochelle Roberts
Tidewater Transit Company
Alban K. Barrus
Mary M. Beam
Vermillion
NationsBank
Elizabeth Jenkins
Fred Hunneke
Rose Pully
Rudolph I. Mintz

Businesses and Organizations

Ruritan Clubs of Lenoir County (7)
Kinston Junior Womens Club
Kinston Evening Rotary Club
Barrus Construction
Branch Banking & Trust
Carolina Power & Light

Jake A. Parrot Ins. Agency
Kinston Laundry Company
Wachovia
Wall Link
West Company

Other Individual Contributors

James D. Bailey
James Blocker
Donald Boldt
Jack Stacy Boone
Bernice D. Bunn
W.A. Chantry
Edwin B. Cooper
Robert F. Corbin
Albert & Virginia Cowper
Sarah Cox
Phil Crawford
Lila Lee Dalton
Martha J. Daughety
John Flournoy
Grace Brown Frizzelle
Wm. & Claire Cannon Foster
Marilynn Ferrell Gay
Irene Grady
Oscar & Betsy Greene, Jr.
Ray M. Hardy
George & Anna Harper
Claire W. Herring
W. I. Herring, Jr.
Oscar Herring
Janie Hickock
Mary Higginbotham
Carolyn Hodges

John & Evalyn Hood, Jr.
Valerie Jones Howell
Tommy & Jo Ann Ipock
Burwell Jackson
M. Doug James
John & Nola Jenning
Rupert & Francis Jilcott III
Kenneth & Grace Jones
Linda West Little
Maylon E. Little
Garland & Hazel Loftin
Martha Mewborn Marble
George & Millie Matthis
Jesse L. & Joyce McDaniels
Cameron McRae
Betsy Mewborn
James H. & Susan Miller
Mina Dail Miller
Bollin & Shirley Millner
William H. Moore
Ed & Catherine Mooring
William & Carolyn Moxley
Bob & Sue Nielsen
Nell S. Noble
Jack & Jean Overman
William & Marie Page
Frances Parker

James Parrott, Jr.
W.T. Parrott, Jr.
Eugene W. Pate
Simmons I. Patrick
Guy Peterson
James & Ruth Privette
Charles & Irma Randell
Buddy & Mary Mac Ritch
June & Sara Rose
Walter R. Sabiston
Charlotte Stewart Servis
Dorothy Shackelford
Ossie Shackelford
Keats Sparrow
Jim & Catherine Stewart
Allyson Bullock Sugg
Julia & Randall Sutton
Charles E. Taylor
James E. & Betsy Todd
George E. Vick, Jr.
Laura Ellen McDaniel Walker
Mahlia Walters
Carey B. & Fern Washburn
Dale & Carolyn Wooten Warner
G. Herbert Whitfield
Rachel Whitfield
Joyce Wooten Witherington

Chapter One

"Bid Fair to Flourish" in the Eighteenth Century

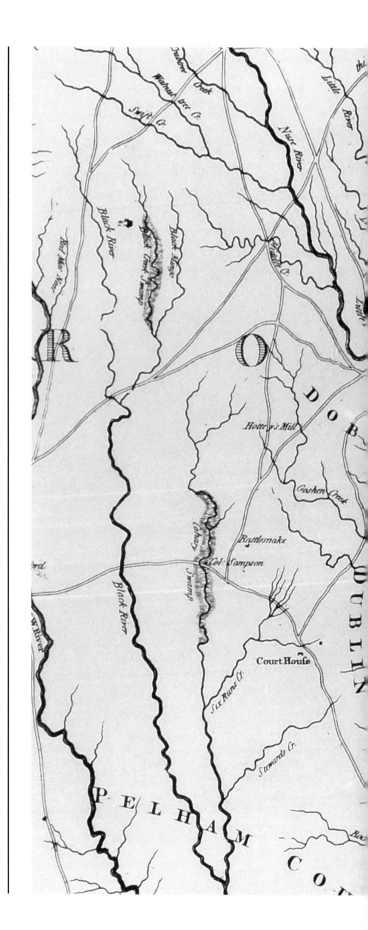

Fig. 1.2. 1770 Collet Map showing Dobbs County, Kinston and Tower Hill (North Carolina Division of Archives and History)

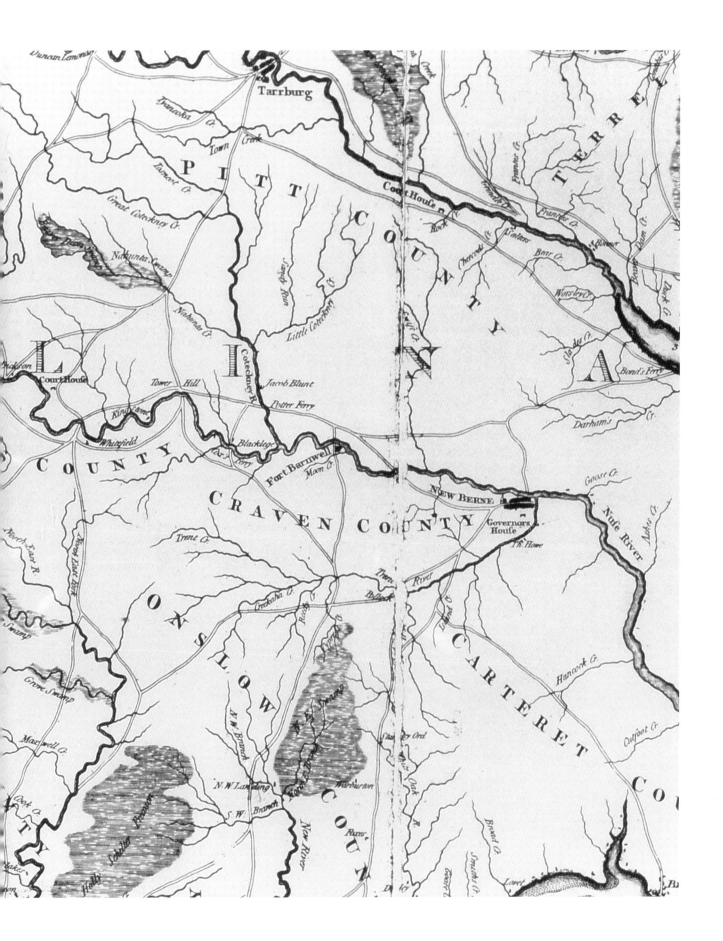

This Is Lenoir County

The land that is present-day Lenoir County, blessed with abundant natural resources and energetic and farsighted settlers, "bid fair to flourish" in the eighteenth century, its formative political period. Located in the North Carolina Coastal Plain, it contains 399 square miles of land area, characterized by a nearly level plain dissected by shallow valleys, with elevations ranging from about 25 feet in southeastern Lenoir County to about 125 feet in the western part. The county is blessed with abundant water, with the Neuse River flowing east through the central area and nearly every farm connected to smaller streams, intermittent gullies, or man-made ditches. The climate is mild, warmed by ocean breezes that moderate seasonal changes in temperature.[1]

As with the other inland counties of the Coastal Plain of North Carolina, much of the land that would become Lenoir County was owned in the eighteenth century under absentee ownership, by speculators who resided in early coastal communities. Such individuals obtained large grants, often of thousands of acres. That was the case, for example, with the land on which the town of Kinston was later established. On December 16, 1729, Robert Atkins acquired this land as part of a 640-acre tract *(Fig. 1.1)*. It then lay in the old Craven Precinct, but it would belong to four different counties before the century ended: Craven County from 1729 to 1746, Johnston County from 1746 to 1758, Dobbs County from 1758 to 1791, and Lenoir County from 1791 to the present.[2] For many years, a large bend in the Neuse River within the area's boundaries was referred to as Atkins [Adkins] Bank. In the vast frontier that would become Lenoir County, a few large

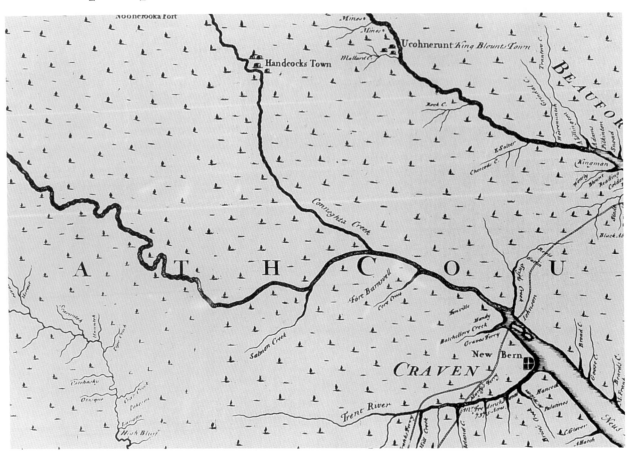

Fig. 1.1. Moseley Map of 1733, showing the area that would become Lenoir County about the time of the Atkins purchase. The map shows New Bern and the "Neus" River. (North Carolina Division of Archives and History)

landowners shaped the future, often from afar. It is said that Robert Atkins lived about forty miles west of New Bern, about halfway between the present cities of Kinston and Goldsboro, where he ran a trading post.[3] Atkins had no heirs, and prior to 1731, when he died without a will, he had assigned his Neuse River patents to his attorney, a young lawyer named William Herritage.[4] Not until 1744 did Herritage acquire title to Atkins Bank, due to problems in the settlement of Atkins's estate. Herritage did not move to Atkins Bank but continued to live near New Bern at his Springfield plantation.[5]

In 1746, when Johnston County was created from Craven, the future site of Kinston fell into the new county. About 1748 a chapel was established at Atkins Bank, and a tobacco warehouse was built there in 1758, when Johnston was split into two counties, the western part retaining the name Johnston and the eastern section becoming Dobbs County. The assembly ordered that the Dobbs County seat be established on Walnut Creek and authorized one of three tobacco inspection warehouses for the new county to be built at Atkins Bank on the land of William Herritage. [6]

North Carolina did not yet have a permanent capital, and if Governor Arthur Dobbs had gotten his way, the seat of government would have been established in Lenoir County. Dobbs, royal governor of the colony from 1754 to 1765, attempted to establish a permanent capital in present-day Lenoir County, on 850 acres at Tower Hill, on the north side of the Neuse River about three miles east of the present location of Kinston, which site Dobbs purchased for this purpose. Dobbs had a particular interest in public architecture, having been supervisor of construction of public buildings in Ireland and a promoter of new public architecture during his tenure in North Carolina. In 1758 he proposed that a complex of public buildings, to be known as George City, be built at Tower Hill. Detailed specifications both for the plan of the new town and the design of the public buildings were included in the "Act for erecting a City on Neuse River, upon the Plantation called Tower-Hill, fixing the Seat of Government therein, and building a Governor's House, and public Offices in the same." These were to include a two-story statehouse, a secretary's office, and a governor's residence, all of two-story brick construction, arranged in a formal Palladian composition with connecting colonnades. The act noted that Tower Hill "hath been found to be healthy and agreeable, having the natural Advantage of a pleasant temperate Air, high and dry-Land and wholesome Spring."[7] The act was passed but never executed, in part because of sectional rivalries regarding the location of the seat of government. In 1766 New Bern was selected as the capital. The George City Governor's House plan foreshadowed by a decade the tripartite Palladian style Governor's House at New Bern, known as Tryon Palace, completed in 1770.

Establishment of Kingston

By 1762 sufficient settlement had occurred in the eastern section of Dobbs County to support establishment of a town. In December of that year Governor Dobbs approved an act of the assembly establishing Kingston, named in honor of King George III (In 1784 the g was dropped and the town's name became Kinston) *(Fig. 1.2 See page 10)*. The first provision of the 1762 act read:

> Whereas, it has been presented to this Assembly, that the land of William Herritage, lying on the north side of the Neuse River, at a place called Atkin's Banks, in Dobbs County, is a pleasant and healthy situation, and commodius for trade and commerce; and the said William Herritage having acknowledged his free consent to have one hundred acres of the said land laid off for a town, and fifty acres for a town common, which will greatly promote the trade of the said river. . . .[8]

The assembly reserved one and a half acres for the warehouse and an Anglican chapel, the only existing buildings within the proposed town. The remaining property was to be sold in half-acre lots. The trustees, Francis MacElwean, Richard Caswell, Simon Bright Jr., John Shine, and David Gordon, took subscriptions for the purchase of a total of fifty lots.[9] Any purchaser owning two or more contiguous lots was instructed to build a brick or well-framed house at least sixteen feet square with a nine-foot height and a chimney of brick or stone.[10] This standard provision was intended to promote settlement of the town, and the trustees may not have enforced it, since apparently few early houses were erected. [11]   Most initial purchasers were landowners who were already established in the vicinity of the new town. The families of the Caswells, the Cobbs, the Herritages, and the MacElweans, all related by marriage, acquired the majority of lots through initial purchase and additional purchases.[12]   Richard Caswell's first wife was Mary MacElwean, daughter of James MacElwean. Her brother Francis MacElwean was one of the original trustees. Caswell's next wife was Sarah Herritage, daughter of William Herritage. Sarah Herritage's sister Elizabeth married Jesse Cobb, from Bertie County, who had moved to Dobbs County around 1767. [13]   John Herritage, a son of William Herritage and brother-in-law of both Richard Caswell and Jesse Cobb, also loomed large in early Kinston. [14]   According to historian Jerry Cross, "the first thirty-seven years of Kinston's development could legimately be described as a family enterprise; therefore, it is not really surprising that few buildings were erected despite the law."[15]

The head of this family enterprise and the central figure in the story of early Kinston was Richard Caswell (1729-1789), who emigrated to North Carolina from Maryland in 1745 and became an apprentice to the surveyor general, James MacElwean *(Fig. 1.3)*. For several years he lived with the MacElwean family on their large plantation, Tower Hill, located at Stringer's Ferry on the Neuse River near present Kinston. Caswell received an introduction into state politics from MacElwean, long-time member of the General Assembly, and from Dr. Francis Stringer, a neighbor and fellow assemblyman. In 1747 Caswell received his first land grant and built a home, called The Hill for his elderly parents, who had moved from Maryland.[16]

Caswell was intimately involved in Lenoir County's political affairs until his death in 1789. As early as 1764 he tried unsuccessfully to have Kingston named as the seat of Dobbs County. In 1779, while Caswell served as governor, Wayne County was created out of Dobbs, and Kingston was finally established as the county seat of Dobbs.[17]   In 1784, when Caswell served both as state comptroller and Speaker of the state senate representing Dobbs County, the General Assembly passed an act amending the original law that founded Kingston.   Caswell likely drafted that amendment, which changed the name from Kingston to Kinston (in order to disassociate the town from British royalty), appointed new trustees, set off the southern half of Lot 76 for the county jail, and established regulations for governing the town. The new trustees were Richard Caswell and two of his sons (William and Richard Jr.), Jesse Cobb, Isaac Wingate, John Herritage, and John Sheppard. Except for Wingate and Sheppard, the new board of trustees were all members of the same family.[18]   In 1791 Dobbs County ceased to exist and the counties of Glasgow (later changed to Greene) and Lenoir (named for Revolutionary War hero William Lenoir) were created in its place.[19]

The closely connected nature of the political affairs of Lenoir County and Kinston from the 1760s to the end of the century, when the influence of the Caswell family declined, shows up in the roster of political officeholders. Richard Caswell served in the General Assembly for eighteen years, his son William Caswell served for four years, and his son Richard Caswell Jr. served for one year. Richard's brother-in-law Jesse Cobb served in

Fig. 1.3. Alleged Portrait of Richard Caswell (1729-1789), first governor of the state of North Carolina. (North Carolina Division of Archives and History)

14

the assembly for three years, his other brother-in-law, John Herritage, for five years, and his son-in-law, William White, for five years. In 1783 the entire Dobbs County delegation to the General Assembly consisted of Caswell family members. From 1762 to 1797, all of the registrars of deeds were Caswells. Except for 1762 and part of 1763, all of the clerks of court for Dobbs, later Lenoir, County, were Caswells. Benjamin Caswell (Richard's brother) was sheriff of Dobbs and Lenoir Counties for eleven years during this time. [20]

Because the Caswell family had such strong control over local affairs, and because he was governor of the state for seven terms, Richard Caswell dominates accounts of the early history of Lenoir County. Richard Caswell begat eight children who lived to adulthood, all of whom married into other prominent families. They produced such a large clan that any white resident of the county during the late eighteenth century likely had a Caswell connection.[21] In the 1770s and 1780s while Richard Caswell was governor of North Carolina, Kinston functioned as the unofficial capital of the state. As John Washington, remembering the heady political environment of the late eighteenth century, put it in 1810, "This town once bid fair to flourish."[22]

In Lenoir County, as elsewhere in North Carolina during the eighteenth century, the scale of early land grants, the economics of a plantation economy, and the lack of urban amenities created a far-flung society. Its members lived on large estates and used the county seat primarily for trade and government business. Most early Kinston property owners were merchants and planters and probably spent more time on their plantations than in Kinston, which was the market town. Wives and children probably enjoyed life in Kinston much more than life on the plantation, since their relatives and friends were available for socializing in town.[23] Perhaps families spent a good portion of the winter in Kinston and stayed at the plantation during the growing season of the summer, when crops needed to be managed.

Another attraction of life in Kinston was religious services held in the Anglican chapel. The first record of a permanent minister at the Anglican chapel, on the bluff near the tobacco warehouse in Kingston, dates from 1767, when the Reverend William Miller was serving the church. Miller tutored some of the town's youth.[24] Around the time of the Revolution, Miller left Kinston, and the chapel remained open under lay leadership. Not only Anglicans, but also other denominations used the building.[25]

The original town plan of Kinston, square in shape, contained some twenty-five blocks with a grid of streets oriented east-west and north-south, extending out from the river bend *(Fig. 1.4)*. The principal streets were named King and Queen Streets; the boundary streets North, East and South Streets; and the intermediate streets after the town commissioners and William Herritage. The town commons were located along the river at the west edge of town and along the east edge of town.   A composite map of early Kinston, based on research by Jerry Cross, shows the extent of construction in the village in the late eighteenth century *(Fig. 1.5)*. The original courthouse, a frame building, was constructed in the intersection of King and Queen Streets in 1784–1785, and the town jail was built nearby on the east side of Queen Street at the same time. The first block of King Street was a commercial area, with Richard Caswell Jr.'s store built about 1783.[26]

The earliest residents of Kinston did not build along Herritage Street, the street that fronted on the Neuse River, but preferred to build on Bright Street, which ran east from the river. Some half-dozen town houses, each occupying an entire block, were built along Bright and Shine Streets after 1762.[27] John Herritage built "a large mansion" beside the river, at the southwest corner of Herritage and Bright Streets. Herritage also owned a plantation near Woodington in south Lenoir County known as Harrow.[28] In the next block of Bright Street, on the south side between Herritage and Queen Streets, Jesse Cobb (ca.1728-1807) built a two-story house that became a hotel and a temporary prison during the Civil War and was known in later years as the "old castle."[29] Cobb also owned several plantations, including his home plantation of nearly 4,000 acres on Southwest Creek, southeast of Kinston.[30]

The location of the Kinston dwelling of Richard Caswell has been a controversial subject during much of the twentieth century. The strongest traditions pointing to the location of Caswell's town house are the reminiscences of several Kinston women in the twentieth century.   Harriet

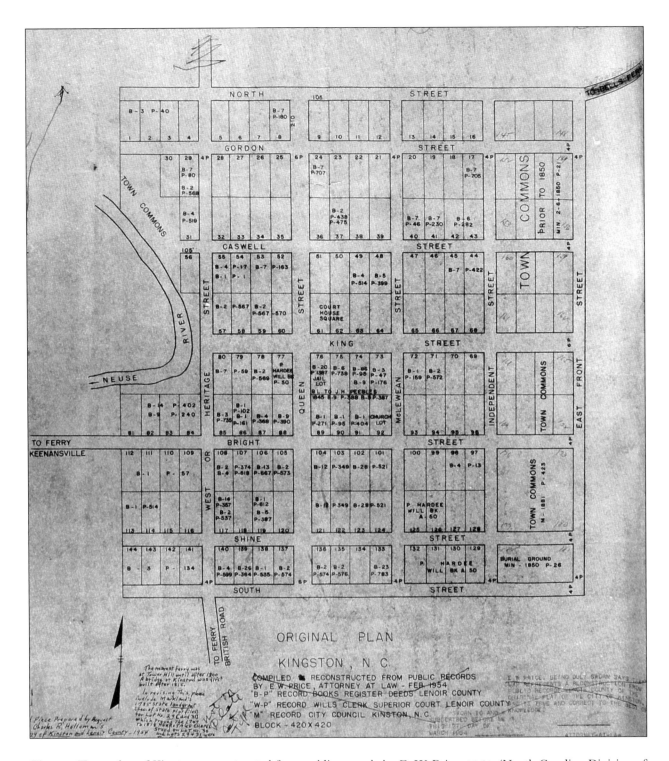

Fig. 1.4. Town plan of Kinston, reconstructed from public records by E. W. Price, 1954. (North Carolina Division of Archives and History)

C. Lane recalled in 1913 that Caswell's house stood on Bright Street. [31] In 1962 Marguerite A. Dyer declared that "on the South side of Bright Street there stood a tall red house of Revolutionary architecture. It was the oldest house along this street. . . . From generation to generation people have always known through their families that this was one home of Gov. Caswell."[32] The house is gone, demolished in the 1960s as part of an urban renewal project.[33] Thus it appears that the three wealthiest residents in Dobbs County before the Revolution, Caswell, Cobb and Herritage, occupied the three western blocks of Bright Street.

16

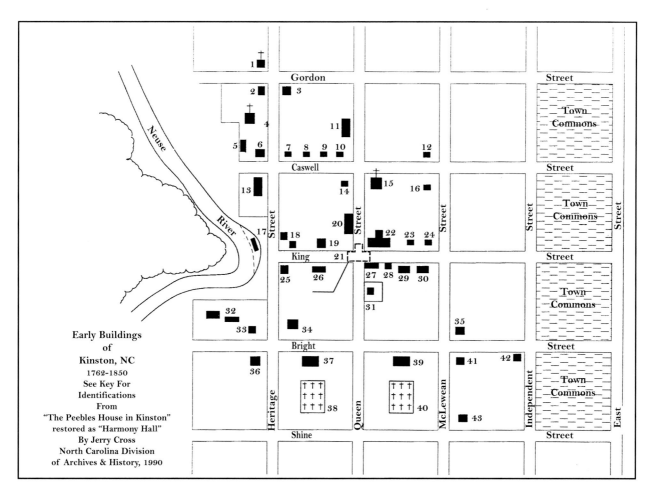

Fig.1.5. Early buildings in Kinston (drawing by Robin J. Stancil after original by Dr. Jerry Cross, North Carolina Division of Archives and History)

Key

1. Christian Church, ca. 1843
2. John Washington's store, after 1810. (later known as Blount Store, King Store)
3. John Washington House, after 1810. (later the St. Charles Hotel)
4. possible site of Anglican chapel, 1762
5. possible site of tobacco warehouse, 1762
6. Dibble Brothers Carriage and Buggy Factory, 1850
7. Nichols Store, ca. 1836
8. Moses Patterson Store, 1850
9. R. L. Collins House, 1850
10. R. L. Collins tailor shop, 1850
11. W. J. Pollock Hotel, 1850
12. Dallam Caswell House, after 1810
13. Market House, 1850
14. Dr. John L. Taylor House and office, 1850
15. St. Mary's Episcopal Church, 1840s
16. possible site of Ambrose Jones House, 1800
17. possible site of wharf, 1762
18. Dr. William A. Holland House and Store, 1830s
19. R. W. King Store, 1845
20. W. C. Loftin Hotel, 1850. (possible site of Thomas King House in 1800)
21. First courthouse, 1784–1785
22. Second courthouse, 1830
23. possible site of William McBean House, 1800
24. possible site of Joseph Elliot House, 1800

25. Store possibly operated by Richard Caswell Jr., 1783–1783; Jesse Cobb, 1790s; Davis, Kornegay and Hunter in 1835
26. Mrs. Perry's Boarding House, 1850
27. Store, pre-1845, possibly run by John Washington in early 1800s; run by John H. Peebles by 1850s
28. John H. Peebles's office
29. John Washington House, early 1800s
30. Bright-Peebles House, ca. 1790 (now known as Harmony Hall)
31. County jail and stocks, 1784
32. Steam mill, 1849
33. Blacksmith shop, 1849
34. John Lovick House, ca. 1796. (probable house of Richard Caswell, Jr. 1782–1784)
35. John Gatlin House, after 1810
36. John Herritage House, ca. 1770
37. Jesse Cobb House, ca. 1770
38. Cobb Graveyard
39. "Red House," early home of Richard Caswell. Sec. of State James Glasgow lived here from 1777-1779.
40. Early cemetery, perhaps associated with Caswell family
41. Alexander Nicol House, 1836
42. Walter P. Allen House, ca. 1835
43. Dallam Caswell House, 1790s (later the Pinkney Hardee House)

During the 1780s and 1790s a few other dwellings were built on Bright and Shine streets. Across Bright Street from the Cobb House Richard Caswell Jr. probably built his house in the 1780s. In the fourth block of Shine Street Caswell's son Dallam Caswell built a house in the 1790s.[34] Later in the eighteenth century King Street became a popular residential street. In 1800 the census taker enumerated two houses on the south side of King Street between Queen and McLewean: the house of John Washington (demolished) and the house of Simon Bright III, later the Peebles House.[35] The house, known since the 1960s as Harmony Hall, still stands at 206 East King Street. As the sole remaining eighteenth-century building in Kinston, Harmony Hall is the only memorial of Kinston's first century *(Fig. 1.6)*.[36] The house lost its eighteenth-century appearance through enlargements and remodeling during the antebellum period. Only the two mantels, of Georgian design, in the low-ceilinged bedchambers upstairs recall Simon Bright's initial occupancy.

The primary residences of most of the families who owned town houses in Kinston were on their plantations. In his 1810 sketch of Lenoir County for the Raleigh *Star*, John Washington praised the "beautiful places for building" that the countryside of Lenoir County offered. All of the plantation seats of the founding fathers of Kinston are gone, but their names, such as Newington, Woodington, and Harrow, conjure up intriguing images of colonial estates. Richard Caswell owned and lived at several plantations around Kinston before settling at Newington, his last home plantation, about 1776. With his first wife, Mary, Caswell lived at the Red House, a plantation northwest of the original town, believed to have included the present Caswell-Neuse State Historic Site. With his second wife, Sarah, he lived at Woodington, a plantation south of Kinston near that of his brother-in-law John Herritage, and owned a town house in

Fig. 1.6. Bright-Peebles House (Harmony Hall), 109 East King Street, Kinston, ca. 1790. (Photo, M. Ruth Little, North Carolina Division of Archives and History)

Kinston.[37] By 1780 he had become the largest landowner in Dobbs County, with his family members Jesse Cobb and John Herritage close behind. All three owned vast tracts in the county and each held a sizable number of town lots.[38] William Herritage, Simon Bright, Richard Caswell, Lewis Whitfield, and other grand planters of the eighteenth century moved in an elite economic and social sphere in which one large landowner sometimes owned numerous plantations and operated them as satellite farms.

Richard Caswell moved to The Hill in 1776, after the Revolutionary War got under way and shortly before he became the first governor of the state. He resided at the plantation, where he farmed and ran an indigo works and tannery, until his death.[39]   His house stood beside the Kinston-Snow Hill road, on top of the prominent ridge north of town.   (The house was later rebuilt or remodeled for John Cobb Washington when he acquired the plantation about 1840, renaming it Vernon Heights.[40]) Records show that Governor Caswell maintained his country home and rode daily into town to perform his duties, since he had transferred much of the state's business from the state capital in New Bern to Kinston because he felt that it was safer. In 1784, Caswell ordered some glazing and painting materials from merchant John Gray Blount in Washington, North Carolina.

> I want some Articles in the Building way and a few for my Family's use, if you can procure them for me you will oblige me, I will make you payment in produce delivered at Newbern or paper Money Hard Cash I cannot engage, the articles are as follows
> 200 feet glass 8 x 10
> 200 feet ———— 10 x 12 or 9 x 11
> about 12 Gal Linseed Oyl
> 100 tt white lead
> 100 tt Spanish Brown
> 20tt Yellow Oaker
> 2 Casks of Nails
> 1 Doz. paint Brushes
>   Your Most obed. Serv't,
>   R. Caswell
>   Kingston 18th 1784[41]

Caswell was building or refurbishing a structure, perhaps in Kinston or at The Hill plantation, which he intended to paint Spanish brown and yellow ochre, popular colors in the eighteenth century. Since 1776, during his years as governor and state comptroller, Caswell's wealth had begun to erode. Rapid wartime inflation outstripped his salary, and he could not devote sufficient time to manage his plantations.[42] Sterling was scarce during the Revolutionary period, thus it is not surprising that he could not produce "Hard Cash" to pay Blount.

Eighteenth-Century Houses in the County

The houses at The Hill, Harrow, and the other seats of the era are gone, but a handful of surviving eighteenth-century houses represents eighteenth-century life in the county. Any house of this period that stands in its original form has enormous significance. Such a landmark is the Leary-Stroud House near Pink Hill. In a traditional "homeplace portrait" of the late nineteenth century, the Stroud family displays its homeplace (*Fig. 1.7*). Nothing is known of the Leary family, who apparently built the house about 1790, but by the 1800s Isaac Stroud and his family lived here. This two-story wooden house, like many rural houses, had apparently never been painted. The front door opens into the main living room (known as the hall), and the smaller room beside it (known as the parlor or chamber) was probably the main bedroom. These rooms still contain some of their eighteenth-century unpainted wall sheathing, raised panel wainscoting, and mantels. A few of the eighteenth-century raised panel shutters still survive. Their hand-carved raised panels represent craftsmanship typical of Georgian architecture, named for the King Georges who sat on the throne of Great Britain during the eighteenth century. The classical style evolved out of

Fig. 1.7. House Portrait, Leary-Stroud House. In this photograph taken in the 1890s Mrs. Jonas Stroud, whose husband Jonas (1846-1889) was Isaac Stroud's son, sits in front with two of her children, India and Dortch. (North Carolina Division of Archives and History)

the Renaissance preoccupation with the buildings of ancient Rome. Georgian buildings had simple, symmetrical forms decorated with heavy classical moldings and paneling. At the Leary-Stroud House the shed-roofed front piazza with its decorative sawnwork railing has been replaced by a newer porch.[43]

Another eighteenth-century house that survives in relatively intact condition is the Richard Noble House near Jonestown in south Lenoir County, probably built about 1795 *(Fig. 1.8)*. According to tradition Richard Noble II (1769-1853), who married Mary Ann Kinsey about 1790, built this house. He was the son of Richard Noble I, who had moved from New Bern to present Lenoir County. Later his son Richard Noble III (1808-1882) lived here. Richard Noble III ran Noble's Mill in the mid-1800s; presumably his father operated it previously. Like the Leary-Stroud House, the two-story wooden Noble House has a main room, heated by a gable-end chimney, and a smaller room beside it. The Noble family employed skilled artisans to build this well-crafted house. The chimney is laid in fine alternating header-stretcher bond, known as Flemish bond, and the shoulders are finished with flat brick paving. The flush boards that finish the interior walls have beaded edges, and some of the original beaded weatherboards outside still survive. The mantels have simple classical pilasters framing the arched fireboxes *(Fig. 1.9)*. Across the front of the house, carpenters created a sturdy shed-roofed piazza. On the west end a breezeway connects a significant early semidetached kitchen to the main house.[44]

Fig. 1.8. Richard Noble House, circa 1795. (Photo, Robbie D. Jones, North Carolina Division of Archives and History)

Fig. 1.9. Mantel, Richard Noble House. (Photo, Robbie D. Jones, North Carolina Division of Archives and History)

Chapter Two

The Antebellum Face of
Lenoir County

At the turn of the nineteenth century, no abrupt break in Lenoir County's economy or social system occurred; an ever-growing slave labor force supported larger farms and the production of corn, hogs, naval stores, and rice. Until the arrival of the railroad in 1856, Kinston remained a village of little more than a courthouse, a few stores, and some fifty dwellings—a place to sell crops, buy provisions, conduct government business, and then return to the farm, where the county's main activities took place—full-time agriculture and part-time occupations such as harvesting naval stores, milling, or crafts such as barrel making. The centers of everyday activities were the hundreds of farms, averaging a few hundred acres and ten slaves. County residents developed a network of churches and private and public schools, including the well-known Lenoir Collegiate Institute. When the Atlantic and North Carolina Railroad line rumbled through town, Kinston woke up.

Yet as the influence of the Caswell circle waned at the turn of the nineteenth century, with the deaths of Richard Caswell Jr. in 1784, Richard Caswell in 1789, Simon Bright III in 1802, and Jesse Cobb in 1807, Kinston had nearly ceased to exist. The 1800 census of Lenoir County listed only ten households in Kinston, containing a total of thirty-eight white persons and sixty-nine Negro slaves.[1] Between 1800 and 1810 all but a few of the original town residents died or moved away. Indeed John Washington (1768-1837), a Virginia native and merchant who moved to Kinston in the 1790s and married Jesse Cobb's daughter Elizabeth about 1798, was the only head of household listed in the 1800 census who still remained in Kinston in 1810 when the census was taken. Washington was a planter, merchant, and one of Lenoir County's leading citizens throughout his long life *(Fig. 2.1)*.

In an informative description of Lenoir County published in 1810 in the Raleigh newspaper the *Star*, Washington frankly assessed the decline of Kinston from its late-eighteenth-century peak as a promising village to 1810, when only a few of the eighteenth-century inhabitants remained. "This Town once bid fair to flourish, but from County commotions, and no doubt other causes perhaps the badness of navigation, it dwindled and became very low, as indeed it now is, as will appear by the number of inhabitants, which is comprehended in ten Families, though it certainly is mended from what it has been."[2] The "County commotions" Washington mentions refer to the civil disobedience of numbers of Lenoir County men, both during the Revolution and into the late 1780s. Among the disturbances were resistance to the draft, military desertion, and the burning of the Comptrollers House in Kinston.[3]

At the turn of the nineteenth century, both town and county remained sparsely settled, with 4,005 people in the county, 107 of whom lived in Kinston. Kinston's problems were shared by most inland North Carolina settlements. Too far from the ocean to benefit from coastal commerce and with unpredictable navigation on the Neuse River, Kinston was also not quite far enough away from New Bern to compete as a trading center with that town, only thirty miles east (sixty miles by river).[4] The port of New Bern, the colonial state capital and unofficial capital of the new state for a few years after independence, was a political and commercial center, serving as a magnet for Lenoir County trade and social affairs.

For the gentry, life in Lenoir County revolved around both plantation and town. The wealthiest citizens, like John Washington and his son John C. Washington, owned one or more plantations and a house in town. John Washington was a merchant who had moved to Kinston about 1790 and married Elizabeth Cobb, daughter of Jesse and Elizabeth Herritage Cobb, in the late 1790s. Washington built his first town house about 1800 in the second block of King Street near the jail. Across the street the houses of William McBean and Joseph Elliott were probably built about the same time.

Fig. 2.1. Portrait of John Washington (1768-1837), Lenoir County planter, merchant and leader. (Heritage Place, Lenoir Community College)

Like the Bright-Peebles House (Harmony Hall), these were probably of frame one- or two-story construction with touches of stylish Federal decoration around the entrances and porches.

Like eighteenth-century Kinstonians, Kinstonians of the early 1800s may still have resided chiefly on the plantations and used their town houses for business. Such was certainly the case for John and Elizabeth Washington. Plantation affairs were uppermost in their lives, Kinston being the market where Washington operated a store. During her husband's frequent absences Elizabeth served as the plantation manager, a complicated job given the extent of the Washington family lands (they owned at least three separate farms: the home farm, White's farm, and the Bond place.) In letters written to his wife during the 1810s while on buying trips up North, John Washington gave careful instructions regarding crop planting and harvesting. In 1814, on a buying trip in Petersburg, Virginia, he wrote Elizabeth instructing her to have the corn and potatoes gathered and informing her that he was traveling on to Richmond. In 1815 Washington was in Philadelphia, where he purchased goods and shipped them to Kinston by vessel. In 1817 he wrote Elizabeth from Raleigh, asking her to harvest the corn and "break up the field at Whites, also the wheat ground and all Bond place broken up." He also told her to "get the wood out of the new ground."

In the last two decades of his life Washington stayed close to home, conveying news about home life to his daughter, Eliza. In letters written in the 1820s to Eliza at school in Raleigh, he discussed news about the family, including their slaves. In 1822 he related that the whole family had been sick from an unnamed malady, that one of the black children died, and that "the black ones" were still sickly. By the early 1830s Washington discussed his plantation Egypt, whose location is unknown, in letters to Eliza in Washington, North Carolina, where she was living with her husband, Richard Grist.[5]

"Few counties can boast of fuller crops"

As a planter John Washington was vitally interested in Lenoir County land, and he began his county sketch with a detailed appraisal of topography and productivity. He stated that the higher land north of the Neuse River was "pleasant and good corn land" and that land south of the river was low, flat, and less productive. In praise of his fellow county farmers Washington wrote, "such is the industry and exertions of the Farmers, that few Counties in the State . . .can boast of fuller crops or a greater product to the hand." Lenoir farms produced corn, peas, sweet potatoes, wheat, rye, cotton, pork, and naval stores. Tobacco would not become a significant crop until the late nineteenth century. Farmers carted their surplus goods, particularly pork, corn, flour, cotton, and naval stores, to market in Virginia or floated them down the Neuse River to New Bern on flat-bottomed boats called scows.

Agriculturally, Lenoir County occupied the middle eastern section of the state, neither the wealthiest nor the poorest region during the antebellum period. Large areas of the county were in staple crop production under a profitable slave-labor plantation system, as well as the small family farm system. While the Roanoke Valley counties along the Virginia border to the north specialized in tobacco, and rice was the staple crop of the Lower Cape Fear counties in the southeast region, the staple crops of the middle region, including Lenoir County, were corn, pork, and naval stores. Cotton was cultivated but had not yet become a leading crop *(Fig. 2.2)*.[6]

County farmers accumulated wealth by amassing a large amount of land and putting it into cultivation by the use of slave labor. Antebellum farms required a year-round intensive labor force to keep them in operation. Slaves began preparation for a crop a year in advance. By mid-December all crops had been harvested. About mid-January workers began to plow the fields with horse-drawn plows. At the same time they composted manure and plant material and used them to fertilize the fields, as well as to refresh the soil in the cattle and hog lots. This work lasted until the end of April. Cotton was generally chopped once and hoed three times. After 1840, when fields had been overcultivated, large amounts of fertilizer had to be used.[7]

Fig. 2.2. Antebellum farmhouse near Kinston that served as a field hospital during the First Battle of Kinston, 1862. Its severe form and the multiplicity of fences were probably typical of many farmhouses in the county of the era. William G. Reed, a Union soldier who fought in this battle, took this photograph when he returned to Lenoir County in 1884 to revisit the scenes of his war experience. (North Carolina Collection, University of N.C. Library at Chapel Hill)

Slavery

Farmers who did not have slaves generally could not rise above the level of subsistence farming. As in the rest of eastern North Carolina, slavery was intertwined with the history of settlement in Lenoir County, and the importance of slaves increased during each decade. In 1800 one-third of the county's population was slaves. By 1820 the number of slaves was approximately equal to the number of whites.[8] By 1830 slaves slightly outnumbered whites (blacks continued to do so until the 1880s). In 1850 there were approximately 3,500 whites in the county, 4,100 black slaves, and 145 free blacks.[9] In 1860 approximately 4,900 whites, 5,100 slaves, and 178 free blacks resided in the county *(Fig. 2.3)*.[10] At this time Lenoir was one of sixteen counties in North Carolina, concentrated mostly in the eastern section, in which slaves outnumbered free citizens. Other majority-slave-population counties nearby were Jones County, which bordered Lenoir on the southeast, and Greene and Pitt counties, which abutted on the north *(Fig. 2.3)*.[11]

Distribution of plantations and slaves corresponded to the productivity of the land, which was more fertile north of the Neuse River. In 1810 John Washington particularly praised the fertility of the Falling Creek area, located northwest of Kinston. So it is not surprising that the Bear Creek (later known as Moseley Hall) District of northwest Lenoir County, which including Falling

PICKING COTTON NEAR KINSTON, N. C.

Fig. 2.3. Picking Cotton near Kinston, date unknown. (Postcard collection of Sarah Pope, Goldsboro)

Creek, held the largest number of plantations with slaves in 1860. In the entire state in 1860 only 133 slaveholders owned more than 100 slaves, and two of them lived in Lenoir County—Council Wooten, who owned 133 slaves on three different farms in Bear Creek District, and John Tull, who owned 148 slaves in the Kinston District. Other large slaveholders in Bear Creek District were James Wood, Thomas J. Kennedy, Shade Wooten, Jesse Lasseter, Bright Kennedy, and Parrott M. Hardy. In the Kinston district large slaveholders were John C. Washington, S. C. Desmond, and Walter Dunn. The largest slaveholders in the Contentnea district in northeastern Lenoir County were William W. Carraway, John H. Coward, and Curtis Phillips. Districts south of the Neuse River—Sand Hill, Trent, and Woodington—had far fewer families who owned slaves, and those who did owned fewer slaves per family. In the Sand Hill District W. L. Kilpatrick, and in the Trent District Aretis Jones, James Davis, Richard Noble, and Wiley Rouse, owned significant numbers of slaves. Most slaveholders throughout the county, as in the entire state, owned fewer than ten slaves.[12] Slaves in Lenoir County, as elsewhere, show up in census records only as marks in the appropriate columns of age categories. Of the thousands of slaves numbered in the Slave Schedule of 1860, only one is identified by a name. This is Sukie, a slave belonging to Jesse Lasseter in the Bear Creek District, who was one hundred years old. Apparently the census taker recorded her name in honor of her advanced age.[13]

The River and the Railroad

Throughout the 1830s and 1840s Lenoir County struggled with the lack of dependable transportation to nearby markets. A convention of counties along the Neuse River met in Kinston in 1833 to discuss ways to improve transportation and decided that improving the "blocked up and foul" Neuse River was impractical and that it would be more sensible to construct a railroad.[14] But it was many years before this happened. Numerous attempts were made to utilize the river for regular transportation, although small craft navigated its fluctuating water levels more dependably than larger craft. James and Franklin Dibble, owners of a Kinston carriage factory, began running a steamboat on the Neuse River about 1840 and in 1850 built a wharf on the riverbank at Kinston.[15]

By the mid-nineteenth century, Washington's praise for Lenoir County farms, "few Counties....can boast of fuller crops," would have been even more apt than when he wrote it in 1810. Agriculture remained the pride and joy of the county. In the 1840s Lenoir County planters, along with their counterparts throughout North Carolina, embraced agricultural reform. The introduction of commercial fertilizers about 1845 increased the productivity of Lenoir County farms. Efforts at agricultural reform in eastern North Carolina included the establishment of local agricultural societies and periodicals such as the *Farmer's Journal*, published in Bath in the 1850s. In 1852 the editor, John F. Tompkins, visited Lenoir County and obtained a list of seventy-five new subscribers who were solicited by local farmer and industrialist John C. Washington, son of John Washington. Tompkins also saw in Lenoir County "the finest specimens of marl that we ever saw any where, many of the beds containing a large quantity of phosphate of lime, which is highly valuable as a fertilizer."[16]

During the later antebellum years improved transportation, including plank roads, railroads, and steamboat navigation; an increase in capital; and agricultural reform led to agricultural prosperity for farmers in Lenoir County and across the state. Lenoir farmers obviously invested in both equipment and slaves and reaped the benefit at harvest time. Lenoir County was not a major cotton county in the first half of the nineteenth century, and most farmers who raised cotton produced three bales or less per year. But during the 1850s cotton cultivation exploded, from 185 bales in 1850 to 4,283 bales in 1860. Cultivation of rice and other crops declined correspondingly. Almost 45,000 more acres of land were in cultivation in 1860 than in 1850, most of this presumably planted in cotton. Between 1850 and 1860 farm values rose from approximately $1.2 million to approximately $2.5 million. The cash value of farm implements and machinery more than doubled.[17]

"Though there are some wealthy men in this County, they are not numerous"

Among the approximately six hundred farms in the county in 1860 there were stark contrasts between plantations covering thousands of acres and small farms of fewer than one hundred acres. Council Wooten owned the largest plantation, near LaGrange in the Bear Creek District, with 3,000 acres cleared land and 10,000 acres of woodland, valued at $65,000.[18] Another of the largest plantations in the county was Monticello, one of the seats of Lewis Whitfield and later his son-in-law Snoad B. Carraway and his grandson William W. Carraway. By 1850 Monticello consisted of 3,000 improved acres and 7,000 unimproved acres valued at $100,000. Three-fourths or more of the acreage of plantations and farms was typically "unimproved," but that did not mean that it was unused. John Washington mentioned the "extensive oaken swamps which affords [sic] excellent range for Hogs and cattle." The oak, hickory, longleaf pine, shortleaf pine, and dogwood trees of the woodland were harvested for firewood and hunted for wild game. Pine trees provided tar, pitch, and turpentine, which were packed into barrels and taken downriver to market. Woodland provided expansion possibilities for new fields. In the days before scientific farming with fertilizer, fields were allowed to lie fallow and were often sown with small grain which replenished the soil. New fields could be cleared out of the woodland as needed.

Just as men like William Herritage and Richard Caswell had operated in a regional economic sphere that transcended county borders in the previous century, men like Lewis Whitfield did so in the nineteenth century. Whitfield (1765-1849), a legendary character in Lenoir County history, is credited with owning over 50,000 acres of land and a number of plantations, including Monticello and LaFayette. According to family tradition Whitfield was raised at Whitehall, his father's plantation in nearby Wayne County. Early in his life he became a Baptist minister, but he occupied himself primarily with agricultural pursuits. He married three times, first in 1782, then in 1800, and finally in 1816.[19] Whitfield acquired Monticello plantation about 1790. When he died in 1849, he had residences in both Lenoir and Carteret counties and owned land in five southeastern North Carolina counties. In Lenoir County, in addition to Monticello plantation on Wheat Swamp, Whitfield owned LaFayette plantation on Beaver Dam Branch, Carmon plantation on Wheat Swamp, lands in the fork of the Neuse River and Stonyton Creek, the Clark Place, the Walter Jackson Plantation, and lots in Kinston. His will mentions that his plantations Nature's Beauty, Baptist Hall, and Rich Island were located in both Lenoir and Wayne counties, thus the boundaries must have crossed county lines. In Carteret County Whitfield owned the Cooks Hammock land near Beaufort, which had been subdivided into lots for a development called Paradise, and land on Turners Creek called Florida. He also owned Sloop Point plantation in New Hanover (now Pender) County and land in Sampson County.[20]

Monticello is one of the best documented and best preserved plantations in Lenoir County. Although reduced from thousands of acres to 157 acres by the twentieth century, the plantation retains several important features. Monticello occupies well-drained land along Wheat Swamp at the northern edge of the county. The mansion house stands at the end of a cedar allee *(Fig. 2.4)*. The east half of the center hall plan, two-room-deep house has some Georgian interior features, indicating an eighteenth century construction date, but the house apparently reached its present appearance in the early 1800s. A well-preserved Federal-style interior features a large upstairs bedchamber said to have been a ballroom.

Shown in an early-twentieth-century plat map, rectangular fields stretch to the rear, drained by a hand-dug canal and by Wheat Swamp *(Fig. 2.5)*. Canals were and still are major topographic features in the farm landscape of Lenoir County. With fifty-two inches of rainfall annually, county fields required drainage ditches, sometimes called canals. Many of the original canals were proba-

Fig. 2.4. Monticello, early 1800s. (Photo, M. Ruth Little, North Carolina Division of Archives and History).

30

bly dug by slaves and measure well over six feet deep and six feet wide.

Monticello's ninety-three slaves produced 71 bales of cotton of the total of 185 bales produced in the county in 1850.[21] By that time, Whitfield's daughter and son-in-law, Harriet and Snoad Carraway, ran the plantation. Monticello must have had its own horse-powered cotton gin. One early horse-powered cotton gin still stands in the county, on the Rountree-Askew-Moseley Farm on Stonyton Creek north of Kinston *(Fig. 2.6)*. Before its conversion to a barn, the gin house was open at the first level to allow for the gin machinery, which stood in the center, and was powered by a horse or mule that walked in a circle to turn the gin. After the cotton was ginned, it was pressed into bales in a cotton press much like this one photographed in the Lenoir County region *(Fig. 2.7)*.

In addition to the large amount of cotton grown at Monticello in 1850, the plantation also produced almost 6,000 bushels of Indian corn, 300 bushels of oats, 150 pounds of wool, 1,000 bushels of peas and beans, and lesser amounts of Irish potatoes, sweet potatoes, and wheat and rye. A herd of 240 pigs, a flock of 60 sheep, 27 beef cattle, and various milk cows, horses, mules, and oxen also roamed Monticello.[22]

With many plantations owned by absentee landlords, overseers managed the operations. In 1850 there were fourteen overseers in the county, and by 1860, at the peak of the plantation economy, the number had increased to thirty-five. Most of them worked in Moseley Hall, Bear Creek, and Kinston Districts.[23] The Tull Plantation, the fourth largest plantation in the county in 1850, a few miles north of Kinston, illustrates the rapid expansion of acreage and slave force in the decade before the Civil War. In 1850 Henry Tull owned 6,200 acres of land and 98 slaves. His thousand acres of cleared land produced primarily Indian corn, peas and beans, and sweet potatoes. During the 1850s his son John Tull became master and increased the acreage to 7,500, making the plantation the second largest in the county. John and his family built a new house (now destroyed) on the plantation, and John hired an overseer and allowed him to live in his father's old house. By 1860 Tull's overseer was supervising 148 slaves living in twenty-five dwellings (all traces of these slave houses are gone). The slaves still cultivated Indian corn as a primary crop, but they also produced 125 bales of cotton as a cash crop. Tull's numbers of horses, mules, and oxen increased significantly during the 1850s. Tull also had a steam-powered sawmill, a blacksmith shop, and a corn mill on the plantation, probably run by slaves. Another source of cash was the $4,000 earned from the sale of turpentine produced from his 5,000 acres of woodland.[24]

Overseers' housing conditions probably varied greatly from one farm to another. Sometimes overseers lived in their employer's household; sometimes they resided in a separate dwelling with their own family. On his plantation near LaGrange, planter Council Wooten kept his twenty-five-year-old overseer, E. H. Oxly, in his household. A separate overseer's house still stands on the John Sutton Farm near LaGrange. The side-gabled dwelling apparently had a loft, and probably a porch, although it is now used as a packhouse and is much altered.[25]

Large farms and plantations often had commissaries, combination offices and stores where provisions were sold and wages were paid out to farm workers. One example, a one-room board-and-batten commissary believed to have served the farm of John D. Hodges, whose house stood across the road, still stands in the county *(Fig. 2.8)*. [26] The building has a front door and window, an attic with a gable-end opening, and exposed joist tails.

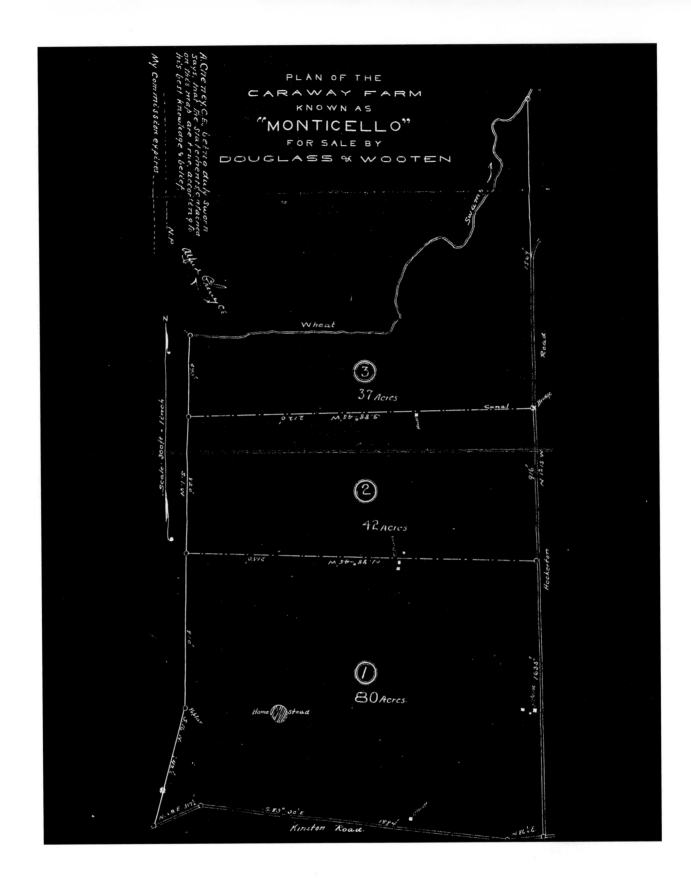

Fig. 2.5. Monticello Survey Map, drawn by Alfred Cheney, civil engineer, circa 1918. (Collection of Benjamin Franklin Scarborough, III)

Fig. 2.6. Antebellum cotton gin, now a barn, on the Rountree-Askew-Moseley Plantation. (Photo, M. Ruth Little, North Carolina Division of Archives and History)

Fig. 2.7. Cotton press in Lenoir County region. William G. Reed, photographer, 1884 (North Carolina Collection, University of N.C. Library at Chapel Hill)

Fig. 2.8. John D. Hodges Farm Commissary, middle nineteenth century, Institute vicinity. (Photo, Robbie D. Jones, North Carolina Division of Archives and History)

Naval Stores

The production of naval stores—tar, turpentine, and pitch made from pine tree resin—was the premier eastern North Carolina industry from the colonial period to the mid-1800s. On turpentine plantations, from November to March workers (usually slaves) began cutting the boxes into which the liquid dripped. Each worker managed about a half acre of pine trees. The next step was to go from tree to tree with a barrel and dip out the resin, or sap. Coopers (barrel makers) usually worked right on the farm or plantation, fashioning five barrels a day.[27]

Turpentine demand increased dramatically during the early 1800s. Most Lenoir County farmers shipped their naval stores down the Neuse River and sold them at New Bern. John Washington described a type of flat-bottomed scow that had come into use on the Neuse and Tar Rivers in the late eighteenth century and that held between fifty and two hundred barrels, probably of naval stores. Men poled individual boats down the river, but occasionally mechanization allowed collection on a larger scale. In the year 1845, for example, two steamboats hauled numbers of rafts, each containing six hundred barrels of naval stores, from Wayne, Johnston, Lenoir, and Greene Counties down the Neuse River to New Bern.[28] By 1850 Lenoir County had at least fifteen turpentine distilleries which employed forty-four men to produce almost 6,700 barrels of turpentine spirits annually. All of these were small operations that earned less than $1,500 per year except the distillery of Einstine and Brothers, which produced $15,000 worth of turpentine. The owner must have been Moses Einstine, a young merchant from Bavaria who operated a store in Kinston. In the same year John C. Washington's barrel factory employed ten men to produce 2,000 barrels, most of which were probably used for turpentine.[29] In 1860 the industrial census listed only two turpentine distilleries, that of Chauncey Gray in the Woodington District, which employed four men and produced approximately 6,000 barrels of turpentine per year, and a smaller one owned by H. N. Croom, also in Woodington District. Even so, dozens of men listed their employment as turpentine farmer, turpentine distiller, and turpentine laborer in 1860, indicating that turpentine production was still a major occupation in the county, though largely unreported in the census's Industrial Schedule.[30]

"Generally of that happy medium which qualifies them to be useful"

In John Washington's words most Lenoir County farmers belonged to "that happy medium" in terms of wealth, and there were few wealthy men in the county in the early nineteenth century. Although the later antebellum period saw the accumulation of some considerable fortunes in the county, by far the majority of white men were subsistence farmers who struggled to raise enough corn and pork and vegetables to feed their own families, enough cotton and wool to make their own clothes, and perhaps some extra to earn a little cash.

To supplement their farming income, many rural residents of Lenoir County worked in a trade. Some worked in the building trades as shingle drawers, carpenters, painters, or masons, some as wheelwrights, coopers, tanners, gunsmiths, or buggy trimmers, and others as shoemakers, hatters or seamstresses. Some were millers, some harvested naval stores, and some were fishermen. The amount of money earned from fishing in Lenoir County paled in comparison to the large fisheries in adjacent Craven County, closer to the Atlantic Ocean, where the wide, deep creeks held bountiful supplies of shad, mullet, and herring. Nevertheless, seining for fish in the larger creeks and in the Neuse River provided an important dietary supplement for rural families in the antebellum years.[31]

With a relatively small amount of cleared land and one family of slaves, Frederick Green Taylor's farm on Lousin Swamp, north of the Tull Plantation, belonged to the "happy medium." But like his neighbor, planter John Tull, Taylor was aggressively increasing production during the 1850s. In 1850 Taylor owned 60 acres of cleared land and 140 acres of woodland valued at $1,000. Taylor's valuation increased to $5,000 by 1860, when he was farming 150 cleared acres and 243 acres of woodland. His biggest crops were 700 bushels of Indian corn and 150 bushels of sweet potatoes. Taylor and his wife had a small swine herd, one horse, and one milk cow. Although many middling farmers raised a small amount of cotton, the Taylors raised none. With only a few slaves, they apparently did not have sufficient land nor field hands to cultivate cotton.[32] The Taylor family's compact antebellum cluster of house, attached kitchen, storage building, and, across the road, family cemetery has survived decades of use as a tenant farm *(Fig. 2.9)*. The heavy-timber storage building, probably built about 1850 along with the house, has a main room, a loft, and a rear shed room, all probably used for general storage.

On their 250-acre farm in the sandy landscape of south Lenoir County, Richard Noble and his wife ran a diversified, self-sufficient operation that is another example of the middling farmer in Lenoir County. Living on the family farm in a house built by Richard's father about 1790, the Noble family had assets in 1850 consisting of eight slaves (four male, four female), $100 worth of farm machinery, and $665 worth of livestock. Noble cultivated 100 acres, keeping 150 acres of woodland. In the woods the family raised pigs and sheep and kept milk cows, mules, horses, and cattle for food and to work the fields. The Nobles produced Indian corn, wool, sweet potatoes, oats, peas and beans, Irish potatoes, butter, honey, and fruit from an orchard. Although the farm was valued at only eight hundred dollars, the Nobles were obviously able to feed their own household, including slaves, and to earn some cash through the sale of excess products at market.[33]

The major rural industry in the county was milling. One of the farm tasks John Washington delegated to his wife in his absence was having the wheat ground at the neighborhood grist mill to make flour. In 1810 Washington counted in Lenoir County some seventeen grist mills, either water powered or horse powered. In 1860 that number had declined to seven water-powered mills and three steam-powered flour mills.[34] One of the early mills was probably Kelly's Mill on Southwest Creek, said to have commenced operation in the early 1700s. The mill building itself was rebuilt in the early twentieth century, but the mill pond has probably changed little since antebellum times.

Richard Noble's grist mill, located near his farm on the Trent River, was almost certainly counted in Washington's list, since Noble's Mill is said to have been established in the late eighteenth century as a rice mill. [35] Rice was the staple crop of the Lower Cape Fear region during the antebellum period. Lenoir was one of the few counties elsewhere in the state where the grain was grown, and in 1850 the county produced 94,000 pounds of rice. The swampy fields along the Neuse

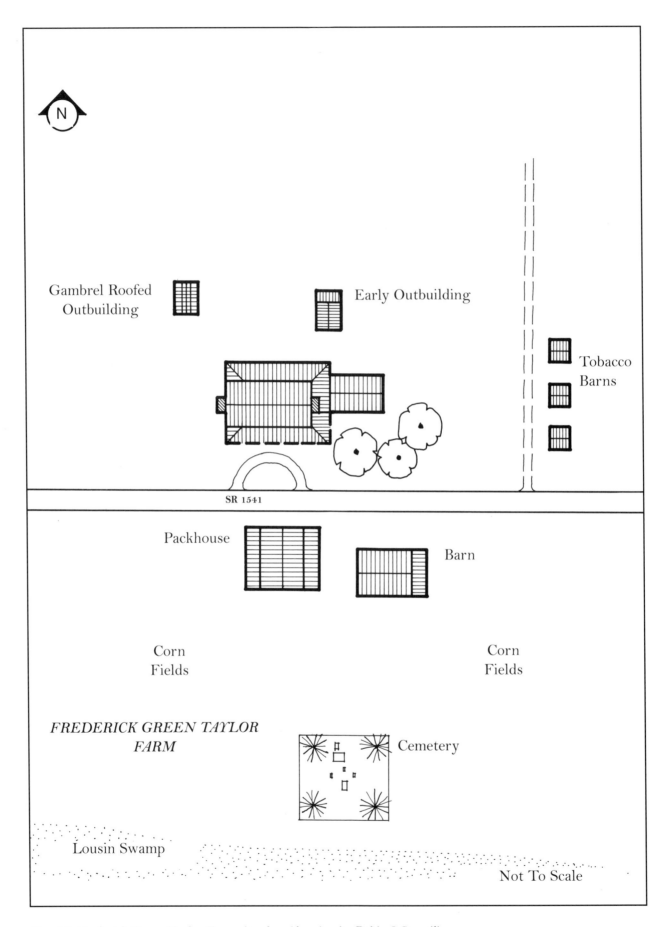

Fig. 2.9. Frederick Green Taylor Farm site plan. (drawing by Robin J. Stancil).

and Trent Rivers and numerous creeks were well suited to rice production.[36] Rice cultivation was primitive and laborious and done almost exclusively by slaves. The following description of rice culture is not of Lenoir County in particular but represents the general pattern in North Carolina. Slaves hand-dug ditches to divide the rice fields into one-quarter-acre sections. In March slaves hoed the fields and dug trenches for the seeds. From then until September the fields were alternately flooded by letting water into the ditches through flood gates, then drained and weeded. Slaves had to work for long hours in wet fields, and the prevalence of malaria in southeastern North Carolina caused considerable sickness among the slaves. In September slaves cut the ripe rice with sickles, left it to dry out for a day in the fields, then gathered it into shocks. In colonial times slaves pounded the grain with a pestle in a deep mortar, but by the early nineteenth century rice mills such as Noble's Mill had begun operating. The final winnowing, sifting, and polishing of the rice grains were often done by mechanical power, but even late in the antebellum period much of this work was still done by hand.[37] Noble's Mill later became a corn mill and is still in operation, although the present water-powered mill was rebuilt in the early twentieth century.

Education

During the antebellum period a network of both private and public schools developed in Lenoir County. The earliest academy in Lenoir County to start operation was Spring Hill Seminary of Learning, chartered about 1802 in western Lenoir County near the Neuse River. By 1806 it had a regular teacher, and by 1810 the academy had more than forty students. One of its most famous alumni was William D. Moseley of LaGrange, who served in the state legislature and later moved to Florida, where he was elected the first governor.[38] Fairfield Academy was organized in 1817 at Mewborne's Crossroads, Kinston Academy by 1822, Cambridge Academy in 1826, Moseley Hall Academy in 1828, and Union Academy in 1842. The planter class often sent their children outside the county to be educated. John Washington sent his daughter Eliza to Miss White's School in Raleigh in the 1820s; his son George trained in New York and Paris to be a physician. Jesse Jackson II entered Wake Forest College in 1835. John and Harriet Peebles sent a daughter to Saint Mary's School in Raleigh in the 1850s.[39] In 1839 the North Carolina General Assembly enacted a statewide free public school law. By the mid-1850s Lenoir County had twenty-two school districts, with nineteen schools and close to 1,000 children enrolled.[40]

The most famous antebellum private school in the county was the Lenoir Male and Female Seminary—also called the Lenoir Collegiate Institute, but generally referred to as the Institute—established under the direction of a Methodist minister, the Reverend W. Henry Cunningghim in 1853 in northwest Lenoir County. This short-lived college preparatory school officially opened in 1855, with the Reverend Levi Branson as the first principal of the male department, and Sarah L. Hampton in charge of the female department by 1856. By 1857 campus buildings worth $3,000 had been erected. Sixty boarding students, an unknown number of day students, and four male and four female teachers were participating. The school served the planter class of Lenoir and surrounding counties. In its 1857-1858 catalogue the staff noted that

> This Institution has a beautiful location, eleven miles northwest of Kinston, twenty miles east of Goldsboro, eight miles south of Snow Hill, and within less than an hour's travel of Mosely Hall Depot [later named LaGrange], on the Atlantic and N. Carolina Railroad. Students and others coming by Railroad, should stop at the Depot, then take the Tri-weekly Hack, which runs to and from the Depot and Hookerton, by way of Lenoir Institute and Snow Hill, every Tuesday, Thursday, and Saturday."[41]

In 1860 Branson left the school and the Institute closed, probably due to a combination of factors, including the loss of Branson.[42] The buildings became private residences and the community is still known as Institute.

At least five Institute buildings still stand on both sides of the Institute road, State Road 1541, constituting the most impressive cluster of Greek Revival buildings in Lenoir County *(Fig. 2.10)*.

About 1855 the main building, a two-story frame, front-gable building, was constructed to house the newly established Methodist academy. The first floor was used for public worship and school assemblies and the upper floor served as the female department classroom *(Fig. 2.11)*. In 1887 the Lenoir Collegiate Institute building was deeded to the Methodist Episcopal Church South at Lenoir Institute and eventually became the Institute United Methodist Church. It has been greatly altered by the removal of the upstairs windows and the addition of large stained-glass windows in the lower level of the building.[43]

About the same time the main building was built, Institute staff arranged for construction of the Lenoir Collegiate Institute female dormitory next door *(Fig. 2.12)*. This large, handsome, and simply finished house stands two stories tall and has four rooms, each with a fireplace, on each floor and a central stair hall lit by a transom and sidelights around the double front door. The two-story front piazza is a replacement of the original piazza. After the Institute closed, this became the house of the Reverend Henry H. Gibbons.[44]

A short distance away, the staff had a male dormitory built for the Lenoir Collegiate Institute. An early-twentieth-century photograph, taken when the dormitory had become the home of the Logan Donald Hardy family, shows the dormitory almost unaltered from its original appearance. It housed male students at Lenoir Collegiate Institute from about 1855 to the closing in 1860 *(Fig. 2.13)*. Instead of the center hall plan customary for Greek Revival-style houses, the dormitory had two front doors, which open directly into the two front rooms. The simple front piazza had square posts and a decorative sawnwork railing. Another male dormitory for the Institute stands nearby and is now known as the Cunningghim-Patrick-Bryan House, for the families who have lived here since the Institute closed. The earliest occupant following the closing was the Reverend W. Henry Cunningghim, the Methodist minister who founded the school. This two-story frame house has a center hall, four rooms on each floor, and an original one-story piazza with Doric posts stretching across the entire front elevation.[45] Another of the Institute's buildings was the residence of the Reverend George W. Venters, one of the school's founders. The Venters-Hardy House, as it is now known, follows the same form as the school dormitories, although it has a replacement classical

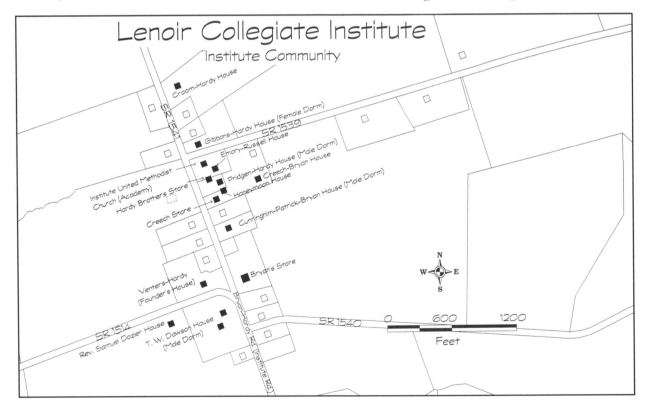

Fig. 2.10. Institute stretches along both sides of S.R. 1541 northeast of LaGrange. (map, Kinston Planning Department)

Fig. 2.11. Methodist Academy, Lenoir Collegiate Institute, circa 1855. This building became the Institute United Methodist Church after the Institute closed. (from R. Bruce Pate, *The History of Lenoir Collegiate Institute*)

Fig. 2.12. Female Dormitory, Lenoir Collegiate Institute, circa 1855. This later became the Rev. Henry Gibbons residence. (Photo, Robbie D. Jones, North Carolina Division of Archives and History)

Fig. 2.13. Male Dormitory, Lenoir Collegiate Institute, circa 1855. This later became the Logan Donald Hardy residence. (Documentary photo, early 1900s, Heritage Place, Lenoir Community College)

Fig. 2.14. Staircase, Venters-Hardy House, 1850s. This was the residence of Rev. George W. Venters, a founder of the Institute (Photo, Robbie D. Jones, North Carolina Division of Archives and History)

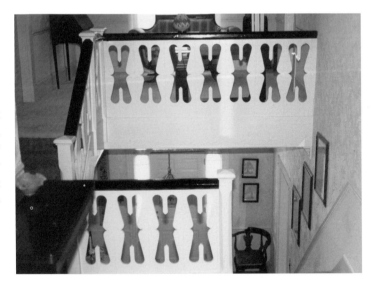

portico in place of its original Greek Revival porch. In addition to graceful Greek Revival mantels and interior moldings, the house has an eccentrically decorated stair railing, a flat sawnwork balustrade with balusters and intervening pendants *(Fig. 2.14)*.

Fraternal Lodges

The oldest Masonic lodge known to stand in the county is the Rountree Masonic Lodge, later known as the Bethel Lodge, located near Bethel in northeastern Lenoir County *(Fig. 2.15)*. The two-story side-gable frame building was built about 1850 and used exclusively by the Masons until

Fig. 2.15. Rountree Masonic Lodge (Bethel Lodge), Bethel vicinity, circa 1850 (Documentary photo, circa 1935, North Carolina Division of Archives and History)

around 1880, when the lower floor began to be used by students of the Bethel Academy, organized by the Bethel Masonic Lodge. The building continued to house both the Masons and schoolrooms until the 1920s, when school consolidation eliminated the need for it as educational space. The Masons finally moved out in the 1930s, and the building was renovated as a private dwelling. The door in the center of the gable end accessed the first floor; the door in the long elevation probably led directly upstairs. The simple Greek Revival effect created by the corner posts, front cornice, gabled eave returns, and large six-over-six sash windows befits a Masonic lodge. The narrow, two-story form is traditional for rural Masonic lodges throughout North Carolina during the nineteenth century.[46]

Religious Buildings

By 1810 two different Baptist sects, the United Baptists and the Anabaptists or Free Will Baptists had established churches in Lenoir County, while the Methodists, having no church, worshiped in the court house at Kinston.[47] The only recognizably antebellum church building standing in the rural portion of the county is the Croom Meeting House at Sandy Bottom, which prob-

Fig. 2.16. Croom Meeting House, Sandy Bottom, early nineteenth century (Photo, Robbie D. Jones, North Carolina Division of Archives and History)

ably resembles others of the era now lost *(Fig. 2.16)*. The Baptists established a congregation here about 1803. Local citizens believe that farmer Lott Croom built the little rectangular frame building of side-gable form, with nine-over-nine sash windows and board-and-batten doors, in the same year. Its severely plain finish, with weatherboards and neatly boxed eaves, and its original floor plan, with a single door in three sides, link it to other early rural meetinghouses and indicate an early-nineteenth-century construction date. The front door was originally located on the long side, with side doors in the gable ends and the pulpit in the center opposite the front door. Local people say that the rear entrance was the slave entrance during the antebellum period. Later the plan was rearranged so that the front door is in one gable end and the pulpit stands at the opposite gable end, yet the original pews, clerk's table, and pulpit are still used.[48]

Two other antebellum church buildings have survived, although much altered,. in rural Lenoir County. In the 1830s a Methodist Episcopal Church South congregation formed in the community of Institute, in northwest Lenoir County. About 1855 this congregation built a Methodist academy building—a combination church and academy (already mentioned in the discussion of early schools)—that still stands at Institute, although much altered. The Wheat Swamp Free Will Baptist congregation, which was established in the eighteenth century and affiliated with the Christian Church in 1843, continued to use its eighteenth-century church building until 1858, when they built a new building. The Wheat Swamp Christian Church sanctuary, a simple rectangular frame building with a gable front with double door, was remodeled in 1908 and enlarged in the 1970s *(Fig. 2.17)*.[49]

Fig. 2.17. Wheat Swamp Christian Church, Wheat Swamp, 1858. This 1969 documentary photograph shows the original church building, although the stained glass windows and other additions have obscured its form (North Carolina Division of Archives and History)

"Some Instances of Good Wood Buildings. . . by no means eligant"

These words of John Washington, a frequent traveler familiar with the elegant early-nineteenth-century architecture of Petersburg, Virginia, Philadelphia, and New York, where he went to purchase goods for his Kinston store, describe the houses and other buildings in Kinston and Lenoir

County in 1810. Washington noted that there were no brick buildings and that most edifices were simple frame structures. He observed that most citizens did not desire a stylish house but had a "spirit of accumulation."[50] They might have been accumulating material possessions, land or slaves or simply working so hard at self-sufficiency that they had no time to go beyond serviceability when they built their houses.

Most of the houses in the county were, no doubt, one- or two-room log or frame houses that fell below Washington's threshold of "good wood buildings." The county is not known today for log dwellings as are Piedmont counties such as Orange or Caswell, but log houses constituted a fundamental construction type in many Coastal Plain counties, such as adjacent Onslow County, which has been extensively investigated. Enough antebellum log houses are documented in Lenoir County to suggest that they constituted a significant portion of historic houses in the county that have disappeared. For example the house of farmer James Tindal, who subsisted on a small farm containing twenty acres of cleared land and fifty acres of woodland in Trent Township in south Lenoir County in 1860, has disappeared but was probably of log.[51]

To build the Stroud-Chambers Log House near Betty Wooten's Crossroads in southwest Lenoir County in the early 1800s, woodmen sawed logs into planks and finished them with full-dovetail corner notching, forming such a house so well fitted that it remained functional well into the twentieth century *(Fig. 2.18)*. A mud-and-stick chimney is thought to have heated the one-room house. The openings might have been fitted with wood shutters since the building probably lacked glass windows. Lenoir citizens continued to use plank-log construction in the later 1800s, but primarily for outbuildings, such as smokehouses, rather than dwellings.

Christopher and Nancy Turner's log house stood in Woodington township until the 1990s *(Fig. 2.19)*. The couple probably built the log house about 1850, when Christopher Turner, a teacher,

Fig. 2.18. Stroud-Chambers Plank Log House, Betty Wooten's Crossroads vicinity, early 1800s (Photo, 1969, North Carolina Division of Archives and History)

Fig. 2.19. Christopher and Nancy Turner Log House, Woodington Township, circa 1850 (Photo, Fred Whitaker, circa 1950, Heritage Place, Lenoir Community College)

married Nancy Stroud. In 1860 their farm was valued at five hundred dollars.[52] Built of round logs set on lightwood blocks, the house had a mud-and-stick chimney at each end. The gabled roof sheltered each chimney to protect the mud from the weather. The kitchen occupied a separate building. By 1870 Christopher and Nancy were raising eight children between the ages of one and seventeen in the small house. Christopher must have spent most of his time teaching, because only 12 of his 162 acres were cleared. The farm produced small amounts of Irish potatoes and sweet potatoes, butter and milk from two cows, and meat from a herd of fifteen pigs.

The Federal Style

John Washington might have numbered some of the town houses in Kinston among the "good wood buildings" in the county. Certainly the Bright-Peebles House, the only pre-1810 house in Kinston that survives, would have fit into this category. Good buildings would have had not only durable construction but also some architectural ambition. From the late eighteenth century to the 1840s, North Carolinians who desired up-to-date architecture built in a style later named Federal, for the early years of America's independence. Federal-style architecture was based on the eighteenth-century Georgian architecture of England, itself derived from ancient Rome and the European Renaissance. However, the Federal style favored lighter, more delicate details than did the Georgian style. Federal buildings possessed balanced facades and elegant detailing, including glass fanlights over doors, decorative moldings around openings and along roofs, brickwork laid in ornate patterns, beaded weatherboards, slender classical porch columns, and delicate railings. A handful of "good" plantation houses survive in Lenoir County, perhaps not "eligant" compared to those in Philadelphia or New York, but equal to other plantation houses in the Coastal Plain. Graceful Federal forms with finely detailed classical moldings and ornament characterize most of the merchant-planter houses of the early nineteenth century.

If Lenoir County merchants and planters needed models to follow when they wanted to build "good" houses, just thirty miles away in New Bern they could find many stylish town houses. One of the most distinctive types of Federal house in New Bern was the side-hall plan, a two-story house, usually of brick, with a side-gable roof. The entrance, set in the side bay of the main facade, was emphasized with elaborate woodwork and an ornate porch. Perhaps Stonyton Creek planter and grist mill owner Charles Wilson Tilghman was imitating New Bern architecture when he built his large, frame side-hall house in the early 1800s *(Fig. 2.20)*. The tall round-arched sash windows in the attic gables added a surprisingly stylish feature to the otherwise plain exterior treatment.[53]

Only one New Bern-type side hall still stands in the county, expanded and transformed into a Victorian mansion in the late 1800s and now known as Cedar Dell. The core of the main block of Cedar Dell was built in the early 1800s, apparently by Henry Herring, and may have been the first brick house in the county. The plantation passed to his son George W. Herring in 1845. The original two-story house, consisting of the center hall and southern rooms finished with elegant Federal woodwork, constitutes one of the few New Bern-type side-hall-plan brick houses found outside the port town.

The two-and-one-half-story Needham Herring House, located in the LaGrange vicinity, probably exhibits the best-preserved elegant Federal finish in Lenoir County *(Fig. 2.21)*. The single-pile house has a later Victorian-style porch and rear additions. Its main block displays the craftsmanship of the early-nineteenth-century house carpenter and joiner in Lenoir County through the carefully executed decorative moldings, pegged doors, sash windows, paneling, and other features. The big frame house sits on a full Flemish bond foundation and has Flemish bond chimneys. One of the chimney bricks bears the date 1801. Such a marking usually represents the date of construction of a house. But the mature Federal design and finish of the house suggest a construction

Fig. 2.20. Charles Wilson Tilghman House, Stonyton Creek, early 1800s, demolished. (Photo, North Carolina Division of Archives and History)

Fig. 2.21. Needham Herring House, LaGrange vicinity, 1820s. (Photo, Tony Vaughn, 1970, North Carolina Division of Archives and History)

date in the 1820s, thus the dated brick may have been reused from an earlier house. The boxed cornices at the front and rear are embellished with a modillion cornice. Probably built for Edward Herring (1755-1825) or his son William Herring (1779-1830), the house is remarkably stylish for Lenoir County. The Herring family took advantage of the most up-to-date room arrangement, featuring a spacious center hallway displaying paneling more ornate than that of the rooms themselves. The hall contains the stairs to the second floor and affords privacy to the two downstairs parlors. Original woodwork, including dentiled cornices, tripartite mantels with delicate gougework, windows and door moldings, and a second-floor built-in hall press, is still in place *(Fig. 2.22)*.

Around 1820, in southern Lenoir County near the Duplin County border, farmer John Davis built a large two-story frame house with equally impressive Federal-style interior appointments. The unknown craftsman who carved the mantels demonstrated less restraint than did the artisan of the Herring mantels, and he embellished the central tympanum and corner blocks of the parlor mantel with large sunburst decorations *(Fig. 2.23)*. Now known as the Wooten-Davis House, the dwelling stands at Betty Wooten's Crossroads. Like the Needham Herring House, it has tall windows resting on paneled wainscots, with plastered walls and high ceilings completing the tasteful interiors. To add a further note of sumptuousness, an unknown painter grained the six-panel doors in an imitation of mahogany, a more desirable wood than pine, the staple construction material.

Small houses often had finishes as decorative as those of large houses. The "good wood building" built about 1810, probably for Thomas Harvey Sr., in the northern end of the county near Taylor's Crossroads is now known as the Harvey-Mewborne House *(Fig. 2.24)*. The carefully finished one-and-one-half-story dwelling with front dormer windows, gable end chimneys, and rear shed rooms recalls colonial cottages of the eighteenth century. An early, perhaps original, detached kitchen connects through a rear breezeway. Such delicate finish as the dentiled cornices on the dormers and the Flemish bond brick of the chimneys represents the fine craftsmanship of the Federal era. The little frame house has two main rooms, a hall and a parlor. This hall-parlor room arrangement was the most common room arrangement in early North Carolina houses. The rooms

46

Fig. 2.22. Stair hall, Needham Herring House (Photo, Robbie D. Jones, North Carolina Division of Archives and History)

Fig. 2.23. Parlor mantel, Wooten-Davis House, Betty Wooten's Crossroads, circa 1820 (Photo, 1976, North Carolina Division of Archives and History)

Fig. 2.24. Harvey-Mewborne House, Taylor's Crossroads vicinity, circa 1810 (Photo, 1976, North Carolina Division of Archives and History)

are finished with wainscot, paneled doors, and stylish Federal mantels. An enclosed winder stair rises between the hall and parlor. The present porch is a replacement of an earlier attached porch.[54]

Big House-Piazza-Little House"

The piazza, locally pronounced "PI-zah" with a long *i*, was a regional feature linking the county to the rest of the Tidewater region of North Carolina and the South. A piazza was a covered open porch or veranda supported by columns or posts and attached to the outside of a building. American usage of this term appeared in South Carolina by about 1730 and moved up the seaboard. By the end of the eighteenth century, use of the term *piazza* had become common throughout the South. On dwellings piazzas provided cool, shady reception areas for visitors.[55] In 1790 a visitor to New Bern remarked on the proliferation of piazzas in the town. "There are to many of the houses Balconies or Piazzas in front and sometimes back of the house, this Method of Building is found convenient on account of the great Summer Heats here."[56] To this day, Lenoir County people call their porch a "pizah" or "pizer," a local variation of *piazza*.

In Tidewater North Carolina a distinctive house type incorporating or engaging the piazza under the main roof proliferated. This house form, known among architectural historians variously as coastal cottage, raised cottage, Creole house, or Tidewater house, contained a front engaged piazza, two main rooms with a loft, and small shed rooms, all covered by one roof. The use of a shed room, instead of a gabled rear ell, to gain extra space is a distinguishing feature of the piazza house. A shed room is created by adding a sloping roof and three walls along the front or rear or sometimes the side of a house. Two-story Tidewater houses tended to be enlarged with sheds rather than with gabled ells. Early examples of the house form rest on a high foundation. The house with engaged piazza is called the Creole cottage in the Deep South of Alabama, Mississippi, and Louisiana, where it was the house of choice for families of French, Spanish, and Cajun origin in the 1700s and early 1800s. In Lenoir and the adjoining counties of Craven, Duplin, and Onslow, the piazza house was the house form of choice for most middling and wealthy homeowners until the mid-nineteenth century.[57] A persistent method of house enlargement in the region during the antebellum period was to link new house to old house with a piazza, and use the old house as a kitchen and dining annex—a configuration which could be called big house-piazza-little house.[58]

The Rountree-Askew-Moseley House at Mewborne's Crossroads exemplifies the big house-piazza-little house pattern *(Fig. 2.25)*. In the late eighteenth century the owner of this plantation, probably Robert H. Rountree, built a house consisting of two rooms with a central chimney, an engaged piazza, and a rear shed. About 1820 Rountree or the next owners, the Askews, added a two-story side wing (the big house) and extended the original piazza across the front of the new wing, linking big house and little house. About 1850 the owners needed even more space and built two bedrooms, with Greek Revival finish, behind the big house. An even more common enlargement was to construct the big house in front of the little house, allowing the little house piazza to serve as a breezeway between the two buildings.

The exquisitely finished Davis-Robinson House, Sandy Bottom vicinity, is a piazza house built about 1810 *(Fig. 2.26)*. It is five bays wide, with a fully engaged front piazza and two front dormer windows. The louvered shutters that flank the piazza windows may be original and represent a rare survival of this type of shutter, which originally performed the dual function of providing privacy and security without blocking air circulation. The hall-parlor plan is finished with original paneled doors, paneled wainscot, moldings, and a magnificent Federal-style mantel in the parlor with fluted pilasters, paneled frieze, and double shelf with gougework moldings.

The Wright Nunn House, in the Liddell vicinity, was a classic example of the form but has been converted to a packhouse and lost much of its finish *(Fig. 2.27)*. Built about 1825, the compact house contained six rooms: hall (with fireplace and enclosed stair), parlor, loft, two shed rooms, and a front porch room (removed). Such intricate Federal features as beaded weatherboards, six-panel doors, flush sheathing with chair rails and baseboards, and hand-forged hardware indicate how

Fig. 2.25. Rountree-Askew-Moseley House, Mewborn's Crossroads, late 1700s, circa 1820, circa 1850 (Photo, Jim Shell, 1969, Heritage Place, Lenoir Community College)

Fig. 2.26. Davis-Robinson House, Sandy Bottom vicinity, circa 1810 (Photo, Jim Shell, 1969, Heritage Place, Lenoir Community College)

carefully finished the house was. Wright Nunn, born in 1800 and said to have descended from Swiss Protestants who settled in New Bern in the eighteenth century, lived here in 1850 with his wife and six children.[59]

Like those in many other areas of North Carolina during the early 1800s, homeowners in Lenoir County hired artisans to add special decorative finishes that turned even small farmhouses into works of art. The front piazza at the Davis-Grady House near Jonestown has the only plastered ceiling found on a porch in the county. As was the tradition in the nineteenth century, the ceiling is painted light blue, said by old-timers to represent the sky and to keep away flies. Some shutters with original strap hinges still hang on the 1830s house. The hall and parlor room arrangement is enriched by a fancy Federal-style mantel with a sunburst, and one six-panel door is decorated with feather painting to create the illusion of an elegant wood grain.

The most impressive house with piazza in Lenoir County is the Whitfield-Dunn-Wiggins House, also known as LaFayette *(Fig. 2.28)*. Much confusion exists over the identity of the builder and the construction date of this significant house. County legend links it to the Reverend Lewis Whitfield, reputed to have presided over a plantation that stretched from this house near Stonyton Swamp west to Wheat Swamp, where Monticello stands. Other house legends describe its use as a tavern and as a Masonic lodge in its early years. Available historical documents suggest that much of the tradition is true. In the 1860s the plantation was still known as LaFayette.[60]

Whitfield family genealogy describes the house at LaFayette plantation as having stone pillars, solid porch columns, built-in porch seats of heavy timbers, and eight-foot-tall doors.[61] The Whitfield-Dunn-Wiggins House corresponds to this description in every respect, for it rests on high stone and marl (a seashell conglomerate found locally) foundation piers; the front entrance sits within a flush-sheathed recessed porch with solid porch posts, apparently original; and built-

Fig. 2.27. Wright Nunn House, Liddell vicinity, circa 1825 (Photo, Robbie D. Jones, North Carolina Division of Archives and History)

in benches originally flanked the front door. The piazza railing, a Chinese Chippendale lattice design, has been removed. Perhaps Whitfield had a particular affinity for this house type, since he owned Sloop Point, a well-known coastal cottage that was built in the early and mid-eighteenth century. Whitfield acquired Sloop Point in the mid-nineteenth century.[62]

What is indisputable is that LaFayette is the largest and finest piazza house in the county. Prior to its adaptation and alteration for modern living about 1980, the house was unaltered and presented a pristine example of a commodious and well-appointed plantation house. LaFayette's room arrangement is unique in the county and perhaps in North Carolina: a center hall with flanking large rooms; smaller porch rooms entered only from these large rooms and flanking a recessed porch; and three rear shed rooms, with an open winding stair from the center shed room leading upstairs *(Fig. 2.29)*. The upstairs contains three bedchambers separated by a narrow center hall. The chamber above the parlor is the same size as the parlor, and according to family tradition, served as a ballroom. The original interior treatment features simple and elegant Federal plastered walls and ceilings, door and window moldings, tripartite mantels, sheathed wainscots and chair rails, and flat-paneled doors. The "ballroom" had the most elegant finish of any room in the house, although usually the first-floor parlor would have been given this treatment. The room had a flat-paneled wainscot and Adamesque-style mantel with sunbursts and a dentil cornice. Other unique features of LaFayette are the original, attached kitchen and an unusually large transom that ventilated an upstairs bedroom.

Fig. 2.28. LaFayette (Whitfield-Dunn-Wiggins House), Graingers vicinity, circa 1830 (Photo, Jim Shell, 1969, Heritage Place, Lenoir Community College)

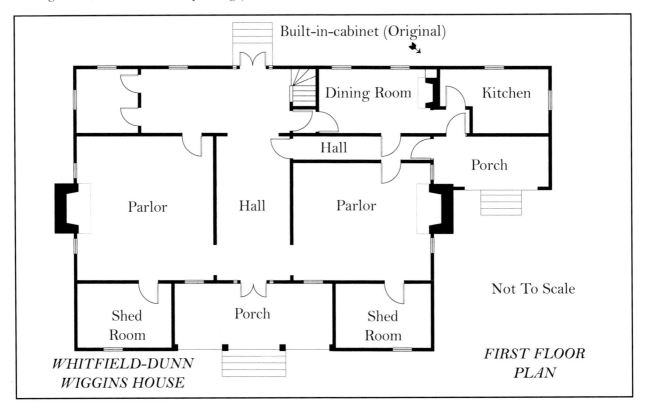

Fig. 2.29. LaFayette Floor Plan (Drawing by Robin J. Stancil after Robbie D. Jones)

The Greek Revival

The architectural style that symbolizes the plantation house not just in Lenoir County but throughout North Carolina and the South is the Greek Revival. This style, introduced into North Carolina by such landmarks as the State Capitol at Raleigh, built in the 1830s, reached into the Lenoir County countryside by the 1840s. Aided by pattern books such as Asher Benjamin's 1830 *Practical House Carpenter*, which translated the form and Grecian orders of ancient Greek temples into simple decorative schemes for house construction, carpenters created classical porches with columns or posts supporting pediments, wide cornices and baseboards, corner boards, and corner block accents at windows and doors. Orienting the roof gable to the front created the Greek temple form desired for the style, but few North Carolina houses approached this ideal. Only one surviving Lenoir County house, the John Council Wooten House, has the temple form. Built near Southwood about 1860, the house features a full-height portico supporting the pedimented front gable of the facade *(Fig. 2.30)*. A shallow balcony runs across the upper facade. While some Deep South plantation houses had a portico extending completely around the house, as did some Greek temples, Wooten contented himself with a one-story porch extending down both sides and around the rear to the detached kitchen.

Fig. 2.30. John Council Wooten House, Southwood vicinity, circa 1860 (Photo, Robbie D. Jones, North Carolina Division of Archives and History)

A sizable group of Greek-style houses in north Lenoir County, where the richer soil encouraged the development of large plantations, marks the most pretentious expression of the slave economy. The houses sit far apart, with the exception of a concentration at Institute, where the Methodist academy operated in the late 1850s. Numerous houses were not only two stories high, but were also two rooms deep. Such houses tended to have hipped roofs, a center hall arrangement, and double front porches.

The Jesse Jackson House, sited on a ridge overlooking the Neuse River about five miles south of Kinston, illustrates the transition of the Federal style into the Greek Revival *(Fig. 2.31)*. Built about 1840 for Frederick Jones, the Jackson House has the tall two-story form, one room deep, of such Federal style-houses as the Needham Herring House, built earlier in the century. The original Greek Revival detailing features wide gable eave returns; large transoms and sidelights illuminating the front, back, and upper level porch entrances; wide, simple moldings; and mantels that resemble the front of a temple: Doric pilasters supporting a frieze, cornice, and shelf. A Doric-style entrance porch on the front overlooks the Neuse River. According to Jackson family tradition, Jesse Jackson, a planter, acquired the house and 1,000 acres about 1850. His descendants still own the place.[63]

With its large size and exuberant detailing, the Moore-Heath House, built about 1845 for planter Jesse Moore in the Taylor's Crossroads vicinity, was one of the most interesting Greek Revival plantation houses in the county *(Fig. 2.32)*. It was destroyed by fire about 1990. The two-story house, five bays wide and two rooms deep, had a hipped roof, a hipped front porch with Doric posts, and a double front door with transom and sidelights. The refined moldings with corner blocks around the front door hinted at the creative Greek Revival finish that embellished the

Fig. 2.31. Jesse Jackson House, Kinston vicinity, circa 1840 (Photo, Collection of Jim and Catherine Stewart)

interior. Rather than displaying the standard decoration limited to mantels and door and window moldings, Jesse Moore's interior finish encompassed the entire public area: the center hall and flanking parlors. Baseboards, window aprons, moldings, mantels, doors, and hallway arch created a unified and highly individualized Greek Revival ensemble. The parlors were treated with high baseboards, molded aprons beneath the windows, and moldings with corner blocks around the windows. Behind the decorative hall arch lay the rear hall, with a graceful stair and a smaller room on each side with simpler finish.

For many of their well-to-do clients in Lenoir County, builders built updated versions of the practical and popular piazza house with Greek Revival porches and woodwork. Wiley Joel Rouse (1818-1883) was a prosperous planter in the Strabane community, and he and his wife Frances, who were married in 1843, probably had The Sycamores built at that time *(Fig. 2.33)*. The five-bay-wide, side-gable house with inset piazza and rear shed rooms features the up-to-date Greek Revival style. Around the front door, letting sunlight into the central hall, are the trademark transom and sidelights. Molded corner blocks accent the corners of the windows and doors, and square Doric posts, pilasters, and a dentiled cornice turn the piazza into a facsimile of a Greek temple. Throughout the interior the house carpenter continued the Greek Revival theme with post-and-lintel mantels, corner block moldings, and paneled aprons beneath the window sills. When the house was restored, the original orange and turquoise feather paintings were repainted on the doors and window aprons. The details are Greek Revival, but the overall form is local, with the piazza leading to a semidetached side kitchen with an exposed-face chimney recalling chimney-construction in antebellum New Bern.

54

Fig. 2.32. Moore-Heath House, Taylor's Crossroads vicinity, circa 1845, demolished (Photo, Jim Shell, 1969, Heritage Place, Lenoir Community College)

Fig. 2.33. Wiley Joel and Frances Rouse House (The Sycamores), Strabane community, circa 1843 (Photo, Robbie D. Jones, North Carolina Division of Archives and History)

Fig. 2.34. Will Sutton House, Falling Creek vicinity, circa 1850 (Photo, Robbie D. Jones, North Carolina Division of Archives and History)

Although smaller and plainer than the Wiley Joel Rouse House, the Anthony Davis House, built about 1850 near Pink Hill, incorporates Greek Revival details into its localized piazza house form. Exaggeratedly large paneled posts support the piazza roof, and two front doors lead into the interior. The piazza wraps around the side to provide access to the semidetached kitchen located in a side wing. A twentieth-century owner added the prominent latticework decorating the piazza.

Surprisingly, some of the most sophisticated Greek Revival finish in the county appeared on one-story Greek Revival cottages. Will Sutton apparently had his house in the Falling Creek vicinity built about 1850. The center hall plan, hipped-roof Will Sutton House has two interior chimneys and four rooms *(Fig. 2.34)*. The wide Doric corner boards, pedimented lintels topping large six-over-six sash windows, double front door with transom and sidelights, and pedimented entrance porch supported by tapering fluted Doric posts and with a flush-sheathed porch wall all create a bold Greek Revival finish. The Miller-Nunn House (demolished) had an elegant center hall plan and flanking rooms with tall windows, wide surrounds extending to the floor and enclosing paneled aprons, and stately mantels *(Fig. 2.35)*.

Sometimes Greek Revival stylistic features appeared in only a few touches, such as an entrance or mantels added to an otherwise traditional house. Jeremiah (Jerry) Sutton (1834-1900), in the Bucklesberry vicinity, had a frame house with piazza built for his family about 1860. The Sutton House

Fig. 2.35. Parlor, Miller-Nunn House, Elm Grove vicinity, circa 1860, demolished (Photo, North Carolina Division of Archives and History)

was plainly and sturdily constructed, with gable-end brick chimneys and a large piazza with plain posts and railing. The transom and sidelights around the double front door brought a bit of style to the otherwise vernacular dwelling. An 1898 family photograph shows Jerry, his wife, two sons, two daughters, and the family dog standing on both sides of the front picket fence. A luxuriant flower garden blooms inside the fence *(Fig. 2.36)*. Sutton married three times, and this wife is believed to be Sarah Croom Sutton. In 1860 the family owned seven slaves; a small building at the far right is said to have been a slave quarters. Two black girls, one named Rose and one whose name is unknown, stand in front of this structure.

By the 1850s architectural trendsetters in the nation and in North Carolina had begun to incorporate the arches, towers, and heavy Renaissance details of Italianate buildings into their town houses and country estates, often in combination with Greek Revival elements. In Lenoir County, the most eclectic combination of the Greek Revival and Italianate styles appears at the James Wood House *(Fig. 2.37)*. The two-story, double-pile frame house with a hipped roof, built in the 1850s by James Wood (1815-1875), a planter in the Bucklesberry section on the Neuse River, has a number of remarkable features. Like some of the largest plantation houses in the county, it has four chimneys, but these are unique in displaying ornate and eccentric separated twin flues and pointed-arch panels. The front elevation features a perfectly preserved two-story Greek Revival entrance porch and heavy bracketed eaves. Window surrounds taper to a crossetted pediment at

Fig. 2.36. Jerry Sutton House, Bucklesbury vicinity, circa 1860, demolished (Photo, 1898, North Carolina Division of Archives and History)

Fig. 2.37. James Wood House, Bucklesbury vicinity, 1850s (Photo, Jim Shell, 1969, Heritage Place, Lenoir Community College)

the top and have paneled aprons at the first and second-story levels. In contrast to the exterior, the center hall plan interior is finished not with eccentric woodwork but with sedate, classically beautiful Greek Revival trim, including corner block surrounds, classical-style mantels, and a heavy polygonal newel post and ramped stair railing. James Wood's plantation on the Neuse River was a stopping point for steamboats on the way to Seven Springs, a resort just over the Wayne County line. Fearful for his family's safety during the Civil War, James reportedly bought a house in Greensboro and moved there during the war. When he returned to his plantation, he found that it had escaped damage.

Another blend of Greek Revival and Italianate architecture is seen on the Rouse-Edmondson-Wilson House in the LaGrange vicinity *(Fig. 2.38)*. The two-story double-pile form and double piazza that extends almost completely across the front elevation represent the Greek Revival style, but the unconventional jigsawn decoration of the piazza (a local version of the sheaf-of-wheat balustrade pattern), large square posts, and curvilinear drip course beneath the eaves are Italianate in style. Planter Noah Rouse, born in 1830 and owner of a large plantation with eighteen slaves and three slave houses in 1860, is believed to have built this large plantation house.[64]

Fig. 2.38. Rouse-Edmondson-Wilson House, LaGrange vicinity, circa 1860 (Heritage Place, Lenoir Community College)

Outbuildings

On all farms, from the largest plantations to the smallest homesteads, daily activities took place in specialized buildings that stood apart from the dwelling house, such as the kitchen, the smokehouse, and the wash house. The kitchen had almost as much significance as the main house, for women, children, and female slaves of the household spent many of their waking hours in this building. Fear of fire, aversion to cooking odors and heat, and the general use of slaves or servants made detached kitchens practical and desirable, both in town and out in the country. In Lenoir County kitchens were generally detached or semidetached until the twentieth century. Detached kitchens stood in close proximity to the main house but were not connected. Semidetached kitchens were connected to the main house by a porch or breezeway. Twentieth-century residents usually enclosed the breezeway or added a new kitchen that connected directly to the living rooms. Even then the old kitchen's life was not over, for the little building was often moved to a new site for use as a dwelling or part of a dwelling, often a tenant house. In Lenoir County a building could go full circle, from use as a dwelling to use as a kitchen and then back to use as a dwelling.

The first form of kitchen construction in the county, as throughout North Carolina, was the detached kitchen, a separate building that stood near the dwelling but not so close that a fire in the kitchen would burn down the dwelling. One such building is the Phillips Log Kitchen, a sawn-plank structure with full-dovetailed corner notching probably built in the early nineteenth century *(Fig. 2.39)*. The kitchen stands in the Edwards Bridge community (also known as Fountain Hill) of northeastern Lenoir County, although the adjacent house has been destroyed.[65] A kitchen building sometimes predates the main house because it was the original house, relegated to use as a kitchen when a larger house was built adjacent to it. The kitchen form in Lenoir County often

Fig. 2.39. Phillips Log Kitchen, Fountain Hill vicinity, early 1800s (Photo, Robbie D. Jones, North Carolina Division of Archives and History)

contains an engaged piazza. The Smith-Blizzard Kitchen near Deep Run in south Lenoir County may have originally served as a dwelling *(Fig. 2.40)*.

A later form of Lenoir County kitchens was the semidetached kitchen, often placed beside the main house and connected to the front piazza. Kitchens in other parts of North Carolina were usually connected by a breezeway extending out the back door of the hallway. At the Wiley Joel Rouse House, for example, the family walked from the front piazza directly into the kitchen. The place-

ment of the kitchen's chimney inside the room, with its brick face exposed on the exterior wall, is characteristic of early house chimneys found in nearby New Bern. Exposed-face chimneys added a distinctive visual effect to the exterior of a building.

Other types of antebellum domestic outbuildings, especially smokehouses and washhouses, have largely disappeared from the landscape. A storage house at the Horace Fields Plantation near LaGrange demonstrates, through its high level of craftsmanship, just how valuable such storage houses were in antebellum days. The Fields storage house, of heavy-timber construc-

Fig. 2.40. Smith-Blizzard Kitchen, Deep Run vicinity (Photo, Robbie D. Jones, North Carolina Division of Archives and History)

Fig. 2.41. Brandy House, Horace Fields Plantation, LaGrange vicinity, early 1800s (Photo, Robbie D. Jones, North Carolina Division of Archives and History)

Fig. 2.42. Smokehouse, Howard-Williams House, Kinston vicinity, nineteenth century (Photo, Robbie D. Jones, North Carolina Division of Archives and History)

tion with a brick cellar, beaded weatherboards, rosehead nails, fully sheathed interior, and a floored loft, was probably built in the early 1800s *(Fig. 2.41)*. A rare example of a well-preserved smokehouse constructed of neatly notched log planks, with a cantilevered roof over the front door, stands behind the Howard-Williams House near Kinston *(Fig. 2.42)*. County residents remember with great fondness the hams, sausage, and other meats that cured in such smokehouses all over the county in more self-sufficient times.

The Village on the Neuse

As farms and plantations expanded in the countryside, what became of the village on the Neuse? Periodic attempts to increase Kinston's status occurred throughout the early 1800s. In 1826 a charter of incorporation was granted to the little town, but the appointed board of officials did not qualify for office and the incorporation lapsed.[66] About 1830 the original eighteenth-century frame courthouse, which stood in the center of the intersection of King and Queen Streets, was moved and a new brick courthouse was built on the northeast corner of the intersection, where the present courthouse stands. The 1830 courthouse stood until it was destroyed by fire in 1878. No image of it has survived.[67] In 1833, in an attempt to trade on its past glory, the town was renamed Caswell, but citizen objections resulted in a return to the name Kinston the following year.[68] During the 1830s the county, like much of the state, experienced a net loss of population as people migrated, often going south to Georgia, Alabama, Mississippi, and Texas. They left in search of more land, in search of land that had not been worn out by overcultivation, and a healthier climate where malaria, typhoid, and yellow fever did not threaten.[69] Apparently almost no construction occurred between 1810 and 1830, and Kinston survived primarily because it was the county seat.[70]

By the mid-1830s a new wave of building began, with houses built by Walter Allen in the fourth block of Bright Street, by Scottish merchant Alexander Nicol on South McLewean Street, and by Dr. William Holland on Herritage Street. Holland also constructed a store on Herritage Street, as did the merchant Nicol. In the first block of King Street merchant Richard W. King built a store in the mid-1840s. In the late 1840s a steam mill, a blacksmith shop, a market house, and Franklin Dibble's carriage factory were built along the banks of the river and along Herritage Street.[71] The Episcopalians worshiped in the old 1760s Church of God Chapel, discussed previously, until 1832, when the congregation constructed a new sanctuary at the southeast corner of Caswell and Queen Streets called Saint Mary's Episcopal Church. The number of worshipers in the little town was so small that Baptists and Methodists shared the building.[72]

Kinston was governed by the Lenoir County commissioners until 1849, when a new charter of incorporation was issued, allowing a younger generation of townspeople to take over the government. By this time the town had a white population of a little over two hundred, and things were looking up. The 1849 Board of Aldermen consisted of Virginia native and lawyer John F. Wooten, farmer Pinckney Hardee, Virginia native and merchant John H. Peebles, farmer James W. Cox, and William C. Loftin, a merchant who operated one of the hotels.[73] In 1850 the first town officials—mayor Moses Patterson, town clerk Dr. Thomas Woodley, town treasurer Richard W. King, and town sergeant James B. Weeks—subdivided parts of the old town commons into lots for sale.[74]

The generation that came to power in Kinston in the 1840s was the first generation whose loyalties were not split between plantation and town. As in earlier years, Kinston remained a community of merchant-planters, men with plantations in the county and stores and town houses in Kinston, but the town had begun to acquire a stable year-round population as artisans, lawyers, and doctors located there and as planters found it more socially congenial to live in town than in the country. Planter Walter Dunn, who owned a plantation with fifty-two slaves near Kinston, lived in town and founded the town's first newspaper, the *American Advocate*, in the 1850s.[75] John C. Washington, a son of prominent merchant-planter John Washington, owned a plantation on the Herritage lands in northern Kinston, where he built a brick house, Vernon Heights, about 1850.[76] Queen and Herritage Streets were extended north in the early twentieth century on each side of the estate, now known as Vernon Hall. John C. Washington was an urban industrialist and entrepreneur who helped to develop Kinston into an industrial center. Washington was a progressive planter, and in 1852 the editor of a new state agriculture journal visited his farm and reported that Washington "is making fine improvements upon his farm, which is beautifully situated near Kinston."[77]

Carriage factory owner Franklin Dibble, who served as census taker for Kinston and Lenoir County in 1850, enumerated 184 white inhabitants and 19 free blacks living in forty-six dwellings in the village of Kinston. Approximately 253 slaves lived in town. All but a few of these households were located west of McLewean Street in the compact twelve-block area along the river.[78] They were filled with a mixture of merchants, artisans, service workers, a few wealthy farmers, wives, children, mothers-in-law, servants, and others, who made Kinston an exciting place to live. Obviously the young men who had moved their families to town heard opportunity knocking. A number of households included one or more unrelated individuals who were young artisans or professionals, probably boarding with the family. No fewer than nine merchants, most of them in their thirties and forties and owning a considerable amount of real estate and personal property, operated in Kinston in this year. In addition to Virginia merchant John H. Peebles, who moved to town in 1834, there were New York merchant Moses Patterson (who served as mayor); North Carolina natives Stephen White, William Loftin, and Richard W. King; and two merchants who were born in Germany. These merchants often had boarders, usually younger men such as clerks, who probably worked for them, or artisans or professionals. "Botanic physician" Randal Nobles (who would now be called a pharmacist), from New Hampshire, lived in the house of Moses Patterson. Anthony Seapark, a young Virginia watchmaker, young teacher Alexander Strong, and young clerk Simon B. Taylor lived in merchant Stephen White's house. John F. Wooten was the only attorney in town, but there were four physicians: Heritage W. Blunt, John L. Taylor, Thomas Woodley, and a young doctor who lived in Richard W. King's house. About 1850 Dr. John L. Taylor built himself a house and office on Caswell Street.[79]

Heads of household reported a wide variety of occupations in 1850. A number of carpenters, masons, and painters were in town to build new structures and repair old ones; coachmakers and wheelwrights built and repaired wagons and carriages; harness makers outfitted horses; shoemakers and tailors supplied clothing; and watchmakers and peddlers sold jewelry and other specialty items. One of the tailors, R. L. Collins, built a house and shop on Caswell Street about 1850.[80] Taking care of transportation were William W. Whitfield, the stage proprietor, and David Eudrick, the stage driver. Richard W. King served as sheriff, Alexander Strong was a teacher, and Loftin Nethercut was barkeeper. While most Kinston residents were born in North Carolina, a significant number listed their birthplaces as Virginia, Georgia, New York, New Hampshire, Germany, or Ireland. Of course there were proportionate numbers of women and children in town, for all but the youngest traveling artisans and professionals had families. A few households were headed by widows such as Rachel Graw and Ann King.[81]

By 1850 there were several places for itinerants to lodge. A Mrs. Perry ran a boarding house, and two hotels, the Pollock Hotel and the Loftin Hotel, stood along Queen Street. Merchant William Loftin, proprietor of the Loftin Hotel, across the street from the courthouse, housed his son, a clerk, as well as four other young men: two tailors, a harness marker, and an overseer. Such rooming houses allowed skilled craftsmen and professionals from out of state and from foreign countries to establish a base of operations in towns such as Kinston with limited housing opportunities.

The river-oriented town of this era was described as

> a village of remarkable beauty and sterling business integrity. . . . the northern half of the town was a black-jack thicket, and much of the eastern portion a chinquapin orchard, when the steamboats coursing the waters of the Neuse between Kinston and Newbern furnished the only means of transportation, and the wooden structures of antiquated style were prized as unique mansions. . . .[82]

All Aboard the Shoo Fly

In 1852 a private company was organized to build a railroad between the port of Beaufort, on the Atlantic Ocean, through Kinston to Goldsboro. In 1854 Lenoir County approved a bond issue of $50,000 to support the project. The next year the Atlantic and North Carolina Railroad was completed from New Bern to Kinston, and in 1858 it was extended to Goldsboro on the west, where it connected with the North Carolina Railroad, which opened from Goldsboro to Charlotte in 1856. Local industrialist John C. Washington served as contractor for the railroad tracks between Kinston and Goldsboro, which he built at a cost of $340,000.[83]

As the Atlantic and North Carolina Railroad sliced a diagonal swath across the northeast corner of Kinston, the riverside village slowly began to reorient itself. By midcentury Queen Street had already become the institutional avenue, with the courthouse, jail, and Episcopal church, as well as the two primary hotels, the Loftin Hotel and the Pollock Hotel.[84] The railroad depot was built where the tracks crossed Queen Street, at the corner of Blount Street. Gradually merchants moved their businesses from Herritage Street, along the river, one block east to Queen Street, and by the 1870s Queen had become the "main street." An unknown observer, remembering Kinston landmarks from around 1860, focused on Queen Street:

> The railroad station [was] at the corner of Blount and Queen. . . .near it was the St. Charles Hotel; down at the northeast corner of King and Queen Streets was the new brick courthouse; on the southeast corner of Caswell and Queen streets was the Episcopal chapel; opposite the chapel on the northwest corner. . . .was the Pollock Hotel; next to the hotel and south of it was the shop of R. L. Collins. . . .fashionable tailor; further down the [Caswell] street was the carriage and buggy factory of the Dibble brothers; just below it was the market house.[85]

Kinston's position on the major east-west trunk line connecting coastal and Piedmont towns of the state would transform Lenoir from a county of mostly self-sufficient farmers to one with a prosperous market-oriented economy. The town's continuing viability was now assured. A new spirit of enterprise swept Lenoir County between 1850 and 1860, much of it undoubtedly due to the arrival of the railroad. The first trains on the line were the day passenger train the Shoo Fly and the night passenger train the Cannon Ball.[86]

In 1860 census enumerator Alex Fields found 1,333 free inhabitants living in 136 households when he made the rounds of Kinston, almost triple the population of a decade earlier. This included 662 whites, 635 slaves, and 36 free blacks.[87] Kinston had become one of thirteen North Carolina towns with a population of over 1,000. A number of new merchants had joined those operating in 1850, including German merchants Aaron Baer and K. Baer, Bavarian merchant Moses Einstine, J. G. Herring, Evan Williams, S. B. West, and others. In addition to John F. Wooten, three other lawyers practiced in Kinston, including John Washington's son George Washington, a lawyer who had moved back to Kinston from New York. Besides physician Thomas Woodley, four other doctors and one dentist practiced in Kinston. Walter Dunn published the town newspaper, housing in his household three young printers who probably worked for him. The town had four jewelers: Leonard and Edward Friend, born in Bavaria, and Joseph and E. F. Gilbert, born in Connecticut. Two female milliners, Narcissus Syndam and Amanda M. F. Lee, created finery for the ladies. One confectioner, one cabinetmaker from Maryland, one silver plater from Maryland, and even an artist, E. H. Chadwick, worked in town. In addition to established farmers Pinckney Hardee and Richard W. King, four other well-to-do farmers lived in town: Amos Harvey, Reuben Barrow, William Fields, and John Stubbs. Three railroad employees, agent Thomas Blakely, ticket agent A. C. Wadsworth, and section master M. W. Albertson, resided in Kinston.[88]

Evidently the largest industry in town was the coach and carriage business, with eighteen coachmakers, some of whom worked at the Dibble Carriage Works, as well as five harness makers, three coach trimmers, and two coach painters. A number of these artisans, including James H. Dibble himself, were born in Connecticut. In 1858 brothers John C. and George Washington opened a shoe factory, where, according to tradition, they employed slaves and Yankees. They are said to have built employee housing on Tower Hill Road, northeast of town, which became known as Yankee Row.[89] Bookkeepers, clerks, blacksmiths, wheelwrights, postmen, the town clerk, a druggist, hotel keepers, tinners, master carpenters, carpenters, house painters, and shoemakers all lived and worked in town.

During the decade the Baptists and Methodists finally built their own churches (they had been sharing the Episcopal church prior to this period). In 1852 the Methodists constructed the Caswell Street Methodist Church, believed to have been the first Methodist sanctuary built in the county. After it burned in 1858, the Methodists began a new frame sanctuary at the southeast corner of Caswell and Independent Streets. The frame Greek Revival-style building has a front pedimented gable, but its original windows have been replaced and an entrance portico added. Old-time town residents claimed that the building served as a hospital during the Civil War.[90] In 1858 the Missionary Baptist congregation built a frame church at the corner of Bright and McLewean streets and a parsonage next door at 211 South McLewean Street. In the early twentieth century, after the Baptists had built a new sanctuary, an African American congregation had the old sanctuary moved to the northwest corner of Tiffany and

Fig. 2.43. White Rock Church, 516 Thompson Street, Kinston, 1858. This was originally the Missionary Baptist Church. (Photo, M. Ruth Little, North Carolina Division of Archives and History)

Thompson Streets, where it is still in use and known as the White Rock Church *(Fig. 2.43)*. Henry and Lillie Archbell purchased the parsonage in the 1890s and made their home there, thus it is better known as the Archbell House.[91] The Disciples of Christ denomination organized their first North Carolina Sunday school in Kinston in 1849, known as the Church School of the Kinston Church of Christ.[92]

"Wooden Structures of Antiquated Style"

The "wooden structures of antiquated style" noted by visitors to the bustling town of Kinston on the eve of the Civil War were gradually replaced by new frame and brick buildings during the transformation of the next one hundred years.[93] Not only is the antebellum landscape physically lost, but almost no architectural legacy survives. From available information, it seems that a wide variety of modestly stylish residences graced the streets of the village. In addition to the Bright-Peebles House, built in the 1790s, three antebellum houses still stand. The two-story wooden house at 300 South McLewean Street was built in the 1830s for Scottish merchant Alexander Nicol. In the early twentieth century contractor R. L. Blalock transformed it into an ornate Queen Anne-style dwelling by adding arched chimneys, richly detailed moldings, and a wraparound porch with a corner gazebo. Blalock's residence demonstrated his building skills, but the house lost all traces of its original appearance.[94] Across the street at 211 South McLewean Street, the parsonage's quietly dignified Greek Revival styling reflects the reserve proper for a Baptist minister's house *(Fig. 2.44)*. The third survival is a two-story hipped-roof frame house said to have been General P. G. T. Beauregard's headquarters during the Civil War. It originally stood at the corner

Fig. 2.44. Missionary Baptist Church Parsonage, later the Archbell House, 211 South McLewean Street, Kinston, 1858 (Photo, M. Ruth Little, North Carolina Division of Archives and History)

Fig. 2.45. General Beauregard's Headquarters, 210 East Blount Street, Kinston, circa 1860 (Photo, M. Ruth Little, North Carolina Division of Archives and History)

of King and McLewean streets, but was moved a few blocks north to 210 East Blount Street *(Fig. 2.45)*.[95] The main block has a Greek Revival character similar to that of the Baptist parsonage; the front wing is probably a post-war addition.

John C. Washington's Vernon Heights survives only in a documentary photo *(Fig. 2.46)*. This mid-nineteenth-century rural villa located north of Capitola Street was a two-story brick house with a hipped roof and probably had a Greek Revival-style front porch before Jesse Grainger remodeled it in the Italianate

Fig. 2.46. Vernon Heights, home of John C. Washington and later Jesse Grainger, 117 West Capitola Avenue, Kinston, 1850s (Heritage Place, Lenoir Community College)

style in the 1890s. Prior to Washington's ownership, Richard Caswell's plantation house, The Hill, stood here. The house in the photograph betrays no hint of eighteenth-century construction; apparently Washington completely rebuilt the earlier house.

Railroad Gothic

The Shoo Fly and the Cannon Ball not only carried people and goods to Raleigh, New Bern, and points beyond; they also brought the outside world of trade, ideas, and fashion to Lenoir County, which had long been an isolated area with utilitarian architectural traditions. Lenoir County looked west to the newly emerging urban centers for the latest fashion in architecture. In Raleigh, in the late 1840s, Christ Episcopal Church went up on Capitol Square in the Gothic Revival style, built of stone with a tower and pointed windows. Saint Mary's School for Girls built a new wooden chapel in the Gothic style in 1856. For houses, the style was spread by builders' pattern books such as *The Architecture of Country Houses* by New York architect Andrew Jackson Downing. During the 1850s the tasteful new picturesque style appeared in North Carolina in towns and along the railroad lines linking urban areas. In eastern market centers such as Edenton and Tarboro a few sophisticated clients had picturesque residences adapted from the new pattern books.

Perhaps it is not surprising that one of the first houses built in the depot settlement of LaGrange is a Gothic-style cottage *(Fig. 2.47)*. This section of LaGrange was part of Moseley Hall plantation, a portion of which was subdivided and sold in 1848. Council Wooten received this parcel and is believed to have built the house soon after the railroad came through in 1858.[96] Perhaps the builder hired by the Wootens to build their new house at the LaGrange depot in western Lenoir County had one of the new architectural pattern books. The house uses the cottage form—one-story with an attic—and board-and-batten exterior siding made popular in the books. The win-

Fig. 2.47. Wooten-Timberlake House, 204 West Railroad Street, LaGrange, circa 1860 (Photo, Tony Vaughn, North Carolina Division of Archives and History

dows have pointed caps, and the steeply pitched roof is accented with spiky wooden trim supplied by a sash and planing mill. The decorative mantels inside the center hall plan house, containing Italianate ornament, were probably ordered from a mantelworks and shipped by rail to the house site.

Chapter Three

Civil War, Reconstruction, and the Days of "King Cotton"

Fig. 3.1. "The Battle of Kinston, fought 14th December, 1862." engraving by E.P. Forbes, *Harper's Weekly* (North Carolina Collection, University of N.C. Library at Chapel Hill)

The years of the Civil War, from 1861 to 1865, and Reconstruction, from 1865, when Federal troops occupied the South, to 1877, when they withdrew, profoundly affected every Lenoir County resident, white and black, rich and poor. When the war began in 1861, Kinston benefited economically, as businesses such as the Washington shoe factory, the Queen Street bakery, and Webb Carriage Works shipped shoes, hardtack, and horseshoes by rail to the Confederate army. But the war's ultimate effect was destructive. Because it was a strategically located Confederate supply depot, Kinston was occupied for a short time in December 1862 by the troops of Union general John Foster. By the time Foster's soldiers arrived, almost all of the local white men of working age had been conscripted into the Confederate army, and much of the rest of the population had fled to safer locations. For example, Kinston residents John and Harriet Peebles evacuated to Goldsboro, and planter James Wood and his family, who lived on the Neuse River in the Falling Creek section, went to Greensboro, North Carolina.

A depiction of the so-called First Battle of Kinston, which took place on December 14, 1862, illustrates the character of the countryside around Kinston *(Fig. 3.1 See previous page).* The Confederates had built fortifications south of town along the north bank of the Neuse River but were driven back after sporadic fighting.[1] Not only had many of the whites left the area, but a good many slaves had run to freedom behind the Northern lines after Union forces captured New Bern in March 1862. Outside of Kinston, the countryside of Lenoir County was devastated by the war, for the slave labor on which its agricultural economy depended gradually ceased, and a great deal of military activity occurred in the area *(Fig. 3.2).* By the end of 1862 both large and small farmers were affected. The county was dotted with abandoned farms, empty fields, and plundered buildings. The effect of Foster's Raid, described by a Union army chaplain, was that "Signs of war were visible on every side. The fences had been destroyed by our men as they marched and bivouacked. The fields were tracked and torn by artillery or army wagons."[2] Another Union soldier wrote that "Wide fields remained uncultivated, and in not a few cases ripened crops were left to perish unharvested. Vast barns and granaries were left entirely empty. On the most extensive plantations but few signs of life were visible."[3] Agricultural operations, especially on the larger farms, had almost ceased by the end of the war, the result of both neglect and the ravages of soldiers.[4]

The ironclad vessel, CSS *Neuse,* built at Whitehall in nearby Wayne County, was brought by Confederate troops to Kinston in November 1863 for finish construction. In April 1864 the vessel embarked on a voyage on the Neuse River and was grounded on a sandbar, where it sat until the spring of 1865, when the river level rose enough to allow it to travel. At that time Union forces were within five miles of Kinston, and in order to keep the ironclad from falling into Union hands, the Confederates loaded it with explosives and set it afire. It sank and remained in the river until 1963, when the hull was raised and moved to a site west of Kinston, where it remains on display *(Fig. 3.3).*

On March 8, 1865, Lenoir County underwent its final battle of the war, known variously as the Battle of Wyse Fork and the Battle of Southwest Creek *(Fig. 3.4).* Confederate forces successfully defended themselves against portions of General John M. Schofield's Union army but then retreated to Goldsboro to await orders from General Joseph Johnston. Kinston was thus left to be occupied by Union troops once again. Dr. John Cobb's house, known as the Cobb-King-Humphrey House, on U.S. Highway 70 near Kelly's Mill Pond, was used as a headquarters and field hospital by Union troops. The attic of the two-story frame farmhouse, which still stands, has soldiers' names scratched into the plastered walls *(Fig. 3.5).*[5]

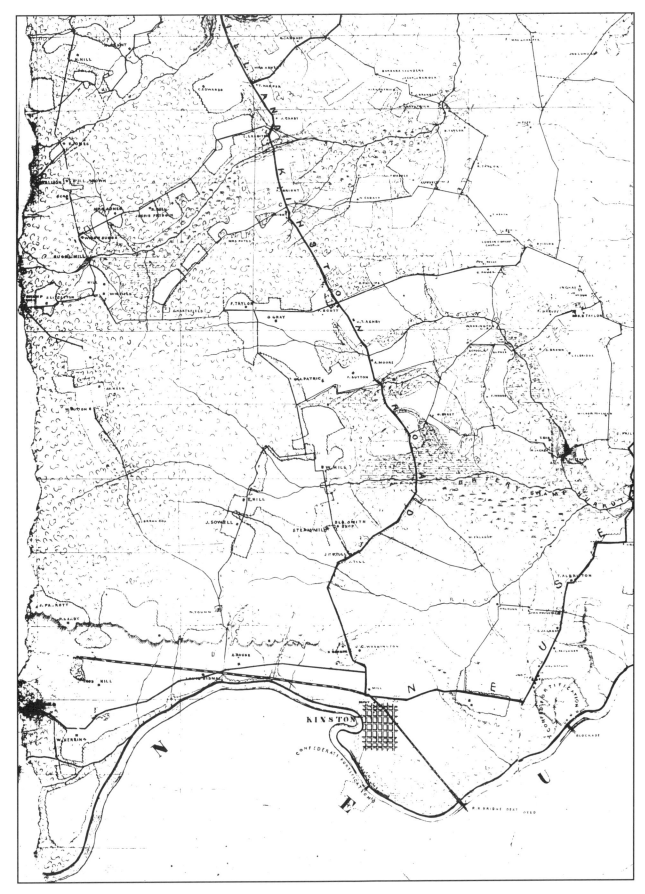

Fig. 3.2. Detail of 1863 Koerner Military Survey Field Map of central Lenoir County, drawn for the Confederate Army (North Carolina Collection, University of N.C. Library at Chapel Hill)

Fig. 3.3. Model of the Ram Neuse, Ram Neuse Historic Museum, Kinston (Heritage Place, Lenoir Community College)

Fig. 3.4. Battle of Wyse Fork near Kinston, March 8, 1865. Engraving from *Leslie's Civil War in the United States 1861-1865.* (North Carolina Collection, University of N.C. Library at Chapel Hill)

Fig. 3.5. Cobb-King-Humphrey House depicted in Leslie's engraving, Southwood vicinity, mid-nineteenth century (Photo, Jim Shell, 1969, Heritage Place, Lenoir Community College)

One Lenoir County family's experience at the end of the war evokes the experiences of many others. A foraging party raided John Tull's plantation near Kinston in 1865. Tull was nearly bankrupt after the war but managed to retain ownership of most of his property. He later submitted a claim to the Federal government stating that twenty-one horses and mules, 1,000 bushels of corn, and a number of other goods valued at $4,300 were taken from him. His agricultural production fell from 10,000 bushels of Indian corn in 1860 to 1,000 bushels in 1870 and from 125 bales of cotton to 30 bales during the same period. In 1869 Tull sold off 2,000 acres of his plantation, including the overseer's house, and moved away.[6]

Agriculture

Just as the largest plantation in the county, the Tull Plantation, was subdivided after the war, throughout the remainder of the nineteenth century Lenoir's other plantations were slowly split up into small farms as the county adjusted to the nonslave economy. Farms continued to increase in number and decrease in size as more and more families became tenants. In 1860 there were approximately 600 farms; by 1870, 641 farms, valued at less than one-third the value of farms in 1860. In 1880 slightly more than half of the approximately 1,500 farms in Lenoir County were tenant farms. The census statistics do not separate white and black tenant farmers, but they do state that 211 farms in Lenoir County were being rented for cash and 637 were being rented for product shares.[7] Landowners after the Civil War usually did not have the resources to hire more than a few laborers to work their farmland, so they rented the land to tenant farmers either for cash or for a share of the crops, a system known as sharecropping. By 1900 slightly more than one-third of the county's farms were owner cultivated. About one-third were farmed by white tenants, and the other one-third by black tenants.[8]

After the war, the value of many farms hit rock bottom. The value of Frederick Greene Taylor's farm, for example, plummeted from $5,000 value in 1860 to $400 in 1870. The number of county acres under cultivation dropped from 111,000 acres to 72,000, about one-third less than in 1860. Surprisingly, however, agriculture recovered rapidly in Lenoir County, and by about 1870 optimism and cash were once again available to at least some county farmers who had adjusted to the postwar economy, which centered on "King Cotton," the cash crop of the period. Farmers gradually became part of the cash economy. More farms raised a cash crop than in the antebellum era, and nearly every farm grew some cotton for sale. Total crop production in the county had nearly recovered to its 1860 levels by 1870. Although the production of large farmers such as John Tull and middling farmers like Frederick Greene Taylor suffered, the number and productivity of small farms increased. Almost 5,000 bales of cotton were produced in 1870, only about 500 bales fewer than in 1860. Rice production actually went up to 27,600 pounds, from the 12,270 pounds grown in 1860. A small amount of tobacco was also grown.[9] Production of rosin and turpentine was an important industry until about 1880, when the resources were exhausted. By 1880, 23 percent of the tilled land was in cotton production, generating more than 8,000 bales of cotton.[10]

Cotton remained "King" during the 1880s, but few farmers prospered. From 1872 to 1878 an average of more than 5,500 bales of cotton were shipped out of Kinston each year. By 1878 the annual amount had doubled from that shipped out before the Civil War. Yet declining prices of crops kept farmers from getting ahead, causing large numbers of them to lose their farms and keeping many of them as tenants on farms owned by others. Cotton prices dropped from twenty-five cents a pound in 1868 to twelve cents in the 1870s, to nine cents in the 1880s, and finally to five cents a pound in 1894. Costs of fertilizer and other farm essentials stayed high, as did railroad freight charges.[11] Cotton remained the main cash crop on Lenoir County farms until the late 1880s, however, with Indian corn, rice, and truck farming of fruits and vegetables of secondary importance. In 1880 a little more than 8,000 bales of cotton was produced, and almost 96,000 pounds of rice. Tobacco had increased from a trace amount in 1870 to 13,500 pounds on forty-five acres.[12] The crop lien system, under which a merchant sold a farmer farm supplies and provisions on credit and then was repaid, with interest, at harvest time, perpetuated the farmers' dependence. Constant debt compelled farmers to grow cash crops—cotton and tobacco—instead of growing subsistence crops such as corn and vegetables, which would feed their families. Consequently the subsistence farm of earlier times, which produced nearly everything the family needed, gave way to the cash crop farm, which forced families to sell their products to buy food.

Country stores, which supplied farmers with seeds, fertilizer, food, credit, mail delivery, and a link to the community, stood all over Lenoir County in the late nineteenth century. A period store still standing is the Hardy Brothers Store at Institute (*Fig. 3.6*). Arden W. Taylor built the one-and-one-half-story frame building with a gable front as a general merchandise store about 1892. Taylor had moved to Institute from his home near Hookerton, in Greene County. During most of the twentieth century the store was operated by the Hardy brothers and also served as the Institute post office. Although the store was moved across the road from its original site about 1975, it is still in commercial use, until recently as an office for Hardy Oil Company, and retains its chamfered support posts, board-and-batten front door, and counters made of heart pine.[13]

Farmers made a determined effort to improve their lot. The Lousin Swamp Agricultural Club was organized in north Lenoir County in the late 1870s. Its activities were published in the Kinston Journal. In the 1880s a number of farmers excavated their marl deposits, which had been praised for their high lime content since the antebellum era, for use as fertilizer. Local chapters of the Grange and the Farmer's Alliance, national organizations, were established in the late nineteenth century to share information on the latest agricultural innovations and to improve farmers' business practices. William Henry Worth, purchaser of part of the Tull Plantation when it was broken up in 1869, was active in all three organizations. By 1889 Worth had become the state business agent for the Farmer's Alliance and supervised purchases of fertilizer, household and farm equipment for Alliance members throughout the state. J. M. Mewborne of Lenoir County belonged

Fig. 3.6. Hardy Brothers Store, Institute, circa 1892 (Photo, Robbie D. Jones, North Carolina Division of Archives and History)

to the state Farmer's Alliance executive committee.[14]

Reconstruction Housing

During Reconstruction most farm families made do with their prewar dwellings, and the few new houses reflected the diminished circumstances of the time. After the war some veterans lucky enough to own land built new houses and started families. Others moved into new tenant houses constructed by landlords. Likely the construction boom caused by the increasing number of separate tenant households changed construction methods, favoring house forms that could be constructed more quickly and with less-complicated roof joinery than earlier house types.

Whether owner built or built for tenants, homes of log construction remained a cheaper alternative to sawn frame houses. Using the easy technique of round-log construction with saddle-notched corners, which took less effort than hewing the logs to a square shape, one family in the Pleasant Hill area built their one-room log house, now known as the Sally Taylor House, about 1870. Perhaps typical at one time, log houses, especially round-log ones, are now rare in the county. As in many earlier Lenoir houses, fat lightwood blocks (whose sap made them resistant to rot and termites) support the house.[15] Although the gable-end chimney, probably of mud-and-stick construction, has disappeared and the house has been adapted for use as a barn, this is one of the best-preserved examples of late log dwelling construction in Lenoir County.

Another round-log house standing in Lenoir County is the Amos Stroud Log House near Pink Hill, apparently built by Amos Stroud (1842-1894) in the third quarter of the nineteenth century. The roof of the side-gabled house extends in front to engage a piazza and in the rear to cover the shed rooms *(Fig. 3.7)*. The generous overhang on the chimney end would have sheltered the original mud-and-stick chimney, but when the house was moved a short distance in the early 1900s, a brick flue replaced this original chimney. The round logs are fitted together tightly and saddle-notched at the corners. For further stability, vertical locking strips are pegged into the logs at the corners. All the walls except the porch wall are covered with weatherboards.[16]

Lenoir County people continued to build Greek Revival-style houses, more often associated with the antebellum era, for some ten to fifteen years after the war. The Sutton-Ivy-Dawson House, a Greek Revival cottage, is virtually identical to cottages, such as the Will Sutton House, built before the war in every respect but the decorative trim *(Fig. 3.8)*. The front door with its Gothic-arched panels and the pedimented caps over the windows are features that borrow from the fascination with Gothic Revival and Italianate architecture that had just begun to reach Lenoir County on the eve of the Civil War. Family tradition holds that Thomas Sutton built the house in the 1870s for his daughter Katie.[17]

Fig. 3.7. Amos Stroud Log House, Pink Hill vicinity, circa 1860 (Photo, Robbie D. Jones, North Carolina Division of Archives and History)

Fig. 3.8. Sutton-Ivy-Dawson House, LaGrange vicinity, 1870s (Photo, Robbie D. Jones, North Carolina Division of Archives and History)

New sawn-frame houses often resembled antebellum houses, with some important differences. The piazza house, a form that could accommodate housing at both ends of the economic spectrum, lost its most distinctive feature, the engaged piazza, during the 1870s and 1880s. Builders began to construct the piazza as a separate attachment to the house rather than as an integral part of the main roof. The resulting cottages with attached porches perhaps reflect the changes in construction methods. Elias Liverman Hazelton (1845-1920), a native of Pitt County, fought in the Civil War, then worked in a printing shop in Kinston. In 1871 he married Betty Coward of Greene County, and they settled on a farm located near the Greene County line in northeast Lenoir County. He is said to have named the nearby crossroads Hugo after his favorite author, Victor Hugo. Known as the Squire of Hugo, Hazelton farmed, taught school, and served as a justice of the peace.[18] The cottage he and his wife built is a one-and-one-half-story house with a hall and parlor plan heated by exterior end chimneys, with smaller unheated rear shed rooms and an attached front porch. The stairway to the attic rooms rises from the rear shed.

The Will Worthington House, built about 1870 near Graingers, is a stylish and functional version of the attached-porch cottage, with a central front gable and flanking dormer windows, which give it a picturesque Gothic Revival appearance *(Fig. 3.9)*. The main front rooms are heated with exterior gable-end chimneys and the rear shed rooms are unheated. The kitchen and dining room ell, located on the side and reached by the hipped front piazza, illustrates the continuation of traditional kitchen placement in late-nineteenth-century Lenoir County houses.

A popular new type of farmhouse in the postwar period was the gable-and-wing house, consisting of a side-gable main block with a front-gabled wing projecting from the facade. Seth West built such a house at West's Crossroads, in northeast Lenoir County, on his 1,500 acre farm in 1876 *(Fig. 3.10)*. The expansive two-story single-pile house with a hipped roof reflects his affluence as a farmer, entrepreneur, and merchant. An attached porch wraps around the projecting front wing, containing the entrance hall. Seth West, born in 1851, raised corn, cotton, and tobacco on his farm and operated a general store, which still stands beside the house. The one-and-one-half-story store has a gable front, a batten door, and a single window in the front *(Fig. 3.11)*. West, who engaged in the lumber business on his farm, later moved to Craven County to start up a lucrative sawmilling business.[19]

Another popular type of farmhouse in this period was the I-house. Farmer John Samuel Davis and his wife, Mary Carr Davis, had their Victorian I-house built in the Moss Hill vicinity about 1882, although John died before the house was complete. The I-house, so named in the twentieth century, is a two-story, one-room-deep house type built by prosperous North Carolinians in the late nineteenth and early twentieth centuries.[20] The tall, boxy form of the Mary Carr Davis House is enhanced by the pedimented two-story entrance porch. Such simple trim as the turned porch

Fig. 3.9. Will Worthington House, Graingers vicinity, circa 1870 (Photo, Robbie D. Jones, North Carolina Division of Archives and History)

posts, the diamond-shaped ventilator in the front gable, the louvered shutters and the transom and sidelights around the front door gives the residence middle-class respectability *(Fig. 3.12)*.

No doubt the most ostentatious estate created in Lenoir County during the "King Cotton" era was Cedar Dell. In 1876 William LaFayette Kennedy purchased an elegant side-hall brick house built by the Herring family in the early 1800s. W. L. Kennedy became one of the largest landowners in Lenoir County, director of two banks, and the owner of Coahoma Mill, a water-powered grist mill. About 1885 he transformed the stately antebellum house into a richly ornamented Victorian mansion worthy of his planter and financier status and named the estate Cedar Dell.[21] He added balancing rooms on the other side of the hall, with a large bay window, an Eastlake Gothic-style

Fig. 3.10. Seth West House, West's Crossroads, 1876 (Photo, Robbie D. Jones, North Carolina Division of Archives and History)

Fig. 3.11. Seth West Store, West's Crossroads, circa 1900 (Photo, Robbie D. Jones, North Carolina Division of Archives and History)

Fig. 3.12. Mary Carr Davis House, Moss Hill vicinity, circa 1882. The house was attractively landscaped with a picket fence, small trees, and a profusion of vines climbing up the turned porch columns. Mary Carr Davis stands in front, holding onto the front gate, and her children and one grandchild are ranged along the fence. The small building at the far right was apparently the detached kitchen. (Photo, 1895, North Carolina Division of Archives and History)

front porch with wrought-iron roof cresting, Eastlake-style false dormer windows across the front roof, a slate roof, and paneled and crenellated chimneys *(Fig. 3.13)*. Leaving intact most of the elegant Federal-style mantels and woodwork of the original house, Kennedy had the interior of the new addition and the old side hall—now a center hall—finished with a heavy Eastlake-style staircase, an elliptical arched screen separating the front and rear halls, and Eastlake mantels and mirrored overmantels in the new rooms *(Fig. 3.14)*.

As in the antebellum period, many specialized outbuildings still clustered around the farmhouse. People spent a good deal of the day out of doors or in outbuildings cooking, eating, washing, churning, and performing many other tasks. People even took naps out of doors. James Lewis Jones, who grew up on a farm near Pink Hill, fondly recalled the sycamore trees that stood across the road from his house when he was a boy about 1880.

> They made a most wonderful shade and this was called the coolest place in the whole yard. It must have been for there each one of us boys would enjoy an hour of good sleeping just after [midday] dinner every day. At that time we usually had one hour from work to rest and relax. Each one of us had a wide plank we used as sleeping boards. We would place one end of the plank on a large root of a sycamore, thereby putting the board in a fine, slanting position and creating a wonderful spot in which to rest, relax and sleep.[22]

"Cedar Dell"
House of Mr. & Mrs. Wm. Kennedy *1911*

Fig. 3.13. Cedar Dell, Seven Springs vicinity, early 1800s; circa 1885. In 1912 the William LaFayette Kennedys donated the estate to the Baptists for use as an orphanage. Now known as the Kennedy Home, it is still a children's home. (Photo, 1911, North Carolina Division of Archives and History)

In the late 1800s, as the area was being transformed with new dwellings, new churches and schools were under construction at crossroads throughout the county. One of the best-preserved country churches of the era is Daly's Chapel Free Will Baptist Church, near Strabane in southwest Lenoir County. Its gable-front form, frame construction, and lack of a steeple are common in church construction of the period. Pedimented surrounds embellish the double front door and the windows, and pilasters accent the corners of the building *(Fig. 3.15)*.

Many small wooden schools were built in the county in the later years of the nineteenth century to replace one-room log schoolhouses. Typical of these was the Moss Hill School , established about1868 in the Moss Hill community of western Lenoir County. In 1890, when the log schoolhouse burned, the school moved into a sturdy two-room frame building which continued in use until 1917, when the school closed. Many other one-room schools, for both white and African American children, were in use into the 1930s.

Fig. 3.14. Center Hall of Cedar Dell. (Photo, 1911, North Carolina Division of Archives and History)

Fig. 3.15. Daly's Chapel Free Will Baptist Church, Strabane vicinity, late 1800s (Photo, Robbie D. Jones, North Carolina Division of Archives and History)

A Parallel Reality: African Americans in the Countryside

What became of the more than 5,000 slaves in the county who were set free by President Abraham Lincoln in 1863? Some of them left the county, never to return. Many African Americans emigrated to the Plains states—particularly Kansas—to buy land and establish farms. It is said that thousands of blacks, termed Exodusters, left North Carolina for Kansas and Indiana in the 1870s.[23] By 1879, according to a story in the *Kinston Journal*, the exodus to Kansas was subsiding: "I. F. Aldridge, a colored teacher near Kinston, writes us an article opposing the Kansas movement, but as the feeling seems to be dying out we omit the publication."[24] Others moved to settlements specifically founded for blacks, such as James City near New Bern, established during the Civil War.[25] Closer to home, Kinston's growth as a mercantile and industrial center drew blacks as well.

But many African Americans stayed on the farms where they had been slaves, working at the same jobs—cook, gardener, agricultural laborer—that they had performed as slaves, but now working for wages or just to earn their keep *(Fig. 3.16)*. Many others moved to new farms, seldom as owners, mostly as tenants. A small 1860s tintype once in the Whitfield Grady family's possession, shows "Silvia," who, according to family history, was born a slave on Grady's six-hundred-acre plantation in Woodington Township and remained with the family after the war *(Fig. 3.17)*. Silvia's right arm rests awkwardly on the photography studio's corner tableau as she stands in middle-class dress before a romantic backdrop of branches and mist. Who was Silvia? In 1850 Whitfield Grady owned ten slaves, six of whom were female; the six females included mulatto girls aged sixteen and eighteen and an eight-year-old child. Perhaps Silvia is one of them. After the war no Silvia is listed in Grady's household nor in the households of his sons Lewis and Durham.[26] Silvia may have married or gone to live with one of Grady's daughters, possibly Sarah; or, contrary to Grady family lore, she may have moved on, leaving only a tintype to mark her presence.

Most county blacks spent their lives as tenant farmers. One such family was the Doves in Woodington Township, who worked the Jesse Harper Farm. A descendant of Wiley Dove, who married Mary Jarman about 1880, described Wiley as

> fortunate enough to learn how to read but not to write. The toil and tasks of the farm drew sweat from his brow. He toiled from sunrise to sunset, and gave praise to God as he retired the mule and plow. He wore overalls and chewed Brown Mule Chewing Tobacco most of the time. Mary wore high necked blouses, long skirts and laced up shoes. She always wrapped her long hair in a ball on top of her head. Mary was best noted as the farm's midwife. She delivered the landlord's children, her grandchildren, and some of her great grandchildren. She also enjoyed dipping Sweet Lori-Lords snuff.[27]

Other African Americans moved to Kinston or LaGrange to find community and work. Those who remained in the country worked as tenant farmers and farm laborers and sometimes were able to buy property. They established communities and by the 1880s were building churches, Masonic lodges, and houses for themselves.

Property ownership among African Americans was extremely rare. The only Lenoir County black landowner listed in *Branson's North Carolina Business Directory* in the 1890s was Allen Arnold, who lived in Kinston Township. It is not known how many acres Arnold owned, but statistics for North Carolina farms in 1910 list white farmers as owning an average 116.7 acres per farm. African Americans who owned their farms had an average of only 55.8 acres per farm. In communities like Sand Hill and Falling Creek there were many African American residents, but African American land ownership was limited in both places. In Sand Hill blacks owned a mere 848 of the township's 12,319 acres. In Falling Creek, in spite of there being ninety-six black polls and seventy-six white polls, whites owned nearly 20,000 acres of the township, and blacks only 376 acres.[28]

The few African Americans who owned their farms usually divided the acreage among their descendants. The resulting parcels were known as heir land. In some cases the grantor would include a caveat forbidding the sale of the land outside the family. Eliza Dawson, a former slave who bought sixty-eight acres north of Kinston in 1872, saw heir land as a way to ensure family

Fig. 3.16. Uncle Ike Davis (1864-1952), lived on the Jesse Jackson Plantation throughout his life and cared for the Jackson children (Heritage Place, Lenoir Community College)

Fig. 3.17. Silvia, a former slave (1860s tintype from the Smith-Grady Family Papers, J. Y. Joyner Library, East Carolina University Manuscript Collection)

harmony and perpetual ownership of land. Eliza Dawson's 1894 will stipulated that the land could never be sold, and that her daughters were to receive a lifetime interest in the part of the property where they had built houses. Eventually, with successive generations, the security of this type of ownership was overshadowed by the resulting family disputes over usage of the land.[29] A few African American heir land estates, including Eliza Dawson's tract and the Moore family estate near Institute, still exist in Lenoir County.

In addition to farming, rural African Americans in Lenoir County diversified their livelihoods with other businesses. Shinglemakers Tony Wells and John Hatch went into partnership and sold their shingles in New Bern. Wells borrowed Hatch's canoe one winter day in 1880 and paddled to Duck Creek in Craven County to get a load of wood for shingles. He was seen on his way to New Bern that afternoon but, according to reports, never reached there and was presumed to have drowned.[30] For Wells and Hatch and the other blacks who ventured beyond farming, entrepreneurship, whether it meant gathering lumber miles from town, traveling by water in flimsy boats, or obtaining marl for fertilizer from the beds near the Neuse River, could be perilous.

African American Architecture

By 1906 African Americans had established twelve schools and three churches in Lenoir County's townships.[31] A handful of these important community centers have survived, one of which is the Sand Hill Free Will Baptist Church in Sand Hill Township. The West family, white landowners in the area, sold the church lot to the African American congregation in 1888. The church, said to have been built in 1889, has a distinctive front facade with a cluster of three towers influenced by Gothic Revival design *(Fig. 3.18)*. A prominent characteristic of many African American sanctuaries in North Carolina is the use of large front corner towers. In 1972 the frame walls of Sand Hill Church were covered with brick veneer. Behind the church lies the cemetery, lined with twentieth-century whitewashed concrete vaults. The vaults bear inscriptions of birth and death dates and, occasionally, epitaphs by Herman Dunn, who was the church sexton for over sixty years.

Another important rural African American landmark is the Capstone Lodge in Graingers, the only turn-of-the-twentieth-century black Masonic lodge known to survive in the county *(Fig. 3.19)*. The two-story front-gable frame building still has its Masonic insignia at each gable end. It also has original leaded stained-glass windows at the second story, denoting the former prestige of this building. The African American community in the Graingers vicinity, as in other areas of the county, owned only a fraction of the 21,162 acres comprising Graingers and Contentnea Neck Township yet was substantial enough to support a fraternal lodge.[32]

Rural freedmen settled in Woodington, Falling Creek, and the other communities in farmhouses of four types: converted slave dwellings, tenant cottages built by whites for black tenants, houses built by blacks themselves, and houses originally built for white families and later bought or occupied by blacks. No slave dwellings are known to have survived. Most of the tenant houses were small frame and log cottages, many with mud-and-stick chimneys, now demolished or greatly altered. Some African American familes were able to buy property in the decades after the Civil War, but few of their stories are known outside their own family circles. One family whose story and house have survived is the Daughetys, who built the Alonzo Daughety House in the Rivermont area south of Kinston in the late 1800s *(Fig. 3.20)*. The weatherboarded "story-and-a-jump" house has one brick chimney and no windows on the ends. The kitchen and dining room are located in the rear ell. Large outbuildings on the property—a two-story pack barn and a mule barn—remain, showing the early-twentieth-century prosperity of this family. The Daughetys owned the farm for several generations.

At the turn of the twentieth century Johnny and Ninnie Bryant contracted Will Donald, an African American builder, to construct a two-story frame house for them on their farm outside Grifton *(Fig. 3.21)*. The Bryant

Fig. 3.18. Sand Hill Free Will Baptist Church, Sandhill vicinity, 1889 (Photo, Robbie D. Jones, North Carolina Division of Archives and History)

Fig. 3.19. Capstone Masonic Lodge, Graingers, circa 1900 (Photo, Robbie D. Jones, North Carolina Division of Archives and History)

Fig. 3.20. Alonzo Daughety House, Rivermont vicinity, late 1800s (Photo, Robbie D. Jones, North Carolina Division of Archives and History)

Fig. 3.21. Johnny and Ninnie Bryant House, Grifton vicinity, circa 1900 (Photo, Robbie D. Jones, North Carolina Division of Archives and History)

House, which is still owned by the family, has lost its original porch but retains many of its exterior features, particularly the two-story projecting front bay window and the high-hipped standing-seam metal roof capping the house. A frame pack barn and a concrete-block pump house are still in place.[33]

Kinston's Bustling Depot and Shady Streets, 1865-1900

Kinston was occupied by Union forces from the end of 1862 into 1863 and again in 1865. One Union soldier described the town in a letter to his cousin on June 9, 1863, as "a charming little place situated on the Neuse River and beautifully laid off. The streets are wide with beautiful shade trees on either side. The houses are mostly of cottage style with large flower gardens in front."[34] Townsfolk bitterly resented the occupation, and some of the spirited citizens resisted indignities. Capturing memories of local resistance, Harriet Lane recalled years later:

> My aunt Harriet Peebles was a woman of great spirit and the Yankees found her difficult to subdue. She was recently widowed and her husband had been buried in a bricked-up grave. The grave was kind of a vault under the ground, and it was bricked across the bottom, the sides, and the top. The Yankees searched all such graves for treasure and this one had not escaped their notice. It contained the body of Mr. John Peebles, but it did not escape. The Yankees put the coffin of another man into this grave on top of the coffin of Mr. Peebles. Mrs. Peebles indignantly moved the dead Yankee from the tomb, and had it bricked again. The next day the coffin of the Yankee was again put into her grave. Again she removed it, and still again, but when she removed the Yankee coffin from above her dead husband the third time she sent word to the officer in command that if she found the dead Yankee in her husband's grave again, she would have the Yankee's coffin thrown into the river. The offense was not repeated **(Fig. 3.22)**.[35]

Fig. 3.22. Photo of Harriet Cobb Peebles (1822-1898). (Lenoir County Historical Association, Kinston)

Although Kinston was not plundered like much of the countryside, the community suffered much property damage and disruption from the Civil War. As the market for the county's agricultural products, Kinston felt the impact of the war profoundly. The census taker counted 1,100 people in 1870, a decline in population from the 1,333 white and black inhabitants in 1860, yet these people lived in 235 households, some 100 more than were listed in 1860. Many of these new households may have been set up by recently freed African Americans.[36]

The war's bitter legacy reverberated well into the twentieth century. The Confederate cause continued to be championed by southerners, including a notable Kinstonian, Lillie Vause W. Archbell, who came to Kinston during the war at the age of eight with her family, refugees from New Bern, which had been occupied by Union soldiers. They lived with her aunt Harriet Peebles in the Bright-Peebles House (Harmony Hall). In 1884 Lillie married Henry Archbell, a candy maker in Kinston, and they raised a family in the old Baptist parsonage on McLewean Street, where Lillie operated a school in later years. As a fervent member of the United Daughters of the Confederacy, she published the official state magazine for the organization from 1912 to 1914. *Carolina and the Southern Cross* was "dedicated to our busy people who always have time to make history but never time for research." Lillie Archbell, driven like others in the organization by the sense that many history books contained only the "Northern" version of the war and its aftermath, summed up her mission in this statement from the magazine:

> Every foot of ground around Kinston was the scene of some event in history. . . .These things will not stay forgotten. They come back like ghosts in distorted forms clothed in a garb that is only part the truth. . . . Daughters and Veterans can not afford to be silent about the painful past. Let our descendants have a truthful account of that awful time as far as written words can give it. We have put away all bitterness and evil speaking and both North and South should know the truth of the war. It will help us to a better understanding of each other.[37]

The town's physical fabric and the railroad survived the war, allowing growth to resume by the end of the 1860s. When the first statewide business directory was published in 1869 by Levi Branson (who had served as the first principal of the male department at Lenoir Collegiate Institute before the war), it listed in Kinston three churches, two hotels/boardinghouses, a dentist, nine physicians, seven lawyers, eight grist mills, two shoe factories, one harness maker, twenty-seven merchants, three carriage works, and the Kinston Female Academy. Some of the men who listed their occupations in 1870 as banker, bar keeper, cotton broker, steam mill operator, horse trader, fireman, telegraph operator, and railroad conductor had jobs that did not even exist in town before the war. Several white men of means in their fifties, such as Q. L. Brock and Isaiah Wood, were designated as "gentleman at leisure," apparently a euphemism for retiree.[38]

Rooming houses and hotels functioned in every North Carolina town not only as shelter, but also as a refuge and orientation for newcomers. Kinston had a number of such lodging establishments for whites from the 1840s on. J. H. Stevenson ran a hotel on Queen Street in 1870. In addition to Mrs. Stevenson and five school-age children, in that year it housed eleven male boarders and one female boarder. Among the men boarders were a butcher born in Switzerland, a Bavarian merchant, a Massachusetts merchant, a watchmaker, the town sheriff, a barkeeper, and several clerks *(Fig. 3.23).*[39]

The decade of the 1870s brought solid growth to Kinston. The population rose from 1,100 in 1870 to over 1,700 in 1880. By 1872 the town had six schools, three churches, one hotel, one boarding house, one dentist, two turpentine distilleries, and forty-eight merchants in addition to those listed in the 1869 business directory. Most of the merchants operated out of one-story frame stores along North Queen and Herritage Streets and extending up to the passenger and freight depots at Queen and Blount Streets. During the decade Lemuel Harvey's agricultural implement and fertilizer business opened, and Dave, Abe, and Sol Oettinger settled in Kinston and opened a furniture store.[40] In 1878 the county's second courthouse was destroyed by arson; in the same year the new courthouse was completed *(Fig. 3.24).* In 1882 mapmakers O. W. Gray & Son, of Philadelphia, drew a detailed town map that depicts individual buildings and owners' names *(Fig. 3.25).* The Gray map shows Kinston's growth up to Peyton Avenue on the north, two blocks beyond the original North Street boundary. Dwellings extended beyond East Street along Blount Street, Tower Hill Road, and Bright and Shine Streets. On the west houses had been built along West North and West Gordon Streets near the river. Along the river stood J. M. Parrott's sawmill and a turpentine distillery. Queen Street, an unusually long main street for a small town, had an almost solid row of frame buildings extending from Bright Street north to Blount Street. Outside of the business district large and small houses occupied large lots throughout town, with a few estates set outside the town limits.

The Caswell Monument, one of the first in a long tradition of memorials to Richard Caswell in Lenoir County, was unveiled at the center of the intersection of Queen and Caswell Streets in 1881.

Fig. 3.23. Tavern on Main Street, Kinston. This 1920s documentary photo apparently shows the King Hotel, located on the southwest corner of King and Queen streets on Gray's 1882 Map. It may have been Stevenson's Hotel in 1870. (Mary Grace Canfield Photo Album, North Carolina Collection, University of N.C. Library at Chapel Hill)

Fig. 3.24. Third Lenoir County Courthouse, northeast corner of Queen and King streets, Kinston, 1878, demolished in 1930s (Heritage Place, Lenoir Community College)

The tall granite and marble obelisk, dedicated in a ceremony with local and state dignitaries, military regiments, and the Masons, was one of the earliest public monuments erected in North Carolina. It preceded the movement to erect monuments to Confederate soldiers in civic squares that began in the 1890s. The Caswell Monument stood in the center of Queen Street until 1934, when it was moved to the courthouse lawn.[41]

As in the antebellum period, Kinston's economy at this time was based upon the products of the countryside. The majority of businesses in Kinston in the mid-1880s sold fertilizer and agricultural implements and bought cotton and turpentine. The firm of Dawson and Mewbourne, farm agents, bought cotton and sold guano. W. F. Stanley was a general merchant who also bought cotton and sold fertilizer. Lemuel Harvey was a general insurance agent and a dealer in fertilizers and naval stores (tar and turpentine). Harvey owned the only turpentine still in Kinston and shipped 5,000 barrels of spirits and rosin annually to New York. The Kinston Machine Works, G. E. Miller and E. S. Laughinghouse, proprietors, sold such agricultural implements as plows, cultivators, and cotton gins. A. R. Miller operated a general merchandise store and sold fancy groceries and dry goods. Queen Street developed some swank establishments. Marston's Drug Store, built by Dr. R. H. Temple and E. B. Marston in 1888 on the northwest corner of Queen and Gordon Streets, was a modern, luxurious building with a famous white onyx soda fountain, where ladies loved to meet their friends *(Fig. 3.26)*. [42]

The railroad had not yet gained a monopoly on transportation in town during this period, thus riverboat traffic continued to carry goods. The Dibble brothers steamboat company gained a competitor, the Caswell Steamboat Company, in 1873. Up to the late 1880s steamboats remained as important as the railroad, and Kinston was apparently the westernmost town on the Neuse River with some navigability all year round *(Fig. 3.27)*. The Neuse and Trent Steamboat Company served Kinston in the late 1880s.[43] For a time, these companies competed to carry goods to market.

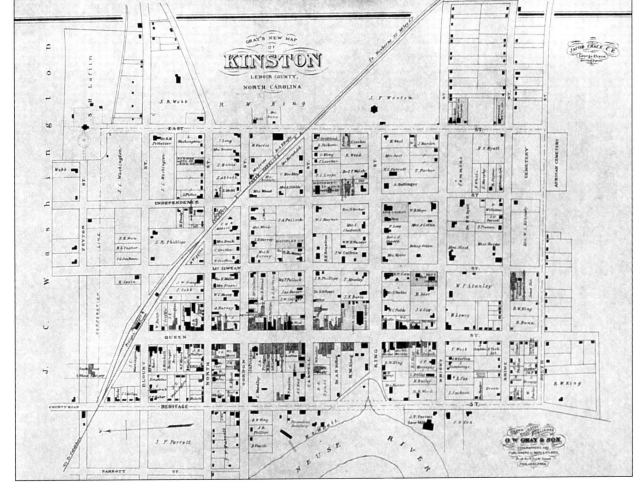

Fig. 3.25. Gray's 1882 Map of Kinston (Heritage Place, Lenoir Community College)

By the mid-1880s Kinston's self-image was changing from that of an antebellum village to that of a beautiful and bustling modern town. Comparing antebellum Kinston to the current town, one writer observed

> a forcible contrast . . . . as one now notes the bustle at the depot, and scans the length and symmetry of the streets and sidewalks, the beautiful shade trees and luxuriant shrubbery adorning the many aesthetic residences, the blocks of brick stores on Queen Street, the Opera House, the spacious new Court House, with its mammoth four-faced town clock on its tower, all having partaken largely of the modern style of architecture.

> The whites have four churches, representing the most dominant religious sects of the day, each having a regular pastor, and the colored people also have several church buildings. The educational facilities are equal to those of any similar town in the State, having a graded school, and a first-class college—Kinston College.[44]

The writer also delighted in the new iron bridge across the Neuse River south of town, new steel jail cells, a new market house, the new Caswell Monument, and a new bridge built from Caswell Street across the river to provide access to a town park created by local citizen J. F. Parrott. Travel writer George Nowitzky in 1888 admired the business buildings on Queen Street "built mostly of brick, with iron columns, caps, cornices and other ornaments." He thought the Hotel Tull, a three-story brick building with a mansard roof with numerous windows, the most imposing building in Kinston. Although he praised the neat cheerful appearance of the town's churches, he declined to describe them because, "as they are all built of perishable material (wood), it is not within the province of this book to give them a special description."[45]

Fig. 3.26. Marston's Drug Store, northwest corner Queen and Gordon streets, 1888 (Photo, early 1900s, Heritage Place, Lenoir Community College)

The "May Belle" hauled both passengers and freight.

Fig. 3.27. "May Belle," Neuse River, date unknown. (Kohler, *200 Years of Progress*)

A Kinstonian who had been a small boy in the 1880s recollected not architecture but the food at the new market house on Queen Street.

It was a large frame building situated on the west side of the street and boasted several stalls, or eating places. The food was largely sea food and everybody coming to town was crazy about fish and oysters. I want to say right here that the best fish and oysters I ever ate were prepared in the old Town Market in the village of Kinston during the early eighties. I want to say, too, that it was the favorite eating place of the lawyers and judges, especially during court terms, which lasted for one week only twice a year **(Fig. 3.28)**. [46]

Growth of the railroad network in and around Lenoir County in the 1890s continued to increase the attractiveness of the rails over horse and wagon or river transport. The Atlantic and North Carolina Railroad from Morehead to Goldsboro, known as the old Mullet Road for the boxcars of salted fish brought inland from the coast, grew more important every year.[47] In 1891 the second railroad to serve Kinston, the Wilmington and Weldon Railroad, completed a branch to the town from Greenville and was later incorporated into the Atlantic Coast Line. [48] Stations built along the tracks in Kinston, LaGrange, Graingers and other train stops in the 1800s are gone. Kinston's depot, rebuilt in the early 1880s at the corner of Queen and Blount Streets, was of brick construction with pilasters between the windows and doors and a wide roof, supported on decorative wood-

Fig. 3.28. "The water pump in front of the courthouse was and had been for many years the only place on the grounds where you could quench a thirst. Many were the farmers and pedestrians who stopped at the old pump to exchange views on different matters such as the weather and politics, if it happened to be an election year." (James Lewis Jones Manuscript) (Photo, circa 1890, North Carolina Collection, University of N.C. at Chapel Hill).

Fig. 3.29. Passenger Depot, Queen Street, Kinston. Thirty years after the tracks first came by the edge of Kinston, the depot still sat at the edge of town, with a farmhouse, barn and fields visible in the background. The cotton bale on the platform symbolized Kinston's status as one of the largest cotton markets in North Carolina. (Photo, William G. Reed, 1884, North Carolina Collection, University of N.C. at Chapel Hill)

Fig. 3.30. Orion Knitting Mills, Atlantic and North Carolina Railroad tracks, Kinston, 1890 (Photo, early 1900s, Heritage Place, Lenoir Community College)

en brackets, overhanging the train platform *(Fig. 3.29)*.

The decline of cotton prices in the 1880s, due in part to an oversupply of cotton at northern knitting mills, prompted a group of businessmen in Kinston, including Dr. Henry Tull, to establish the Orion Knitting Mills in 1890 to provide a local market for Lenoir County cotton. A two-story brick building, constructed in southeast Kinston along the Atlantic and North Carolina Railroad line in the block between East, Caswell, Gordon, and Tiffany Streets housed the firm, which began knitting cotton stockings in 1891 with forty employees. By 1893 the mill employed 210 workers *(Fig. 3.30)*. [49]

But cotton growing and textile manufacturing were not destined to define Kinston's future. As cotton prices sank lower and the cost of freight rose in the 1880s and 1890s, farmers in Lenoir County and the rest of the Coastal Plain sought alternative money crops. The public, including railroad officials, large landowners, local bankers, other businessmen, warehouse owners, and local newspapers, pressured farmers to grow tobacco. The "Old Bright Belt," located in the northern Piedmont along the Virginia border, had emerged earlier as the center of tobacco cultivation in the mid-nineteenth century and had prospered. In Lenoir County, bright-leaf tobacco was successfully introduced near LaGrange in the late 1870s by farmer Council S. Wooten. Dissatisfied with his poor tobacco production in 1877, when he earned only $125 from a fifteen-acre planting, Wooten hired J. T. Burch from Person County, in the Old Bright Belt, to manage his farm for one year. Burch spared no expense in cultivating Wooten's tobacco fields, preparing the soil carefully and fertilizing it well. When Wooten sold his tobacco harvest at the market in Durham the next year, he earned $705. In 1878 the Harvey family built the first tobacco factory in the county, the A. Harvey and Company Tobacco Company in Kinston, which produced smoking tobacco. [50] Tobacco cultivation increased slowly until 1895, when a sweeping agricultural revolution brought large-scale tobacco cultivation to Lenoir County, a story told in the twentieth-century chapter of this book. Throughout the Coastal Plain and in nearby counties such as Nash and Pitt a similar switch to tobacco culture occurred at the same time.

Stylish Houses on Shaded Streets

In the early 1880s city government planted oak trees along all of the principal streets, and the resulting shade was noted with gratitude in numerous descriptions of the town in later years. An observer of Kinston during the decade praised the broad streets shaded by two lines of trees and, on King Street, an additional line of trees in a central median, which "casts a grateful shade over travelers in vehicles and their weary beasts." [51] The piazza, so prominent a feature of antebellum architecture, continued to be a valued appendage to a house. One observer taking the readers of the *Kinston Journal* on a street tour in 1880 remarked that "Elder C. W. Howard's cottage embowered in grateful shade invites us to enter and cool off in its broad piazza." [52]

With the increasing prosperity of the 1880s, Kinston's enterprising men built themselves handsome new houses embellished with the latest architectural fashion. One such house was erected about 1883 by merchant and banker B. W. Canady. He built an Italianate Revival house on North Queen Street, in a block filled with other new dwellings *(Fig. 3.31)*. A center wing with a gable decorated with an intricately carved rosette ventilator projects from the facade. The piazza wraps around the front, entrance wing and down the side elevation. Heavy pendant brackets decorate the roof eaves. On the interior an arched screen divides the front hall from the staircase, and Italianate mantels continue the style.

Walter Dunn LaRoque, who operated a livery stable on West Gordon Street, had a smaller house built for his family in the 500 block of North Queen Street about the same time *(Fig. 3.32)*. The one-story house with its front-gabled wing with bay window and large piazza would no doubt have been called a cottage by Kinstonians of the 1880s. Its turned posts decorated with Eastlake-style sawnwork brackets epitomize the localized version of the Queen Anne style popular in Kinston in

Fig. 3.31. B.W. Canady House, 600 North Queen Street, Kinston, circa 1883. The business district has now surrounded the house. (Heritage Place, Lenoir Community College)

Fig. 3.32. W. D. LaRoque House, 115 East Washington Street, Kinston. The house was moved twice, arriving at this site in 1937. (Photo, M. Ruth Little, North Carolina Division of Archives and History)

the 1880s and 1890s. This nationally popular style, a revival of early eighteenth-century British architecture, featured bay windows, turrets, cupolas, decorative chimney stacks, and ornate woodwork. Kinstonians achieved the Queen Anne look by breaking away from restrained house forms into asymmetrical shapes, including wings and bay windows, and by embellishing their piazzas with turned and sawn woodwork, often referred to as "gingerbread."

Few of these self-confident expressions of Kinston's late-nineteenth-century prosperity have survived, for such houses were built as close to the business district as possible in these days before the advent of suburban neighborhoods, and were razed as the commercial district expanded. Those that still stand, like the Canady House and the Laroque House, are treasures.

A Parallel Reality: African Americans in Kinston

In 1860, on the eve of the Civil War, a small community of free blacks lived in Kinston, including artisans such as mattress maker Richard Budd, blacksmith Anderson Dunk, and seamstress Louisa Byrd. Joseph Dunk was a hotel servant, and a few free African Americans lived in residential households. For example, county court clerk Nicholas Hunter kept a ten-year-old black girl named Edney Tyler in his household, probably as a servant. In the home of wealthy farmer William Fields, in addition to his wife and nine children, were Warren Tyler, a fifteen-year-old black boy, and Sallie Tyler, a ten-year-old mulatto girl.[53]

A number of the African Americans listed in the 1870 census in Kinston still lived and worked as servants in the white households where they had been slaves, such as Mary Whitfield, a cook in merchant John Coleman's house, and Cora Gansey, a fourteen-year-old black nurse (children's nanny) in the same household.[54] More often, black cooks or washerwomen or domestic servants or laborers lived in separate households in between white households, possibly still in the slave quarters. Most African Americans in Kinston worked at the same types of jobs that they had held in slavery. In addition to serving as laborers, cooks, house servants, washers, and nurses, African Americans worked as hostlers (horse grooms), drayman, brick masons, hotel waiters, distillers, barbers, roofers, woodcutters, basket makers, and gardeners. Black children were employed at very young ages. One seven-year-old boy and an eleven-year-old girl worked as "nurses." A few Kinston African Americans held positions of authority in 1870. Richard Whitfield was a constable, Lewis H. Fisher a merchant, and sixty-four-year-old Argeant Morriss a midwife.[55]

The rural blacks who began moving to Kinston after emancipation encountered a stable African American community. By 1872, only nine years after emancipation, Branson's directory listed a small but substantial group of blacks doing business in Kinston. Wiley Lowery, L. H. Fisher, Henry Fisher, and Richard Whitfield had general stores. Black Kinstonians Lewis Green, a barber (and upholsterer); Anthony Blount, a baker; and "M. Lynch, Painter," operated businesses along South Queen Street. Blount, Green, and Lowery were still in business in 1877, as was Charles Dunn, who owned a small grocery store.[56] In 1888 a mention in the April 19 issue of the *Kinston Journal* acknowledged the black community's growing importance. "Kinston has a number of prosperous colored citizens, who own property. Peter Borden and Holland Cobb are building dwelling houses on North Street."[57] Holland Cobb, an elderly woman, had worked as a cook. At the time of the previous census she had lived with her husband Eli, a farmer, and their grandson Peter.[58]

The three most prominent African American businessmen, Peter Borden, Charles Dunn, and Joseph C. Hargett, were former slaves of Lenoir County families. Peter Borden was born a slave about 1855 on John Cobb Washington's plantation near Kinston. He was probably the son of Joshua Borden, a carpenter who was instrumental in founding the Saint Augustus African Methodist Episcopal Zion Church. Peter, also a carpenter, managed to raise himself to the level of merchant.[59] His biography in the 1899 Industrial Issue of the *Kinston Daily Free Press* elaborates upon his steady progress which began in the 1880s:

He bought the lot he is now on, on North Street, two doors east of the Webb building and paid $25 cash on it, built a little shop and had $45 to buy stock. He has built three times, the last time, in '96, a brick store. He expects to erect a brick warehouse in the rear of his store this fall.

He carries a nice line of dry goods, shoes and groceries. He has a very pretty soda fountain and a cool drink counter, over which he dispenses all sorts of cool drinks in season.[60] *(Fig. 3.33)*

Besides Borden and Cobb, other African Americans were buying—and apparently developing—property in the East North Street area into the 1910s. One was Charles Dunn, a young entrepreneur who in 1895 was appointed as a justice of the peace for Lenoir County. A few years later he founded the first African American bank in Kinston:

Charles Dunn was born January 31, 1856, and was a slave of John Dunn, a Lenoir County preacher. He located in Kinston in 1878 and opened a little store on Tuckahoe. . . . He was burned out in March, 1895. Immediately he purchased from W. L. Kennedy the site where G. E. Kornegay did business before the fire. It had a frontage of 60 feet on Queen Street, and Charles erected thereon two brick stores. He merchandised for awhile after the fire, but having opened the "Dime Bank" July 7, 1897, he discontinued his mercantile business and now devotes his entire attention to the bank. . . He had eighty depositors within two weeks from the beginning, showing that the colored people appreciate having a place where they can make small deposits of their earnings, subject to check or get interest thereon after 30 days not subject to check. The bank has a 5,000 pound Mosler-Bahmann safe of latest pattern time lock.[61]

Fig. 3.33. Peter Borden and family, apparently in front of their house at 306 East North Street, Kinston. Borden and his wife stand on the right of a seated older woman who may have been his mother or mother-in-law. (Industrial Edition, *Kinston Free Press*, 1906)

Dunn was lauded by the white establishment as a businessman who "encourages his race by precept and example to habits of frugality and to lay aside frivolous things and acquire land, goods, and money."[62] In 1900 Dunn took a major step in expanding his commercial realm.

> Lumber is being hauled in front of Charles F. Dunn's lot on Queen Street for the new brick hotel for colored people, which this enterprising colored man will soon have built. As soon as brick can be procured, work will be commenced on the building. The hotel will be 75 x 45 feet with an annex for a kitchen 14 x 20 feet. The building will have 2 stories.[63]

Another prosperous businessman was Joseph C. Hargett, an African American whose grocery and dry goods store was located on Queen Street. Like Charles Dunn and Peter Borden, Joe Hargett had been born a slave. Hargett's family had been owned by the John and Harriet Cobb Peebles family on King Street in Kinston. After teaching in the rural black schools, Hargett returned to Kinston in the 1880s and started his grocery.[64] At one time Hargett was considered for an appointment as Kinston's postmaster. In 1899 the *Kinston Daily Free Press* reported admiringly that

> He is today the biggest merchant of his race in Kinston. He carries a stock ranging from $3,500 to $4,000. . . . it is probably just to say that J. C. Hargett carries a larger stock, does a bigger business, and is the best qualified merchant of any man of his race that has ever done business in Kinston.[65]

Starr Hicks was one of many African American farm laborers who decided to try his luck in Kinston. In 1880 the twenty-year-old Hicks lived in Woodington Township with his father, Henry, a forty-six year-old farmer; his mother, Ella; and eight siblings. Starr, who could read and write, moved to Kinston between 1880 and 1898 and became a prominent member of the African American business community. By 1898 Hicks was captain of Kinston's black fire-fighting brigade, a prestigious position in the African American community. He was also a successful grocer and in the 1930s had Hicks Street in the Tower Hill neighborhood named after him.[66]

African American businesses in the heart of Kinston's white commercial district catered primarily to white customers, one example being Green's Barber Shop on East Gordon Street, which advertised:

> 1898: NEW BARBER SHOP—I have opened a nice, clean Barber Shop on Gordon Street between THE FREE PRESS office and Temple's corner.
> Thanking all my friends for the past patronage, I hope for a continuance.
> Thos. H. Green[67]

In another advertisement, Thomas Green promised parents sending their children for haircuts that "We will cut the hair all right, and treat your children kindly and politely."[68]

Tuckahoe and Tower Hill

Although many of Kinston's black citizens continued to live among whites, two distinct black neighborhoods developed during this era. Tuckahoe, located at the south end of Queen Street below King Street, derived its name from Tuckahoe Creek, a small tributary of the Neuse River in this vicinity. An 1880 description of Tuckahoe mentions new construction in the area: "Going West from the country along Moon Street [now South Street] we notice four or five new and neat residences built for colored tenants within twelve months past. . . . Wiley Lowery has built a large two-story store and residence at the [northeast] corner of Bright and Queen Streets."[69]

At the northeast edge of the Kinston town limits, along North, Blount, and Peyton Streets, the Tower Hill area developed in the 1880s with the entrepreneurship of African American citizens like Peter Borden. The center of the Tower Hill neighborhood at that time was East Blount Street, in the 400 and 500 blocks between East Street and Tiffany Avenue. Before 1880 this area had been the property of John Cobb Washington. By the turn of the twentieth century, East Blount Street was home to African American laborers and middle-class businessmen such as Nelson Physic, a porter at 402 East Blount Street, and E. E. Pittman, a bottler at 406 East Blount Street. To the north, along the Atlantic Coast Line railroad tracks, lay a network of smaller streets—Beasley's Alley, Thompson Street, Dennis Street, and Carraway Street—lined with one- and two-story frame dwellings. Carraway Street was home primarily to laborers. Farmers such as Emperior Croom and Peter Codgell also lived on Dennis Street.[70]

Within these new neighborhoods churches grew up to serve Kinston's growing African American population. Kinston's African American churches provided a sure sign that a large black population, drawn by the promise of work and a better life, was moving into the town. According to oral history the earliest African American churches in the area were "bush shelters," open spaces in woods where slaves, and later freed African Americans, worshiped. Vine Swamp Church, First (Colored) Baptist Church (which initially met on the banks of the Neuse River), and Saint Peter's Disciple Church of Christ in Lincoln City are three of the many Lenoir County black churches that began as bush shelters. Longtime Lincoln City resident Edna Speight recalled the origins of Saint Peter's Church in the early twentieth century:

> I remember when they built St. Peter's Church. My grandmother and grandfather were the old founders of that church. They belonged to Hickory Grove Church out in the country when they moved. Uncle Ed Hill was one of the preachers; Rev. C. R. D. Whitfield was the pastor. . . . Won't no churches out here. They got together and decided to build a Disciple Church. The nearest church to them was Hickory Grove, so they decided to build a church in Lincoln City. They had a bush shelter. They cut those bushes down that had growed up and made a bush shelter and put those bushes on top of it. . . . I remember when the church was built, a one-room church, won't much bigger than my dining room. And it was high up from the ground because it was built on a low place.[71]

Other African American churches in Kinston were formed as mission outposts fostered by white churches, the Saint Augustine Episcopal Church being one example. The original small, front-gable frame chapel, heated by a wood stove and lit by oil lamps, stood on the east side of South Independence Street near East Shine Street. Lawn parties and Easter egg hunts at the Saint Augustine Episcopal Church were periodically announced in the Kinston papers.[72] The present Saint Augustine Episcopal Church stands in the 700 block of East Washington Street.

Some churches organized after the Civil War that did not originate as bush shelters or as white-sponsored missions but rather as self-initiated places of worship built by Kinston's African American community. In the 1870s and 1880s the fire of religious zeal must have burned particularly bright in black Kinston; Branson's 1877-1878 business directory lists seventeen African American ministers in Kinston, three in LaGrange, and two in Falling Creek.[73] One of the new churches was the Saint Augustus American Methodist Episcopal Zion Church. The Saint Augustus Church, which began in the mid-1860s as the Yankee Row Methodist Church at 506 East Blount Street, moved to 318 East North Street in 1881. The frame church built there, "a good substantial building," measured thirty feet by sixty feet and had an eighteen-foot-pitch ceiling "and a recess in the rear 12 x 15 feet." Church members were assiduous in collecting the funds needed to raise the building. The contractor for the new church, I. H. Fisher, was quoted as saying "they owe only $17 on it having raised and paid out over $100."[74] In 1905 the Reverend H. H. Wells and the congregation built a second church at 318 East North Street. The new building was a brick Romanesque and Gothic Revival structure with twin castellated towers, polychromed buttresses, and a projecting brick gallery over the entrance *(Fig. 3.34)*. Other "self-made" churches—Saint John's Free Will Baptist, White Rock Presbyterian, Saint James African Methodist Episcopal—followed. Of these, Saint John's Church and the White Rock Presbyterian Church, a frame Greek Revival building that was formerly Kinston's white First Baptist Church, still stand.

African American congregations cultivated support from Kinston's white citizens by involving whites in their enterprises. The *Kinston Journal* gave notice in June 1881 that "The members of the A.M.E. Church of Kinston are erecting a handsome building on the corner of East and Shine

Fig. 3.34. St. Augustus A.M.E. Zion Church, 318 East North Street, Kinston, 1905, demolished. (*St. Augustus A.M.E. Zion 50th Anniversary Program*, 1919)

Streets. It is 32 x 56 feet with 20 feet pitch. The pastor, R. H. W. Leak, says there will be but little debt against it when completed."[75] Several weeks later the newspaper reported on a public benefit held to raise money for the new building: "The entertainment given by our colored citizens for the benefit of the new church building, St. James, at the Court House on Friday and Saturday night, June 3rd and 4th, netted $45.00. The pastor, R. H. W. Leak, returns thanks to the public for their patronage."[76]

The earliest documented school for Kinston's black children is said to have been started by Union soldiers in John Washington's shoe factory on Tower Hill Road. The teacher, Sarah Keys, was a white woman who died during Reconstruction. Another white teacher, Mary Baker, took Sarah Keys's place before John Washington regained his property.[77]

Isaac Best and J. H. Carey, two African Americans, are known to have been teachers in Kinston in 1884. In 1888 the black community received its first permanent school, the former white graded school. Period maps show that the school was a two-story gable-and-wing frame building sited on the southwest corner of East Shine and South McLewean Streets. A small frame chapel extended from its east elevation.

> The old graded school building was bid off by the colored public school committee of this district at $1,000. The arrangement allows several years for them to pay for it. It will be rented out and run as a pay school until paid for. C. T. Williams and Violet Parrott commenced teaching in it Monday.[78]

In addition to churches and schools, African Americans in Kinston began building fraternal lodges in their neighborhoods. In 1879 the *Kinston Journal* announced that "The colored people of the I.O. of G.S. and D.S. [Independent Order of Good Samaritans and Daughters of Samaria] are preparing to build a Samaritan Hall on a lot purchased of Mr. Washington, on the West side of Independent Street, and adjoining the corner lot on North Street."[79] Starr Hicks became one of the organization's leading members, along with J. H. Fisher, a grocer, John E. Davis, and O. R. Hicks.[80] The Samaritan Hall is no longer standing.

By the end of the nineteenth century, in a span of only thirty-five years since African Americans had been held in slavery, blacks in Kinston had achieved a remarkable feat—the creation of a complete new life for themselves in a number of prosperous communities, filled with dwellings, black-owned businesses, churches, fraternal lodges, fire-fighting companies, and schools. African Americans had earned the respect of white citizens and were even being appointed to public office.

Chapter Four:

A Century of Rural Progress

Fig. 4.2. Knott Brothers Warehouse, 100 block East Washington Street, Kinston. early 1900s, demolished. This was one of the earliest tobacco warehouses in Kinston. (Heritage Place, Lenoir Community College)

In Lenoir County, the twentieth century—the tobacco century—can properly be considered to have started in 1895, when Jesse Willis Grainger, with five hundred dollars worth of tobacco seeds, became the Johnny Appleseed of tobacco in the county by inaugurating tobacco cultivation *(Fig. 4.1)*. Cotton prices had dropped to their lowest point in many years, and farmers were desperate for a new cash crop. Grainger distributed the seeds to county farmers, promising that he would provide an auction warehouse in Kinston for their tobacco if they would cultivate and cure it. Farmers responded enthusiastically, and Grainger built the Kinston-Carolina Warehouse at the corner of Herritage Street and Vernon Avenue that fall, the first tobacco warehouse in the county *(Fig. 4.2 See previous page)*.

In the first year tobacco sales exceeded 800,000 pounds.[1] One week after the first sale of Lenoir County tobacco, the newspaper crowed:

> A new era for Kinston! That is what the opening of a tobacco market here last week meant. We believe it means greater prosperity for Kinston and the surrounding country. . . . Our business men are united and enthusiastic for making Kinston a great tobacco town. They must say so, and put forth every effort to induce the farmers in all the country surrounding Kinston to plant tobacco next year, and use all their influence to induce farmers from a distance to bring their tobacco to Kinston. With united effort on the part of our citizens Kinston will be the leading town of Eastern Carolina.[2]

In the second year of tobacco sales, production reached between 2 and 3 million pounds. Lenoir County formed part of the New Bright Belt, an arc of Coastal Plain counties that adopted tobacco in the last two decades of the nineteenth century. Bright-tobacco cultivation had come to Nash and Pitt Counties in the 1880s, and by 1888 the region already bore the name "New Bright Belt." In the year following Lenoir's 1895 marketing experiment with tobacco, the Kinston Chamber of Commerce boasted that "barns sprung up as if by magic throughout Lenoir, Duplin, Jones, Onslow, and Greene Counties."[3]

Rural life in the county underwent a total transformation during the first half of the twentieth century. Changes included not only a large population increase but also startling improvements in such areas as agricultural technology, home construction, and roads, as well as problems caused by a rise in tenant farming. In the first quarter of the century, tenancy increased from two-thirds to three-fourths of all farmers. Although much of the population increase occurred in the two major

Fig. 4.1. Jesse Grainger (1845-1910) was raised in neighboring Greene County and educated at Trinity College. He moved to Kinston in 1879, bought the Washington estate north of town and became a truck farmer and a distributor of fertilizer and farm machinery. One of the most influential men in the county, Grainger served in the state legislature and was the Kinston agent of the Atlantic and North Carolina Railroad. (Heritage Place, Lenoir Community College)

towns of Kinston and LaGrange, more people lived in the country as well. In 1900 the county contained 18,639 people. By 1910 the population had increased 22 percent, to 22,769, and by 1920 it had increased almost 30 percent, to nearly 30,000. By 1960 Lenoir County had 55,000 inhabitants. In the 1920s approximately 55 percent of the inhabitants were white and 44 percent African American; by 1960 the ratio was 60 percent white to 40 percent black. Although industrialization began in the rural areas of Lenoir County in the early 1950s, farming continued to dominate. In 1959 more than 90 percent of the land in the county was still devoted to farming. Of the 2,429 farms, fewer than one-third were operated by owners, over one-half by tenants, and the remainder by farm managers. More than 83 percent were tobacco farms; the rest produced livestock, poultry, or cotton. In some cases farms belonged to both categories.[4]

Spread over the county in 1925 was a network of more than 3,000 farms. As in the nineteenth century, the farm remained the center of life, families continued to be large, and communities were made up of close-knit, extended-family networks. What had changed since the previous century was that tenants now operated three out of four farms. About one-half of the county's land area was cleared and under cultivation. The average farm contained fifty acres. Farms had many outbuildings and many mules. A number of farms had tractors, but most still relied on mules to pull the plows and wagons, with horses of secondary importance. Farmers spent an average of $217 a year for fertilizer in 1925.[5]

The naturally rich Lenoir County soil and mild climate grew a wide variety of crops, but farmers, especially tenant farmers, relied on cash to pay their bills. Of the two major cash crops, greater acreage was planted in cotton, but tobacco brought higher revenues. In 1920, 11,843 bales of cotton were grown on 23,611 acres (twice as many bales as were produced on the same acreage in 1890, evidence of the benefits of improved cotton plants and farming techniques). In the same year more than 12 million pounds of tobacco were grown on 16,125 acres. Despite the reliance on cotton and tobacco, the majority of farms were diversified. Farmers grew corn mainly as feed for work animals, but also for food. Fields were planted with rye and oats for grazing for the animals in the winter, then plowed under in the spring. Sweet potatoes, potatoes, cabbage, collards and other vegetables were grown for home use. Nearly every farmer kept chickens and other fowl. Farmers who owned their farms were more likely than others to cultivate fruit trees and grapevines, as well as to tend a pen of ten or twenty hogs for their own meat consumption, as well as for sale. Many of these farmers kept between one and four milk cows, although very few beef cattle. A few farmers kept herds of sheep and goats.[6]

Since cotton production declined in the 1920s, the major cash sources for county farms have been tobacco, trucking, livestock and timber products.

Tobacco Production

The first history of the county, published in 1954, attributed the success of the New Bright Belt to the Coastal Plain's unique soil and climate: "The tobacco planted in eastern North Carolina soil not only grew larger leaves but also leaves that were brighter and of more delicate texture than those anywhere else in the world" *(Fig. 4.3)*.[7] The long dominance of tobacco in the county produced a landscape dotted with tobacco curing barns with wood-burning flues, packhouses, and tenant houses. Lenoir County tobacco barns are of frame or log construction, surrounded and sometimes connected to each other by open sheds, where the tobacco was strung on drying sticks for curing inside the barns *(Fig. 4.4)*. In 1929 Kinston resident Forrest H. Smith invented an oil-fired tobacco furnace to replace the labor-intensive wood-fired brick furnaces and flues with which farmers had previously cured tobacco.[8] In the 1950s mechanized processes were introduced. By the 1970s bulk barns, low metal containers in which the tobacco is cured, were becoming commonplace in Lenoir County. Now that tobacco is no longer cured in log or frame barns, many of these buildings have disappeared. The rest stand empty, their sheds sheltering farm equipment such as trucks, plows, and tractors.

Fig. 4.3. Mr. Isaac Lane in his tobacco field, 1935 (North Carolina Collection, University of N.C. Library at Chapel Hill)

Fig. 4.4. Typical tobacco barns, N.C. 11, Graingers vicinity (Photo, Scott Power, North Carolina Division of Archives and History)

Produce Trucking

County farms have long had a reputation for the high quality of their produce. The *Kinston Free Press* in 1906 described Jesse W. Grainger's 250-acre truck farm, known as Vernon Farm, located along the Hill at the north edge of Kinston, as "a beautiful, a charming and bewitching place—of which there are so few left. He has the broad acres surrounding the hill under the best cultivation in strawberries, beans, peas, cabbage, asparagus, cantaloupes, etc."[9] Although Vernon Farm apparently specialized in produce, most of the larger farmers in the county grew at least some produce. Other notable truck farms were the McAthur Farm, the Tull Hill Farm, and the Patterson Farm. The Kinston Chamber of Commerce bragged in 1917 that "Trucking is extensively engaged in, and the excellence and quantity of the product bespeak the intelligence of the farmers, as well as the generosity of the soil. Lettuce, asparagus, beans, cabbage, white and sweet potatoes, tomatoes, cucumbers, all kinds of berries, pecans and nuts, and other truck are produced in large quantities, while hay, grain, clover, alfalfa, corn, and peanuts do not claim less attention from farmers," *(Fig. 4.5)*.[10]

Fig. 4.5. Sweet potatoes grown at the Caswell Center, circa 1924 (North Carolina Collection, University of N.C. Library at Chapel Hill)

Livestock: Cattle and Hogs

In 1920 Lenoir farmers kept the fifth highest number of dairy cattle among the state's one hundred counties, and by 1927 there were twenty-eight dairies in the county. One of the largest, the Cedar Dell Dairy in the Falling Creek section, sold its products primarily to Kinston retail dairies and ice cream plants. In the early twentieth century, as they had in the nineteenth century, farmers continued to ship much of their livestock out of the county for processing. For example, in 1927 thirty train-car-loads of Lenoir County hogs were shipped to Richmond, Virginia. But by mid-century Lenoir became a leading meat market, with the 1945 construction of a meat processing plant in the county by a group of Kinston businessmen. This facility was the first meat plant in the state to receive federal approval.[11]

Timber Products

As longleaf pine forests were exhausted in the late nineteenth century, the importance of naval stores—tar and turpentine—declined, setting the stage for the economic significance of raw lumber. The development of railroad logging lines allowed raw lumber to be transported to Kinston for processing in local lumber mills or to the railroad terminals in Kinston for shipment throughout the state. These lines were a significant impetus to rural growth, transporting not just wood but farm products, fertilizer, and even people. In 1897 the Hines Brothers Lumber Company built a logging railroad through northern Lenoir County to Snow Hill, in adjacent Greene County, to facilitate collection of timber. The line became a passenger line as well, and a depot was built at Dawson's Station in north Lenoir County. About 1900 the Gay Lumber Company of Kinston constructed a logging railroad, the Kinston and Carolina Line, to the south section of the county, where the town of Pink Hill grew up around the terminus. The line became a freight and passenger general service in 1917, when a line from Chinquapin, in Duplin County, connected to it. Competition from newly constructed highways led to the discontinuation of the passenger service in 1926, and the line closed in 1929.[12]

Small frame depots grew up at railroad stops around the county, such as Graingers in Contentnea Neck Township *(Fig. 4.6)*. The railroads provided employment to many Lenoir County residents. The Graingers Section House is the only railroad-worker lodging still standing in the county *(Fig. 4.7)*. Built in the 1890s, the one-story side-gable building covered with board-and-batten siding is a reminder of the days when work crews often spent a good part of their time on the job and away from their families.

Fig. 4.6. Graingers Depot, Graingers, 1890s, demolished (Heritage Place, Lenoir Community College)

Fig. 4.7. Graingers Section House, Graingers, 1890s (Photo, Robbie D. Jones, North Carolina Division of Archives and History)

Owner-Occupied Farms

Farms ranged in size and prosperity from the thousands of acres of Cedar Dell, owned by businessman William LaFayette Kennedy in the Falling Creek Township, to fifty-acre tenant farms. Kennedy also owned the Coahoma Feed Mill in Southwest Township. The lyrical picture painted of Cedar Dell in the 1906 Industrial Issue of the *Kinston Free Press* epitomizes the gentleman farmer's estate.

> The Berkshire pigs rolling in fat, produced by peanut-feasting, the flock of mammoth turkeys, of choice Kentucky breed, the covey of haughty pea-fowls, the herd of 50 sleek fat Jerseys, the long row of stables, suggesting a number of horses and mules, neat and commodious outbuildings on the terraced green give evidence of the smiling plenty that is enjoyed by Capt. Kennedy and his attractive, refined and travelled wife.[13]

The typical Lenoir County owner-occupied farm lacked the "smiling plenty" of Cedar Dell but provided a satisfying existence. The small Rouse-Suggs Farm, with its house, five outbuildings, and one tenant house set in a compact cluster on both sides of a county road, is typical of county farms during this era *(Figs. 4.8, 4.9)*. Walter Rouse established a small farm near Dawson's Station, in northern Lenoir County, in the early twentieth century. He built a farmhouse, a small one-story gabled house with a detached kitchen, directly on the road. Luther Suggs purchased the farm about 1929 and raised his family here. His daughter still owns the property. In the west rear yard stands a smokehouse. Strung along the farm lane east of the house are a barn, a packhouse, and two tobacco barns. In the 1930s the Suggses moved the kitchen across the road and converted it to a tenant house. They added a new kitchen ell to the back of their dwelling.

Fig. 4.8. Rouse-Suggs Farm, Dawson Station vicinity, early twentieth century (Photo, M. Ruth Little, North Carolina Division of Archives and History)

Fig. 4.9. Rouse-Suggs Farm, Dawson Station vicinity, early twentieth century (Photo, M. Ruth Little, North Carolina Division of Archives and History)

Tenant Farms

The tenant system had evolved slowly since the Civil War, increasing from approximately 50 percent of all farms in 1880 to 75 percent in 1925. By 1925 three out of every four farms in Lenoir County were tenant farms, with only 1/2 of 1 percent operated by managers. [14] A small number of tenants paid cash rent and so could use the land any way they wanted as long as they paid the rent and their share of the taxes. But most tenants in the county sharecropped, with the landlord furnishing land, work animals, and one-half the fertilizer and receiving one-half the crop profits.

African Americans were disproportionately tenants. In the 1900 census a new category, "Farms of Colored Farmers," reported that one-third, or 715, of the 2,179 farms in Lenoir County were owned, rented, or, in a few cases, managed by African Americans. Of these 715 farms, 35 were owned outright by black farmers, 35 more were part-owned, 139 were rented to blacks, and 504 employed black sharecroppers. By 1920 the number of African American-owned farms in Lenoir County increased to 111, but the combined number of black tenant farmers and sharecroppers reached 1,289. [15]

Many tenant houses stand, some still occupied by tenants, but most are abandoned. They were usually small, side-gable houses of a few rooms, with a detached kitchen in the rear connected by a breezeway. Few had any decorative additions, although some have front porches with millwork columns and brackets. The tenant house often had its own encircling outbuildings—outhouse, smokehouse, packhouse. Some tenant farms were subdivisions of established family farms. Others were new operations set up by newcomers who purchased land in order to establish tenant farms. E. Norman Dickerson, a tobacconist from Oxford, in Granville County, was one of a number of Old Bright Belt men who came to Kinston in the 1890s to participate in the introduction of tobacco to the section. In addition to acting as a tobacco dealer, he got involved in tobacco cultivation by purchasing a number of tracts of land in the county, building tenant houses, and renting them to tenants who grew tobacco *(Fig. 4.10)*.

Tenancy declined precipitously in the county after World War II, as tobacco cultivation became mechanized. In recent decades big farms have leased the small farms that used to be tended by tenants, cultivating crops with mechanized equipment and using migrant workers for labor.

Throughout the twentieth century state and local agencies have worked intensively with county farmers to improve their farm income and quality of life. Decade by decade modern amenities have come to the countryside. Following the establishment of the North Carolina Agricultural Extension Service in the early twentieth century, the first farm extension agent started working in Lenoir County in 1909. Rural telephone service arrived during the same decade. The first home demonstration agent began work prior to 1935. In the mid-1930s much of the county received electricity from the Tidewater Power Company, which ran power lines from Kinston out into the countryside. In 1939 the federal Rural Electrification Administration ran lines in the south end of the county. Families began to acquire such modern amenities as electric lights, electric refrigerators, and electric stoves. Households gradually acquired indoor plumbing as electricity became available and community water systems were built. By the mid-twentieth century modern farming methods, mechanized equipment, and commercial fertilizers enabled Lenoir County farmers to greatly increase the yields of their acreage. Land that would produce ten to twenty bushels of corn in the days of John Washington in 1810 yielded one hundred bushels or more by the 1960s. [16]

Fig. 4.10. Dickerson Tenant House, Taylors Crossroads vicinity, early 1900s (Photo, M. Ruth Little, North Carolina Division of Archives and History)

Education

Like other counties in North Carolina, Lenoir County educated its children for four or five months a year in public schools, small frame buildings containing one or two classrooms. In 1906 there were forty schools for white students and twenty-four for African American students in the county. By the mid-1920s 5,500 white students attended thirty-four white schools, and 4,000 black students attended twenty-eight African American schools.[17] Several of the pre-consolidation-era schoolhouses still stand, some converted to houses, some used as barns, and some abandoned. Airy Grove School, the best-preserved wooden school building in Lenoir County, stands near Taylors Crossroads. The school lot was acquired by the county Board of Education in 1887, but the original one-room, front-gable building was probably built in the early 1900s. W. Chester Forrest recalled attending Airy Grove in 1914, when he was in the second grade. The classroom had no electricity, was heated by a wood stove, and had two privies, one for the girls and one for the boys. The next year a side wing containing a second classroom was added. At its peak Airy Grove School had seven grades in which forty-three children were enrolled. In 1924, when Contentnea School, a consolidated school, was built in Graingers, Airy Grove School was abandoned. Although now used as a packhouse, the school retains its weatherboards, sash windows, original front porch with turned posts, and cloakrooms and folding doors between classrooms on the interior *(Fig. 4.11)*. [18] One of several other schoolhouses that still stand is Fairfield Schoolhouse, built about 1910 at Mewborne's Crossroads, although it has been moved a short distance.

Fig. 4.11. Airy Grove School, Taylors Crossroads vicinity, early 1900s. (Photo, Robbie D. Jones, North Carolina Division of Archives and History)

African American students benefited from the Rosenwald Fund, a program established by Julius Rosenwald, president of Sears, Roebuck and Company, to contribute private money to combine with local and state public money in the construction of schools for black students.. From 1928 to 1929 Rosenwald schools were built at Bank's Chapel, Grifton, Kinston, and LaGrange.[19] Apparently none of these schools survive today. African American schools were not consolidated until the 1950s, beginning with the construction of the Frink Union School in LaGrange in 1951, and the Savannah School and Woodington School in 1952.[20]

In the early twentieth century a number of private white schools continued to operate in the rural county. Near Dawson's Station in north Lenoir County, a private Disciples of Christ school, Tyndall College, educated students in the primary and secondary grades from 1907 to 1929. Many of them were day students, but a number boarded at the school in large frame dormitories. Only the abandoned girls' dormitory and the frame houses of two of the staff members still stand.[21] Holy Innocents Episcopal Church established the Holy Innocents Parish School in 1903-1904 in Strabane, and by 1906 the school had about forty students. The plain, front-gabled frame building, its facade originally sheltered by a porch that has been enclosed, resembled a number of the public school buildings of the period *(Fig. 4.12)*.[22]

The most famous educator in the county was James Yadkin Joyner (1862-1954). He was born in Davidson County, where his parents had fled during the Civil War, but the Joyners returned to their native Lenoir County and raised young James in Kinston. After attending the University of North Carolina, Joyner became principal at LaGrange Academy in 1882, then superintendent of Lenoir County Schools from 1882 to 1884. From 1902 to 1919 he served as state superintendent of public instruction, presiding over the greatest period of educational development in the state's history. More than 3,000 public school buildings were built in the state during Joyner's tenure. In 1919 he retired to his farm at LaGrange, where he engaged in a variety of civic activities until his death in 1954.[23]

No doubt due in part to the political influence of James Y. Joyner, Lenoir County became one of the first in the state to begin consolidation of its white public school system.[24] One of the first consolidated schools constructed in the county was the Moss Hill School, built in 1917 to consolidate the old Moss Hill, Sandy Bottom, Blands, and Byrds frame schools. The two-story brick building has Neoclassical styling and a flat roof *(Fig. 4.13)*. Contentnea School was completed in 1924 in Graingers. Other brick consolidated schools were built in LaGrange, Wheat Swamp, Pink Hill, Deep Run, and Southwood during the 1920s. These schools, generally two stories tall, brought together the students of numerous one and two-room rural schools. Wilmington architect Leslie Boney, a prolific specialist in school design, designed a number of these brick Neoclassical-style consolidated schools.

Fig. 4.12. Holy Innocents Parish School, Strabane, 1903-04 (Heritage Place, Lenoir Community College)

Fig. 4.13. Moss Hill School, Strabane vicinity, 1917. Additions were made in the 1950s and 1970s, and the school is still in use (Photo, Robbie D. Jones, North Carolina Division of Archives and History)

Religion

In the first two decades of the twentieth century, most rural churches continued to build simple, wooden Gothic-Revival style buildings like those of earlier decades. But by the 1920s some congregations had the prosperity and the ambition to build stylish brick sanctuaries, such as the Pink Hill United Methodist Church, erected in 1928 by the white Methodist congregation in Pink Hill. The Colonial Revival-style two-story brick church featured a pilastered steeple, clipped-gable roof, and arched windows *(Fig. 4.14)*. Ebenezer Missionary Baptist Church in LaGrange was built in 1920 by one of the county's oldest African American congregations, established in the 1870s. The brick building is the finest example of Romanesque Revival design in the county *(Fig. 4.15)*.

Fig. 4.14. Pink Hill United Methodist Church, Pink Hill, 1928, demolished 1996 (Photo, Robbie D. Jones, North Carolina Division of Archives and History)

Fig. 4.15. Ebenezer Missionary Baptist Church, LaGrange, 1920 (Photo, Robbie D. Jones, North Carolina Division of Archives and History)

State Institutions

In 1910 the county failed in its campaign to have East Carolina College located in Kinston when a site in nearby Greenville was selected. Soon afterward state officials selected a site just west of Kinston for the new State School for the Feebleminded. The school opened in 1914, and in 1915 the name was changed to Caswell Training School. Since 1956 Caswell Center, as it is now known, has served thirty-one eastern counties. Architects of statewide renown designed buildings for the new school, including Hook and Rogers of Charlotte, C. E. Hartge of Raleigh, Benton and Benton of Wilson, and Mitchell Wooten of Kinston *(Fig. 4.16)*.[25]

The county received another state institution in 1927 when the Women's Industrial Farm Colony located on a rural site north of Kinston. In 1943 the facility became the State Training School for Negro Girls, the first such school for African American females in North Carolina, although Samarcand School for white girls had been established in 1917. The State Training School, now known as Dobbs School, currently serves as a training school for teenage boys.[26]

Fig. 4.16. Caswell Chapel and eight surrounding cottages, Caswell Center, 2415 West Vernon Avenue, Kinston. A. Mitchell Wooten, architect, 1936 (Photo, M. Ruth Little, North Carolina Division of Archives and History)

The Country Store

The hub of social life in rural Lenoir County until recent years was the country store. Small frame store buildings stood at every major crossroads in the county, supplying the farmer with basic food and agricultural supplies—fertilizer, seeds, fuel. Often the storekeeper and his family lived in a residential wing at the back of the store, upstairs, or in a house next door. Sometimes prosperous farmers built stores beside the highway, with their farmhouse sited far to the rear, away from the road. For farmers who needed credit, especially tenant farmers, the store owner usually sold goods under the crop lien system. Throughout the growing season the farmer bought seeds and fertilizer, as well as foodstuffs and other goods, putting up his crop as collateral for the amount of credit extended. At harvest time, when he had sold his tobacco, cotton, or corn, he paid the merchant out of his profits. In 1923, P. T. Smith built the Liddell Cash Supply, a general merchandise store in the Liddell community near Deep Run. Like dozens of his fellow merchants across the county, Smith sold groceries, clothing, plows, fertilizer, and feed *(Fig. 4.17)*. [27] Smith's gable-front wooden store building has a front door recessed between two sets of display windows. A deep front porch, where local farmers surely spent many leisure hours, shelters the storefront.

Fig. 4.17. Liddell Cash Supply, Liddell Crossroads, 1923 (Photo, Robbie D. Jones, North Carolina Division of Archives and History)

Recreation

Rural residents spent most of their leisure time visiting relatives and friends, fishing, hunting, and swimming at millponds. Family tales handed down through the generations bring to life the inventive amusements of the early twentieth century and help to explain life in Lenoir County during this period of rapid progress. People's first reactions to such newfangled inventions as ice-cream cones (invented at the Saint Louis World's Fair in 1904) and elevators (developed in the mid-1800s but not seen in the Lenoir County region until the 1900s) and mirrored restaurants (products of the 1920s and 1930s) were so startling that they have been memorialized in family stories.

A favorite excursion spot for western Lenoir County people was Seven Springs, a spa on the Neuse River just over the Wayne County line. People went there to drink water from the seven different springs that bubbled up on the south bank of the Neuse River and were believed to have health-giving properties. They ate at the Maxwell Hotel or had picnics amid the tall oak trees draped with Spanish moss. One summer Sunday in 1912 two young men from the country near LaGrange, Garland and Earl Walters, rode their ponies to Seven Springs to spend the day. Ice cream was being sold in a new type of container, a sort of inverted cone-shaped tube, so the boys decided to try some. They paid their nickels and started eating. Earl ate the ice cream off the top of his tube, then scooped the rest out with his fingers. Garland began eating so quickly that before he knew it, he had eaten the tube along with the ice cream. When they got home that night, Earl could hardly wait to tell his parents about their trip.

"Ma, you awake?"
"Yes, son."
"We had a good time today," he began, standing in the bedroom doorway.
"I'm glad you did, son."
"Ma, I want to tell you what Garland done."
"Well, what did he do, son?"
"While we wuz down at the Springs we bought us some ice cream, and that man that was sellin' it put it in a funnel. An, an, you know what?"
"What, son?"
"Well, Garland, he eat the funnel."
"Well I declare! It's a wonder it didn't make him sick."[28]

Trains took Lenoir County citizens on business and pleasure trips. Ruth Rouse White, who grew up in the 1880s and 1890s in Moseley Hall Township, sometimes took a Sunday morning excursion train from Lenoir County through New Bern and on to the Atlantic Hotel in Morehead. There vacationers took a ferry to the beach, changed into their bathing suits, and frolicked in and out of the water. In the evening they returned home on the train. Ruth told her children about a dream in which, on the way to Morehead, she got off the train in New Bern to use the rest room. Returning to the track, she discovered that the train had pulled away without her. All the other beachgoers were on board. So, in her dream, she flew all the way to Morehead. When she awoke, she was tireder than she had ever been in her life![29]

A trip to the city of Raleigh held many wonders for a Lenoir County woman. One day in the 1930s Ruth Rouse White of LaGrange spent the day with her daughter in the state capital. They had lunch at the S & W Cafeteria, an elegant place with mirrored walls on the ground floor of the Sir Walter Hotel. As they were eating, Ruth leaned over and whispered into her daughter's ear, "You know, there's somebody over there that keeps looking at me. Every time I look up I see her staring at me. My goodness, she has on a hat exactly like mine." In a little while, she looked again and started laughing. "Law, it's me. There's a mirror over there and I'm looking at myself!"[30]

Millponds such as the Davis Millpond near Strabane, Kelly's Pond near Kinston, Maxwell's Millpond near Pink Hill, Noble's Millpond near Jonestown, and Walters Millpond near LaGrange were favorite recreational destinations for boating, fishing, picnicking, and swimming *(Fig. 4.18)*. John N. Walters and Lou Rouse Walters had a large pond on their farm about two miles from LaGrange. John built a grist mill beside the mill dam. He also constructed two bathhouses (one for

Fig. 4.18. View of Kelly's mill pond, Kinston vicinity. (Photo, Robbie D. Jones, North Carolina Division of Archives and History)

Fig. 4.19. Fishing at Walters Mill Pond, LaGrange vicinity, circa 1928. Clockwise from top left: Ruth Rouse White, her daughters Hazel Ferris and Virginia Dare, and niece Lora Walters. (Collection of M. Ruth Little)

the ladies and one for the gentlemen), a dance hall, and a "concession" that sold sodas and snack food. The pond and grist mill still exist, but the pleasure buildings are gone. People who grew up in the 1910s and 1920s in the vicinity have fond memories of Walters Millpond *(Fig. 4.19)*.

The Queen Anne Farmhouse

The new century brought no immediate shift in architectural design to the county. Most people continued to build the traditional I-house (the two-story, one-room-deep house with a side-gable roof) or the one-story house (one-room-deep with side-gable roof). But availability of cheap sawn lumber and store-bought architectural ornamentation gradually began to change the stolidly conservative, plain character of farmhouses around 1900. The Queen Anne and Italianate Revival styles, popular since the 1880s in the two principal towns of Kinston and LaGrange, appeared sporadically in the countryside. The turn of the century witnessed the peak of popularity of the Queen Anne style. This style displayed ornate millwork such as porch railings, posts, cornices and brackets, gable-end decoration, decorative wooden shinglework, fancy staircases, and mirrored mantels. Queen Anne houses broke out of their nineteenth-century boxes to form front wings, bay windows, wraparound porches, balconies, and porte cocheres. Local industries, such as the Kinston Mantel Company, established in 1913, catered to architectural tastes with mantels, columns, balusters, porch railings, screen doors, windows, storefronts, and all kinds of wooden interior finish. W. H. O'Berry, the owner, also operated a lumber mill that turned out dressed lumber and shingles.[31]

The new house that John H. Rouse, buggy manufacturer, cabinetmaker, and casket maker, built in LaGrange for his large family around 1900 is a commodious, two-story frame dwelling in the Queen Anne style *(Fig. 4.20)*. The side-gable main block has a two-story front wing with a two-story bay window, and a spacious wraparound front porch with a cornice accented with brackets resembling wheel spokes. John Fields Jr., a substantial farmer in Moseley Hall Township, and his wife, Betty Pope Fields, had a large and well-appointed Queen Anne-style farmhouse built about

Fig. 4.20. John H. Rouse House, 206 West Washington Street, LaGrange, circa 1900 (Photo, Robbie D. Jones, North Carolina Division of Archives and History)

1906 next to Fields Station, east of LaGrange. The large two-story house, capped by a deep hipped roof, features roof gables, bay windows, and a wraparound porch with a balcony above the front entrance. The interior is lavishly finished with an ornate staircase, fancy mantels with mirrored overmantels, and an intricate wooden hall screen with turned and sawn ornament *(Fig. 4.21)*.

The Queen Anne style was equally adaptable to smaller houses, whether appearing merely in decorative trim or breaking out into wings and bays. In 1906 the *Kinston Free Press* described the new house built for Dr. Richard Williams Wooten in Southwest Township as a "comfortable and attractive cottage home" *(Fig. 4.22)*.[32] Wooten was a prominent farmer and rural doctor whose practice included both Lenoir and Jones counties. He cultivated seventy-five acres in crops and kept a large garden. His "cottage" utilized the simple side-gable form that had been popular in the county for many years, but its front gable with colored-glass window and brightly painted sunburst evoked the Queen Anne style found in much bolder form in the towns of Kinston and LaGrange. In 1908-1909 Stephen Nathan Gilbert built a Queen Anne cottage for his family near Hugo. Using lumber sawn at his father's nearby Gilbert Sawmill, he spent five hundred dollars for his materials and paid five hundred dollars to the carpenters.[33] The one-story house has a front-gable wing with a bay window, decorative cross gables, and a wraparound front porch with turned posts with decorative sawnwork brackets *(Fig. 4.23)*. The Johnny Hill House, built in 1918 near Deep Run, is a one-story gable-and-wing frame house with a wraparound front porch with turned columns, a railing with turned balusters, and sawnwork trim. The gable ends contain stained-glass windows.

Many people throughout the county built compact one-story houses with deep hipped roofs that resemble pyramids. These pyramidal-roofed cottages were built from the turn of the century to about 1925. Like many houses in the county, these cottages had tall ceilings, which combined with the high roof to keep the rooms comfortable during summer heats. Noah Small Sr. bought thirty

Fig. 4.21. Interior of the John and Betty Fields House (Photo, Robbie D. Jones, North Carolina Division of Archives and History)

acres in the Wheat Swamp vicinity about 1925 and had a pyramidal-roofed cottage built for his family. A bracketed front porch shelters the front door, which opens to a high-ceilinged hallway leading straight to the back door. The back door opens onto a porch alongside the dining room and kitchen wing *(Fig. 4.24)*.

Fig. 4.22. Dr. Richard Williams Wooten House, Southwest Township, circa 1906 (Heritage Place, Lenoir Community College)

Fig. 4.23. Stephen Nathan Gilbert House, Hugo vicinity, 1908–1909 (Photo, Robbie D. Jones, North Carolina Division of Archives and History)

Fig. 4.24. Noah Small Sr. House, Wheat Swamp vicinity, circa 1925 (Photo, M. Ruth Little, North Carolina Division of Archives and History)

120

The American Foursquare House

Although Victorian styles remained popular for several decades, early in the twentieth century increasing numbers of citizens began to experiment with two new house types, particularly the American foursquare and the Craftsman bungalow. Charles A. Broadway Sr., Graingers Store owner and railroad stationmaster, had his large house built beside the railroad tracks in the depot community about 1915 *(Fig. 4.25)*.[34] The square, two-story wooden house is covered by a low hipped roof, has interior chimneys, and features the four-room floor plan typical of the American foursquare, with the front door opening directly into the living room. To adapt this house type to Lenoir County, Broadway had a porch with heavy classical posts built across the entire front and down one side of the house. Inside, Broadway added such modern features as pocket doors and brick mantels, not found in earlier farmhouses.

Prefabricated houses ordered from catalogues were popular in Lenoir County, as they were throughout the nation. In 1918 young farmer Simpson Waller and his wife, Minnie Williams Waller, ordered a new house from the Aladdin Homes catalogue. They selected the Charleston model, at a cost of $2,604.[35] The Michigan-based Aladdin Company had a manufacturing plant in Wilmington, North Carolina, at this time, and Waller's house may have been shipped from there. The American foursquare house has two stories, a hipped roof with a dormer window, a front bay window, and a classical front porch. Waller located his house near Woodington, and it has survived with little alteration *(Fig. 4.26)*. The house kit came complete with hardware, and the trademark doorknobs and brass door knocker in the shape of a genie still adorn the building. The house has a small front porch with classical posts, and shallow bay windows projecting in the front and sides. In 1918 Claude Douglas Brown purchased a Sears and Roebuck house through the company's

Fig. 4.25. Charles A. Broadway Sr. House, Graingers, circa 1915 (Photo, Robbie D. Jones, North Carolina Division of Archives and History)

Fig. 4.26. Simpson Waller House, Woodington vicinity, 1918 (Photo, Robbie D. Jones, North Carolina Division of Archives and History)

Modern Homes catalogue for $2,365 and assembled it on U.S. Highway 70 near Kelly's Mill.[36] The large, two-story, double-pile frame house has a hipped roof and conforms to the American foursquare type. It contains a parlor, a dining room, a kitchen, four bedrooms, two bathrooms, and a full basement and large attic.

The Craftsman Bungalow

The Craftsman style, an architectural manifestation of the Arts and Crafts movement, a glorification of hand craftsmanship, was the most popular house style in Lenoir County during the 1920s through 1940s. When farmer Redding Jackson built his new house near Fountain Hill Crossroads in 1917-1918, family tradition holds that he had the lumber brought from New Bern to Grifton by boat, then hauled by mule wagon to the site *(Fig. 4.27).*[37] The frame two-story farmhouse still reflects the architectural form of turn-of-the-century farmhouses, with its front-gable wing, two decorative front cross gables, and front door with transom and sidelights. Yet Redding built a porch that wraps around the front facade, with posts in the new Craftsman style, consisting of thick brick bases supporting tapering Doric posts.

The bungalow, a one-story house form, is the hallmark of the Craftsman style. Stylish bungalows were introduced in Kinston by 1920 but were not limited to towns. In the north end of the county, farmer Carl Jones had a bold bungalow built for his family in 1924 *(Fig. 4.28).*[38] The low, horizontal one-story house has a shed dormer recessed into the roof to create a balcony. The slate roof extends out to cover the front porch, supported by massive brick posts and a brick railing. The most dramatic feature is the heavy wooden arch that stretches the full width of the porch. Balancing the porte cochere on one side is a matching porch on the other side; both have heavy brick posts. The spacious interior features French doors, a hall screen, and four mantels.

Fig. 4.27. Redding Jackson Farm, Fountain Hill crossroads, 1917-1918 (Photo, Robbie D. Jones, North Carolina Division of Archives and History)

Such large bungalows were exceptional; far more typical were modest Craftsman houses such as the one built for Adair Kennedy and his wife, Mary Harper Kennedy, in the vicinity of Woodington when they married in 1932.[39] The side-gable roof shelters an engaged front porch with Craftsman posts, and the front shed dormer and roof brackets resemble those on more flamboyant bungalows, yet there is no porte cochere, and the windows are small sash windows with Craftsman-patterned upper muntins *(Fig. 4.29)*. Many Craftsman houses in the county have front-gabled forms featuring minimal ornamentation: porches with the typical brick bases supporting tapering wooden posts, and triangular eave brackets.

During the later popularity of the Craftsman style, in the 1930s and 1940s, modern amenities such as indoor plumbing and electrified kitchens were incorporated into houses during construction. The functions of the old detached kitchens, smokehouses, and washhouses became integrated into the main house, and domestic outbuildings largely disappeared. Owners of old houses with detached kitchens found that the breezeway between the main house and the kitchen made a perfect place for an indoor bathroom.

Housing in Lenoir County has changed radically since World War II. The introduction of such housing alternatives as the "ranch house," a low, one-story dwelling often built of brick; the mobile home; the manufactured house; and the subdivision has changed the traditional landscape. The use of new synthetic materials such as vinyl siding, and the standardization of design, heighten appreciation of the architectural value of both simple and fancy older farmhouses still standing in the countryside.

Fig. 4.28. Carl Jones House, Taylors Crossroads vicinity (Photo, Robbie D. Jones, North Carolina Division of Archives and History)

Fig. 4.29. Adair Kennedy House, Woodington vicinity, 1932 (Photo, Robbie D. Jones, North Carolina Division of Archives and History)

124

Chapter Five:

Kinston in the
Twentieth Century

Fig. 5. 1: Tull Hotel, Kinston, circa 1896, demolished.
(Duke University Rare Book, Manuscript, & Special
Collections Library)

Two watershed events in 1895—an awful fire and the introduction of a great new crop, tobacco—inaugurated Kinston and Lenoir County's modern era. On February 28, 1895, a fire broke out in a stable and destroyed two central blocks of Kinston's business district, the blocks facing Queen Street between Caswell and Gordon Streets on the south and north, extending back to Herritage and McLewean streets on the west and east. Nearly two dozen additional fires, apparently a spate of arson, between February and June of 1895 burned many other Kinston businesses and dwellings.[1]

Occurring during an optimistic decade, the disastrous fire of 1895 slowed but did not stop Kinston's growth. Old wooden stores along Queen Street, identified with the nineteenth century, gave way to modern commercial buildings. Looking back in 1921, Kinston's mayor described the town as a phoenix rising from the ashes: "What many then thought was Kinston's finish proved to be only the beginning of the greater Kinston of which we are so proud today. The burnt district was rebuilt with brick buildings of modern construction and its rebuilding became contagious."[2] Dr. Henry Tull rebuilt the Tull Hotel at the northeast corner of Queen and Caswell Streets. A round turret with an onion-shaped dome at the corner of the large, two-story brick building led Kinstonians to praise the hotel's "Moorish flair" *(Fig. 5.1 See previous page)*.[3] The year after the fire the town built a new brick fire station next to the courthouse, which is now a firehouse museum.[4]

Tobacco Town

Beginning in 1895 tobacco drove the Kinston economy, with textiles and carriage manufacturing adding to the market vitality. The early tobacco warehouses stood at the edge of the business district, on Herritage Street near the river. Jesse Grainger expanded his first tobacco warehouse, the Kinston-Carolina Warehouse, at the corner of Herritage Street and Vernon Avenue in 1896 and hired Roxboro native and tobacconist Luther P. Tapp, from the Old Bright Belt, to manage it. Tapp stayed in Kinston, acquired part ownership in several other warehouses, and eventually built Tapp's Warehouse at the corner of Herritage and King Streets. Other Old Belt tobacconists, including R. L. Crisp of Caswell County and E. Norman Dickerson of Granville County, settled in Kinston in the mid-nineties. Hardware merchant B. W. Canady opened Kinston's second warehouse, the Atlantic Warehouse, at the corner of Herritage and Washington Streets in 1896 *(Fig. 5.2)*.[5] By 1906 four more tobacco warehouses stood around the business district: the Eagle Warehouse (1898), at 200 East Lenoir Street; the Central Warehouse (1899), at the corner of Herritage and North Streets; the Farmers Warehouse; and the Knott Brothers Warehouse (early 1900s), in the 100 block of East Washington Street.[6]

Tobacco processing facilities were constructed as well. The John R. Hughes Tobacco Company built a large factory on Herritage Street. In 1898 Hoge Irvine built a stemmery. Six large tobacco prizeries, where the tobacco was packed into hogsheads for shipment, were constructed in the 1890s, one by the American Tobacco Company. By 1902 the Imperial Tobacco Company had built a processing plant.[7] In the early 1910s the tobacco warehouses enlarged their spaces, and the factories of C. R. Dodson, E. V. Webb and the Imperial Tobacco Company doubled their capacities. By 1914 Kinston had become one of the largest bright-leaf tobacco markets in the world, selling over 12 million pounds the previous year.[8]

Some of the new tobacco buildings strutted flashy architecture—brick walls with decorative parapets, or sprawling frame construction with multiple-gable roofs. The Atlantic Warehouse and the Knott Brothers Warehouse had false fronts with jaunty curves. The Imperial Tobacco Company's ca. 1925 office on the railroad tracks at North Herritage Street features ornate brick crenellated parapets with diamond-shaped accents along the roofline *(Fig. 5.3)*.

During the 1930s more than ten tobacco buildings, mostly brick, sat north, west, and east of the business district. In 1942 Kinston's nine tobacco warehouses sold 50 million pounds of leaf. Liggett and Myers, R. J. Reynolds, and the American Tobacco Company, the big three tobacco producers, bought tobacco in Kinston but did their processing elsewhere. Five firms that processed tobacco had plants in town: E. V. Webb and Company, L. B. Jenkins and Company, Dixie Leaf Tobacco Company, Imperial Tobacco Company, and Export Tobacco Company. By the early 1950s the facilities had grown to include fourteen tobacco warehouses and seven processing plants. During the 1960s there were twelve auction warehouses and six processing plants in business.[9]

The other major tobacco market towns in the Coastal Plain, Rocky Mount, Wilson, and Greenville, had slightly larger marketing facilities and gradually, during the first half of the twentieth century, surpassed Kinston in volume of tobacco sold. Wilson claimed to be the largest bright-leaf market in the United States by the mid-1960s.[10]

Fig. 5.2. Atlantic Warehouse, corner of Herritage and Washington streets, Kinston, 1896, demolished (Heritage Place, Lenoir Community College)

Fig. 5.3. Imperial Tobacco Company Office, 420 North Herritage Street, Kinston, circa 1925 (Photo, M. Ruth Little, North Carolina Division of Archives and History)

The Making of Modern Kinston

Kinston attracted other new businesses and population throughout the 1890s. The population more than doubled during the decade, from 1,762 in 1890 to 4,106 in 1900. The Quinn and Miller Furniture Company, D. V. Dixon and Son Hardware, and the Bank of Kinston were established. Businessmen such as J. A. McDaniel, merchant, hotel proprietor, and East Kinston developer; N. J. Rouse, attorney and entrepreneur; and druggist J. E. Hood moved to town. People from surrounding counties who used to shop in New Bern, Goldsboro, Raleigh, or Fayetteville now came to Kinston.[11]

Kinston's growth as a retail center was due in part to its Jewish community. By 1872 Eastern European Jewish families began to settle in Kinston. They were part of a wave of immigrants who had begun arriving in the United States in the mid-nineteenth century, and some moved into the South, where they opened cash stores in many small towns. Among Kinston's early Jewish families were Dave, Abe, and Sol Oettinger, who opened Oettinger Brothers store. Morris Pearson opened a dry goods store about 1900. Hyman Stadiem started a clothing store, H. Stadiem, that still operates. Other early familes in Kinston included the Foxmans, Blooms, Adlers, and Kanters. Tiphereth Israel Temple, Kinston's first Jewish congregation, formed in 1904.[12]

In addition to the tobacco industry, carriage factories, textile mills, and lumber plants were established in town. Kinston had had an important carriage manufactory since before the Civil War, when the Dibble Carriage Works flourished. More men worked in this trade than in any other in Kinston in 1860. Although interrupted by the war, Kinston's carriage trade regained its central role in the southern United States. The Ellis Carriage Works opened in 1886 and soon developed a business that extended from Virginia to Florida. The company built an assembly building at 126 West Blount Street, then erected a new building on the same site about 1910. It still stands,

130

although it was converted in the 1930s to an automobile showroom. In 1890 C. T. Randolph opened his carriage factory in Kinston and was soon making more than seven hundred vehicles a year. After the Randolph Carriage Factory was destroyed by the 1895 fire, C. T. Randolph immediately built a new, three-story brick building at the southeast corner of Queen and Gordon Streets. In LaGrange, John H. Rouse opened a buggy and casket factory in the 1890s.[13]

The textile industry, which had begun in 1891 with the Orion Mill, continued to prosper. The Orion Mill's success led to the construction in 1898 of the Kinston Cotton Mills, which produced cotton yarn from baled cotton to supply Orion Mill. The two-story brick building was constructed adjacent to Orion Mill. Built in the simple Italianate Revival style that had become standard among textile mills in North Carolina, the building had a four-story entrance tower and large windows *(Fig. 5.4)*.[14] The Caswell Cotton Mill (now known as Glen Raven Mill) was erected on the riverbank west of the business district in 1909. The company built forty-two substantial frame mill houses on its property.[15]

Timber processing also fueled Kinston's growth at the turn of the century. About 1897 the Hines Brothers Lumber Company was established to provide materials for the booming construction industry in town. Harvesting lumber from the pine forests in the region, the company produced railroad crossties, heavy bridge timber, house sills, fence posts, moldings, tobacco sticks, bed slats, and other products. The company became one of the largest manufacturers of wood products in eastern North Carolina and remained a strong force in Kinston's economy until after the Great Depression.[16] Several other lumber companies, including the Kinston Lumber Company, also operated in the town.

By 1900 Kinston's booming economy, and particularly its position as a wholesale grocery distribution point for surrounding counties, prompted the Atlantic and North Carolina Railroad to construct a large brick freight depot just off Queen Street *(Fig. 5.5)*. The railroad used the depot until the 1980s.[17]

The first two decades of the twentieth century continued the boom of the Gay Nineties, with new industries, commercial enterprises, and population growth. By 1910 there were 6,995 people in Kinston; by 1920, 9,771. The business district filled in with brick buildings from one to four sto-

Fig. 5.4. Kinston Cotton Mills, Atlantic & North Carolina Railroad tracks, Kinston, 1898 (Heritage Place, Lenoir Community College)

Fig. 5.5. Atlantic & North Carolina Freight Depot, south side of Blount Street between Queen and McLewean Streets, Kinston, 1900. (Duke University Rare Book, Manuscript, & Special Collections Library)

ries high. The Hotel Caswell, built by J. A. McDaniel, opened in 1906 at 108-114 South Queen Street near the courthouse. Its fifty rooms all had electric lights and call bells.[18] The flat-roofed three-story brick building with stone window trim still stands on Queen Street. In 1914 the United States Post Office, a Roman-appearing limestone and granite landmark, was built on the northeast corner of Queen and North Streets.

If banks are an indicator of an economy's vitality, then the three banks at the corner of Queen and Gordon Streets, which created "Banker's Corner," the focus of the business district, tell Kinston's tale *(Fig. 5.6)*. About 1900 B. W. Canady built his brick Romanesque Revival-style hardware and agricultural implement store, with rows of round-arched windows, on the southeast corner. During the next few years the other three corners filled up with banks. In 1906 the First National Bank erected their three-story up-to-date Beaux Arts style office, with terra cotta trim and a dome at the northeast corner. Two years later the National Bank of Kinston built its Neoclassical Revival-style office on the southwest corner; the structure was expanded in 1925. In 1924 the Farmers and Merchants Bank built, on the northwest corner, an impressive six-story Renaissance Revival bank designed by Benton and Benton, Architects, of Wilson.

By the early twentieth century Herritage Street, which had been the main street of the antebellum, river-oriented era, had metamorphosed into the tobacco and transportation district, full of warehouses and stables. Queen Street became the main business street during the railroad era. In the mid-1910s horse-drawn wagons and autos shared the newly paved streets of Kinston and the dirt roads of the county *(Fig. 5.7)*. By the 1920s automobile garages and salesrooms had moved onto Herritage Street.

Good schools were a significant factor in Kinston's turn-of-the-century growth. The most famous educator in Kinston was Dr. Richard Henry Lewis. From 1877 to 1882 Lewis headed the Kinston Collegiate Institute. From 1882 to 1889 he operated a second school, Kinston College, and from 1893 to 1902 a third institution, known as "Dr. Lewis's School" *(Fig. 5.8)*.[19]

Fig. 5.6. Banker's Corner, intersection of North Queen and Gordon Streets, Kinston (Sarah Pope Postcard Collection, Goldsboro)

Fig. 5.7. Inscore & White's Livery & Sale Stables, Herritage Street, Kinston, circa 1914. Co-owner John Hughes White holds the horse's reins in the center. (Collection of M. Ruth Little)

Kinston began to offer the amenities of a city. A 1903 bond referendum to improve the electrical system and the waterworks, to create a new sewer system and fire alarm system, and to pave Queen Street was passed. By 1906 Queen Street was paved with vitrified bricks. During 1915-1916 twelve miles of Kinston's city streets were paved with asphalt, and a complete sewerage system was installed. Lenoir County taxpayers went into debt to finance one of the earliest paved road systems in the state. Beginning in 1919, hard-surfaced roads were built toward New Bern, Trenton, Greenville, Goldsboro, Kenansville and Snow Hill. These roads extended to the county borders to await linkage with roads in adjacent counties. The Central Highway, which paralleled the tracks of the North Carolina Railroad from Morehead to Asheville, was built in the 1910s, passing through Kinston on Queen Street and Vernon Avenue. It later became U.S. Highway 10 and then U.S. Highway 70. In the late 1960s a four-lane highway was constructed on the south side of the Neuse River to bypass town.[20]

Health care available to Kinston and Lenoir County residents improved gradually. Dr. Henry Otis Hyatt (1848-1922) operated the Hyatt Eye Hospital and later the Hyatt Sanatorium, a private hospital, in a large frame house on North Queen Street in the 1890s and early twentieth century. Brothers Dr. James M. Parrott and Dr. W. Thomas Parrott set up a hospital in 1905 in J. A. and Laura McDaniel's stylish frame house way out on East Gordon Street. Because the McDaniels had donated the house as a hospital, it was named the Robert Bruce McDaniel Memorial Hospital for their son, who died in infancy. In 1914 the Parrotts enlarged the house into a modern two-story brick building, which they named Parrott Memorial Hospital *(Fig. 5.9)*.[21] By 1925 Kinston's growth necessitated a second hospital. This new, thirty-bed institution, the first public hospital, stood in the northwest section of town at the corner of Rhodes Avenue and College Street and was known as Memorial General Hospital. This hospital was replaced by a larger facility, a three-story brick International Style building, about 1950. Both Parrott Memorial and Memorial General Hospitals continued to operate until 1973, when they were replaced by the large Lenoir Memorial Hospital.

Fig. 5.8. Lewis School, 300 block East King Street, built circa 1893, demolished (Duke University Rare Book, Manuscript, & Special Collections Library)

134

Fig. 5.9. Parrott Memorial Hospital, East Gordon Street, Kinston, 1914, demolished (Heritage Place, Lenoir Community College)

The eleven-story Moorish Revival-style Hotel Kinston marked the apogee of Kinston's downtown development and has remained the tallest building in the town *(Fig. 5.10)*. This hotel was erected in 1928 at the northeast corner of North Queen Street and Peyton Avenue, establishing the northern boundary of the business district until after World War II. A colonnade formed of polychrome Moorish arches forms the main entrance of the brick building. J. Herman Canady, who worked with his father in the B. W. Canady hardware business, managed an unusual campaign to raise public funds to build the hotel. For many years the Hotel Kinston was the hub of civic and social activities, with wedding receptions, dances, banquets, and other events taking place in its ballroom. Following its closure in the late 1960s, the building was leased in 1969 to the Kinston Housing Authority, which converted the one hundred guest rooms to apartments for the elderly.[22]

During the Great Depression, which began in 1929 and lasted until the late 1930s, local banks and businesses closed, industry halted, and Lenoir County agriculture fell to its lowest point since the Civil War. In Kinston the Orion Mill closed its doors. Kinston's oldest bank, the First National Bank, shut down in April 1931; soon afterward the National Bank of Kinston closed. Yet even in the depths of the depression there were hopeful developments. A group of local businessmen, including H. I. Gross, and New York entrepreneurs bought the Orion Mill and converted it to a shirt factory, which became known as Hampton Industries. The Farmers and Merchants Bank remained open, and in 1933 the Branch Banking and Trust Company opened an office in the First National Bank building.[23]

Businesses and individuals recovered slowly in the later 1930s. A number of substantial houses and at least one church were built in Kinston during this period. In the business district some sophisticated renovations modernized the early twentieth-century-storefronts. The Laroque and Hewitt Building at 105 West Gordon Street received a sophisticated new facade of black glass panels. The Grand Theatre at 211 North Queen Street was remodeled and renamed the Paramount. In 1935 the Carolina Theatre at 121 North Queen Street was created out of an old building by adding an Art Deco facade with cream and black tile accents. The Smart and Thrifty Clothing Store building at 123 North Queen Street gained a Moderne-style facade of large white and pink

Fig. 5.10. Former Hotel Kinston, 501 North Queen Street, Kinston, 1928 (Photo, Allison Black, North Carolina Division of Archives and History)

marble tiles in 1938.[24]

In 1940, with Works Projects Administration funding, the old county courthouse was replaced with a bold modern courthouse designed in 1939 by local architect A. Mitchell Wooten and his associate, John J. Rowland. The four-story limestone building features plaques adorned with low-relief sculpture featuring Indians with peace pipes and tobacco leaves *(Fig. 5.11)*.

Fig. 5.11. Lenoir County Courthouse, northeast corner of King and Queen Streets, Kinston, 1940. A. Mitchell Wooten, architect (Heritage Place, Lenoir Community College)

Fashionable New Suburbs

Kinston's bustling business district—block after block of neat frame dwellings, cotton mills, tobacco warehouses, and factories—served as a powerful magnet drawing rural residents. By the mid 1890s the original core of Kinston had been largely developed, and landowners who held large tracts around the town limits began subdividing their acreage and selling building lots to accommodate expansion. The development of Trianon into one of Kinston's fashionable new sections, as well as the development of Mitchelltown on the west side of the town limits and the Grainger Hill area on the north side into middle-class white suburbs, is a story that unfolded from the 1890s through the first third of the twentieth century.

James A. McDaniel (1867-1928), who had moved to Kinston from Jones County in the 1870s and received his education at Wake Forest College and the Eastman Business School in New York, was ready to help Kinston break out of its eastern boundaries. In 1893 he bought three hundred acres of the old Richard W. King plantation and

> built far out in the field a beautiful residence. It was considered that the young man had put his money to a foolish use. But he had thought before he leaped. He began cultivating and improving a portion of it and laid the balance off into lots and extended the streets from the town through the farm, set out trees and began to offer all kinds of inducements to parties wishing to build. That beautiful residence, once far out in that old field, for a while looked lonely, but now has drawn the town right up to it and around it *(Fig. 5.12)*. [25]

McDaniel named his East Kinston development Trianon. His own house was a rambling frame Queen Anne-style cottage with a piazza with a turreted central gazebo. By the late 1890s fashionable houses had been built near McDaniel's house by M. H. Wooten, a schoolteacher, and Carl W. Pridgen, a merchant.

On the west side of Kinston, a farmer became a developer. Adolphus Mitchell (1851-1906), a Granville County native, purchased two hundred acres in 1882 and raised cotton and corn for some years. In 1894 he began to sell building lots at the south end of the property adjacent to the Atlantic and North Carolina railroad tracks along Mitchell Street and West Peyton Avenue. Early deeds refer to the area as Mitchell Town, and Mitchell began to call himself a "Home dealer."

Fig. 5.12. James A. McDaniel House, later Parrott Memorial Hospital, East Gordon Street, Kinston, circa 1893, demolished (Heritage Place, Lenoir Community College)

Mitchell continued to lay out streets, including College and Pollock Streets, and sell off lots until his death. In 1913 his family sold the remainder of the land to the Atlantic Coast Realty Company, a Greenville development company, which developed smaller, more standardized lots through the early 1920s. Dwellers who built in Mitchelltown before 1900 included postmaster J. C. Wooten, jeweler Kleber Denmark and James Ellis, owner of the Ellis Carriage Works. In the new century sheriff and mayor Dal F. Wooten, tobacco warehouseman G. P. Fleming, tobacconists Luther P. Tapp and William Knott were among many people who built houses in the neighborhood.[26]

Up on the Hill north of town, prominent merchant, industrialist, and civic leader Jesse Grainger acquired sole interest in John C. Washington's estate, Vernon Heights, in 1892. Grainger lived in the main residence and began to lay out streets and sell off lots for homes on what became known as Grainger Hill. He also built houses for both speculation and rental. The area grew slowly and continued to develop long after Grainger's death in 1910. Large houses were built on expansive lots along the Hill, and smaller lots and houses appeared on the flatter terrain to the north and south.

Kinston's late-nineteenth-century developers built some of the finest houses in town for themselves. After donating his first Trianon house for use as a hospital in 1905, James A. McDaniel constructed two more homes for himself before the Great Depression. One block away at 702 East Gordon Street he built a larger, even more stylish two-and-one-half-story frame Queen Anne-style house, enriched with such sophisticated details as pebbledash stucco gables, a Palladian window, and Ionic porch columns. In 1914 McDaniel and his wife retired to their large farm in the Falling Creek township, to a frame Colonial Revival-style country home that they named Maxwood *(Fig. 5.13)*.[27]

Some Kinstonians could afford to hire architects to design their homes. In 1905 Jesse Grainger hired New Bern architect Herbert Woodley Simpson to design a home for his daughter Capitola and her husband, Daniel T. Edwards, publisher of the *Kinston Free Press*. Contractor S. M. Harrell

Fig. 5.13. Maxwood, residence of Mr. and Mrs. James A. McDaniel, Falling Creek, circa 1914 (Photo, Robbie D. Jones, North Carolina Division of Archives and History)

built the massive Neoclassical Revival-style brick residence, located on the Hill east of Grainger's home, Vernon Heights *(Fig. 5.14)*. Inspired by the popular image of an antebellum Deep South plantation house, the home's most prominent feature is a massive, classical curved portico with six fluted Corinthian columns that shelters the front entrance and the ornate wooden balcony above it. The house, named Sarahurst, stood at the termination of Queen Street until 1914, when it had to be moved aside to extend the street, but even without its original imposing site it remains the grandest residence in the Grainger Hill neighborhood. Sarahurst is typical of the architect Simpson's large houses for wealthy clients in New Bern and other eastern North Carolina towns. Simpson also designed an only slightly less imposing brick Neoclassical Revival house on the Hill, at 108 Park Avenue, for Mrs. Alice Fields, widow of W. C. Fields, a cotton broker and developer who had been a business partner of Grainger.[28]

One of the finest houses of the late 1920s built in Kinston is the Harvey C. Hines House on North Queen Street. Hines was the local Coca-Cola distributor and also owned Hines Ice Cream Factory. Designed by High Point architect Herbert Hunter, Hines' striking brick Tudor Revival-style house features a picturesque assemblage of shapes, casement windows set in stone trim, and huge chimneys with chimney pots, all set behind a matching brick wall that creates an unusually private enclave amid the open streetscape of Kinston *(Fig. 5.15)*.

Some Kinstonians ordered their homes through the mail and received them in a railcar shipment. J. T. Pratt erected The Carolina, a mail-order house from Aladdin Homes, on his lot on East Capitola Avenue. He built The Virginia, another Aladdin Home, on the adjacent lot, apparently as a rental dwelling.[29] Aladdin probably shipped the houses from its plant in Wilmington, North Carolina. Both of these models are American foursquare homes, compact two-story houses with the simple, bold trim made popular by the Arts and Crafts movement of the early twentieth century.

Suburban growth often draws energy away from older neighborhoods, and in Kinston the growth of Trianon, Mitchelltown, Grainger Hill, and other new developments gradually displaced

Fig. 5.14. Sarahurst, residence of Daniel T. Edwards and Capitola Edwards, 1201 North Queen Street, Kinston, circa 1905 (Photo, M. Ruth Little, North Carolina Division of Archives and History)

Fig. 5.15. Harvey C. Hines House, 1118 North Queen Street, Kinston, late 1920s, Herbert Hunter, architect. (Photo, Allison Black, North Carolina Division of Archives and History)

the original residential area of Bright, King, and Herritage streets, which had become "south Kinston." The streets where stood the old town houses of founding fathers Richard Caswell, Simon Bright, John Herritage, and others sank into shabby gentility in the early twentieth century.

One of the most prominent members of the building trades whose skill and industry transformed Kinston during the first third of the century was Robert L. Blalock. Blalock, born in nearby Johnston County in 1870, became a building contractor, working in various North Carolina cities until 1906, when he moved to Kinston. Until his death in 1929 he operated a large construction company in Kinston that employed some of the best local craftsmen. He designed and engineered all of his buildings in handsome classical and other revival styles. His work includes a number of former landmarks now demolished: the Quinn and Miller Furniture Store at Queen and Caswell Streets, Lewis School on East King Street, Hines Ice Cream Factory at the southwest corner of Gordon and Herritage Streets, and Union Station on East Caswell Street. Among his works still standing are several buildings at the Caswell Center, the Hunter Building at 103 South Queen Street, and the J. C. Penney Building at 300 North Queen Street.[30]

A. Mitchell Wooten (1905-1940), apparently Kinston's first formally trained architect, grew up in Kinston; studied architecture at Georgia Tech, in Europe, and in New York City; and then returned to Kinston, where he designed several dozen buildings in the late 1930s. These were primarily Colonial Revival-style residences but also included the courthouse, an impressive complex of buildings at the Caswell Center (the former Ehringhaus Building and a circle of cottage dormitories), and the first two public housing projects in Kinston: Simon Bright Housing, for whites, and Mitchell Wooten Housing, for blacks.[31]

Wooten brought to Kinston the design concepts of the Art Moderne, or Modernistic style of the 1920s and 1930s, which he had absorbed in Europe and New York. He especially admired the integration of sculpture into architecture that became popular in the Art Deco and Art Moderne styles of the 1920s and 1930s, particularly on commercial and institutional buildings. Wooten introduced the Art Moderne style to Kinston with two of his last commissions, the courthouse and the housing projects, both designed shortly before his sudden death in November 1940. The public housing features flat-roofed brick buildings illuminated by windows that wrap dramatically around the corners and decorated with cast concrete plaques showing children at play. At the same time Wooten and his associate, John J. Rowland, designed two public housing complexes in New Bern: Trent Court, for whites, and Craven Terrace, for blacks. These projects feature the same modernist style and sculptural panels of children at play.[32]

Wooten's residential work in Kinston reflected his clients' taste for conservative Colonial Revival forms. Only two of his house designs reflect his modernist inclinations: the Henry Johnson House at 2111 North Queen Street and Wooten's own home at 1003 West Road. The Johnson House is a streamlined brick house with a modernist staircase lit by a large multipaned window. The Wooten House, which Wooten himself described as "Nassau Colonial," is an elegant Art Moderne-style ranch house, one of few in eastern North Carolina *(Fig. 5.16)*. The one-story painted brick house encloses an atrium with a granite fountain. Wooten's untimely death in 1940 sadly deprived Kinston of the further development of his bold synthesis of tradition and modernism in public buildings.[33]

Fig. 5.16. A. Mitchell Wooten House, 1003 West Road, Kinston, 1939-1940 (Photo, Penne Smith, North Carolina Division of Archives and History)

Kinston's African Americans during the Jim Crow years

At the turn of the century Kinston's African Americans, like blacks throughout North Carolina and the South, lost many of their political rights, including the right to vote. The Jim Crow laws and social codes enforced during the early twentieth century, which continued in use until the 1960s, had the effect of solidifying separate white and black commercial and residential districts. In some ways the control of such regulations, through enforced separate public facilities for whites and blacks, was blatant; in other ways, through deed covenants and town ordinances, the control was less obvious, although just as constricting.

Segregation evolved naturally in Kinston even before Jim Crow laws took effect. In nineteenth-century Kinston blacks had lived in close proximity to whites, first in enforced slavery and later as paid servants. In the later years of the century black businesses, such as Thomas Green's barber shop, shared the white business district. But by the 1880s blacks had begun to create their own neighborhoods of Tuckahoe, Tower Hill, and Lincoln City.

In 1919 the African Americans who had made their homes in the areas of East Bright and Shine Streets, Lincoln City, and Tower Hill went about their business cautiously, as these words of the Reverend R. S. Oden, minister of the Saint Augustus A.M.E. Zion Church, indicate:

> As a watchman on the wall, I can say to the colored citizens of Kinston, that we have some splendid friends among the white people of the city, and we do well to act in such a way as not to cause them to become fearful as to our position in this our community. We want to be industrious, manly, respectful, and producers of things, and a sentiment that will cause our friends to know that we stand for those things that assure peace and construction and the growth to this our city.[34]

Segregation forced African Americans to do most of their shopping and dining on South Queen Street and in East Kinston. Small black businesses, including those of launderers and dry cleaners, barbers, grocers, mechanics, taxi companies, sign painters, masons, bricklayers, and hoteliers, catered to their own communities.

In 1902 Starr Hicks's grocery operated at 221 South Queen Street, and its competitors in the immediate area included Fred Nunn at 327 South Queen Street and S. F. Gorham at 302 South Queen Street. Other African American businesses at that time included Jesse Hawkins's shoe shop at 304 South Queen Street, Harriett Linker's restaurant at 324 South Queen Street, and Nancy Parker's oyster business at 208 South Queen Street. Charles Dunn's bank and hotel also stood in the 200 block of South Queen Street. The commercial area spurred residential growth. Blacks, many of them laborers, began to settle along nearby East Shine and East Bright Streets.[35] By 1920 Kinston's main African American commercial area was located along South Queen Street below West King Street. In spite of competition from smaller commercial areas in Tower Hill and Lincoln City, South Queen Street remained preeminent into the 1950s.

The businesses of some previously successful black businessmen in Kinston failed during this era, perhaps as a result of racial repression. Of three successful African American entrepreneurs in Kinston in the late nineteenth century—Charles Dunn, Joseph Hargett, and Peter Borden—only Borden continued his businesses into the early twentieth century comparatively unscathed. Borden's close ties to the Saint Augustus A.M.E. Zion Church, where he was chairman of the Board of Trustees by 1919, provide some insight into his mercantile stability. Borden's grocery, on the edge of Lincoln City at East Bright and South East Streets in 1919, was in an area settled predominantly by African Americans. Joseph Hargett's grocery, opened in the 1880s, was no longer listed in the Kinston directories by 1902. In 1904 Charles Dunn (1856-1929), who had founded the Dime Bank in 1897 and opened the Hotel Charles next door in 1900, went into bankruptcy and lost the hotel *(Fig. 5.17)*. In 1916 South Queen Street had two other African American-owned and -operated hotels: William Murphy's hotel at 304 South Queen Street and the Hotel Williams at 410 South Queen Street.[36]

South Queen Street remained a vibrant commercial district well into the twentieth century. In the 1990s Cozelle Wilson and Clarence Moye retained vivid memories of shopping there in the 1930s.

> There was Lewis Rowland, ran a cafe down there, [at 344 South Queen Street] very profitable. Mr. Baker's funeral home. Brother Beech—Harvey Beech's brother—had the nicest soda shop, pavilion, and you'd go down there and eat banana splits and things. Mack Millan ran a barbecue stand. Then there was Kinston Wholesale in that building [309-311 South Queen Street].[37]

> When we lived at East Washington Street, I went to a store called the Yellow Front; it was the cheapest store in town. It was on the South Queen Street. . . . I'd go to save a little money. Fatback meat was three cents a pound. . . . And then I used to shine shoes on the street. And there wasn't any refrigeration at that time. So when the stores closed at twelve o'clock at night, I'd get eight pounds of fish for a quarter and eight pounds of neckbone for a quarter, you see. I'd take that home and Mother would fix the fish for the breakfast and the neckbone for dinner. It was during the Hoover time, now. She'd put pastry in it. . . like pastry and chicken. Fix it so we'd have a good dinner.[38]

Fig. 5.17. Hotel Charles, 200 block South Queen Street, Kinston, circa 1900, 1930s (North Carolina Division of Archives and History)

African Americans continued to work on farms, as well as in lumber mills and on railroads. Tobacco was another industry that increasingly employed blacks. As prizeries, stemmeries, and tobacco warehouses opened in Kinston, some skilled African Americans came from other towns to process the cured leaves for markets and factories. In 1898 the Randolph Mead Company's stemmery brought black workers in from Danville, Virginia.[39] In that same year there was a strike at another Kinston stemmery, the H. J. Bass and Company facility.

The people, mostly colored, working in the tobacco stemmery of Mess. H. J. Bass & Co. have struck for higher wages. Most of the strikers are from Durham and have been in Kinston about a week. They claim that they were promised 75 cents per hundred pounds for stemming tobacco. They were only paid 60 cents per hundred.[40]

By 1920 Kinston's tobacco manufactories were major employers of African Americans. The tobacco processing facilities drew rural black sharecroppers, including the Moye family, into town in the early twentieth century. Clarence Moye recalled in 1994: "I've lived in Kinston since I was five years old. I was born in Jones County, about fifteen miles from here, in Pleasant Hill. . . . I'm seventy-five. My family came here for a better way to live. . . . They were sharecroppers down there. They come over here, looking for something better. When they first came over here, they worked for a tobacco factory—Export Tobacco Company. They were getting a dollar and a quarter a day" *(Fig. 5.18)*.[41]

A small group of early-twentieth-century African American entrepreneurs served the real

Fig. 5.18. Black workers in stemmery, Kinston, 1935 (North Carolina Collection, University of North Carolina Library at Chapel Hill)

Fig. 5.19. People's Bank, 242 South Queen Street, Kinston, circa 1924 (Photo, M. Ruth Little, North Carolina Division of Archives and History)

estate, banking, and commercial needs of the black community. Merchants Thomas B. Holloway, Peter Borden, and Starr Hicks founded a bank between 1902 and 1908. The Holloway, Murphy, and Company Bank was organized in 1916 at 101 East Bright Street. In 1919 the bank advertised "$25,000 worth of bonds to sell to enable the Company to take care of more farmers while growing crops and to build a modern Bank."[42] The bank was officially chartered in 1921; by 1924 a new bank building, a handsome, two-story Classical Revival brick structure, stood at 242 South Queen Street *(Fig. 5.19)*.

For some five years in the 1910s African Americans managed and staffed a silk mill in Kinston. Thomas W. Thurston managed Ashley Silk Mills, located in the former Kinston Furniture Factory at 800 Park Avenue, from about 1914 to 1919. One of the buildings, a two-story brick structure, still stands. The mill employed about eighty-five men, women, and boys.[43]

Even during the height of segregation, some white businesses—L. Harvey and Son, Barrett and Hartsfield, H. Stadiem Clothiers, and the Caswell Pharmacy—advertised in Kinston's black publications, and African Americans were made welcome in some stores on North Queen Street. Cozelle Mills Wilson recalled those days: "You couldn't go to a white soda shop and things in the first place, and we didn't go. There was the bank down there [South Queen Street], and the grocery stores and meat market. . . . We bought clothes at the white stores, some of them, now. When I was growing up, we bought most of our clothes here on Queen Street from the stores."[44]

Tower Hill, at the northeast corner of Kinston, had a thriving neighborhood commercial district. Lloyd Patrick's Meat Market, a two-story, rock-faced, concrete-block store at 916 Tower Hill Road that was built between 1919 and 1925, was one of the area's landmarks. The building was built by automobile mechanic Lloyd Patrick, who repaired cars in the rear first floor, had a soda shop in the front section of the first floor, and rented apartments upstairs *(Fig.5.20)*.[45] Another landmark was Patterson's Store at 929 Tower Hill Road, at the corner of Tower Hill and Adkin Roads, known as Patterson's Corner. Later there was a soda shop in the building. "All the kids in school and everywhere went to the soda shop. If parents wanted you or anything, you were always around there. We'd go round there, we'd listen to Nat King Cole, and we'd eat. Everybody would sit around, we'd get out the homework. It was a hangout for all the kids. Adults would come."[46]

During this era Kinston's African American communities had their own doctors, undertakers, architect, builders, and teachers. One of the first African American doctors known to have settled in Kinston was Dr. Leonidas A. Rutherford, who lived at 408 South Queen Street at the turn of the twentieth century. His house, demolished some years ago, was a two-story frame dwelling on the east side of South Queen Street, next to the Williams Hotel. In 1902 Dr. Rutherford sent his daughter, Anna, to nursing school at Raleigh's Saint Agnes Hospital with the intent that she would practice in Kinston. By 1908, according to Kinston's city directory, Anna Rutherford was doing just that.[47] By 1920 Rutherford was gone, but Charles H. Bynum, whose office stood at 205 North

Fig. 5.20. Lloyd Patrick's Meat Market, 916 Tower Hill Road, Kinston, circa 1920 (Photo, M. Ruth Little, North Carolina Division of Archives and History)

Independence Street, and Joseph P. Harrison, who practiced at 228 South Queen Street, were Kinston's African American physicians into the 1940s. Cozelle Mills Wilson recalled that "Dr. Bynum was our doctor. His office got burned down. It was up there on Independent and North Street. His wife was my fourth-grade teacher, and his daughter was my teacher at Adkin High School. The two-story house (I think it's torn down, now) was right off Independent where the railroad track is. We had another doctor, J. P. Harrison."[48]

Undertakers, who enjoyed a prestigious position in African American society, were often able to build substantial houses. Clyde Albritton, an early-twentieth-century Kinston undertaker, built his Colonial Revival dwelling at 500 Quinerly Street in the Tower Hill neighborhood in the late 1920s. Albritton was also a realtor and developer between 1920 and 1945. In the 1930s he developed lots on Fields, Quinerly, Thompson, Washington, and North Adkin Streets, all in northeastern Tower Hill near Adkin High School.[49]

Only one African American architect is known to have worked in Kinston between 1900 and 1945. Will G. Lewis could build in steel, stone, and frame as well as brick *(Fig. 5.21)*. He considered his specialty, however, to be "Artistic Stone Work." Only one of Lewis's buildings is known to remain in Kinston, but it is probably his most monumental work. Saint John's Free Will Baptist Church at 405 East Blount Street was built in 1914 and has retained its Gothic- and Romanesque-

Revival-influenced design and polychromed vitality, from the whitewashed stringcourses and keystones to the variegated pointed-arch and rectangular window openings *(Fig. 5.22)*.

Building was an important profession in African American Kinston. Between 1900 and 1930 a number of black contractors worked in town, including G. Everett Morris; Charles Perry, who lived on Lincoln Street; Mitchell and Byrd; and J. L. Hodges. The firm of Mitchell and Byrd operated at 809 Chestnut Street in a one-story gable-and-wing frame cottage. In 1936 John K. Byrd, one of the partners, resided at this address. J. L. Hodges, a contractor for brick work and stonework, had an office at 223 South Queen Street. Cozelle Mills Wilson remembers him as the person "we called Bud Hodges, and he's been dead for years, but he owned a place on Lincoln Street and he was a stone manufactor, and his daughter taught in the city schools for years."[50]

Blacks also worked in large numbers in other building trades—as bricklayers, carpenters,

Fig. 5.21. Will G. Lewis, architect. (*St. Augustus A.M.E. Zion 50th Anniversary Program*, 1919)

Fig. 5.22. St. John's Free Will Baptist Church, 405 East Blount Street, Kinston. 1914. Architect, Will G. Lewis (Photo, M. Ruth Little, North Carolina Division of Archives and History)

masons, and plasterers. Stanley Parks, a plasterer, is listed in the 1916 Kinston city directory as living at 519 East Shine Street. Bricklaying, traditionally a predominantly African American trade, was taught in Kinston's black schools into the 1970s. Many bricklayers, Casey Hill, Isom Copeland, and Simon Fields, to name a few, plied their trade in Kinston between 1900 and 1945. Black bricklayers often worked for white contractors. Simon Fields, for example, was the principal bricklayer for Robert Blalock's early-twentieth-century Classical Revival buildings.

Black service workers—domestic servants, railroad porters, street vendors, and bus station attendants—regularly interacted with white Kinston as a part of their livelihood. African Americans were employed by white families to clean houses, maintain lawns, and cook. Some of these families built servants' apartments over their garages, but blacks usually commuted to work from their homes *(Fig. 5.23)*. Other service jobs were connected with the railroad; for example, William Moore, who lived in Tower Hill, worked as a porter for the Atlantic Coast Line Railroad from 1910 to 1940.

African Americans who had access to horses and carts worked as draymen or street vendors, hauling things or selling goods along the streets *(Fig. 5.24)*. Clarence Moye happily recalled the 1930s and 1940s, when street vendors with horses and wagons were still commonplace.

> Way back, you used to have a horse pulling a wagon, vegetable wagon. Used to come through every evening selling vegetables. Had all the kinds of vegetables you could name—rutabagas, turnips, celery, collards, cabbage, you name it, peas, butter beans, smoked ham, meat, all that stuff would be on there. He'd be going down the street, selling it and ringing a bell.
> He'd be out there, "The vegetable wagon's coming by." The meat wagon. He had all that on there. Fresh from the country. Horse would be pulling it. Yeah, sometime. . . the fish man would come by, he'd be doing it. He'd be, "Fish...just caught." Most any kind you can name. They went out that night and caught them. People used to go someplace or another in the nighttime before day in the morning, and bring them back in the morning and sell them. . . . Or they'd go down to the Sound, and take the boat when they come in. . .you'd get them cheap, and you'd come back and make a profit off them. . . . But they used to go all over town, with the mule pulling the wagon or the horse. . . . Everything around here used to be pulled by some kind of animal—the trash truck. . . . I know when the mailman used to come by twice a day. . . . in the '30s, not the '40s. See, the war broke out and after the war broke out that dried it all up. It was all in the '30s.[51]

Within Kinston's black community, barbers proliferated. In 1919 seven barber shops were listed in the city directory, offering "Hairstraightening, Singeing, Shaving, and Haircutting." Many black barbers also worked in white barber shops *(Fig. 5.25)*.

The Great Depression hit Kinston's black communities as hard as it did the white communities. To provide decent affordable housing to the working urban poor, a federal public housing program began in 1933. North Carolina passed an act authorizing cities to establish local public housing authorities in 1935. Kinston was one of numerous cities across the state that began to set up such authorities; the first city, Wilmington, set up a housing authority in 1938.[52] The Kinston Housing

146

Fig. 5.23. Waitman Hines and his servant John display their catch, Kinston. (Heritage Place, Lenoir Community College)

Fig. 5.24. Mr. Stewart, the vegetable man, Kinston, 1994 (Photo, Penne Smith, North Carolina Division of Archives and History)

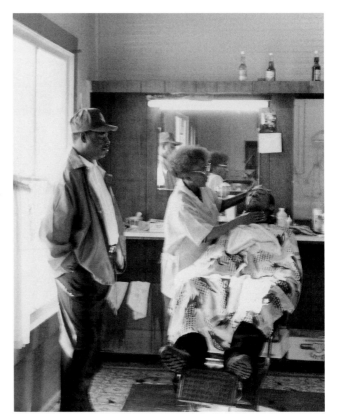

Authority's first two projects were Mitchell Wooten Housing, for African Americans, and Simon Bright Housing, for whites, designed in 1939 and built in 1940-1941. Both projects were placed in East Kinston, approximately six blocks from each other. Each campus, planned to provide a safe and attractive environment for low-income families, contained rows of apartment buildings built around courtyards, with play areas for children and a community building *(Fig. 5.26)*.

Families who worked for Kinston's tobacco factories were hit hard by the depression, as their jobs did not always exist year-round. Some, like Clarence Moye's father, diversified their income by working a variety of jobs throughout the year.

Fig. 5.26. Mitchell Wooten Housing, 700 block East Washington Street, Kinston, 1940-1941, A. Mitchell Wooten, architect (Photo, Penne Smith, North Carolina Division of Archives and History)

Well, one thing about my daddy was that he was a mechanic and he kept a pretty good steady job. He could do almost any kind of work, you know? But it was hard, though. . . . He kept working at the tobacco factory part-time. Then when the factory would close up, they'd let him do repairing work. He worked nearly year-round. My mother worked there during the season time. Before then, she'd do a lot of work like washing for different people, cook, housecleaning, stuff like that.[53]

In the later 1930s opportunities for blacks in East Kinston expanded when the Orion Mill, which had become the Gross Shirt Factory, began employing African American workers. One of Cozelle Mills Wilson's first jobs was at this factory.

Black people started working in the shirt factory. One time they couldn't do anything but press shirts. During that time, they started buying houses. . . . The economy grew. After the union came in the late 1930s and Mr. Gross sold out, Mr. Schecter and Mr. Fuchs came in. I remember them. After school, they'd let us go up there and starch collars for money. I was about fourteen . . . . You had children going to school, to college, they always had a job when they came home, at the shirt factory. Then they'd get professional jobs and teach school.

We'd starch collars right alongside Mrs. Schecter, Mrs. Pearlie Mae. . . . The shirt factory was different. The Schecters were different. Mr. Gross and them were different. It wasn't as much of a racial thing to them. They didn't look at color.[54]

African American Education and Social Organizations

In 1896 there were eighteen African American teachers in Kinston, nine in LaGrange, one in Falling Creek and one in Institute. Kinston College, an African American Free Will Baptist school that included grades one through nine, existed as early as 1890 (not to be confused with the school of the same name operated by R. H. Lewis). In that year, Branson's business directory listed a "Kinston College (col.), Kinston, J. Carey (col.); teachers Isaac Best & J. H Carey." Best and Carey had been schoolteachers in Kinston since 1884.[55] By 1919 Kinston College, located on University Avenue, had a two-story dormitory and had added more grades. The Reverend Levi Rasbury, pastor of the Antioch Free Will Baptist Church, supervised the school. A 1919 advertisement described the college as "A High Grade Institution of Learning for both sex [es]. Located in East Kinston, NC, about fifteen minutes walk from the post office and business center of the city. Healthy location, ideal home life, modern equipment. Good accommodations for boarding students. Good wholesome food. [The curriculum includes] Theology, Kindergarten, Primary, Grammar, Normal and College, Domestic Science, Domestic Art and Music."[56] Kinston College remained open until the 1930s, when it became a casualty of the Great Depression and closed permanently.

Developer James A. McDaniel donated land on the Adkin Branch between Desmond and East Shine Streets for a school, and the large frame building erected there is remembered by some East Kinston residents as the McDaniel College.[57] The McDaniel School was listed in the 1916 Kinston city directory, with the Reverend Allen A. Smith as its principal.

With the expanding African American population in Tower Hill after 1900, the Tower Hill Elementary School, a two-story frame building, was constructed at the corner of Tower Hill Road and Tiffany Avenue by 1919, and a secondary school, Adkin High School, was built in 1928. Adkin High School, a one-story brick school located a few blocks east of Tower Hill Elementary School, was built with local funding matched by a grant from the Rosenwald Fund, a philanthropic program that matched private money with local and state money for the construction of schools for black students *(Fig. 5.27)*. In 1942 Tower Hill Elementary School burned. Adkin High School then moved its students south to the old Kinston College building on University Avenue, and grades one through five occupied the Adkin High School building. When Tower Hill Elementary School, transformed into the brick J. H. Sampson School, opened again in 1948, Adkin High School returned to its original site, adding a new two-story annex. A gymnasium, a library, and additional classrooms were added in the 1950s. The original one-story school building was demolished when the school closed in 1979.

Fig. 5.27. Adkin High School, Kinston, 1928, demolished 1979 (Collection of Ellen E. Berry)

African Americans had many social outlets: fraternal and civic organizations, local baseball teams, church gatherings, and music clubs flourished. Masonic Hall, located at Webb's Alley off North Independence Street, provided a meeting place for various African American fraternal organizations. In 1916, orders meeting there were the King David Lodge, the Pride of Kinston Lodge, and the Eastern Star, a Masonic women's organization that still meets today. Other fraternal orders were the International Order of Odd Fellows, whose hall was on Golden Progress Alley off Queen Street, and the International Order of Good Samaritans, whose meeting place at 302 North Independence Street was built in the 1880s.

The Hotel Charles reopened in 1916 and operated into the 1950s. Because of segregation black entertainers who performed in Kinston stayed here. Cozelle Mills Wilson remembered the excitement of this era.

> During that time, with the strict segregation, the bands would come in and go to the warehouse. We'd all go to watch. Ella Fitzgerald, Les Henderson. . . . Right down the street here [at 500 Quinerly Street], in this brick house, Mr. Joe Williams had a pressing club [dry cleaners]. He would press their clothes for them. They were staying at the Dunn's Hotel down there. We'd get up early that morning and we'd run by there and, you know, hang around and ask them if they wanted or needed any clothes done. Then we'd take the clothes back to Joe. They'd always give us a tip. I remember Ella Fitzgerald gave me fifty cents. I thought I was rich! I was twelve, thirteen, fourteen years old. We didn't think about autographs or anything like that. . . . I remember Louis Armstrong gave us a dollar.[58]

East Kinston Architecture

The most historic African American neighborhoods are Tower Hill and Lincoln City, established in the nineteenth century and now part of East Kinston, the largely African American section of Kinston east of East Street, the original town boundary. The earliest surviving houses are single-family houses built by black professionals and businessmen in the early twentieth century. Blocks of rental housing, both shotgun houses (a one-room wide house with rooms one behind the other) and two-story front-gable houses, built in the 1920s and 1930s stand along the streets and alleys throughout these neighborhoods.

A few of the stylish houses built by Kinston's most successful African Americans still stand as landmarks of black achievement during the early years of segregation. Thomas B. Holloway, merchant, realtor, and banker (a founder of the Holloway, Murphy, and Company Bank on South Queen Street) and his wife Kate owned a house at 412 East Shine Street, near Lincoln City. The two-story gable-and-wing late Queen Anne residence, built about 1910, is set within mature trees. The weatherboarded Holloway House is graced by diamond-shaped gable ventilators, sawnwork decoration on the gables, and a bungalow-style wraparound porch added in the 1920s *(Figs. 5.28, 5.29)*.[59] Next door, at 416 East Shine Street, stood the longtime residence of Dr. J. P. Harrison.

Fig. 5.28. Thomas B. Holloway, merchant and banker. (*St. Augustus A.M.E. Zion 50th Anniversary Program*, 1919)

Harrison's two-story house was also built in the Queen Anne style, with a front wing with a two-story bay window and a wraparound front porch *(Figs. 5.30, 5.31)*. Black contractor G. Everett Morris lived there from 1902 to 1917; he may have built the house and been its first occupant.[60]

Ezekiel K. Best, born around 1880 near Ballards Crossroads in Pitt County, came to Kinston at the turn of the twentieth century when he married his wife, Addie, a teacher who had grown up on North Alley (now Short Street) near Tower Hill Road. Like many Kinstonians both white and black, he lived in town and owned a farm in the country. The Bests were among the first homeowners on Chestnut Avenue, a dirt lane south of Tower Hill Road just east of North Adkin Street. They built a two-story frame Queen Anne–style house at 1015 Chestnut Avenue (now Hicks Avenue) in 1911 *(Fig. 5.32)*. Across the street at 1012 Chestnut Avenue stands a virtu-

Fig. 5.29. Thomas B. Holloway House, 412 East Shine Street, Kinston, circa 1910 (Photo, M. Ruth Little, North Carolina Division of Archives and History)

Fig. 5.30. Dr. J. P. Harrison, physician (*St. Augustus A.M.E. Zion 50th Anniversary Program*, 1919)

ally identical two-story Queen Anne-style frame house built by the Reverend Matt Dawson and his wife, Ida Brown Dawson, Ezekiel Best's sister-in-law, in 1913 because, as Best's son stated, "she liked our house so well." The two houses, still standing, are comparable to the Queen Anne style-houses built in the white neighborhoods of Mitchelltown and the Trianon district. Ezekiel Best sold real estate, and his real estate holdings included commercial properties on Tower Hill Road and a row of shotgun houses built on Golden Progress Alley, off South Queen Street, in the 1930s.[61]

William Moore, longtime porter for the Atlantic Coast Line Railroad, and his wife Bertha owned a large, two-story Queen Anne-style dwelling at 1214 Macon Street in Tower Hill, built between 1910 and 1915 *(Fig. 5.33)*. The house still has its original wraparound front porch decorated by turned porch supports and a turned-rail balustrade. The corbel-cap interior brick chimneys are still in place, as are the prominent gables pierced with dia-

Fig. 5.31. Dr. J. P. Harrison House, 416 East Shine Street, Kinston, circa 1902, demolished 1980s (North Carolina Division of Archives and History)

152

Fig. 5.32. Ezekiel K. Best House, 1015 Hicks Avenue, Kinston, 1911 (Photo, M. Ruth Little, North Carolina Division of Archives and History)

mond-shaped louvered ventilators. Like the Holloway, Harrison and Best families, the Moores lived in a spaciousness and comfort unavailable to most African Americans in Kinston.

Clyde Albritton, an early-twentieth-century Kinston undertaker, built his Colonial Revival dwelling at 500 Quinerly Street in the Tower Hill neighborhood in the late 1920s *(Fig. 5.34)*. Albritton's cousin, Cozelle Mills Wilson, now lives in the house and appreciates its construction quality: "If you notice, in the 1920s, the ceilings were high, notice the moldings. And this house is built out of pure hardwood, everything in it. Every sixteen by sixteen and every four by four in this house is doubled. You don't ever have to have any repair work done for decaying."[62]

In the 1930s and 1940s most of Kinston's African American neighborhoods had dirt roads and smaller streets and alleys behind principal avenues. Clarence Moye's family, sharecroppers who had moved to Tower Hill to make a better life for themselves, were, like most African American families, renters instead of homeowners and moved frequently between these side streets and alleys.

> In the 1930s we moved to—it's changed its name about two or three times now—Rowena Street [south of 400 Tower Hill Road]. We lived in a three-room—what you call a shotgun—house. In the 1940s we were living on Thompson Street, 704 Thompson Street. The house has been tore down. It was a five-room house— two rooms up the stairs, and three down the stairs. Two-story. The rent was three dollars a week. The light bill was about eighty cents a month, and the water bill was sixty cents a month. Kinston had its own water plant and its own light company then.[63]

Shotgun houses comparable to the Moye family's house on Rowena Street stand in long rows in East Kinston *(Fig. 5.35)*. A two-story house comparable to the one Clarence Moye lived in during the 1940s, representing more spacious and private living conditions for the family, stands in the 600 block of Fields Street *(Fig. 5.36)*. At the typical two-story front-gable house, the front door opened into a small stair hall with a living room, bedroom, and kitchen on the first floor, and two bedrooms on the second floor.

Fig. 5.33. William Moore House, 1214 Macon Street, Kinston, circa 1912 (Photo, M. Ruth Little, North Carolina Division of Archives and History)

Fig. 5.34. Clyde Albritton House, 500 Quinerly Street, Kinston, late 1920s (Photo, M. Ruth Little, North Carolina Division of Archives and History)

154

Fig. 5.35. Shotgun Row, 600 block Fields Street, East Kinston, 1920s-1930s (Photo, M. Ruth Little, North Carolina Division of Archives and History)

Fig. 5.36. Two-story shotgun house, 600 block Fields Street, Kinston, 1920s-1930s (Photo, Penne Smith, North Carolina Division of Archives and History)

From World War II to the Present

A seminal event in the industrial history of the county was the purchase, about 1940, by Kinston and Lenoir County of 640 acres near the Dawson's Station community, for twenty-five dollars an acre, to develop an airport. Local pilots and City of Kinston employees, assisted by Works Projects Administration funds and labor, cleared a small area as a landing site. When World War II began in December 1941 the airport was taken over by the federal government as an emergency landing field to serve both Cherry Point Marine Air Station at Havelock and Seymour Johnson Air Force Base at Goldsboro. Several million dollars were invested in runways and buildings to accommodate military personnel. The base became known as Stallings Field in honor of two pilots, Kinston brothers, killed during the war in 1945. When the war ended the facilities were turned over to the city and county to be developed as a civilian airport. From 1951 to 1957 the Serv-Air Corporation operated a flight training school at the airport for the United States Air Force, training some 4,000 Air Force pilots there.[64] The pilots and their families, many of them from other countries, provided a boost to the local economy as well as lively cultural experiences to local citizens who befriended them. The Serv-Air Hangar of 1954, a steel-frame building covered with corrugated metal and illuminated by skylights, is a well-preserved remnant of Cold War history (*Fig. 5.37*). In recent years a number of industries have built plants near the airport. In the early 1990s the state began planning and construction of a large industrial complex, known as the Global Transpark, around the airport, designed to provide convenient air transportation for industrial cargo.

World War II affected Lenoir County greatly. Some 4,072 of its young people saw service during the conflict. Food was rationed; travel was restricted. In 1941, just as the region was recovering from the Great Depression, World War II cut off foreign markets for American tobacco. On the positive side, enlisted men from the military bases of Camp Lejeune and Cherry Point in nearby Craven and Onslow Counties stimulated the economy by their frequent visits and purchases of goods and services in Kinston.[65]

The war and its repercussions changed Kinston's residents profoundly. Men who had never been outside the South enlisted in the military, and some traveled overseas and saw combat. Those who stayed saw small and large transformations in their communities.

> There were so many servicemen here, you could hit a one on every corner. I bet there was 20,000 in East Kinston. It was Camp Davis, the airport here, Seymour Johnson, and Jacksonville. . . . everybody was coming back here to Kinston. The town was full of them. There was so many Marines, servicemen, until they were patrolling the streets like the policeman were. Military police had offices here. . . all over town. I was working at the bus station during the time. There were so many people down to the bus station, it stayed open twenty-four hours day and night. And you could never miss them—and there was a bus going down every hour in the day, there was a bus going down to the bases. . . . Well they had clubs, and dance clubs and joints. Down on the corner of McLewean, the USO.[66]

> People were coming from a lot of places. . . a lot of servicemen. I used to go out on my porch at Hicks Avenue sometimes, and it would be full all the way across. My mother was a minister and, being religious, she was so glad. She hauled all the men, all of them, to church in droves. People understood that, because most of their boys were gone, too. 'Round Saturday, they'd buy and cook and cook because they were expecting servicemen to come on Sundays. They'd just come up early—it got to be a habit. They'd come up early, sometimes twelve or fifteen, and they'd sit on the porch. You'd invite them in to dinner. And they'd always go to church. Then they would come back; sometimes they would come regularly, or another group would come . . . . People were very cordial; they did everything they could for those boys for they were young, eighteen, nineteen, and away from home.[67]

The postwar boom resulted in population growth and increased job opportunities in both Kinston and the county. Kinston became a center of shirt manufacturing, with the Kinston Shirt Company, the nearby Atlas and Lenoir Shirt Company, and the North Carolina Shirt Company employing about 750 workers by 1951.[68]

The song refrain about returning World War I veterans, "How you gonna keep 'em down on the farm after they've seen Paree" was particularly appropriate after World War II in Lenoir County.[69]

Fig. 5.37. Serv-Air Hangar, Stallings Field, Kinston, 1954 (Photo, M. Ruth Little, North Carolina Division of Archives and History)

The event that began the large-scale employment shift from agriculture to factory jobs came early in the 1950s. The beginning of modern industrialization in eastern North Carolina was the construction of the E. I. DuPont de Nemours and Company Dacron Fiber Plant in Lenoir County. In 1951 the company purchased from the Canady family 635 acres of farmland on U.S. Highway 11 seven miles east of Kinston. The new plant, which opened in 1953, was the first plant in the world to produce the new synthetic fiber Dacron polyester. By the mid 1970s the plant employed 3,600 people.[70]

Kinston's progressive recreational amenities formed part of its attraction for the DuPont company. In 1938 the Works Progress Administration had partially financed construction of a new wooden grandstand and fence for a baseball field in the 400 block of East Grainger Avenue. The present stadium, one of the finest minor-league stadiums in the state, was completed in 1952.[71] The city's first public park, Emma Webb Park, which included a large municipal swimming pool, was completed in 1936 in the north end of town *(Fig. 5.38)*. In the late 1930s a frame dance hall was built there with funding from the Works Projects Administration. Emma Webb Park served as a hub for the growing middle-class suburbs in north Kinston.

During the 1950s Kinston began its biggest period of growth since the 1890s. Many of the architecturally distinguished early-twentieth-century brick stores on Queen Street received modern face-lifts of shiny metal and glass. Long praised as one of the widest main streets in eastern North Carolina, Queen Street became known as the "Magic Mile." By 1951 new houses were being built as fast as local labor and materials would permit. Older houses were divided into apartments; mobile home parks sprang up. After World War II local architect William A. Coleman created landmarks of Neo-Gothic and Neo-Georgian design that symbolize this period of growth—the Saint Mary's Episcopal Church, the Home Federal Savings Bank Building, the Kinston Country Club, and his own residence on Walker Drive. Contractors George Dubose and W. Roy Poole helped satisfy the demand for new houses for the DuPont employees who moved into town. Contractor Oscar L. Shackelford was active during the 1940s and 1950s, executing many local projects, including the Simon Bright Housing, the First Presbyterian Church, the Kinston Laundry, and the New Dixie Warehouse.[72]

At the end of World War II life in East Kinston changed as well. The black commercial areas began to decline. Some residents left the neighborhoods to try their luck in cities like New York. Many black military veterans returned to Kinston, however, and were able to build new houses at the eastern edge of Tower Hill, off Adkin Street. White developers and contractors, including Eli Perry and Oscar Shackelford, built small, affordable "ranch houses" in the 1950s, which veterans purchased with Veterans Administration loans.[73] In the late 1940s racial integration of public facilities began to improve the lives of African Americans.

The taxi business opened up for black entrepreneurs after World War II. A lone frame building on the north side of 900 Tower Hill Road is the last of the taxi stands once scattered through the streets of Lincoln City and Tower Hill *(see Fig. 5.20)*. Small black-owned taxi companies, such as Eagle Taxi at 102 Shine Street owned by W. K. Dudley and James Kilpatrick, and Globe Taxi at 315 South Queen Street remained profitable businesses in Kinston as late as the 1960s.[74]

SWIMMING POOL, KINSTON, N. C.

Fig. 5.38. Municipal Swimming Pool, Emma Webb Park, North Queen Street, Kinston, 1936 (Post Card, Heritage Place, Lenoir Community College)

Epilogue

In spite of industrialization, during most of the twentieth century Kinston retained the feeling of a farm and tobacco center, characterized by the warehouse districts, the late-summer influx of tobacconists, and the fall upsurge in employment, retail business, and social life.[75] The warehouses stood mostly empty throughout the year except during tobacco auction season, in August and September, when farmers and buyers crowded the city to trade the season's golden leaf *(Fig. 5.39)*.

At the end of the twentieth century Kinston has lost the atmosphere of a tobacco market town. Tobacco's momentous impact on Kinston is no longer evident in the city's architectural fabric. The only three tobacco-related buildings remaining in the city's core are the old American Tobacco Company prizery at 619 North Herritage Street (now known as the Nantucket Warehouse), the Imperial Tobacco Company office building at 420 North Herritage Street (now an apartment house), and the Jenkins Redrying Plant at 211 East Lenoir Street (now Kinston Building Supply). All of the other downtown warehouses and processing plants have been demolished since the 1960s. Tobacco warehouses began moving to the outskirts of Kinston after World War II to avoid traffic congestion and to construct larger, more modern facilities with concrete floors and improved lighting. In 1997 a total of five warehouses auctioned about 60 million pounds of tobacco.[76] While the tobacco market is still important to Kinston, many new and more diversified industries have moved into the city and county in the past thirty years, creating a more stable economy.

Though increasingly urbanized, Lenoir County and Kinston are fortunate to retain many rural communities, urban neighborhoods, and historic buildings. The social fabric, anchored by traditional farmhouses and farm buildings, community churches, schools, and stores, is intact. On the brink of the twenty-first century the goal of county citizens is to achieve growth and an improved quality of life without sacrificing the small-town and rural values that have made the county a wonderful place to live for three centuries. Interest in Lenoir County's rural and town heritage thrives, fostered by the Lenoir County Historical Association, Pride of Kinston, the Kinston Historic District Commission, and other public and private groups. As John Washington said so many years ago, Lenoir County and Kinston "bid fair to flourish."

Fig. 5.39. Tobacco warehouse scene, Kinston, 1960s (Heritage Place, Lenoir Community College)

Notes

Chapter One. "Bid Fair To Flourish"

1. R. C. Jurney and W. A. Davis, *Soil Survey of Lenoir County, N.C.* (Raleigh: North Carolina Department of Agriculture, 1927), 1-6.

2. The majority of the documention in this chapter was compiled by historian Jerry Cross, North Carolina Division of Archives and History, in a carefully researched essay, "The Peebles House in Kinston: A Research Report for the Structure Restored as Harmony Hall," Research Branch, North Carolina Division of Archives and History, Raleigh, 1990. The following footnotes generally cite Cross's essay for documentation rather than the original sources that Cross used. In some instances where the original sources may be of particular interest to the reader, those are cited. Where Cross's analysis is presented in the text, Cross is footnoted.

Craven Precinct was divided into a number of counties. For county formations see David Leroy Corbitt, *The Formation of the North Carolina Counties, 1663-1943* (Raleigh: State Department of Archives and History, 1950).

3. See Charles R. Holloman's sketch of Robert Atkins in William S. Powell, ed., *Dictionary of North Carolina Biography*, vol. 1 (Chapel Hill: University of North Carolina Press, 1979), 59-60, hereinafter cited as Powell, DNCB.

4. Powell, DNCB, I, 59-60. According to Cross, "Peebles House in Kinston," records show that the Herritage family nearly always spelled the name with a double r.

5. Cross, "Peebles House in Kinston," 36-37.

6. Cross, "Peebles House in Kinston," 37.

7. Walter Clark, ed., *The State Records of North Carolina*, 16 vols. (11-26) (Raleigh: State of North Carolina, 1895-1906), 25:373-378. Detailed specifications for the Tower Hill complex, probably developed by Governor Dobbs himself, are given in the published records of the colony. See Catherine W. Bishir, *North Carolina Architecture* (Chapel Hill: University of North Carolina Press, 1990) , 41 and 469 n. 77; A. R. Newsome, "Twelve North Carolina Counties in 1810-1811," pt.2, *North Carolina Historical Review*, 6 (April 1929): 189 n. 21.

8. Clark, *State Records*, 25:468.

9. Cross, "Peebles House in Kinston," 37-38. According to Cross, MacElwean is spelled many different ways in the records. Cross prefers MacElwean. The Kinston street, however, will be designated McLewean, as it appears on current town maps.

10. Clark, *State Records of North Carolina*, 25:468-470.

11. Cross, "Peebles House in Kinston," 38.

12. Cross, "Peebles House in Kinston," 39.

13. Cross, "Peebles House in Kinston," 54-55.

14. Cross, "Peebles House in Kinston," family trees following 38, 39, also 40, 45 (n.9).

15. Cross, "Peebles House in Kinston," 39.

16. Powell, *DNCB*, 342-355.

17. Powell, *DNCB*, 342-344; Clark, *State Records*, 24: 290-292.

18. Cross, "Peebles House in Kinston," 39-40.

19. William S. Powell, *Annals of Progress: The Story of Lenoir County and Kinston, North Carolina* (Raleigh: North Carolina Department of Archives and History, 1963), 14-15.

20. Cross, "Peebles House in Kinston," 40.

21. Cross, "Peebles House in Kinston," Caswell family tree following 39.

22 Newsome, "Twelve North Carolina Counties," 184.

23. Jerry Cross, communication with the author, 1996.

24. Cross, "Peebles House in Kinston," 83.

25. Talmage C. Johnson and Charles R. Holloman, *The Story of Kinston and Lenoir County* (Raleigh: Edwards and Broughton Company, 1954), 146.

26. Cross, "Peebles House in Kinston," following 43.

27. Cross, "Peebles House in Kinston," following 43, 58.

28. Cross, "The Peebles House in Kinston," following 43, 58; *Kinston Free Press*, August 18, 1897, cited in ibid., 57.

29. Harriet C. Lane, "Historic Buildings in and near Kinston," in *Carolina and the Southern Cross*, 1 (November 1913):12; Cross, "Peebles House in Kinston," 10, 57; *Kinston Free Press*, August 18, 1897. This newspaper contains an article by E. L. Miller in which Ann Dibble and Harriet Peebles, believed to be the oldest native residents of Kinston in 1897, stated that these houses on Bright Street were the oldest homes in Kinston back when they were young, and that the houses were probably built by the founding fathers.

30. The 1,500 acres that he purchased from Richard Caswell in 1783 were apparently the start of this Southwest

Creek estate. Cross, "Peebles House in Kinston," 78, n.32.

31. Lane, "Historic Buildings in and near Kinston," 12. Lane noted that Caswell's residence was then the residence of Harold Stanley.

32. *Kinston Free Press*, August 31, 1962. Dyer was the daughter of Lillie V. Archbell, founder and editor of *Carolina and the Southern Cross*, published from 1912 to 1914 as the official organ of the North Carolina Division of the United Daughters of the Confederacy. The publication included a number of personal narratives of the Civil War years. Kinston resident Reginald Stroud recalls the demolition of the house in the 1960s.

33. The Bright Street residence was probably the house that in 1777 became the temporary home of secretary of state James Glasgow and from which much state business was conducted. Caswell may well have shared office space in the house. Apparently other arrangements had been made by the secretary of state by 1779. In that year the General Assembly created Wayne County out of Dobbs but directed that the Dobbs court meet in Kinston "at a house lately occupied by Col. James Glasgow" and continue meeting there until a courthouse could be built. The house probably also served as the unofficial courthouse until the mid-1780s, when the courthouse was built (Cross, "Peebles House in Kinston," 64, 66). After Caswell's death the house was owned in turn by Kinston residents John Gatlin, William Lovick, and Abner Pearce. During the Civil War Confederate generals Braxton Bragg and Robert F. Hoke had their headquarters in the house (Lane, "Historic Buildings in and near Kinston," 12).

34. Cross, "Peebles House in Kinston," map and key, following 43.

35. Cross, "Peebles House in Kinston," 83.

36. Bright moved into Kinston about 1790 and probably built the house at 206 East King Street soon afterward. He lived there until his death in 1802. Cross, "Peebles House in Kinston," 83-84.

37. Powell, *DNCB*, 342-344; Johnson and Holloman, *Story of Kinston and Lenoir County*, 37-41; *Kinston Free Press*, September 2, 1899, August 31, 1962. The last issue cited was the first in a series of articles written by Marguerite A. Dyer and found collectively in the files of Heritage Place, Lenoir Community College, Kinston.

38. Cross, "Peebles House in Kinston," 53.

39. Martha A. Dreyer, "Kinston's Architecture 1762-1930: An Inventory and History" (research report, City of Kinston and North Carolina Division of Archives and History, Raleigh, 1981), 14.

40. Powell, *DNCB*, 342.

41. Richard Caswell to John Gray Blount, 1784, William Blount Rodman Collection, East Carolina University Manuscript Collection, Greenville, N.C.

42. Cross, "Peebles House in Kinston," 76, n. 22.

43. Notes by Quentin Stroud, Leary-Stroud House survey file, Archaeology and Historic Preservation Section, North Carolina Division of Archives and History, Raleigh.

44. Richard Noble House survey file, Archaeology and Historic Preservation Section, North Carolina Division of Archives and History, Raleigh; *The Heritage of Lenoir County, North Carolina* (Kinston: Lenoir County Historical Association, 1981), entries 638, 639, 640.

Chapter Two. The Antebellum Face of Lenoir County

1. Cross, "Peebles House in Kinston," 41; Second Census of the United States, 1800, Lenoir Co., Population Schedule, microfilm, A&H. Kinston's listings after Lenoir County's listings. There were no free blacks in Kinston at this time.

2. Newsome, "Twelve North Carolina Counties," 184.

3. Newsome, "Twelve North Carolina Counties," 182.

4. Cross, "Peebles House in Kinston," 42.

5. John Washington to Elizabeth Washington and Eliza Washington (Grist), 1810s-1830s, Elizabeth Washington Grist Knox Papers, Southern Historical Collection, University of North Carolina, Chapel Hill.

6. Hugh Talmage Lefler and Albert Ray Newsome, *North Carolina: The History of a Southern State* (Chapel Hill: University of North Carolina Press, 1963), 299.

7. Guion Griffis Johnson, *Ante-bellum North Carolina: A Social History* (Chapel Hill: University of North Carolina Press, 1937), 481-482, 484.

8. Second Census of the United States, 1800, Lenoir Co., N.C., Population Schedule; microfilm, A&H; Fourth Census of the United States, 1820, Lenoir Co., N.C., Population Schedule, microfilm, A&H. In 1820 the county had 3,405 whites, approximately 2,939 slaves, and 114 free blacks.

9. Powell, *Annals of Progress*, 5; Seventh Census of the United States, 1850, Lenoir Co., N.C., Population Schedule, microfilm, A&H. See the last page for cumulative enumeration.

10. Powell, *Annals of Progress*, 5; Eighth Census of the United States, 1860, Lenoir Co., N.C., Population Schedule,

microfilm, A&H.

11. Lefler and Newsome, *North Carolina*, 399.

12. Eighth Census, 1860: Lenoir Co. Slave Schedule. Curtis Phillips lived in the Phillips-Moseley House near Mewborne's Crossroads.

13. Eighth Census, 1860: Lenoir Co. Slave Schedule.

14. Newsome, "Twelve North Carolina Counties," 188.

15. "Brief History of Kinston," *Kinston Free Press*, 18 August 1897, quoted in Allison Black, "Historic and Architectural Resources of Kinston, North Carolina" (research report, State Historic Preservation Office, Raleigh, 1989), B.5.

16. "Our Recent Visit, *Farmer's Journal*, 1 (May 1852): 50, (quoted in Dru Haley York, Tull-Worth-Holland Farm National Register of Historic Places nomination form, 1992, 8.15.)

17. York, Tull-Worth-Holland Farm nomination, 8.15-8.16; Eighth Census, 1860 Lenoir Co. Agriculture Schedule.

18. Seventh Census, 1850: Lenoir Co. Agriculture Schedule; Eighth Census, 1860: Lenoir County Agriculture Schedule.

19. Emma Morehead Whitfield, *Whitfield, Bryan, Smith, and Related Families*. vol. 1: *Whitfield*. (Westminster, Md.: privately published, 1948), 75-76.

20. Will of Lewis Whitfield, March 6, 1848, *W. C. Fields vs. W. B. Whitfield, North Carolina Reports* 101: 305. On the Cooks Hammock land stood the "Hammock House," one of the oldest houses still standing in Beaufort today.

21. Seventh Census, 1850, Lenoir Co. Agriculture Schedule.

22. Seventh Census, 1850, Lenoir Co. Agriculture Schedule.

23. Eighth Census, 1860: Lenoir Co. Population Schedule.

24. York, Tull-Worth-Holland Farm nomination, 8.7-8.9.

25. John Sutton Farm survey file, State Historic Preservation Office.

26. John D. Hodges Farm survey file, State Historic Preservation Office.

27. Johnson, *Ante-bellum North Carolina*, 487-488.

28. Emerson's Directory, 32, as cited in Peter B. Sandbeck, *The Historic Architecture of New Bern and Craven County*, (New Bern: Tryon Palace Commission, 1988), 97.

29. Seventh Census, 1850: Lenoir Co. Industrial Schedule; Eighth Census, 1860: Lenoir Co. Population Schedule. Moses Einstine lived in household no. 819.

30. Eighth Census, 1860: Lenoir Co. Industrial and Population Schedules.

31. Newsome, "Twelve North Carolina Counties," 185.

32. Seventh Census, 1850: Lenoir Co. Population and Agriculture Schedules; Eight Census, 1860: Lenoir Co. Population and Agriculture Schedules.

33. Seventh Census, 1850: Lenoir Co. Agriculture Schedule; Richard Noble House survey file, State Historic Preservation Office.

34. Eighth Census, 1860: Lenoir Co. Industrial Schedule.

35. *Heritage of Lenoir County*, 329.

36. Seventh Census, 1850: Lenoir Co. Agriculture Schedule.

37. Johnson, *Ante-bellum North Carolina*, 488-489. When the American Anti-slavery Society sought a testimonial against slavery in North Carolina, it described conditions on a rice plantation near Wilmington.

38. Powell, *Annals of Progress*, 77.

39. Elizabeth Washington Grist Knox Papers; *General Catalogue of Wake Forest, North Carolina* (Raleigh: C. E. Taylor:1892); Cross, "Peebles House in Kinston," 4.

40. Powell, *Annals of Progress*, 77-79.

41. *Catalogue of the Officers and Students of Lenoir Collegiate Institute, Male and Female*, 1857-58 (Kinston: American Advocate Office, 1858), 12 (copy in Lenoir Collegiate Institute survey file, State Historic Preservation Office).

42. R. Bruce Pate, *A Moment in Time: The History of Lenoir Collegiate Institute* (Durham, N. C.: Carolina Academic Press, 1981).

43. Lenoir Collegiate Institute survey file.

44. Gibbons-Hardy House survey file, State Historic Preservation Office.

45. Pridgen-Hardy House survey file, State Historic Preservation Office.

46. Willard B. Gatewood Jr., *Eugene Clyde Brooks: Educator and Public Servant* (Durham, N.C.: Duke University Press, 1960), 14-17.

47. Newsome, "Twelve North Carolina Counties," 187.

48. Croom Meeting House survey file, State Historic Preservation Office.

49. Wheat Swamp Christian Church survey file, State Historic Preservation Office.

50. Newsome, "Twelve North Carolina Counties," 184.

51. Eighth Census, 1860: Lenoir Co. Agriculture Schedule.

52. Notes attached to documentary photo of Turner Log House, Heritage Place, Lenoir Community College, Kinston; Eighth Census, 1860: Lenoir Co. Agriculture Schedule.

53. Charles W. Tilghman House survey file, State Historic Preservation Office.

54. Harvey-Mewborne House survey file, State Historic Preservation Office.

55. Carl R. Lounsbury, *An Illustrated Glossary of Early Southern Architecture and Landscape* (New York: Oxford University Press, 1994), 269.

56. Bishir, *North Carolina Architecture*, 114.

57. Sandbeck, *Historic Architecture of New Bern and Craven County*; J. Daniel Pezzoni, "The Historic and Architectural Resources of Onslow County" (research report, State Historic Preservation Office, 1989); Jennifer Martin, "The Historic and Architectural Resources of Duplin County," (research report, State Historic Preservation Office, 1992).

58. This is the author's own term, inspired by an analysis of the "stepped" or "telescope" pattern of house enlargement traditional to Maryland's Eastern Shore in Paul Baker Touart's *Along the Seaboard Side: The Architectural History of Worcester County, Maryland* (Worcester County, Md.: 1994). Such houses were built with a stepped profile, sometimes decreasing in height from the main block to the kitchen, and connected by enclosed passageways. Architecturally, Eastern Shore housing has little in common with Lenoir County housing. The same logic for the construction of additions in Lenoir County is found elsewhere in North Carolina, although breezeways link additions more often than do piazzas in other areas. A piazza differs fundamentally from a breezeway. A breezeway is an open connection, a covered walkway; a piazza forms an integral part of a house.

59. Wright Nunn House survey file, State Historic Preservation Office.

60. Lenoir County Road Overseers' Report, 1840, cited in Ruth Little-Stokes, "LaFayette Documentation Report," (research report, State Historic Preservation Office, 1973); H. S. Lee to his cousin, Dec. 15, 1867, copy in Whitfield-Dunn-Wiggins House survey file, State Historic Preservation Office.

61. Whitfield, *Whitfield, Bryan, Smith, and Related Families*, 75-78.

62. Sloop Point National Register of Historic Places nomination form, State Historic Preservation Office.

63. Jesse Jackson House survey file, State Historic Preservation Office.

64. Moore-Heath House survey file, State Historic Preservation Office.

65. Phillips Log Kitchen survey file, State Historic Preservation Office.

66. Cross, "Peebles House in Kinston," 42.

67. Mike Kohler, *Two Hundred Years of Progress* (Kinston: Kinston-Lenoir County Bicentennial Commission and Lenoir County Board of Commissioners, 1976), 70.

68. Powell, *Annals of Progress*, 38.

69. Black, "Historic and Architectural Resources," B.3.

70. Cross, "Peebles House in Kinston," 42.

71. Cross, "Peebles House in Kinston," map and key, 44.

72. Powell, *Annals of Progress*, 72.

73. Black, "Historic and Architectural Resources," B.3.

74. Powell, *Annals of Progress*, 38.

75. Black, "Historic and Architectural Resources," B.5; Eighth Census, 1860: Lenoir Co. Slave Schedule.

76. See Koerner Military Survey Field Map of Lenoir County, 1863, A&H.

77. "Our Recent Visit," *Farmer's Journal*, 1 (May 1852): 50 (quoted in York, Tull-Worth-Holland Farm nomination.)

78. Seventh Census, 1850: Lenoir Co. Population and Slave Schedules. The enumerator tallied up the figures on the last page of the Kinston section, at the end of the county population census.

79. Cross, "Peebles House in Kinston," map and key, 44.

80. Cross, "Peebles House in Kinston," map and key, 44.

81. Seventh Census, 1850: Lenoir Co. Population Schedule.

82 John Latham, ed., *Historical and Descriptive Review of the State of North Carolina*, (Charleston, S.C.: Empire Publishing Company, 1885), 2: 98.

83. Johnson and Holloman, *Story of Kinston and Lenoir County*, 98.

84. Cross, "Peebles House in Kinston," map and key, 44.

85. Johnson and Holloman, *Story of Kinston and Lenoir County*, 98-99.

86. Powell, *Annals of Progress*, 41.

87. Eighth Census, 1860: Lenoir Co. Population and Slave Schedules. (Kinston is listed at the end of the Population Schedule.)

88. Eighth Census, 1860: Lenoir Co. Population Schedule.

89. Dreyer, "Kinston's Architecture," 18.

90. Black, "Historic and Architectural Resources," B.5.

91. Black, Former Baptist Parsonage National Register of Historic Places nomination form; Kinston Baptist/White Rock Presbyterian Church National Register of Historic Places nomination form, State Historic Preservation Office, 1989.

92. Powell, *Annals of Progress*, 74. This building stood at the corner of Gordon and Herritage Streets.

93. *Historical and Descriptive Review of North Carolina*, 98.

94. Dreyer, "Kinston's Architecture," 116.

95. Lillie V. Archbell, "Historic Buildings in and near Kinston," *Carolina and the Southern Cross*, 1 (November 1913): 12.

96. Wooten-Timberlake House survey file, State Historic Preservation Office.

Chapter Three. Civil War, Reconstruction, and the Days of "King Cotton"

1. Powell, *Annals of Progress*, 43-50; *Kinston Free Press*, 1897 Industrial Edition, 1.

2. Memoirs of Clay Trumbell, quoted in Clifford Tyndall, "Lenoir County during the Civil War" (master's thesis, East Carolina University, 1981), 21.

3. Memoirs of Clay Trumbell, quoted in Clifford Tyndall, "Lenoir County during the Civil War."

4. York, Tull-Worth-Holland Farm nomination, 8.16.

5. Cobb-King-Humphrey House survey file, State Historic Preservation Office.

6. York, Tull-Worth-Holland Farm nomination, 8.9-8.10.

7. *Report on the Productions of Agriculture, 1880* (Washington, D.C.: Government Printing Office, 1880), 79.

8. Richard L. Zuber, *North Carolina during Reconstruction* (Raleigh: State Department of Archives and History, 1969), 52-53; York, Tull-Worth-Holland Farm nomination, 8.17-8.18.

9. Jerry Cross, letter to author, April 17, 1996; York, Tull-Worth-Holland Farm nomination, 8.17-8.18; Ninth Census of the United States, 1870: Lenoir Co. Agriculture Schedule, microfilm, A&H.

10. Jurney and Davis, Soil Survey, 3; *Tenth Census of the United States, 1880.* vol. 6, *Cotton Production* (Washington, D.C.: Government Printing Office, 1884), 3; *Compendium of the Tenth Census of the United States*, pt. 1 (Washington, D.C.: Government Printing Office, 1883), 720.

11. Powell, *Annals of Progress*, 53; Lefler and Newsome, North Carolina, 493.

12. *Ninth Census of the United States, 1870* (Washington, D.C.: Government Printing Office, 1880).

13. Hardy Brothers Store survey file.

14. Newsome, "*Twelve North Carolina Counties*," 183; York, Tull-Worth-Holland Farm nomination, 8.10, 8.11, 8.17.

15. Lightwood blocks were created by girdling a pine tree. Lounsbury, *Illustrated Glossary*, 212.

16. Lutson Stroud Log House survey file, State Historic Preservation Office.

17. Sutton-Ivy-Dawson House survey file, State Historic Preservation Office.

18. Elias Hazelton House survey file, State Historic Preservation Office.

19. Seth West House survey file, State Historic Preservation Office.

20. Geographer Fred Kniffen named the type after the letter I because it was prevalent in such midwestern states as Indiana and Illinois.

21. W. L. Kennedy purchased the house from his father, Thomas Jefferson Kennedy, who had bought it in 1855. Cedar Dell survey file, State Historic Preservation Office.

22. James Lewis Jones, "A Brief Description of the Old Home," James Lewis Jones Manuscript, 1947, 1, East Carolina University Manuscript Collection, East Carolina University, Greenville, N.C.

23. Jeffrey J. Crow, Paul D. Escott, and Flora J. Hatley, *A History of African Americans in North Carolina* (Raleigh: Division of Archives and History, 1992), 93.

24. *Kinston Journal*, July 24, 1879.

25. Crow, Escott, and Hatley, *History of African Americans*, 92.

26. Seventh Census, 1850: Lenoir Co. Population Schedule; Eighth Census, 1860: Lenoir Co. Population Schedule; Ninth Census, 1870: Lenoir Co. Population Schedule; Tenth Census of the United States, 1880: Lenoir Co., N.C., Population Schedule, microfilm, A&H. There is also no listing of a black or mulatto female named Silvia in the 1880 Woodington census.

27. *The Heritage of Lenoir County*, 208. Wiley Dove is listed in the Tenth Census, 1880: Lenoir Co. Population Schedule as living in Woodington Township with his sister Jane and her two children (nos. 284,298).

28. *Branson's North Carolina Business Directory, 1896* (Raleigh: Levi Branson, 1896), 381. There were no African American landowners listed in the 1870s or 1880s directories. *Thirteenth Census of the United States*, vol. 6 (Washington, D.C.: Government Printing Office, 1910), 222-223; *Kinston Free Press*, 1906 Industrial Issue, 95, 104.

29. Claire Cannon Foster, interview by Louvenia Walker, Kinston N.C., 1993.

30. *Kinston Journal*, January 6, 1881.

31. *Kinston Free Press*, 1906 Industrial Issue, 85, 87, 89, 104, 107, 108, 109.

32. *Kinston Free Press*, 1906 Industrial Issue, 109.

33. Bryant House survey file, State Historic Preservation Office.

34. Dreyer, "Kinston's Architecture," 20.

35. Lane, "Historic Buildings," 17. The writer was Harriet Cobb Lane, niece of Harriet Cobb. John Peebles had died in 1864.

36. Ninth Census, 1870: Lenoir Co. Population Schedule; Powell, *Annals of Progress*, 5.

37. Lillie V. Archbell, "Editor's Column," *Carolina and the Southern Cross*, 1, (January 1914), 10; *Carolina and the Southern Cross*, 1 (February 1914), 8.

38. *Branson's Business Directory, 1896*; Ninth Census, 1870: Lenoir Co. Population Schedule.

39. Ninth Census, 1870: Lenoir Co. Population Schedule.

40. Latham, editor. *Historical and Descriptive Review*, 2: 101-108.

41. Kohler, *Two Hundred Years of Progress*, 52.

42. Latham, *Historical and Descriptive Review*, 2: 101-108; Powell, *Annals of Progress*, 65-66.

43. George I. Nowitzky, *Norfolk Marine Metropolis of Virginia, and the Sound and River Cities of North Carolina* (Raleigh: the author, 1888), 178.

44. Latham, *Historical and Descriptive Review*, 2: 98.

45. Nowitzky, *Norfolk and the Sound and River Cities*, 179-181.

46. James Lewis Jones, "Stirring Events of the Early Eighties in Lenoir County," 6-7, James Lewis Jones Manuscript.

47. "Stirring Events of the Early Eighties," 6.

48. Black, "Historic and Architectural Resources," B.11.

49. Kohler, *Two Hundred Years of Progress*, 101.

50. Powell, *Annals of Progress*, 55; Nannie Mae Tilley, *The Bright-Tobacco Industry, 1860-1929* (Chapel Hill: University of North Carolina Press, 1948), 141.

51. Nowitzky, *Norfolk and the Sound and River Cities*, 179.

52. *Kinston Journal*, September 9, 1880.

53. Eighth Census, 1860: Lenoir Co. Population Schedule.

54. Ninth Census, 1870: Lenoir Co. Population Schedule; Powell, *Annals of Progress*, 5.

55. Ninth Census, 1870: Lenoir Co. Population Schedule.

56. *Branson's North Carolina Business Directory: 1877-1878* (Raleigh: Levi Branson, 1878), 136-137, 174-175.

57. *Kinston Journal*, April 19, 1888.

58. Tenth Census, 1880: Lenoir Co. Population Schedule.

59. Tenth Census, 1880: Lenoir Co. Population Schedule. See also *Kinston Daily Free Press*, November 23, 1957; *Kinston Daily Free Press*, 1897 Industrial Issue.

60. *Kinston Free Press*, 1899 Industrial Issue, 6.

61. *Kinston Free Press*, 1899 Industrial Issue, 6; Lenoir County deeds place the bank on the west side of Queen Street.

62. *Kinston Free Press*, 1899 Industrial Issue, 6.

63. *Kinston Daily Free Press*, June 13, 1900.

64. *Kinston Free Press*, 1899 Industrial Issue, 6.

65. *Kinston Daily Free Press*, 1897 Industrial Issue, quoted in Kohler, *Two Hundred Years of Progress*, 108.

66. Tenth Census, 1880: Lenoir Co. Population Schedule, Woodington Township; *Kinston Daily Free Press*, May 30, 1898.

67. *Kinston Daily Free Press*, April 7, 1898.

68. *Kinston Daily Free Press*, June 7, 1898.

69. *Kinston Journal*, September 9, 1880.

70. Gray Map of Kinston, A&H, 1882; *Kinston City Directory* (Charlotte: Interstate Directory Company, 1902), 91-117.

71. Edna Speight, interview by Mavis Anderson, quoted in Anderson, *A Lincoln City Celebration* (Kinston: Black Artists' Guild, Inc., 1985), 5-6.

72. *Kinston Daily Free Press*, June 15, 1904.

73. *Branson's North Carolina Business Directory*, 1877-1878, 174-176.

74. *Kinston Journal*, June 2, 1881; *Kinston Free Press*, November 23, 1957. Yankee Row was the nickname of industrial housing built along Tower Hill Road before the Civil War for the Washington Shoe Factory. In 1957 the Yankee Row church had been demolished for some time; its site was given as the Reverend John Louis Borden's home.

75. *Kinston Journal*, June 2, 1881.

76. *Kinston Journal*, June 16, 1881.

77. According to tradition white Kinstonians detested Miss Keys for publicly parading in the street with her pupils and for the fact that "her school was conducted in Mr. Washington's Shoe Factory without paying Mr. Washington for the use of it." When Miss Keys died, it was arranged that she would be buried temporarily in the town cemetery until her friends or family claimed her, but her body, with a tombstone, still rested at Maplewood Cemetery in the early twentieth century. (G. B. W. and Mrs. F. H., "Kinston in the Sixties," *Carolina and the Southern Cross* 1 (November 1913): 2.

78. *Kinston Daily Free* Press, September 13, 1888; *Branson's North Carolina Business Directory,1884* (Raleigh: Levi Branson, 1884), 416-418.

79. *Kinston Journal*, July 24, 1879.

80. Lenoir County Deed Book 22:429, 1898, microfilm, A&H.

Chapter Four. A Century of Progress

1. *Kinston Free Press*, August 18, 1897.

2. *Kinston Free Press*, August 22, 1895.

3. Tilley, *Bright-Tobacco Industry*, 144; *Illustrated City of Kinston, Lenoir County, North Carolina* (Kinston: Kinston Chamber of Commerce, c. 1914), 2.

4. *Survey of the Public Schools of Lenoir County* (Raleigh: State Superintendent of Public Instruction, 1924), 9-11; Powell, *Annals of Progress*, 5, 90, 92; Johnson and Holloman, *Story of Kinston and Lenoir County*, 181.

5. Jurney and Davis, *Soil Survey*, 1-6.

6. Jurney and Davis, *Soil Survey*, 1-6; *Eleventh Census of the United States, 1890: Report of the Statistics of Agriculture* (Washington, D.C.: Government Printing Office, 1895), 395.

7. Johnson and Holloman, *Story of Kinston and Lenoir County*, 123.

8. Powell, *Annals of Progress*, 92.

9. *Kinston Free Press*, 1906 Industrial Issue, 67.

10. *Kinston and Lenoir County, North Carolina* (Kinston: Kinston Chamber of Commerce, 1917), 4.

11. Bill Sharpe, *A New Geography of North Carolina*, 4 vols (Raleigh: Sharpe Publishing Company, Inc., 1954-1965), 3:1384-1385; Jurney and Davis, *Soil Survey*, 4-5; Powell, *Annals of Progress*, 92.

12. Jurney and Davis, *Soil Survey*, 3; M. Ruth Little, "North Carolina Global Transpark Historic Architecture Report," research report, State Historic Preservation Office,1993. The Kinston-Snow Hill line operated until 1929, and the tracks were removed in the 1940s. *The Highway, the Motor Vehicle, and the Community* (Washington, D.C.: National Highway Users Conference, 1938), 45.

13. *Kinston Free Press*, 1906 Industrial Issue, 106.

14. Jurney and Davis, *Soil Survey*, 1-6.

15. *United States Census Office, Twelfth Census Reports*, vol. 5, *Agriculture Statistics* (Washington, D.C.: Government Printing Office, 1900), 110-111; *Fourteenth Census of the United States*, vol. 6 (Washington, D.C.: Government Printing Office, 1920), 236-237.

16. Powell, *Annals of Progress*, 91; Isabelle Fletcher Perry, interview by M. Ruth Little, September 1997.

17. *Kinston Free Press*, 1906 Industrial Issue; *Biennial Report of the Superintendent of Public Instruction for North Carolina for 1924-1926* (Raleigh: State Superintendent of Public Instruction, 1926), 157.

18. *Survey of Public Schools*, 127; W. Chester Forrest, notes about Airy Grove School, August 15, 1989, copy in Airy Grove survey file, State Historic Preservation Office.

19. Thomas W. Hanchett, "The Rosenwald Schools and Black Education in North Carolina," *North Carolina Historical Review* 65 (October 1988): 436.

20. *Heritage of Lenoir County*, 51-53.

21. Charles Ware, *A History of Atlantic Christian College* (privately printed, 1956), 98-100.

22. *Kinston Free Press*, 1906 Industrial Issue; *Heritage of Lenoir County*.

23. Powell, *Annals of Progress*, 83-86. See also the J. Y. Joyner House survey file, State Historic Preservation Office.

24. Powell, *Annals of Progress*, 83-86.

25. Kohler, *Two Hundred Years of Progress*, 147; Dreyer, "Kinston's Architecture," 54.

26. Kohler, *Two Hundred Years of Progress*, 146.

27. Liddell Cash Supply survey file, State Historic Preservation Office.

28. Eliza Walters Magill, *Fool John and Other Stories* (n. p., 1975), 143-144.

29. Virginia White Little, interview by the author, Raleigh, 1995.

30. Virginia White Little interview.

31. *Illustrated City of Kinston*, 12.

32. *Kinston Free Press*, 1906 Industrial Issue, 97.

33. Stephen Nathan Gilbert House survey file, State Historic Preservation Office.

34. Charles A. Broadway House survey file, State Historic Preservation Office.

35. Simpson Waller House survey file, State Historic Preservation Office.

36. Brown-Gates House survey file, State Historic Preservation Office.

37. Redding Jackson Farm survey file, State Historic Preservation Office.

38. Carl Jones House survey file, State Historic Preservation Office.

39. Adair Kennedy House survey file, State Historic Preservation Office.

Chapter Five. Kinston in the Twentieth Century

1. Black, Kinston Commercial Historic District nomination, 8.2; Kohler, *200 Years of Progress*, 71.

2. Joe Dawson. "Realty Changes in Kinston Are Very Important." *Kinston Daily News*, 24 September 1921, 1.

3. Dreyer, "Kinston's Architecture," 29; 107. The hotel stood until 1930 when it was demolished to make way for the Commercial National Bank, currently Wachovia Bank.

4. 118 S. Queen St. Firehouse Museum.

5. Kohler, *200 Years of Progress*, 93; Powell, *The Story of Lenoir County and Kinston*, 56; "Kinston Tobacco Market," *Kinston Free Press*, 18 August 1897, 2.

6. "City's Tobacco Factories are Boost for Local Sales," "Tobacco Is King in Kinston and Eastern Carolina," *Kinston Daily Free Press*, 23 November 1957, B.9-10.

7. "Kinston Tobacco Market," *Kinston Free Press*, 18 August 1897, 2; Powell, *Annals of Progress*, 57.

8. *Illustrated City of Kinston*, 2.

9. *The State*, "Industry in Kinston," August 14, 1943, 20-24; *The State*, "Kinston Has Everything," August 18, 1951, 6-7, 19-21; Sharpe, *A New Geography of North Carolina*, 3, Lenoir County.

10. From 1933-1974 period, as seen in Table 2, T. E. Austin, "Tobacco Marketing Warehouses and Their Location in the Urban Landscape of the Eastern Flue-Cured Belt of North Carolina (M.A. Thesis, East Carolina University, 1977). During this period, Kinston sold an average of about 49 million pounds, Rocky Mount an average of about 52 million pounds, Greenville an average of 53 million pounds and Wilson an average of about 69 million pounds; see also Sharpe, *A New Geography of North Carolina* 1 (1954), 2 (1958), 3 (1961), 4 (1965).

11. Black, "Historic and Architectural Resources of Kinston," B.12; Powell, *Annals of Progress*, 62, 66.

12. Eli N. Evans. *The Provincials: A Personal History of Jews in the South.* (New York: Atheneum, 1973); Powell, *Annals of Progress*, 65; *The Heritage of Lenoir County*, 116, 342, 90, 381; *Illustrated City of Kinston*, 8.

13. Powell, *Annals of Progress*, 55; Kohler, *200 Years of Progress*, 100.

14. Kohler, *200 Years of Progress*, 101, 104. Since the early twentieth century these two mills have changed owners and names several times. Additions have merged the two buildings, and neither original mill is distinguishable.

15. Dreyer, "Kinston's Architecture," 45. A few of the mill houses still stand, but most were moved to other locations.

16. Kohler, *200 Years of Progress*, 102.

17. Black, (former) Atlantic and North Carolina Railroad Freight Depot Nomination, 8.2.

18. Powell, *Annals of Progress*, 5; *Kinston Free Press*, 1906 Industrial Issue.

19. Powell, *Annals of Progress*, 80-81.

20. Dreyer, Kinston's Architecture," 38-39; Powell, *Annals of Progress*, 68; Kohler, *200 Years of Progress*, 85, 88.

21. Delia Hyatt Collection, A&H; Black, Trianon Historic District National Register Nomination, 1989, SHPO. A portion of the house is said to have been saved and used for hospital purposes, but the entire complex was later demolished.

22. *Builders of Eastern North Carolina* (Kinston: Eastern Carolina Chamber of Commerce, Inc., 1931), 115; Kohler, *200 Years of Progress*, 157.

23. Dreyer, "Kinston's Architecture," 59.

24. Black, Queen-Gordon Streets Historic District Nomination, 8.3; Scott Power, Colin Ingerham, Queen-Gordon Streets Historic District (Boundary Increase), 1994, 7.3.

25. *Kinston Free Press*, September 2, 1899, 26.

26. Dreyer, "Kinston's Architecture," 144; 1900 Census of the United States, Lenoir County, Population Schedule; Black, Mitchelltown Historic District Nomination, 8.2-3.

27. Black, Trianon Historic District Nomination, 8.1-4.

28. Black, Hill-Grainger Historic District Nomination, 8.3.

29. Ibid.

30. Black, Robert L. Blalock House Nomination, 8.1-2.

31. Research in progress by Penne Smith, Abstract for A. Mitchell Wooten Thesis, University of Delaware, 1997.

32. Ibid.

33. Ibid.

34. Rev. R. S. Oden, "Sketch of Kinston," for the *Programme and Directory of the Fiftieth Anniversary and Jubilee and the Fifty-Sixth Session of the North Carolina Conference, November 23-30, 1919* (Kinston, St. Augustus A.M.E. Zion Church, 1919), 13. Hereinafter referred to as *Fiftieth Anniversary Program*, St. Augustus A.M.E. Zion Church.

35. 1902 Kinston City Directory: Sampling of "Colored Directory," 91-117.

36. By 1916, the Hotel Charles was back in business but it is not certain that Charles Dunn was the proprietor. Dreyer, "Kinston's Architecture," 43. Taken from Dreyer's interview with John Sparrow, Kinston, May 1981.

37. Rev. Cozelle Mills Wilson, interview by M. Ruth Little and Penne Smith, 1994.

38. Clarence Moye, interview with Penne Smith, 1994.

39. Crow, Escott, and Hatley, *A History of African-Americans*, 121; *Kinston Daily Free Press*, August 30, 1898, 4.

40. *Kinston Daily Free Press*, August 29, 1898, 4.

41. Moye interview.

42. Black, Peoples Bank National Register Nomination, 1989, SHPO, 8.0-1; *Fiftieth Anniversary Programme*, St. Augustus A.M.E. Zion Church, 17.

43. *Kinston Daily Free Press*, February 21, 1914, 4; *Kinston Free Press*, June 11, 1919, 4; also Kinston Sanborn Fire Insurance Maps, 1919 (page 6), 1925 (page 20).

44. Wilson interview.

45. Ezekiel K. Best, interview with Penne Smith, 1996.

46. Kinston City Directories; Wilson interview.

47. *Kinston Daily Free Press*, July 11, 1900, 4.

48. Wilson interview.

49. Wilson interview.

50. Wilson interview.

51. Moye interview.

52. Kristin Szylvian, "Public Housing Comes to Wilmington, North Carolina," *North Carolina Humanities*, 3, No. 1 (Spring-Summer 1995), 52-53.

53. Moye interview.

54. Wilson interview.

55. *Branson's North Carolina Business Directories*, 1890, 1896.

56. *Fiftieth Anniversary Programme*, St. Augustus A.M.E. Zion Church, 42.

57. Mavis Anderson, *A Lincoln City Celebration* (Kinston: The Black Artists' Guild, Inc., 1985), 3.

58. Wilson interview.

59. *Fiftieth Anniversary Programme*, St. Augustus A.M.E. Zion Church, 6. Mr. Holloway's speech, not reprinted in the programme, was "The Church's Place in the Community." Also Kinston City Directories.

60. Wilson interview.

61. Best interview; HUD Grant Files, Golden Progress Alley Rehabilitation Project, Kinston, N.C., 1976-1978: File 621-648; 1890, 1896 *Branson's Business Directory*; 1920s-1930s Kinston City Directories.

62. Wilson interview.

63. Moye interview.

64. Kohler, *200 Years of Progress*, 86.

65. Black, "The Historic and Architectural Resources of Kinston," B.19.

66. Moye interview.

67. Wilson interview.

68. *The State*, "Industry in Kinston," August 14, 1943, 20; *The State*, "Kinston Has Everything," August 18, 1951, 6-7, 19-21.

69. This is the title of a 1919 song by Sam Lewis and Joe Young.

70. Kohler, *200 Years of Progress*, 103; Powell, *Annals of Progress*, 95-96.

71. Kohler, *200 Years of Progress*, 148.

72. Jack Rider, "A Partial History of Lenoir County," *The Lenoir County News*, Special Edition, 1952; Dreyer; "Kinston's Architecture," 62; Johnson and Holloman, *The Story of Kinston and Lenoir County*, 279-282.

73. Wilson interview.

74. Ted Dawson, interview with Penne Smith, 1995.

75. Sharpe, *A New Geography of North Carolina*, 3, 1387-1388.

76. Jim Stewart interview with Billy Brewer, former Kinston warehouseman, May 1997; Statistic provided by Isabelle Fletcher Perry, May 1997.

CATALOGUE OF HISTORIC STRUCTURES

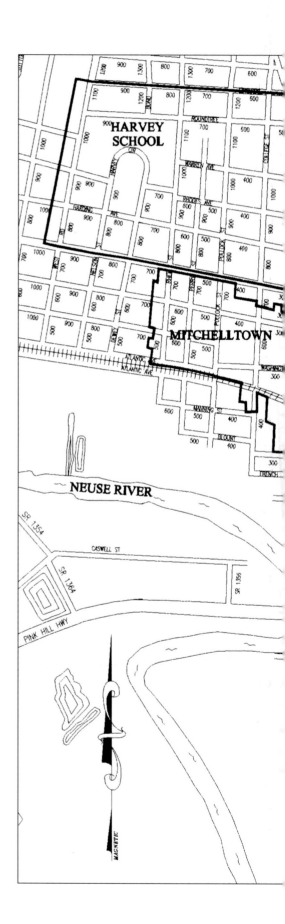

City of Kinston

Written by
Penne Smith

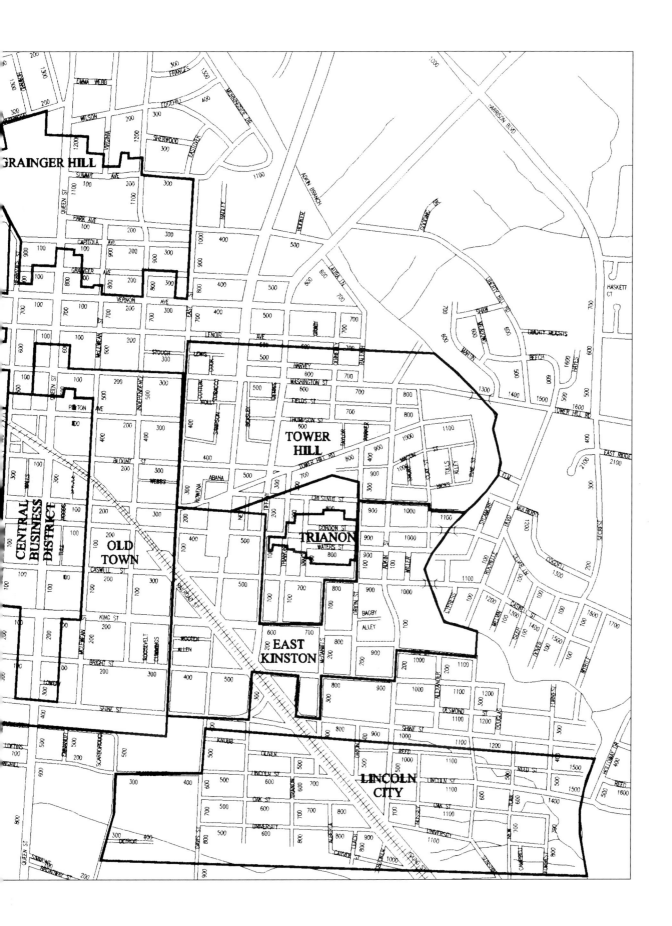

Early twentieth century view of Queen Street (Postcard Collection of Sarah Pope, Goldsboro)

Kinston Central Business District

Kinston's central business district, with North Queen Street as its heart, begins in the African American commercial district of South Queen Street (known in the nineteenth century as part of Tuckahoe) and runs north along North Queen Street to the intersection of busy Vernon Avenue. The tributary Streets of King, Caswell, Gordon, North, and Blount, and Washington and Lenoir Avenues, run east to west; sections of McLewean, Herritage, and Independence Streets also form part of the commercial district. With its dense concentration of early-twentieth-century buildings, this area represents Kinston's explosive growth at the turn of the twentieth century, when the town became a prime tobacco and cotton market for eastern North Carolina. As a result of this growth, there was an expansion of building, including new churches executed in popular period architectural styles and sophisticated, substantial public buildings. This expansion continued into the 1920s and 1930s, particularly on West Blount Street, North Herritage Street, West North Street, and parts of North Queen Street. In these areas there are examples of restrained versions of Victorian and Art Deco styles. Downtown Kinston, known locally as the Magic Mile, has retained many period buildings with remarkable integrity.

As early as 1879 Kinston had envisioned itself as a vital commercial center. Its transformation from village to bustling small town separated Kinston from comparable settlements like Trenton in Jones County and Snow Hill in Greene County. The editor of the *Kinston Journal* mused in that year that "there seems to be some magic connected with the presence of steam and electricity, which pervades every one living near them, creating a vim and push that begets and encourages enterprises of all descriptions."[1] Manufactories and general stores were opening in Kinston. In 1878 the A. Harvey and Company tobacco company, located on the south side of North Street between McLewean (then listed as McIlwaine) and Queen Streets, was the first small tobacco factory in Kinston. There were also Lemuel Harvey's successful agricultural hardware and fertilizer business and the Oettinger family's furniture store at 114-116 North Queen Street. In 1885 the east block of Queen Street between Gordon and Caswell Streets included four saloons, three groceries, three barbershops, two machinery shops, a cobbler shop, a dry goods store, a hardware store, a general store, a post office, and an insurance office.

All of the buildings on Queen Street described above were casualties of the 1895 fire. The fire broke out in Bryan Fields' stables, located behind a grocery and feed store on the south side of East Gordon Street, in the middle of a February night. Within five years, however, Kinston resurged; the new buildings were, for the most part, brick instead of the former "shabby wooden buildings with their over-reaching sheds."[2] Among structures from that group of early-twentieth-century buildings still standing today is Burwell Westbrook Canady's two-story Romanesque Revival brick commercial complex at 131-135 North Queen Street, completed in 1900.[3] Immediately after the 1895 fire destroyed his building on the corner of North Queen and Gordon, Canady built a temporary annex at 105-107 East Gordon Street to maintain his agricultural supply and hardware business until a larger new building could be finished; the annex is still standing. Another merchant, Jesse Grainger, built a two-story late-Victorian brick commercial building at the southeast corner of North Queen and North Streets, at 215 North Queen Street, which still stands.

Other turn-of-the-twentieth-century commercial buildings in this immediate area include the Citizens Bank Building at 201 North Queen Street and the former Sumrell and McCoy Wholesale Grocery, built circa 1909 at 400 North Queen Street. The Beaux Arts/Romanesque Revival-style Citizens Bank, built in 1903, has a distinctive corner bay surmounted by a convex metal dome; old photographs show that the first-floor voussoir corner arches were supported on sturdy, but diminutive, pilasters and one projecting pier. Another bank built prior to 1910 was the bold Neoclassical Revival-style National Bank of Kinston. The Farmers and Merchants Bank on the northwest corner of Queen and Gordon Streets, a towering Renaissance Revival structure designed by the architectural firm of Benton and Benton of Wilson, was then the tallest building in town and helped to draw most of the city's banking institutions to this immediate central area. These banks were patronized by Kinston citizens and the county's farmers alike.

Tobacco manufactories began appearing in Kinston in the 1890s. The earliest one that has survived is the former Export Leaf Tobacco Company, in the former American Tobacco Company building, a large two-story brick facility constructed between 1901 and 1908 at the southeast corner of West Lenoir Avenue and Herritage Street.[4] Other brick tobacco warehouses that have survived in Kinston include the former L. B. Jenkins Tobacco Warehouse, an attractive two-story structure on East Lenoir Avenue built circa 1930, and the 1925 Imperial Tobacco Warehouse, located by the railroad tracks off East Lenoir Avenue. Most of Kinston's famous brick tobacco warehouses—the Eagle, located at the northeast corner of East Lenoir Avenue and North McLewean Street; the old Central Warehouse, spanning the north block of 200 West North Street; and others—were located within the commercial district and no longer exist. These warehouses, which served as sites for assemblies, pageants, dances, and political rallies outside tobacco season, were important community centers.[5]

Other landmarks at the turn of the twentieth century in the commercial district included Thomas H. Green's barbershop at 105 East Gordon Street and George Kornegay's grocery at 100 South Queen Street, recalled as the "first store encountered on entering the town from that direction [south]."[6] J. E. Hood's brick drugstore stood at 203 North Queen Street, and Skinner's

Confectionery at 115 North Queen Street served oysters in season. For citizens like W. D. LaRoque, Luther Tapp, and J. E. Hood, conversation over cigars and oysters at Skinner's was a popular after-work pastime.[7] Green's barbershop and Hood's Drug Store still stand.

Even as commerce and industry expanded in and around the central business section, the area remained the location for many of the city's major churches. By the late nineteenth century congregations had outgrown their earlier facilities, and at the turn of the twentieth century they had begun constructing new and larger churches. At 118 East Gordon Street the Gordon Street Christian Church, an unusual Romanesque Revival brick building, was built between 1912 and 1915. The Queen Street United Methodist Church at 500 North Queen Street, a magnificent Victorian brick building, was built in 1910. At the northeastern edge of Kinston's commercial district, at 613 North McLewean Street, stands the former Universalist Church. This church, also built circa 1910, has both Romanesque Revival and Gothic Revival features; the heavy massing of the building is balanced by the crenellated crossing tower (now altered) and the lancet-arch windows. Isaac Rochelle, a local contractor who developed a good deal of the early-twentieth-century Grainger Hill neighborhood, was one of the Universalist Church's builders. He had the help of a patented cement-block machine, which made blocks on site.[8]

Other institutions, primarily public, were operating in Kinston's commercial district, including the United States Post Office. As in other early-twentieth-century towns, Kinston's post offices operated out of commercial buildings, often occupying a corner of a store, until the second decade of the twentieth century, when dedicated post office buildings became more common. The Kinston Post Office, on leaving its Grainger Building office at Queen and North Streets, moved to 112 East Gordon Street, where it remained until the 1915 construction of the limestone Neoclassical Revival-style Post Office-Federal Building at 301 North Queen Street.

Robert Blalock, a prominent early-twentieth-century Kinston builder, employed Classical Revival stylistic elements when he constructed the (former) J. C. Penney, Inc. building at 300 North Queen Street in 1927 and the (former) Brown's Wholesale Grocery at 109 West North Street. Both two-story buildings have sheet-metal cornices below facade parapets. Blalock was noted for his design and construction of commercial and civic buildings. His commissions included many of Kinston's most significant early-twentieth-century buildings, such as the old Central Tobacco Warehouse, Kinston Garage (which received an Art Deco facelift in the 1930s) at 105 West Blount Street, and Union Station, which was completed in 1924.

Blalock's Union Station opened in March 1924 to much local fanfare. The masonry Mission Revival-influenced building was hailed as commodious and comfortable, well-equipped, adequately lighted and architecturally attractive.[9] Located at the southeastern intersection of East Caswell and Davis Streets, the station was conveniently sited for business, transport, and passengers. The station, which no longer stands, might be said to symbolize Kinston's continued assertive progress. Four years later the Hotel Kinston towered over North Queen Street. This building was the triumphant culmination of local efforts to establish a first-class modern hotel to accommodate visitors and businessmen. The hotel was especially lively during the tobacco warehouse season between the end of August and mid-September, and the Moorish Revival-influenced ballroom saw many parties during this time. The Imperial Tobacco Company's brick office building on North Herritage Street, built in 1925, was a stylish unique addition to the Herritage streetscape, then composed primarily of plain one-story brick stores and large tobacco warehouses. The Imperial Tobacco Company office's exterior combined an unusual battlemented cornice with lively Art Deco details, such as diamonds within the cornice's panels. It is similar to Greenville's Imperial Tobacco Company office, located thirty minutes north of Kinston.

Farther south below King Street, the swampy south end of Queen Street known as Tuckahoe had been drained in the late nineteenth century and became home to African American businesses. As such it was distinct from the predominantly white Magic Mile, and there were few commercial buildings comparable to those at Banker's Corner in Tuckahoe. One exception is the 1920s Peoples Bank, at the northeast corner of Queen and Shine Streets. The bank, a small Classical Revival building of ribbon brick and limestone details, was the second African American bank established in Kinston.

During the 1930s building activity in the business district was restricted principally to remodeling a number of buildings there. The Grand Theater was remodeled and renamed the Paramount; its 1930s marquee survives at 211 North Queen Street. The LaRoque and Hewitt Building at 105 West Gordon Street, an early-twentieth-century masonry structure, had its facade sheathed by Art Deco-inspired pigmented structural glass panels about 1930.[10] The local branch of the Works Progress Administration and the National Resettlement Administration operated at 133-135 West North Street, a two-story brick building, with little exterior decoration other than contrasting brick window surrounds, built in the mid-1920s. Notable examples of the few commercial buildings constructed in the 1930s include the terra-cotta-and-tile-facaded Montgomery Ward building at 324 North Queen Street and the Lenoir County Courthouse, an impressive Art Moderne limestone building with Art Deco details. The courthouse, designed by A. Mitchell Wooten, was completed in 1939-1940. Smaller 1930s Kinston buildings are Hines Barbeque, a one-story brick building at 218 North Herritage Street, and a Tudor Revival-influenced former service station at the southeast corner of McLewean and East Caswell Streets.

The former Kinston Steam Laundry at 208 West Gordon Street, built in 1947, completes the varied range of architectural styles in Kinston's commercial district. The laundry (which replaced an earlier building) has large vertical windows, minimal exterior decoration, and curving brick surfaces, which indicate the popular amalgamation of the International style and Art Moderne by the late 1940s. Such streamlined details appeared on period objects, from toasters and automobiles to theaters and early shopping centers.

Since the Second World War few new buildings have been added to Kinston's Magic Mile; business owners conservatively chose to remodel stores or cover them with more-modern facades. Today Kinston participates in the national Main Street Program and consequently championed downtown revitalization by working through such active local organizations as the Pride of Kinston. There are a number of successful adaptations of earlier buildings for new uses, most notably the Arts Center, now housed in the old Sumrell and McCoy Grocery, and the Hotel Kinston, which has become a retirement community for elderly citizens. Underlying the rehabilitation and restoration of Kinston's many early-twentieth-century commercial buildings is the town's love of the past, combined with its continuing ambitions for future growth.

Notes

1. *Kinston Journal*, February 7, 1879.

2. *Kinston Daily Free Press*, September 24, 1921.

3. *Kinston Daily Free Press*, May 16, 1900.

4. Sanborn Fire Insurance Maps of Kinston: 1901, 1908, 1914, North Carolina Collection, University of North Carolina, Chapel Hill; Kinston City Directories 1902-1916. The American Tobacco Company had moved to 300 East Vernon Avenue by 1914.

5. Tilley, *Bright-Tobacco Industry*, 203. Some 1890s issues of the *Kinston Daily Free Press* mention gatherings to be held at the warehouses.

6. Jones, "James Lewis Jones Manuscript," 5-6.

7. Marianna LaRoque Lewis, interview by Penne Smith, Kinston, December 8, 1995.

8. Marianna Rochelle Pressly, interview by Penne Smith, Kinston, November 23, 1994.

9. *Kinston Daily Free Press*, March 3, 1924.

10. Black, Queen-Gordon Streets Historic District Nomination, 7.10.

1. (former) Travellers Gas Station

built circa 1958
301 South Queen Street

This small gasoline service station is significant as one of the highly endangered urban gas stations built in the 1940s and 1950s, which are rapidly disappearing. The building is a dramatic example of the Moderne style popular for service stations, with a flat-roofed, narrow service block and a narrow office wing projecting to the front, covered by a flat roof that slopes dramatically upward to become a broadly cantilevered porte cochere in the front. The office has an angled glass display window wall. Steel posts support the front porte cochere. The entire structure is made of concrete block with a veneer of porcelainized enamel panels. The gas station was one of many built in the late 1950s for the Travellers chain, then headquartered in Wilmington, North Carolina.

2. Peoples Bank

built circa 1923; listed in the National Register of Historic Places, 1989
242 South Queen Street

The Peoples Bank, a two-story brick-veneered building in the Classical Revival style, is a significant Kinston landmark. It is one of two banks established by a group of African American businessmen at the turn of the twentieth century, and the only one still standing. Between 1902 and 1923 the Peoples Bank, then known as Holloway, Borden, Hicks, and Company, was located in a two-story frame building at the southeast corner of Bright and Queen Streets. In 1921 the company was granted a charter to operate as the Peoples Bank. The resulting new bank across the street from the old one is a tribute to the proud and prosperous African American community that financed it.

The bank's exterior is rich in classical-inspired details combined with 1920s stylistic elements. The raised parapet at the building's front and south elevations is decorated by brick panels with diamond lozenges, and below it is a sheet-metal boxed cornice with a plain frieze. The front facade has a limestone sign panel with foliated borders, placed between a three-part, one-over-one sash window and a large arched opening to the recessed entrance. The sign panel is blank, but the borders have rich ornamentation. At the south elevation the space between the first- and second-story windows is defined by a row of recessed limestone panels. Other classical-inspired details are the brick corner quoins, the brick mock water table at the front and south elevations, and the arch's stone surround with a stone eagle adorning the keystone. Set into the tile floor of the entrance are the letters *T P B*.

The Peoples Bank continued to prosper until the

Great Depression. In 1931 the North Carolina Commissioner of Banks sold the building. After 1933 the building had many African American occupants, including Coy Turner's dry-cleaning business and a branch of the North Carolina Mutual Life Insurance Company. The first floor had a barbershop for many years. Although the area immediately surrounding the bank comprises vacant and/or demolished buildings, the former Peoples Bank remains the most architecturally sophisticated building in the South Queen Street commercial district.

3. (former) Dr. Joseph P. Harrison Office
built circa 1900, 1930s
235 South Queen Street

The west side of 200 South Queen Street was part of Kinston's thriving African-American business community at the turn of the twentieth century, as white commerce moved further north on Queen Street. 235 South Queen Street, a well-preserved two-story concrete-block building, is one of a handful of buildings that have survived from this period. This was the office of Dr. Joseph P. Harrison, one of Kinston's premier African American physicians, during the first half of the twentieth century. It also served as the office of Elijah Rasberry, a realtor, in the 1930s.

4. Lenoir County Courthouse
built 1939-1940; listed in the National Register of Historic Places, 1979
128-130 South Queen Street

The Lenoir County Courthouse, one of eastern North Carolina's premier transitional Art Deco-Art Moderne buildings, was designed by Kinston architect A. Mitchell Wooten, AIA, and his associate, John J. Rowland, AIA, in 1939. The courthouse was built with financial assistance from the Works Progress Administration, which, with the earlier Public Works Administration, assisted in constructing numerous public buildings throughout the nation in the 1930s. The contractor for the building was either Norman Rouse Sr. of Goldsboro, North Carolina, or T. A. Loving of Kinston. During the Great Depression many city halls and courthouses and even some schools were built in the same style, synthesizing the bold surface decoration of Art Deco with the more volumetric emphasis of Moderne design.

The four-story H-shaped building is faced with a limestone veneer and carries, along its front elevation, five deeply recessed bays behind square fluted columns, forming an in-antis portico. The main entrance, centered behind this portico, has an overhead relief plaque showing a Native American, as well as bronze geometric grilles lining the transom and sidelights, quintessentially Art Deco motifs. Exterior decoration includes innovative Art Deco-style front-facade bas reliefs of Native Americans with peace pipes, and tobacco leaves. Tobacco leaf plaques were an especially apt symbolic motif, given that the bright leaf was the backbone of Lenoir County's economy. The building's windows, arranged in vertical rows, have at the projecting end bays and side elevations metal spandrels decorated with reeding and chevrons—another feature more Art Deco than Moderne. At the southwest corner of the building stands the Caswell Monument, a tall obelisk honoring Governor Richard Caswell, which was moved to this site about 1940. Near the obelisk is a modernistic water fountain, a small column of fluted limestone with symmetrical fountain niches. In 1983 the courthouse was expanded with a four-story rear addition, also veneered with limestone and with similar bands of windows, by Barnstudio and Jenkins-Peter Architects, with the assistance of the Dale

Blosser and Associates construction firm.

The courthouse's interior is, in keeping with the exterior, sparingly decorated, an identifiable trait of Mitchell Wooten's synthesis of Art Deco and Moderne design. The wide streamlined halls have tan marble veneering, and the atrium, which now connects the new wing to the 1930s building, has its original geometric light fixtures and bronze stair railing. The courthouse itself is a reduction of Wooten's initial vision of the complex; in his presentation drawing, the courthouse complex included a large plaza and a similar limestone edifice for Kinston City Hall, at the approximate location of the Caswell Fire Station.

5. Caswell No. 1 Fire Station

built circa 1896
118 South Queen Street

The Caswell No. 1 Fire Station at 118 South Queen Street is a two-story brick building with a one-story extension at the north elevation. A documentary photograph from the 1906 Industrial Issue of the *Kinston Free Press* shows the fire station (established circa 1896) nearly as it exists today. In the early years of the twentieth century the City of Kinston Board of Aldermen held their regular meetings on the second floor of the fire station.

The building is now a local museum. The extension, which had hinged wooden doors, has been rehabilitated into an office; the main block of the building still has its large two-over-two double-hung sash windows, three raised-stretcher stringcourses, and dogtooth brick course of the plain cornice. The entrance, originally recessed, is now flush with the round-arch openings, which have been remodeled into transomed doors.

6. (former) Hyatt Clinic

built circa 1896
117 South Queen Street

117 South Queen Street was one of the first buildings constructed after Kinston's devastating 1895 fire. Dr. H. O. Hyatt and his son, Dr. A. L. Hyatt, operated a clinic for indigent patients in this building. According to Delia Hyatt, H. O. Hyatt's daughter, her father called the clinic "my Sunday School class," because they generally congregated at the clinic early on Sunday mornings for treatment. Family lore relates that Dr. Hyatt once aspirated a patient's stomach contents to counteract a laudanum poisoning, an unprecedented procedure at that time. Hyatt was practicing in Kinston as early as 1898, but not at 117 South Queen Street. *The Kinston Daily Free Press*, citing Dr. Hyatt's sanatorium as one of two private hospitals in North Carolina then recognized by the Medical and Surgical Register of the United States, mentioned that "Dr. Hyatt has his office in the building and his family lives there also." The building, illustrated in Dr. Hyatt's brochure as a large two-story frame house, was at 330 North Queen Street and was previously known as the Nunn Hotel. Eventually Dr. Hyatt abandoned his residential practice. By 1916, Dr. H.O. Hyatt and his son, Anderson, established their office at 117 South Queen Street, which was then listed as 115 1/2 South Queen Street. Mrs. Hyatt converted the former sanatorium at North Queen Street into a boardinghouse.

The Hyatts practiced medicine at 117 South Queen Street into the 1940s. Apart from small alterations to the front facade, the clinic's original brick pilasters and mullioned display transoms are intact.

7. A. J. Sutton and Sons Store
built circa 1908
109 South Queen Street

The former A. J. Sutton and Sons' early-twentieth-century dry goods store is a brick two-story, two-bay building whose front facade has a monumentality more often found in rusticated stone Renaissance Revival banks or offices. The building is surmounted by a paneled parapet, the projecting corners and center part of which resemble battlements. Below the parapet and its pressed-metal cornice are two wide windows with stone sills, then a stringcourse. A large display space on the first floor, now enclosed, is framed by brick pilasters striated, like the rest of the front facade's brick courses, to form quoining. At the second-story windows the striated courses meet between the cornice and the lintels to form stylized voussoirs.

The 1914 *Illustrated City of Kinston* states that Sutton's successful general merchandise store was known as the One Price Cash Store. Twenty years later W. H. Caroon had taken over Sutton's building and was operating a grocery there.

8. (former) Hotel Caswell
built 1906
108-114 South Queen Street

Presently an office complex known as Court Square, this impressive three-story brick building was erected as the Hotel Caswell in 1906. Known as the handsomest hotel in Kinston, the Hotel Caswell had fifty rooms, each with electric lighting and call bells. On the front exterior, pressed-metal pilasters support a pressed-metal canopy with a rounded entrance pediment, on which "1906," enclosed by foliate scrolls, is embossed. This original entrance bay has remained intact, although the first-floor facade has been modernized. Other original exterior elements that have survived are the Italianate pressed-metal cornice and brackets, and the projecting central bay that is symmetrically flanked by single and paired windows. The windows all have stone voussoir lintels and flat brick sills.

9. Commercial Building

built circa 1901; remodeled 1920s
102 South Queen Street

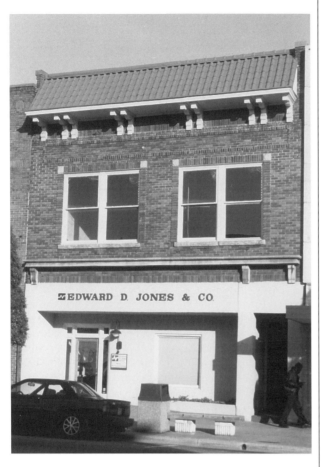

102 South Queen Street, a two-story brick commercial building with a Mission-style pent-roof cornice supported by decorative brackets, was the C. H. Larkin Clothing Store in the 1930s. The building has a signage panel made of brick headers below the cornice, beneath which are paired one-over-one double-hung sash windows. The window surrounds are brick stretchers at the lintels and sides, rusticated stone corner blocks above, and rusticated stone sills. Above the remodeled ground floor is a bracketed pressed-metal cornice. The law firm of Rouse and Rouse (N. J. Rouse, Robert Rouse, and Charles Rouse) had its offices on the second floor during the early years of the twentieth century.

10. Miller Furniture Company

built circa 1915-1920
103 South Queen Street

The Miller Furniture Company, a two-story brick commercial building at 103 South Queen Street, was originally known as the Hunter Building and is said to have been designed by local contractor R. L. Blalock between 1915 and 1920. This richly detailed two-story brick Classical Revival building has four brick pilasters dividing the front into three symmetrical blocks, which support a stone cornice surmounted by a plain brick and stone parapet. Below the cornice and between the pilasters are three window units, each consisting of a patterned brick course with diamond-shaped tiles, above which is a band of four one-over-one windows. The West Caswell Street elevation of the building carries the same detailing, in addition to glass-block spandrels.

By 1920 many lawyers—including the firms of Moore and Croom, and Powers and Elliott—had offices in the Hunter Building at 103 South Queen Street.

11. B. W. Canady Building
built circa 1899
131-135 North Queen Street

12. (former) National Bank of Kinston
built circa 1908 (altered 1925)
136 North Queen Street

This three-section, two-story brick Romanesque Revival-style commercial building was built for Burwell W. Canady's hardware business, which extended to two sections of the building, in 1899. Canady (1854-1905), a prominent Kinston merchant, sold builders' implements, saddlery, guns, agricultural supplies, cookstoves and food choppers, and "Delft and Granite Ware" from this corner store, which operated from 1899 into the 1960s. Canady's two sons, James Herman (1878-1953) and Henry Westbrook (1898-1963), ran the hardware store in succession.

The front facade and north elevation of the building have remained remarkably intact through the years. Of the three sections, 135 North Queen Street has retained the most original exterior decoration, including its recessed entrance, paneled display windows, and metal entrance step with the imprint "B. W. Canady 1899." Across the second story's front facade are twelve round-arched windows, paired at the end sections and the center, surmounted by granite lintels. Above the windows are recessed brick panels, followed by an elaborate brick arched, corbeled architrave painted white to echo the granite rounded window surrounds. The brick pilasters framing each section still have their recessed panels and corbeling.

The third section of the building, 131 North Queen Street, was leased to Fields and Becton by 1906. William C. Fields and Edward J. Becton dealt in a variety of businesses at this office, from cotton brokering and fertilizer to real estate and insurance. By 1920, 131 North Queen Street was Allison's, a millinery shop; in 1936, 131 and 133 North Queen had combined to house Rose's five-and-ten store, and B. W. Canady and Sons's business limited itself to 135 North Queen Street.

The handsome two-story, three-bay tan brick building at the southwest corner of North Queen and West Gordon Streets was built in 1908 for the National Bank of Kinston (established 1897). Well-known architect Herbert Woodley Simpson of New Bern is believed to have designed the building. In 1914 several prominent Kinstonians were on the bank's board of directors—Plato Collins, R. L. Crisp, W. C. Fields, T. W. Mewborne, and R. C. Strong, the bank's president. At that time the bank was quite successful, with a surplus of over 93 million dollars. The building's stately appearance, with its connotations of power and stability, echoed the banking industry's efforts toward fiscal strength and civic pride.

When the National Bank of Kinston expanded in size in 1925, the building's north elevation along West Gordon Street remained untouched. On that side the six projecting flat pilasters continued to rest on projecting rusticated stone bases, and the recessed windows kept their original surrounds—flat, rusticated stone lintels at the first floor, round-arch stone surrounds at the second, with a raised brick panel between the two stories. Alterations at the front facade were significant but in keeping with the Neoclassical character of the exterior.

There were professional offices on the second floor in the 1920s, including the Dawson, Manning and Wallace law firm. The office entrance was at the Gordon Street elevation. The National Bank of Kinston failed during the Great Depression. Branch Banking and Trust Company of Wilson opened a temporary bank in the building, which office eventually became an established branch of that organization.

13. Farmers and Merchants Bank

built circa 1924

200 North Queen Street

At the northwest corner of North Queen and West Gordon Streets stands the former Farmers and Merchants Bank, a five-story Italian Renaissance Revival ashlar limestone building. Benton and Benton, Architects, of Wilson, North Carolina, one of the most prominent architectural firms in the region, designed the bank in 1924. The building's elegant design and grandness of scale are perhaps indicative of the grand streetscape envisioned by twentieth-century citizens, a towering "City Beautiful" that never completely materialized on North Queen Street.

The building is divided vertically into three parts, after classic Italian Renaissance design. Each division—the spacious first floor, then the second to fourth floors, and finally the fifth floor—is demarcated by prominent cornices wrapping around both the North Queen and West Gordon elevations. At the first section five large first-floor windows framed by columned pilasters are spaced alongside the West Gordon Street facade. The banking patron enters the main entrance on North Queen Street, between Ionic columns and through a tall arch with a carved stone shield and metal grille. At the corner of the building, by the entrance, is a rare surviving large metal lantern clock with a ball finial. The middle three

stories have single and paired sash windows. The top section of the building has windows with cartouche and foliate reliefs in their lunette panels, surrounded by a console keystones and molded heads and jambs. Along the West Gordon Street elevation these windows alternate with stone relief panels. A plain denticulated frieze and a remarkable overhanging flat-roof cornice with elaborate brackets crown the building.

The Farmers and Merchants Bank failed during the Great Depression. About 1935 a branch of the First Citizens Bank and Trust Company of Smithfield opened in the building.

14. Citizens Bank

built circa 1903

201 North Queen Street

The Citizens Bank was founded in 1901 by a number of prominent Kinston citizens including N. J. Rouse, Lemuel Harvey, J. E. Hood, Dal Wooten, and David Oettinger. In 1903 it moved from its original location at 134 North Queen Street to 201 North Queen Street. The new bank was an imposing commercial palace of eclectic style, combining exterior decorative elements then familiar on Kinston's commercial buildings, such as the third story's round-arch granite window heads, with more sophisticated treatments. The corner-bay tower shelters the original entrance and projects slightly from the building, separated by flat pilasters that rise to paired colonnettes with composite terra-cotta capitals. The pilasters enclose single window units and decoration repeated on the rest of the building, except for the second story's narrower paired windows. The plain classical entablature and parapet are offset dramatically by the tower's metal convex dome and paneled battlements. On both sides of the tower the construction date 1903 appears in a tympanum below the dome. Above the dome is a tall crowning finial.

Excepting the ground floor, the building has remained virtually intact through the years. The East Gordon Street elevation's first floor was converted to a storefront after 1940, but the original Gordon Street entrance to the building, with its classical surround, is still at the east end of the south elevation. The front facade and tower's second- and third-story windows are still separated by terra-cotta relief panels decorated with laurel swags. All second-story windows have granite sills and rusticated flat-arched heads; all third-story windows have granite sills. The third-story lunettes and second-story window transoms are now enclosed.

In 1908, the Citizens Bank changed its name to the First National Bank. It remained an important center of commerce for Kinston into the 1920s. An advertisement in the 1919 *Programme and Directory of the Fiftieth Anniversary and Jubilee* of the Saint Augustus A.M.E Zion Church describes the First National Bank as operating with a capital and surplus of $200,000, stating that "Business" was "Solicited From Both Black and White."

15. J. E. Hood and Company Drug Store
built circa 1903-1904
203 North Queen Street

John Ezekiel Hood (1867-1921), the scion of a pharmacist family with roots in Wayne and Johnston Counties, came to Kinston in 1893 after attending the Philadelphia College of Pharmacy and receiving a license from North Carolina's pharmaceutical board in 1889. After working for ten years at John E. Parrott's drugstore at the southwest corner of Queen and Caswell Streets, Hood built an imposing three-story brick building in an L-plan, wrapping around the newly established Citizens Bank to a side entrance at 102 East Gordon Street. "The store is furnished throughout," noted the 1906 Industrial Issue of the *Kinston Free Press*, "with plate glass counter cases of the handsomest construction," in addition to the prescription counter's giant plate-glass mirror, which gave "a complete view of the whole store from any point of view." Following

a trend at many prosperous turn-of-the-century pharmacies, Hood installed a soda fountain that dispensed, along with other popular soft drinks, Coca-Cola. The pharmacy operated at 203 North Queen Street for more than seventy years, with offices on the second floor and a private club on the third.

The Hood's Drug Store's facades on North Queen and East Gordon Streets have been altered, most notably through the enclosing of the first-floor entrances with a brick wall and the removal of the second-story oriel window on the Queen Street elevation. However, much original exterior decoration does remain. The building is still surmounted by its original pressed-metal cornice at both elevations.

16. Barrett and Hartsfield Store
built circa 1905
205-207 North Queen Street

This pair of two-story brick buildings at 205 and 207 North Queen Street was built in 1905. In 1909 the two buildings housed the Barrett and Hartsfield clothing store, which provided Kinston with women's and men's apparel for nearly twenty years. Belk's department store took occupancy of the building in the late 1920s. By 1936, 205 North Queen was the A. J. Sutton and Sons Dry Goods store and 207 North Queen the J. H. Mewborn and Company Jewelers and Cut-Rate Variety Store.

Both buildings' first floors were altered and have later awnings, but the second floor windows—two round-arch windows flanking a paired double-hung sash window—in each building have rusticated stone heads. Both structures are framed by plain brick pilasters that rise to the corbel table frieze. 205 North Queen Street still has much of its original decorative metal cornice; it is also said to retain Kinston's first elevator and the original oak flooring on its second floor.

17. D. V. Dixon and Son Hardware Store
built circa 1896
215-217 North Queen Street

This two-story, two-section corner commercial build-ing was built for Jesse W. Grainger in 1895, following the Kinston fire. After a brief tenancy at 215 North Queen by the post office and at 217 North Queen by the C. T. Randolph Carriage Factory, Grainger started a hardware store in the building with David V. Dixon in 1898. Two years later John F. Hooker took Grainger's place, and the business became known as Dixon and Hooker, then, by the 1920s, as D. V. Dixon and Son. 215 North Queen Street's front facade has been altered on the second floor by stucco and replacement windows. 217 North Queen Street's storefront facade, like 215 North Queen's, has been enclosed; the second story's front facade, however, has remained intact, from the brick corbeled cornice and recessed signage panel to the three segmentally arched windows below that are surmounted by a continuous brick hood mold. Longtime occupants of 217 North Queen Street include Christopher's Restaurant.

18. J. C. Penney Department Store
built circa 1927
300 North Queen Street

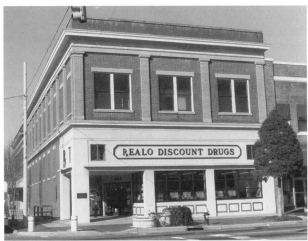

Robert L. Blalock, who built many of Kinston's early-twentieth-century commercial buildings, was the con-tractor for this two-story classical-inspired brick struc-ture for the J. C. Penney Department Store chain. The ground floor has been altered several times, but its stone signage cornice with mezzanine casement windows is original to the building. The first- and second-story win-dows along the West North Street elevation have been enclosed but retain their stone lintels and sills. The sec-ond story's rhythmic "colonnade" of tan brick pilasters with simple stone capitals also remains. At the second story of the front elevation, three paired, double-hung sash windows, also with plain stone lintels and sills, are separated by wider-spaced pilasters. There is a simple brick parapet above the sheet-metal cornice that wraps around the building. The second story of the former J. C. Penney building housed doctors' offices for a time in the mid-twentieth century.

19. United States Post Office
built circa 1914
301 North Queen Street

The former United States Post Office, an imposing Neoclassical Revival ashlar limestone one-story building with basement, at the northeast corner of North Queen and East North Streets, was designed by Oscar Wenderoth, supervising architect for the United States Treasury, circa 1915. The hexastyle Tuscan portico at the building's center section is flanked by symmetrical end sections, each consisting of a large casement window with paneling, above which is a projecting belt course and a plain frieze with a recessed panel over the window bay. Along the entrance facade behind the portico are tall windows, with elaborate metal grilles with fleurons and palmettes at the window transoms, separated by pilasters. Later occupants of this building have included the Lenoir County Library and the Lenoir County Chamber of Commerce.

20. Montgomery Ward Building
built circa 1930-1935
322-324 North Queen Street

This two-story, three-bay masonry and tile building replaced the one-story frame late nineteenth-century house of S. H. Loftin in the early 1930s. From the mid-twentieth century until recently, 322-324 North Queen Street's decorative terra-cotta front facade was enclosed in metal, but its architectural elegance is once again visible. Unusual decorative features of the original front facade include the terra-cotta acanthoid plaques on either side of the signage panel above the store awning, and the rounded-arch three-part windows across the second-story facade, set between pilasters crowned with laurel swags at the shaped-gable parapet. Each parapet crest has a round terra-cotta tile with a rosette; below each rosette and between the swagged pilasters is a recessed tile panel. Below the multipaned glass transom windows at the mezzanine level are the recessed entrance and store display windows.

The Montgomery Ward Company had instituted a uniform design for its early flagship stores. 322-324 North Queen Street is nearly identical to the former Montgomery Ward Store at 114-116 East Fifth Street in Greenville, North Carolina, built in 1929.

21. Mewborn Building
built circa 1900
333-337 North Queen Street

The two-story, six-bay brick building at the southeast corner of North Queen and East Blount Streets was built for the T. W. Mewborn and Company Wholesale Grocery at the turn of the twentieth century, the site having previously contained the H. E. Ellis Carriage Works. The northeast corner of the building, at the West Blount elevation, was angled alongside the neighboring Norfolk and Southern Railroad tracks. Proximity to the nearby freight depot and railroad accessibility were no doubt advantageous to the wholesale grocery, which became the T. W. Mewborn and Company Retail Grocery by 1920. Mewborne further diversified his business by selling men's furnishings and apparel.

The former Mewborn building has retained its original brick quoins and its second-story corbeled cornice with mousetoothed lower course, as well as its double-hung sash windows, plain except for the brick jack arches with keystones overhead. The first floor of the front facade was later rehabilitated into three small storefronts.

22. Sumrell and McCoy Building

built circa 1909; listed in the National Register of Historic Places, 1989
400 North Queen Street

23. Hudson Buggy Factory

built circa 1910
433 North Queen Street

This large two-story brick commercial building with a basement was built for the Sumrell and McCoy Wholesale Company in 1909 at a site adjacent to the Atlantic and North Carolina Railroad tracks, where it was served by a spur siding. At the time of construction of the store, George Sumrell and Henry McCoy had been partners for ten years. Their stock ranged from "a complete line of Flour, Meat, Lard, Sugar . . . and all other goods usual to a first-class, up-to-date Wholesale Grocery Business" to a small bottling plant on the premises, which bottled Pepsi-Cola and "the famous 'Buffalo Lick Ginger Ale'" for local consumption. The building's exterior decoration is minimal and seen mainly at the North Queen Street elevation. There the building is crowned by a plain brick parapet flanked by corner battlement posts, below which is a projecting brick cornice. The second story has two three-part, nine-twelve-nine double-hung sash windows, crowned by molded brick lintels with cast-iron keystones. Other exterior decorative elements are corner brick quoins and brick stringcourses above and below the second story. The cornice and upper stringcourse adorn the south and north elevations, and the north elevation is further enlivened by contrasting courses of brick. The first-floor front facade has its original prism-glass transom over the two North Queen Street display windows and two entrances (one of which has been enclosed and covered in a lively mosaic). The main entrance is still the clipped-corner southwest entrance, supported by an iron column.

The wholesale grocery business was a significant aspect of Kinston's early-twentieth-century prosperity, which continued into the 1930s. In 1936, 400 North Queen Street was listed as the H. H. McCoy, Inc., bottlers and wholesale grocers. In 1989 the Kinston Community Council for the Arts renovated this former wholesale grocery as a gallery and performing space with studios. It was individually listed in the National Register of Historic Places in the same year.

This large brick building is a significant remnant of Kinston's flourishing carriage industry. The Hudson Buggy Factory was the original occupant of this three-story structure comprising two sections. In later years it became the Hudson Apartments, the Kinoca Hotel, and, by 1936, Taylor's Cash Grocery. At the front elevation three brick pilasters rise to a brick corbeled cornice with two recessed panels. This scheme is reflected along the Peyton Avenue elevation, except that the eight pilasters on the former factory do not rise to a recessed corbeled panel. The upper-story windows are segmentally arched, with rounded brick window heads and plain sills. The North Queen Street ground-floor facade and the back part of the Peyton Avenue elevation have been altered by replacement display windows and green glass and ceramic tile paneling.

24. Queen Street United Methodist Church
built circa 1910
500 North Queen Street

25. Hotel Kinston
built circa 1928; listed in National Register of Historic Places, 1989
501 North Queen Street

Dedicated in 1911, the Queen Street United Methodist Church is Kinston's grandest high Victorian church. The designer is thought to be Charles Hartge, a German architect who settled in Raleigh; Hartge built other major churches in Wilson and Wilmington. This cruciform-plan brick edifice vigorously combines Victorian and Romanesque elements in a marvelously eclectic design. The massive three- and four-story bell towers form entrances to the interior and are decorated by a series of belt courses, three-part round-arched and Palladian-influenced windows, quoining, and a flared modillion cornice. They are surmounted by four-sided caps around and below gabled and turreted ornamentation. The entrances and three-part second-level stained-glass windows have stepped rounded-arch surrounds. The Queen Street Methodist Church, as emphatically imposing as its neighbor the Hotel Kinston, has an early-twentieth-century two-story brick administrative building and a well-designed addition by the East Group.

Queen Street United Methodist Church was built to accommodate the growing number of Methodists in early-twentieth-century Kinston. It was needed also because the Caswell Street Methodist Church was no longer in the center of town.

The eleven-story Hotel Kinston, a brick and cast-stone Art Deco building with elegant Moorish Revival details at the front and rear elevations, is not only Kinston's sole skyscraper but also the only skyscraper in eastern North Carolina outside Wilmington except Elizabeth City's 1920s Virginia Dare Hotel. A tangible and visible sign of 1920s Kinston in all its affluence, this impressive, well-appointed hotel was built to accommodate trade, as well as to serve as a showplace.

In 1926 several Kinston businessmen, led by Harvey C. Hines, J. Herman Canady, and H. H. McCoy, organized the Community Hotel Corporation and hired High Point architect Herbert B. Hunter to design the Hotel Kinston. The resulting building, which towers over downtown Kinston, was framed with steel and reinforced concrete beneath its restrained Art Deco decoration and form. There are two two-story stepped side elevations flanking the arcaded recessed entry; the elevations were designed for, and still contain, small shops and offices. Alternating brick and stone sections comprise the lancet-shaped Moorish-style arches, supported by composite-style columns. The entrance is lit by three bull's-eye windows positioned over the two windows and the center double door. Above the ninth floor the central section of the building rises to form a two-story tower with recessed arched panels decorated with tiles and stucco, above which runs a contrasting brick stringcourse. Asphalt tiles have replaced the original Spanish-style tiles covering the high hipped roof. Surviving interior details are the former lobby's wooden ceiling beams and plaster lighting fixtures. Also, the "Moorish-Mission"-style ballroom on the mezzanine level still retains its wooden ceiling beams, its wrought-iron-and-glass lantern chandeliers, and some of the original windows.

The Hotel Kinston managed to stay in business for over forty years. Its decline has been attributed to the rise of motor hotels in the 1950s and, to the changing tobacco economy after the Second World War. In 1960 the Kinston Housing Authority bought the Hotel Kinston, and the former hotel has become housing for low-income residents and retirees.

26. Hunter Building
built circa 1915
106-108 West Caswell Street

The Hunter Building, a brick two-story, four-bay commercial structure built in 1915, was a doctor's office at that time; it still retains the office's original marble tile floor and drain. There were also apartments in the building for single working-class people. Most people in Lenoir County are familiar with this building from its 1960s incarnation as Wilder's Art Shop.

The front facade of the building was altered in 1964, when one of the flanking end-bay entrances was enclosed. However, its rhythmic articulation of space—recessed openings with segmentally arched windows and stone sills, and dentilled brickwork at the cornices and above the recessed signage panels—indicates the understated Victorian style of this commercial building in its prime. In 1997 Jarman Construction Company restored the interior and occupied the upper level as its office.

27. Dr. Victor E. Weyher Office
built circa 1902; current facade added circa 1920-1925
107 East Caswell Street

Dr. Victor E. Weyher's office was in this two-story brick commercial building in 1902. Today the exterior, thought to have been remodeled in the 1920s, still displays a wealth of details, from the Mission-style parapet outlined in sandstone at the top of the building to the brickwork surrounding the recessed sign panel and windows. The three second-story windows are separated by brickwork pilasters. Before he established his practice at 107 East Caswell Street, Weyher, an anesthesiologist and pediatrician, was a partner in Dr. H. O. Hyatt's sanatorium at 330 North Queen Street in the 1890s.

28. (former) Kinston Steam Laundry (Lenoir Oxygen Supply Company)
built circa 1947
208 West Gordon Street

The frame building initially on this site was the Kinston Steam Laundry, built in 1908. It was a part of the manufactory/automobile-livery-service corridor of early-twentieth-century Herritage Street. After a 1947 fire the demolished Kinston Steam Laundry building was replaced by the current brick structure, one of a very few Moderne-style commercial buildings in Kinston. Kinston builder O. L. Shackleford constructed the building for owners George and Marvin Vick. Although apparently no architect was involved with the building, the streamlined Moderne design, with its minimal, flat exterior decoration, rounded corners, and bands of metal casement windows, represents the latest in commercial architecture of the time. The building was converted to the Lenoir Oxygen Supply Company and appears to be unchanged. The surrounding commercial district, however, has declined in terms of its commercial importance in recent years.

29. Parrott-Foxman Office
built circa 1920
107 West Gordon Street

The Parrott-Foxman Office is one of Kinston's most striking diminutive commercial buildings. The three-bay brick Tudor Revival front facade is framed by two

engaged piers with quoining and faceted sandstone pilasters and further punctuated by two bracketed sandstone stringcourses. The second stringcourse encloses a stepped sandstone frontispiece with a crest; the crest appears to either be a Gothic *f* or a *p* that was altered to create an *f*. Between the piers is a low sandstone arch sheltering the yellow pressed-glass transom of the entrance bay. The office of Dr. Albert Parrott, cousin of Drs. Jim and Tom Parrott, was in this building in the early 1920s. By 1936 Ben Foxman, optometrist, occupied the office. The Tudor Revival facade was added to this building during Dr. Parrott's tenure; possibly, Ben Foxman altered the original *p* to an *f* when he took occupancy of the building.

30. LaRoque and Hewitt Insurance Office
built circa 1900; altered 1930s
105 West Gordon Street

The LaRoque and Hewitt Insurance Office is a one-story plain brick commercial store building with an exterior enlivened by Moderne details. The sleek facade covering of black-glass panels, made of a pigmented structural glass popular in the 1930s, was no doubt novel to most local citizens. This black-glass, common to Art Deco and Moderne theaters and shops in larger urban areas, was not extensively used in Kinston. The Moderne style of the facade is further defined by the asymmetrical composition of a six-light metal casement display window and a three-light vertical metal casement window beside the transomed entrance.

Before LaRoque and Hewitt's occupation transformed this modest building into its Moderne incarnation, 105 West Gordon Street was the office for the Lenoir Oil and Ice Company in 1920.

31. Green's Barber Shop and Store (B. W. Canady Building Annex)
built circa 1895
105-107 East Gordon Street

A pair of one-story, brick double-common-wall commercial buildings located around the corner from the old Canady Building contains one of the most intact and best-preserved storefronts of Kinston's 1890s Victorian commercial structures. The buildings' exteriors have typical late-nineteenth-century decoration, such as a simple corbel table cornice below which, on either side of the center projecting brick pilaster, are recessed scalloped panels. Below the panels is a corbel frieze over the large display windows, both double-door entrances are recessed, and the bases of the windows are paneled.

In 1895 these two commercial buildings housed one hardware store; B. W. Canady had them built immediately after the 1895 Kinston fire to serve as a temporary hardware store until the Canady Building, at 131-135 North Queen Street, was finished. In 1920 this complex was still an annex of the B. W. Canady and Sons store. Today 105 East Gordon Street is home to Green's Barber Shop, which has had this address for over sixty years. 107 East Gordon Street, listed as Abbott's Dry Cleaners in 1936, has also been the address of Noble's Bakery, a community institution.

32. Dr. W. Thomas Parrott Office
built circa 1903; enlarged circa 1920
109 East Gordon Street

The first typhoid serum inoculation in North Carolina was administered in this two-story brick building, the office of Dr. W. Thomas Parrott, at the turn of the twentieth century. The second floor was added between 1919 and 1925. The building's four-bay front facade was altered in the 1930s, creating a yellow-brick-veneered exterior combining Beaux Arts stylistic elements (such as the small composite-order columns on high plinths supporting the recessed entrance) with a pent tile roof supported by knee braces and a parapet more in keeping with the Mission style. This treatment is similar to that of a neighboring building, the former office of Dr. Parrott's brother, Dr. James M. Parrott, at 111 East Gordon Street. Two metal steps at the entrance of 109 East Gordon Street still bear the Parrott brothers' names and the date 1903. In recent years the office was occupied by Marion A. Parrott, attorney, the younger son of W. Thomas and Jeannett Johnson Parrott.

33. Dr. James M. Parrott Office
built circa 1903; enlarged circa 1920
111 East Gordon Street

34. (former) Kinston Post Office and Office Building
built circa 1915
112-116 East Gordon Street

111 East Gordon Street, a brick two-story, three-bay commercial building built at the turn of the twentieth century, was, like 109 East Gordon, originally a one-story doctor's office. It was built and occupied by Dr. James M. Parrott, who had bought the property next door to his brother's office at 109 East Gordon Street.

The building was raised to two stories between 1919 and 1925. The late Dr. Rachel Davis, a prominent mid-twentieth-century Kinston physician active in civic and state affairs, treated patients at this office for many years. The building's front facade has a recessed entrance fronted by a Renaissance Revival-style arcade supported by paired Ionic columns, over which are paneled spandrels. Paired wooden curvilinear brackets support a pent-roof cornice similar to the Mission-style cornice at the adjacent Parrott office, though the original tiles have been replaced with modern composition shingles.

Next to the Gordon Street Christian Church are two two-story brick buildings constructed by 1915 as an extension of North Queen Street's busy commercial district. 112 Gordon Street, Kinston's post office from 1910 until 1915, has lively exterior details, including decorative brickwork under the parapet cornice and a large paneled oriel window, a later addition covering a large arched opening. 114 and 116 East Gordon Street also have two second-story oriel windows, though they are plainer than that of the old post office. After 1920 both buildings were insurance and law offices. The Kinston Insurance and Realty Company was one of 114 East Gordon Street's longtime tenants and may have attracted more such firms to the building. By 1936 at least four real estate and insurance companies were operating at 114 East Gordon Street, while 116 East Gordon Street housed several offices for the city of Kinston. Dr. Daniel Worth Parrott, dentist, had his office at 116 East Gordon for a few years prior to his death about 1925.

35. Gordon Street Christian Church

built circa 1915
118 East Gordon Street

The Gordon Street Christian Church is an exceptional building, possessing a sophistication in its structure and details rarely found in eastern North Carolina churches during the early-twentieth century. This tan brick church has Romanesque- and Byzantine Revival-style elements, such as heavy, low massing; granite stringcourses; flanking capped octagonal towers; and a large, two-tier lantern dome. Other unusual features include the front facade's paired ogee-shaped entrance arches and the unusual tripartite window arrangement—two small windows centered with a large Gothic-style lancet stained-glass window with tracery—in the front gable.

The interior of the church was designed following the Akron plan, a mid-nineteenth-century innovation quickly adopted by Protestant churches. In the Akron plan, Sunday school classrooms adjoined the sanctuary, separated by flexible partitions that could be opened at specific times for children to join the regular church service. Another innovation further separated religious worship and education by using annexes. Gordon Street Christian Church's 1969 educational annex replaced an earlier semidetached building from 1922.

36. (former) United States National Resettlement Administration Office

built circa 1925
133-135 West North Street

133-135 West North Street, a two-story brick store with understated stretcher-brick decoration at its second story, has a five-bay ground floor with two transomed entries between glass bay display windows. This building was home to the local branch of the Works Progress Administration and the Resettlement Administration during the 1930s. Of the two government programs the former is probably better known; the jobs it generated for thousands of unemployed people resulted in public buildings, parks, and documentation of historic landmarks. The short-lived Resettlement Administration, a mid-1930s program aimed at relocating farmers impoverished by the Great Depression, was replaced in 1937 by the Farm Security Administration, which continued to assist poor farmers who wanted to improve—and own—the land they worked on.

37. Brown's Wholesale Grocery
built circa 1925
105-107 West North Street

This two-story Classical Revival brick commercial building was Jesse Brown's 1920s expansion of his on-site wholesale grocery. Jesse Brown, the son of wholesale grocer Thomas B. Brown, worked at his father's establishment at 131 South Queen Street before going into business for himself around 1915. The first story of Jesse Brown's grocery has been altered, but most of the front facade's exterior is original and intact. Above the storefront opening is decorative stretcher-brick and stone ornamentation, with stringcourse directly below the second-story windows. The second-story windows, all replacements, are surmounted by stone lintel plaques with foliate scroll reliefs. The facade, combining Adamesque-derived decoration with straightforward commercial design, is completed at the top by a pressed-metal cornice with modillion blocks. Brown's Wholesale Grocery is similar in its robust form to commercial buildings that Robert L. Blalock was constructing in Kinston at this time and may possibly be one of his buildings.

38. Commercial Buildings
built circa 1920-1925
107 and 109 East North Street

The 100 block of East North Street is composed mostly of two-story brick commercial buildings built within the first quarter of the twentieth century. 107 East North Street, the former West Building, is a three-bay building with an open-brickwork-patterned parapet, a herringbone cornice punctuated by cement diamonds on the frieze, and an arched center first-floor window between the two entrance bays. This was built for Dr. C. F. West, who occupied it until he retired in the 1950s. 109 East

North Street's plain brickwork veneer is enlivened by a contrasting brick stretcher stringcourse, below which another stringcourse outlines the lintels of the paired second-story windows.

39. Overland Garage Company
built circa 1914-1919
129 West Blount Street

Unquestionably the most architecturally enriched building in the immediate area of West Blount Street, this three-story brick building was first known as the Overland Garage Company. Several surrounding buildings shared its links to the automotive industry. By 1928 the building housed the Harvey Motor Company, and by 1936 the Spence Motor Company. Distinguished principally by its commodious size and interesting decorative embellishments, it has a rusticated first story on its two primary elevations. Concrete bands delineate the first and third stories, as they do on nearby buildings. Arched windows on the third floor and a corbeled brick cornice add a decidedly Victorian appearance to what is, otherwise, a standard commercial design. The shopfronts have modern windows with signage covering the transom windows. The Herritage Street side is pierced by double doors with an original transom, three double-hung sash windows, and two garage doors, one of which is arched.

40. (former) Ellis Carriage Works
built circa 1908-1914
126 West Blount Street

The H. E. Ellis Carriage Works, founded in 1886, grew from a small building at the northeast corner of Blount and North Queen Streets to 118-122 West Gordon Street in 1902. By 1919 the Ellis Carriage Works's large manufactory and salesrooms were located at 315 North Herritage Street in a large two-story brick building whose warehouse and woodshop wrapped around to Walnut Alley to the east. In 1919, according to Kinston's Sanborn Fire Insurance Maps, 126 West Blount Street was then 116-118 West Blount Street and housed a grocery and store. However, it abutted the Ellis Carriage Works and, judging from a 1914 drawing of the manufactory, was probably built at the same time.

Most of this two-story brick commercial building was converted to an automobile garage and showroom early in its history and continued in related uses until the late twentieth century. 126 West Blount Street was updated in the mid-1930s with the addition of new facings on the north and west street elevations by the W. H. Jones Motor Company, a Ford dealership that occupied the building after the carriage works. The overall original treatment of the elevations included segmentally arched, wood double-hung sash windows, now found only on the second floor of the building's rear and alley sides. The front facade of the West Blount Street entrance is divided into three bays, with the two outer bays having two windows on the second floor above a large three-pane display window with transom lights on the first. The Herritage Street facade of the building has fifteen metal windows on the second floor above a first floor with five metal windows, three large display windows, and two entrances.

41. (former) Kinston Garage
built circa 1910; facade altered 1928
105 West Blount Street

A prolific local contractor, Robert L. Blalock, designed and built this large brick two-story, eight-bay garage, located behind the Sumrell and McCoy wholesale grocery, in 1910. By 1928 the Kinston Garage was an automobile dealership that sold Cadillac and Hudson motorcars. During this time the front facade of the building was remodeled. In 1936 the Kinston Garage became the City

Garage, and since 1958 it has been the Kinston Auto Parts store. The front facade is one of Kinston's best expressions of the commercial Art Deco style; the building is framed with vertical towers at each end, which are defined with stuccoed caps. At the second floor a wide stucco band fitted with red brick and tile diamonds traverses above the six paired replacement jalousie windows. Above the replacement awning and below the raised stucco stringcourse is a plain decorative brick panel with a stucco band. The ground floor of the building has been modernized with an applied modern brick facade and new display windows.

42. (former) Pure Oil Gas Station
built circa 1935
201 North McLewean Street

This narrow one-story brick-veneered service station is a 1930s commercial adaptation of the Tudor Revival style, with two end chimneys with disproportionately large corbeled caps. Two receding angled side extensions flank the service station's office, the north extension apparently a bathroom. The extension to the south, which originally contained two service bays, was altered after 1981.

This building apparently was built as a station for the Pure Oil Company, which favored a picturesque cottage image as opposed to the streamlined modern stations of other gas companies. These Tudoresque stations once stood throughout North Carolina and can still be seen occasionally.

43. (former) Gas Station
built circa 1935
210 North McLewean Street

This former gasoline service station stands on the site of an earlier, 1920s service station set diagonally at this corner. It is possible that the current station was J. Floyd Daughety's 1936 service station. The narrow Moderne-style office and projecting two-bay service garage are of stuccoed brick, "streamlined" and unified by the reeded stringcourse that wraps around the projecting pilasters flanking the office and garage, and the flat canopy extending from the office that is supported by a T-shaped Moderne-style pier. Some of the original windows have been enclosed. This station, now an automobile repair shop, has not otherwise been changed but remains an excellent example of the once-numerous gasoline service stations of the second quarter of the twentieth century.

44. Atlantic and North Carolina Railroad Freight Depot
built circa 1900, listed in the National Register of Historic Places, 1989
302 North McLewean Street

The Atlantic and North Carolina Railroad Depot is a brick front-gable building, curving slightly to parallel the adjacent railroad tracks, that is capped by a monitor roofline. This utilitarian Romanesque Revival depot is the only building left in Kinston and Lenoir County to indicate the importance of the railroad to Kinston from the mid-nineteenth to the mid-twentieth century. In 1899 the state railroad commission moved that Kinston's dilapidated frame freight depot be replaced by a new brick warehouse with dimensions of 220 feet by 40 feet, 18 feet high. The new freight depot was in place, just below the intersection of East Blount and North McLewean Streets, by 1900. The building has changed little in its more than ninety years of use, and retains its interior truss roofing and still-visible painted sign at the west elevation. Along the north and south elevations, segmentally arched openings are framed by projecting brick pilasters united by a stringcourse over each arch. Each gable end has a molded belt course and, at the apex, a small oculus.

The passenger depot stood just west on North Queen Street, but by 1930 it was replaced by Union Station on East Caswell Street.

45. (former) Imperial Tobacco Company Office
built circa 1920-1925
420 North Herritage Street

A striking two-story brick office built by 1925 is the only surviving structure of the Imperial Tobacco Company's early-twentieth-century manufactory complex, located at North Herritage and West Peyton Streets. The former Imperial Tobacco Company Office's most striking exterior feature is its elaborate corbeled cornice consisting of crenellated battlement posts, corbeled stops, and recessed panels decorated with diamond shapes. The liveliness of the cornice anticipates the Art Deco style that became popular in the 1930s. Below are two front entrances, one with a round-arch door hood supported by decorated consoles, the other with paired columns, rondelles, and a classical cornice. The building is lit by paired and single double-hung sash windows, all with stone sills. The office, still in excellent condition, was rehabilitated into apartments. A counterpart to this office is Greenville's Imperial Tobacco Company Office, built in 1916, which has a similar cornice treatment.

46. (former) American Tobacco Company Prizery (Nantucket Warehouse)
built circa 1901
619 North Herritage Street

The two-story brick building dominating the east side of 600 North Herritage Street and Lenoir Avenue is one of a very few early-twentieth-century brick tobacco buildings left in Kinston. Its stepped-parapet roofline, brick belt courses, and bands of segmentally arched windows are no longer commonplace to Kinston's commercial landscape, and its survival is a testament to the tobacco industry that was once such a vital presence in this city. Constructed as a prizery for the American Tobacco Company at the turn of the twentieth century, the building was sold to the Export Leaf Tobacco Company between 1908 and 1914. The Export Leaf Tobacco Company (whose painted sign is still visible along the West Lenoir Avenue elevation) expanded the space; by 1925 it had added a compatible five-bay, two-story brick extension along the North Herritage Street elevation. This new extension also housed a coal bin and a cooper shop. In recent years, after 619 North Herritage Street was no longer a tobacco warehouse and prizery, the building became known as the Nantucket Warehouse.

47. L. B. Jenkins Tobacco Warehouse
built circa 1930
211 East Lenoir Street

The L. B. Jenkins Tobacco Warehouse and Re-Drying Plant, a low brick building with two stories and nine bays on the south side of East Lenoir Street's 200-block face, is one of three early-twentieth-century tobacco buildings left in downtown Kinston. Like the Nantucket Warehouse on North Herritage Street, the Jenkins Warehouse, in form and decoration, recalls the days of Kinston's ascendancy in the tobacco industry. Sited at the edge of the commercial district, the building is decorated by a wide false-front parapet on which, at the top, the painted signage "L. B. Jenkins" is still decipherable. Below the parapet a scored belt course wraps around the front facade. Below the belt course are five square projecting pilasters that divide the front of the building into four units. The two former entrance bays, where tobacco would have entered the large warehouse receiving room "full of sky-lights," have been enclosed, one as a door, the other as a window.

Within the former warehouse the steel-truss roof is still in place, and the concrete floor is still demarcated by painted grids for placement of tobacco baskets. The rehandling and redrying plant extension, which fronted on North McLewean Street, has been razed.

L. B. Jenkins, a prominent tobacco merchant in early-twentieth-century Kinston, had a larger tobacco plant outside town on the Neuse River, and a small farm near the site of the current Rountree Avenue neighborhood, in addition to his Grainger Hill residence.

48. Kinston Power Plant
built circa 1903-1906; altered 1925-1930
900 Atlantic Avenue

The first Kinston power plant, the small Kinston Electric Light and Water Works, built at the southeast corner of West Bright and South Herritage Streets in 1897, provided the town with incandescent arc lighting. In 1903 Kinston's growth had outstripped this small power plant's capacities, and the town voted for extensive public improvements for lighting, water, and sewers. By 1906 these improvements had resulted in a pumping station and power plant on Atlantic Avenue, described in the *Kinston Free Press* as "two brick buildings, very complete, and of the very latest type both as to design and equipment." The plant provided lighting to eighty-three of Kinston's intersections and, at ten cents a kilowatt, to residents.

The two one-story, side-gable attached brick buildings surviving from 1906 are typically utilitarian, their decoration being found in the multipaned round-arched windows with brick surrounds and plain stone sills, and the round-arched transom over one of the doors. The later two-story brick extension, added to the old power station between 1925 and 1930, has brick pilasters framing second-story round-arched windows and first-story paired casement windows, each decorated with a keystone. The roofline of the extension has a paneled parapet and a corbeled frieze punctuated by pendant stops. The artesian-well-water reservoir, analyzed periodically, has remained untreated and supplies all of the city's needs.

Thomas Outlaw in his bean patch, circa 1900 (Heritage Place, Lenoir Community College)

Old Town Kinston

Old Town Kinston—some twenty-five residential blocks wrapping around the business district on the north, east, and south—contains a well-preserved collection of houses and churches built from the late eighteenth century to the early-twentieth century. Bounded by Herritage, South, East, and Washington Streets, the area retains its residential character in places. Bright Street is no longer residential, but King Street, with the Peebles House (Harmony Hall), and South McLewean Street, with the Archbell House and the Nicol-Blalock House, comprise a visual vestige of the former tree-lined residential character of the area.

In 1962 Marguerite Archbell Dyer, who had grown up in Old Kinston, recalled:

> At one time [Bright Street] was the fashionable and best-shaded street in Kinston. Perhaps more important people and their families lived on Bright Street than any other street in this little town. Six doctors, a lawyer (whose son became a lawyer), men of outstanding politics and men of local business made their homes here.[1]

198

Among the six doctors cited by Mrs. Dyer were John Pollock, whose house was at the northwest corner of Bright and Queen Streets, and Henry Tull, who was also a landowner and entrepreneur. Alexander Nicol, a cotton broker and businessman who had emigrated from Edinburgh, Scotland, built a two-story frame house at the southeast corner of Bright and McLewean Streets in 1836. After the turn of the twentieth century Robert Blalock expanded the Nicol house, transforming it into a Colonial Revival residence. A house whose exterior has remained intact is the former Baptist Parsonage at 211 McLewean Street; Henry and Lillie Archbell lived in this 1850s two-story dwelling with their daughter, Marguerite, at the turn of the century.

Most of the cultural institutions that anchored prominent corners are now gone. The Caswell Street Methodist Church at the corner of Caswell and Independence Streets still stands. The First Baptist Church at the corner of South McLewean and East Bright Streets was moved to Thompson Street in 1899. Saint Mary's Episcopal Church, which stood at the southwest corner of South Independence and East King Streets in the 1880s, was destroyed by fire, then rebuilt at the turn of the century. The congregation later built a new church at the southwest corner of North Rhem Street and Rountree Avenue. One of the earliest schools, Kinston Collegiate Institute, stood in the intersection of East King and South East Streets until the early-twentieth century when King Street was extended. The Lewis School, the now-demolished brick building where many older Kinstonians attended grammar school, stood at the northeast corner of North Independence Street and East Peyton Avenue.

Industrial development encroached upon the residential areas of Old Town Kinston during the late nineteenth century. In 1885 Jacob F. Parrott's sawmill stood on the river at the west terminus of Bright Street. By the turn of the twentieth century the Atlantic Coast Line Railroad had built a track along Bright Street, which linked it to the Gay Lumber Company on the Neuse River. The Kinston Electric Light and Water Works plant stood at the southeast corner of West Bright and South Herritage Streets. The Lenoir Oil and Ice Company and the Kinston Mantel Company were located along the east end of Bright Street in 1901. By 1925 East Bright Street and Shine Street held boardinghouses and "Colored Tenements." Between 1919 and 1925 a railroad track was laid on Shine Street. The grand old houses of Kinston's forefathers began to disappear. Dallam Caswell's house, at the northeast corner of McLewean and Shine Streets, was converted to a tenant house at the turn of the century and was torn down for the Simon Bright Apartments in the late 1930s.[2]

Houses were still being built in Old Town Kinston during the early-twentieth century. In 1900 Plato Collins, Lenoir County's clerk of court in the early-twentieth century, built the two-story gable-and-wing house at 300 East Caswell Street. In 1905 Walter Dunn LaRoque Jr. built a two-story frame Neoclassical Revival house at 112 East Caswell Street (demolished circa 1980). Caswell and King Streets continued to be residential into the 1950s. Yet suburban developments like Mitchelltown were already luring families away from Old Town, and the residential decline had begun.

Notes

1. *Kinston Free Press*, August 31, 1962.
2. Sanborn Fire Insurance Maps, 1896, 1901, 1925; *Kinston Free Press*, August 31, 1962.

1. Norwood Evans House
built circa 1908-1915
110 West Bright Street

Although a house of similar form appears on the 1885 Sanborn Fire Insurance Map, this hipped-roof frame cottage, where Norwood Evans, Kinston's 1930s chief of police, resided with his wife, Ida, and their three children, appears to have been built no earlier than 1908. Evans's house is located in what was once the very center of Kinston's late-nineteenth-century residential district. Notable exterior features include the attached hipped-roof wraparound porch supported by Tuscan posts, the distinctive center entrance with sidelights and transom, and the twin brick interior chimneys.

2. Nicol-Blalock House
built circa 1855; renovated circa 1910, listed in the National Register of Historic Places, 1989
300 South McLewean Street

The core of this house is a two-story side-gable frame residence built for Alexander Nicol (1824-1884), a Kinston businessman and city commissioner, sometime in the late 1850s. Nicol, who had emigrated from Scotland to the United States and married Kinstonian Susan McKinne, became a wealthy cotton broker. The house was substantially remodeled in the Colonial Revival style

by Kinston contractor Robert L. Blalock (1870-1929), who lived here from 1914 until his death. Today it is more appropriately identified as a Colonial Revival-style dwelling. Blalock, who designed and built many of Kinston's early-twentieth-century public and commercial buildings, created the unique exterior features now associated with the house. They include the second story's round-arch, double-hung sash windows, positioned within the two exterior end chimneys at the house's north elevation. There is a domed, circular corner gazebo balanced by a porte cochere at the opposite end of the brick wraparound front porch. The front dormer's three-part window is centered by a Colonial Revival-style round-arch surround.

Inside the house Blalock's surviving touches include two unusual Classical Revival brick mantelpieces, one with a massive keystoned arch and decorated cornice at its overmantel. One early-twentieth-century decorative element is the anaglypta wallpaper wainscoting along the house's staircase wall. Anaglypta, an embossed commercial wall covering made from rag stock and linseed oil, was popular in the late nineteenth and early-twentieth centuries and has some similarities to linoleum.

The Nicol-Blalock House has, in recent years served as the House of Best Mortuary, an African American funeral home. When Ezekiel K. Best established the mortuary in the 1940s, the interior of the house was altered.

3. (former) First Baptist Church Parsonage; Archbell House
built circa 1850-1860; listed in the National Register of Historic Places, 1989
211 South McLewean Street

The two-story, three-bay frame hipped-roof house at 211 South McLewean Street was built in the 1850s as a parsonage for the neighboring former First Baptist Church (now the White Rock Presbyterian Church, moved to 516 Thompson Street in 1900). Like the church, the exterior of this house exhibits simple, well-proportioned Greek Revival design, especially in its low hipped roof, twin interior chimneys, wide and unadorned frieze band, and corner pilasters. This residence was occupied between the late nineteenth and early-twentieth century by Henry Archbell, local confectioner, and his wife, Lillie Archbell. Lillie Archbell was the editor and publisher of *Carolina and the Southern Cross*, the North Carolina United Daughters of the Confederacy magazine, which ran from 1912 until 1914. The house is now owned by the Lenoir County Historical Association.

4. Harmony Hall (Peebles House, Bright-Pearce-Peebles House)
built circa 1790, 1840s; listed in the National Register of Historic Places
109 East King Street

The fine residence that has been known since the 1970s as Harmony Hall, located on the south side of King Street between Queen and McLewean Streets, is apparently the only eighteenth-century building to survive in Kinston and undeniably the finest antebellum house in town. The landmark was saved by the Kinston Woman's Club in 1937 and used as a library until the 1950s, then as a clubhouse until 1975, when the Woman's Club turned it over to the Lenoir County Historical Association. In 1979 L. R. Thomas and Sons of New Bern restored the house under the guidance of the North Carolina Division of Archives and History. Furnished with period antiques, it has been open to the public as a house museum since 1984. No original outbuildings remain on the spacious grounds, which now contain an antebellum smokehouse and schoolhouse moved here from out of town. Numerous prominent Kinstonians have resided in the house. The following history is drawn from a research report on the house by Dr. Jerry Cross, N. C. Division of Archives and History, 1990.

Simon Bright III, Owner circa 1790-circa 1801

The house apparently was built about 1790 by Simon Bright III as a two-story hall-and-parlor-plan house with a hipped roof and exterior end brick chimneys. An enclosed staircase rose between the hall and parlor to the two upstairs bedrooms. Within this section handsome Federal-style mantels decorate the first floor and heavily molded Georgian-style mantels with concave-curved friezes adorn the bedrooms. Throughout the house are examples of the work of early artisans of Kinston, such as the Flemish-bond brickwork on the original chimneys, beaded weatherboarding, moldings, mantels, doors, and windows. The style, large size, and high-quality construction suited Bright, who apparently moved to Kinston from his family plantation on Briery Branch in north Lenoir County and served one term in the state senate. Bright suffered a mental breakdown in 1799 and killed a slave of Jesse Cobb, then died while under house arrest about 1801.

Jesse Cobb, Owner 1801-1807
Elizabeth Cobb, Owner 1807-1820

Jesse Cobb, who lived on Bright Street, appears to have acquired the Bright House from the estate of Simon Bright III about 1801. He and his wife, Elizabeth Cobb, had built a large house on the south side of the street between Herritage and Queen Streets, where he was living at the time of his death in 1807. This was later known as the "old castle," served as a hotel and then a Civil War hospital, and was demolished sometime after the Civil War. After she was widowed, Elizabeth moved into the Bright House, remaining there until her death in 1820.

Abner Pearce, Owner 1824-1827

Young merchant Abner Pearce, who arrived in Kinston about 1819, purchased the Bright property by 1824. In 1827 Abner died and is buried behind the house. His daughter Susan, born in 1827, died in 1844 and is buried beside her father.

Phoebe Pearce, Owner 1827-1834
Phoebe and George Lovick, Owners 1834-1845

In 1834 Abner Pearce's widow, Phoebe, married George Lovick. They lived at Harmony Hall until their deaths about 1845.

John and Harriet Peebles, Owners 1846-1898

In 1846 merchant John Henry Peebles bought the property at public auction. Peebles had moved to Kinston in 1834 from Virginia and set up a general store. He married Harriet Cobb, daughter of John Cobb and granddaughter of Kinston patriarch Jesse Cobb. The Peebleses lived and prospered in Harmony Hall. Peebles ran a plantation south of town, where he kept twenty-one slaves, and operated a store located at the corner of King and

Queen Streets. He was one of Kinston's first town commissioners, in 1849, invested in the Atlantic and North Carolina Railroad when it came through in the mid-1850s, and was an active member of Saint Mary's Episcopal Church. Perhaps the Peebleses expanded the house in the fashionable Greek Revival style when they purchased it, adding one-story wings and a two-story transverse front stair hall. The present stair rises in two flights with a landing at one end of the front hall, with Greek Revival-style doors leading from each end of the hall to the wing rooms, finished with Greek-style mantels. The two-story front entrance porch, with its square posts, latticework railing, and transom and sidelights around the main door and upstairs porch door, must have been added about this time. A rear one-story addition contains a room known as the office and an enclosed stair.

John and Harriet's happiness was tragically marred by the deaths of ten of their twelve children born between 1846 and 1864. The children's graves dominate Harriet's family graveyard, the Cobb graveyard, on Bright Street one block south. In 1862, when many Kinstonians deserted the town for fear of Union invasion, John and Harriet fled to Goldsboro, where they rented a house until 1863. By 1864, perhaps despondent over the ruined state of his store and plantation, John Peebles died, some say by suicide. According to local tradition the Peebles House was used as a hospital during the war, perhaps while the Peebleses were living in Goldsboro. In dire financial straits, Harriet took in two seamstresses as boarders, and later Harriet and her son Henry Cobb Vance Peebles shared the house with a family named Herring. Harriet reopened the store shortly after the end of the war and ran it until about 1897. In 1898, at the age of seventy-six, she died. Harriet's spunk and courage inspired her descendants to describe her as the "matriarch of the 1850s."

Henry C. V. Peebles, Owner 1898-1920s

The only child who survived Harriet was Henry Cobb Vance Peebles, known as Zeb, who served as deputy clerk of the county superior court for some years. He lived in the old family home until the early 1920s and then moved out of state. In 1925 the house was sold to John F. Stricklin, then to the Woman's Club.

At some point, probably when the building became a library or a clubhouse, the partition wall that separated the two rooms of the original first floor was removed, creating a single large room.

In the 1970s the house was given the name Harmony Hall, taken from an 1846 newspaper article that stated that an infant son of John and Harriet Peebles died at "Harmony Grove."

5. House
built circa 1890-1910
312 East King Street

312 East King Street is a one-story frame Victorian cottage with twin interior chimneys, a low hipped roof, and a spacious attached hipped-roof front porch, making this a typical example of Kinston's early-twentieth-century middle-class domestic architecture. 312 East King Street, now across the street from Kinston's City Hall, has retained its turned porch posts and balustrade, as well as its low brick wall, shrubbery, and mature trees framing the house. At the turn of the twentieth century J. C. Wagner, the proprietor of the Kinston Bottling Works plant at 120 North Queen Street, was living in this house, then listed as 310 East King Street.

6. Rayner House
built circa 1925
211 East Caswell Street

This frame three-bay, two-story American Foursquare dwelling, built in the mid-1920s, boasts a rich combination of stylistic features common to eastern North Carolina towns during the period. The simple exterior surface of the house and bungalow-style wraparound front porch and porte cochere, as well as the hipped-roof dormer at the front facade, are in keeping with the popular Craftsman style. On the other hand, the curvilinear cornice brackets at the dormer, roof, and porch are, with the paired Ionic posts over the porch's brick piers, Colonial Revival elements. The dormer, hipped roof, and porch are all covered by clay tiles, introducing yet another influence, the Spanish Mission style. Other distinctive exterior features include the front entrance's two-tiered sidelights and transom. C. Eugene Rayner, a partner in the Hunter and Rayner Bicycle Shop at the turn of the twentieth century, was living in this house by 1936. Earlier Rayner had resided at 216 East Caswell Street.

7. Caswell Street Methodist Church
built circa 1860
Corner of Caswell and Independence Streets

This front-gable frame church was the second to be erected on this site. Building commenced in 1860, but the Civil War interrupted progress on the second church. However, the basic structure may have been in place by that time, because local history holds that this building was used as a hospital by the Confederate army. When Kinston's Methodist congregation moved to the newly built Queen Street United Methodist Church in 1911, the Caswell Street Methodist Church continued as the Second Methodist Church for thirteen years. In 1924 it was bought by Kinston's Jewish community, who converted it to a synagogue. Since 1954 the church has been used by different Christian denominations.

The overall form of the church, which rests on a high brick foundation, is that of a basic gable-front Greek Revival sanctuary. Victorian changes include paired stained-glass lancet windows at the north and south sides of the church. The original louvered bell tower with its octagonal spire has been reduced to a smaller octagonal capped belfry.

8. Plato Collins House
built circa 1900
300 East Caswell Street

Plato Collins (1870-1942), clerk of Lenoir County's superior court at the turn of the twentieth century, and his family lived in this frame two-story, gable-and-wing house. A Kinston native, Collins was the son of John Wesley Collins, who, after serving as postmaster in Morehead City during the Civil War, owned a hardware store at 14 Queen Street in the 1880s and 1890s. Plato Collins received his law degree from the University of North Carolina at Chapel Hill in 1892 and was elected twice as the secretary of the Kinston Chamber of Commerce. He is remembered by his descendants as an ardent Democrat and also as a baseball devotee. He was a president of Kinston's first semiprofessional baseball team.

The dwelling's front projecting bay, crowned by a gable with a two-light window, has original diminutive half-timbering. This particular timbering with pebbledash infill is a feature, often seen in early-twentieth-century pattern books, used on stylish yet practical houses throughout the country but rarely used in eastern North Carolina. The Collins House's exterior is further enlivened by a hipped dormer in the wing section of the front facade. The attached hipped-roof, full-facade front porch retains such early Colonial Revival details as its turned Tuscan posts and turned balustrade.

The Collins House, once part of central Kinston's residential district, is now part of East Kinston's African American neighborhood.

9. House

built circa 1880
302 East Caswell Street

Next to the Plato Collins House is a frame two-story, four-bay house built sometime in the last quarter of the nineteenth century. The two exterior end, single-shouldered brick chimneys once were the principal heat sources for this house. The house has a raised two-bay, one-story hipped-roof front porch supported by chamfered posts, and later rear extensions. The two-over-two double-hung sash windows probably date from the early-twentieth century.

10. House

built circa 1890-1910
109 North East Street

109 North East Street is a one-story frame Victorian cottage with twin interior chimneys, a low hipped roof, and a spacious attached hipped-roof front porch, making this a typical example of Kinston's early-twentieth-century middle-class domestic architecture. The house retains its chamfered posts and pilasters but no longer has its sawnwork and bracketed porch decoration.

11. E. C. Rountree House

built circa 1905
307 East Blount Street

E. C. Rountree, of the early-twentieth-century Rountree and LaRoque Insurance Company, once resided at 307 East Blount Street, a one-story frame gable-and-wing dwelling. The front porch was enclosed by wooden latticework in recent years but has retained much of its unusual exterior decoration. The two interior brick chimney stacks are decorated with corbeling and castellated tops, and the unusual hipped-roof balcony projecting from the front gable wing has lost its original supports and floor.

12. Beauregard-Nunn House

built circa 1850
210 East Blount Street

Tradition asserts that this frame two-story, two-bay house was the Civil War headquarters for General Beauregard before the Union occupation, and that the house was moved from 114 East Blount Street. This hipped-roof house has a two-story front wing with an attached hipped-roof front porch that has an enclosed porch room. The wide frieze band, cornerboards, and large transomed and sidelighted entrance represent simple Greek Revival decoration that may date to the Civil War period. At the turn of the twentieth century 210 East Blount Street was the home of Joseph Park Nunn, Lenoir County's sheriff. Nunn, his wife, and seven children lived in this house when they were not at Nunn's farm in Woodington Township. In 1936 Mrs. Mattie L. Nunn, Nunn's widow, still resided at this house.

13. W. D. LaRoque House

built circa 1880-1886
115 East Washington Street

According to Walter Dunn LaRoque's descendants, he and his wife, the former Annie Parrott Mewborne, moved into this one-story gable-and-wing house in the 1880s when it stood at 517 North Queen Street. LaRoque (1851-1911), who operated a livery stable at 111-113 West Gordon Street, lived in this house for the rest of his life. After LaRoque's death his son, Frank, lived in the house into the 1930s; Frank LaRoque is listed in the 1910-1920 Kinston city directories as a tobacconist. The LaRoque House, which was moved to 115 East Washington Street in 1937, has remained one of the most intact Victorian cottages in Kinston. It is also the best documented. W. D. LaRoque's granddaughter, Mrs. Meriwether Lewis, has preserved the original written specifications for the house.

The paneled bay window in the house's prominent front gable was once sheltered by a porch that wrapped around to what was then the north elevation. The surviving element of the porch shelters the two-bay-wing front facade of the house and is supported by slim turned posts decorated with Eastlake-style sawnwork brackets. Exterior elements—the large two-over-two double-hung sash windows, the plastered interior chimneys, the small pilastered cornerboards and the wide transomed entrance—are original, and mature oak trees frame the dwelling.

14. B. W. Canady House

built circa 1883; listed in the National Register of Historic Places, 1989
600 North Queen Street

The frame two-story Italianate residence of Burwell Westbrook Canady (1854-1905) at the northwest corner North Queen Street and West Washington Avenue is the finest surviving house of this style left in Kinston. Exterior decorative details of the house, from the projecting gabled bay's carved pendant brackets and intricately carved rosette ventilator to the tall paneled chimney stacks with corbeled caps and the molded woodwork of the peaked-arch window lintels, express the prosperity that came to Canady in the late nineteenth century. Much of the interior is intact and original, including paneled wainscoting, a double-archway gallery dividing the stairway from the center hall, and three Italianate-style mantelpieces on the second floor. The house was partially remodeled in the Colonial Revival style by Canady's heirs (the house remained in the family for almost ninety years) in the early-twentieth century.

Canady moved to Kinston in 1873 from his nearby family plantation, Quebec, and operated a hardware and building supply store on Queen Street. He invested in the local textile mills, owned the Atlantic, the second tobacco warehouse built in Kinston; and held a number of civic and county positions, including town mayor, alderman, and county commissioner. In his obituary Canady was remembered as a "farmer, merchant, public man and a devoted husband and father" to whom "is largely due the industrial progress of Kinston."

15. Fields House

built circa 1919; porte cochere added by 1925
607 North Queen Street

In recent years this spacious frame and rubblestone bungalow has been used as a commercial building, but it is one of only two residences still in place on 600 North Queen Street. According to the Kinston Sanborn Fire Insurance Maps, 607 North Queen Street—a weather-boarded story-and-a-half dwelling with a wide shed dormer and gabled side extensions—was in place by 1919. This would make the Fields House, along with the E. J. Becton House in the Grainger Hill Historic District, one of the first Craftsman bungalows to have been built in Kinston. Like the Becton House, the Fields House has retained its original narrow weatherboarding, decorative knee braces and exposed rafters, and wide engaged front porch supported by massive rubblestone piers. Usage of such stone, frequently seen in bungalows located in the Piedmont and in western North Carolina, was unusual in Kinston. The porch extends to a patio at the south end of the front elevation, and at the north end a porte cochere, supported by rubblestone piers, was in place by 1925. In 1936 William C. Fields was living in this house.

Orion Knitting Mills, Atlantic and North Carolina Railroad tracks, Kinston, 1890. (Photo, early 1900s, Heritage Place, Lenoir Community College)

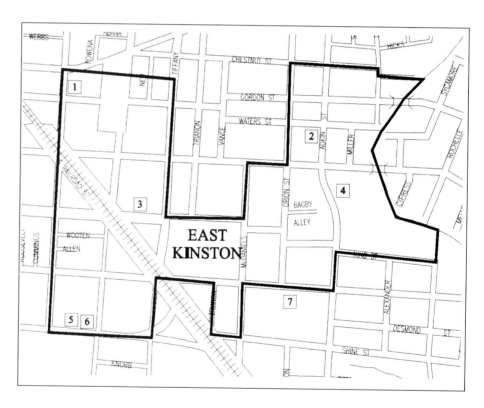

East Kinston

The physical area of East Kinston was never a consciously planned residential neighborhood like the Trianon District but rather the result of gradual residential and industrial growth east along the railroad lines. East Kinston occupies some twenty-five blocks, with East Street as its western boundary and the Adkin Branch below East Chestnut Street as its easternmost boundary. Lovit Hines Park on East King Street's 1000 block takes up a good deal of the eastern edge of this area. East Kinston's northern and southern boundaries are more irregular, as the Trianon District sits squarely in the middle. The southern border, beginning at the northeast corner of South East and

East Shine Streets above Maplewood Cemetery, travels east to include the 1940-1941 Simon Bright public housing project before terminating at the intersection of East Bright and South Adkin Streets. Within this area are a variety of house types—Queen Anne-style one- and two-story dwellings, rental housing for mill and factory workers, and Craftsman-style houses. One significant church remains in East Kinston—the former Christian Science Church at 400 East Gordon Street.

Industry provided the incentive for East Kinston's growth. By 1901 the Hines Brothers Lumber Company stood beside the Atlantic and North Carolina Railroad tracks along the south side of East King Street, between South Tiffany Avenue and McDaniel Street. Behind Hines Brothers, at the northwestern corner of East Bright and South Trianon Streets, stood the Lenoir Oil and Ice Company, another major employer. Neither complex stands today. The first two textile mills in Kinston, the former Orion Knitting Mill and the Kinston Cotton Mill, still stand side by side along the tracks between East Caswell and East King Streets. Gradual enlargement joined the two buildings and has obscured their original forms.

With these factories, the need for worker housing was immediate. Mill houses were built, in uniform lots, along South Trianon and South McDaniel, South Orion, Mill, and Waters Streets. By the 1920s North and South Adkin Streets near the Adkin Branch had been developed. By 1925 the 100 block of South Adkin Street had been built up, with six shotgun houses on the west side and four on the east side, all inhabited by whites who worked mostly for Kinston mills and factories. This working-class white neighborhood extended further east to the 900 and 1000 blocks of East King and Desmond Streets, which had white homeowners and renters as late as 1936. East King Street's inhabitants, like the white residents of South Adkin Street, were employees of the Hines Lumber Company, the Neuse Mantel Company, and other Kinston manufactories.

The mill neighborhoods grew to incorporate older areas of the town into East Kinston. These older residential areas, mainly along East Shine and East Bright Streets, were in place as early as the 1880s. An 1882 map shows that, in the years following the Civil War, the town had expanded its residential areas east of McLewean Street. Dwellings are indicated along both East Bright and East Shine Streets outside the town limits, along with Dr. H. O. Hyatt's small clinic at the northeast corner of East Bright and South East Streets. A middle-class African American neighborhood had developed, distinct from Lincoln City, in this immediate area by the turn of the twentieth century. The *Kinston Journal* of June 2, 1881 reported that "the members of the A.M.E. Church of Kinston are erecting a handsome building on the corner of East and Shine Streets." Another African American church in this area at the time was the Episcopal Church Mission, on the east side of South Independence Street just above East Shine Street. Prominent late-nineteenth-century black Kinston citizens resided in this neighborhood, including the merchant banker Thomas B. Holloway, at 412 East Shine Street, and Starr Hicks, a businessman who formed an African American fire fighters group, at 308 East Shine Street.

When East Gordon, East Caswell, and East King Streets were extended beyond East Street in the early twentieth century, houses quickly followed, some positioned along the railroad corridor of South Atlantic Avenue, which cut diagonally through the southeast corner of East Caswell and South East Streets. All of the significant railroad buildings in East Kinston have been demolished. Within this area East Gordon Street remained a residential—and white—area to its terminus at 915 East Gordon until after World War II. After 1945 East Kinston gradually became an African American residential area.

1. (former) First Church of Christ, Scientist

built circa 1914
400 East Gordon Street

Built in 1914 for Kinston's small group of Christian Scientists, this cross-gable brick structure at the northeast corner of East Gordon and North East Streets was poised between the white middle-class East Kinston residential area and the African American neighborhood along Tower Hill Road. The church, which later became the Gateway to Heaven Pentecostal Holiness Church, has an attractive early-twentieth-century eclectic design. The shaped parapets of the cross gables are lobed like Dutch gables and have glazed header courses, but the rectilinear stained-glass windows and the rosette gable windows recall both the Gothic and Mission styles. At the intersection of the cross gables is a two-story corner entrance tower, capped by a pyramidal tile roof with flared eaves, with two entrance doors at the base.

2. Bungalows

built circa 1925
900 block of Waters Street, South side

The four frame, one-story, front-gable bungalows lining the south blockface of 900 Waters Street are just outside the Trianon Historic District but are instructive of a later phase of residential development in that district. All four dwellings appear on the 1925 Kinston Sanborn Fire Insurance Map. They were probably built as housing for middle-class whites in the mid-1920s. They have retained much of their initial character, including, on each house, the front-gable roof extending to form the porch.

3. (former) Orion Knitting Mill and Kinston Cotton Mill (Hampton Industries)

built circa 1891 (Orion), 1898 (Kinston); established 1937 (Hampton Industries)
Northwest corner of King and Tiffany Streets

Within the rambling two- and three-story brick building at the northwest corner of King and Tiffany Streets encompassing nearly the whole city block are the original buildings of Kinston's two successful turn-of-the-twentieth-century textile enterprises. The Orion Mill, founded in 1891, and the Kinston Cotton Mill, founded seven years later, were the earliest textile mills in Kinston. The Orion Mill was a two-story brick industrial building with dimensions of forty by eighty feet, having a twenty-four-by-forty-foot one-story annex sited in the northern half of the block. In 1906, 225 people—apparently all whites—were employed at the mill. The chief product at that time was colorfast black hosiery, sold to "ladies and misses." The Kinston Cotton Mill, a larger two-story brick building with two annexes for a "picker room," engine, and boiler, was financed and built to provide the Orion Mill with cotton yarn. There was a two-story tower on the premises, equipped with sprinklers for fire protection that has been torn down. The original buildings have been obscured by successive additions. In the early-twentieth century there was a small Orion Mill annex at the northeast corner of East Bright and South Davis Streets near the Carolina Duntile concrete-block manufactory (now demolished).

In later years, when the Orion and Kinston Cotton Mills combined to form first the Kinston Shirt Factory and then, in 1937, Hampton Industries, the mills continued to be a substantial employer for the community. African American high school and college students became an important source of part-time labor in the 1930s and 1940s. Employment at Hampton Industries in turn provided these students with the means to finish their education and move into the professional working classes.

4. Shotgun Row

built circa 1915
100 block of South Adkin Street, east side

Between 1915 and 1925 a double row of shotgun houses was built on South Adkin Street between East Caswell and King Streets. There were seven houses on the west side and four on the east side. The houses were rented by whites who worked for the Kinston Cotton Mill, the Orion Knitting Mill, and the Hines Lumber Company. Although the shotguns on the west side of South Adkin Street no longer stand, the shotgun houses on the east side have survived with their original exterior integrity largely intact. The street is still lined with large oak trees and some cedars.

Below the 1950s brick grocery store at East Caswell and South Adkin Streets is the shotgun row of 112, 114, 116, and 118 South Adkin Street. All four of these weatherboarded dwellings are one-story, two-bay frame shotguns on raised brick foundations, with replacement standing-seam metal roofs and attached hipped-roof front porches. Except for 112 South Adkin Street, each has the original diamond louvered ventilator in its front gable. South Adkin Street, which was inhabited by white residents as late as the 1940s, is now an African American residential area.

Mill workers and artisans lived on 100 South Adkin Street in the first decades of the twentieth century. The west row's 1910s-1920s white occupants resembled those on the east side of the street. In 1916 J. Tase Monroe, a carpenter, lived at 109 South Adkin Street; by 1920 Harper Register, who worked for the Orion Knitting Mill, lived there. In 1920, 113 South Adkin Street was the home of Haywood Jones, a mill hand. In 1916 Annie Dunn, the widow of Noah Dunn, lived at 116 South Adkin Street. Noah Crain, another mill worker, lived at 117 South Adkin Street in the later 1910s. Behind the shotgun at 119 South Adkin Street, where Kim Holland, employed by the Kinston Cotton Mill, resided in the 1930s, was a small shotgun positioned in the middle of the block between South Adkin and South Orion Streets. This was the home of Charles C. Hardison, a night watchman for the Hines Lumber Mill in the 1910s and 1920s.

5. T. B. Holloway House

built circa 1900
412 East Shine Street

The frame, two-story, gable-and-wing house at 412 East Shine Street was the home of T. B. Holloway, an early-twentieth-century African American banker and merchant, whose office was at 302 South Queen Street. In the 1919 *Programme and Directory* for the Saint Augustus A.M.E. Zion Church's fiftieth anniversary, Holloway is listed as "the oldest merchant doing business on Queen Street." Holloway was also one of the founders of the African American People's Bank at the turn of the century. His house is comparable or identical to houses built and owned by successful middle-class white Kinston businessmen. Original Victorian exterior elements of Holloway's residence are mostly intact. Both the front and side gables still have diamond-shaped ventilators, simple scalloped vergeboard decoration, and, at the front gable, cutaway corners where the second-story bay windows begin. The wraparound, attached hipped-roof front porch was "updated" in the 1920s, with tapered bungalow-style wooden posts over brick piers replacing the original turned wooden posts.

6. Simon Bright Apartments

built circa 1940-1941

Between South McDaniel, East Bright, East Shine, and South Adkin Streets

In August 1940 the plan for the Simon Bright Apartments called for twenty residential buildings, a community building, and two large play areas all within the block encompassed by East Bright, East Shine, South McDaniel, and Adkin Streets. Simon Bright Apartments was developed for lower-income white families by the United States Housing Authority through its local agency, the Kinston Housing Authority. A. Mitchell Wooten was the architect and Oscar Shackelford the contractor. Shackelford and Wooten also collaborated on a residential complex for lower-income African American families located nine blocks north. This complex, completed in 1941, was named Mitchell Wooten Courts for Wooten, who died before it was finished.

Simon Bright Apartments, executed in the spirit of the International style with corner casement windows and minimal exterior detail, has identical two-story brick apartment buildings with hipped roofs, interior chimney stacks, and paired and corner windows that originally were metal casement but have been replaced by double-hung sash. The simple facades are enlivened by plain concrete sills and brick stringcourses. As with the Mitchell Wooten Courts, the most memorable feature of the Simon Bright Apartments is the cast-concrete relief plaques over the paired apartment entrances, depicting children at play with various instruments and toys. Wooten designed similar low-income housing projects in New Bern, North Carolina, and Portsmouth, Virginia, before his sudden death in November 1940. More apartment buildings were added to the Simon Bright Housing project in the 1950s. After World War II residency within the complex shifted to African Americans.

Ezekiel K. Best House, 1015 Hicks Avenue, Tower Hill, built circa 1916.

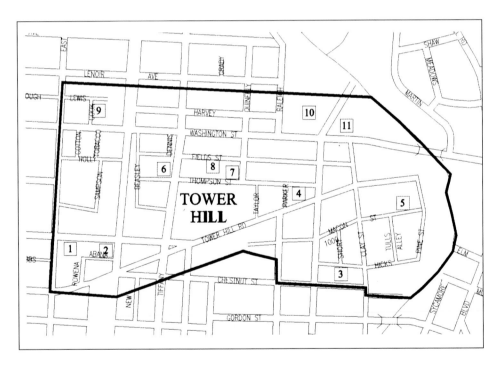

Tower Hill

Tower Hill, an early-twentieth-century African American neighborhood, lies in East Kinston, with Tower Hill Road as its spine. This thoroughfare, an early road once leading to the antebellum plantation of Tower Hill, runs northeast from the corner of North and East Streets, the original town limits. This neighborhood grew after the Civil War with the assistance of late-nineteenth-century black businessmen and speculative developers; it originated, however, in the second quarter of the nineteenth century.

The area encompassing Tower Hill consists of approximately forty-five small blocks a half mile east of downtown Kinston, bounded by Lenoir Avenue on the north, Chestnut Street on the south, Adkin Branch on the east, and East Street on the west. Older streets in the western part of Tower Hill include Abana Alley, Beasley Street, Thompson Street, Dennis Street, and 400-500 East Blount Street. These streets combine turn-of-the-twentieth-century African American neighborhoods with early-twentieth-century rental shotgun houses and deserted industrial areas along Davis Street. East of Highway 11 (Tiffany Avenue) Tower Hill has tree-framed turn-of-the-century African American residences on Macon Street and Hicks Avenue. Also within the Tower Hill neighborhood are 1930s and 1940s residential and institutional complexes: the Mitchell Wooten Courts and the former Our Lady of the Atonement Catholic Mission on East Washington Avenue, the old Adkin High School grounds on Tower Hill Road, and the J. H. Sampson Elementary School at the intersection of Tower Hill Road and Tiffany Avenue.

Tower Hill has two of Kinston's most significant African American churches. The first, Saint John's Free Will Baptist Church at 405 East Blount Street, a late Romanesque Revival-style brick church, is the premier landmark in the immediate area. Built in 1914 by Will Lewis, an African American builder, the church is his only known surviving building. The antebellum White Rock Presbyterian Church, which moved to 516 Thompson Street at the turn of the twentieth century when its African American congregation bought it from the First Baptist Church, is a handsome Greek Revival-style frame sanctuary.

Gray's 1882 map of Kinston indicates that the blocks now comprising the western end of Tower Hill Road, along with 400 East Blount Street, were once the property of John Cobb Washington, an early-nineteenth-century landowner. Washington built the first dwellings along Tower Hill Road for his shoe factory employees in the mid-nineteenth century; these white laborers, who had emigrated from the North, prompted the name Yankee Row. By the turn of the twentieth century, African Americans had built homes, churches, and stores on the surrounding areas of East North and East Blount Streets, as well as along Tower Hill Road. Within Tower Hill's Streets west of Tiffany Avenue, well-to-do African American merchants like Peter Borden resided on wide streets. Behind these streets were smaller alleys containing rental shotgun housing for tobacco factory workers, domestic servants, and lumber mill workers. The Cook's Alley and Abana Alley shotguns are typical of these areas.

Like Lincoln City, early-twentieth-century Tower Hill was a place where African Americans could buy lots and build houses. Between 1915 and 1945 Hicks Avenue was home to African American barbers, grocers, firemen, cooks, laundresses, and farmers. Most Tower Hill inhabitants were less reliant upon the seasonal income of the tobacco factories than were the residents of Lincoln City. Residency in Tower Hill often indicated African American upward mobility in the early-twentieth century. One of many examples of this is Paul A. Hodges, who first appeared in the city directory in 1909 as a laborer living in a one-story frame house beside the railroad tracks at 305 North Railroad Street (now North Davis Street). By 1916, Hodges lived in a two-story frame shotgun house (now demolished) at 1019 Macon Street, one block south of Tower Hill Road, and operated Hodges Tailoring Company. By 1936 he had achieved substantial success—he owned his house and had become the Reverend Paul A. Hodges.

White developers, particularly James A. McDaniel, sold lots on Chestnut Avenue, near the Adkin Branch, in the early-twentieth century to African American families, who built substantial houses and remained in the area for decades. Three families—the Beasley, Best, and Blount families—resided on Chestnut Avenue from the 1910s until the 1970s. In 1915 Tony and Sarah Beasley bought a 40-by-130-foot parcel of land at the northwest corner of North Alley (now Short Street) and Chestnut Alley (now 1012 Hicks Avenue) from J. T. Whitfield for one thousand dollars. Beasley, a house carpenter, operated a grocery next to his Queen Anne-style house. He died sometime between 1936 and 1946, after which his widow continued to live in the house into the 1950s. [1] In 1916 Ezekiel K. Best, a farmer, bought a 55-by-125-foot lot on the south side of Chestnut Avenue from James A. and Laura McDaniel and probably built the two-story Queen Anne-style frame house at the site, 1015 Chestnut Avenue. On the north side of Chestnut Avenue, across from the Beasleys, Marcellus and Lena Blount bought a lot from T. E. Stainbeck in 1916 (along with a small parcel of land in 1918 from Richard C. Green), where they built a one-story frame house at 1016 Chestnut Avenue. When Marcellus Blount died, his daughter, Mrs. Walter Dawson, moved into the house and established a laundry, which had the first washing machines in East Kinston.[2]

Chestnut Avenue, a comparatively well-preserved example of Tower Hill's early-twentieth-century African American prosperity, was renamed Hicks Avenue for prominent black Kinstonian businessman Starr Hicks in the 1940s. The narrow street runs east from the 300 block of North Adkin Street, bends slightly north at the intersection of Clay Street, and terminates at Pine Street, just below Tower Hill Road. Of the twenty-four buildings on Hicks Avenue, twenty were built before 1940 and, for the most part, retain their original character of one- and two-story frame late Victorian and Craftsman-style dwellings.

On Hicks Avenue and Macon Street, one out of three residents in 1936 owned his or her own home. To understand how exceptional such ownership was at that time, it should be noted that one out of seven residents on nearby Pine Street was a homeowner, and only two out of eleven families on Clay Street owned their homes. Eleven families rented the shotgun houses built on Tull's Alley; seven families rented in Short Street (also known as North Alley). Tower Hill Road east of Trianon Street also had a high percentage of homeowners, but a majority of the residents were renters. In 1936, of the twenty-one dwellings on Fields Street just north of Tower Hill Road, only two were owned by their residents. Thompson Street east of Dennis Street only had sixteen owners, as compared to twenty-six renters. The majority of tenants rented shotgun houses built by white developers.

The Tower Hill neighborhood is clearly divided between the remnants of a middle-class African American 1920s to 1940s community and more transitory developments along North Adkin Street, Tower Hill Road, and Macon Street. The early-twentieth-century frame houses that have survived recall the pleasant residential streets that once characterized this African American neighborhood. There are oak, pecan, pine, and smaller flowering trees alongside and behind the houses on Macon, Hicks, Clay, and parts of Tower Hill Road. Gardens are few, but there are some examples of creative gardens, such as the arbor in the 1200 block of Tower Hill Road, the wave-like topiary in the 1100 block of Macon Street, and the lush screen of sasanquas, cacti, camellias, and vines at 1012 Hicks Avenue.

Two schools were built in the neighborhood, the Tower Hill Elementary School at the corner of Tower Hill Road and Tiffany Avenue, in the 1920s and the Adkin High School in the 1940s, a few blocks east on Tower Hill Road. When the frame elementary school burned about 1940, a two-story brick-veneer school was built on the site and named J. H. Sampson Elementary School in honor of J. H. Sampson, pastor of nearby White Rock Presbyterian Church from the 1930s to the 1950s. Sampson's wife taught at the school in the 1930s. Adkin High School, a two-story brick building, closed in the late 1970s. A portion of it was demolished, but a 1940s two-story brick wing has operated as a retirement home since 1978, and its 1950s brick gymnasium is used for community events.

Notes

1. Lenoir County Register of Deeds, 51:417 (Whitfield>Beasley, 1915); Kinston City Directory, 1953.
2. Lenoir County Register of Deeds, 65:249 and 65:250 (Green>Blount and Stainbeck>Blount, 1919 and 1918); Ted Dawson, interview by Penne Smith, Kinston, January, 1995.

1. Saint John's United African Free Will Baptist Church
built circa 1914
405 East Blount Street

The lively early-twentieth-century, Gothic Revival, brick Saint John's United African Free Will Baptist Church is the only building designed by local builder Will Lewis known to survive. Lewis was an early-twentieth-century African American brickmason. Saint John's two crenellated bell towers, with their corbeled brickwork and recessed panels, flank the front-gabled nave, in which an elevated arcaded entrance has been incorporated. The concrete water table along the ground elevation of the church extends to form a prominent stoop, which still holds the original decorative metal lamp fixtures that illuminated the church by evening. Lancet-arched and rectangular stained-glass windows, as well as buttresses, complete Lewis's masterpiece.

2. Duplex
built circa 1914
415 East Blount Street

This frame one-and-a-half-story duplex, sheltered by an attached hipped-roof porch, represents a dwelling type that once formed a cohesive row along 400 East Blount Street. Each unit has a separate entrance flanked by a six-over-six double-hung sash window. The duplex also has a central brick chimney for each interior fireplace or stove. The 1914 Kinston Sanborn Fire Insurance Map shows six such duplexes on the south side of 400 East Blount Street.

3. Ezekiel K. Best House
built circa 1916
1015 Hicks Avenue

This frame two-story late Queen Anne-style house in East Kinston's Tower Hill neighborhood is a surviving indication of prosperous African American homeownership in the early-twentieth century, when the Tower Hill area was being developed by middle-class African American farmers, barbers, bankers, and store owners. In 1916 Ezekiel K. Best, a farmer, bought a 55-by-125-foot lot on the south side of Chestnut Alley (now Hicks Avenue) from James A. McDaniel. By 1927 the lot and its two-story gable-and-wing house with one-story rear kitchen ell were completely in Ezekiel and Addie Best's possession [Lenoir County Register of Deeds (McDaniel>Ezekiel Best, 46:600, 1916; 71:528; 93:273) 1916-1927]. The Best House, still owned by the family, is, although plainer on the exterior, comparable to houses built at the time in Mitchelltown and Trianon for middle-class white merchants. The attached hipped-roof wraparound porch, with its Tuscan columns and pedimented entry, and the roofline's pedimented gables indicate early Colonial Revival influence, something that would be more obvious if the small gable Palladian window in the front facade were restored.

4. Commercial Building and Taxi Stand
built circa 1920; taxi stand circa 1938
910-914 Tower Hill Road

At 910-912 Tower Hill Road are an early-twentieth-century, two-story, four-bay commercial building and attached one-story, two-bay side extension, all constructed with rock-faced concrete block; this commercial building, known as Lloyd Patrick's Meat Market in the 1930s, is comparable to the now-demolished Isaac Sparrow Grocery in Lincoln City, documented by Martha Dreyer in her 1981 study of Kinston's architecture. The inset signage panel over the second-story double-hung sash windows is intact, as are the plain cornice and raised side-parapet rooflines of both the former meat market and the one-story extension, known in 1936 as the East Royal Cafe.

At the west side of 914 Tower Hill Road stands a frame, one-bay, enclosed front-gable building on concrete-block piers that was a taxi stand for nearly fifty years. The taxi stand still retains its six-over-six front window, smaller side window, front door, furnace flue, and light meter. This taxi stand, one of many once dotted throughout Lincoln City and East Kinston/Tower Hill in the mid-twentieth century, is the only known taxi stand left in Kinston. It was operated by one man, Elijah, from the 1930s until his death in the early 1990s. The late Ted Dawson, whose father, Walter Dawson, was a Kinston sign painter in the 1930s and 1940s, recalled that the elder Dawson painted logos for the approximately five white taxi companies in Kinston, and also for two African American taxi companies, operated respectively by Jerry Perkins and Willie Mills. Perkins and Mills each had a fleet of five cars, according to Dawson; it is not known how many Elijah had.

5. William Moore House
built circa 1915
1214 Macon Street

At 1214 Macon Street is a large four-bay gable-and-wing late Queen Anne house, its overlapping offset front gable meeting a pedimented side-gable extension, built for William Moore, an African American passenger train porter, and his family. This house is a surviving indication of prosperous African American home ownership in the early-twentieth century, when the Tower Hill area was being developed by middle-class African Americans. Although the Moore House would be modest by Mitchelltown or Trianon standards, it is comparable to white middle-class residences of the period. The two interior corbeled-cap chimneys, the attached hipped-roof wraparound porch supported by plain columns between a turned-rail balustrade, and the pedimented gables pierced by diamond-shaped louvered ventilators indicate the Moore family's prosperity. According to the 1920 census, Moore's wife, daughter, son-in-law, teenage son, and boarder, Mollie Jones, who worked at one of Kinston's tobacco manufactories, shared this house. In 1936 Miss Jones, who had become a nurse, continued to share the house with the Moores. Bertha Moore, William Moore's wife, is remembered by older Tower Hill residents as the woman who kept track of everyone's birthdays. Once a month there was a birthday party for the neighborhood children at the Moores' house, in addition to ice cream suppers (mentioned in Mavis Anderson's 1985 *Lincoln City Celebration* as a particular treat in early-twentieth-century African American Kinston) on Sundays.

6. First Baptist Church of Kinston; White Rock Presbyterian Church

built 1858; listed in the National Register of Historic Places, 1989
516 Thompson Street

The handsome temple-front Greek Revival church now at 516 Thompson Street was erected in 1858 at the northwest corner of Bright and McLewean Streets as the First Baptist Church of Kinston, the earliest church building erected for Kinston's Baptist denomination. The Greek Revival parsonage still stands at 211 South McLewean Street, around the corner from the church's original site. The church has been moved twice. The first move occurred in 1891, to the northeast corner of Gordon and McLewean Streets, then considered a more central location. In 1900, when the First Baptist congregation decided to build a new building, the frame church was sold to the White Rock Church, an African American congregation, who moved it to its present location. Above the simple pedimented gable is a pilastered lanternlike belfry with a low hipped-roof cover and wide cornice. The belfry was originally capped by a steeple; the present roof, with its exposed rafters, is a replacement. The rather sophisticated design features a hexastyle in-antis portico with enclosed end bays serving as vestibules. Inside, the church has retained much of its mid-nineteenth-century character, including a simple beaded chair rail, under which is a wide flush tongue-and-groove wainscot, and some of the original box pews. The White Rock Presbyterian Church remains an important landmark for Kinston's African American community.

7. Clyde Albritton House

built circa 1925
500 Quinerly Street

The frame two-story multigabled Colonial Revival house towering over the shotgun row west of the Quinerly and Thompson Street intersection was built by Clyde Albritton, an African American mortician and developer, after 1925; Albritton bought his corner lot from the W. C. Fields estate in 1923, but his house does not appear on a Kinston Sanborn Fire Insurance Map until 1930. The house is a 1920s Craftsman adaptation of the late Queen Anne-early Colonial Revival-style frame houses seen in Kinston's white neighborhoods, for example, Mitchelltown (particularly on Mitchell Street) and the Trianon District. The roofline is a combination of the two-story crossgable forming the main block of the house, from which extend the pedimented false gables and the offset front gable at the front elevation, and the one-story side-gable extension. All of the front facade, including the side extension, is encompassed by a large bungalow-style wraparound porch with pediments at the entrance and porte cochere. The frame two-bay garage behind the porte cochere has retained its standing-seam metal hipped roof and ball finial. In 1930 Albritton's house was one of only three in this neighborhood. Albritton himself was instrumental in developing the immediate area of Thompson, North Adkin, Quinerly, and East Washington Streets with speculative and rental housing.

8. Shotgun Houses
built circa 1925-1935
600 block of Fields Street, south side

The south blockface of 600 Fields Street, off busy Tiffany Avenue in the East Washington neighborhood of East Kinston, comprises seventeen dwellings, sixteen of which are one- and two-story frame front-gable shotgun houses built between 1925 and 1935. This blockface is an unusually well-preserved and intact example of a 1930s shotgun house development built exclusively for African Americans working in Kinston's tobacco manufactories and mills. Comparable developments built at roughly the same time, such as Tull's Alley and Short Street (whose streets were never paved) off Hicks Avenue, are nearly obliterated. The three weatherboarded two-story shotguns at 639, 635, and 631 Fields Street all have attached hipped-roof bungalow-style front porches with brick piers and one-story rear shed extensions. The one-story shotgun houses have a little more variety in terms of form and decoration, indicating a less uniform pattern of speculative development. At the west end of Fields Street stand 619, 617, and three altered shotgun houses, all of which were smaller than the houses at the east end of the block and have, instead of brick-pier foundation posts, wedge-shaped concrete-blocked supports. The overall front of this blockface is bare and relatively uncultivated, mainly because the houses are so close to the street. In fact, this block of Fields Street was not paved until the 1980s.

9. Cook's Alley
built circa 1934
North side of 400 East Washington Avenue

About 1934 a local developer built seven frame shotgun houses here. His cook, who had been living with his family, moved into one of them. She named it Cook's Alley because she and several other residents worked as cooks for families in the white neighborhoods of Mitchelltown, East Kinston, and Grainger Hill. The front-gable frame shotgun houses have been rehabilitated and the original porch supports and balustrades replaced. Cook's Alley, with its well-maintained yards and plant-filled porches, is one of the few intact shotgun rows left in the lower Tower Hill area.

10. Mitchell Wooten Courts

built circa 1941
700 block of East Washington Street, north side

Mitchell Wooten Courts, located on the north side of the 700 block of Washington Street and across from the former Our Lady of the Atonement Catholic Mission, is the second of two lower-income housing projects designed by A. Mitchell Wooten and Associates in Kinston. Both housing projects—Simon Bright Apartments, built for lower-income whites, and Mitchell Wooten Courts, built for lower-income African Americans—were influenced by the International Style of the late 1920s and 1930s, particularly in the siting of the apartments and their large landscaped areas. In the basic design of each, Wooten and the Kinston Housing Authority, who assisted with the project, were reaching for a "livable and moral" alternative to crowded tenements and shotgun rows. Both Simon Bright and Mitchell Wooten had space specifically allotted for play areas and a detached community center building (the Mitchell Wooten Community Center has been an outpost for the Kinston police in recent years), and the buildings were designed to be appealing in appearance, yet easy to maintain.

The eighteen buildings at Mitchell Wooten Courts built between 1940 and 1941 (two buildings were built later) are all brick, two-story, hipped-roof, side-gable apartments, each ten, fourteen, or sixteen bays across. Exterior details include brick stringcourses, corner windows, modern interior brick chimney stacks, and, on most of the apartments' entrances, relief plaques of children at play with various instruments and toys. The entrances beneath the plaques are sheltered by cantilevered door hoods with brick supporting pilasters. The Mitchell Wooten Courts, designed in an amphitheater format, as opposed to the more rectilinear layout of the Simon Bright Apartments, have had some alterations since 1941, but the apartment exteriors are identical to the Kinston Housing Authority's 1941 presentation drawing, now at the former community building.

11. (former) Our Lady of the Atonement Catholic Church Mission

built circa 1939-1952
800 block of East Washington Street

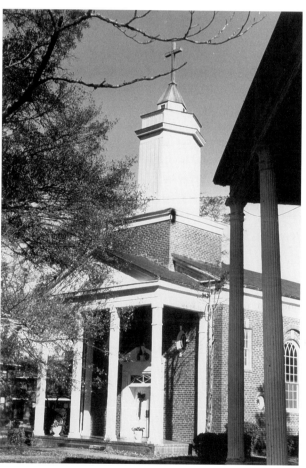

The former Our Lady of the Atonement Catholic Church Mission began with the Reverend David Gannon's purchase of a five-acre site above East Washington Street in the late 1930s to serve as a mission for East Kinston's African American community. The architects who designed the complex are not known; according to local history, they were not Kinston residents. In 1939 a brick two-story late Colonial Revival-style rectory, with a flat-roofed, full-facade two-story front portico, was built. Three years later the front-gable brick Colonial Revival church, whose octagonal steeple has been altered, was built; the church, lit by four large recessed arch windows at each side of its nave, is sheltered at its entrance by a pedimented portico. The other significant original building at the complex is the brick two-and-a-half-story hipped-roof Colonial Revival-style convent/school building, begun in 1947 and completed in 1952. The mission school, administered by the Order of the Sisters Adorers of the Most Precious Blood, closed in 1969 after having operated for over twenty years. The convent/school building has, at its east elevation, a one-story brick rear extension with a shaped parapet connecting the older building to a 1960s one-story classroom building that served, in recent years as a day-care center.

All of the buildings have retained their original tile roofs. The grounds are landscaped with trees and some shrubbery, and sidewalks run between the buildings.

Shotgun Houses, 700 block of Oak Street, Lincoln City, circa 1920.

Lincoln City

Lincoln City was one of the first concentrated African American neighborhoods to develop in Kinston. The earliest published mention of Lincoln City was in 1914, but settlement in the neighborhood was under way at the turn of the twentieth century and possibly before. This area, directly southeast of Kinston's central business district and just east of Maplewood Cemetery, the final resting place of white Kinstonians, has been described throughout its history as a small neighborhood of no more than twelve streets, including Lincoln, Oak, Olive, and Davis Streets, and University Avenue.[1] Lincoln City has remained much like it has always been—a small residential African American area with a few churches and grocery markets. In the early part of the twentieth century the Lincoln City School and Kinston College, both of which no longer exist, were the grammar and high schools for African American residents. The people of Lincoln City worked for the Hines Brothers Lumber Company and the Lenoir Oil and Ice Plant, as well as working as porters, bricklayers, barbers, grocers, and domestic servants for white families. Kinston's tobacco manufactories provided additional employment. One indication of this is Lincoln City's former 1920s Durhamville Road, now known as Sunshine Street. The road may have been named for the

African American workers who were sent, or came, to Kinston during tobacco season from as far away as Durham or even Danville, Virginia.[2]

The beginnings of Lincoln City are evident in the southeastern boundaries of the 1882 O. W. Gray map. On the map, Kinston's "African Cemetery," just outside the city limits, lies near present-day Lincoln Street. There is no indication on the Gray map of a settlement in the present Lincoln City area. The 1902 *Kinston City Directory's* "Colored Directory" appendix lists a number of African American laborers residing along the 300, 400, and 500 blocks of East Bright and East Shine Streets, but there are no listings for Lincoln City streets.

Lincoln City's emergence began with James A. McDaniel, the prominent late-nineteenth-century Kinston businessman who developed the Trianon neighborhood for whites from his 350-acre farm. At the turn of the twentieth century McDaniel subdivided another portion of his farm and sold lots to African American developers and homeowners. One of the earliest known inhabitants of Lincoln City was Lincoln Barnett [Bonnet]. Barnett purchased a one hundred-by-two hundred-foot lot on Lincoln Street on January 6, 1902, from James McDaniel and shortly afterwards built a two-story house that is no longer standing.[3] Edna Speight recalled the turn of events for *A Lincoln City Celebration*:

> Why this was named Lincoln City, well, when they started selling this area out, they sold it in acres. Mr. Jim McDaniel sold it in acres, cause it was out in the country, nothing but woods. The people could buy an acre and clear it up. . . . People started buying the lots fast. Then Mr. McDaniel decided he'd run it off in streets.[4]

In 1914 the American Realty and Auction Company announced the sale of "50 Nice Residence Lots In Lincoln City on Both Sides of the Railroad—for White or Colored People."[5] The railroad mentioned was probably the Norfolk and Southern Railroad, bisecting Lincoln Street and University Avenue.

By the late 1910s a stable neighborhood composed of African American homeowners existed in this area, and schools were being built in Lincoln City. The 1919 Kinston Sanborn Fire Insurance Map shows the United American Free Will Baptist College, a two-story frame building, on University Avenue at the railroad tracks. The 1925 Sanborn map shows two freestanding buildings added to the campus. The United American Free Will Baptist College, a secondary school also known as Kinston College by 1919, offered courses in primary education, theology, and "domestic science."[6] The 1930 Sanborn map showed that the original building had been brick veneered. By 1925 Lincoln City had its own grammar school, the Primary Graded School, at the corner of Lincoln and Adkin Streets.

This historically significant African American neighborhood contains early houses, grocery stores, and churches, including Saint Peter's Church, the site of which was originally a brush arbor for outdoor worship services at the turn of the twentieth century. The houses in Lincoln City are modest one- and two-story frame dwellings, including some shotguns, many now brick veneered, and late Craftsman bungalows. At the east end of Lincoln City, bounded by Sunshine Street, housing was developed for black veterans returning from World War II. Into the 1960s this neighborhood continued to develop as a stable middle-class black area with neatly kept brick ranch houses. In these postwar areas yards are well landscaped with grass lawns, trees, shrubs (sometimes trimmed into topiary forms), vegetable gardens, and some flower gardens.

Notes

1. Anderson, *A Lincoln City Celebration*, 1.

2. Sanborn Fire Insurance Maps, 1925, 1930. Also see *Kinston Daily Free Press*, August 29, August 30, 1898.

3. Anderson, *A Lincoln City Celebration*, 3; Lenoir Co. Register of Deeds, 26:766 (J. A. and Laura McDaniel>Lincoln Barnett, 1902).

4 Anderson, *A Lincoln City Celebration*, 3.

5 *Kinston Free Press*, January 10, 1914.

6 *Fiftieth Anniversary Programme*, Saint Augustus A.M.E. Zion Church, 42.

1. Saint Peter's Disciple Church of Christ

built early twentieth century; 1946
710 Lincoln Street

Saint Peter's Disciple Church of Christ, the oldest church in Lincoln City, began as a brush shelter built by local residents who had moved to the area from nearby rural settlements; two rural areas with African American neighborhoods were Georgetown to the northeast and Hickory Grove to the east. The Reverend C. R. D. Whitfield, with a group of congregants from the Hickory Grove Disciple Church of Christ, founded Saint Peter's Church sometime between 1909 and 1915. According to Edna Speight, who remembered the construction of the church, platforms and lecterns were fashioned out of fish boxes, and lanterns were strung about for lighting. Mrs. Speight remembered the first church building as a one-room church on a high foundation, so high that she could walk between the piers.

Saint Peter's Church is now a small, wide front-gable building, still on a high foundation, that is encased in rock-faced concrete block. There are a large oculus window over the three-part entrance and light fixtures at each side of the curving stoop entrance stairs. A cornerstone identifies the building as the Antioch United African Free Will Baptist Church, another Lincoln City congregation that apparently moved to this building in 1946.

2. House and Grocery

built circa 1930
808 Lincoln Street

This frame two-story, front-gable building in Lincoln City beside the Atlantic and East Carolina Railroad tracks is a good and quite intact example of the type of grocery store that existed in Lincoln City during the first half of the twentieth century. Neighborhood stores were community hubs. Schoolchildren, teenagers, elderly neighbors, and others congregated outside to exchange news and socialized. Often groceries like these served a dual function, with the store below and living quarters above, extended by a wide front porch.

The grocery's attached hipped-roof, full-facade porch on the second story, screened by houseplants, is supported by plain posts and secured by a plain-rail balustrade. The occupants' living space thus extends over both the sheltered storefront entrance and the door to the upstairs rooms, while the cover of plants affords some privacy. 808 Lincoln Street does not appear on the 1925 Kinston Sanborn Fire Insurance Map but was probably built soon after 1925.

3. Shotgun Houses

built circa 1920
700 block of Oak Street

In contrast to the one-story, front-gable Craftsman cottages along the 600 block of Oak Street are the shotgun houses lining the north and south blockfaces of 700 Oak Street. The shotgun, usually a one-story, two-bay frame house one room wide and two to three rooms deep, was seen by early-twentieth-century speculative property developers as an ideal form for rental complexes. Such houses were built throughout Kinston's African American neighborhoods, as well as in a few of its working-class white residential areas. 700 Oak Street contains one of the largest intact original shotgun rows in Kinston; most of the houses have retained their attached shed- or hipped-roof porches supported by plain wooden posts. A great deal of period landscaping—mature pecan trees, shrubbery, and trained vines—also appears to have survived.

Vernon Hall, 117 West Capitola Avenue, Grainger Hill, circa 1914.

Grainger Hill

The Grainger Hill District rises above North Queen Street north of Vernon Avenue, its neighborhood streets lined by towering oak trees planted at the turn of the twentieth century. This district, bounded by North Herritage and North Independence Streets to the west and east, and Vernon and Highland Avenues to the south and north, contains about twenty blocks. Within

Grainger Hill are some of Kinston's most magnificent residences, a municipal park, the first "modern" shopping center in the city, a 1940s apartment complex influenced by the International Style, and streets containing Queen Anne-style houses, Craftsman bungalows, and early ranch-style houses. At the southeast border is Grainger Stadium, a municipal baseball park built in 1953 on the site of an earlier Works Projects Administration-built stadium, and Kinston's small industrial corridor. To the north and west is more residential and commercial development.

Most of the neighborhood comprises the Hill-Grainger Historic District, listed in the National Register in 1989. The following overview and individual entries are edited from Allison Black's district nomination, with additional research by Penne Smith. An east-west ridge called the Hill or Grainger Hill extends through the neighborhood with Summit Avenue on the north side of the Hill and Park Avenue on the south side. A desirable location for a house since the eighteenth century, the Hill contains the largest lots and grandest homes in the neighborhood.

Before there were mansions along Queen Street or smaller, early-twentieth-century dwellings on Virginia, Summit, Capitola, and Grainger—and long before the construction of the 1950s Parkview Shopping Center or Emma Webb Park—Grainger Hill was "the country." The Grainger Hill neighborhood began with John Cobb Washington in the mid-nineteenth century. Washington's father, John Washington, had left the Tidewater of Virginia for the small village of Kinston by 1800.[1] John Cobb Washington owned an extensive tract of land along the ridge just north of town, said to be the site of Richard Caswell's plantation, the Hill. On the Hill stood the mansion, Vernon Heights, where the Washington family lived and farmed. A 1906 photograph of Vernon Heights, taken after the estate had passed out of the family and the house had been partly remodeled, shows the dwelling—a brick two-story hipped-roof residence—and, behind the house, farm buildings visible through tall trees.

Prominent late-nineteenth-century merchant, civic leader, and industrialist Jesse W. Grainger acquired sole interest in a 257-acre tract of the Caswell-Washington land north of Kinston in 1892. Vernon Heights, part of the tract, became Grainger's residence. At that time Grainger began building rental and speculative housing, then proceeded to sell lots in the area for residential development. The acquisition of Vernon Heights and its environs was the culmination of a thirteen-year enterprise. Grainger, a native of Greene County, had moved to Kinston in 1879, where, in addition to engaging in successful business ventures in truck farming and agricultural supply sales, he formed a partnership with Lemuel Harvey and William C. Fields to purchase this large tract of land. In addition to residential development, Grainger carried out a large truck farming operation at Vernon Heights. After Grainger's death a massive brick Neoclassical Revival-style house was built on the site of Vernon Heights in 1914 by Charles Felix Harvey, one of Lemuel Harvey's sons. The younger Harvey bought Vernon Heights from Jesse Grainger's heirs and demolished it to make way for his own imposing residence, known as Vernon Hall, which had become a bed and breakfast known as The Bentley by the mid-1990s.

Grainger developed his property in small sections, laying out grid-patterned streets and small urban lots, with the exception of the lots along the Hill, which were of a grand size. One of Grainger's first developments below the Hill sat on the flat terrain between Lenoir and Grainger Avenues, extending from North Independence to North Herritage Streets. An early renter was Grainger's own protege, Luther P. Tapp, an Orange County warehouseman whom Grainger had recruited for Kinston's burgeoning bright-leaf tobacco market. Grainger's earliest speculative houses were either large frame Queen Anne dwellings, with their projecting bays and multiple gables, or traditional side-gable houses. Grainger continued his speculative activities into the early twentieth century and hired two local contractors, S. M. Harrell and D. H. Taylor, to build houses for rent or sale.

Sophisticated examples of the Neoclassical Revival style also appeared in the district at this time. Herbert Woodley Simpson, a noted architect from New Bern, designed and built two Neoclassical Revival showplaces in Grainger Hill, Sarahurst and the Fields-Rasberry House. Sarahurst, featured in the 1906 Industrial Issue of the *Kinston Free Press*, is an impressive brick two-story mansion with a full-height curving portico sheltering the massive entrance and balcony. Sarahurst stood on the Hill at the head of North Queen Street for twelve years. In 1914, to facilitate the extension of Queen Street, Sarahurst was carefully rotated ninety degrees to its current location at 1201 North Queen Street. Simpson's other Grainger Hill residence is the large brick Neoclassical Revival house built for W. C. Fields's widow, Alice, in 1907. This house, now known as the Fields-Rasberry House, sits at 108 Park Avenue.

American Foursquare and bungalow house forms were harbingers of the Craftsman style in Grainger Hill. The earliest evidence of this very popular style in the neighborhood is the E. J. Becton House (circa 1915) at 1006 North Queen Street, a handsome frame bungalow with battered-rubblestone corner piers and chimney. Two American Foursquare residences in Grainger Hill are mail-order houses from the Aladdin Homes company, a Michigan firm that had a factory in Wilmington, North Carolina. The J. T. Pratt House at 307 East Capitola Avenue is one of Aladdin's 1918-model houses, called the Carolina. The Pratt House has retained much of its early-twentieth-century character and many original elements, including the finial crowning its pyramid roof. Its neighbor at 312 East Capitola is the Aladdin Company's 1918 Virginia, an American Foursquare dwelling with a Craftsman-like bracketed cornice and multipaned upper-story sash windows. Many of the early bungalows in Grainger Hill were built on speculation for prospective homeowners. Two charming examples of early bungalows are the clipped-front-gable bungalows with corner porches located at 213 and 215 East Capitola Avenue, built circa 1921. A. D. Sugg, a butcher, lived at 213 East Capitola and may have rented 215 East Capitola to tenants.

Several families contributed a distinctive aspect to Grainger Hill's development. Local building contractor Isaac S. Rochelle built houses for his two sons and himself in the early 1920s on Grainger Avenue. This section of the neighborhood, now bordering Grainger Stadium, was composed of small front-gable and gable-and-wing cottages and cotton fields.[2] Rochelle also built houses further north, near Highland Avenue, in the 1930s: one for himself at 1305 Holman Street and one for his daughter and son-in-law at 1302 Holman Street, both Victorian-style dwellings with comfortable porches.

In the early 1920s a number of substantial and architecturally sophisticated houses were built in Grainger Hill, as Kinston's population became increasingly prosperous. Some members of the community familiar with current architectural styles seen in larger towns hired architects and builders to provide them with fashionable houses. The Colonial Revival style, however, was already evident in Grainger Hill at the turn of the twentieth century. Lawrence Cobb, founder of the Cobb and Johnson Wholesale Grocery at 403 North Queen Street, resided in a large frame house built around 1906 at 1003 North Queen. Now known as the Cobb-Sams House, this two-story dwelling is a good example of Grainger Hill's early Colonial Revival houses. The Colonial Revival style became increasingly popular over the next twenty years, although more 1920s examples had brick-veneer than frame finishes.

One of the finest representations of the Tudor Revival style in eastern North Carolina is Harvey C. Hines's second house, built in 1929 at 1118 North Queen Street. The Hines House influenced the spread of the Tudor Revival style into Kinston's residential neighborhoods and, particularly, influenced builder-contractor Oscar Shackelford. After assisting architect Herbert Hunter with the Hines House, Shackelford went on to design and build smaller Tudor-style houses in the area. One of Shackelford's Tudor houses was the one-and-a-half-story brick and half-timbered house built at 1002 North Queen Street for Rachel Tull, founder of the R. S. Tull and Company Insurance Agency, in 1934.

Grainger Hill even has an example of the Prairie style, the simple and emphatically horizontal architectural style developed by Frank Lloyd Wright in the early twentieth century. George Carter's unusual stucco house, at 1014 North Independence Street, was built in 1935 and is Kinston's only example of the style.[3]

In addition to residential development, Jesse Grainger initiated the building of schools. Kinston's first public school was the Kinston Graded School, a combined grammar and high school on East Lenoir Avenue between North Independence and North East Streets built on land donated by Grainger.[4] This school is not to be confused with the Lewis School, the lively Romanesque-

Classical Revival brick building that was also known as the Kinston Graded School before 1919. By 1919 Grainger's weatherboarded school was replaced by Kinston's first high school, a brick building on a lot running from Lenoir to Vernon Avenue just west of North East Street and known as the Grainger School.[5] When this second building burned in 1924, it was replaced by Grainger High School, a large brick late Neoclassical Revival building designed by Wilmington architect Leslie Boney, a noted designer of school buildings. Grainger High School, located at the northeast corner of Park Avenue and North Independence Street, became first Kinston High School, in the 1970s, and then Kinston Junior High, by 1982. The school closed in the 1980s.

As it did in all of Kinston, construction in Grainger Hill slowed during the Great Depression. During this time new houses in the neighborhood continued to be relatively modest. Most of these new houses were examples of Colonial Revival and Tudor Revival residences typical of early-twentieth-century neighborhoods across eastern North Carolina. Grainger Hill was almost completely developed by 1941, with few vacant lots remaining in the area bounded by North Herritage and North East Streets, and Lenoir and Summit Avenues. At the northern fringes of the district lie suburban neighborhoods developed largely in the 1940s and after. For example, one neighborhood developed around Highland Avenue east of North Herritage Street between the 1930s and the 1950s. This neighborhood, consisting of Queens Road, Howard Street, Holman Street, Glenwood Avenue, and part of North Queen Street, still has doctors' clinics, bungalows, Cape Cod cottages, and ranch-style houses. This northern area also contains the early-1950s Parkview Shopping Center and Emma Webb Park.

Emma Webb Park, built in 1935-1936, contributed to this suburban area's self-sufficiency. The park, a magnet for the growing middle-class neighborhood of Parkview in the 1940s and 1950s, offered Friday night dances in its WPA dance hall building. Across from Emma Webb Park are the Kinston Apartments, an International Style complex developed by 1941.

Parkview Shopping Center, situated on the triangular island formed by the convergence of Queens Road, North Queen Street, and Highland Avenue, was the first suburban shopping center in Kinston. Initially owned by the H. S. Stadiem estate, the modern brick complex was designed and built by Kinston contractor E. R. Smith circa 1951-1952. The 1951 deed for Parkview stipulated that the two-story cinema structure be as identical to Charlotte's Center Theater as possible, considering available finances and prescribed dimensions.[6] The 1953 Special Edition of the *Lenoir County News* featured photographs of Parkview's streamlined complex, juxtaposed with an aerial shot of the empty lot in the 1940s. The caption reads: "Although some citizens in the area originally objected to commercial buildings in one of the town's nicest original areas, the objections have faded away and the modern functional building has been readily used and accepted by the neighborhood as well as the entire Kinston Trading Area."

The area of Wilson and Virginia Avenues was developed around the park between the late 1930s and early 1940s as a residential area for middle-class white professionals and doctors and was linked to the older residential areas on North Independence Street and Summit Avenue. The area east of 300 Wilson Avenue, however, was never fully developed until the 1950s and 1960s, when brick and frame housing—Colonial-style cottages and ranch houses—was built. Overall, most buildings in Grainger Hill have remained single-family dwellings, with few having been converted to apartments, so that the district clearly retains its character as an early-twentieth-century middle-class residential neighborhood.

Notes

1. *The Heritage of Lenoir County*, 21.
2. Pressly interview.
3. *Kinston Free Press*, May 9, 1995.
4. *The Heritage of Lenoir County*, 124.
5. Sanborn Maps, 1914, 1919; *The Heritage of Lenoir County*, 124. The two-story brick building known as the Lewis School was, around 1900, called the Kinston Graded School and stood at the northeast corner of North Independence and East Peyton Streets.
6. Lenoir County Deed Book 329:547 (Stadiem Estate>General Realty and Management, 1951).

1. Dawson-Hodges-Tull House
built circa 1901
900 North Queen Street

2. Grainger Stadium
built 1952
400 block of East Grainger Avenue

The two-story frame Queen Anne-style house at 900 North Queen Street is one of Jesse Grainger and S. M. Harrell's turn-of-the-twentieth-century speculative houses on the Hill. It is also the only house left on this blockface, due to expanding commercial development. From the shingled and pedimented cross gables extending from the high hipped roof to the spacious Eastlake-style wraparound, attached, hipped-roof front porch with a spindle frieze and slim turned porch posts, the house's exterior has been little altered since its construction at the beginning of the twentieth century.

The first three owners of this house were active in city and county government. John H. Dawson, a farmer and city of Kinston treasurer, first owned the house, in 1901. Dawson's son-in-law, Paul Hodges, then owned the house in the later 1920s. Hodges was a member of the Lenoir County Board of Education, as well as the North Carolina State Highway Commission. Isaac Tull, who had grown up at Tower Hill, the Tull family farm and eighteenth-century estate, was living at 900 North Queen Street by 1935. Tull died in July 1935.

During the early twentieth century the site of the future Grainger Stadium comprised cotton fields and small farmhouses. Baseball was already a popular pastime in Kinston, and the *Kinston Daily Free Press* reported regularly about the town's white and African American teams. The first professional Kinston baseball team was organized during the 1920s and was known as the Kinston Eagles. It formed part of what was known as the Virginia League. The playing field was located directly across the railroad tracks from the Kinston municipal power plant. The playing field moved to its present location during the early 1930s.

The white baseball team, a member of the Coastal Plain League, is now known as the Kinston Indians. In 1952 Grainger Stadium was built, framed by earlier-twentieth-century one- and two-story houses on Grainger Avenue and East Street and the former silk mill on Park Avenue. John J. Rowland, who took over A. Mitchell Wooten's architectural firm in 1940, was the stadium's architect. In 1994 the Kinston Indians' home stadium was rehabilitated by Hickman and Loving, P.A., with a new brick office and iron gates with a striking motif of a baseball. Rowland's enclosed tiered bleachers were updated with a red-and-turquoise paint scheme, but the older part of the stadium was not radically altered. The baseball field is enclosed by a six-foot concrete-block wall.

3. Turnage-Hooker House
built circa 1906
106 West Capitola Avenue

Mary M. Laws House
built circa 1906
108 West Capitola Avenue

In 1906 Edgar Moseley, a farmer, built two frame, two-story, Queen Anne-style houses for his daughters, Eva Moseley Turnage and Mary Moseley Laws, at 106 and 108 West Capitola Avenue, on lots adjacent to his own house. Peyton Hooker, owner of the P. A. Hooker Meat and Fish Market, bought 106 West Capitola Street from the Turnages in the 1920s. Mary M. Laws was the wife of Herman F. Laws, who ran the Kinston Buick Company before becoming manager of Tapp Tobacco Warehouse.

Both houses, exemplary of the late Queen Anne style, have high hipped roofs with pedimented cross gables and tall corbeled chimney stacks. The pedimented cross gables and false side gables all have patterned shingles and large louvered ventilators. Both attached hipped-roof wraparound porches are still intact. 108 West Capitola Street has a uniquely staggered porch line, following the line of the house's projecting sections, with Eastlake-style scalloped brackets and large turned porch posts.

4. Rochelle and Pratt Houses
built circa 1922
307 and 310 East Capitola Avenue

The two frame, two-story, hipped-roof houses at 307 and 310 East Capitola Avenue represent the American Foursquare style. The American Foursquare, a popular early-twentieth-century house form, utilized a double-pile, consolidated floor plan; a center hall entrance; many windows; and features such as hipped-roof dormers and attached bungalow-style porches. Elements of the American Foursquare persisted in later Craftsman and Colonial Revival houses. 307 Capitola Avenue has retained many original exterior features, including the small windows on either side of its exterior brick chimney with corbeled shoulders, and the finials atop the hipped roof and dormer. Contractor Isaac Rochelle built this house for his son, B. H. Rochelle, in the early 1920s.

310 Capitola Avenue has retained its curvilinear cornice brackets, original double-hung nine-over-one sash windows, and small side bay window. Built for J. T. Pratt circa 1922, this house is thought to be The Virginia, one of the houses manufactured by the Aladdin Homes company.

5. E. J. Becton House
built circa 1919
1006 North Queen Street

E. J. Becton, an early-twentieth-century real estate broker who was a partner in the Becton and Fields insurance company on North Queen Street, lived in this exceptional one-and-a-half-story Craftsman bungalow, one of the earliest Craftsman-style houses in Kinston. North Queen Street, the heart of one of Kinston's most fashionable early-twentieth-century neighborhoods, no doubt made an ideal location for a real estate broker. Becton was also involved, through the Atlantic Coast Realty Company, in the 1920s and 1930s development of Mitchelltown. With the Craftsman exterior elements of his house are found more classical features, such as the porch's entrance surmounted by a bracketed front gable with a keystone. The house also employs rubblestone instead of brick. Battered-rubblestone posts over piers support the porch, carrying over to the stoop and exterior chimney. The interplay of gables—the deep eaves of the side gables juxtaposed with the overlap of the front-gable porch and the similarly bracketed front-gable dormer—combined with the original exterior tracery of the double-hung sash windows and narrow weatherboarding, contributes to the intactness of this unique and early example of the Craftsman style in Kinston.

6. Leo Brody House
built circa 1935
1008 North Queen Street

Leo Brody, who operated H. Brody and Sons department store in Kinston starting in 1928, lived in this handsome one-and-a-half-story brick and frame Tudor Revival house. The Brody House, built in 1935, is a good example of the Tudor Revival style in the early to middle twentieth century. The house's steep cross gables employ traditional half-timbering against stucco infill and are pierced by casement windows. The entrance of the house, like those of many Tudor Revival houses, is a recessed arch incorporated into a sloping front gable. Other distinctive exterior elements are the tall paneled exterior end chimney stacks, the stucco and timber front-gable dormer windows, and a side extension, probably a solarium, covered by an unusual balloonlike hipped roof.

7. Vernon Hall
built circa 1914
117 West Capitola Avenue

Vernon Hall, an impressive two-and-a-half-story Neoclassical Revival residence of tapestry brick, was built at the crest of a small rise north of West Vernon Avenue. Charles Felix Harvey Sr., a prominent Kinston businessman and the son of Lemuel Harvey, built Vernon Hall in

1914. The colossal front-gable, full-height Ionic portico is pierced by a fanlight gable window. Other details of the elegant classical design include the modillion-block cornice, classical-inspired front-gable dormers with arched windows, and center entrance with its fanlight transom and sidelights. The interiors contain elaborate classical detailing and Italian marble mantelpieces. The house is now a bed and breakfast called the Bentley and owned by the J. Ward McConnells.

Before 1914 a two-story brick mansion occupied the site of Vernon Hall and was known as Vernon Heights. It was first the home of John Cobb Washington and later of Jesse A. Grainger.

8. Canady-Sutton House
built circa 1925
1101 North Queen Street

1101 North Queen Street, a two-story brick house capped by a low-pitch hipped green tile roof, is a handsome example of 1920s Renaissance and Colonial Revival design. The house has semicircular-arched sash windows and a recessed sidelighted entrance sheltered by a flat portico with Tuscan columns and battlements, just under the center second-story paired windows. Like on many 1920s and 1930s Colonial Revival houses, symmetry is maintained by the flanking porte cochere and frame solarium. This house was built for J. Herman Canady, son of B. W. Canady, in 1925. The builder is believed to have been Captain William Kennedy. Fred I. Sutton Jr., a prominent Kinston realtor, acquired the house in 1950.

9. Fields-Rasberry House
built circa 1907
108 Park Avenue

Framed by mature magnolia and hardwood trees on the crest of Park Avenue's north slope, this handsome two-story brick Neoclassical Revival residence was designed by New Bern architect Herbert Woodley Simpson. It was for many years the home of Alice Fields, the widow of William C. Fields. W. C. Fields was a prominent landowner and businessman in early-twentieth-century Kinston and president of the Kinston Cotton Mill. The house was later owned by Joseph C. Rasberry, who established an insurance company in Kinston at the turn of the twentieth century and went on to serve as the National Bank of Kinston's president.

The Fields-Rasberry House is sheltered by a dramatic full-height tetrastyle portico with Corinthian columns, which spans the house's three-bay front facade. The porte cochere's balustrade is echoed in the balcony above the center entrance; both the balcony and center entrances have impressive leaded-glass transoms and sidelights. Above the portico is a returned front gable pierced by a round-arch window. There is a one-story rear wing. Outbuildings on the two-acre tract include a concrete-block smokehouse and a one-story garage constructed of rock-faced concrete block.

10. O. W. Greene House
built circa 1920
202 Park Avenue

Blackwood-Jenkins House
built circa 1920
204 Park Avenue

The two-story brick Georgian Revival house at 204 Park Avenue and the two-story-with-attic brick and frame Dutch Colonial-style house at 202 Park Avenue are good examples of Colonial Revival design in 1920s Kinston. 202 Park Avenue, the former O. W. Greene House, has a tiled gambrel roof with a large shed dormer pierced by shuttered double-hung sash windows, above which is a smaller attic shed dormer. The Greene House has an open columned side porch at its east elevation and a solarium—a small sun porch with bands of windows—at its west elevation. O. W. Greene was a manager of the Carolina Telephone and Telegraph Company who later operated the Kinston Electric Company and Greene Gift Shop.

Like the Greene House, the Blackwood-Jenkins House has a small side porch and side solarium, and a prominent entrance above which are paired small windows. The Blackwood-Jenkins House's entrance is particularly well executed, with a pineapple finial within its broken pediment, and fluted pilaster jambs. L. B. Jenkins, Luther Tapp's son-in-law, established his own tobacco warehouse. Jenkins bought the house from Robert A.

Blackwood, president of Carolina Gas and Electric Company, in the 1930s.

11. Grainger High School
built 1926
300 Park Avenue

Leslie Boney, an early-twentieth-century Wilmington architect whose 1920s Colonial Revival brick schools are still seen throughout eastern North Carolina, designed this three-story classically detailed brick building on Grainger Hill overlooking Park Avenue and North Independence Street. This monumental building replaced the previous Grainger School, a smaller brick-veneered building at the northeast corner of East Lenoir Avenue and North East Street, that burned in 1924. During the years that Kinston was building a new public high school, the Harvey School changed its schedule to accommodate the influx of temporary students. At the Harvey School, grammar school classes ran from 8:15 A.M. until noon, and then high school students had their classes from 12:30 until 4:00 P.M. The new Grainger High School constituted part of Grainger Hill's transformation from an area of lofty and simple country houses to a verdant suburb of Kinston. The school was built on the site of Isaac Rochelle's former sawmill and overlooked cotton fields soon to convert to streets and cottages.

The flat-roofed three-story main block of the former Grainger High School is flanked by two-story wings with covered entrances and finished by two east and west temple-front wings. The auditorium (west) and gymnasium (east) wings are two-story side extensions distinguished by tetrastyle porticoes with Corinthian columns, and large round-arched windows with keystones at the side elevations. Overall the school has remained a stately example of the academic Colonial Revival style, the only building of its type in Kinston.

12. Harvey C. Hines House

built circa 1925
1118 North Queen Street

This magnificent Jacobean-influenced residence on the west side of North Queen Street shows the Tudor Revival movement of the 1920s to be a more scholarly interpretation of English medieval forms and motifs than those found with earlier revivals. It was built for Harvey C. Hines, a Kinston businessman who founded a wholesale grocery establishment and operated Kinston's Coca-Cola Company bottling works in 1929. Hines also organized an ice cream business in the early 1920s and shipped ice cream throughout a large portion of eastern North Carolina.

The slate-roofed house is secluded within a high curved brick wall surrounding the grounds. Exterior details of the Hines House include multiple triangular gables (some of which enfold small shed side extensions), clustered rectangular mullioned windows, stone trim, Tudor-style grouped chimney pots, and patterned brickwork. The entrance is an imposing Tudor-style stone arch with a recessed parapet. Whimsically, the decorative copper gutterwork incorporates a Coca-Cola bottle motif. Herbert Hunter of High Point, North Carolina, was the architect, and the building contractor was T. A. Mitchell of Kinston. Construction of the Hines House proved to be a formative experience for one of Mitchell's assistants, Oscar Shackelford. Shackelford, a 1930s-1950s Kinston contractor, would eventually design smaller Colonial and Tudor Revival residences with equally imaginative and meticulous details.

13. Sarahurst (Daniel and Capitola Grainger Edwards House)

built circa 1902
1201 North Queen Street

Designed by Herbert Woodley Simpson of New Bern between 1902 and 1904, Sarahurst remains one of Kinston's most impressive Neoclassical Revival residences. It was first the home of Daniel T. and Capitola Grainger Edwards. Capitola Edwards was the daughter of Jesse A. Grainger and the person for whom Capitola Avenue was named. Daniel T. Edwards, a North Carolina native who received a Ph.D. from New York University in 1899, was editor of the *Kinston Daily Free Press* when the house was built. The house was named for the Edwards' young daughter, Sarah Grainger Edwards, who married Clifford "Pat" Crawford, Kinston's first superintendent of recreation. The Crawfords founded Camp Morehead by the Sea, one of North Carolina's most renowned seaside summer camps, in 1936.

This two-and-a-half-story brick edifice originally stood at the head of North Queen Street. Although the house seems too massive to have been moved, Sarahurst was turned ninety degrees to its current location in 1914, when Queen Street was extended beyond the Hill. The house's impressive curved portico has a prominent modillion cornice, which wraps around the house, and is supported by fluted Corinthian columns on brick plinths. Within the portico is a large trabeated entrance, over which is a balcony with a turned-rail balustrade supported by large curvilinear consoles. Around the corner of the portico is a side-gable, hipped-roof porte cochere. Above the portico are pedimented front-gable dormers that, from a distance, add to Sarahurst's palatial quality. Other exterior elements are the double-hung sash windows with flat-arched sandstone lintels and granite sills, and curvilinear Art Nouveau-style muntins.

14. Liston Nash House
built circa 1937
1302 Holman Street

Liston Nash's former house, a frame one-and-a-half-story side-gable dwelling, sits in the heart of the neighborhood that grew between Glenwood and Highland Avenues from the late 1930s until the 1950s. On this particular block early-twentieth-century frame Craftsman houses coexist with 1950s Minimal Traditional-style cottages and ranches. Among these contrasting styles, the former Nash House adds an interesting twist, that of a pleasant anachronism.

Isaac S. Rochelle, a Kinston farmer and builder-contractor originally from Falling Creek, and his son-in-law, Liston Nash, built the house at 1302 Holman Street in the late 1930s. The exterior elements, however, from the steeply pitched standing-seam metal roof with two front-gable pedimented dormers to the front-gable porch entrance supported by square-in-section column posts, make the house appear to have been built at least ten to twenty years earlier. This is because Rochelle and Nash salvaged building materials and decorative elements from earlier houses that were to be razed and applied them to this house.

Other houses in this neighborhood also employed elements from earlier buildings. Isaac Rochelle's later house at 1305 Holman Street, a frame one-story gable-and-wing cottage, is also thought to have been built from salvaged material. Another example is at nearby 1306 Howard Street, where a wrought-iron balcony and supporting brackets that once graced a now-demolished house in central Kinston are positioned over the entrance to a 1950s double-pile two-story house.

15. Emma Webb Park
built circa 1935
100 block of East Highland Avenue, south side and 1300 block of North Queen Street, east side

In the 1936 *Kinston City Directory* is a photograph of the impressively large Kinston Municipal Swimming Pool, taken at the June 1935 dedication ceremonies for Emma Webb Park, named after a primary school teacher at the Lewis School. Emma Pittman Webb was the wife of George Webb, a Kinston buggy manufacturer. The pool and neighboring tennis courts were built between 1935 and 1936 at a cost of $50,000. The park was a hub for the growing middle-class neighborhood of Parkview in the 1940s and 1950s. It offered Friday night dances in the since-altered two-story side-gable dance hall building, constructed with Works Projects Administration assistance in the late 1930s. The wooden gazebo bandstand, with its slanting-lattice frieze and foundation sheathing, was also built in the late 1930s. Kinston tradition holds that sections of the park's walkways were fashioned from bricks that once paved Queen Street.

16. Kinston Apartments

built circa 1941

1300 block of McAdoo Street, east side

The five-building, two-story brick complex of Kinston Apartments is sited around a courtyard of tall oak trees on the east blockface of 1300 McAdoo Street, which faces Emma Webb Park. The apartment buildings, built by 1941, combine the exterior features of traditional row housing with Moderne-style treatments. The low hipped-roof buildings have rounded metal dormers, corner casement windows, and projecting hipped-roof two-story side extensions with large metal casement windows. The entrance to each apartment unit comprises a flat-roof one-story portico with latticed decoration, sheltering an Art Deco-style metal door, enclosed by a reeded surround, with three octagonal glass panes. Centered directly above the portico is a tall metal casement window with a decorative brick surround. The designer of these buildings has not been confirmed, but the overall style is very similar to the residential architecture of A. Mitchell Wooten (1905-1940), particularly that of the Caswell Center and the Mitchell Wooten and Simon Bright housing projects. The original residents of Kinston Apartments were white middle-class professionals who worked for local businesses. A sampling from the 1946 *Kinston City Directory* indicates that this residential complex was home to Walter C. Cox, manager of the Freezer Locker Plant; Doris Pratt, a cashier at L. Harvey and Sons retail store; and Ralph Shell, a podiatrist who resided in the apartments with his wife, Mildred.

17. Charles McDevett House

built circa 1941

400 Wilson Avenue

Wilson and Edgehill Avenues, just east of North Independence Avenue beyond the fringe of the Grainger Hill Historic District, were developed in the early 1940s as housing for white middle-class professionals and their families. Charles McDevett, then the managing editor of the *Kinston Free Press*, built his one-and-a-half story brick and frame late Tudor-Colonial Revival house in 1941, at the point formed by the convergence of Wilson and Edgehill Avenues. Probably one of residential Kinston's most pleasant sites, the point forming the house's front yard is landscaped with mature oak trees. The McDevett House, which has remained in the family, has an inset corner porch sheltering an entrance, at the side of a large, two-bay, two-story, brick front gable with a flush chimney.

Harvey School, 400 block Rhodes Avenue, built circa 1924, demolished 1990 (Postcard Collection of Sarah Pope, Goldsboro)

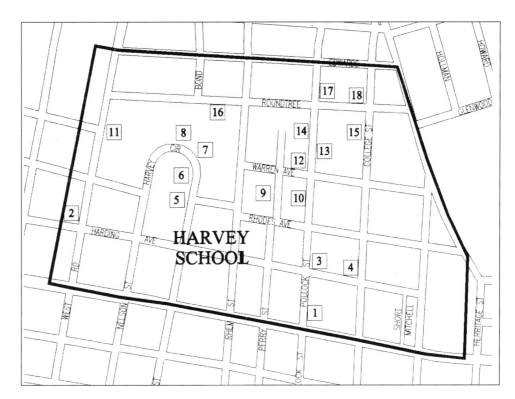

Harvey School Neighborhood

The Harvey School neighborhood covers about thirty blocks and is bounded by Vernon Avenue to the south, Rountree Street to the north, North Mitchell Street to the east, and North West Road to the west. The neighborhood, originally anchored by the Lemuel Harvey School, represents growth extending north from Mitchelltown and west from the Hill-Grainger neighborhood. The school, named for Kinston merchant Lemuel Harvey, operated on this site between 1924 and 1974. Harvey School, which constituted the entire 400 block of Rhodes Avenue, was demolished in 1990. Harvey Gardens, a park, now occupies the block. Small bungalows and the former Lenoir Memorial Hospital surround the park.

The Harvey School neighborhood is made up of three development areas: the Harvey School area, the Harvey Circle area, and the Rountree Avenue area. The latter two areas, Harvey Circle and Rountree Avenue, represent the extension of Kinston westward in the 1920s and 1930s. Harvey Circle, planned in the 1930s, is a semicircular road sited on a gentle rise beginning at Perry Park Drive and Nelson Street and ending to the east at Rhodes and Dewey Streets' intersection. Directly north of the Circle (in fact, sharing a common paved service alley between North Rhem Street and West Road) is Rountree Avenue. Although houses were built in the area as early as 1925, the bulk of Rountree Avenue's development took place fifteen to twenty years after that of Harvey Circle. The areas' differing concepts—Harvey Circle as an exclusive address with large lots and impressive mansions, and Rountree Avenue, with its smaller lots and middle-class housing, as part of 1940s and 1950s expansion from nearby Perry Park Drive and West Road—resulted in two variations on the early-to-mid-twentieth-century suburban development theme.

Harvey School was not the first school in northwest Kinston. The Rhodes Military Academy, a monumental three-story weatherboarded edifice with twin turrets, was built one block east of the future Harvey School between North College and North Mitchell Streets in 1902.[1] Its superintendent, Colonel W. H. Rhodes, ran the school with the objective of teaching "young people higher and better ideals of life and thus helping give to the State a citizenship with right conceptions of their civil and religious duties."[2] The school, a successful operation in 1906, ran into financial difficulties. By 1909, after the Rhodes Military Academy had closed, the monumental building was demolished. Today all that remains of the former academy is the name Rhodes Avenue.

Harvey School was a three-story Classical Revival brick building. Behind the impressive brick and stone facade were two rear wings and a small auditorium. The school could accommodate one thousand students, thereby eliminating the "doubling-up and short school hours" system that the Kinston City Schools had previously endured.[3]

The person most closely associated with Harvey School throughout most of its fifty-year existence was Miss Scotia Hobgood (1883-1957), principal from 1925 until 1957. She was the sister-in-law of G. W. Knott Sr., of the Knott Brothers Tobacco Warehouse, and had taught school in the Kinston area as early as 1903. Most of her twenty-two years before she worked at Harvey School were spent at the Lewis School, first as a teacher and later as assistant principal.[4]

The neighborhood that grew around the Harvey School was outside Kinston's city limits in 1925. The Sanborn Fire Insurance Maps show that thirty-seven new dwellings were built in the area immediately surrounding the school between 1925 and 1930. Besides the Harvey School neighborhood's large number of bungalow-style houses, there were Colonial Revival-style residences, one being Dr. Floyd P. Wooten's two-story house at 1114 North College Street. Many of the Harvey School neighborhood's inhabitants were businessmen. Courtney Mitchell, one of Adolphus Mitchell's sons, founded the Mitchell Oil Company in 1929 and by 1936 was living at 1115 North College Street. Alex Gross, who ran the Kinston Shirt Factory, resided at 811 North College Street.

The expansion of this area also brought Kinston's first public hospital. By 1920 Kinston discovered that its hospital was as crowded as its schools. The increasing population of both city and county was creating a strain on Parrott Memorial Hospital, and the area had another problem—new doctors coming to the county found themselves with no facility in which to practice, as Parrott was a private hospital with a closed staff. Memorial General Hospital opened in 1925 at the northeast corner of Rhodes Avenue and College Street, across from the Harvey School. The thirty-bed hospital was designed by L. L. Mallard, with T. A. Mitchell and Oscar Shackelford acting as the contractors. Memorial Hospital even had a small nursing school on the premises.[5] After the new Lenoir Memorial Hospital was built in 1973, the former hospital was rehabilitated as a retirement home.

By 1941 the neighborhood surrounding the Harvey School was largely complete, with block after block of Craftsman bungalows and some Colonial Revival-style houses. The neighborhood has changed little since then. One late-nineteenth-century farmhouse, the L. M. Broome House at 1002 North Perry Street, stands as a reminder of the farmland that this pleasant area used to contain.

The houses along Harvey Circle consist of nine Tudor and Colonial Revival dwellings built between 1935 and 1955, with two 1930s two-story houses that appear influenced equally by elements of the Tudor, Prairie, and Art Deco styles. All the houses have wide front lawns bordered with pine trees, oaks, dogwoods, ivy, and shrubbery.

The Harvey Circle area was initially planned by two early-twentieth-century Kinston businessmen—Ely J. Perry, whose house still stands at the southwest corner of Perry Park and West Road, and Charles Felix Harvey Sr. Both the Perry and Harvey families had their nineteenth-century farms in this area. Charles Felix Harvey was the son of Lemuel Harvey, one of Kinston's late-nineteenth-century magnates. Lemuel Harvey began operating in the 1860s as a merchant and insurance agent but then diversified into fertilizer and farming implement sales and cottonseed oil processing. A 1906 advertisement for the L. Harvey and Son company lists such diverse items for sale as crockery, dry goods, hats, shoes, cottonseed meal and hulls, buggies, wagons, and five different types of guano for cotton and tobacco cultivation. Harvey's Department Store and the L. Harvey and Son Oil Company are two surviving arms of this enterprising gentleman's businesses.

Charles Felix Harvey, in addition to running all of the family businesses, was a real estate developer. He had begun plans for an upscale development called West End (of which Harvey Circle was a part) just east of Perry Park Drive when he died in 1931. Development of Harvey Circle, already under construction, was frozen between 1931 and 1935 because of legal matters regarding Harvey's estate. During this time Harvey Circle's unpaved dirt road became, according to local residents, a "lover's lane."

A 1935 map of the Harvey Circle development, drawn by Kinston surveyor Meriwether Lewis from a 1931 survey, indicates that the Harvey Circle that exists today is only a portion of C. F. Harvey's intended plan. The actual drive was originally planned as an ellipse, with a small park and smaller terraced lots along two roads below the Circle—East and West Harvey Drive—leading from the prominent thoroughfare of Vernon Avenue.

In 1935 development recommenced on Harvey Circle, and the first house built was Alban Barrus's Kingsley Hall, a two-story frame and brick structure with an attached two-story Mount Vernon-inspired front porch. The two lots that the Barrus family bought cost $1,200. The Barrus deed gives further details about the Harvey Circle development. First comes the stipulation that "No residence erected on any lot in West End shall cost less than $2,500.00," clearly signaling the upscale white neighborhood that Harvey and his Circle's prospective residents envisioned. The deed goes on to describe further divisions of wealth and means: the materials and construction for buildings on the lower part of Harvey Circle were to cost not less than $4,500, but the houses at the upper part of the circle (one of which was the Barrus House) could cost not less than $6,500. Finally, there was the then-standard caveat for white residential neighborhoods, a covenant restricting residency to whites only, except for domestic servants who would live on the premises.

Ely J. Perry, an early-twentieth-century Kinston lawyer and developer, owned land west of Harvey Circle—in the vicinity of Walker Drive, West Road, Carey Road, and Perry Park Drive—together with his mother, the former Lillian Sutton, and his sisters Bliss (Mrs. John P. Carey) and Susie (Mrs. C. F. West). The C. F. West House, a large Colonial Revival brick residence at the southwest corner of West Road and Walker Drive, was one of the first houses built in the neighborhood (approximately 1927-1928), as was Ely Perry's smaller Colonial Revival house. R. Thornton Hood's two-story late Neoclassical Revival house at the northeast corner of West and Perry Park, built in 1928, was a source of civic pride to Kinstonians and was described, with the Barrus House (and Vernon Hall on Grainger Hill), as one of "Just three of the many beautiful homes that make Kinston so attractive" in a 1942 promotional brochure.

Below the Circle the Harvey Circle area, in its slope to Vernon Avenue, is a mix of 1920s to 1940s smaller brick and frame houses, particularly on West Road between Perry Park and Harding Street.

This appears to be partly an extension of the area that had developed around the Harvey School from 400 Rhodes Avenue. It is said that in the 1930s these houses were considered remote from the rest of Kinston. Supposedly the small 1932 Norman-Tudor Revival house at 1001 Harding Avenue was sold by its first owners because, after living there for two months, they decided that the house was too far out of town for their liking.

The lower ellipse of Harvey Circle and the two flanking roads of West and East Harvey Drive were never constructed. Instead, 800 West Vernon and Harding Avenues between Dewey and Nelson Streets contain houses, apartment buildings, and commercial structures built after 1950.

The Rountree family, along with the Crisp and Cowper families, owned the land now comprising the Rountree Avenue area just north of the Harvey School area; streets were being laid out or extended by 1925. Rountree Avenue was the site of the Bond-Rountree House, a two-story Greek Revival residence demolished in the early twentieth century. The three families began subdividing the area in 1921, after the Cowper-Hewitt House was moved to the Bond-Rountree site. The newly named streets of Jewell (changed to Rountree in the 1940s), Edwards, and Bond, as well as the extensions of older streets like Pollock, College, West, and Rhem, were created. One longtime resident of the Rountree neighborhood recalled that in the 1930s and 1940s the area was still largely farmland, and that the roads were unpaved into the 1950s. By 1960 the Rountree Avenue neighborhood was completed.

The oldest Rountree Avenue houses were built in the popular 1920s and 1930s Colonial and Tudor Revival styles and are the most highly finished in the neighborhood. Dwellings on Edwards, Bond, the south side of West Highland Avenue, and the intersecting areas of College, Rhem, Herritage, and Pollock are much more modest and are mostly 1940s to 1960s Minimal Traditional cottages and ranches, with some attractive late-1930s and 1940s Tudor Revival brick and frame houses.

This area was settled by many prominent citizens, including tobacconists like Walter C. Jones, whose two-story Colonial Revival house at Rountree Avenue and North Pollock Street was designed by architect A. Mitchell Wooten in the 1930s. Oscar Shackelford, a local builder who contributed significantly to building in Kinston in the 1920s and 1930s, lived at 1108 North Pollock Street in, not surprisingly, a picturesquely eclectic Colonial Revival cottage of his own design. Other residents included long-established Kinston families like the Parrotts, Hodgeses, and Cowpers, and many Kinston families who moved from earlier houses in East Kinston and Mitchelltown.

Other blocks in the Rountree area have buildings with different styles and functions. For example, 1306 North Herritage Street is a 1950s International Style one-story doctor's clinic, where R. T. Hood Jr. had his pediatrics practice. On the same block are a 1920s-1930s front-gable Craftsman bungalow and a two-and-a-half-story late-1920s Colonial Revival house. 1300 North Pollock Street has a similar mix of Craftsman, Minimal Traditional, and ranch housing, mostly rented. Originally this block was the site of a 1930s farm and horse paddock.

The duplex development on the 1300s block of North College and North Herritage Streets recalls the rental housing built for returning World War II veterans in many small cities in the late 1940s. The duplexes' minimal exterior decoration and compact form are in keeping with the Federal Housing Administration's 1940s promotion of simple, economical dwelling units—a contrast to the more elaborate residences on Rountree Avenue and Pollock and College Streets. By 1953 the occupants of these duplexes were families employed by Dupont, Kinston Heating and Plumbing, a local radio station, and Thompson Hosiery.

Notes

1. *Heritage of Lenoir County*, 119.
2. *Kinston Free Press*, 1906 Industrial Issue, 55.
3. *Kinston Daily Free Press*, September 8, 1924.
4. *Heritage of Lenoir County*, 262.
5. *Heritage of Lenoir County*, 62.

1. Bungalows
built circa 1925
803-809 North Pollock Street

Along the 800 block of North Pollock Street are four intact and well-detailed examples of bungalow-style dwellings lining the tidy street. Period exterior details of the houses include tapered and battered exterior end chimneys rising through the roofs' eavelines, bracketed eaves and exposed rafters, front-gable and shed-roof engaged porches, and wooden posts over brick piers as porch supports. 803 North Pollock Street's corner piers and front gable are both covered by wooden shingles, and there is a projecting bay window, supported by brackets, in the front gable. The bungalow also has an unusual pierced-slat balustrade.

2. Hines-Spence House
built circa 1932
900 West Road

At the northwest corner of West Road and Harding Avenue is the Hines-Spence House, a brick one-story cross-wing Jacobean Revival dwelling with a narrow, steep shingled roof. The front facade has original mullioned casement windows and a projecting small, round, one-story turret, also shingled and with mullioned casement windows. The turret, which houses the breakfast room, has been cited as a Norman Revival influence.

Oscar Shackelford built the house for William Hines as speculative housing in 1932. The first occupants reportedly lived there for only three months before moving closer to downtown Kinston. Willis Hines and his family then owned the house for twenty years, after which it was bought by the Spence family.

The exterior of the house has many delightful decorative features, such as the paneled Tudor-style brick chimney stack at the cross wing, and the shed door hood from which hang two lanterns. There are also the brass medieval-style door escutcheons and the landscaped front yard, which has been developed by Mrs. Marvin Spence over the years.

3. House
built circa 1925
413 Harding Avenue

A clipped-gable roof forms the side gable of this one-story three-bay frame cottage. A projecting center cantilevered roof, between paired windows at each end, forms the front porch and is semienclosed by decorative trellis posts. There is a one-room outbuilding at the side yard, which is covered by German siding and has a shed-roof porch and a raised brick foundation.

4. Bungalow
built circa 1925
900 North College Street

At 900 North College Street a large cross gable extends to shelter the full three-bay facade of this neatly detailed frame one-and-a-half-story bungalow. The porch, which shelters two large nine-over-one triple windows flanking a handsome entrance with sidelights and transom, is supported by battered square columns. The front gable is enlivened by a paired nine-over-one double-hung sash window, comparable to the ones beneath the porch.

5. The Reverend Jack R. Rountree House
built circa 1937
1000 Harvey Circle

Like Jonas Weiland's former home at 1006 Harvey Circle, the Rountree House was designed by A. Mitchell Wooten in the mid-to-late 1930s. Both houses combine classical and traditional elements with Art Deco and other early-twentieth-century innovations, creating exceptional buildings that stand apart from the neighboring Tudor and Colonial/Georgian Revival residences. The form of the two-story brick Rountree house, with its asymmetrical board-and-batten-covered second story and low-hipped roof with overhanging eaves, looks back to the form of Prairie houses and ahead to the popular split-level ranch housing of the 1960s and 1970s. The second story's two narrow paired four-light casement windows are reminiscent of the Craftsman style yet are not dissonant with the first story's conventional eight-over-eight double-hung sash windows. Significant features of the house's exterior include the interplay of the alternating hipped roofline, the recessed front porch sheltering a simple transomed entrance, and the glass-block solarium window and a double-leaf door at the back.

Jack R. Rountree, a descendant of Kinston's prominent Rountree family, was an Episcopal minister who decided to build his own house instead of living in Saint Mary's Rectory. According to surviving documentation, Rountree gave Wooten free rein to design his house as the architect wished. However, Rountree played a significant role in the design of the house, from the upstairs library's restrained modern interior treatment to the dining room, whose window faced a semicircular outside fountain with a gargoyle "to be furnished by J. R. Rountree" (the gargoyle is no longer there). Of particular beauty is the center-hall staircase with its Chinese Chippendale fret design.

6. Edwin Oettinger House
built circa 1935
1002 Harvey Circle

Edwin Oettinger's substantial two-story dappled-brick Tudor-style house, built between 1935 and 1936, has been attributed to Charles Gillett of Greensboro. Oettinger's former house sits at the top of the south side of Harvey Circle below Kingsley Hall and is landscaped with ivy, dogwoods, pines, and shrubbery, which further create the ambiance of a Tudor grange. The front facade is enlivened by stuccoed front-gable dormers, a large front-gable two-story cross wing, and, against the cross wing, a sloping front-gable entrance with half-timbering and stucco infill. At the east end of the long front elevation is a side-gabled screened porch. According to older residents, Edwin Oettinger installed the first modern kitchen in Kinston here. The kitchen, designed by General Electric, was briefly on public display and featured wooden and stainless steel counters, a stainless steel sink, and an electric dishwasher and disposal. This combination of revived Tudor and modern convenience was the exception, not the rule, for most 1930s Kinston residences.

7. Brooks-Kanter House

built circa 1936
1007 Harvey Circle

Oettinger-King House

built circa 1937
1005 Harvey Circle

The two brick two-story Georgian Revival side-gable houses at 1007 and 1005 Harvey Circle are excellent examples of A. Mitchell Wooten's understanding of classical ornamentation and the Georgian format, as well as his translation of these precepts into "modern" 1930s dwellings. The Brooks-Kanter House was built for Craven S. Brooks, who was secretary-treasurer of his family's leaf tobacco business, in 1936. Surviving blueprints confirm Wooten's decorative signature throughout the house, from the hipped-roof Regency Revival-style side porch supported by latticed posts and spandrels and the impressive flat-pedimented tripartite front entrance to interior treatments such as the living room mantelpiece's crosset-corner opening and bolection-molding frieze centered by a reeded tablet. The recessed one-and-a-half-story side extension is semivisible because of the mature trees at the crest of the slope on which the house stands. Gerald and Sharon Kanter bought the house from the Brooks family in the 1970s.

Leonard Oettinger of the Oettinger Brothers Furniture Company, established in 1872, also commissioned Wooten to design his house, a brick two-story,

three-bay, side-gable building with flanking side extensions. Direct access to the center entrance, which has a four-light transom and is enclosed by a rounded-pediment with fluted pilasters, is screened by a boxwood hedge, which partly conceals a wrought-iron curved rail at each side. Exterior decoration at the front facade features includes a wide scalloped cornice, paneled aprons beneath the first story's eight-over-eight windows, and rounded dormer windows at a one-and-a-half-story side extension, the upper floor of which was once a servant's room. The other side extension is a solarium that, though it has a more modern treatment (minimal paneling and open glass areas), fits in with the overall design of the house.

8. Kingsley Hall (Alban K. Barrus Sr. House)

built circa 1936
1009 Harvey Circle

The brick two-story five-bay reinterpretation of Mount Vernon that crowns the slope just above Harvey Circle was built for Alban K. Barrus Sr., the owner of a construction business in Kinston, between 1934 and 1936. Charles Gillett of Greensboro is the attributed architect of the former Barrus House, or (as the existing plate on the brick driveway gate is inscribed) Kingsley Hall.

Barrus's residence was one of the first built in Harvey Circle and, with its two-story, full-facade, flat-roofed portico surmounted by a sheaf-of-wheat balustrade, the most visually imposing. The original landscaping of the wide lawn with magnolias and other foliage behind the house and of the property's entrance has remained intact, increasing the visual grandeur of Kingsley Hall. The house was featured in a 1942 brochure as one of the grandest residences in Kinston. The rounded-pediment centered entrance shown in the 1942 photograph was replaced by John J. Rowland in 1948 with a wider classical entrance with overlapping Ionic pilasters surmounted by a modillioned, tripartite, flat pediment. The front-gable brick garage and connecting arcade are reminiscent of A. Mitchell Wooten's more modernistic traditional designs, but no attribution has been established. Wooten himself did not get the commission for Kingsley Hall, but

William A. Coleman, Wooten's draftsman and Barrus's nephew, apparently was involved in the project. Coleman became a prominent Kinston architect in the 1950s and 1960s.

9. L. M. Broome House
built circa 1890
1002 North Perry Street

The frame two-story Victorian house sheltered by trees and a tall wooden fence was the main dwelling for the L. M. Broome estate, a large late-nineteenth-century farm. In the 1940s and 1950s the former farmhouse was used by the Holy Trinity School, a Catholic kindergarten and grammar school. The house was later owned and occupied by J. P. Strother and his family. The Broome House has, despite alterations, retained its original wood flooring and its original center-hall plan with one-story front bay, in addition to the enclosed side kitchen extension. Columns, brackets, and balustrades salvaged from homes being razed were incorporated into this residence. Consequently the house is a virtual museum of Kinston's decorative heritage.

10. Farmer House
built circa 1920
1010 North Pollock Street

Located in a neighborhood consisting predominantly of bungalows, the frame two-story front-gable house was one of the first built in this area, well before there was a Harvey School. The well-maintained three-bay dwelling has its original bracketed front gable and three-light gable window, four-over-one double-hung sash windows, and one-story rear kitchen ell. The attached hipped-roof, full-facade front porch is supported by square-in-section classical columns.

11. A. Mitchell Wooten House
built circa 1939
1003 West Road

A. Mitchell Wooten's brick one-story residence, which he described as "Nassau Colonial" was his one hundredth commission and one of the last buildings he designed. It is an elegant example of an Art Deco- and Moderne-styled 1930s ranch house, one of very few such examples in eastern North Carolina and certainly the most exceptional one in Kinston. It is especially unique because, apart from replacement wall coverings, the house has been virtually unchanged since its inception. Wooten was one of the very few trained native architects working in eastern North Carolina during the 1930s. His Art Moderne and Colonial Revival-styled buildings are comparable to those designed by the Benton and Benton firm in Wilson, North Carolina.

1003 West Road's front facade behind a patterned, low, brick and steel fence designed by Wooten, frames the almost inscrutable front facade. From the north end of the facade projects a front-gable extension with its flush exterior end chimney, positioned beside a recessed side-lighted entrance with its reeded wooden surround. The front facade windows make an asymmetrically harmonious pattern of double-hung six-over-six sash windows alternating with a brick grille window and an octagonal window with a reeded surround. The white exterior paint (indicated in Wooten's sketches) emphasizes the massing of the house and the variegated openings; such detail would have been lost with unpainted brick.

Inside 1003 West Road the elegantly spare front hall, its main decorative finish being reeded doorway surrounds with Greek key corner blocks (in addition to the recently restored black-and-white 1930s linoleum tile floor), wraps around to a corridor—the solarium/atrium, which is lit by a band of metal casement windows and glass doors. The solarium leads to a small flagstone courtyard, the centerpiece of which is a granite fountain designed by Wooten, which is situated within a small curvilinear parterrelike granite border.

With the hall and solarium Wooten clearly anticipated a more casual, naturally ventilated, and light-filled interior than was the norm in 1930s Kinston. Nevertheless, 1003 West Road is as structured as any Georgian-style dwelling, with the solarium-great hall as the link between the sleeping and living quarters of the house. The north wing of the house below the living room is divided into spaces for a dining room, a kitchen and a service wing. At the northwest corner of the front yard the original front gate "for servants" (as indicated in the building specifications) is still in place, as is part of the original walkway. The south wing of the house—and the rooms on the east side off the solarium—include a bath, bedrooms, and a small room that was Wooten's study.

Wooten's presentation drawings for the house indicate that landscaping was to be restrained so as not to obscure the form of the house. A small boxwood hedge was suggested to run along the south side of the driveway. Otherwise, landscaping is limited to small shrubbery around the house's front facade and, at the back, small shrubs bordering the driveway, the attached garage, and the north wall of the courtyard.

1003 West Road and 1000 Harvey Circle (designed in the late 1930s for the Reverend Jack Rountree, who had married Mitchell Wooten's aunt, Clara Wooten) probably best reflect Wooten's own personal tastes, undiluted by any patron's preferences. Both houses, with their restrained decorative details and elegant Moderne form, integrate private exterior courtyards with interior plans in the manner of the California bungalow ranches designed by the well-known architectural firm of Greene and Greene.

[Information in this entry was drawn from the private papers of A. Mitchell Wooten, in the collection of Verna Wooten Ewell, Kinston, North Carolina; and from interviews with Verna Wooten Ewell and Frances Langrall (A. Mitchell Wooten's secretary), conducted by Penne Smith in 1994.]

12. Frank Marston House
built circa 1922
1100 North Pollock Street

One of the earlier homes in the Harvey School neighborhood is the frame one-and-a-half-story Craftsman-style house at 1100 North Pollock Street, with its attached shed-roof bungalow-style front porch. Over the porch is a large shed dormer with two paired six-over-one double-hung sash windows. The bungalow-style porch is supported by brick piers and shelters two three-part windows flanking the front door. Frank Marston, who operated Marston's Drug Store, formerly resided in this house.

13. House
built circa 1925
1105 North Pollock Street

1105 North Pollock Street is another good example of the Craftsman houses that dominate this neighborhood. It has a front clipped-gable dormer bay incorporating the entrance, whose front door is sheltered by a small trellised portico. According to local sources this house reportedly had the first metal lath used to hold plaster in Kinston. The house, screened by trees and a picket fence, has multipaned paired windows and a conservatory.

14. Oscar Shackelford House
built circa 1928
1108 North Pollock Street

The one house in the Rountree neighborhood definitely built before 1930 is Oscar Shackelford's former home at 1108 North Pollock Street. The one-and-a-half-story house, of ribbon brick and frame, is an elegantly understated combination of Colonial Revival and Craftsman exterior elements. The second story's front-gable shed dormer is flush with the first floor of the house, from which projects a pedimented and enclosed portico/vestibule entrance. The portico has paneling and a dentilled frieze over the sidelighted front door. The enclosed solarium at the south elevation of the house also has a pedimented side gable and denticulation. Brick decoration at the base of the house suggests a water table, a classical-inspired feature of eighteenth- and early- to mid-nineteenth-century residences. Shackelford (1889-1954), a major early-twentieth-century Kinston builder, began his career with T. A. Mitchell, a general contractor, and then went on to take a hand in many of Kinston's most significant twentieth-century buildings, particularly the Hines House on North Queen Street and the Hines-Spence House at 1001 Harding Avenue.

15. Dr. F. P. Wooten House

circa 1925
1114 North College Street

One of the earlier Colonial Revival-style residences in the Harvey School neighborhood is the frame two-story, five-bay house built for Dr. F. P. Wooten in the 1920s. The Wooten House carries the traditional side-gable roof, exterior end chimney, and shuttered six-over-six double-hung sash windows. The house also has a pent roof separating the first and second floors, creating a gambrel-roof profile at the side elevations. The front elevation is centered by a front-gable portico that shelters an elegant fanlight-transomed entrance. There are two flanking small one-story side extensions, and the house is framed by mature trees at the edge of the front lawn.

16. "Starter" Garage Houses

built circa 1946
805 and 810 Rountree Avenue

805 Roundtree Avenue

For some post-World War II families the "starter" garage, a two-story hipped-roof garage apartment later appended to a house and/or enclosed with extensions, was a popular way to build a new home in stages. The final result could take a complex form, such as a split-level ranch; in other cases, the starter garage merely enclosed the garage bays or remained a garage apartment. On Rountree Avenue, there are four such houses—709, 805, 810, and 908 Rountree—in varying stages of development. 805 and 810 Rountree Avenue are the two strongest examples, for one has changed little since it was built, while the other has undergone substantial additions but has the format of the original house still visible.

The core of 805 Rountree Avenue, a two-story, two-bay hipped-roof garage apartment, was built in 1947 for Frances and Edward Phillips. In the 1950s a one-story side extension and front porch were added, and the garage was enclosed. There were later extensions at the back of the house. The former garage's original second bay is visible but has a door and picture window incorporated under a pagoda-shaped copper awning. The original paved driveway remains. Frances Phillips's sister, Dr. Rose Pully, later inherited the house.

Across the street from this "mature" starter garage house is 810 Rountree Avenue, next to Saint Mary's Episcopal Church. The house at that location was built for Benjamin Roark, a Kinston jeweler, in 1946. Like the Phillips House, the Roark House is located farther from the street than most of the Rountree Avenue houses. Roark and his family moved into this two-story hipped-roof house with the intent, no doubt, of eventually adding to the house and enclosing the downstairs garage bay. The garage was eventually enclosed and has a center entrance flanked by two shuttered double-hung sash windows. However, possibly because of Roark's untimely death soon after he moved into the house, extensions were added. For students of postwar housing, these two buildings provide excellent examples of the starter garage house.

17. Tyler-Gurley-Suddreth House
built circa 1937
605 Rountree Avenue

18. Rountree-Cowper-Hewitt House
built circa 1925
1200 North College Street

The brick one-and-a-half-story Colonial Revival side-gable house at 605 Rountree Avenue, was built in 1937 by Oscar Shackelford, a prominent local builder who had been Kinston's premier local "architect" until A. Mitchell Wooten set up his architectural practice in 1934. The house, originally owned by John Tyler, manager of the Kinston Belk-Tyler clothing store, was later owned by Foster Gurley, who operated Kinston's Pontiac dealership in the 1940s, and then by the Suddreth family. 605 Rountree Avenue has unusual exterior decoration, such as the enclosed front-gable portico entrance with six-over-six double-hung sash windows at each side of the vestibule, corner quoins, and a plaster urn relief surmounting the three-part pilastered doorway. The first-floor windows are unusually large, with twelve-over-twelve double-hung sash; the size and number of panes may be intended to imitate the Williamsburg Colonial Revival style. The two-bay garage side extension, with two front-gable pedimented dormers like the main block of the house, has arched paneled wooden bays. There is also a screened side porch. The classical details of the house and its manicured shrubbery and mature trees complete the impression of the gracious appropriations Shackelford made from the Georgian style.

This brick two-story side-gable mansion built for Kinston lawyer G. V. Cowper stands on the site of the Bond-Rountree House, a two-story frame Greek Revival residence that was demolished in the early twentieth century. The Rountree family originally owned the surrounding land, which has since been developed into suburban residences. Cowper's impressive new house was moved to the center of the lot when North College, Rountree, and Bond Streets were cut through the original front yard in the 1930s. The house is one of Kinston's grandest and most intact 1920s Colonial Revival residences. Its enclosed front-gable portico, one-story porch side extensions, and flush end chimneys decorated by corbel tables, are comparable to features of other high-style Colonial Revival residences being built throughout the country at this time. In 1950 the Hewitt family bought the house.

200 block of West Lenoir Street, north side, Mitchelltown.

Mitchelltown

Mitchelltown, a tree-lined neighborhood along the north side of Atlantic Avenue, offers a range of late-nineteenth-century and early-twentieth-century architectural styles within a setting of well-tended front lawns and quiet residential streets. Atlantic Avenue's railroad tracks, still in place, separate the north part of Mitchelltown from its smaller southern half along Mitchell and West Blount Streets. Of Kinston's surviving late-nineteenth-century neighborhoods, the twenty-odd blocks of Mitchelltown comprise the most intact collection of Victorian houses, as well as excellent examples of Classical Revival, Colonial Revival, and Craftsman-style dwellings of the early twentieth century. The neighborhood comprises the Mitchelltown Historic District, listed in the National Register of Historic Places in 1989. The following overview and entries are edited from Allison Black's nomination, with additional research by Penne Smith.

Set just two blocks west of Queen Street, Mitchelltown was planned as a convenient retreat for Kinston's middle class, and wealthier citizens, its grid street plan constituting an extension of the existing town streets. The Knott family of Mitchelltown, for example, established its tobacco warehouse in 1902 at McLewean and East Washington Streets, a short distance east. Eventually Mitchelltown and the other early residential developments superseded the residential areas at the center of town as the most desirable places to live. In 1925 Henry B. W. Canady could stand on the front porch of his massive bungalow at 508 Mitchell Street and see the back of his father's 1880s Italianate frame mansion at 600 North Queen Street, an address that found itself in the middle of Kinston's commercial center. By 1930 Mitchelltown's varied houses and streets were so enmeshed with the town that it must have been difficult for some residents to recall that their verdant neighborhood had been farmland less than fifty years before.

Mitchelltown, developed primarily between 1885 and 1930, embodies a significant aspect of Kinston's history, for it—like the Trianon and Grainger Hill Districts—represents the rise of late-nineteenth-century middle-income residential neighborhoods throughout small southern towns and cities. After the Civil War Kinston's population, commercial establishments, and industry increased. Consequently, building was intensive to accommodate the new citizens. A brief 1890s editorial stated, "There are a huge number of dwelling houses, mostly small ones, in course of erection in Kinston. And yet the demand is not supplied."[1] Prosperity and its rewards created a broad middle class, whose members wanted to build new houses in the popular styles touted by periodicals and to live more comfortably than had their parents.

The neighborhood known today as Mitchelltown was part of a two-hundred-acre tract, north of the Neuse River and northwest of Kinston proper, owned by the Parrott family by the late nineteenth century. Jacob F. Parrott, a farmer who also operated a sawmill just west of Herritage Street on the Neuse River, sold the tract to Adolphus Mitchell, a Granville County native, in 1882. Mitchell had established a livery business in Kinston by 1884; in 1891 Mitchell's Livery was in J. Lassiter's former stables at 9 North Queen Street.[2] In 1884, soon after his first residence burned, Mitchell built a large three-story Queen Anne-style frame house at the southeast corner of the present neighborhood at the corner of Atlantic Avenue and Mitchell Street, above the Atlantic and North Carolina Railroad tracks. Ten years later, around 1895, Mitchell ceased large-scale farming of the former Parrott lands and began selling the farmland as lots in response to Kinston's influx of new citizens. The first lots sold bordered the 1890s town limits (now, roughly, in the 400 block of Mitchell Street and the 200 block of West Peyton Avenue). Deeds of the period referred to the area as "Mitchell town."

Mitchelltown's residents were prominent in Kinston's burgeoning tobacco industry and included G. W. Knott (of first the Eagle Warehouse and then Knott Brothers Warehouse) and Luther P. Tapp, who, after working for Jesse Grainger, established his own tobacco warehouse in 1923 on the northwest corner of Herritage and West King Streets.[3] Tapp's grand Neoclassical Revival residence at 611 Mitchell Street, circa 1916, is a superb example of that style's combination of spacious light-filled rooms and elegant classical-inspired details. Mitchelltown also had merchants, including Errol P. Dixon, who managed his family's hardware business at 217 North Queen Street and built his one-story Queen Anne cottage at 311 West Washington Avenue in 1904. Dal Wooten, who served as Kinston's mayor and a Lenoir County sheriff, lived in the frame two-story early Classical Revival house at 412 Mitchell Street. Mitchelltown was also home to doctors, industrialists, and ministers.

Adolphus Mitchell deeded lots to his three oldest children. Wayne A. Mitchell, the eldest son and a lawyer, built a house on the northwest corner of College Street and Atlantic Avenue. The two oldest daughters, Wita and Bessie, received lots when they married. Wita, who married Harry C. Wooten, Dal Wooten's nephew, was the mother of Adolphus Mitchell Wooten (1905-1940), a locally prominent architect. The Wootens' house, now demolished, was at 306 Atlantic Avenue.[4] Wayne Mitchell, executor for his father's estate, continued selling lots in the Mitchelltown area between 1906 and 1913.

In 1913 the Mitchell family sold the remainder of their undeveloped Mitchelltown property to Atlantic Coast Realty Company; most of this land was located west of College Street, where Pollock, Rhem, and Perry Streets now exist. The Atlantic Coast Realty Company, after dividing the parcel of land into more-uniform lots, made eighteen sales in Mitchelltown in 1913 and twenty-four in 1914, after which sales gradually declined.

The Mitchells and Atlantic Coast Realty were not the only developers of Mitchelltown. J. F. (Jack) Parrott and his siblings, Dan, Willis, and Hattie Parrott, were involved in speculative housing along the 200 block of West Lenoir Avenue and South Mitchell Street, particularly two-story frame side-hall-plan houses ideal for young families.

Mitchelltown's buildings were primarily residential. There was, however, the early-twentieth-century Harper's Grocery at 412 Atlantic Avenue, which was operated by Mrs. Claudia Harper in the 1930s.[5] Most schoolchildren in Mitchelltown attended the Harvey School, located just north of Vernon Avenue.[6] There were only two churches in Mitchelltown—Holy Trinity Catholic Church, built in 1921, and the circa-1935 First Presbyterian Church (now the First Free Will Baptist Church of Kinston). In recent years some Mitchelltown residences have been rehabilitated into restaurants and other businesses. But the heart of Mitchelltown remains little changed from the quiet neighborhood of the 1920s and 1930s.

Notes

1. *Kinston Daily Free Press*, Aug. 17, 1898.
2. *Branson's Business Directory, 1884*, 416; Sanborn Fire Insurance Map, 1891.
3. Johnson and Holloman, *Story of Kinston and Lenoir County*, 307; Sanborn Fire Insurance Map, 1930.
4. *Kinston City Directory*, 1920, 1936.
5. *Kinston City Directory*, 1936. Dreyer, *Kinston's Architecture*, 147.
6. Dr. Rose Pully, interview by Penne Smith, Kinston, November 1994.

1. Houses
built circa 1905
304-312 West Blount Street

The 300 block of West Blount Street contains frame one-story single- and double-front-gable dwellings. These houses, possibly a speculative development at the turn of the twentieth century, were designed for middle-class families. The gable fronts and the variety of sawnwork exterior decoration on the houses, in addition to the small landscaped front yards and mature trees lining the street, give the streetscape an attractive and cohesive quality. One longtime resident was Joseph F. Ballard, who lived at 308 West Blount Street between 1908 and 1936. Ballard was the foreman at the *Kinston Free Press*. Other early-twentieth-century residents included Macon Pully, who ran Pully's Barbecue with his mother, Inez Pully, and brother between 1929 and 1962. Pully was living at 306 West Blount Street in 1936.

2. Trippe-Whitaker House
built circa 1901
410 Mitchell Street

Guy Trippe, a traveling salesman, was living in this two-story late Queen Anne house between 1902 and 1909. This house, however, is best known for having been the home of Dr. F. Stanley Whitaker, a Kinston physician, between 1916 and 1928. By 1936 Mrs. Florence Humphrey was living at 410 Mitchell Street and running part of it as a boardinghouse.

The gable-and-wing-plan front of the Trippe-Whitaker House incorporates an additional bay beyond the two-story three-sided projecting gable bay and a wide one-story rear ell, also with a three-sided bay window at its south elevation. The large wraparound front porch, supported by turned posts with sawnwork brackets, shelters the transomed center-hall entrance, which has two round-arched vestibule windows on either side. The delicate gable vergeboard has survived, as well as the sawnwork brackets at the gabled bays' cutaway corners.

3. Dal F. Wooten House
built circa 1901
412 Mitchell Street

The residence of Dal F. Wooten is a frame two-story side-gable building with a center projecting front gable pierced by a fanlight ventilator and, at the second story, a tripartite Craftsman-style two-over-one and three-over-one double-hung sash window. A wraparound hipped-roof porch supported by paneled square posts over brick piers shelters both the entrance, with its multi-paned transom and sidelights, and a transomed side entrance. The center staircase, with its large newel post and turned rails, has remained in place, but the center hall of the house has been substantially altered and the original mantelpieces have been removed. Dal Wooten, in addition to being an early-twentieth-century mayor of Kinston, was president of the First National Bank of Kinston, a former Lenoir County sheriff, and a director of a number of Kinston enterprises including the Caswell Training School, the Hotel Kinston, and the Caswell Cotton Mill.

4. Harper's Grocery

built circa 1915
412 Atlantic Avenue

The former Harper's Grocery at 412 Atlantic Avenue, a small frame three-bay structure with a shed-roof porch that once extended over the sidewalk, was moved to a site in the backyard of 419 South Pollock Street. The small, quaint grocery that served the Mitchelltown neighborhood for decades was operated by George Green Harper. It is one of only a few early-twentieth-century neighborhood stores left in Kinston. The unchanged store has vertical tongue-and-groove exterior walls, two four-over-one double-hung sash windows, a small "false front," and a large double-door entrance.

5. Adolphus Mitchell House

built circa 1885; moved and remodeled circa 1940
307 West Atlantic Avenue

Adolphus Mitchell, the livery stable owner who developed Mitchelltown into a prosperous middle-class and upper-middle-class suburb, built this large, frame, two-story, hipped-roof Queen Anne-style dwelling in 1885. Apart from the projecting pedimented cross-gable bays, the large transomed entrance with sidelights, and the multipaned upper sash windows, there is little decorative about the exterior. There are, however, prominent shingled gables that curve inward at the unusual wide four-

over-one gable windows. Before 1930 the Mitchell House had a wide porch that wrapped around its front and north elevations, with a corner gazebo. The house was remodeled between 1930 and 1950; at that time, the entrance was revised and a one-story pedimented portico supported by square-section classical posts was added. The Mitchell House was also moved forty-five degrees to its current site in the 1940s, changing its siting so that the front did not face the railroad but, rather, the eastern edge of Mitchelltown and the commercial district.

6. H. B. W. Canady House

built circa 1923
508 Mitchell Street

On the west side of 500 Mitchell Street, within viewing distance of B. W. Canady's two-story Italianate-style residence at 600 North Queen Street, is a frame one-and-a-half-story Craftsman bungalow built for Canady's son, Henry Burwell Westbrook Canady (1898-1963), in 1923. The H. B. W. Canady House is as impressive as the Queen Street residence, built nearly forty years earlier. The first visual impression of 508 Mitchell Street is of the massive full-facade one-story bungalow porch, its low front-gable roof decorated with nonfunctional exposed rafters at its tympanum and supported by brackets and large battered fieldstone piers. The porch extends to a porte cochere, also supported by fieldstone piers, with an overhead pergola. Over the porch is a large front-gable shed-roof dormer, replete with exposed rafters, brackets, and a large four-part Craftsman-style window sheltered by a shed hood. Two interior chimneys are of fieldstone with cement coping. The house's exterior was restored in the early 1990s, but some mysteries persist. At the north elevation of the house facing West Washington Street are fieldstone steps presently leading nowhere; it is possible that originally there was either a service entrance here or a service bay where groceries were regularly left for the Canady family. Henry Burwell Westbrook Canady supervised the family's farms and, later in his life, the B. W. Canady and Son store, upon the retirement of his brother, James Herman Canady, after the Second World War.

7. Wayne A. Mitchell House
built circa 1905
500 College Street

Wayne A. Mitchell, a son of Adolphus Mitchell and a director of the Atlantic and North Carolina Railroad, was the first resident of this massive frame two-and-a-half-story Colonial Revival-influenced dwelling. The main block of the house is topped by a high-hipped roof, which carries pedimented dormers on the north and front elevations and joins the two-story front-gabled rear ell (there is also a one-story rear extension), which has a front-gable dormer at its south elevation. All dormers have pebbledash infill within their tympana. The Mitchell House's exterior has other intact elements, such as patterned shingles at the second story of the main block; a two-story pedimented circular bay projection at the south elevation, which has a band of four paired mullioned casement windows at each story; and large plate-glass sash windows (the living room window has an overhead transom) on either side of the sidelighted front entrance. The low-hipped-roof front porch, which is raised, has a dentil cornice and is supported by tapered square columns over posts.

8. William Allen Knott House
built circa 1915
508 College Street

William Allen Knott, a Knott Brothers partner, lived in this frame two-story Classical Revival-style house. Bridging the Queen Anne and Colonial Revival styles, this house combines projecting front-gable bays extending from a high-hipped roof (whose finial is intact) and irregularly placed windows with pedimented gables, plain eaves, and cornices. The simple attached wraparound front porch has a pedimented entry and corner gazebo supported by Tuscan posts over brick piers. The entrance has a transom, and sidelights above paneled aprons. William Allen Knott's house stood across the street from 310 West Washington Street, where his brother, George, lived. The Knott brothers built, owned, and operated Knott Brothers Tobacco Warehouse downtown. They moved to Kinston during the 1890s from the "Old Belt" of Granville County. According to family history the two men discussed business and events of the day from their respective porches on summer evenings.

9. George Knott House
built circa 1923
310 West Washington Street

This brick two-story Colonial Revival residence was built for George Knott, a partner in the Knott Brothers Tobacco Warehouse, around 1923. At the time it was built, George Knott's house offered a striking contrast to the earlier Victorian houses in Mitchelltown surrounding it. Characteristically Colonial Revival features of the house include the side-gable roof, with its wide-modillioned eaves and cornice. Modest yet stylish is the front-gable portico supported by Tuscan posts. The flanking one-story wings, a screen porch and a solarium, were a common feature of Colonial and Georgian Revival houses between the 1920s and 1950s. More 1920s-type features of the house include the stretcher-bond flat arches over the windows and the detailed shoulders of the nearly recessed single-shoulder exterior end chimney.

10. Moore-Edwards House
built circa 1905
600 Mitchell Street

Built for Needham Moore, production manager for the Lenoir Oil and Ice Company, this one-and-a-half-story house typifies the modestly elegant turn-of-the-twentieth-century eastern North Carolina town house. The Moore-Edwards House, like many earlier Mitchelltown residences, has elements of both the Victorian and Neoclassical Revival styles. The crest finials crowning the high-hipped roof have survived; below are pedimented projecting gables over a spacious wraparound porch, decorated by Tuscan columns and a turned-rail balustrade. The three-sided center entrance has a transom and is flanked by small rounded-arch vestibule windows. Eugene Edwards, the proprietor of Edwards' Men's Clothing at 109 North Queen Street, owned this house after Moore.

11. James F. (Jack) Parrott House
built circa 1908
500 Pollock Street

The frame two-and-a-half-story Colonial Revival residence at 500 Pollock Street, with the unusual juxtaposition of a hipped-roof main block with a front-gable gambrel roofline at the Pollock Street elevation, was built for James F. (Jack) Parrott, an early-twentieth-century Kinston insurance agent and grocery store owner, and his wife, Mattie Kennedy Parrott. Parrott, who previously resided at 804 North Queen Street, was living at "Pollock, head of West Washington" by 1908. The main hipped roof of Parrott's house is cut by various cross gables, including the two-story projecting pedimented bay at the north elevation and the centered gable at the south. The front porch is supported by Tuscan posts and shelters the transomed and sidelighted entrance, as well as two asymmetrically sized double-hung sash windows.

Sidney Andrews, a nephew of Jack Parrott, and a naval draftsman in Newport News, Virginia, designed this unusual house. Andrews subsequently located in Raleigh, where he worked as a draftsman of maps for the State Highway Commission until his retirement.

12. Fleming House
built circa 1908
401 West Washington Street

George Fleming, who operated the Eagle Tobacco Warehouse with his sons, owned this frame two-story Queen Anne-style gable-and-wing house in the 1920s. As with most Queen Anne houses, the gabled front bay extension and the side-gable wing of the house project from the main block's high-hipped roof. The interplay of volumetric forms is heightened by the shingled gable dormers across the front elevation, the second-story balcony porch over the first floor's transomed entrance, and the spacious attached hipped-roof wraparound porch. The porch's turned posts and rail balustrade are further complemented by the posts' paired drop-pendant sawn-work brackets and the framing landscape of mature shrubbery and trees.

13. J. O. Miller House
built circa 1905
608 Mitchell Street

This two-story side-hall-plan house was built at the turn of the twentieth century for J. O. Miller, a founder of the Quinn and Miller Furniture Company on Kinston's North Queen Street. As with most late Queen Anne-style side-hall-plan dwellings, there is little exterior decoration apart from the attached full-facade one-story porch's turned balustrade and posts and the plain cornice and cornerboards. The facade of the Miller House, like those of similar houses lining the west side of Mitchell Street, is enlivened by an offset gable window with a leaded-glass casement. At the back of the house is a frame two-car garage with a standing-seam metal hipped roof.

14. J. H. Evans House
built circa 1910
606 College Street

The J. H. Evans House, a frame two-story tri-gable, side-gable dwelling, is simpler than its neighbors in exterior form and ornamentation and is more in the tradition of the classic I-House of farmsteads throughout eastern North Carolina. The house was built for Jesse Hallock Evans, a contractor, and later owned by Palmer Sugg, a farmer. The center and side gables are pedimented and pierced by rectangular windows, and a full-facade attached hipped-roof porch with turned posts, sawnwork ornamentation, and a pedimented entry shelters the two first-story windows and the center transomed entrance.

15. Bland-Fort House
built circa 1922
606 West Lenoir Avenue

The Bland-Fort House, a frame two-story front-gable Craftsman-style house, is nearly identical to Aladdin Homes's Shadow Lawn model and may have been one of the many premanufactured "houses by mail" that Aladdin and Sears, Roebuck and Company produced during the early twentieth century. The wide front gable, supported and decorated by large knee brackets, shelters the shingled second floor, below which is a three-quarter attached shed-roof bungalow-style porch extending to form a porte cochere. J. Thomas Bland, the first owner of this house, was a superintendent for Carolina Gas. A later occupant was Mrs. Henry Fort, whose husband had been a supervisor for the Orion Knitting Mill.

16. Edward Stroud House
built 1916
406 West Lenoir Avenue

John Smith and Robert L. Blalock built a frame, two-story, hipped-roof, Classical Revival-style house in 1916 for Edward (Eddie) Stroud, a partner in the Stroud Brothers Grocery, at 406 West Lenoir Street. The Stroud residence shows the synthesis of Mitchelltown's Victorian and Colonial Revival houses. The form of the house—pedimented cross gables emerging from the hipped-roof main block, and an attached hipped-roof wraparound porch—is Victorian, but the exterior elements are sparer and more inspired by the classical than the Queen Anne style. The irregular massing of the house, fanciful screen door, and intricate leaded glass nevertheless combine easily with the porch's square-in-section columns, the molded window cornices, and the small diamond-pattern frieze.

17. First Presbyterian Church
built circa 1935
314 West Lenoir Avenue

A brick-veneered Colonial Revival-style church, with its pedimented portico and octagonal-in-base spire, was built in the mid-1930s for Kinston's First Presbyterian Church. From the round-arched center entrance and side windows decorated by stone keystones, alternating with jack-arched double-hung sash windows, to the modillion cornice and the pilastered steeple belfry, the former First Presbyterian Church is aesthetically pleasing in its restrained Georgian Revival exterior details. The two-story brick-veneered rear extension is an educational building designed by A. Mitchell Wooten and John Rowland in 1940. It is possible that Wooten, who began his architectural practice in Kinston in 1934, also designed the church. In 1957 the First Free Will Baptist Church bought the building.

18. Luther P. Tapp House
built circa 1915
611 Mitchell Street

Luther Tapp, a Person County tobacco merchant, was lured to Kinston by Jesse A. Grainger, to aid in developing Kinston's bright-leaf tobacco market. By 1923 Tapp had his own warehouse and had built this two-story frame Neoclassical Revival house with a double-pile, center-hall plan and a two-story rear ell. A full-height Ionic portico and full-facade attached hipped-roof front porch supported by Ionic colonnettes shelter the front facade of the house but do not obscure the fluted cornerboards or the center pedimented gable projecting from the high hipped roof. The gables have Palladian-style windows, contrasting with the plain one-over-one sash windows below. With its period details, such as narrow weatherboarding, the Tapp House has remained a magnificent example of a grander early-twentieth-century Kinston house.

19. John Hughes White House

built circa 1916
601 West Lenoir Avenue

John Hughes White, co-owner of Inscore and White Livery and Sales Stable, and later general agent for Reserve Loan Life Insurance Company, had this house built for his wife, Ruth and their five children about 1916. Virginia White Little, the youngest child [and the mother of the author, M. Ruth Little], recalls hearing bells and a lot of noise coming from downtown, about seven blocks away, one day in 1918 when she was playing on the front porch. What the four-year-old heard was the celebration of the ending of World War I. Although lots were fairly small in the suburb of Mitchelltown, Ruth Rouse White managed to continue such rural activities as making soap in an iron pot in her backyard.

The up-to-date bungalow features a pyramidal roof with a large dormer window projecting from each side, allowing for commodious upstairs bedrooms, as well as a good-sized front porch with classical posts and a wooden railing. It retains its original weatherboarding, Craftsman-style window sash, and three tall chimneys with corbeled caps.

20. Bungalow

built circa 1920
507 West Lenoir Avenue

This frame story-and-a-half residence was executed in the bungalow style, which developed in California at the turn of the twentieth century and moved rapidly eastward in the 1920s. The side-gabled roof with its centered large front-gable dormer extends into the massive front-gable bungalow-style porch, which is supported by battered brick piers. Both dormer and porch gables share the low, sloping quality characteristic of early-1900s California bungalows. This house, no doubt quite exotic alongside earlier Queen Anne and Classical Revival houses when it was built, has two one-story side extensions, one of which is a porte cochere also supported by battered brick piers. Knee brackets decorate the wide eaves of the gables, side porch, and porte cochere. The twin interior chimneys, in contrast to the tall corbeled-cap chimney stacks of earlier Mitchelltown houses, are battered in a fashion similar to the piers below.

21. Charles Mangum House

built circa 1925
303 West Lenoir Avenue

An intriguing combination of revival styles is found in this two-story brick-veneered house built for Charles Mangum, a pediatrician and founder of Memorial General Hospital. The Spanish Mission Revival style, in the form of the first floor's paired arched windows and segmentally arched balcony opening within the parapeted central front-facade bay, combines with the Colonial Revival to form an eclectic yet simple exterior. Classical elements include the parapeted central broken pediment with its urn finial, and decorative brickwork with quoining and a stretcher-bond stringcourse. An almost anachronistic corbel chimney cap, more at home with the Victorian style, emerges from the slate hipped roof, but there is no documentation indicating that the Mangum House was built earlier than 1925. A screened side porch with a three-part window/entrance completes the facade.

22. Holy Trinity Catholic Church

built circa 1921
506 West Vernon Avenue

Small in scale yet rich in Gothic-influenced details, this brick Catholic church is an excellent example of the type of Gothic ecclesiastical designs erected by small Catholic parishes during the early twentieth century, then enhanced by later alterations. A crenellated two-stage tower, added in the 1950s, abuts the front-gable brick facade, from which projects the random-coursed ashlar- stone narthex, which was also added in the 1950s. A stone belt course forms the base of the tower's second stage, which has tracery over louvered Gothic-arch openings. Stepped buttresses at the outside of the nave, and the narthex's handsome wooden door set in a pointed arch, above which is the nave's round stained-glass window, complete the medieval motifs of this 1920s structure.

With the building of Holy Trinity, Kinston's Catholic families finally had a church to worship in. In previous years, beginning in 1914, services had been held either in the Whitaker Building on North Queen Street or in private homes. With permanence came outreach; the Reverend Louis Ruth, who came to Kinston in 1933, began a mission for Kinston's African Americans that eventually became the Our Lady of the Atonement Catholic Church on East Washington Street. Holy Trinity Catholic Church has seen a marked increase in the number of congregants in its seventy-five-year existence. What was a handful of families in 1921 has grown to more than three hundred families in this Catholic parish.

McDaniel-Sutton House, 702 East Gordon Street, Trianon, circa 1905.

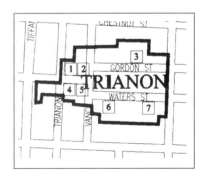

Trianon

The Trianon district lies about one-half mile east of Kinston's central business district, and one block northeast of the former Orion Knitting Mill and Kinston Cotton Mill. Developed largely between 1893 and 1930, this neighborhood is historically and physically focused around a 1.9-acre rectangular tract of open land. The one- and two-story houses along the tree-lined streets are typical of working-class and upper-middle-class housing in Kinston during the early twentieth century. The following overview and entries were edited from Allison Black's 1989 National Register nomination for the Trianon Historic District, with additional research by Penne Smith.

By the mid-1890s, when the population began to grow as a result of the town's development as a cotton and tobacco market and a mercantile and industrial center, Kinston's original core was largely developed. Local entrepreneurs who owned substantial tracts of land outside the town limits began subdividing their acreage and selling building lots. Adolphus Mitchell was subdividing farmland into residential lots in Mitchelltown; Jesse Grainger was doing the same thing in the future neighborhood of Grainger Hill. Trianon's entrepreneur was James A. McDaniel.

James Alexander McDaniel (1867-1928) was born in Jones County but moved to Kinston in the 1870s with his mother, sister, and stepfather, Richard W. King. King, who died in 1883, was a major landowner in Kinston who possessed a large tract east of the town, as well as several lots within the town limits, and land in Lenoir County and New Bern. Tiffany West, King's great-niece, inherited most of the home plantation east of Kinston and continued to farm the land for another ten years. James McDaniel was educated at the Kinston School (operated by Dr. R. H. Lewis), Wake Forest College, and the Eastman Business School in Poughkeepsie, New York. After returning to Kinston he purchased three hundred acres of Tiffany West's lands in 1893. By 1899 McDaniel had built a stylish Queen Anne house in the center of a large field, platted streets and lots around it, and other houses were being constructed.

Among those who purchased building lots in the Trianon area was attorney T. C. Wooten, whose two-story frame Queen Anne residence (now demolished) on the northeast corner of Gordon and Tiffany Streets appeared in the 1897 Industrial Issue of the *Kinston Free Press*. In 1898 Wooten's house was struck by lightning one May afternoon; according to an eyewitness, "the dining room chimney was split open" and Wooten's wife narrowly escaped electrocution. At the time it was thought that had it not been for the Wootens' telephone wire, which conducted the electricity, the family would have been killed and the house burned.[1] Another Trianon resident was schoolteacher M. H. Wooten, whose large frame Colonial Revival house at 607 East Gordon Street, built in 1896, still stands. A later owner of the house was Maine native James W. Black, the vice president and general manager of Caswell Cotton Mills. George W. Sumrell, cofounder of the wholesale grocery firm of Sumrell and McCoy, lived at 701 East Gordon Street in a two-story frame house (still standing) built in 1899. The *Kinston Daily Free Press* announced on June 17, 1898, that "Mr. Carl W. Pridgen has purchased a lot on the corner of Vance and Gordon streets, and is preparing to build a six-room residence." Pridgen, a merchant who also operated a brokerage firm, was one of Lenoir County's registrar of deeds; his house, a frame gable-and-wing Queen Anne dwelling with decorated gables, sits at 705 East Gordon Street.

Many of the houses built along East Gordon and Waters Streets facing the McDaniel residence tract appear to have been either speculative or rental housing built by McDaniel and others. McDaniel built a speculative frame Queen Anne cottage across the street, at 801 Waters Street, about 1912 and sold it to assistant chief of police, J. C. Heath. Walter Dunn LaRoque Jr., who operated the Rountree and LaRoque Insurance Company, purchased a tract of land on Waters Street from McDaniel in 1915 and divided it into eight lots, most of which he sold within the next three years. Jesse G. Brown, a wholesale grocer, purchased three of these lots, building rental houses at 815 and 817 Waters Street.

Most of these rental and speculative houses are smaller than the dwellings at the west end of Trianon, and architecturally less varied. The earlier speculative houses follow traditional forms— L-plans, or three-bay one-room-deep plans with rear wings—but are embellished with a variety of decorative devices. Defining elements include turned porch posts and balusters, sawn brackets, spindle friezes, ornamental wood shingling, sunbursts, classical columns, and entrances with transoms and sidelights. Later Trianon houses, dating after about 1910, exhibit Craftsman-style influences such as triangular knee braces and exposed rafter ends. The occupants of these houses typified Kinston's growing middle class and included barbers, postal carriers, watchmakers, salesmen, members of the building trades, insurance agents, and police officers.

In 1905 McDaniel deeded his house at the end of East Gordon Street to Drs. James M. and W. T. Parrott. According to the deed the Parrotts agreed to "equip and maintain a hospital [in the house] for the treatment of medical and surgical cases." The hospital was named the Robert Bruce McDaniel Memorial Hospital in memory of McDaniel's infant son, who died of dysentery in 1904.[2] Nine years later the Robert Bruce McDaniel Memorial Hospital was renamed the Parrott Memorial Hospital, when the Parrotts bought out McDaniel's remaining interest in the property.

A clause in the contract between McDaniel and the Parrotts stipulates that the doctors set up additional wards to provide care for not only indigent white medical and surgical patients but "indigent colored patients" as well. The Parrotts built a two-story hipped-roof Renaissance Revival brick building with broad bracketed eaves and arched second-floor windows. The 1930 Sanborn Fire Insurance Map shows that a two-story brick-veneered nurses' dormitory was built after 1925 at the southeast corner of the Parrott Hospital tract. In 1973, when the present Lenoir Memorial Hospital opened, Parrott Hospital closed. Its buildings were demolished later in the 1970s. Even though James McDaniel's first house and the Parrott Hospital complex are gone, their presence has remained strong in the memories of neighborhood residents. McDaniel's 1904 house at 702 East Gordon Street, an impressive two-and-a-half-story Classical Revival dwelling, has survived, as have neighboring houses built along the streets flanking the former hospital tract.[3]

That Parrott Memorial Hospital, Kinston's first hospital, was built in Trianon—as well as the different types of speculative development in the neighborhood—raises an interesting idea. It is possible that Trianon was a conscious attempt on McDaniel's part to create a self-sufficient neighborhood, not just a residential suburb. Furthermore, Trianon's formal central common, surrounded by regular grid blocks, possesses a more planned design than does either the Grainger Hill or the Mitchelltown neighborhood.

Most of the houses in the 700 and 800 blocks of East Gordon Street were in place by 1910. On the other hand, the majority of the houses along Waters Street were built between 1917 and 1935. By 1930 development in Trianon was nearly complete. Only one house, a gable-front frame bungalow at 811 Waters Street, was built after that time. Few changes have occurred within the district since 1930. Several of the larger houses have been converted to multifamily use, but the majority remain single-family dwellings, both rental and owner occupied. Many of the trees planted by McDaniel have survived and grown to mature, shady heights. The general character of the area remains intact, reflecting the efforts of late-nineteenth- and early-twentieth-century local entrepreneurs to provide good-quality housing amidst pleasant surroundings for the growing population of Kinston.

Notes

1. *Kinston Daily Free Press*, May 27, 1898.
2. Lenoir County Register of Deeds, 30:427 (McDaniel>Parrott, 1905); *Kinston Daily Free Press*, May 23, 1904.
3. Lenoir County Register of Deeds, 30: 427; *Lenoir County Heritage*, 62.

1. Parrott-Coleman House
built circa 1900
700 East Gordon Street

The Parrott-Coleman House, a one-and-a-half-story triple-pile frame Queen Anne cottage, has some elegant detailing, such as the hipped roof's dormers with triangular carved sunbursts. Staggered-patterned shingles in the projecting gables, and the large entrance with its fanlight transom, sidelights, and paneled aprons, are also typical of Victorian design. The original narrow weatherboarding has been replaced by aluminum siding. 700 East Gordon Street was built for Dr. W. Thomas Parrott at the turn of the twentieth century, conveniently close to the Parrott Hospital. William B. Coleman, clerk for the city of Kinston, and his son, architect William Coleman, resided at this house after Parrott.

2. McDaniel-Sutton House
built circa 1905
702 East Gordon Street

The McDaniel-Sutton House, at 702 East Gordon Street bordering Trianon Park, is a large two- and-one-half-story frame Queen Anne-style house. Exhibiting a mixture of Victorian and Colonial Revival elements, the dwelling has pedimented two-story bays projecting from the central pyramidal-roofed main block, large corbeled interior chimney stacks, and a hipped-roof corner dormer with its original upper sash with hexagonal panes. This

was James A. McDaniel's second residence in the Trianon District; McDaniel deeded his previous house to the Parrott brothers to house the Parrott Memorial Hospital. Except for the loss of the attached wraparound front porch, which was supported by paired Ionic colonnettes over brick piers, the house's exterior remains virtually identical to its 1906 photograph in the Industrial Issue of the *Kinston Daily Free Press*. The modillion cornices at the eaves and the raking modillioned cornices are still in place, as are the pebbledash and curving timber in the pedimented gable ends. The elegant Palladian window within the front facade's projecting pedimented gable is intact, as are the chimney stacks. Frederick Isler Sutton Sr., a local attorney and former Kinston mayor, later owned this house.

3. Houses
built circa 1900
812-816 East Gordon Street

Other variations of cottages developed by James A. McDaniel for speculative housing appears along the 800 block of East Gordon Street. 812 East Gordon Street, a frame one-story L-shaped dwelling, was built at the turn of the century by E. W. Chadwick and by 1908 had become the residence of Robert Scott, partner in the Scott and Waller roofing company. 814 East Gordon Street is an L-shaped one-story frame house with a front pedimented gable, an attached hipped-roof porch now supported by replacement posts over brick piers instead of the original wooden columns, and an interior corbel-cap chimney stack. E. R. Waller, who operated the E. R. Waller Sheetmetal Company, lived at 816 East Gordon Street, a one-story frame tri-gable, side-gable house, in the early twentieth century. 816 East Gordon Street has retained much of its original exterior decoration, particularly its attached hipped-roof front porch supported by turned posts, which are decorated by sawnwork brackets.

4. George W. Sumrell House

built circa 1899
701 East Gordon Street

George Sumrell, cofounder of the Sumrell and McCoy wholesale grocery on North Queen Street, was the original owner of the frame two-story transitional Queen Anne-style house at 701 East Gordon Street. The three-sided projecting central bay of the front facade houses the entrance, displays a second-story window, and is surmounted by a steeply pitched front gable decorated by returns, sawnwork brackets and pendants over the cutaway corners, and a louvered diamond-shaped ventilator. The full-facade attached hipped-roof front porch, supported by Tuscan columns and projecting at the steps with a pedimented entry, wraps around to the west side of the house.

5. Carl Pridgen House

built circa 1898
705 East Gordon Street

The L-shaped frame one-story Queen Anne-style house at 705 East Gordon Street has a high hipped roof at the center of the two cross wings—which is at the entrance of the house—and a smaller hipped-roof front extension joining the wraparound front porch at its pedimented entrance. The gable at the front facade is enhanced by a carved diamond-shaped sunburst, below

which is a Queen Anne-style sash window bordered by small rectangular panes and patterned wooden shingles. Carl Pridgen, an early owner of this house, was a Kinston merchant, broker, and, at one time, Lenoir County's registrar of deeds.

6. McDaniel-Heath House

built circa 1900
801 Waters Street

The one-and-a-half-story frame L-plan Queen Anne-style dwelling at 801 Waters Street was built by James A. McDaniel as speculative housing and later owned by J. C. Heath, Kinston's assistant chief of police. Even with its wider replacement siding, it remains an interesting example of Victorian architecture, from the front projecting gable's imbricated shingles and pendant sawnwork over the first floor's cutaway corners to the small six-light window eccentrically adjacent to and below the front-gabled wall dormer's sill. The attached three-quarter hipped-roof front porch still has its original turned-spindle frieze, and most of the windows are double-hung two-over-two sash.

7. Jesse G. Brown House

built circa 1900
815 Waters Street

This one-story frame dwelling, thought to be another of James McDaniel's speculative houses, carries delicately balanced front gables pierced by scallop-trimmed louvered ventilators. The three bays of the front facade are sheltered by an attached hipped-roof porch supported by replacement square-in-section wooden posts and a replacement plain-rail balustrade. Jesse G. Brown, an early-twentieth-century resident, operated a wholesale produce grocery on Queen Street.

Caswell Center

established 1911; enlarged 1920s, 1930s, 1950s

2415 West Vernon Avenue

The Caswell Center was founded in 1911 for the care and specialized training of mentally retarded children, through the efforts of Dr. Ira Hardy of Kinston. In 1912, after Mrs. Carrie E. Schweikert's property was acquired for the center, Hardy supervised construction of the first buildings. The Hardy Building, also known as Central, was designed by Hook and Rogers of Charlotte. Charles E. Hartge of Raleigh designed dormitories for the male and female residents. The dormitories were destroyed by two separate fires in 1918 and 1919.

Because of the loss of the dormitories and the pressing demands of increasing enrollment, the 1920s and 1930s were a period of considerable growth for Caswell. On nearby Hull Road, frame houses were built for Caswell employees from designs by James A. Salter, the state architect. Eleven residential and administrative buildings and a plumbing and heating plant were constructed between 1921 and 1928. The 1925 Kinston Sanborn Fire Insurance Map shows that the Caswell Training School for the Feeble Minded had thirty-one buildings, including an industrial school, a laundry, a "shoe shop," and a domestic science building.

Caswell Chapel (formerly Ehringhaus Chapel), a large Art Deco brick and stone building, and eight surrounding residential cottages form the centerpiece of the

Caswell Center's campus. These nine buildings were designed by local architect A. Mitchell Wooten in 1936. The cottages, picturesquely known as Elm, Maple, Willow and other tree names, are one-story brick Moderne-style buildings with bands of casement windows and minimal fluted brick and stone decoration. The connecting walkways are later additions. Caswell Chapel, although recently altered, retains dramatic large window bays and a fluted belt course, as well as fluted recessed surrounds at the front entrance and flanking windows.

The 1950s and 1960s brought more facilities to Caswell. Most of these buildings—including dormitories, administrative buildings, and a new heating plant—were designed by Benton and Benton, Architects, of Wilson. Today the Caswell Center, which has metamorphosed from an institutional facility to an outpatient center providing services to eastern North Carolina's mentally challenged citizens, is a sizable complex with residences, a hospital, a gymnasium, offices, clinics, and a number of agricultural buildings.

CATALOGUE OF HISTORIC STRUCTURES

Lenoir County

Written by
Robbie D. Jones
Penne Smith
Scott Power
M. Ruth Little

D. W. Hamilton Store, Grainger community

MOSELEY HALL
TOWNSHIP

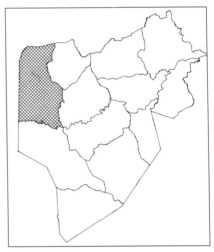

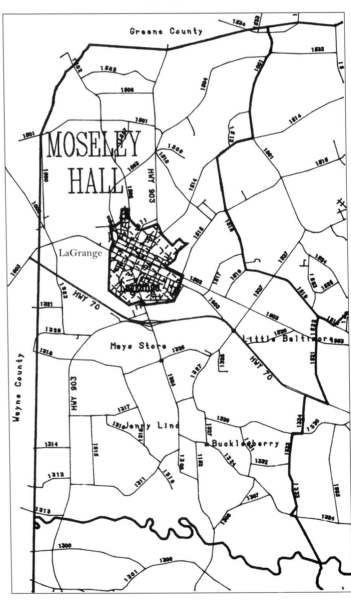

Hugh Emery Hardy Tenant House

built first decade of the twentieth century
Institute vicinity

Colloquially known as a story-and-a-jump farmhouse, this building provides an excellent example of a type of farm dwelling common to tenant and small farmers in the late nineteenth and early twentieth centuries. This house is attributed to Hugh Emery Hardy (1884-1968), a life-long landowner and farmer in Lenoir County who also held farmland in neighboring Greene County. Hardy attended Rhodes Military Academy in Kinston in his youth and was an active member of the Wheat Swamp Christian Church and Institute Methodist Church. The tenant house he constructed on his farm was plain, but more substantial than most in the early twentieth century.

Identifying the three-bay house as a story-and-a-jump form are the truncated windows, which have squarish proportions, just beneath the eaves of the roof. The less-than-full-height windows signify a "near" second story, one not of full height. Except for this "jump," the farmhouse is rather typical in appearance, with an attached hip-roof front porch (now screened) supported by turned posts. This type of house was often illustrated in period publications on farm life such as *The Home and Farm Manual*, printed in 1884, which shows a similar treatment in one of its drawings. In typical fashion an ell and later additions project from the rear of the house. The two chimneys, one an interior chimney between the main block and rear ell, the other an interior rear chimney, are original, and the rear ell has a brick flue.

Following Hardy's death, his son Hugh Holton Hardy inherited the tenant house and continues to own his father's farm.

Abner S. Fields House and Store and Horace E. Fields Store and Cafe

house built 1917-1918; store built 1916; store and cafe built 1930-1940
LaGrange vicinity

This small enclave of residential and commercial buildings set in the isolated western section of the county is a vestige of the once-common family enterprisies that dotted the rural countryside, providing social gathering spots as well as mercantile exchanges. At the center of this community sits the charming and well-maintained one-story Victorian dwelling built in 1917-1918 for Abner S. Fields (1860-1935). Fields and his wife, Georgiana Coker Fields (1870-1921), resided in their store—an age-old tradition that survived well into the twentieth century—until Georgiana persuaded her husband to build a house across the road to provide the couple with their own dwelling and a measure of privacy. The main feature of the modest gable-and-wing dwelling is the decorative wraparound front porch supported by turned posts.

Fields built his typical rural store in 1916, a year before he constructed a dwelling for his family. Distinguished by a false parapet concealing a gable-front roof, the store utilizes a ubiquitious building form and has a small shed-roof front porch and shuttered windows. Abner Fields operated a store in the northern half of the one-story building while residing in the southern section.

Located within site of the Fields Store is another small frame store building, constructed by Abner's youngest son, Horace Earl Fields (1906-1938). The two-section building was constructed in phases, with the southern portion built first, about 1930, for use as a general mercantile business and the northern portion, where Horace Fields operated a cafe, built a few years later. Like his father's store, this early-twentieth-century example is typical for the region and distinguished by a hip roof that incorporates a pass-through. It shares many similarities to the nearby Pelletier's Store. Connected to the store is the cafe, which features a stepped false facade and side-elevation parapets.

Horace Fields Storage Building
built early nineteenth century
LaGrange vicinity

This small, finely crafted outbuilding is the only remaining building from an early-nineteenth-century farm, shown as H. Fields on the 1863 Koerner Military Survey Field Map. Local tradition holds that the building was used as a storage cellar for the large antebellum house that stood very near it. The two-story dwelling, thought to have been constructed in the early 1800s, was known as the Horace Fields House and was demolished decades ago.

The attenuated form of the one-room outbuilding is enhanced by the four-foot-high brick foundation that creates a cellar, an extremely uncommon feature for outbuildings. The foundation is similar to those of the nearby Federal-style dwellings of Joshua Herring and Langhorne Hardy, dating from the first decade of the nineteenth century. Details such as heavy mortise-and-tenon construction, fully sheathed interior, exposed ceiling beams, and some beaded siding verify such an early construction date for the cellar building as well. A small window opening, originally covered with a wooden shutter, and a board-and-batten door with rosehead nails and strap hinges are the only fenestration. Fine craftsmanship, including a fully floored loft and small pegged

rafters, is found throughout this rare surviving outbuilding of an early Lenoir County farm. One theory is that the building functioned as a brandy house, in which jars of fruit syrup were stored for fermentation.

Thomas H. and Huldah Dawson House
built circa 1851
Institute vicinity

This exceptional two-story transitional Federal/Greek Revival-style house is one of only a few dwellings remaining in the county that have their original two-story rear ells. Tradition states that the central-hallway I-house was constructed in 1850-1851 by Thomas Herring Dawson (1820-1883) and Huldah Truett Daniel Dawson (1824-1900), who were married in 1846. The Dawsons are said to have added the rear ell in 1865-1870. Thomas worked 350 acres of improved land and 210 acres of unimproved land, worth $10,000 in 1860. The Dawsons owned several slaves, 3 horses, 4 mules, 4 milk cows, 2 oxen, 15 cattle, 35 sheep, and 150 swine. On his farm Dawson produced, in 1860, 60 bushels of wheat, 2,000 bushels of Indian corn, 50 pounds of wool, 15 bushels of peas and beans, 30 bushels of Irish potatoes, 200 bushels of sweet potatoes, 100 pounds of butter, 21 tons of fodder, and an impressive 29 bales of cotton (400 pounds each). One unusual crop raised in this section of the county was rice, and Dawson produced 520 pounds in 1860, probably along the swampy land near Groundnut Creek on the rear side of the farm. Thomas's wife, known as "Aunt Huldah," grew an herb and flower garden with boxwood-lined paths to the rear of the house, many of which still exist.

Two open stairs, one in the center hall of the main block and one in the rear ell, feature simple Federal-style newel posts. An enclosed winder stair with a board-and-batten door leads to the attic. Deeply molded mantels, window and door surrounds with crossettes, two-panel doors, and flat-paneled window aprons all contribute to the Greek Revival character of the house.

The house was altered in the mid-twentieth century with the removal of the original central-bay one-story portico, the original front entrance, and the second-level door (which led to the roof of the portico). These details were reconstructed in the circa 1980 restoration by Henry

Warren Brothers III and his wife, Beverly Kearney Brothers, using a historic painting of the dwelling for reference. The present three-panel front door with transom and sidelights and the second-level two-panel double doors were salvaged from the Henry Warren Brothers House (now demolished), located in nearby Institute. During restoration of the house numerous historic items were discovered in the attic floorboards, including Confederate currency and a deed dated 1790.

The exterior of the house was originally embellished with some of Lenoir County's most elaborate Greek Revival-style detailing, including molded window and door surrounds with small corner blocks. But perhaps the most unusual architectural detail was the decorative gougework on the corner pilasters near the cornice of the front facade. Fortunately, this rare and impressive woodwork was placed in storage when the house was covered in vinyl siding.

The Dawson family cemetery, including a number of African American graves, is located on the farm. Outbuildings include tobacco barns, a packhouse, a barn/stable, a pump house, a smokehouse, and a garage.

Pelletier-Hines Grocery Store
built circa 1934
Pelletier's Crossroads

Built by Oscar and Marvin Pelletier circa 1934, this small frame commercial store has been in continuous operation ever since, although the current owner serves only "soda and smokes." Typical of early-twentieth-century rural stores, this building is distinguished by its unusually small size. Common features include a pass-through with hip roof. The rear and side shed additions were built later.

Rouse-Edmondson-Wilson House
built late 1850s
LaGrange vicinity

Exhibiting an intricate two-tier porch, this double-pile central-hall house is an impressive example of Lenoir County's antebellum Greek Revival architecture. The second level of the handsome porch has lost most of its original sheaf-of-wheat balustrade but retains the unique overhead spandrels and original square columns. The large corner pilasters with capitals and double front entries on both stories are characteristic of the Greek Revival style, but rare in Lenoir County. A wraparound rear porch is supported by chamfered posts. Other details indicative of the fine nature of the dwelling are flush beaded porch ceilings and a foundation that features brick latticework between piers.

Though the history of the plantation is relatively unknown, the dwelling appears as "Noah Rowse" on the 1863 Koerner Military Survey Field Map, and census research reveals a probable construction date of circa 1855-1860. Noah Rouse Sr. operated an extensive antebellum plantation with eighteen slaves and three slave houses in 1860, and Noah Rouse Jr. was a prominent businessman in LaGrange in the late nineteenth century. Subsequent owners have been the Edmondson and Wilson families.

James Yadkin Joyner House

built 1919
LaGrange vicinity

The humble character of Dr. James Yadkin Joyner's retirement cottage speaks little of his stature in the annals of the public education movement in North Carolina. Born in 1862 at Yadkin College, Davidson County, where his family fled from advancing Federal troops in coastal areas of the state at the beginning of the Civil War, Joyner returned to Lenoir County to live with his grandfather after the conflict. His parents, John and Sallie A. (Wooten) Joyner, both died before he turned the age of one. Joyner was educated locally at LaGrange Academy, graduated from the University of North Carolina in 1881, and returned to Lenoir County to become principal of the academy and superintendent of county schools. In 1884 he was appointed superintendent of Winston schools in Forsyth County, returning only a year later to his native eastern North Carolina to practice law in Goldsboro and to act as chairman of the Wayne County Board of Education. Joyner returned to education from 1889 to 1893, becoming superintendent of the Goldsboro Schools. Later that year he was appointed professor of English literature and dean of the State Normal School at Greensboro (now the University of North Carolina at Greensboro). Joyner's accomplishments in Greensboro included election to an alderman's seat, to the board of directors of the Agricultural and Mechanical College (now North Carolina A & T State University), and as chairman of the North Carolina Textbook Commission.

Perhaps Joyner's greatest contributions came when he was appointed by Governor Charles Brantley Aycock to the post of state superintendent of public instruction in 1902. The task of overhauling the state's system of public education was formidable, considering that North Carolina spent only 50 cents per capita annually on public education. More than 5,000 of the schools in the state were one-teacher facilities. Only thirty high schools existed in the entire state, and all were supported by local taxation. No school libraries existed, school terms lasted only seventy days, and a teacher's salary was a mere twenty-four dollars per month. Under Joyner's leadership a renaissance in public education ensued and charac-

terized the remainder of his superintendency. Accomplishments included increased state aid to local school boards, lengthened school terms, increased teacher salaries, establishment of school libraries, and, perhaps Joyner's greatest contribution, consolidation of schools on an unprecedented scale. The many architecturally striking school buildings designed by architects across the state in the 1910s and 1920s are lasting reminders of Joyner's and his associates' contributions to the advancement of public education in North Carolina.

Joyner was secretary and later president of the Association of the Southern States Superintendents (1903-1907) and was president of the National Education Association in 1910. He was also president of the North Carolina Teacher's Assembly and of the Summer School for Teachers, as well as conductor of the Teacher's Institute in the state. Farming and rural education were primary interests of Joyner, which fact was reflected in his presidency of the North Carolina Convention of Farmers and Farm Women and his directorship in the Tobacco Growers Cooperative Association.

Following Joyner's retirement as superintendent of public education in the summer of 1918, he returned with his wife, Effie E. Rouse of LaGrange, to an ancestral farm of the Wooten family just outside LaGrange. Early in 1919 Joyner contracted with builder Fred Fields of LaGrange to construct a "little cottage on the old site of Mrs. Joyner's grandfather, that will be shaded by the same old elms that shaded the ancestral home." In a letter to Fields dated February 7, 1919, Joyner explains, "The porches to the cottage are to be built on the east and west side, the front porch facing the road and grave-yard, and the back porch on the side next to the big elms. I hope to be down at the farm Thursday and Friday of next week. The order for all the shop work including the balusters and the crown molding has been sent to Wilson's Mills and will be ready for you I am assured before you need it. Please push the work as rapidly as you can as we are anxious to get in the house as soon as possible." The "little cottage" built for the Joyner's was just that, a small, rather unadorned one-and-a-half-story house with engaged porches on the front and rear and a one-story kitchen ell extending from the east elevation. A simple slat balustrade and French doors mark the level of sophistication associated with this comfortable but unpretentious design.

Joyner lived until 1954, when he died suddenly on January 24. *The Greensboro Daily News*, in an editorial on Joyner's contributions, summed up the feelings of his admirers by stating: "As Dr. Joyner returns to the soil from which he came, his creed, his philosophy, and his faith are reincarnated in every school child in North Carolina. The State which he and his fellow crusaders inspired looks forward, its faith, its hope and its investment centered in its children . . . Dr. Joyner was a dreamer spared long enough to see his dream come true."

Herring House

built 1801
LaGrange vicinity

Arguably one of Lenoir County's earliest and finest Federal-era plantation dwellings, the Herring House was built by one of the earliest families to settle in the area. Well preserved, with restrained yet inventive detail typical of the more ambitious vernacular dwellings of the period, this example presents an early expression of the domestic style that swept the nation following the American Revolution. The two-story frame dwelling was built with beaded weatherboards and set on a Flemish-bond brick foundation. Facing south, the five bays of the main facade are broken with a central entrance surmounted by a four-light transom. The original porch configuration is unknown, since a single-story hip-roof porch, which carries around the front and the east gable end, was added in the twentieth century. The house is buttressed on the gable ends by chimneys laid in Flemish bond with stepped shoulders. The west chimney contains a brick dated 1801. It is from this brick that the date of construction is assumed.

The overall scale and proportion of the house, including the attenuated nine-over-nine-light sash windows on the first floor and nine-over-six on the second, hail defining attributes of the Federal style. Likewise the handsome modillioned cornice with applied bed molding speaks of Federal design.

A center passage marks the plan of the house, with a large parlor on either side and an open-string stair rising in two flights from the left side of the hall. Curvilinear brackets and a simple balustrade with posts and balusters, square in section, define the stair design. Illustrating the sophisticated nature of the house is a secondary enclosed stair in the east parlor, which ascends to the second floor.

The Federal style is most evident in the mantelpieces adorning fireplaces throughout the house. Finely executed designs, each individualized with gouged and carved ornament, create wonderful vernacular expressions. The most elaborate has a modified three-part form, with the center tablet no wider than the end blocks, and fluted pilasters beneath a horizontal lower frieze band adorned with gougework scallops. Of particular note is

an early cupboard located at the head of the secondary stair next to the partition wall. Federalist in composition, the floor-to-ceiling case piece is capped by a dentil cornice and accessed by a diminutive six-panel door above a two-panel unit.

The Herring family had settled in Lenoir County by the 1730s and had a background in public service, as well as farming. John Herring (1684-1760) served in the colonial Assembly in 1749, and his son, Joshua (1725-1801), was a justice of the peace by the time of the Revolutionary War. Although family tradition asserts that Joshua Herring completed the house in the year of his death, his advanced age would suggest that either his son Edward Matchet Herring (1755-1825) or his grandson William Herring (1779-1830) constructed the dwelling. Needham Whitfield Herring (1856-1942) was the fourth- or fifth- generation Herring to inherit the house. Needham Herring's son Bryan was the last Herring to own the house. In the 1940s it was purchased by Ely Perry and later sold to Lillian Burton. At her death in 1997 the property passed to her nieces Jodie Kyser and Bliss Kite.

Moseley Hall (destroyed)

built circa 1840; destroyed 1917
LaGrange vicinity

Moseley Hall plantation comprised the ancestral lands of the prominent Moseley family, which by the late eighteenth century settled near what was to become the town of LaGrange in western Lenoir County. The area where the Atlantic & North Carolina Railroad came through in the mid 1850s, creating a depot stop, was originally known as Moseley Hall (after the plantation). Matthew Moseley moved to former Dobbs County in 1777 from Princess Anne County, Virginia, and married Elizabeth Herring, daughter of Joshua and Elizabeth Herring, prominent landowners in the county, in 1783. Over the next seventy-five years members of the Moseley family spread throughout surrounding counties, including Greene and Duplin.

The house that marked the seat of the Moseley Hall plantation survived until 1917, when it was destroyed by fire. A photograph taken in 1912 shows a spacious two-story double-pile frame dwelling, which may have been either an overbuilt earlier home or a house constructed at one time. Lack of documentary evidence only breeds speculation as to the dwelling's history. From all indications in the photograph, Moseley Hall was a substantial Greek Revival-era house probably built about 1840. William Dunn Moseley was the last family member to live in the house. He moved to Florida sometime during the early 1840s after suffering a narrow defeat for the governorship of North Carolina. He became the first elected governor of the state of Florida and served from 1845 to 1849. The property was sold to the T. R. Rouse family by the Moseleys.

Other than its overall five-bay width, central projecting portico, and four exterior side chimneys, little is known about the house's appearance. The photograph suggests that a polychromatic paint scheme had been employed on the house and that such decorative elements as corner pilasters and a second-story patterned balustrade on the portico embellished an otherwise unadorned dwelling. Typical of the landed gentry of the antebellum era, Moseley Hall was a testament to the prosperity of the region's agriculture and the conservative tastes shared by the majority of planters.

James F. Britt Sr. House
built first quarter of the twentieth century
LaGrange vicinity

Commodious in size and above average in ornamental woodwork, this two-story side-gable single-pile I-house represents the prosperous nature of farming in early-twentieth-century Lenoir County. Long associated with the James F. Britt family in the LaGrange area, the farmhouse is distinguished on the exterior principally by a centered false gable above a full-width hip-roof porch. Conforming to the traditional center-hall plan with a one-story rear ell extension, the house faces south on a slope above the old Kinston-Goldsboro highway, which is still a dirt road. The three-bay exterior facade provides little by way of introducing the unexpectedly ornate interior. A handsome Victorian staircase with paneled understair, turned balusters, and heavy handrails and newel posts characterizes the well-appointed interior. Contributing to the decorative appeal are five-panel doors and Neoclassical Revival door surrounds and mantels.

Deciduous plantings surround the farmhouse, including oaks, pines, and magnolias. The traditional grape arbor and an early-twentieth-century frame smokehouse next to a well complete this intact farmstead. The most recent occupant of the dwelling was Lorraine Britt Bell, the original owner's daughter, who was a schoolteacher and died at the age of ninety-nine.

Alphonzo Walters Mill
built 1917-1919
LaGrange vicinity

Located on one of the largest and most scenic bodies of water in the county, Alfonzo Walters Mill is one of only a handful of remaining grist mills in Lenoir County. It was built by Alphonzo Walters, son of John N. and Lou Rouse Walters, who owned a large farm nearby. Of particular significance is the mill's intact appearance. Most of the original mill pieces are intact, including the millstone that was manufactured by B. F. Starr and Company in Baltimore. The huge chamfered posts remain functional, turning 360 degrees on axis. The dates "1921-24" are visible on the sides of the cast-concrete foundation, possibly indicating dates of additions. The millpond was the site of a dance hall/pavilion in the 1920s that served folks from the LaGrange area. The pond was a popular swimming and fishing spot for many years. At approximately fifteen acres, the millpond is one of Lenoir County's largest bodies of water and is thought to be much older than the mill itself, maybe even dating to the antebellum era.

John Thomas Haywood Walters House
built 1840s
LaGrange vicinity

John Thomas Haywood Walters (1814–?), a nineteenth-century farmer, is the first recorded owner of this one-and-a-half-story timber-frame hall-and-parlor-plan coastal cottage, probably built sometime in the 1840s. The roof pitch is lower than on earlier coastal cottages, and the full-facade engaged porch with its square wood posts appears to be a vernacular interpretation of Greek Revival precepts. The house has some original elements, such as the nine-over-six sash windows on the first floor and the six-over-six in the attic, and the engaged front porch still supported by its large wooden posts, although the balustrade is now gone. The original single-shoulder end chimneys are both gone, one having been replaced, and there is a later rear ell extending from the now-enclosed 1840s back porch. There are no surviving period outbuildings, but there are an early-twentieth-century packhouse and tobacco barn on the property.

Sally Whitted House
built late nineteenth century
LaGrange vicinity

The Sally Whitted House is a well-preserved one-story vernacular late Victorian frame farmhouse with later rear and side extensions, connecting an originally detached frame kitchen at the back of the house. Certain features, such as the wraparound hip-roof front porch supported by wooden posts with sawnwork brackets with star motifs, give the farmhouse a picturesque appeal. The sidelighted and transomed entrance has a peaked lintel, as do the elongated four-over-four sash windows—a prominent feature on many Victorian houses, which infuses a hint of Gothic design. A bay window at the front ell has Queen Anne stained-glass windows, which add a level of sophistication to the otherwise typical period farmhouse. Inside, the house is plastered with patterned beaded tongue-in-groove board ceilings—an exemplary use of a standard building material. Paneled mantelpieces, possibly ordered from a catalogue, add to the overall Victorian flavor of the dwelling. Later outbuildings include a shed, a chicken house, barns, a smokehouse, and a tenant house a small distance away. A grape arbor and mature pecan trees are sited around the house.

Nathan George Sutton House
built third quarter of the nineteenth century
LaGrange vicinity

The two-story frame weatherboarded Nathan Sutton House is a substantial Greek Revival I-house with the county's only example of a circular staircase located in the spacious center hall. On the exterior the center pedimented portico, as evidenced in an old photograph, has lost its original second floor with sawnwork trim. The original square columns have been replaced by two single fluted columns, which carry from the porch floor to the cornice of the porch roof. The gable-end chimneys are unusually narrow in the breast, and the three-bay facade is marked by four-over-four sash windows—both features that suggest that the dwelling could have been constructed after the Civil War. A long shed and large gable-roof ell protrude from the dwelling's rear elevation.

On the interior, mantels on the first floor are replacements from a house on Queen Street in Kinston, while simply rendered mantels on the second floor are original to the house. The elegant curved staircase, from its curvilinear wall to its walnut handrail and turned balusters (more Victorian in feel), is a feature found more often in urban town houses than in even comfortably affluent country farmhouses. The cinder-block packhouse and frame smokehouse are twentieth century and are the only surviving outbuildings on this farm.

Fields-Sugg House
built circa 1906
LaGrange vicinity

John Fields, one of the most substantial farmers of Moseley Hall Township, had this large two-story Victorian-style dwelling constructed circa 1906 next to Fields Station on the Atlantic and North Carolina Railroad just east of LaGrange. The 1906 Industrial Issue of the *Kinston Free Press* featured an article on the new home. Purchased by Albert Sugg Sr. circa 1933, the double-pile central-hall-plan house features a high hip roof with two small projecting side bays, two interior central chimneys (removed above roof level), and one-over-one sash windows. A wraparound front porch with an entrance-bay projection is supported by Doric columns and originally featured a second-level central-bay deck with balustrade (removed).

The interior retains some of the best preserved and most sophisticated Victorian detailing in the county, featuring such elements as an open-string stairway with molded newel posts, pocket doors, columned overmantels with mirrors, molded window and door surrounds with decorative corner blocks, and an intricate hall screen. Stained-glass windows are intact in the second-level hall.

The farm retains a large number of original ancillary buildings including a smokehouse, a Delco building, a garage, a servant dwelling (used by the owner while the main house was under construction), and numerous tobacco-related outbuildings. Also noteworthy are the cast-concrete foundation piers of the original waterworks and a very old fuel pump.

Hill-Sutton House
built circa 1820
LaGrange vicinity

Located on a hill and facing south toward the Neuse River is the two-story hall-and-parlor-plan Federal-style dwelling believed to have been constructed by Richard Hill (1792-?) about 1820. The attenuated three-bay asymmetrical facade has nine-over-six sash windows on the first floor and six-over-six sash on the second. Both of the original single-shoulder chimneys are intact and exhibit such unorthodox construction details as an off-center shaft and asymmetrical shoulders, characteristics commonly associated with vernacular buildings. Details such as beaded and tapered rake boards on the gable ends and front shed porch, two-part molded window and door surrounds, and molded cornice trim exemplify the Federal style.

The rear kitchen/dining ell was constructed circa 1915-1920 and features a hip roof, uncommon for this period. Two large transverse barns and a toolshed are remaining outbuildings. The family cemetery is located in an adjacent field and retains a very old wooden grave marker.

Jerry and Agnes Sutton House
built 1906
Falling Creek community

Jerry and Agnes Sutton had this finely detailed, one-story, vernacular Queen Anne-style cottage constructed in 1906. A front projecting bay window and wraparound front porch with sawnwork brackets define the well-maintained house—a style not generally found as well developed in Lenoir County as in this nicely rendered example. A five-pane transom and three-pane sidelights flank the front entrance of the central-hall gable-and-wing plan, which retains an original rear ell. Completing the Victorian character are variegated shingles in the gable end, and cross gables with star-shaped ventilators set in circles.

Sutton-Ivy-Dawson House
built third quarter of the nineteenth century
Jenny Lind vicinity

Just south of "Buckleberry Poquosin" in the rich agricultural lands fronting the nearby Neuse River is the Sutton-Ivy-Dawson House, an exceptional example of the pervasive Greek Revival style. This one-story dwelling was likely built on the eve of the Civil War and exhibits traditional elements commonly identified with its antebellum counterparts. A low hip roof, the double-pile center-hall floor plan, two interior chimneys, and a handsome central-bay portico are all traditional Greek Revival details predominant in northern Lenoir County. Remarkable for surviving this late in the twentieth century, the small portico features a full pedimented gable supported by plain square columns. Certain traits such as pedimented window surrounds, unusually small corner pilasters, and arched panels in the front door point to a postbellum construction date, though the actual date for the house is unknown.

The area where the Sutton House is located was, during the antebellum period, a farming community associated with numerous members of the Sutton family, all living within a short distance of the Neuse River and the mid-1850s railroad connecting Raleigh with Kinston. T. Sutton was found at this location on the 1863 Confederate Engineer's Field Map. The house is thought to have been owned by an Ivy family by the 1870s. Katie Ivy, daughter of the second owner, married Richard Jeter Dawson on the grounds of the house circa 1904. Their son, Fred Dawson, presently owns the farmhouse.

Unlike many other mid-nineteenth-century farm dwellings, the Sutton House retains a smokehouse and detached kitchen—original outbuildings remaining on the farm. The heavy mortise-and-tenon smokehouse has recently been reroofed but retains an excellent board-and-batten door with strap hinges. The porch/breezeway that originally connected the kitchen to the house was enlarged and enclosed circa 1950 to create more interior space, constituting the dwelling's only exterior alteration. An early- to mid-twentieth-century feed production facility that distributed Nutrena Feeds to local farmers also remains.

Sutton-Barwick House (demolished)
built circa 1820-1830; demolished early 1990s
Bucklesberry vicinity

This oddly proportioned two-story frame house was believed to have been constructed for a John Sutton (1779-?) sometime during the 1820-to-1830 period. Sutton appears in census records as early as 1810 as the head of a family with one white male ages 26-45 (possibly a family member) and one white female aged 16-26 (presumably his wife). He is also credited with owning two slaves. By 1840 John Sutton had established a large family, with nine children, his wife, and one grown male living in his household, as well as having twenty-one slaves. The two-story Federal-style dwelling attributed to Sutton would have provided the space necessary for such a sizable family, as well as projecting a status of prominence befitting a planter financially enriched enough to own twenty-one slaves.

Demolished in the early 1990s, the Sutton House was one of the county's most intact plantation dwellings, as well as one of the most unusual, with its truncated second floor and enclosed end bay on the front porch. Often referred to as a peddlers or preachers porch, the enclosed room with a single door leading to the porch would have been offered to traveling drummers or circuit preachers for lodging. Paneled corner pilasters and chamfered porch posts with a simple balustrade completed the exterior. Interior treatments were plain but well-executed Federal motifs, such as the center-hall open-string stair with square newel and balusters, and the first-floor mantels with applied cornice moldings and unadorned pilasters.

The only surviving remnant of the nineteenth-century plantation is an outbuilding traditionally referred to as the plantation office. This one-story, heavily framed, gable-end building had, in its original configuration, one large room with opposing doors on the sides, a single window, and a gable-end chimney. The doors are board and batten as is a shutter that covers the window opening. The interior walls and ceiling appear never to have received any finish other than the patina rendered by years of smoke from the fireplace. Some woodwork is beaded, lending credence to the tradition that this building functioned as something other than an agricultural dependency.

George and Zenobia Fields House
built 1890s
Jenny Lind vicinity

Located at the end of a long dirt lane is the one-and-a-half-story house that Daniel Hines (1813-?) built for his daughter, Zenobia (1878-1962), who had recently married George Fields, in the 1890s behind his own house. The small central-hall-plan dwelling epitomizes the typical farmhouse of the era found throughout Lenoir County. Such features as a central-hall plan, wraparound front porch, and manufactured tongue-and-groove interior were up to date, but such traditional details as flush gable ends, a rear shed addition, a detached kitchen, nine-over-six sash windows, and tree stump foundation piers had been used since the early nineteenth century.

An impressive collection of outbuildings has been retained, including a smokehouse, mule stables, a workshop, tobacco barns, and a rare log crib. The log corncrib, with a cantilevered entrance and side shed, is almost identical to one found on Daniel Hines's neighboring farm.

Hines-Warters-Adkinson House
built circa 1860
Seven Springs vicinity

At the center of a modest farm complex constructed by Daniel Hines in the mid-nineteenth century is a one-and-half-story dwelling that is a variation of the coastal cottage house form. This form features a roof that encompasses the main rooms along with the front and rear shed rooms. Between the house's front porch rooms are a small recessed front porch featuring board-and-batten detailing and two front entrances. About 1900 an attached front porch was added in front of the recessed porch. The uncommon floor plan is centered around a rare central chimney and an enclosed stair that rises across the front wall. Though the interior has been modernized on the first floor, the second floor retains an original chamfered newel post and board-and-batten ceilings with plastered walls. Original board-and-batten and four-panel doors are retained throughout the house, along with the original rear kitchen/dining ell.

A wide range of outbuildings is intact, including a washhouse, workshop, log corncrib, and nineteenth-century outbuilding whose original use is unknown.

The farm was inherited by Alice Hines Warters who later rented it to the Adkinson family. This African American tenant farming family, who had rented the farm since the 1930s, purchased the house in 1971. Needham Adkinson is the present owner.

Raymond Jones House

built third quarter of the nineteenth century
Jenny Lind vicinity

This significant two-story Greek Revival-style farmhouse is illustrative of postbellum construction attainable by a small number of planters who survived the ravages of the Civil War relatively unscathed. Long associated with twentieth-century black tenant Raymond Jones, the house originally belonged to an unknown owner. The imposing siting of the dwelling suggests a continuation of pre-Civil War traditions. The picturesque and prominent location of the Jones House, along with a retention of much (though seriously deteriorated) physical integrity, makes the dwelling one of Lenoir County's most impressive sites.

Built in an era when most farmers, suffering from financial collapse following the Civil War, could afford only modest dwellings, this house stands out as an anomaly. Several architectural details, such as the low hip roof, board-and-batten ceilings, and two-story portico with a pediment supported by large square columns, are Greek Revival in nature and thus carryovers from the antebellum period. Other traditional elements, such as an enclosed stair and rear shed rooms, are more reminiscent of vernacular, homegrown ideas. The rear detached kitchen/dining ell trimmed with exterior board-and-batten siding (a late Greek Revival-era treatment) is connected by a rather large breezeway to the rear of the house. This arrangement was constructed nearly universally after the Civil War, though few examples as intact as this one remain. The front porch configuration is original, but surviving reused slats from the first-floor balustrade suggest that the first-floor porch was enlarged in the late nineteenth century.

An antebellum construction date would normally be assumed for a dwelling with such thorough Greek Revival finish, but several features suggest a construction date in the immediate postwar period. In addition to rather unskillfully constructed details, the inclusion of sawn sills and factory-made four-panel doors, mantels, and shutters—with hardware manufactured by Lull and Porter—as well as severely plain post-and-lintel mantels and undecorated door and window surrounds, indicate postbellum construction. Simple and crudely fashioned

trim on such a substantial dwelling was uncharacteristic of the plantation economy of antebellum Lenoir County. Evidently the owner lacked the money necessary to build in a manner consistent with the properous antebellum years. The house does not appear on the 1863 Confederate Engineer's Field Map, further evidence of a postbellum date of construction.

No outbuildings have survived, and the house, which is now surrounded by crops, was never updated with electricity or plumbing.

Rockford Chapel Free Will Baptist Church

built circa 1915
LaGrange vicinity

Consistent with traditional African American churches built throughout eastern North Carolina during the early twentieth century, this vernacular frame church was constructed for the Rockford Chapel Baptist Church congregation circa 1915. According to nearby resident Raymond Elijah Sutton, the name derives from the nearby eighteenth-century Rockford plantation, owned by the Whitfield family. The overall form of the church resembles that of a front-gable meetinghouse with an applied three-stage bell tower. Unadorned on the exterior, the church rests on a brick foundation and is capped by a standing-seam metal roof. Replacement siding and windows as well as a modern rear addition denote the church's active use during the second half of the twentieth century.

Benjamin Franklin Sutton House

built circa 1860; wing added circa 1900
Jenny Lind vicinity

Standing as the centerpiece of an outstanding ensemble of farm buildings, this vernacular one-and-a-half-story farmhouse evolved over at least two major building periods. The earlier portion of the house is an excellent example of a late Greek Revival-era dwelling. Simple yet large Greek Revival mantels, beaded board-and-batten ceilings, two-panel doors (one retaining its original robust paint scheme), and a central hall are details that place the house in the late antebellum era, probably circa 1860. Other architectural elements found in the house persisted from the earlier Federal era, such as an enclosed hall stair and nine-over-six sash windows. A rear kitchen/dining ell, dating to the original house construction, was initially detached, but the breezeway was enclosed in the mid-twentieth century for bathroom space.

Between 1899 and 1901 a large wing was added to the front of the house, containing some of rural Lenoir County's finest Victorian detailing. Comprised of a large side hall and two rooms with tall twelve-foot-high ceilings, the addition retains two vigorous Victorian mantels, corner closets, and a wraparound porch supported by chamfered columns. The most striking architectural detail is the hall curtain framework—chamfered posts that mimic the porch columns, and a ceiling lintel with a small keystone element. This traditional Victorian feature would have supported a drapery that separated the rear hall from the front hall, where visitors entered.

The extraordinary collection of well-maintained outbuildings includes a rare example of a two-story smokehouse and a large barn, both of which probably date to the third quarter of the nineteenth century. The construction technique of these two buildings is a unique combination of heavy mortise and tenon with exterior flush sheathing. The barn (originally located very near the road) has horizontal strips that cover the cracks in the sheathing, similar to board-and-batten sheathing, and the smokehouse was weatherboarded. Completing the ensemble of outbuildings are a very rare potato house, mule stables, silos, tobacco barns, and a farm equipment shed. The family cemetery is prominently located near the front of the house.

Benjamin Franklin Sutton (1838-1897) is credited with the construction of the original portion of the house. Sutton married four times, and all of his wives are buried beside him in the family cemetery. His wives were (in order of marriage) Henrietta (1846-1878), Laura (1858-1881), Elsie Ann (1853-1886), and Mary Frances (1864-1910), who married G. W. Wynne in 1899, after Benjamin F. Sutton died in 1897. The Victorian addition to the house is credited to Wynne and his bride, Mary Frances. Clifton Rinehart Sutton Sr. (circa 1896-1984), Benjamin F. Sutton's son, inherited the farm and resided there until his death. The house has remained vacant since. Clifton Sutton Sr. recalled that the Victorian addition was constructed when he was four years old, validating the circa 1900 date.

Wood-Sutton House

built 1840s
Jenny Lind vicinity

An important example of the late Federal-style farmhouse, this prominent dwelling is thought to have been constructed by Dempsey Wood (1815-1880) in the 1840s. The large two-story house features an attenuated form with asymmetrical facade, two tall exterior end chimneys, and a hall-and-parlor floor plan, hallmarks of Federal-era architecture. One original, deeply paneled mantel, of transitional Federal/Greek Revival design, has survived many modernizations and helps date the house to the late Federal period.

A large array of outbuildings contributes to the large farm's strong sense of place and includes a rare granary, packhouses, a garage, tobacco barns, tenant houses, and modern bulk barns. Located in a small grove of trees to the rear of the farm is the original family cemetery, which contains the graves of Dempsey Wood, his wife, Elizabeth, and their son Thomas H. Wood (1849-1880).

The present owner, Alton Sutton, inherited the farm from his father, Marcus Sutton, who purchased it in 1931 from the Creech family. How the farm was passed to the Creech family from the original Wood owners is not known.

John Aldredge Sutton House

built circa 1875
Bucklesberry vicinity

John Aldredge Sutton (1840-1915) was the son of Hardy and Anna Hill Sutton. He is buried, with his wife, Martha A. Sutton, in a family cemetery adjacent to this one-story three-bay vernacular farmhouse. Probably built in the midst of Reconstruction, the center hall-plan house has several traits linking it to its antebellum Greek Revival predecessors, such as the four-pane sidelights surrounding the entrance, which is sheltered by a Greek Revival portico with chamfered posts. A testament to the enduring influence of this most pervasive style, the house also has hewn sills with circular-sawn joists, four-panel front and rear doors, and simple brick piers. The frame smokehouse at the rear of the house is twentieth-century in origin, as are the tobacco barn and shed. The Sutton House represents what was likely the most common house type constructed in the county during the economically depressed years of Reconstruction, when most families could not afford to build elaborate houses.

LaGrange: "A Good cotton and tobacco market . . . containing quite a number of pretty homes"

Circa 1904 View of Railroad Street, LaGrange, looking east from Caswell Street. The freight depot and warehouse of the Atlantic and North Carolina Railroad stand along the tracks, and stores appear in the right foreground. The distinctive turret of Col. A. C. Davis' house on East Railroad Street, beside the site of the Davis Military Academy in the 1880s, is visible in the background. The Davis House still stands, but the academy buildings are gone.

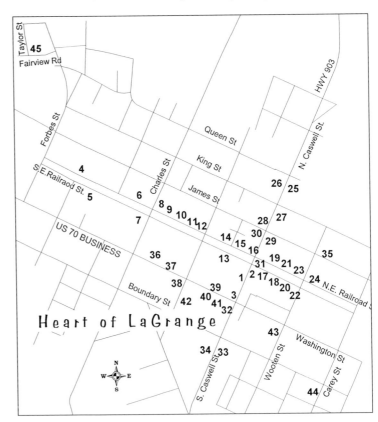

LaGrange, praised in 1906 as "a good cotton and tobacco market . . . containing quite a number of pretty homes," owes its existence to the railroad, whose tracks were laid through this section of rural Lenoir County from 1855 to 1858 when the Atlantic and North Carolina Railroad was built from Morehead City to Goldsboro.[1] In 1848, shortly before the tracks came through, Col. William D. Moseley had sold off the portion of his plantation that the railroad would traverse to local farmer Council Wooten, and it is he who apparently took advantage of the situation to develop a town. LaGrange was nicknamed the Garden Spot in the late 1800s because of its verdant streets lined with trees. The heritage visible today along the quiet streets is architecture—several hundred dwellings, churches, and stores in their historical styles of Queen Anne with its bays, porches, and gingerbread trim; Gothic Revival with its richness; and others. The block-long business district on Caswell Street contains the second-generation, fireproof brick stores that succeeded the frame stores.

LaGrange enjoys a strategic location twelve miles by rail from the county seat, Kinston, and fourteen miles from Goldsboro, the county seat of adjacent Wayne County. According to tradition, the railroad tracks from the two county seats joined at LaGrange; to celebrate, a multitude feasted at a big dinner where "oysters and Whiskey were plentiful." [2] A train depot, known as Moseley Hall Depot for the largest plantation in the vicinity, was built at this time. Moseley Hall plantation had been the post office and stagecoach stop for this section for a number of years. The plantation house, at the northern end of North Caswell Street, burned about 1917.

The land north and south of the tracks was laid out in grid-patterned blocks and subdivided into lots, presumably soon after the railroad came through. The developer apparently was Council Wooten, who owned this tract of land. The principal street, Railroad Street, flanks the tracks, with the section on the north side of the tracks called North Railroad Avenue and the one on the south side South Railroad Avenue, on early maps. The street is now known as West Railroad Street west of Caswell Street, and East Railroad Street to the east. Crossing the tracks at the original depot, a principal north-south street, Caswell Street, was laid out. James Street and Washington Street were laid out to the north and south; Center Street and Wooten Street to the west and east. This core contained the densest growth for many years; in fact, the Sanborn Fire Insurance Company mapped only these six blocks until 1914.

The community, like the rest of Lenoir County, suffered the turmoil of the Civil War from 1861 to 1865, with a number of town youth fighting in the Confederate army. The army encamped only four miles from town. After the war Moseley Hall Depot, set in the middle of Falling Creek Township, one of the most fertile agricultural regions in the county, became an important shipping and receiving point for farm products and supplies. Tradesmen and professionals moved to town to supply goods and services, but the majority of the population remained connected to rural farms. Residents often drove herds of swine and cattle to Richmond, Virginia, to market. [3]

The town was incorporated in 1869 and renamed LaGrange. There had been some confusion in mail delivery because another town had the name Moseley Hall. The origin of the name LaGrange, French for barn and also the name of a national agricultural association, is unknown, but the name may have seemed suitable because the town was a rural village in which the chief occupation was agriculture. LaGrange's leading families, doctors, merchants, and tradesmen alike, were also farmers. They lived and practiced their trades or professions in town while supervising farms out in the country, often with the aid of overseers.

The commercial district initially developed along Railroad Street with the construction of stores by Drew Murphy and Colonel F. Whitfield. In 1872 there were three factories in town: Obadiah Pearce's buggy and cart factory, Freeman Smith's boot and shoe factory, and Asa McCoy's harness and saddle factory. Nearly a dozen merchants had general merchandise, grocery, or liquor stores by that year.[4] LaGrange had grown into a genteel town by the 1880s, with a newspaper, the Spectator, and a parklike cemetery, known as Fairview Cemetery, on the northwest edge of town.[5] By 1893, the first year that the Sanborn Fire Insurance Company mapped LaGrange, the 100 block of Caswell Street between Railroad and Washington Streets had become "downtown." The block was approximately half full of one-story wooden groceries and general merchandise stores. Robert

B. Kinsey's General Store, a two-story brick showplace with stained-glass transoms, and his equally fancy one-story grocery next door, had already been erected on the west side of the block. By 1911 the block had a nearly solid row of mostly wooden stores, including furniture stores, banks, barbershops, and printing shops. The district was becoming such a desirable place to do business that old buildings were being demolished to make way for new ones. T. R. Rouse's new Rouse Banking Company was being built at the northeast corner of Railroad and Caswell Streets in 1908, on the site of a frame grocery store that had been there for many years.[6] The bank presents a Roman temple facade to the street, with classical pilasters supporting a modillioned pediment, meant to symbolize the integrity and stability of the business.   LaGrange's importance as a station town and its large number of boarding students from out of town induced many local residents to turn their homes into boardinghouses. Mrs. Henry Fields kept the Fields House, the first hotel, a long wooden building, around the corner from the business district on Railroad Street. In the early-twentieth century the two-story brick Harper Hotel, across from the passenger depot, served travelers.[7]

A series of fires, beginning in 1911, wiped out nearly all the old wooden stores in the business block and other buildings along Railroad Street, such as the Fields House, as well. This cleared the way for the erection of a new and improved brick business district. On the 1914 Sanborn map, the north half of the downtown block was already largely rebuilt, with one- and two-story brick buildings, including a movie theater on the east side. By 1925 the block had assumed the architectural appearance that it largely retains today. The 1880s Kinsey General Store and Grocery, one of the few survivors of the fires, is the oldest store in LaGrange.

Schools and Churches

By the 1870s LaGrange's schools became an inducement to farming families to move to town. The earliest schools in town were said to have been operated in residences, including the home of Council Wooten. The first school open to the general public was started about 1870 by Dr. Preston Wooley in a building on West James Street, later the site of the Kinsey Seminary, one block north of the railroad tracks and three blocks west of the business district. In 1874 Joseph E. Kinsey and his brother Robert B. Kinsey moved to LaGrange and taught in this school.

During the decade of the 1880s two private schools of high reputation, one for boys and one for girls, operated in LaGrange, serving as magnets for youth from Lenoir and surrounding counties. The Davis Military Academy for boys was established in 1880 on East Railroad Street about one block east of the business district, on a large campus extending for more than a city block. The founder, Colonel Adam C. Davis, had buildings constructed in a quadrangular arrangement. The school flourished, attracting at its peak some two hundred young men from nearby counties, and some from farther away. In the 1889-1890 school year a meningitis epidemic forced the sudden closure of the school. Colonel Davis reopened it in Winston-Salem a short time later.[8]

In 1881 Joe Kinsey established the Kinsey Seminary for girls in the same building in which the Wooley School had operated. Enrollment eventually reached about sixty. This school for girls flourished until 1897, when it moved to Wilson and continued to grow. When Kinsey retired in 1901, the Kinsey Seminary at Wilson became Atlantic Christian College, still in operation and now known as Barton College.[9]

LaGrange High School, a public school, began in the two-story frame Kinsey Seminary for Girls about 1892, operating there until 1907, when a large brick school was built on West Railroad Street. By 1918 the school had twelve grades. The present brick building was constructed in 1928 beside the 1907 building to serve as a consolidated high school. The original building then served elementary-age pupils from LaGrange and the surrounding vicinity. In 1950 the elementary building was replaced with a new building. In 1964, with the construction of a new consolidated rural high school, the entire LaGrange School facility became an elementary school. The oldest school building surviving in LaGrange is the 1928 facility, but Colonel Davis's impressive 1880 house still stands on the old Davis Military Academy site, proof of the high level of architectural taste in town at this time.

As farming families moved to LaGrange to take advantage of town amenities, new church congregations sprang up. By 1877 there were Methodist, Free Will Baptist, and Union Baptist churches for white citizens.[10] The first church erected in town was the First Missionary Baptist Church, built at 201 North Caswell Street on a tract donated to the congregation by Council Wooten. The congregation of Bear Creek Primitive Baptist Church, located a few miles north, actually moved its church building into town about 1880 (it is now the LaGrange Garden Clubhouse at 210 West Washington Street). By 1900 the Methodist, Presbyterian, and Christian denominations had all built churches in town.[11]

LaGrange's African American citizens played an important role in town history. By 1877 they had several Free Will Baptist churches. By 1925 there were approximately seven African American churches, including Moore's Chapel A.M.E. Zion Church on Boundary Street, the grand brick LaGrange Missionary Baptist Church on Carey Street, a Presbyterian church on Boundary Street, and Saint Luke's Free Will Baptist Church on King Street. Most of these were in the southeast section of town, in the black community. [12]

The high quality of LaGrange architecture is particularly visible in its churches. For white LaGrange, the two finest sanctuaries were the LaGrange Presbyterian Church of 1892 (now the Rotary Club building) and the LaGrange Free Will Baptist Church (114 North Caswell Street) of about 1895. Both buildings, covered outside and inside with imaginative Gothic Revival features, are apparently the work of the same builder. An African American congregation built an equally splendid Gothic Revival sanctuary of brick, the Ebenezer Missionary Baptist Church, in 1920. Its towers reflect a long tradition of the twin-towered form in eastern North Carolina black churches.

Cotton and Tobacco Warehouses and Processing Plants

The earliest cotton gin in LaGrange was said to have been built by a man named McIntyre, probably in the late 1800s. In 1919 there were three gins in town: Luby Measley's gin on James Street, Alex Sutton's gin on East Railroad Street, and Jones and Hardy's gin on East Railroad Street.[13] Tobacco warehouses and processing plants appeared in LaGrange in the 1890s, at the same time that Kinston was gearing up as a market for the yellow leaf that Lenoir County farmers had begun to grow. By 1919 LaGrange had six tobacco warehouses with floor space to handle several million pounds of tobacco daily, along with a prizery, a stemmery, and a rehandling house, which processed tobacco for shipment to the factories that would convert it into the finished product. A 1920 fire is said to have burned the warehouses, ending the town's tobacco market era.[14] None of the historic tobacco buildings have survived.

LaGrange had only a few manufacturing facilities. John H. Rouse operated a buggy manufactory and undertaking business in a large complex near the depot on North Caswell Street from the 1890s to the 1920s. Hardy and Newsome operated an iron foundry, which made iron pots and agricultural implements, as well as a celebrated bean "operated" harvester. The brick factory was built about 1918 on West Railroad Street across from the LaGrange Graded School and continued in use as a foundry until recent years. The building still stands, although unused.

Residential Architecture

In 1906 the town had 151 building lots, 82 owned by whites and 69 by blacks.[15] LaGrange has grown so gently since the mid-nineteenth century that many of its original buildings dating from then to the early twentieth century still exist. All along the railroad tracks through the eastern and midland counties of the state, new houses in the latest fashion were being built. Such display was no doubt due to the progressive inclinations of the homeowners, who embraced the future by addressing their residences directly to the tracks, as well as to the new ease of receiving the latest millwork, and sash and blind products from distant factories by rail. Near Moseley Hall Depot Shade Wooten built a stylish Gothic Revival house, at 204 West Railroad Street, about 1860. The George Taylor House at 302 West Railroad Street and the Nan Sutton House at 114 West Railroad Street are Greek Revival-style cottages built around the same time. These are the three oldest houses in LaGrange that have retained their original appearance.

Today the houses lined neatly along the principal thoroughfares of West Washington, Railroad, and Caswell Streets, as well as the intervening streets, present a catalogue of fifty years of historic architecture, from the 1880s to the 1930s. When new construction started up after the economic disruptions of the Civil War, LaGrange embraced the Queen Anne style. This style, which dominated until about 1910, not only met the need of residents to be up to date, but also adapted well to the summer heats. Steep pyramidal hipped roofs acted like umbrellas, shielding high-ceilinged interiors from the hot sun. Wraparound porches shaded windows and created outdoor living rooms.

In the late 1880s businessman and farmer George B. W. Hadley built one of the earliest Queen Anne-style houses still standing in LaGrange, at 108 West Railroad Street. The two-story house reflects the transition in style from the Italianate Revival of the 1870s and 1880s to the Queen Anne style of the 1880s and 1890s. The Hadley House has the gable-and-wing form, a two-story bay window, and wide molded trim. The earliest full-blown Queen Anne-style house still standing, and one of the finest ever built in LaGrange, is Colonel A. C. Davis's two-and-one-half-story house at 131 East Railroad Street. The gable-and-wing form has characteristic Queen Anne features—windows with peaked lintels, stained-glass windows, patterned shingles in the cross gables, and a wraparound porch with fancy millwork trim—but also has a unique tower with a shingled bell-shaped turret sheltering a second-story balcony. The interior is similarly detailed with a grand staircase in the center hall, Eastlake-style spindle hall friezes separating the front hall from the rear hall, and ornate mantelpieces. Other good examples of the Queen Anne style are the Octavius Taylor House at 127 East Railroad Street, the Sutton-Kinsey House at 107 West Washington Street, and the Walter Pace House at 309 North Caswell Street.

By the early years of the twentieth century taste in residential design was shifting to the Colonial Revival and Classical Revival styles, then to the Craftsman bungalow style in the late 1910s and 1920s. When banker Thomas Richard Rouse built a new house at 212 West Railroad Street in 1916 and 1917, the contrast between it and houses of the late 1800s could not have been starker. Rouse's two-story house was square and symmetrical, with bands of large plain windows, a simple classical entrance, and a classical front porch that did not wrap around the corners of the house. In 1920-1921 Thomas Richard Rouse built one of the earliest and most stylish bungalows in the county at 214 West Railroad Street as a wedding present for his daughter, Eliza, and her husband, Atlas B. Windham. The massive roof of the one-and-one-half-story house overhangs the walls, with heavy eave brackets, and shelters the front porch with its heavy masonry posts. Pebble-textured stucco covers the walls, and large windows of upper sash with tiny lights set over single-pane lower sash let in the light. A trellised porte cochere extends from the side. All of these features were characteristic of the bungalow, a style that remained popular in LaGrange until World War II.

Notes

1. *Kinston Free Press*, 1906 Industrial Issue, 101.

2. Nannie Braxton Herring, "History of LaGrange," manuscript, circa 1919, 1955.

3. *Kinston Free Press*, 1906 Industrial Issue, 101-104; Herring, "History of LaGrange."

4. Herring, "History of LaGrange," *Branson's North Carolina Business Directory*, 1872.

5. *News Argus*, Goldsboro, March 29, 1970.

6. Sanborn Fire Insurance Maps, 1893-1908.

7. Herring, "History of LaGrange"; *Kinston Free Press*, 1906 Industrial Issue.

8. Virginia Pou Doughton, "A Bright Spot in LaGrange," *State*, September 1980, 10-12.

9. Ware, *History of Atlantic Christian College*, 32, 62-64.

10. *Branson's North Carolina Business Directory*, 1877-78.

11. Herring, "History of LaGrange;" Sanborn Fire Insurance Map, 1925.

12. Sanborn Fire Insurance Map, 1925.

13. Herring, "History of LaGrange;" Sanborn Fire Insurance Map, 1919.

14. Goldsboro *News Argus*, March 29, 1970. The tobacco buildings appear in the following sequence in the Sanborn Fire Insurance Maps: 1897: LaGrange Tobacco Warehouse on Charles Street; 1904: Banner Warehouse on James Street; 1908: the old LaGrange Graded School on James Street had become a tobacco warehouse; 1914: Parks Warehouse on West Railroad Street, May and Taylor Warehouse on Center Street, Parks and Jones Prizery on James Street; 1919: J. M. Edmunds Stemmery on West Railroad Street, J. E. May Rehandling House on James Street, Farmers Tobacco Sales Warehouse on James Street.

15. *Kinston Free Press*, 1906 Industrial Issue, 101.

1. LaGrange Commercial District

built 1880s-1950s
100 block of South Caswell Street between East Railroad Street and East Washington Street

The densely packed block of one- and two-story brick commercial buildings, which share party walls, that form LaGrange's central business district is an outdoor museum of the town's commercial history. Approximately eighteen store buildings front on each side of the block. A series of fires beginning in 1911 destroyed all of the old frame stores that formed the original business district of LaGrange. But by 1914 the block had been largely rebuilt with one- and two-story brick buildings. Many of these still exist, interspersed with pre-1911 brick buildings that escaped the fire and with more recent commercial buildings.

Few of the buildings underwent the concealment behind metal false fronts that disfigured so many business districts in the 1960s and 1970s. The original upper facades of these commercial buildings still display their ornate metal and brickwork cornices and window openings. The building at 137 South Caswell Street was a grocery store in the 1890s. The store at 117 South Caswell Street still has "Simeon Wooten" inscribed on its facade parapet; in the early twentieth century Wooten supposedly sold everything "from a paper of pins to a pair of mules and a wagon" here. The building at 141 South Caswell Street was a general store in 1908, then a "moving picture theatre" by 1914.

2. (former) Rouse Banking Company

built circa 1919
101 South Caswell Street

Situated at the pivotal corner where LaGrange's business district along South Caswell Street adjoins the railroad tracks along Railroad Street, Thomas Richard Rouse's Rouse Banking Company is one of the oldest and most architecturally distinctive stores in LaGrange. The Neoclassical Revival-style building, one bay wide and two stories tall, extends nine bays to the rear along Railroad Street. The main facade features a classical temple form of full-height Ionic pilasters, a tall paneled frieze, and a pediment with a modillion cornice. The first-floor entrance is a modern replacement, but the band of three windows across the second story is original, as is the triglyph-and-metope frieze separating the two stories. The building has a flat roof and a plain side elevation, whose second-story windows have been infilled.

T. R. Rouse, a prosperous farmer, was cashier of Rouse Banking Company during the early twentieth century. According to the 1906 Industrial Issue of the *Kinston Free Press*, "the large clientage of the bank is a tribute to [Rouse's] fidelity to his trust, to his unfailing courtesy, and to his excellent business methods." Rouse's first bank, built about 1914, burned in 1919 and was rebuilt. The building has served as a branch for Mutual Savings and Loan Company and for Branch Banking and Trust.

The interior was remodeled in the 1960s, although the pressed-tin ceiling is still visible in a portion of the interior. The bank is now owned by the LaGrange Restoration Commission.

3. Kinsey General Store and Grocery
built circa 1880
140 South Caswell Street

Robert B. Kinsey, a native of Jones County, came to LaGrange with his brother, Joseph, in 1874 to teach at Dr. Preston Wooley's new public school. Joseph Kinsey was to take over Wooley's school, which became the Kinsey Seminary in 1881. Robert, however, decided that his future lay in the mercantile, rather than the academic, sphere. By 1884 Branson's business directory lists R. B. Kinsey as the owner of a general store. Kinsey's handsome brick, two-story, five-bay Italianate style general store and its brick one-story three-bay side extension, listed as a grocery on LaGrange's 1893 Sanborn map, are both thought to have been built in the early 1880s. To have two brick structures of such high exterior and interior finish in a small settlement like LaGrange was quite unusual, and indicative of Kinsey's prosperity. LaGrange's commercial center from the 1880s to the early twentieth century consisted primarily of one- and two-story, frame buildings, which had plank sidewalks

and shed pass-throughs along the fronts. In 1911, according to the contemporary account of a LaGrange citizen, "a series of fires . . . wiped out all the old wooden buildings," and brick ones took their place. The Kinsey family owned the general store and grocery as recently as 1976.

Both the grocery and the general store have retained their exterior physical integrity remarkably. Both have exceptional period exterior decoration, which rivals that on surviving contemporary buildings in nearby Kinston, such as the B. W. Canady Building on North Queen Street. To begin from the top, the pedimented cast-iron cornice crowning the general store is missing an end finial, but the tympanum's sunburst decoration is as impressive as it must have been over a century ago. The cornice's brackets are repeated just over the first-floor entrance's stained-glass windows. Below these brackets are three recessed panels (for either decoration or signage). A raised brick stringcourse wraps around the building just below the second-story windows' raised lintels. The five second-story windows, which are now boarded, have concrete sills, and peaked lintels with an incised S-scroll motif often seen in Victorian Italianate decoration.

The first floor of the general store consists of a double-leaf center entrance, flanked by a large bay display window on each side, and a paneled double-leaf side-hall entry, where stairs rise to the second floor. Above the doors and display windows and below the cast-iron brackets are eight exceptional (and incredibly well preserved) stained-glass windows, accented by an overhead frieze of smaller clear-glass panes. The design of the windows, a kaleidoscopic pattern centered in each window by a round, painted, stained-glass design of birds and flowers, is in keeping with the Eastlake-influenced decoration, a fusion of orientalism with the Arts and Crafts movement, of the 1880s. One of these stained-glass windows is the side entrance's transom.

The grocery's centered double-leaf entrance, with its large plain two-light transom, is flanked by a large two-over-two display window on each side. Below the doors and windows are wooden panels. There is a simple bracketed cast-iron entablature/architrave above the windows and transom, but the pilasters framing the entrance are plain brick, instead of slim decorated cast-iron pilasters like those framing the general store's entrance and display windows. Above the entablature are a frieze, consisting of three recessed brick panels, and a stepped brick cornice.

The stores have had a series of connected and detached outbuildings, the development and eradication of which can be easily traced through the LaGrange Sanborn Fire Insurance Maps from between 1893 and 1925. The first known outbuilding was a one-story kitchen, connected to the rear of the general store by a covered breezeway in 1893. There was also a small warehouse (apparently frame) located behind the grocery at that time. In 1897 the warehouse and two small outbuildings were still in place (a long shed beside the warehouse, possibly a stable, had been torn down by 1897), and the kitchen, according to the 1893 and 1897 Sanborn maps, may have been expanded. In 1904 the kitchen, still connected to the store (the store now described as "dry goods, B&S and clothes"), had been converted to a one-and-a-half-story dwelling. The warehouse and outbuildings had been expanded. In 1908, with South Caswell Street's commercial area being further expanded and developed, there were also some notable changes at R. B. Kinsey's general store. A brick one-story double store ("furniture and stoves") to the north side had added two connected warehouses where part of the Kinsey store's dwelling had stood. The dwelling, then a one-story building with an attached porch, was located directly behind the Kinsey store, and this arrangement continued in 1914. By 1919 the dwelling had been moved a short distance west and converted into another warehouse. In fact, it is tempting to speculate that an abandoned frame one-and-a-half-story triple-A cottage, its windows boarded but its original standing-seam metal roof in place (the cottage now sits a short distance behind the general store), could be the "store dwelling," a supposition that could possibly be confirmed or refuted by documentary photographs. The only known surviving outbuilding behind the general store, a two-bay brick hipped-roof warehouse built circa 1908 for the furniture/stove double store, was later said to have been used for storing tobacco.

4. LaGrange Elementary School
built 1928
300 block of West Railroad Street

The two-story brick building used since 1964 as the LaGrange Elementary School is significant as one of the oldest and best-preserved schools in Lenoir County. Well-known school architect Leslie Boney of Wilmington designed the building in the academic Colonial Revival style. The long rectangular school, containing twelve classrooms, features a flat roof with low parapet walls, a prominent brick stringcourse, and bands of windows. The focus of the facade is the arched, recessed entrance sheltered by a gabled portico with slender fluted classical columns. In the 1950s the Works Projects Administration gymnasium, known as the Tin Can, was replaced by a brick gymnasium addition to the rear of the building. The interior of the school was completely renovated in the 1970s.

LaGrange had several earlier public school buildings.

In 1907 the school moved from West James Street to a new brick building at this site. By 1918 this school had twelve grades and eleven teachers. In 1928 superintendent E. E. Sams consolidated the elementary schools in the LaGrange vicinity into the 1907 building and built this new building to serve as a modern high school with twelve classrooms, a library, and laboratories. In 1950 a new building for grades one through eight was completed behind the 1928 school, and the 1907 building was demolished. In 1964 a new high school was completed at another site, and the LaGrange School became an elementary school.

5. Hardy-Newsome Manufactory
built circa 1918
300 block West Railroad Street

About 1918 two prosperous landowners of this section of Lenoir County, Herman Hardy and a Mr. Newsome, built the Hardy-Newsome Bean Harvester Factory, a two-story gable brick building with a stepped parapet facade facing the railroad tracks on Railroad Street. All the openings are segmentally arched, including three large loading doors on the main facade. Iron tie rods with star-shaped ends strengthen the brick walls. The company prospered, necessitating a flat-roofed two-story addition with segmental-arched windows and doors at a later date.

By 1925 the manufactory incorporated an adjacent industrial complex, the J. M. Edmunds Company, located east on Railroad Street, into its operations. This was a tobacco stemmery, built in the early twentieth century, that employed several hundred people by 1919. This sprawling one-story brick complex was enlarged and altered during later years but retains its common-bond brick walls and segmental-arched windows.

A small, one-story frame store with a false front, built as a company store, still stands behind the old stemmery complex on the east side of School Street. The storefront retains two-over-two flanking display windows, now sheltered by an aluminum awning. The store has since become a neighborhood grocery.

Writing in 1919, local school-girl Nannie Braxton Herring described the factory as "the largest, if not the only bean harvester factory" apparently in the state. The harvester was invented by a man named Suggs, from

Greene County, who was the overseer of Herman Hardy's farm. In the early 1950s, during the Korean War, the factory made camouflage and ammunition boxes for the federal government. The foundry continued to operate until the 1980s. The complex is presently unused.

6. George Taylor House
built circa 1868
302 West Railroad Street

One of the oldest houses in LaGrange, this one-story frame Greek Revival-style cottage is known as the George Taylor House because of its long association with members of the George Taylor family, who lived here from 1900 to 1982. The side-gable dwelling, three bays wide, is two rooms deep. The builder imitated a Greek temple by applying wide Doric corner posts and a wide frieze, which wraps around the gable ends. The center-bay door has a classical-style transom and sidelights and is sheltered by a well-proportioned pedimented portico with square Doric posts. A vernacular sawnwork balustrade encloses the porch. The well-preserved house retains plain siding on the exterior. On the interior the house retains original pine flooring, mantels, heart pine pegged doors, and high ceilings.

J. P. Walters III purchased the property from Taylor descendants in 1982, and he and his family reside there.

7. Smithwick-Stanton House
built circa 1900
301 West Railroad Street

One of numerous stylish and commodious residences built facing the railroad tracks in LaGrange at the turn of the century, this two-story frame house has the gable-and-wing form that was popular during the period. The main block has a side-gable roof, with a projecting front-gabled wing. Characteristics of the popular Queen Anne style are the bay window with a paneled wainscot projecting from the wing, and the porch nestled beside the wing, with chamfered posts, sawnwork brackets, and a turned balustrade. The four-over-four sash windows are surmounted by peaked lintels that reflect the Victorian interest in Gothic architecture. The well-preserved house retains its plain siding and rear kitchen-dining room ell, capped by a hipped roof and a bracketed cornice.

The house may have been built for J. M. W. Smithwick, who was living there by 1905. Smithwick, one of three doctors in town at this time, taught chemistry, physiology, and physics at LaGrange High School, and had the added distinction of being the first person in LaGrange to own an automobile. Later the Stanton family owned and resided in the house. In the 1970s it became the property of B. Eugene Taylor.

8. A. B. and Eliza Windham House

built 1920-1921
214 West Railroad Street

The Windham House, LaGrange's most impressive example of the Craftsman bungalow style popular throughout the United States during the early twentieth century, was built as a wedding present for Eliza Rouse Windham and her husband, Atlas Bernice Windham, by Eliza's father, Thomas Richard Rouse. Rouse had been cashier of the Rouse Banking Company for many years and was also a prosperous farmer. Rouse deeded the half-acre lot to his daughter and son-in-law. The house later was bought by Willie Gray Britt soon after his marriage to Dr. Smithwick's daughter Inez. They renovated the home and made the attic into bedrooms. Mr. and Mrs. Leroy Martin reside there now.

The Windham House stands apart from the more typical Craftsman-style houses in LaGrange because of its pebbledash stucco walls, its unusual twenty-four-over-one sash lights in the large windows, and dramatically battered porch posts. The one-and-one-half-story house features characteristically Craftsman-style overhanging eaves with eave brackets, an engaged front porch, and a side porte cochere. Craftsman-style light fixtures at the entrance are original.

9. Rouse–Joyner House

built 1916-1917
212 West Railroad Street

Thomas Richard Rouse, prosperous farmer and cashier of the Rouse Banking Company in LaGrange for many years, had this house built as his own residence in 1917. The large two-story frame house exhibits the simple Classical Revival style that was popular in Lenoir County at this time. The center entrance has a classical transom and sidelights. Paired one-over-one sash windows illuminate the large rooms that flank the center hallway at each level. A wide one-story porch, supported by boxed Doric posts, with a simple balustrade shelters the main facade. A hipped roof covers the dwelling, with a hipped dormer window in the center of the facade.

In 1935 noted educator James Yadkin Joyner, who had married T. R. Rouse's sister, Effie Rouse, bought the house. T. R. Rouse, Miss Bessie Rouse, and Dr. Joyner lived in the house until Joyner's death in 1954. Joyner's son, James, then lived there until his death in the 1970s. At that time the house became the property of George R. Rouse, the son of T. R. Rouse. The current owners and occupants are C. E. and Mary Pell Rouse Foster. Mrs. Foster is the daughter of George R. Rouse.

10. McDonald House

built 1867; remodeled circa 1900
210 West Railroad Street

The ornate, architecturally unusual two-story frame house at 210 West Railroad Street was the home of a man named McDonald, a druggist who owned a drugstore in the 100 block of South Caswell Street in the early twentieth century. The original house was constructed, according to a date found in a fireplace, in 1867. The appearance of the original house is not known. About 1900 the house was remodeled to its present appearance, an eclectic blend of Victorian architectural features, probably for Mr. McDonald. The three-bay-wide main block, one room deep, has a side-gable roof with a front decorative cross gable. The center front door and the nine-over-nine (replacement) sash windows have peaked lintels. A two-story pedimented porch, one bay wide, shelters the front door and a second-story door. Clusters of turned posts support the porch, and a turned balustrade and spindle frieze, with curvilinear brackets, decorate the upper porch. A one-story porch with turned posts extends across the entire facade. The gables are finished

with patterned shingles, decorative ventilators, and sawn-work bargeboards.

On the interior the center hall contains a magnificent curved staircase, following the curved plaster wall of the rear of the hall. A heavy turned newel, a molded handrail, and turned balusters form the stair railing. The open string of the stair is ornamented with curvilinear stair brackets.

The McDonald House is an outstanding example of the house builder's skill in LaGrange at the turn of the century. The property is now owned and occupied by Mr. and Mrs. W. H. N. Smith.

The Shade Wooten House, believed to be the oldest building standing in LaGrange, is the town's most architecturally distinctive structure. The house has a one-and-one-half-story frame gable-and-wing form of Gothic Revival design. Perhaps the builder hired by the Wooten family to build their new house had one of the popular house pattern books by New York architect Andrew Jackson Downing, who popularized this style in the mid-1800s. The house uses the cottage form—one story with attic—and board-and-batten exterior siding made popular in the books. The windows have pointed caps, and the steeply pitched roof is accented with decorative wooden trim supplied by a sash and planing mill. The trim imitates in wood the ornamental stonework of Gothic buildings in Europe. Decorative mantels inside the center-hall-plan house, containing Italianate ornament, may have been shipped to the site, along with the other woodwork, on the railroad.

The house apparently was constructed by Council Wooten soon after the Atlantic and North Carolina Railroad came through in the latter 1850s. Council Wooten purchased a large tract known as the Moseley Hall land from Colonel William D. Moseley. When Wooten died, his land was divided in the probate court of

Wayne County. In this division, made May 26, 1874, the Moseley Hall tract was allotted to several claimants as tenants in common. John P. Joyner received lot 3 "containing forty acres more or less including the dwelling and other out buildings." This reference is the earliest evidence for the existence of the dwelling known as the Shade Wooten House. In a deed of January 2, 1889, J. P. Joyner conveyed a lot on the north side of the Atlantic and North Carolina Railroad and fronting on North Railroad Street to S. I. Wooten and J. Y. Joyner. This deed very likely refers to the present structure. Sometime later the house was acquired by Shade Wooten, for whom the house is named. His will of September 27, 1911, created a life estate for his wife, Sarah, in their house and lot on Railroad Street. The will provided that after her death the property pass in fee simple to Wooten's daughter, Ada Wooten Carter. The house was subsequently sold by her to a grandson of Shade Wooten, George Whitfield, from whom it passed into the hands of the present owner, Susan Timberlake.

The Wootens are a long-established family in Lenoir County, claiming descent from Ensign Shadrach Wooten, a Revolutionary War officer. A number of his descendants bear the name Shade, which would appear to be a shortening of Shadrach.

12. House

built circa 1900
202 West Railroad Street

This one-story frame house with a steep, nearly pointed hipped roof is one of LaGrange's best examples of the pyramidal cottage, a house form extremely popular in eastern North Carolina during the first two decades of the twentieth century. The small gabled wing that extends toward the front, and the additional wing extending to the east side, frame a hipped wraparound porch. Slender classical posts, connected by a turned balustrade, support the porch. The house has one-over-one sash windows and plain siding.

13. Harper Hotel (demolished)

built circa 1900
117 West Railroad Street

The Harper Hotel flourished during the early-twentieth-century heyday of LaGrange as a cotton and tobacco market for western Lenoir County. Harper and his wife operated the hotel from 1903 to the mid-1920s. It was described in 1906 as "as good a two-dollar-a-day house as one usually finds." Mrs. Harper, "a refined lady and excellent housekeeper," supervised the hotel's restaurant and the "well-furnished, large and ventilated" rooms lit by large two-over-two sash windows.

The two-story brick building had a flat roof and a two-story porch extending along a portion of the facade. Harper also owned a general merchandise store, in partnership with his brother-in-law, in LaGrange. By 1925 the hotel had closed, and the building had been renovated to house a grocery and another store. It was demolished in the 1980s.

14. Sutton-Fields House

built 1852
114 West Railroad Street, LaGrange

The Sutton-Fields House is one of the three oldest houses retaining their original appearances in LaGrange. About 1852 this small one-story frame house was built along the railroad tracks, apparently for Nan Sutton. The horizontal proportions, three-bay wide side-gable form, Doric cornerboards, and wide plain frieze with gable eave returns strongly resemble the Greek Revival features of another early house along the tracks—the George Taylor House at 302 West Railroad Street. Like the Taylor House, this dwelling has a central entrance with sidelights sheltered by a pedimented portico. Slender clustered Doric columns support the pedimented roof. The sawnwork ornament in the pediment has a vernacular character similar to that of the sawnwork balustrade of the Taylor House portico. The house retains board-and-batten ceilings and a Victorian-style mantel. The much-altered building that now functions as a garage is the original detached kitchen.

In the 1930s Julian William "Spot" Fields Jr. purchased the house from Nan Sutton. His son Johnnie Fields and his wife Judy next owned the property. Judy Fields still resides there.

15. Hadley-Mays House
built circa 1890
108 West Railroad Street

The Hadley-Mays House, now used in part as a thrift shop, is a fine example of a two-story Queen Anne-style residence. Its excellence lies in its Queen Anne "textbook" features, such as the multipaned stained-glass windows in the two-story front projecting bay windows, the original German siding, the segmentally arched paired four-over-four sash windows at the front and sides of the house, and the attached hipped-roof front porch with its slim turned posts and spindle frieze with attached sawnwork pendants.

This house was built by George B. W. Hadley, the son of Dr. J. M. Hadley, one of LaGrange's principal physicians in the 1890s (the other was Dr. Kirkpatrick). George Hadley received his bachelor's degree from Western Maryland College and taught first at LaGrange Collegiate Institute, then at an academy in Enfield, North Carolina, and finally at LaFayette Military Institute in Fayetteville before he returned to LaGrange. He then married Clara Forbes of Greenville, North Carolina, and established himself as both a landowner and a partner in the Rouse Banking Company. The house was eventually bought by the Mays family, who lived there for some time, and is now owned by Mack Cunningham.

A photograph of George Hadley's house appears in the LaGrange section of the 1906 Industrial Issue of the *Kinston Free Press*. A comparison of the 1906 photograph with a current photograph reveals some superficial differences: the house's weatherboards were a darker color in 1906, and the porch supports and frieze, window surrounds, and vergeboard were then painted in contrasting colors. Decorative details, such as the two-story bay window's paneling and sawnwork ornamentation, were defined by darker paint. But it is remarkable how intact the house has remained. The original paneled interior chimney stacks are still in place, as are most of the Queen Anne windows. The porch balustrade and second-floor balcony are now incomplete, but many of the original porch posts and nearly all of the spindle frieze are in place. In 1906 the house was surrounded by pecan and magnolia trees and bounded by a picket fence. Today the fence is long gone, and there is no tree cover at the front of the house. The concrete lot markers are, however, still in place.

16. Commodore and Lela Barrow House
built circa 1905
102 West Railroad Street

Although this one- and two-story flat-roofed brick building appears on the 1908 Sanborn map as a dwelling, its brick construction, with segmental-arched windows and flat roof, is characteristic of commercial construction of the early twentieth century. The building was built by John H. Rouse, who was associated with the Rouse Funeral Home and Carriage Manufactory, as a dwelling for Commodore Barrow. Until 1904 the LaGrange Post Office was located at 102 West Railroad Street in a different building. The post office was moved, the former building demolished, and this building constructed by 1908. It was built with brick walls inside to make it fireproof. A hipped one-story porch supported by slender classical columns nearly encloses the house. On the interior an entry vestibule contains an ornate staircase and an Eastlake-style frieze across the hall ceiling.

17. Commercial Buildings

built early twentieth century
114-122 East Railroad Street

On the south block of East Railroad Street are four one- and two-story brick commercial buildings—modest early-twentieth-century counterparts of the mercantile buildings around the corner of South Caswell Street. Before construction of these buildings the Fields House, built in the 1880s and demolished by 1914, was located on the site where LaGrange's City Hall and 116-118 East Railroad Street stand today.

LaGrange City Hall and Police Station sits at 120-122 East Railroad Street, a one-story building with three recessed panels above the storefront that, in its original state, would have contained signs advertising the store. The City Hall entrance was altered, apparently between 1950 and the 1960s, with a recessed entrance and glass display windows. According to local tradition, what is now City Hall was originally a 1920s dry goods store. The building at 118 East Railroad Street was a tin shop in 1925; appropriately, its one-story facade is ornamented with pressed-metal fluted pilasters. The large two-story building at 116 East Railroad Street was Wood Hardware Store in the 1910s; its smaller two-story neighbor, 114 East Railroad Street, was the rear extension of a department store on South Caswell Street. Today the buildings on this block west of 120-122 East Railroad Street are apparently used for storage.

18. James and Sudie Wooten House

built 1915
122 East Railroad Street

This two-story frame house combines the massive quality of the American Foursquare style with Queen Anne and Craftsman features. The square shape of the house, containing four ample-sized rooms on each floor, is the hallmark of the Foursquare style popular during the early twentieth century. Another feature of this style is the placement of the main entrance in the side bay of the facade, indicating that the house does not have a center-hall plan. The hipped roof with hipped front dormer window is also characteristic of the style, as is the one-story front porch with Craftsman-style wooden posts set on brick piers. The two-story bay window on the east side, with pedimented gable, two small stained-glass windows set in the side wall of the entrance hall, and oriel bay window supported on brackets on the west side of the house are characteristic of the romantic Queen Anne style of the turn of the century. One-over-one and two-over-two sash windows and plain siding complete the exterior finish of this well-preserved house.

The dwelling was built in 1915 for James S. Wooten and his wife, Sudie Taylor Wooten. James Wooten, a prominent merchant, died before construction was completed, but his wife continued with the project. She and their three children made their home in the house when it was finished. In the 1930s the W. P. Hardy estate acquired the property. Angus P. Leach became a later owner.

19. Frazier House

built circa 1910
123 East Railroad Street

Local citizens recall that the Frazier family lived in this two-story frame house facing the railroad tracks in LaGrange. The house follows a form found more often in the countryside than in town in the early twentieth century. Two-story, side-gable, one-room deep houses of this type, known as an I-House, were built throughout Lenoir County as farmhouses between 1890 and 1930. The center front cross gable is a decorative feature that often appears on this house type. The decorative one-story porch that extends across the facade and bows out at the east corner around a one-story bay window lends a stylish note to the otherwise plain facade. Turned posts with sawnwork brackets resembling vernacular Ionic capitals, connected by a turned balustrade, distinguish the porch. The house retains its original four-over-four sash windows and plain siding.

20. Wooten-Williams House

built circa 1900
124 East Railroad Street

The Wooten-Williams House, which appears on the Sanborn Fire Insurance Maps of LaGrange by 1904, is a tall two-story frame house of vernacular Queen Anne style. The main square block is capped by a pyramidal roof, with extremely tall corbelled interior brick chimneys. Two-story pedimented wings project from the front and east elevations. A hipped wraparound porch extends between the two projecting wings. The house has always had three front entrances: the center entrance, a door in the front wing, and a door in the front face of the side wing. Some of the original Queen Anne features have been lost during remodelings: the present porch posts are replacements, artificial siding now covers the walls, and the upstairs window sash have lost their original stained glass.

Shade I. Wooten is said to have been the original owner of this house. The Williams family, who still lives here, bought the house in 1929.

21. Octavius Taylor House

built circa 1895
127 East Railroad Street

Octavius Taylor built this two-story frame Queen Anne-style house on the grounds of the Davis Academy after that illustrious school closed in 1889. One of the largest and most decorative houses in LaGrange during this period, the Taylor House features the picturesque shape that was a hallmark of the Queen Anne style. The main block, five bays wide and one room deep, is side gabled. A large pedimented two-story wing projects from the main facade and terminates in a two-story cutaway bay window. The side gables, the front gable, and a decorative cross gable on the facade are decorated with patterned shingles, a sawnwork bargeboard, and stained-glass windows. One-over-one sash windows, plain siding, and patterned slate roof shingles complete the exterior finish. A marvelous, intact one-story porch wraps across the multifaceted facade. Its turned posts, ornate sawnwork brackets, spindle frieze, and turned balustrade constitute one of the fanciest porches in LaGrange.

Mrs. Octavius Taylor's daughter, May Taylor Allen, maintained ownership and resided in the house until her death in the early 1990s. Since then the house has changed ownership and has been remodeled. It is now known as the Victorian Inn.

22. Leon Rouse House
built circa 1900
130 East Railroad Street

This pyramidal cottage is one of numerous well-preserved dwellings reflecting LaGrange's early-twentieth-century heyday. The frame house has distinctively patterned diamond and square shingles in its two front cross gables and the gable ends of its front and side wings. The hipped front porch has an equally distinctive sawnwork balustrade enclosing original chamfered porch posts. The sash windows and wall siding are replacements. The house apparently was constructed for Leon Rouse.

23. Colonel A. C. Davis House
built 1887
131 East Railroad Street

Located at the northwest corner of East Railroad and Wooten Streets, the frame two-story Queen Anne house built for Adam C. Davis is the only known surviving and intact building of the former 1880s Davis Military Academy. The school, which opened in 1880, was a military preparatory school offering a complete academic curriculum (in addition to a "full course in Book-keeping") to young gentlemen. Local accounts place the number of boys attending at about two hundred. The school's

objective was to provide a superior education that would prepare a young cadet for the greater playing fields of Annapolis and West Point. The Davis School had a counterpart in the nearby Kinsey Seminary for girls. "The boys and girls," according to Nannie Braxton's 1919 essay, "wore uniforms of gray, the color that their fathers had worn during the Confederacy," and apparently socialized under strict supervision.

From 1880 until 1889 A. C. Davis's school flourished. Students came on the railroad from as far north as Petersburg, Virginia, but most were from nearby counties. An 1880s etching of the school grounds shows Davis's house, false turret and all, in the righthand corner, appearing much as it does over one hundred years later. The other buildings, situated around a large quadrangular common where the cadets performed their military exercises, included the commissary and tailor shop, mess hall, business office, and classroom building. As none of these frame buildings correspond to any structure in LaGrange, it appears that they were all either torn down or moved after the school's abrupt closure in 1890. The approximately eight small structures that were the cadets' barracks are no longer on-site, either, but it is possible that they were moved and reutilized as outbuildings. The original campus grounds are said to have extended for more than a full city block. Nannie Braxton wrote that the complex "covered all the land east of O. Taylor's store . . . down Railroad Street for two blocks and on James Street (the small street just north of Railroad Street) for two blocks including Park's baseball grounds."

A. C. Davis's house was later the longtime residence of George Fields, a local historian who maintained the house in nearly its original state. It is now owned by Mr. and Mrs. Richard Poteat, who live in the house and have carried out further sensitive rehabilitation. An attached hipped-roof wraparound porch with a pedimented entrance bay replaced the house's original attached hipped-roof porch, which wrapped around the west side of the house to just below the second-floor balcony, after 1889. The form of the house, a gable-and-wing with a two-story rear ell and an attached rear kitchen ell, is enhanced by the false turret, a small tower with a partly shingled bell-shaped roof, that shelters the center second-floor balcony. This is the only tower of this sort to have survived on a Lenoir County residence. Other decorative exterior features include the small vernacular Diocletian-style window on the turret tower, the Queen Anne stained-glass windows at the balcony and front bay window, the front gable's patterned shingles and three-light window, and the peaked-arch lintels and raised panels of the window surrounds. There are also the porch's turned-rail balustrade and millwork trim, and the transomed doubleleaf entrance with its original wooden screen doors.

The interior of the house has many exceptional decorative elements as well, such as the center-hall staircase with its Victorian-style turned balustrade and substantial wooden newel post. Part of the staircase's spandrel is paneled. The house also has hall screens across doorways, most notably the vernacular Eastlake-style frieze at the center hall. Mantelpieces are in the Victorian style with decorative shelf brackets and raised panels. There is one excellent mantelpiece with an arched firebox opening surmounted by a center raised cartouche; it has a wooden mirrored overmantel painted in the trompe l'oeil manner to resemble marble. The former upstairs balcony door has been converted to a window, but the original reeded three-part window surrounds and Queen Anne stained glass remain in place.

The Davis School had been in operation for nearly ten years when, in the winter of 1889, there was a meningitis epidemic. In spite of almost immediate medical attention (Davis's father, a doctor, quickly realized that the cadets were experiencing something much graver than catarrh or flu), a few of the cadets died. As a result of the epidemic and deaths, parents came for their sons and the school closed. In April 1890 the Davis School relocated to Winston-Salem, where it enrolled two hundred students the following year. Unfortunately the Panic of 1896-1897, which closed many schools and businesses throughout the country, closed the Davis School as well. Today the former Davis School grounds in Winston-Salem contain the Methodist Children's Home. According to Nannie Braxton Herring, Davis gave up his dream of running a school and by 1919 was a lawyer in Goldsboro.

[Two articles by Virginia Pou Doughton contributed to this entry: "Bright Spot In LaGrange," *State*, September 1980, 10-12; "Davis School in Winston," *State*, July 1981, 22-24.]

24. Richard Henry Hardy House
built circa 1900
201 East Railroad Street

The 1910 will of Richard Henry Hardy seems to indicate that he had this house built about 1900. The two-story frame dwelling is a large, well-preserved example of the picturesque house form brought by the Queen Anne style to North Carolina architecture. The main block is surmounted by a pyramidal roof. A two-story gabled wing projects from the main facade, and an additional gabled wing projects from the rear facade. A one-story hipped front porch follows the undulations of the main facade. The porch has turned posts, a plain railing, and a pedimented entry bay. Six-over-six sash windows

and plain siding complete the very well preserved exterior of the Hardy House.

25. Sutton-Jones House
built circa 1885
310 North Caswell Street

The Sutton-Jones House, a frame gable-and-wing one-story cottage on a raised brick foundation, can be judged by its well-maintained exterior as a superb example of a LaGrange vernacular-style Victorian residence. The house, now owned and occupied by Dr. and Mrs. Frank Pisani, has recently been restored, which has given its exterior decoration a rejuvenated quality. Immediately notable decorative elements are the Italianate bracketed raking cornice; the two paneled bay windows, both with bracketed cornices; the small six-light gable windows over the bay windows; and the three-quarter attached shed-roof porch, supported by turned posts and a turned-rail balustrade. The porch shelters a three-bay area with two four-over-four sash windows with peaked lintels and a paneled double-leaf entrance surmounted by a plain glass transom. The standing-seam metal roof of the house is broken by two interior chimneys with corbeled caps and paneled stacks. The roof behind the front facade rises to a higher hipped-roof formation. It appears as if the front facade's gable and wing have been attached to another house, or vice versa. According to Robbie Jones, the Lenoir County architectural survey's principal investigator, the hipped roof is only an attached roof structure; its actual function, if any, has not been ascertained. The house also has a rear kitchen ell with an enclosed porch. There is a frame packhouse at the back of the lot, behind the garden, and some frame tobacco barns sit a short distance from the house.

The house, built in the 1880s, has been linked to Alexander Sutton (1849-?), a local farmer who owned the cotton gin on the south side of East Railroad Street by 1905. The 1910 census lists Sutton, then a sixty-one year-old farmer, as residing at the end of North Caswell Street with his wife, the former Mary H. Walters. Six years before, in 1906, Sutton's daughter Ida had married James Edward Jones, a widower who worked for Sutton before becoming a tobacco warehouseman in 1900. By 1920 James Jones, with his wife and two young daughters, in addition to James Emmett Jones, Jones's twenty-three-year-old son from his first marriage, were living on North Caswell Street.

James Emmett Jones purchased the property at 310 North Caswell Street in 1934 from the Durham Land Bank, which had apparently acquired it during the Great Depression. "Mr. Emmett" never lived here. His daughter sold it to the present owners.

26. Walter Pace House
built circa 1900
309 North Caswell Street

This very stylish Queen Anne cottage was built around the turn of the century near the northern boundary of LaGrange for Walter Pace, a merchant. An elaboration of the basic pyramidal cottage, a one-story square-in-shape house with a high hipped roof, the house has two front cross gables, a third decorative cross-gable in the main facade, and an ornate porch that wraps around the varied wall planes of the facade. Original turned posts with sawnwork brackets, a delicate spindle frieze, and an enclosing turned balustrade create the porch. The cross gables are decorated with fish-scale wood shingles, sawnwork bargeboards, and small arched Queen Anne windows. The center-bay entrance has a transom and sidelights enclosed within a wide surround with a peaked lintel. The windows of the main facade have similar peaked lintels with raised lozenges. A smokehouse and a later shed stand behind the house. Will Hardy Britt and his family now own the property and reside there.

27. Joe Wells House
built circa 1900
204 North Caswell Street

This frame gable-and-wing house is the one-story counterpart of the larger gable-and-wing houses found in LaGrange. Like them, it has a bay window fronting the wing and a decorative porch fitted into the recess formed by the junction of the main block and wing. The original turned posts and sawnwork balustrade are in place, as are original four-over-four sash windows. The center-bay entrance has a transom and sidelights. The original chimney has been removed, and the house has been re-sided with vinyl. A late-nineteenth-century brick smokehouse and early-twentieth-century frame shed stand behind the house.

Joe Wells, a local policeman, owned the house and lived there until his death in the 1930s. After his death Lucy Anderson purchased the house and lived there the remainder of her life. Ola Seymour now owns the house and lives there with her brother, Edward Anderson.

28. First Missionary Baptist Church
built circa 1860; renovated 1888; additions built mid-twentieth century
201 North Caswell Street

"On December 19, 1857, know all men by these presents that I, Council Wooten, for the love I have for God and people do give a donation to the Moseley Hall Missionary Baptist Church a certain tract or parcel of land situated North of the Railroad at Moseley Hall Depot, being four acres." Thus one of the chief landowners in the area where LaGrange emerged as a town deeded this tract of land to the congregation, which built the present frame church shortly afterward. The congregation, founded in the 1750s, was known as the Bear Creek Missionary Baptist Church of Moseley Hall. It had worshiped in a fifteen-by-twenty-foot meetinghouse on land donated by Joshua Herring.

The gable-front sanctuary is three bays wide and seven bays deep. It was renovated in 1888, when the slave gallery was removed from the back of the church and a patterned beadboard ceiling was installed. The round-arched windows and small entrance vestibule may have also been installed at this time. The baptistery and the two-story brick education building were added in the twentieth century.

29. (former) LaGrange Free Will Baptist Church
built circa 1895
114 North Caswell Street

This extremely well preserved vernacular Gothic Revival-style church building is so similar in its richly inventive Gothic Revival features to the LaGrange Presbyterian Church of 1892 that it was undoubtedly designed and built by the same carpenter. The basic configuration, a rectangular frame building three bays wide and six bays deep, with an entrance tower with spire, is identical to that of the Presbyterian Church. The slender lancet windows with hood moldings illuminating the sanctuary and the second stage of the tower are likewise identical. As on the Presbyterian Church, false cross gables with Gothic louvered ventilators accent each slope of the steep gabled roof.

The chief architectural difference is the form of the tower. On the Free Will Baptist Church the main entrance is recessed within the base of the tower, which consists of three open Gothic arches topped by Gothic bracketed hoods. The octagonal spire sits on a polygonal false arcade with applied Gothic arches.

The church is said to have been built by the LaGrange Methodist Episcopal Church. In 1916 the Free Will Baptist congregation rented the church building from the Methodist Episcopal congregation. In more recent years the building has been occupied by several other congregations, including the LaGrange Church of Christ.

30. Pitts-Creech House
built circa 1854; enlarged circa 1910
105 North Caswell Street

The first story of this two-story frame building is said to have served as the Pitts Hotel in the 1850s. About 1910 R. G. Creech reportedly enlarged it to its present appearance, an impressive Neoclassical Revival-style house. Across the three-bay main facade is a monumental flat-roofed Doric portico sheltering a balcony with a turned balustrade. A deep hipped roof with ornamental cross gables and two tall chimney stacks surmounts the house. The central entrance has a transom and sidelights, and plain siding covers the house. Paired one-over-one sash windows illuminate the house. The building has been divided into apartments.

31. LaGrange Cotton Shed (demolished)

built circa 1900
Railroad tracks, at the junction of East Railroad Street and South Caswell Street

Cotton was one of the most important agricultural commodities grown in Lenoir County during the nineteenth century; tobacco superseded cotton in the twentieth century. Located beside the now-demolished LaGrange Depot, this cotton shed was a rare survivor of the pre-World War II era, when such warehouses stood along railroad tracks throughout eastern North Carolina. The one-story frame side-gable building resembled freight depots of the period, with an overhanging roof sheltering a loading dock along both sides. The walls were apparently board-and-batten beneath the artificial siding. The north side of the building had four large openings; the south (track) side probably had similar openings but had been remodeled.

32. (former) LaGrange Presbyterian Church (Rotary Club Building)

built 1892; listed in the National Register of Historic Places
201 South Caswell Street

Construction of the LaGrange Presbyterian Church in 1892 was due in large part to elder Henry Edward Dillon, a prominent LaGrange merchant and civic leader. The frame gable-front church with tall entrance tower is an exuberant vernacular interpretation of the Gothic Revival style. The rectangular building, three bays wide and six deep, is illuminated by lancet windows filled with diamond-paned stained glass, accented by drip molds. The tower rises in two stages, topped with a tall spire. The front entrance, at the base of the steeple, is a double-leaf paneled door with a Gothic-arched transom and a gable hood. The second stage, the belfry, features louvered lancet openings and a bracketed cornice. The eight-sided spire has flared eaves and corner false gables. Plain siding covers the walls.

The most striking feature of the building is on the interior. The walls and ceiling of the sanctuary and chancel are finished with narrow beaded tongue-and-groove sheathing applied in a herringbone pattern. A number of original pews remain, as well as late-nineteenth-century chancel furnishings.

The first Presbyterian congregation in Lenoir County was established in Kinston in the 1860s; however, its church was abandoned in the 1870s. The LaGrange Presbyterian Church was organized in 1883 and met in its early years in the Methodist Church. In 1890 Henry Edward Dillon, longtime mayor of LaGrange, donated the land on which the Presbyterians built their church. Two years later the church was completed at a cost of approximately $1,200. The church maintained a small but active membership throughout most of the twentieth century but experienced a membership decline after 1970. In the 1980s the building was purchased by the LaGrange Rotary Club and is now utilized as the Rotary Club Building. By virtue of its location at the town's busiest intersection and its use as a meeting place by local civic groups, the building continues to be a vital and integral part of the community.

33. George E. Sutton House
built circa 1905
318 South Caswell Street

One of a number of Queen Anne-style gable-and-wing houses built by LaGrange's prosperous middle class at the turn of the twentieth century, the Sutton House still exhibits most of its original decorative architectural features. The house has wooden siding and one-over-one sash windows. The front cross-gables, one topping the wing with its cutaway two-story bay window and one centered in the main block, have decorative wooden shingles, hexagonal louvered ventilators, and delicate sawn bargeboards. The one-story porch, which undulates around the various wall planes of the facade, is supported by original turned posts and has an original millwork pendant frieze. The house was built for merchant and farmer George E. Sutton.

34. Kirby Sutton House and Cotton Warehouse
built circa 1925
319 South Caswell Street

By the 1920s middle-class taste in LaGrange, as throughout the United States, had shifted away from late Victorian styles to the Craftsman style. The house built for Kirby Sutton exemplifies this shift in house design. The one-story dwelling has the form of a pyramidal cottage, with a steep hip roof, but displays such Craftsman details as a wide wraparound porch supported on battered brick piers, with a heavy wooden balustrade. The glazed front door with transom and sidelights is also Craftsman in style.

Beside the kitchen-dining ell is an unusually fine smokehouse with a hipped roof and two front doors. It appears to have been built contemporaneously with the house. At the back of the lot is a cotton warehouse—a one-story side-gable frame building with four doors sheltered by an overhanging roof. It is apparently contemporary with the house as well. Kirby Sutton, merchant and cotton broker, was born and raised in the Bucklesberry section of Lenoir County. He never married. Sutton purchased cotton from local farmers, stored it in this warehouse, then sold it. The property remains in the Sutton family; Kirby Sutton's niece now resides in the house.

35. Joseph Kinsey House (demolished)

built late 1800s; demolished circa 1971
West James Street

In 1870 Joseph Kinsey (1843-after 1929), a descendant of Palatine settlers in Jones County, began the Kinsey Seminary for girls in the L-shaped frame Victorian house that had previously been the LaGrange Academy. The unusually shaped house with its two-story porch with equally unusual Chippendale-style balustrades is clearly visible in an engraving at the front of Kinsey's 1897-1898 catalogue for the school, by then known as the LaGrange High School. Possibly the most famous student of the academy was to be James Y. Joyner, who returned to teach Latin, then began his ascent to his eventual post as state superintendent of public instruction under Governor Charles B. Aycock. The Kinsey Seminary became a boarding school for girls in the fall of 1881; graduation exercises the semester before had featured recitations of "There's Plenty of Room at the Top" by Preston Wooten, "Go and Learn a Trade" by Bettie Kinsey, and "What is the Use of Latin?" by Robert Uzzell and William Reid. The engraving at the front of Kinsey's 1887-1888 school prospectus shows two two-story side-gabled dormitories behind the original academy building. Ninety female students, primarily from Lenoir County (though a sizable percentage came from neighboring Pitt, Wayne, Greene, and Jones Counties, and four students came from Florida), came to the Kinsey Seminary for instruction in English, mathematics, Latin, French, German, penmanship, and drawing and painting.

Kinsey, a certified teacher from the age of seventeen, later wrote of his pupils, "I had an opportunity to find many girls with intellect and little money whom I helped, and their letters to me cause me to feel that my life has been worthwhile." The Kinsey Seminary was moved to Wilson in 1897. The academy building then housed LaGrange High School until classes moved to West Railroad Street in the early twentieth century. The 1897 school prospectus displayed a rigorous academic program, from courses in Latin and Greek to classes in music. The frontispiece lithograph shows the academy and dormitory nearly obscured by mature trees, but the attached two-story porches with their bracketed posts and lattice sawnwork balustrades give the small—and now vanished—campus a pleasant late-Victorian picturesque quality.

36. (former) Bear Creek Primitive Baptist Church (LaGrange Garden Clubhouse)

built circa 1857, 1880
210 West Washington Street

The Bear Creek congregation, one of the earliest Primitive Baptist congregations in Lenoir County, was established about 1750 in the Bear Creek section of Lenoir County, a few miles northwest of LaGrange. In the mid-nineteenth century the congregation built a traditional one-story front-gable frame meetinghouse. In 1880 the building was moved to nearby LaGrange, where it continued to be used by the Primitive Baptists until at least 1925. It appears on the 1925 Sanborn map on its current site, but oriented with its gable front to the street. A December 10, 1987 letter to the *Kinston Free Press* by Virginia Best Hollingsworth explained the building's history. In 1937 the church deeded the property to the trustees of the LaGrange Betterment Club, who converted the sanctuary to a recreation center and library. The building was then reoriented on the lot so that its gable roof sat parallel to the street. At this time a hipped porch was constructed along the long south elevation to shelter the new main entrance. On the grounds a tennis court and playground were built. In 1967 the LaGrange Garden Club took over the property, and it has continued to operate it as a community building to the present.

Although it was moved and has undergone numerous alterations over the years, this simple building possesses considerable significance as one of a handful of early-nineteenth-century church buildings that still stand in Lenoir County. The west gable end, originally the main facade, apparently retains its meetinghouse configuration: a double door with transom, flanked by six-over-nine-pane sash windows.

37. John H. Rouse House
built circa 1900
206 West Washington Street

This large frame two-story gable-and-wing Queen Anne dwelling, built for John H. Rouse at the turn of the twentieth century, is in exceptionally intact condition both inside and out and still retains two original outbuildings. Except for the later enclosure of the porte cochere (circa 1993-1994), some later rear additions, and the removal of the second floor's front balcony (the door was converted to a window), the Rouse House's exterior is still much as it appeared in 1919. The attached hipped-roof wraparound front porch has retained its spindle frieze and turned balustrade; there are the "abacus" vergeboards on the front and side gables, in addition to some of the gables' original patterned shingles. Inside the house a good deal of unaltered decoration exists, including mirrored Neoclassical Revival overmantels with supporting pilasters and the impressive paneled center-hall staircase. There is also an original elongated bull's-eye, or oculus, stained-glass window on the second floor.

John H. Rouse (1862-1953) was a prominent LaGrange businessman who manufactured carriages, cabinets, coffins, and caskets. He is said, in addition, to have sold the first automobile in LaGrange. The Rouse Carriage Works, founded in 1882, was located just north of Caswell and Railroad Streets' intersection and is now the site of the Rouse Funeral Home, owned and operated by John Rouse's descendants until 1985. The Rouse dwelling at 206 West Washington Street, built circa 1900, housed a very large family. When Rouse remarried in 1909, he already had eight living children; with his second wife he was to have eight more. John Rouse was an excellent cabinetmaker who constructed several pieces of furniture for his growing family. Although his furniture is no longer at the house, it is possible that some of the wooden mantelpieces and paneling there were produced by Rouse, with his assistants, at this shop. The house remained in the Rouse family until 1993 and is now owned and occupied by Tom and Rhonda Monses.

There are two outbuildings still standing on the property that appear on the 1919 LaGrange Sanborn map. The first is a frame side-gable garage later converted to a shed. The second outbuilding is a small frame three-bay shed, referred to as a "locker" on the 1919 Sanborn map, that at one time served a variety of functions. It had a laundry room lit by two two-over-four sash windows, a small smokehouse, a smaller stable, and a tiny chicken house. Beside the locker, where the current owners have planted a small garden, is a cast-iron arch; the metal supporting piers are identical to decorative metal pilasters found on many LaGrange commercial buildings constructed between 1880 and 1930 and came from the old Rouse Carriage Works building.

38. A. W. Kennedy House
built circa 1886
201 West Washington Street

A. W. Kennedy, a farmer, apparently had this house built in the 1880s. The Kennedy House is a well-preserved example of the Victorian gable-and-wing form. The main facade, with a one-story Queen Anne-style bay window in the wing and a one-story porch with chamfered posts and delicate sawnwork brackets extending across the facade beside the wing, retains its architectural integrity. The double-door entrance is surmounted by a large four-light transom with a peaked lintel; the two-over-two sash windows have identical lintels. Plain siding covers the house, and a kitchen-dining ell extends from the rear. A. W. Kennedy and his wife resided here during their lifetimes. In the 1970s Mr. Kennedy's grandson sold the property.

39. Leon Fields House
built circa 1918
110 West Washington Street

In the late 1910s a startling new house was constructed in LaGrange—one of the first brick houses in town. Leon Fields, a prominent merchant, had the bricks for this large two-story house shipped to LaGrange on the railroad from Baltimore. With its low hipped roof, hipped front dormer window, and one-story porch wrapping around three sides and executed completely in brick, from its battered porch posts to its solid balustrade, the Fields House resembles the early-twentieth-century Craftsman-style houses being built in the American Midwest at this time in what has been called the Prairie Style. At the west side the porch extends as a porte cochere. The windows have five-over-one sash in keeping with the Craftsman style. The molded brick quoins accenting the corners, flat cement window lintels and sills, pedimented cross gable, and boxed eaves are features from the Neoclassical Revival style also popular during this period. A frame shed shown on the 1925 Sanborn map stands behind the house. The house was later owned by S. P. Hardy of Institute, who sold it to the present owners, the Sidney Myers family, in 1978.

40. Sutton-Kinsey House
built circa 1898
107 West Washington Street

In the late 1890s John Willis Sutton built this exemplary two-and-one-half-story frame Queen Anne-style house. The picturesque massing, with the central hipped-roof core that projects outward into wings with cutaway two-story bay windows, both projecting and recessed porches, and a profusion of decorative gables, exemplifies the interplay of positive and void of the American Queen Anne style. A profusion of original Queen Anne woodwork decorates the house: wood siding, diamond-patterned shingles, a sawnwork bargeboard, turned porch posts with sawnwork brackets, and a spindle frieze. One-over-one sash windows illuminate the main block; delicate fanlight windows accent the cross gables.

The Suttons, a prominent mercantile and farming family in LaGrange, passed the house along to the Kinsey family in later years. Joseph Earl Kinsey, a descendant, and his wife, Barbara, now reside in the house.

41. Sutton-Kinsey House
built circa 1850
105 West Washington Street

John Willis Sutton, a farmer who also operated a steam-powered sawmill in LaGrange in the 1890s, was the original owner of this house. The boxy two-story frame house, two rooms deep, has side gables, a prominent front cross gable, and two interior brick chimneys. The house was apparently remodeled in the Craftsman style in the 1920s or 1930s, and most of the exterior fabric reflects this style. The wide corner pilasters, reminiscent of the Greek Revival style of the mid-nineteenth century, are apparently some of the only remaining original features. The front entrance, the large twelve-over-one sash windows, the front cross gable, and the large two-story front porch were added during the Craftsman remodeling. The porch has wooden posts set on brick piers and a solid wooden balustrade.

In 1915 Sutton deeded the house to Ralph Kinsey, his grandson. Kinsey and his wife lived in the house for the rest of their lives. Kinsey heirs maintained ownership of the property until it was sold in 1980.

42. Dr. L. C. Adams House
built circa 1905
106 Center Street

This large two-story frame house illustrates the transition in LaGrange residential architecture in the early years of the twentieth century from the Queen Anne style, with its profusion of intricately detailed woodwork, to the Classical Revival style, which brought simplified classical forms to house design. The two-and-one-half-story house retains picturesque Queen Anne massing, the gable-and-wing form with a two-story cutaway bay window fronting the wing, surmounted by a cross gable, with additional cross gables on the main facade and at the side elevations. Small Queen Anne-style windows in the cross-gables, along with delicate sawnwork bargeboards, reflect the Victorian style as well. The one-story front porch, however, presents the clean simplicity of the classical style—slender Doric columns support the porch as it follows the changing wall planes of the facade. The house was built for Dr. L. C. Adams, one of three physicians in LaGrange at the turn of the century. He and his family resided here until the 1930s.

43. Dr. J. M. Kirkpatrick House
built mid-to-late 1800s; moved 1969
105 North Wooten Street

Dr. J. M. Kirkpatrick lived in this house and practiced medicine, presumably in the small wing that extends to the side. Kirkpatrick, one of the first doctors in LaGrange, practiced from the late 1870s to the early 1900s. This house stood until 1969 on East Railroad Street where the LaGrange Fire Station now stands. In that year George Fields moved it to 105 North Wooten Street and renovated it as his own residence.

The pyramidal cottage, one of the oldest houses in La Grange, has distinctive tall nine-over-nine sash windows and wide corner pilasters, which are a vernacular echo of the Greek Revival style popular in the mid-nineteenth century. The porch, which extends across the main block and the side wing and wraps around one side elevation, is supported on slender turned posts. It appears to be an early-twentieth-century addition to the house. The side ell currently contains the kitchen, an arrangement not uncommon in Lenoir County. Originally, however, the ell may have been Dr. Kirkpatrick's office. The unusual placement of the side wing, set flush with the main facade, may be evidence that it did indeed contain the office.

44. Ebenezer Missionary Baptist Church
built 1920
209 Carey Street

The cornerstone of this magnificent Gothic Revival-style brick church reads:

> Ebenezer Missionary Baptist Church
> LaGrange, N.C. erected
> 1871 rebuilt 1920 by Rev.
> R. W. Pate Rev. C. H. Brown
> Pastor April 7, 1957

The African Americans who founded this congregation in 1871 probably worshiped in a modest building, perhaps even in a private home, for many years. The construction of this large brick sanctuary in 1920 represented a splendid achievement for the congregation, which benefited from the town's economic boom of the early twentieth century. The rectangular gable-front church, three bays wide and four bays deep, presents twin corner towers to the world. Each tower has two stages, the first stage containing Gothic-arched stained-glass windows, the upper stage Gothic louvered ventilators. A round-arched arcade connects the towers and forms an entrance porch, sheltering two double-leaf doors. Each bay and the tower corners contain buttresses with concrete caps. Similar concrete blocks accent the arches of the windows. The front gable is outlined with decorative stepped brickwork, with a central stained-glass rosette window.

The cornerstone dates from 1957, the year in which the rear apse and education building were constructed. Ebenezer Missionary Baptist Church is one of Lenoir County's most architecturally significant African American churches. Its twin towers reflect a tradition of African American church architecture in North Carolina, but the connecting arcade raises this building above many other examples of this tradition.

45. Fairview Cemetery and Mortuary Building
established 1886; mortuary building built circa 1915-1920
West Railroad Street

In 1886 John H. Rouse and Dr. James Mark Hodges saw the need for a community cemetery in addition to the existing church and family cemeteries in the town of LaGrange. The two men worked with the town to establish Fairview Cemetery as the first town burying ground. Common during the Victorian era, town-sanctioned cemeteries grew in favor over the once-standard family-farm burial plot, and by the early twentieth century nearly every town of consequence had one. Laid out in a typical rectilinear pattern with intersecting paths between quadrants, the Fairview Cemetery is accessed through highly ornate iron gates flanked by sculpted iron posts. Some of the tombstones date back to the 1870s, indicating that part of the cemetery may have originally been a family plot. Many of LaGrange's and western Lenoir County's prominent citizens are interred at Fairview.

Unlike other rural Victorian cemeteries, Fairview contains a mortuary building in the center. John H. Rouse, LaGrange's carriage and casket entrepreneur, had the cruciform-plan, hip-roof cemetery building constructed sometime between 1915 and 1920. Funerals, particularly in bad weather, could be quite difficult to get to in the days of horse-and-buggy transportation, and shelter was often not available. The Fairview Cemetery building, referred to as the Summer House, with its central passage flanked by two covered areas, made it possible for a service to take place inside in case of rain.

Part of the building has since been enclosed, but the cross wings still rest on posts over brick piers—a common feature of houses of the 1920s. The roof still has its patterned slate. The building is currently used to store maintenance equipment. Such mortuary buildings at cemeteries have become rare as people have moved away from the nineteenth-century practices of frequent visitation and social interaction at monuments to the dead. These practices created the picturesque cemeteries and buildings of Laurel Hill in Philadelphia, Pennsylvania, and Cave Hill in Louisville, Kentucky. The Fairview Mortuary Building is the only cemetery building known to exist in Lenoir County outside Kinston.

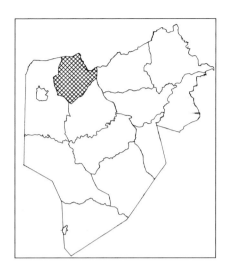

INSTITUTE
TOWNSHIP

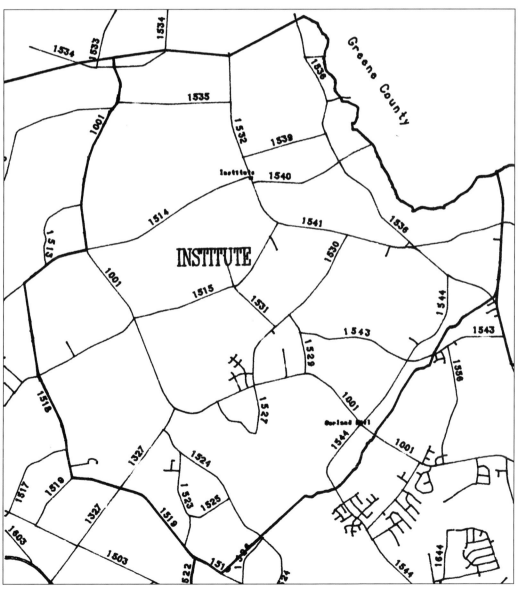

John Thomas Gray House (demolished)

built mid-nineteenth century; demolished 1980s
Institute

Unquestionably influenced by the institutional buildings erected in the 1850s at the nearby Lenoir Collegiate Institute, this commodious two-story plantation house displayed one the county's most impressive vernacular Greek Revival designs prior to its demolition in the 1980s. The early history of the house is not fully known, though family tradition suggests the dwelling was the home of John Thomas Gray (1844-1925). Gray married Mary Pauline Faucette in 1869 and reportedly at that time purchased property in the Institute Township from a Hadley family. Based on the location of the house before it was demolished, and comparisons of that location to Civil War field maps from 1863, the house appears to be the dwelling identified by the name of T. M. Dawson. It may be that the Dawson family constructed the house in the 1850s and sold the property to the Hadleys after the Civil War, and that Gray purchased the farm sometime during the early 1870s, though this is yet to be documented.

Falling within a class of large double-pile side-gable houses that became popular during the late antebellum period, the Gray House exhibited a two-story pedimented front porch with elaborately detailed vernacular treatments in the scalloped bargeboard and stout, square chamfered columns with exaggerated fluting. The five-bay front facade was otherwise undecorated. Whether the porch was original to the house or added by a later owner, perhaps during the Gray family occupancy, is unknown, though the overall Victorian flavor of the decorative motifs suggests a post-Civil War alteration. Sidelights and transoms marked the front and rear entrances. The floor plan is presumed to have been a center hall, and two large interior chimneys provided heat to the numerous rooms.

The association of the Gray House with a group of regional craftsmen working in nearby Institute and LaGrange makes the loss of this dwelling a significant hindrance to garnering a full understanding of the pervasiveness of its vernacular traditions in Lenoir County prior to the Civil War.

Westbrook-Hardy House

built circa 1808
Institute vicinity

Located in the agriculturally prosperous northwest corner of the county near Institute, this early-nineteenth-century two-story farmhouse survives as one of the oldest dwellings in Lenoir County. Believed to have been constructed by the Westbrook family (maybe Moses Westbrook) in 1808—bricks with that date are located in each chimney—this Federal-style plantation house was purchased by Lemuel Hardy III in 1838. Lemuel purchased the farm for his son, Parrott Mewborn Hardy, who moved into the dwelling that year with his bride, Louisa Truitt Daniel. After Louisa died in 1842, Parrott married Sarah M. Aldridge, and by the time of the 1850 federal census the Hardy household included eight children ranging in age from one to sixteen years old. Descendants of the Hardy family have continued to reside in the house. The Hardy family cemetery, surrounded by ancient boxwoods, is located behind the dwelling.

Conforming to the typical two-story single-pile form, with large brick chimneys laid in Flemish bond and a raised brick foundation also in Flemish bond, the heavy-braced frame dwelling depicts standard English building techniques. The basement, used as a root cellar and for storing dried vegetables and preserves, retains wooden foundation grilles, elements referred to locally as "critter guards" or "varmint guards" because they kept unwanted animals out of the cellar. The exterior appearance of the house has been altered somewhat through the years by removal of the original porch and replacement with modern concrete flooring and new brick foundation walls, addition of modern siding, and extension of the roof to form overhangs on the gable ends.

Originally the hall-and-parlor plan featured enclosed winder stairs on both floors. These elements were removed when the house was renovated in the early 1930s by local carpenter Alfred Bush Morris. A partition wall was added, creating a center-hall plan, as well as an open-string stair. The original first-floor mantels were also altered at that time. A number of significant original elements have survived, including beaded chair rails, nine-over-six and six-over-six sash windows, beaded baseboards, a board-and-batten door with hand forged strap hinges, horizontal sheathed wainscoting, and flush vertical-board walls. In the renovation the cracks of the flush sheathing were covered with battens, creating a board-and-batten appearance.

Early in its history the house had a rear kitchen-dining ell and a rear shed room, which was renovated and enlarged circa 1947. The original hall room has a side door leading outside on the east facade–common on houses of this period and often referred to as the fire door, through which firewood could easily be retrieved from the woodpile.

Little of the once-vibrant plantation landscape survives with the exception of an early-nineteenth century smokehouse, constructed of heavy-braced frame with an original board-and-batten door hung on hand-forged strap hinges. A small collection of early-twentieth-century tobacco-related buildings also remains on the farm.

(former) Lenoir Collegiate Institute
built 1853 to 1858
Institute

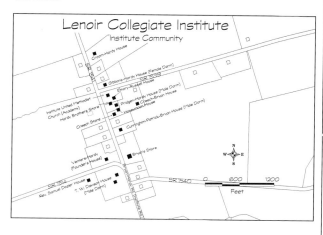

Lenoir Collegiate Institute consists of a small group of buildings constructed along both sides of the Institute Road (now State Road 1541) between 1853 and 1858 for use as dormitories and classrooms for the antebellum coeducational Methodist preparatory school. The present community of Institute includes these buildings, most of which have been renovated for dwelling use, as well as later dwellings and three stores. Most of the original buildings, except for the altered church building, have two stories and vernacular Greek Revival-style elements.

Comprised of center-hall plans, single- and double-pile widths, three-bay facades, and low sloping gable roofs, the buildings were constructed with vernacular Greek Revival-style interior elements such as low paneled wainscots and modest post-and-lintel mantels. Other typical details include molded window and door surrounds with crossettes, two-panel doors, open and enclosed stairs, and square newel posts with molded caps. A few of the buildings were apparently always used as dwellings and exhibit more fashionable interiors with feather painting, molded newel posts, and hand-carved crossettes.

The Institute was formed in 1853 under the direction of the Reverend W. Henry Cunningghim, a Methodist minister, "to foster the spirit of education among the eastern people." The academy officially opened in 1855, with accommodations for 150 students within one mile of the school. The Reverend Levi Branson, who later published almanacs and state business directories in Raleigh, was hired as the principal of the male department soon after his graduation from college, and Sarah L. Hampton was in charge of the female department. Both were hired in the fall of 1856. Some of the original trustees were Blaney Pridgen, John Timberlake, the Reverend John Dozier, Wilson Reed, and Jesse H. Hardy. Soon after the school opened Thomas C. Lamb, a student from Hyde County, died of pneumonia and was buried behind the Creech-Bryan House.

In the 1857 *North Carolina Conference Journal* of the Methodist Episcopal Church, South, the school reported a capital stock of $3,000 in buildings and fixtures, proof that a large number of buildings were already constructed. Sixty boarding students and a number of day students were attending the Institute in 1857 and were taught by four male and four female teachers.

Strict segregation of the sexes, a policy of the Methodist doctrine, was enforced, with separate dormitories and sections in the classrooms, church, and assembly hall. Without written permission from their respective principals, students were forbidden to cross a line in the middle of the road that separated the boys and girls sections of the campus. Many students boarded in the homes of nearby farmers.

The Institute, thought to have been the first two-year preparatory school opened in the eastern section of the state, served mostly the children of planters from Lenoir and surrounding counties. The male students usually transferred to Normal College in Durham (later Trinity College and now Duke University) although they were also prepared to "enter the University [of North Carolina] . . . if desirable." The female students sometimes went on to Greensboro College.

In 1860 Levi Branson left the school to accept the position of principal of a similar institution in Atlantic, North Carolina, and the Institute closed soon after. The Reverend George W. Venters, a cofounder of the academy, purchased the buildings with the determination to keep the school open. Venters renamed the academy Lenoir Male and Female Seminary, but it apparently closed when the Civil War began and never reopened. The buildings remained empty through the Civil War and were not used again until 1869, when the Reverend W. L. Cunningghim opened a private elementary school. Later the school became a public community school, but it closed in 1878. Soon thereafter the buildings were purchased and converted for dwelling use by area farmers, and a few were moved to nearby LaGrange. The assembly hall became the sanctuary of the Methodist Church congregation and, after being deeded to the denomination in 1887, was renovated into a traditional-style church building.

[Several publications contributed to the information in this entry: Raleigh *News and Observer*, February 12, 1950; Raleigh *News and Observer*, February 19, 1955; and Pate, *History of Lenoir Collegiate Institute*.]

Institute United Methodist Church

built circa 1855; remodeled circa 1890
Institute

Originally the Lenoir Collegiate Institute church and classrooms, this building has a very intriguing history. An active Methodist congregation is thought to have been located here as early as the 1830s and 1840s, making this the oldest Methodist congregation in the county. Tradition says that the building was constructed around 1855 and originally had two stories, the lower used for public worship and the upper used as the Female Department classroom. The building continued to be used as a community worship center after the college and subsequent private schools ceased functioning during the Reconstruction era. In 1887 the property was deeded to the Methodist Episcopal Church, South.

The original building was a front-gable form with two floors. After the building began to be used exclusively as a sanctuary, it was renovated to contain only one floor. The renovation, dating to around 1890, converted the church to the more traditional modest Gothic Revival-style that was popular throughout the area. Stained-glass windows, a Colonial Revival front entrance surround, and a patterned tongue-and-groove ceiling were other modifications. The church was enlarged with a rear classroom addition in 1951. A large L-shaped wing, added to the rear facade in 1990, mimics the form and style of the original building.

Gibbons-Hardy House (Lenoir Collegiate Institute Female Dormitory)

built circa 1853
Institute

One of the original Lenoir Collegiate Institute female dormitories, this two-story Greek Revival-style house was later owned and converted to a dwelling by the Reverend Henry H. Gibbons (1818-1887), then purchased by Hugh Emory Hardy circa 1950. Hugh Holton Hardy subsequently inherited the house and remodeled it about 1955.

Like most of the Greek Revival-style dwellings at Institute, this double-pile central-hall-plan house features a low hip roof, two interior chimneys, six-over-six sash windows, double front entry flanked by transom and sidelights, and heavy corner pilasters. A two-story front porch supported by square columns was constructed circa 1951-1952. Interior details include the typical simple mantels, open stair with a square newel post with molded cap, and two-panel doors. Perhaps the most impressive architectural detail is the fully paneled stairwell balustrade on the second level, the only one of its kind in Lenoir County.

Pridgen-Hardy House (Lenoir Collegiate Institute Male Dormitory)
built circa 1853
Institute

Originally used as a dormitory for Lenoir Collegiate Institute, the Logan Donald Hardy house was at one time owned by the Pridgen family. In the early 1900s Logan D. Hardy Sr. and his wife, Ida, purchased the house and raised their family there. Ida Hardy Brown, their granddaughter, is the present owner.

The architecture of the two-story dwelling is the vernacular Greek Revival style associated with the Lenoir Collegiate Institute-related buildings. Exterior detailing includes an original full-facade front porch supported by chamfered columns, flush gables, nine-over-nine and nine-over-six sash windows, a rear ell, and two separate front doors, an unusual deviation from the double-leaf entry of some other Institute buildings. Historic photographs of the house show the original appearance, which featured shuttered windows, a brick pier foundation, and a contrasting paint scheme. Later the shutters were removed, the dwelling was painted white, and a canopy was added to the front porch. When the interior was renovated in 1934, old photographs, believed to be of male students at the Lenoir Collegiate Institute, were discovered behind the original mantels.

Logan Donald Hardy Tenant House (Honeymoon House)
built circa 1930; moved circa 1940
Institute

Located next to the Logan Donald Hardy house is this well-preserved shotgun dwelling. The dwelling was originally located about one mile north on Logan Donald Hardy Sr.'s farm, where it apparently served as a tenant house, but was moved about 1940 for use as an apartment for A. A. Webb, the newly hired agriculture teacher at Wheat Swamp School. In later years the house became affectionately known to locals as the Honeymoon House because of the large number of newlyweds who used the house as a starter home. Architectural details include Craftsman-era eave brackets, a hip-roof front porch, a side addition, and four-over-four sash windows. The house is owned by Leta Hardy.

Cunningghim-Patrick-Bryan House (Lenoir Collegiate Institute Male Dormitory)
Bryan's Store
house built circa 1853; store built 1934
Institute

Originally used as a male dormitory for Lenoir Collegiate Institute, this house was later owned by the Reverend W. H. Cunningghim, the Institute's founder Dr. James M. Patrick resided here by 1867 and sold the farm to R. Pauline and James M. Hines in 1886, who in turn sold it to A. T. Dawson the next month. John Hugh Bryan purchased it from Dawson in 1920. The house is presently occupied by Elizabeth Bryan.

The two-story double-pile house is of the Greek Revival style typical of the Institute buildings, featuring a low hip roof, central hall, and two interior central chimneys. A circa-1937 remodeling replaced several mantels and revealed boys' names and addresses on the walls, apparently from the Institute era. Original architectural details include two-panel doors, six-over-six sash windows, and double front entry flanked by transom and sidelights. Other details commonly found on the dormitory buildings are also present, such as the simple, modest Greek Revival-style mantels. The front facade has five bays on the lower level but only three bays on the upper level and features the original full-facade front porch supported by posts. The rear ell is a later addition.

Outbuildings include two barns, a smokehouse, a garage, and sheds. A family cemetery and an old farmhouse are located behind the dwelling.

Set directly beside the road is Bryan's Store, built for Robert Bryan in 1934. This small store is one of only a handful still operating in Lenoir County. Typical of early-twentieth-century rural stores, this building is distinguished by its unusually small size. Tradition states that a commissary for the African American farmhands of the area was located across the road, and that materials from that building were reused for the construction of the store. Common features include a gable-front roof concealed by a parapet facade over the engaged pass-through. The original storefront and double entry are intact. The store is one of three that operated in the small community at one time.

Venters-Hardy House
built 1850s
Institute

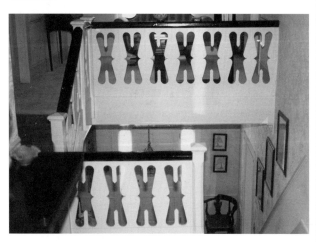

Constructed as one of the original Lenoir Collegiate Institute buildings, this two-story house is one of the most ornately detailed remaining buildings in the community that took its name from the mid-nineteenth-century school. Characterized today by the numerous remodelings it has undergone, this particular dwelling was originally the home of the Reverend George W. Venters, one of the founders of the Institute. During the early twentieth century, the house was owned by Stephen Parker Hardy.

Like other buildings erected in Institute in the 1850s, this dwelling displays vernacular Greek Revival elements from its early history. The unusual configuration of the center-hall-plan house—a two-story L-shaped main block with a two-story ell mimicking a double-pile dwelling—is the only such plan type in the county. A hip roof and two interior chimneys are typical features of antebellum houses. Carved brackets on the cornice and porch suggest post-Civil War changes from the Victorian era, though the porch renovation, to a full two-story height, is said to be a Colonial Revival alteration completed in the early twentieth century. A decorative balustrade now encloses the roof of the porch and sun room. Several additions including a kitchen now protrude from the rear.

Interior renovations in the early twentieth century altered the dwelling's original appearance, but many of the Greek Revival elements, such as molded door and window surrounds with hand-carved corner blocks with crossettes, remain. Of the other surviving details the most spectacular and iconoclastic is an elaborately decorated stair located in the center hall and fashioned with an ornate balustrade composed of sawnwork in an X pattern and terminated by heavily chamfered newel posts. This type of pierced work is more often found in exterior porch treatments.

T. W. Dawson House (Lenoir Collegiate Institute Male Dormitory)
built circa 1855
Institute

An original male dormitory for Lenoir Collegiate Institute, this two-story house was constructed between 1855 and 1858. T. W. Dawson was an early owner, perhaps during the operation of the Institute. The vernacular Greek Revival form matches that of the other original Institute buildings. In 1975 the house was completely remodeled by Kenneth and Ida Hardy Brown, who still live here. Several original architectural details of the single-pile central-hall-plan dwelling were retained, including a two-panel door under the stair, the transom and side-lights flanking the front entrance, six-over-six sash windows, and an original mantel. The original detached kitchen was pulled away from the house and replaced with a new rear addition and is now located to the side of the house. Architectural details of the kitchen include nine-over-six sash windows, two-panel doors, and a boxed cornice.

Emory-Russell House
built circa 1850
Institute

According to local tradition this house served as a male dormitory for Lenoir Collegiate Institute, but this cannot be documented. It is known that Mrs. S. A. Emory resided in the house in 1884. A later owner was Brantley Russell.

The architectural detailing is a curious blend of Greek Revival and late Federal elements. A central-hall plan, very low flush-sheathed wainscot, two-panel doors, and a low-pitched roof are elements of the vernacular Greek Revival style. Other details include an enclosed winder stair, nine-over-six (lower) and six-over-six (upper) sash windows, flush gable ends, and a slightly asymmetrical facade. The two exterior end brick chimneys of common bond are intact, but the mantels on the interior have been replaced. A rear ell and front porch with porte cochere supported by flared columns resting on brick pedestals are later additions.

(former) Hardy Brothers Store
built circa 1900
Institute

Tradition holds that the Hardy Brothers Store was originally operated by Arden W. Taylor and Brother before being purchased by Logan Donald Hardy Sr. in the early twentieth century. Arden W. Taylor came to Institute from Greene County in 1892 to engage in business and apparently built the store at that time. Like many rural stores, the building also housed the community post office. The Hardy family operated the store/post office for nearly seventy-five years before eventually closing it and moving the building across the road from its original location, about 1975.

Basically intact, the building retains its original interior chamfered support columns, board-and-batten door, six-over-six and nine-over-six sash windows, and counters made of heart pine. Important exterior details include a boxed cornice and flush gable returns. Until recent years the building served as offices for Hardy Oil Company and, in addition, functioned as Institute's voting place.

Creech Store
built late nineteenth century; moved early twentieth century
Institute

In the early twentieth century the Creech family moved this front-gable store from nearby Hookerton to Institute on a mule wagon to be operated as a store. Logan Donald Hardy Sr. is said to have operated the store before eventually purchasing the Arden W. Taylor and Brother store. The abandoned building is now known affectionately as "the old red store." Exterior detailing is intact and includes Craftsman-era eave brackets on the front facade, shuttered windows with iron bars, and a board-and-batten front door.

The store is owned by Grace Hardy Rains of Princeton.

Creech-Bryan House
built circa 1855
Institute

Facing a dirt lane close to one of the former male dormitories (Pridgen-Hardy House) of Lenoir Collegiate Institute stands the abandoned Creech-Bryan House, one of the best-preserved examples of domestic Greek Revival-style architecture remaining in the region. Although the house is not known to have been associated with the Institute, it almost certainly served some function for the school, most likely as staff housing.

The one-story central-hall house features common elements such as a low hip roof, two interior central chimneys, and transoms and sidelights flanking the front and rear entrances. A very rare intact feature is the diminutive hip-roof central-bay front portico, supported by large posts and pilasters and sheltering flush facade sheathing. Other exterior details include large nine-over-six sash windows, heavy corner pilasters, a frieze band, a boxed cornice with wide overhanging eaves, a sill skirt, and brick piers. A short, central rear ell appears to be an original wing that was later enlarged with flanking hip-roof rooms and a two-phase kitchen ell extension.

The interior retains some of the best Greek Revival detailing in Lenoir County, including original paint schemes. A transverse arch is located in the central hall (probably added in the late 1800s), as well as a small beaded ceiling beam, which would have supported a light fixture. While the four intact mantels are rather simple in design, the window and door surrounds are some of the most elaborate found in Lenoir County. The deeply molded surrounds found in the parlor are pedimented, while the remaining surrounds feature corner blocks with gougework and hand-carved detailing. Because of the extremely high ceilings, one bedroom features a two-story closet. The original two- and four-panel doors are intact, with several retaining original feather and two-tone paint schemes.

Also located on the grounds are several tobacco-related outbuildings and the Institute cemetery, which contains the grave of a Lenoir Collegiate Institute student who died in 1858.

Croom-Hardy House
built late 1850s
Institute

This small, abandoned one-story dwelling, known locally as the Croom-Hardy House, is located on the edge of the antebellum community of Institute and possibly was connected to the Lenoir Collegiate Institute, though its relationship has not been documented. Bearing resemblance to the Greek Revival-style buildings erected for dormitories and classrooms at the school, the hall-and-parlor-plan house's scale and size suggests that it originally functioned as a residence. A low hipped roof, original rear shed addition, central interior chimney, and later front ell, also with a low hipped roof, define the Greek Revival character of the dwelling. The interior likewise carries a popular mid-nineteenth-century theme, with details such as low horizontal flush-sheathed wainscot and plain post-and-lintel mantels.

Hughes House (demolished)
built circa 1870; demolished in the late twentieth century
Institute vicinity

The Hughes House, located just to the north of Institute until its demolition had been moved from a nearby farm to its site and converted to a packhouse by the Byrd family. The interior detailing of the building had been removed, but intact exterior detailing, such as a boxed cornice, flush gables, and six-over-six sash windows, helped to date the building to at least as early as the third quarter of the nineteenth century. The most interesting aspect of the building was its form: it was a one-story double-pile house with a rear recessed porch that duplicated the coastal cottage except that it lacked the engaged front porch. This modified, or stripped, coastal cottage form was built in other areas of the county during the Reconstruction era.

Only one of the small rooms flanking the recessed porch had a door to the porch. The other room was accessible only from the interior. The double front entrance was uncommon, and only one exterior end chimney placement could be ascertained.

Reverend Samuel B. Dozier House
built 1850s
Institute vicinity

Located just outside Institute is the Dozier House, an excellent example of the transitional Federal/Greek Revival-style dwelling that was being constructed in the area during the 1850s. The two-story central-hall-plan dwelling retains such architectural features as two single-shoulder chimneys, six-over-six sash windows, and a transom and sidelights around the front entrance. Interior details place the house in the Greek Revival era and include original mantels, two-panel doors, and an original dogleg stairway with a chamfered, flared newel-post and scrollwork under the steps. The I-house form with rear shed and low side-gable roof resembles that of the T. W. Dawson House at Institute prior to renovation.

The Reverend Samuel B. Dozier, a small farmer, raised only the amount of food needed to sustain his family. In 1860 Dozier worked fifty-four improved acres and owned another eight unimproved acres of land, worth $3,000. He owned one horse, one milk cow, one other cow, and seventeen swine. On his small amount of land Dozier produced 350 bushels of Indian corn, 5 bushels of peas and beans, 10 bushels of Irish potatoes, 150 bushels of sweet potatoes, 2 tons of fodder, and 3 bales of cotton (400 pounds each). Dozier slaughtered twenty dollars worth of his livestock, most likely his hogs. Although this farm is still the seat of a large tobacco operation, no early outbuildings survive. The farm now uses seven modern

tobacco curing barns, which are arranged parallel to one another, with a flat-roof shed located across their front facades.

Wilson-Brothers House
built mid-nineteenth century; enlarged circa 1899
Institute vicinity

Around 1899 Henry Warren and Ruth Kennedy Brothers enlarged their mid-nineteenth-century dwelling with a two-story addition. The original one-story hall-and-parlor-plan house is thought to have been constructed by the Wilson family and is now the rear kitchen/dining ell of the present house. One of the few Victorian-style farmhouses located in rural Lenoir County, the well-preserved house is distinguished by an open dogleg stairway and a wraparound front porch. Other architectural details include two-over-two sash windows, an exterior end and an exterior rear chimney, seven-panel doors, a transom above the front entrance, a short rear ell, and fish-scale shingles in the gable ends. The rear ell (original house) retains two original mantels and a turn-of-the-century built-in china cabinet.

The house is the seat of an extensive tobacco farmstead and retains many outbuildings, including a smokehouse, a shed, packhouses, tobacco barns, a barn/stable, and an early cook's quarters. The house is now home to Randy and Steva Bledsie.

James William Brothers House

built 1928
Institute vicinity

Located on the site of an antebellum farmhouse of the Hines family is this sturdy brick Craftsman bungalow, built in 1928 for James William Brothers (1895-1948). Substantial for its period, when most rural farmhouses still had frame construction, this well-preserved one-and-a-half-story house features some common elements associated with the style, such as eave brackets, large gable dormers, and four-over-one sash windows. A generous front porch with a central-bay extension and porte cochere is supported by tapered posts set on brick pedestals. Shaded by pecan and pine trees, the Brothers farmstead retains an early-twentieth-century character, with its period smokehouse at the rear of the house, as well as numerous tobacco-related outbuildings.

James Hines House

built mid-nineteenth century
Institute vicinity

This abandoned one-story Greek Revival-style dwelling was originally located on the adjacent site of the James W. Brothers House, prior to being moved in 1928. The house is noted on the 1863 Civil War field maps as "Jas. Hines," though little is known about the early history of this antebellum dwelling. Like the numerous Greek

Revival buildings constructed in nearby Institute, this double-pile center-hall-plan house is noteworthy for its stylistic references to the pervasive idiom. Heavy corner pilasters, an exterior baseboard, a wide frieze beneath a boxed cornice, and a transom and sidelights flanking the front entrance evoke details associated with Greek Revival design. A low hipped roof covers the house, and evidence indicates that a three-quarter-length front porch once shaded the three-bay facade. The modest articulation on the exterior carries to the interior with simple post-and-lintel mantels, plain window and door surrounds, four- and two-panel doors, and six-over-six sash windows.

(former) Dawson Depot

built circa 1900; moved and remodeled 1982
Dawson vicinity

The Dawson Depot was a typical turn-of-the-century rural depot originally located about one and a half miles to the east at Dawson Station. The station served the Dawson community, which grew around a stop on the Kinston and Snow Hill Railroad, which was constructed around 1900. In 1982 Malcolm H. Hill moved and converted the building for use as a dwelling. Although the building is now used as a house, it is the only surviving railroad depot in the county besides the Kinston freight depot.

Exterior architectural characteristics that remain intact include four-over-four sash windows, the standing-seam metal roof, and wide overhanging eaves supported by large curved brackets. The interior retains the original bilevel floor plan and tongue-and-groove wainscoting, as well as the high ceilings.

Wheat Swamp Christian Church
built 1858; remodeled and enlarged 1944, 1954, 1976
Wheat Swamp community

Around 1760 Joseph Parker founded one of North Carolina's original Free Will Baptist Churches at Wheat Swamp. A meetinghouse, located in the vicinity of the present-day North Lenoir High School gymnasium, was constructed at that time. In 1843 the church affiliated with the Disciples of Christ and changed its name from Wheat Swamp Free Will Baptist to Wheat Swamp Christian Church.

On May 21, 1858, a new sanctuary, constructed by John D. Hill, was dedicated. This gable-front frame building, three bays wide and six bays deep, still stands in the center of the present church complex, but its antebellum character has been lost. Little more than the general form and the brick pier foundation indicates the early appearance.

The configuration of the present-day Wheat Swamp Christian Church is the product of numerous additions and remodelings. In 1908 the first major remodeling probably added the stained-glass windows. To accommodate a growing congregation, the church constructed a rear addition and a large side wing in 1944 and 1954. In the 1975-1976 remodeling a front extension and steeple were added. The mid-twentieth-century two-story classroom wing is of concrete-block construction and features gable and shed dormers. Although Wheat Swamp Church has undergone much alteration, the church has great historical significance as one of a handful of surviving antebellum sanctuaries in the county and as one of the oldest congregations in the county.

Dr. Brantson Beeson and Naomi Dail Holder Beeson House
built 1936
Institute vicinity

Dr. Brantson Beeson had this one-and-half-story Craftsman-style house constructed for use as a summer and retirement home in 1936 on his wife's (Naomi Dail Holder's) family farm outside Institute. Naomi Dail Holder was the daughter of Franklin Dail. Beeson was a professor at Washington and Lee University during the 1940s and 1950s. The house's multiple-gabled roof form is uncommon in the county. Eave brackets, sidelights flanking the front and rear entrances, three front gables, and four-over-one sash windows are intact architectural elements commonly associated with the style. The full-facade engaged front porch and porte cochere are supported by flared posts resting on brick pedestals. The house is now occupied by C. L. Herring.

Hines-Aldridge House
built circa 1840
Institute vicinity

Located on a knoll overlooking the surrounding fields near Institute is the Hines-Aldridge plantation house, once one of Lenoir County's finest examples of vernacular Greek Revival architecture. The stately dwelling was built about 1840 by James Madison Hines (1811-1889), Lenoir County's treasurer from 1851 to 1865. One of the county's most prosperous antebellum farmers, Hines had eight slaves and worked five hundred improved and three hundred unimproved acres that were worth $10,000 in 1860. Hines also owned 6 horses, 38 sheep, 10 mules, 10 milk cows, 5 oxen, 6 cattle, and 150 swine. On his land in 1860 Hines produced 125 bushels of wheat, 20 bushels of rye, 2,500 bushels of Indian corn, 20 bushels of oats, 43 bales of cotton (400 pounds each), 80 pounds of wool, 50 bushels of peas and beans, 50 bushels of Irish potatoes, 500 bushels of sweet potatoes, 100 pounds of butter, and 24 tons of fodder. Home manufactures worth $125 and $1,200 worth of slaughtered animals (swine) were produced that year as well.

The two-and-a-half-story central-hall-plan dwelling, of transitional Federal/Greek Revival style, is now in derelict condition but retains much of its original finish, including some extraordinary paint schemes. A two-story central portico embellishes the five-bay facade and appears to have been added sometime soon after construction of the house.

Original exterior architectural details include the nine-over-nine and six-over-six sash windows, roof shingles under the standing-seam metal roof, one shutter, shutter hinges, a double-leaf front entrance with transom and sidelights, an upper front entrance with sidelights, and corner pilasters. The west chimney, now collapsed, featured tumbled shoulders, a decorative Federal masonry design not seen elsewhere in the county. The interior is nearly completely intact, with four-panel doors, transitional Federal/Greek Revival mantels, an open dogleg stairway with scrollwork, a winder stair to the attic, chair rails, and symmetrically molded surrounds with corner blocks. Of particular significance are the original feather painting on the doors, marbleized baseboards, and apparently original paint scheme of the stairway. Other special

features are a hidden wall compartment in the wainscot and a coat rail in the hall.

The rear detached kitchen/dining ell, later attached, features finish like the main house. An interior central chimney serves three fireplaces, two of them corner fireplaces, and the ell retains two original mantels. Other details include nine-over-nine sash windows and an engaged side porch with a porch room with chair rail.

Adding to the significance of the Hines-Aldridge plantation is the large number of extant outbuildings, including an antebellum smokehouse, dairy, and barn. The attenuated two-level smokehouse features a side entrance rather than the traditional gable-end entrance. The one-story front-gable heavy-timber barn exhibits exposed ceiling joists and flush gables. A small front-gable outbuilding with a recessed entry also features exposed ceiling joists and flush gables, although the roof has recently collapsed. This small outbuilding, apparently from the mid-nineteenth century, is thought to have been a dairy. Twentieth-century outbuildings include a barn/stable, three tenant houses, and numerous tobacco barns. Also located on the farm is the Hines family cemetery. A descendant of the Hines family was Harvey C. Hines, notable Kinston merchant.

House
built first decade of the twentieth century
Institute vicinity

A beautiful spindle-and-sawnwork front porch distinguishes this modest though picturesque Victorian farmhouse. By the 1890s decorative architectural elements were readily available through mail-order catalogues or the numerous sash, blind, and door businesses located throughout the region. This example presents an ornate expression found less frequently on modest rural houses than on larger town properties. Built in the traditional one-story triple-A form, the dwelling includes two exterior end chimneys, four-over-four sash windows, and a rear kitchen/dining ell. A smokehouse, a packhouse, a chicken house, and various tobacco barns make up the outbuildings and complete this excellent example of a middle-class farmstead.

Marion Rouse Tenant House
built turn of the twentieth century
Hardison Crossroads vicinity

Located on a tree-filled knoll overlooking agricultural fields is this small Victorian-era farmhouse representing one of the most common dwelling types built throughout Lenoir County. The remarkably unchanged one-and-a-half-story side-gable dwelling is illustrative of a building type constructed for both small landowners and tenant farmers on larger farmsteads. In this example a rarely seen detached rear kitchen connected to the main house by an L-shaped porch survives intact. A central front ell was added to the hall-and-parlor-plan house after its construction. Other identifying details include original four-over-four sash windows, a central chimney, and a brick pier foundation. A feature that was once common on rural farmhouse but rarely survives today is the outside sink on the porch of the rear kitchen. A large packhouse is the only surviving outbuilding. Little is known about the history of this house; however, local tradition suggests that it was erected as a tenant house by local landowner Marion Rouse.

VANCE TOWNSHIP

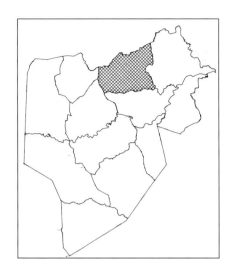

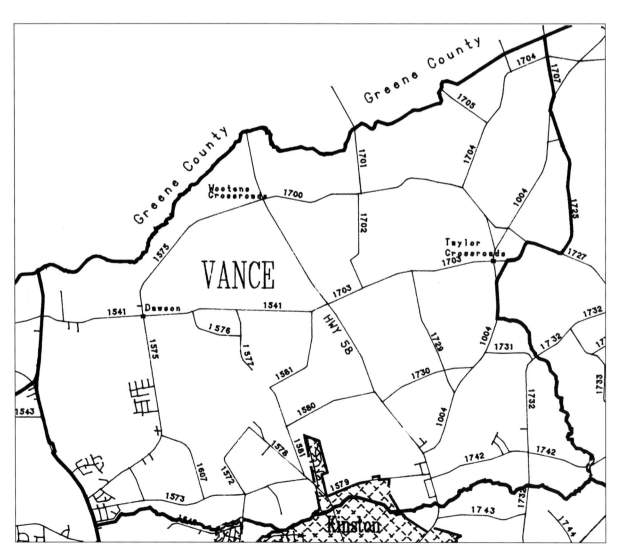

Ossie Taylor House
built circa 1900
Wootens Crossroads vicinity

The Ossie Taylor House was built on Moseley land that was inherited by Addie Moseley. She married Ossie Taylor and they built this house apparently about 1900. They lived here and operated a farm until Addie died about 1934. Ossie then moved away but continued to own the farm until his death about 1956. Thomas Heath bought the farm about 1958, and it is now owned by Henry Heath. It is now a tenant farm. The one-story, frame, three-bay, side-gable house has exterior end brick chimneys, a front door with three-bay transom, a hipped front porch with turned posts, six-over-six sash windows, and wide gable-end eave returns. This is a typical example of the standard vernacular farmhouse of the region during the late nineteenth and early twentieth centuries. The rear ell has a partially enclosed side porch. The house has artificial siding, a replacement front door, and front porch posts that may be replacements. To the rear are a one-and-one-half- story frame packhouse and two sheds.

Post Oak Church Community
built early twentieth century
Wootens Crossroads

Members of the Post Oak Church African American community have been living in this vicinity since the late nineteenth century and may be descended from slaves who worked on nearby plantations. The church is said to have been established around 1890. The first church building burned, and the current church building was constructed circa 1920 or 1930. Elmer Wooten, a son of Robert and Emma Wooten who lived at nearby Wootens Crossroads, is said to have provided the lumber for this church building. Bright's School for black children originally stood across the road from the church. The current settlement contains the Post Oak Free Will Baptist Church, the Sena Mae Bright House located next door, and several nonhistoric residences.

The Post Oak Church is a frame front-gable building with a three-stage Gothic Revival style entrance tower. The building has sash windows of post-World War II vintage and wide Masonite siding.

The Sena Mae Bright House, of vernacular Craftsman style, is a one-story frame house with Craftsman-style sash windows, plain siding, and decorative double front cross gables as well as side gables. This is a variation of the single-front-cross-gable plan that was popular in Lenoir County from about 1910 to 1930. The house has replacement wrought-iron porch posts.

The Post Oak Church community has historical interest as an example of a rural settlement pattern of freedmen in Lenoir County following the Civil War. The basic institutions of church and school provided the nucleus of a black neighborhood here at the turn of the century. This settlement now contains fewer than a dozen houses, although it was probably larger in the early years of the century.

Bright-Hooker-Gray House
built circa 1860; enlarged late nineteenth century
Wootens Crossroads

According to the family tradition of the Gray family, this house was built by Simon Bright before the Civil War. Simon's daughter, Alice Bright, married a Hooker and inherited the house. Hyman Mewborne was the next owner. He sold the dwelling to Neil Gray around 1900. It was inherited by Gray's son Cleveland Gray and subsequently by Cleveland's daughter, Louise Gray

Shingleton, who lives in the house now.

The 1863 Koerner Military Survey Field Map shows a "T. Bright" living at this site. The first Simon Bright in Lenoir County was prominent during the period of earliest settlement, and a line of male descendants named Simon Bright lived in the county at least through the mid-nineteenth century. One document that places Simon Bright as a property owner in this area is a property division of the 1840s that indicates that the lands of Simon Bright adjoined those of Levi Mewborn, whose plantation was to the south near Stonyton Creek.

The 1860 census shows Simon Bright's household as located three households from that of Frederick Greene Taylor, who lived on the next road to the south, State Road 1541. Bright was a twenty-nine-year-old lawyer and farmer. His real estate was valued at $9,000, indicating that he owned a large farm. His personal estate was valued at $7,600. He apparently lived alone, for no one else is listed in his household. The 1860 slave schedule showed Simon W. Bright as the owner of six slaves. It is possible that Bright's School for blacks, originally located a short distance to the west, was named for a freedman named Bright who had been a slave on Simon W. Bright's farm.

It is only a supposition that the 1860 household of Simon Bright was located in this house. In the absence of deeds for this era of Lenoir County history, it is difficult to prove this, but lawyer and farmer Simon Bright certainly lived in this vicinity (and according to Gray family tradition, in this house). The name "T. Bright" on the 1863 map could be a spelling error) or it could refer to a family member of Simon's family. The Gray family has owned the farm for three generations.

The Bright-Hooker-Gray House is a one-story frame Greek Revival-style house, constructed about 1860, with a hip roof, plain siding, six-over-six and four-over-four sash windows, one exterior end chimney laid in common bond, and a rear hip-roofed ell. At the front south facade is a wide Greek Revival-style corner post, and the section of original eave that remains has a wide frieze board. In the late nineteenth century a side wing was added to the north side, with a projecting front gable. At this time the original front porch was probably removed. The addition has plain siding and four-over-four sash windows. The front entrance has wide sidelights and a replacement door.

A good deal of original Greek Revival fabric remains on the interior. The house retains its original center-hall plan, plaster walls, high baseboards, and some vertical two-panel doors, as well as mitred surrounds. The south front mantel survives. It is an idiosyncratic vernacular Greek Revival-style mantel with pilasters supporting a frieze with a shallow segmental arch.

A frame gable-front smokehouse, said to be as old as the house, stands to the rear. There are also a frame garage, a packhouse, and two sheds of early-twentieth-century date. On the south side are two frame tobacco barns built in the 1920s.

Roy Wooten House

built mid-nineteenth century; remodeled and enlarged circa 1890
Wootens Crossroads

The crossroads where the Roy Wooten House stands is known as Wootens Crossroads. The earliest Wootens to live here were Robert D. and Elizabeth Wooten, who moved to Lenoir County in the early 1880s and purchased this tract from Captain William W. Carraway of nearby Monticello Plantation. Their son, Robert Alexander Wooten, married Emma Parrott in 1888, and the couple moved in with his parents. About 1890 the small one-story house was expanded with the addition of the I-house facing the main road, U.S. Highway 58. Robert and Emma eventually enlarged the family holdings to approximately 1,000 acres. One of their sons, Ralph, operated a frame general store (now demolished) at the crossroads. Their youngest son, Roy Wooten, was born in 1910. He continued to operate the family farm after the deaths of his parents. His widow, Sarah Jones Wooten, still lives in the house.

The current Wooten House, built about 1890, is an I-house, the house type probably most favored by Lenoir County's middle-class farmers. It has two rear exterior brick chimneys and large sash windows containing nine-over-nine and nine-over-six sash on the first story and six-over-six sash on the second story. The central entrance has a transom and narrow sidelights. The front hip-roofed porch has square posts covered with vinyl. The exterior siding and trim are covered with vinyl. On the rear are an ell, a shed, and an enclosed rear porch. The rear ell is said to have been built by the Carraway family, probably in the mid-nineteenth century. Its one-and-one-half-story form with flush gable end is the only early feature still visible, for it has been completely remodeled on the exterior and interior. A frame smokehouse dating from the late nineteenth or early twentieth century stands at the rear.

The main section of the house retains its original center-hall plan, with open-string stair with a simple railing and square newel post with molded cap. It also retains some simple late Greek Revival-style mantels, but the remaining interior fabric has been either concealed by newer materials or replaced during extensive remodeling.

Monticello (Whitfield-Carraway-Scarborough Farm)

built late eighteenth century
Wootens Crossroads vicinity

Although the paucity of pre-1878 records hampers investigation into the history of Monticello, its large Georgian dwelling, antebellum graveyard, and impressive setting constitute one of the finest, if not the finest, of the surviving plantation complexes in Lenoir County. The seat of the plantation is a stately two-story frame double-pile house, five bays wide and three bays deep, with a full one-story front shed porch and full rear shed. The house has well-preserved Georgian and Federal details, including flush sheathing beneath the front porch, six-paneled doors, nine-over-nine sash windows, original or early louvered shutters, heavy windowsills, beaded

weatherboards, flush gable eaves, a Flemish-bond brick chimney on the west end, and an interior end brick chimney on the east end. The original or early six-panel front door has a five-pane transom and simple molded surround. The house rests on brick piers and has a steep gabled roof covered with seamed metal.

It is difficult to date Monticello, since legend dates it to around 1740 and early historical records are lost. It appears to have been built in stages. The east dining room has Georgian woodwork, including a mantel with a flat-paneled frieze, a wide surround, and a narrow molded shelf; a high wainscot above the lower, Federal-style wainscot; a built-in cupboard with raised-panel doors; and a raised-panel closet door, indicating a late-eighteenth-century date. A family tradition mentions a secondary staircase (now removed) that rose from the dining room to the second floor. This may have been the stair of the original house. According to tradition the interior was remodeled in 1812, and the house may have been enlarged to its present size at that time.

Since then the dwelling has undergone only minor alterations. The boxed porch posts appear to be replacements. The porch has exposed ceiling joists and replacement sheathing on the underside of the roof. The west rear chimney was demolished and a large six-over-six sash window added in its place on the first story, with a tripartite window added in its place on the second story. Tripartite windows also replaced the original windows on the east gable end. There was originally a recessed porch occupying the center bays of the rear shed, but this has been enclosed. The rear shed wraps around on the east side as a porch. About 1950 the porch was enclosed by owner Eugenia Scarborough, and a large brick chimney with a very tall stack was added.

The interior of Monticello, with the exception of the Georgian dining room, contains well-preserved Federal finish. The center-hall two-room-deep plan is intact on the first floor. The second floor has the same plan now but is said to have contained a ballroom originally. The stair is an open-string stair that rises from the rear hall in a straight run, with a simple newel with molded cap, rounded handrail, and plain balusters. A double-door closet is built into the base of the stair. The hall has wide horizontal-sheathed walls. Throughout the house the ceilings have wide sheathing. Most doors have six flat panels. Except for the downstairs hall, all walls are plastered.

Of the original eight fireplaces in the house, five mantels remain. One chimney with its two fireplaces has been removed, and the corner fireplace in the right rear room of the second floor has been removed. On the first floor the two front rooms flanking the hall have identical tripartite Federal-style mantels with dentil cornices and molded shelves. On the second floor the two front rooms flanking the hall have simple late Georgian-style mantels of similar design. Each has a flat-paneled frieze, a molded surround, and a shallow molded shelf.

A number of outbuildings surround the house, including a well house, a corn silo, sheds, a smokehouse, packhouses, a mule barn, tobacco barns, and a garage. Some of these date from the late nineteenth century; others were built by Eugenia Scarborough in the 1930s. Several tenant houses stand further away. The two most significant accompanying resources are the plantation cemetery and the 1938 house, in which the present generation of Scarboroughs dwells.

The small family graveyard is located just west of the main house in a grove of ancient cedars. It containing three visible grave markers. The oldest visible gravestone is for Harriet G. Carraway, 1832-1834. The second visible marker is a marble obelisk for Harriet Carraway, 1796-1852. The inscription states that she is the daughter of the Reverend Lewis Whitfield and the wife of Snoad B. Carraway. The obelisk is signed by a monument firm whose name is partially illegible: "Bauisi—, McCley—& Wright, Petersburg, Va." The third visible stone is a marble headstone for Captain William W. Carraway, inscribed "Co. E. 3 N.C. Cav. CSA." It has no birth or death date. This marker was erected a few years ago by some Carraway descendants, apparently to replace an older marker. William W. Carraway was born in 1838 and died in 1904.

In the 1904 obituary of Captain William W. Carraway, Monticello was called the old homestead, named the Oak Grove. The house is set at the end of a drive approximately seven hundred feet long that terminates in a large circle in front of the house. The drive is partially lined with cedar trees dating from the early twentieth century, and the house sits in a grove of tall hardwood trees, including an ancient catalpa tree and an osage orange tree said to have been planted in the 1880s by Captain Carraway.

The overall pattern of fields and woodland on the 159 acres seems to be basically unchanged from about 1918, when the property was surveyed by civil engineer Alfred Cheney. The plat shows a division into three lots that correspond to the three fields. The front field, containing the homestead and all outbuildings, goes back to the tobacco barn complex shown on the plat. There are two more fields in the rear, separated by a wooded border. The survey shows a "canal" between the second and third fields. This term apparently refers to a ditch dug from the branch marking the west boundary of the property. The rear boundary, Wheat Swamp Creek, contains heavily wooded wetlands.

According to tradition Monticello was built around 1740 by Lewis Whitfield. Whitfield is said to have owned over 55,000 acres in north Lenoir County during the eighteenth century, and Monticello was his home plantation. Whitfield owned another plantation house, LaFayette, in the east section of his landholdings to use while working the land there. LaFayette still stands to the east of N.C. Highway 11 about seven miles east of Monticello. According to tradition it was built about 1786, but its form and style date it to the early 1800s.

According to tradition a baby boy named Snoad Carraway was left in a basket on Whitfield's doorstep. The child is said to have been named Snoad because it snowed the day he was left at the plantation. The Whitfields raised him, and he married their daughter, Harriet. The 1850 census lists the household of Snoad B. Carraway, a sixty-one-year-old "planter" with a planta-

tion valued at the remarkably high sum of $100,000, indicating that Carraway's plantation may have contained some 20,000 acres located in several different plantations rather than solely at Monticello. Snoad Carraway apparently died during the 1850s.

A biographical sketch of Capt. William W. Carraway appears in *The Heritage of Lenoir County*. Captain Carraway was born at Monticello in 1838, attended Airy Grove Academy, the Bingham School in Orange County, and the University of Virginia. During the Civil War he served with Company E, Third North Carolina Cavalry. The Federal government is said to have confiscated the 5,000 acres of land that were still a part of the plantation and gave a 159-acre homeplace to "Carraway's wife and wards." It is said that Monticello was not burned like many other eastern North Carolina plantation houses because Contentnea Creek and the other creeks in the area were swollen during the time that Federal troops were encamped in the area, and the soldiers could not reach Monticello.

Following the war Capt. Carraway returned to his farm and engaged in agriculture and the mercantile business. By 1880 the farm consisted of seventy acres of cultivated land and fifty acres of woodland and forest, valued at $4,500. The crops were primarily of corn and cotton, with twenty-two acres of corn producing two hundred bushels, and thirty-five acres of cotton producing twelve bales. Carraway paid five hundred dollars in wages to "colored" day laborers during the previous year and produced $784 worth of farm products.

Capt. Carraway led a colorful life, writing articles for the press under the name D. R. Walker, and from 1879 to 1886 traveling as a correspondent for the Raleigh *News and Observer*. Later he served as a post office inspector and traveled to twenty-seven states during his work in that capacity. In 1898 Carraway represented Lenoir County in the North Carolina General Assembly. He was married twice: his first wife was Alice B. Hilliard of Nash County, and his second wife was Mary B. Hilliard. He had thirteen children. Carraway died at his old home, Monticello, and was interred in the "family burying ground at the Oak Grove at the Old Homestead."

The readily verifiable history of Monticello begins in 1919, when the Scarborough family purchased the property. Scarboroughs have lived there since that time and have farmed the acreage continuously. In 1919 the house and 159-acre farm were sold by the Carraways to Hattie Scarborough, widow of Benjamin Franklin Scarborough. Hattie had eight children, John, Nannie, Eugenia, Vivian, Benjamin F., Rachel, Martha and Will, and she moved to Monticello and raised them.

At Hattie's death her children inherited the place. Will, Vivian, and Eugenia Scarborough bought out the other siblings and lived there throughout their lives. Eugenia Scarborough, a schoolteacher, outlived the rest, residing in the house until her death in 1979. Her nephew, Benjamin Franklin Scarborough Jr., inherited the property. He was raised at Monticello in the Colonial Revival brick house that his parents built beside the plantation house in 1938. He and his wife Mary Ann Barlow live in the 1938 house and act as caretakers for Monticello.

Octavius Moseley House
built circa 1875
Kinston North vicinity

Picturesquely located on a small rise, this abandoned house was constructed soon after the Civil War and is one of the only houses in the county with Italianate-style architectural detailing. Built around 1875 by William Octavius Moseley (1851-1918), a prosperous farmer who owned a two-hundred-acre farm and married Launa A. Mewborn about the time he built the house, this handsome dwelling was one of the most stylish in the county. Launa died around 1885, and when Octavius remarried about 1887, he built a new house on Blount Street in Kinston. The country house was occupied by Lemuel Octave Moseley (1878-1951), Octavius's eldest son, until 1920. The house was then occupied by tenants until the 1970s.

Standing in the middle of a field, this two-story, tri-gable I-house was one of the most ornate in the county, but most of the interior and exterior woodwork has been removed in recent years. Historic photographs show that the dwelling featured Italianate architectural details such as molded window surrounds, heavy pendanted eave brackets, and a double-door entrance with a transom set in an ornate surround with a bracketed hood. The dwelling has a rear ell and two facing gable dormers on the rear facade. The now-collapsed full-facade front porch was supported by chamfered columns and originally had a center-bay pedimented gable and heavy pendanted brackets. Most of the original two-over-two sash windows have been removed, but the Italianate window surrounds, which match the front door, survive. The wide boxed eaves carry around the center front pedimented gable and the two rear pedimented gables. The center-hall-plan house has two interior rear brick chimneys with elaborate caps.

Augustus Moseley House
built circa 1860
Kinston North vicinity

Converted to a packhouse and moved a short distance from its original location, this two-story I-house was constructed around 1860 by William Augustus Moseley (1823-1882). It is owned by the B. F. Scarborough Jr. family at the present time.

The frame I-house exhibits a number of vernacular features that are characteristic of nineteenth-century farmhouses in north Lenoir County—a rear shed with a center hall and flanking rooms, a center hall in the main block with the stair ascending from the rear of the hall, and a closet beneath the stair accessible through a door in the left front room. Originally a long breezeway extended between the rear door and the detached kitchen, which had a porch extending around three sides. These features were demolished when the house was moved. The front entrance is a double door with transom and sidelights, and the house retains some of its original six-over-six sash windows. Although the mantels have been removed, the house retains the original stair rail with chamfered newel post and molded cap, the simple molded window and door surrounds, and a Greek Revival style double door.

Packhouses, sheds, and tobacco barns are located on both sides of the house, and a family graveyard remains on the property.

Wylie T. Moseley House

built circa 1850
Kinston North vicinity

Constructed in the antebellum period, this two-story I-house was built by Wylie Thomas (Tom) Moseley (1830-1897). Tom was the oldest son of Tully and Hollon Moseley. After marrying Mary Ann Hardy (1834-1869) in 1850, he bought land near his father and built this house. His first wife died in 1869, and he married Martha Eleanor Harper in 1872. Tom Moseley is said to have been one of the county's most successful farmers, and the house was formerly surrounded by orchards, gardens, pastures, and fields. Tom was also a charter member of the Rose of Sharon Church near Grainger's Station.

This frame I-house with original rear shed and rear ell is of vernacular Greek Revival style, with a double-leaf front door with transom and sidelights, six-over-nine sash windows, flat-paneled corner posts with molded caps, and remnants of Doric porch posts. Both of the original exterior end brick chimneys have been removed.

The interior of the center-hall-plan house features an open-string stair, which rises from the rear hall. The hall extends through the rear shed to the ell porch, just as in the floor plan of Wylie's brother Augustus Moseley's house across the road (both houses may have been built by the same carpenter). But unlike Augustus's house this house has a kitchen and dining room ell extending from the east rear side. The interior has transitional Federal/Greek Revival-style detailing, such as the tapered square newel post with a molded cap. The two mantels in the front first-floor rooms have Doric pilasters supporting scalloped friezes with dentil cornices and molded shelves. The rear first-floor mantels and upstairs mantels are more Federal in style, with tripartite designs and cornices with delicate pierced ornament.

Behind the house are a late-nineteenth-century two-and-half-story frame barn with an open shed on two sides, a group of five tobacco barns, and the family graveyard.

Airy Grove Christian Church

built circa 1895
Kinston North vicinity

Airy Grove Christian Church was established about 1895 on this site, with the sanctuary constructed the same year. The Disciples of Christ, or Christian Church, is a strong denomination in Lenoir County, tracing its roots back to the first county congregation of 1843, known as Little Sisters Church. According to one local resident that church was established nearby. The 1863 Koerner Military Survey Field Map shows the Lousin Swamp Church at approximately this same site. Airy Grove may be the successor congregation to that antebellum church.

Constructed around 1895, the sanctuary is typical of churches in the county—frame, front gable, one bay wide, and three bays deep. It has a small steeple, apparently of recent construction, located on the roof ridge just behind the front facade. The front door is set in a small gabled entrance projection. The building has overhanging eaves with wide eave returns. The rectangular windows are stained glass of recent manufacture. A two-story frame educational wing was added to the rear facade.

The interior of the church has been refurbished with new pews and pulpit furniture, but the walls and ceiling retain narrow tongue-and-groove sheathing that may be original. The balcony is reached by small staircases in the rear corners of the sanctuary.

Sutton-Moore House
built circa 1920
Taylors Crossroads vicinity

The Sutton-Moore house is a good representative of the turn-of-the-century single-story farmhouse. Built circa 1920 for Paul Sutton, this house has a modest Victorian-style front ell with a bay window that enhances the overall plain dwelling—a popular form in the area. Other architectural features include two-over-two sash windows, exterior front and rear chimneys, a wraparound front porch supported by turned posts, and an elongated hip-roof rear ell. An extensive collection of outbuildings remains and includes a packhouse, a garage, a shed, and numerous tobacco barns. In recent years the house has been the residence of Roy Moore.

Carl Jones House
built 1924
Taylors Crossroads vicinity

Standing at the center of this exceptional example of an early-twentieth-century farm enterprise is one of the more sophisticated rural Craftsman bungalows remaining in the county. Built for Carl Jones in 1924, the house exemplifies the bungalow style with such identifying features as large shed-roof front and rear dormers, eave knee braces, scrolled rafter tails and bargeboards, decorative spandrels on the front porch and porte cochere, and

a slate roof. Other architectural features retained are two interior central chimneys, a multipaned transom and sidelights flanking the front door, and transoms over the side and rear doors.

An intact interior features four mantels (some with tile backing), French doors, woodwork, a central-hall ceiling arch, the original kitchen, and original furnishings. The farm has an extensive collection of outbuildings and fences, including a garage, a pump house, a smokehouse, a workshop, a packhouse, a stable, and various tobacco barns.

The house is presently occupied by Doris (Dollie) White of Vanceboro, widow of B. Frank Jones.

(former) Airy Grove School
built circa 1900
Taylors Crossroads vicinity

The Airy Grove School is one of the best pre-consolidation schools remaining in the county. A deed showing that in 1887 Thomas A. Heath sold to the Board of Education of Lenoir County, for $25, one acre of land on which the school was then located indicates that the school predated the deed. The school began as a one-room single-story building with a three-bay facade, gable front orientation, and four-bay side elevation featuring six-over-six sash windows. W. Chester Forrest, who attended the school in 1914, described it as heated by a wood stove, with no electricity, and two outdoor privies. The next year another classroom was added and separated from the original room by folding doors, so that the teacher had privacy. A 1924 school survey indicated that the school contained two classrooms and had an enrollment of forty-three students. In that year the county schools were consolidated and Airy Grove students were reassigned to Contentnea School.

In 1925 J. E. Forrest purchased the lot and building and converted the schoolhouse to a packhouse. His son W. Chester Forrest later moved the school away from the main road to its present location. The well-preserved building is a typical turn-of-the-century schoolhouse. Though still used as a packhouse, the building retains the original front porch supported by turned posts, interior cloakrooms and folding doors, and seven-panel front door.

Felix Hardison House
built 1918-1920
Savannah vicinity

Craftsman bungalows were often chosen for farm-houses during the 1920s and 1930s, and Lenoir County has several sophisticated examples remaining. This particular one represents one of the more ambitious of those built in rural areas of the county and was constructed for Felix Hardison on land inherited by his wife, Martha Virginia Grubbs. According to family tradition the farm upon which the Hardison House stands came from Martha Grubbs's mother, Eliza Fields. Felix Hardison was a farmer and also operated a sawmill. The Hardisons had five children including Daniel, John G., Proctor, Margaret, and Martha.

Conforming to a traditional central-hall double-pile plan, the one-and-a-half-story dwelling includes the archetypal engaged front porch and accent wood shingles in the side gables and front gabled dormer. Setting this example apart from other rural bungalows are the elaborate window and door treatments, composed of full entablatures supported by pilasters, and the shaped exposed rafter ends beneath the porch. A second-story Palladian window in the gable end, eight-over-one sash windows, and nicely detailed bungalow porch columns also add to this house a sophistication rarely seen in rural areas. Evidence of the agricultural function of the property can be found in three surviving outbuildings, including a tobacco barn, tobacco packhouse, and storage barn.

(former) Tyndall College
built circa 1907-1929
Dawson's Station

Tyndall College, established in 1907 and closed in 1929, contained at its peak a seven-acre campus with a three-story boys' dorm, a two-story girls' dorm and two houses for staff members. The boys' dorm has been demolished, but the girls' dorm and the two houses still stand. The girls' dorm and a one-story house are located on the north side of State Road 1575 and are part of the one-hundred-acre Gary Rouse Farm. A two-story house stands across the road and is owned by the F. H. Jarman family.

The girls' dorm is a two-story five-bay-wide frame building with a one-story rear kitchen ell. The main entrance is the extreme west bay of the main (south) facade. The first floor contains a wide T-shaped hall, a large dining room and kitchen, and living quarters for the dormitory supervisor. The second floor contains ten dormitory rooms, five on each side of a center hall, but partition walls have been removed, and now each side of the hall contains one large room. The building has not been used since 1929 and is in deteriorated condition. It has plain siding, six-over-six sash windows, and interior brick chimneys. The interior has narrow tongue-and-groove sheathing, four-panel doors, and a handsome open-string staircase with heavy turned newel posts, molded balusters, and a molded handrail. It is said that the timber for this building was cut at Jasper, in Craven County, and shipped to nearby Dawson's Station.

The one-story house on the north side of the road, just west of the girls' dorm, was built circa 1914 by school president James M. Perry as his residence. The house displays the double-front-gable form so popular in Lenoir County, with two interior chimneys, replacement vinyl siding, one-over-one sash windows, and a hipped front porch with turned posts. The rear ell porch has been replaced by a large shed addition. The front door has narrow sidelights. The center-hall plan has been changed to a hall-parlor plan. One original mantel, a bracketed design with a Neoclassical Revival mirrored overmantel, is still in place in the front east room. The house has been extensively remodeled on the interior. To the rear sits a row of four outbuildings built by Rupert Rouse. These are a small barn, a packhouse, and two sheds.

The two-story house on the south side of State Road 1575 was built for John W. Tyndall about 1907 as his own residence. It is now occupied by the widow of F. H. Jarman. It has a side-gable main block with a front-gable wing, a wraparound porch with Doric columns, interior brick chimneys, one-over-one sash, and the original front door of Neoclassical Revival style. The house now has vinyl siding and an enclosed rear ell. To the rear are a garage and a storage shed.

Tyndall College is an almost forgotten private school operated by three successive Disciples of Christ ministers. John W. Tyndall (1877-1933), a native of Craven County, established the school in 1907 and operated it until 1914. It was named Industrial Christian College. James M. Perry (1880-1952), a native of Windsor, operated it from 1914 to 1916. Then Joseph A. Saunders (1876-1945), a native of Richlands, operated it from 1916 to 1929, when it closed. The school opened with 102 students and had some 200 students by 1911. The most common name for the school was Tyndall College. Most of its students were day students who commuted from the immediate area, some by train.

After the close of Tyndall College in 1929, probably the result of the Great Depression, the land was sold. Rupert W. Rouse purchased the tract containing the girls' dormitory and the Perry House, while the Jarman family bought the tract containing the Tyndall House. The two houses are relatively well preserved because they have continued to be used as residences, but the girls' dormitory is extremely deteriorated because it has been used only for storage.

The old Tyndall College buildings have considerable historical interest as the remnants of a once-thriving Disciples of Christ school that educated many of the young people of Lenoir County during the early twentieth century. The Disciples of Christ, or Christian denomination has been one of the strongest denominations in rural Lenoir County since the early nineteenth century. The three surviving campus buildings are relics of a forgotten institution.

(former) Fairfield Academy School
built circa 1910
Mewborne's Crossroads vicinity

Fairfield Academy was established as a private school in 1817, one of a number of private schools that operated in Lenoir County during the nineteenth century before the advent of public schools in the latter part of the century. But the building itself was probably built about 1910, when the school became part of the public school system. A 1920s publication, entitled *Survey of the Public Schools of Lenoir County*, includes a photograph of the building and describes it as a one-teacher school in poor condition, with an enrollment of forty-six children.

Fairfield Academy schoolhouse is a one-story frame gable-front building, two bays wide and four bays deep. It has a single front door set in the right bay of the facade and a single six-over-six sash front window set at the far left side of the facade. Four six-over-six sash windows were originally located in the right side, but these were removed when a shed room was added. There are no windows on the left side at the present time. The building is covered with plain siding and has a diamond-shaped louvered ventilator in each gable end. All the windows were replaced in 1982. The school once had a hipped front porch, but this apparently was removed prior to 1982.

The interior consists of one open room, with narrow-board wooden floors and tongue-and-groove sheathing on the walls and ceiling. The shed addition on the right side contains a kitchen.

The school is said to have been closed in 1928. The building stood at Mewborns Crossroads, in a field directly north of the Hyman Mewborn House on land owned by Robert Wooten. Wooten gave the schoolhouse to the Hall family in 1982, and the Halls moved it to its present site beside their own house in the same year. The building originally sat on the north side of state road 1541 near NC 58. An open shed was added on the left side, a deck was built across part of the facade, and the interior was restored. The Halls use the schoolhouse as a recreation building.

Benjamin Franklin Scarborough Farm
built 1888
Mewborn's Crossroads vicinity

This land was purchased about 1888 by Benjamin Franklin Scarborough and his wife, Hattie. They had moved from the Falling Creek area of Lenoir County.

They had the house built in 1888 and lived there, raising a family of around eight children, until B. F. Scarborough's death, apparently in the early twentieth century. Hattie Scarborough, a widow, purchased Monticello, a farm located just to the north, about 1919 and moved her family there. The Scarboroughs continued to farm the land around the house until 1983, when they sold the farm to Gladys Gray and her husband Robert T. Gray. Mrs. Gray, now widowed, currently owns the farm.

The one-story frame side-gable house has a central chimney, two front doors, a front porch with chamfered posts, and a rear ell with porch. The corner posts, frieze board, and wide gable eave returns are typical of houses of this period in the area. To the rear is a board-and-batten front gable outbuilding, probably a smokehouse. Stretching in a row down a farm lane behind the house are a frame packhouse that is two-and-a-half stories tall, with a side-gable orientation that may indicate that it originally functioned as a cotton gin, and three tobacco barns.

Noah Small Sr. House

built circa 1925
Wheat Swamp vicinity

The Noah Small Sr. House is a typical and well-preserved example of a pyramidal cottage, with a relatively shallow hip roof, overhanging eaves with exposed rafter tails, four-over-four sash windows, and a hipped front porch with original turned posts with brackets. There is no porch railing. The rear ell retains its ell porch, with posts identical to those of the front porch. The original kitchen pantry is located in the enclosed end bay of the ell porch. The interior has a center-hall plan.

Noah Small Sr. purchased this land and had the house built about 1925. His grandson, James Thurman Tyndall, inherited the house and still lives here. This small farm contains approximately thirty acres of land. Behind the farmhouse are a smokehouse, barn, and privy of traditional frame construction.

Hill Farm

built 1840, remodeled late nineteenth century, circa 1925
Wheat Swamp vicinity

The Hill House has the form of a substantial Federal-style farmhouse but has lost nearly all of the Federal finish on both the exterior and interior, with the exception of the handsome Flemish-bond chimneys. The Federal cottage, one-and-a-half stories high, of frame construction has stepped-shoulder chimneys laid in Flemish bond, plain siding, flush gable eaves, and front and rear boxed cornices. The house has six-over-six sash windows on the first story, set in simple molded surrounds that may be original. The upper gable ends and ell have four-over-four sash windows in plain surrounds. The front porch is a late-nineteenth-century replacement and features turned posts with brackets, a railing with turned balusters, and a hipped roof. The ell contains the kitchen, which was attached to the house and enlarged in the late nineteenth or early twentieth century. A pantry extends from the rear of the kitchen. The ell porch has been enclosed.

The original Federal interior probably consisted of a hall-parlor plan with an enclosed stair. This was apparently removed in the late nineteenth century, when the present stair was built. The stair railing consists of a heavy turned newel, square balusters, and a molded handrail. The center-hall plan and the narrow beaded tongue-and-groove sheathing on the floors, walls, and ceilings may also date from the late nineteenth century. The mantels in the main rooms flanking the center hall are Neoclassical Revival-style millwork with bracketed shelves and appear to date from the 1920s. The attic contains a center hall and flanking bedrooms, all finished in narrow wood sheathing.

The house, in a grove of tall hardwood trees, faces north, with its west side toward U.S. Highway 258. Adjacent to the road at the driveway are three gabled frame buildings that functioned as a steam-powered corn mill operated by Noah Small Jr. These buildings are deteriorated and overgrown with vegetation. Behind the farmhouse are a one-and-one-half-story gable-front barn, with a central runway, and a one-story frame storage shed. Both buildings, dating from the early twentieth century, are covered with metal sheathing.

The 1863 Koerner Military Survey Field Map marks the approximate site of this farmhouse as the home of the Hill family. The house has been known in recent times as the Noah Small Jr. House because it was purchased about 1925 by Noah Small, whose father built the farmhouse just to the north. The farm is owned by Noah Small's daughters, who rent out the house and farmland to tenants. The Hill family graveyard is located in a field north of the house. It contains some twenty-five gravestones for the Hartsfield and Hill families. A newly erected granite plaque notes that some unmarked Hartsfield graves date from 1850 to 1958, while the oldest inscribed stone is that of William R. Hill, 1823-1877. The cemetery is surrounded by a concrete-block wall. As late as 1990 a descendant of the Hill family, David William Hill (1899-1990), was buried in the graveyard.

Josiah A. Suggs House
built mid-nineteenth century
Wheat Swamp vicinity

The original owner of this house and hundred-acre farm was Josiah A. Suggs. According to family tradition his neighbors pitched in to build this house for him during a time when he was sick in bed. The house is said to have a pegged frame. Josiah (Joe) Suggs gave each of his children a portion of his farm, but fifty-six acres still remain with the homeplace. After his death the homeplace passed to his daughter Mary Eliza Suggs, who married a Smith. She died in 1951 at the age of eighty-two. The present owner, Sally Smith, is the widow of the grandson of Joe Suggs, and she lives in the house.

The Josiah Suggs House, apparently built in the mid-nineteenth century, is an interesting example of the coastal cottage form in Lenoir County. Unlike the L. C. (Pomp) Moseley House, which evolved into a coastal cottage when the front porch was added, the Joe Suggs House was apparently constructed with an engaged front porch at the beginning. The house lacks the early Coastal Cottage feature of a recessed porch in the center bay of the rear shed, and it has a center-hall plan instead of the common early hall-parlor plan. The gable roof engages a front porch (now enclosed) and rear shed rooms. A lower gabled wing extends from the east gable end, and its front porch has been enclosed as well. The house has

gable-end brick chimneys, some original six-over-six and some replacement sash windows, and vinyl siding completely encasing the exterior.

The interior has undergone a fair amount of alteration as well. The narrow center-hall plan is barely discernible because of the construction of a bathroom in the center section of the hall. On each side of the hall are two rooms: the front rooms are larger than the rear rooms. An enclosed stair rises from the rear hallway to an unfinished loft. Both front and rear door are replacements, but there are one early six-flat-panel door and two batten doors that appear original. Some original horizontal hand-planed sheathing remains on the walls. Both of the main rooms have turn-of-the-century bracketed mantels of Victorian design. The front and rear doors have four-pane sidelights that are unusual in that there are no decorative panels beneath them.

Dawson's Station Community
established early twentieth century
Kinston vicinity

Walter Rouse House

B. L. Nethercutt Store

Dawson's Station was established about 1900 as a stop on the Kinston-Snow Hill Railroad, built by the Hines Brothers Lumber Company of Kinston as a logging line and "common-carrier." A station was built at the northwest junction of the Institute Road and the Wootens Crossroads Road. This station, a frame building with wide overhanging bracketed eaves, stood on its original location until about 1990, when it was moved to U. S. Highway 258 and remodeled as a residence. The railroad was consolidated with the Kinston-Beulahville Railroad and became the Kinston-Carolina. The railroad tracks were removed in the 1940s.

Dawson's Station crossroads is a small settlement containing a grocery store and seven one-story frame houses located in the four corners of the crossroads. At least some of the houses built at the crossroads were related to the railroad. Dawson's Station was an important commercial center in the early twentieth century.

Many local men worked on this rail line, and the *B. L. Nethercutt Store* was a major source of farm supplies. Now known as Twins Grocery, the one-story frame building built about 1925 has a flat roof, a front shed porch, and a recessed double door with a two-pane transom and flanking display windows set in wooden surrounds. The interior has wood sheathing, wooden interior post supports, and several skylight wells. Across the crossroads, the *Walter Rouse House*, circa 1910, appears to be the oldest building at the crossroads. It is a one-and-one-half story, side-gable, double-pile frame house with interior brick chimneys, plain siding, tall four-over-four sash windows, wide gable eave returns, and a front porch with turned, bracketed posts. The interior retains some late Greek Revival mantels and four-panel doors. The *Dortch Hill House*, circa 1920, is a one-story double-pile frame house with the two front gables and interior chimneys that were popular in Lenoir County during the early twentieth century. The house has plain siding, six-over-six sash, and a front porch with replacement posts. Dortch Hill is said to have been a railroad engineer.

Hartsfield House
built circa 1850; remodeled circa 1890
Dawson's Station

The 1863 Koerner Military Survey Field Map shows "G. Hartsfield" living on this site. Surrounding residents refer to the house as the "old Hartsfield House" and say that it is the oldest dwelling in the vicinity. The frame I-house has six-over-six sash windows, a low gable roof

with flush gable ends and box cornices, exterior end brick chimneys, a rear shed, and a wraparound front porch. The entrance consists of an unusual six-panel door with transom and sidelights. Vinyl siding covers the walls and all trim. The bungalow-style porch posts are 1920s or 1930s replacements. The interior has a center-hall plan and has been refurbished so that little original fabric is visible.

Although this antebellum house has gone through many architectural changes, it still reflects nineteenth-century history.

Moore Community
built circa 1910-1940
Dawson's Station

The Moore settlement, a rural black community, developed in the early twentieth century. The anchor of the community is the eighty-acre farm of Ed and Bertha Moore, a black farm couple who bought the land about 1922, built a house, and raised a large family there. Their children live in newer houses around the farmhouse, but the farmland is owned jointly by all their heirs and is called heir land. The Moore House and four other pre-World War II houses stand in a row on the north side of State Road 1541, just east of Dawson's Station crossroads.

The Moore House, a one-story frame house with front wing and wraparound porch, was built about 1922 for Ed Moore (1876-1938) and Bertha Moore (1873-1964) on some eighty acres of land. Ed hired a contractor to build the house. Ed and Bertha grew tobacco, corn, cotton, and soybeans on their own land, and Ed also farmed "on halves" on land owned by James M. and Pattie Mewborne east of the Moore farm. The Moores raised eleven children, and the youngest, Catherine Moore Smith, owns the homeplace and lives there. The house has a central chimney, four-over-four sash windows, and a rear ell with enclosed porch. One outbuilding, a front-gable frame smokehouse built by Ed Moore after 1922, still stands.

Frederick Greene Taylor House and Farm

built 1849

Mewborne's Crossroads vicinity

The Frederick Greene Taylor House is a late example of the Federal style. The two-story frame side-gable house has exterior end chimneys, a rear shed, and a kitchen-dining room ell located on the east side. The house has plain siding, boxed front and rear eaves, flush gable eaves, and nine-over-six, six-over-six, and six-over-four sash windows. The west chimney has a dated brick underneath the concrete stucco, and "1849" is scratched into the stucco. The front porch was demolished by Hurricane Fran in 1996. Breaks in the siding of the rear shed indicate that the central bay was formerly open, probably as a recessed porch. The kitchen wing has three different areas of siding. It appears that there was an open breezeway between the kitchen and main block that has been filled in.

The hall-parlor-plan interior has retained most of its original Federal-style fabric. Between the two rooms is an enclosed stair, accessible through a door from each room. Some six flat-panel Federal-style doors and some original batten doors survive. Both hall and parlor retain large decorative tripartite mantels, each with paneled pilasters, a frieze with a central paneled block, and a molded shelf. These are late Federal in style. All walls have replacement tongue-and-groove sheathing, but most ceilings retain the original wide beaded sheathing.

One antebellum outbuilding remains, a tall storage building with a hand-hewn and pegged frame and a single door on the west gable end, facing the house. This outbuilding has an original or early shed on the north side, also with an entry door. Although covered with sheet metal, the steep gable roof with exposed roof joists is a telltale feature of an early building. Other outbuildings date from the late nineteenth and twentieth centuries.

The Taylor cemetery, across the road on Stonyton Creek (known as Lousin Swamp in earlier years), contains seven or eight graves enclosed by a wire fence and landscaped with four large cedar trees, one at each corner of the square cemetery plot. The earliest burials are those of Stanton Taylor, (d. 1841) and his wife Nancy (d.1848). Frederick Greene Taylor (d. 1908) and his wife, Jane H.

Taylor (d.1892) are also buried there, along with several of their children who died young. The gravestones are marble headstones and footstones, and a tall marble obelisk marks the graves of Frederick and Jane.

The Taylor Farm is significant for its well-preserved Federal-style farmhouse, the antebellum storage building, and the graveyard. According to a descendant, the farm was owned by three generations of Taylors: Frederick Stanton Taylor, his son Frederick Greene Taylor, and his son John L. Taylor. Stanton Taylor (1784-1841), apparently a land surveyor, was born in Lenoir County near Woodington. He married Nancy Bruton and in 1826 they moved to the plantation of Nancy's father, Simon Bruton, located here. They bought out the other heirs, made this their home, and raised ten children here. Stanton died in 1841. The second son, Frederick Greene Taylor (1820-1908), returned home to help his mother with the farm. His mother, Nancy, died in 1848, and Frederick apparently built the house the next year. He married Jane Hooker in 1850 and later served in the Civil War. Frederick and Jane raised eight children on the farm.

The 1850, 1860, and 1870 census population and agriculture schedules outline the lives of Frederick Greene Taylor and his family on their farm. In 1850 Frederick was a thirty-year old farmer with real estate valued at three hundred dollars. His wife, Jane, was twenty-four years old, and his twenty-three-year-old brother, Guilford Taylor, a farmer, lived with them. By 1860 Frederick was a forty-year-old farmer whose real estate was valued at $5,000. His personal estate was valued at $7,700. He and Jane had five children aged from infancy to nine years. The 1860 agriculture schedule shows that Frederick Taylor was farming 150 improved acres and had 243 unimproved acres. He had three horses, one mule, four cows, two oxen, four other cattle, and seventy swine. He produced 30 bushels of wheat, 5 bushels of rye, 700 bushels of Indian corn, 12 bushels of beans, 15 bushels of Irish potatoes, 150 bushels of sweet potatoes, 4 tons of fodder, 10 pounds of flax, 6 pounds of beeswax, and 100 pounds of honey and slaughtered four hundred dollars worth of animals. He did not produce any rice, tobacco, cotton, or wool. Taylor's farm was typical of other large farms in the area with two exceptions: he did not raise cotton like most of his neighbors, and he had only seven slaves, a grown male and female and five children (probably a family).

The Civil War greatly affected the Taylors' fortune, for their real estate value fell to four hundred dollars and their personal estate value to eight hundred dollars by the 1870 census. Frederick was still farming and had eight children, ages four to eighteen, living at home. The three oldest boys were laborers on the family farm.

Although Frederick Taylor (and most of his neighbors) do not appear in the 1880 agriculture schedule, he must have continued to farm, for *Branson's North Carolina Business Directory* of 1897 lists him as a prominent farmer in the Kinston Township. John L. Taylor (1860-circa 1930), who inherited the homeplace and 102 acres, must have been doing most of the farming by the 1880s, when his father was in his sixties. John raised cotton, tobacco, and corn, but lost the farm about 1926 and moved to Kinston, where he lived with his daughter Bessie Taylor Phillips in his final years. Ely Perry, a large Lenoir County landowner, purchased the farm from the estate of John L. Taylor circa 1926. It has apparently been rental property since that time and is now managed by his son, Ely Perry Jr.

Hyman Mewborne Farm
built circa 1900
Mewborne's Crossroads

Hyman Mewborne built his farm house on the site of the Hebron Christian Church, which stood here by 1888 and burned in the late nineteenth century. Hyman Mewborne built a house, cotton gin, and dairy here, but the only surviving structures are the house and the brick dairy building. Mewborne was apparently a descendant of the Mewborne family that was prominent in this area in the antebellum period. J. Hyman Mewborne (1870-1933) attended Kinsey School in LaGrange and graduated from Guilford College, after which he returned to the family farm. In 1906 he cultivated around three hundred acres, operated a general merchandise store with $3,000 in stock and goods, and operated a large cotton gin that processed twenty-five bales of cotton a day. A photograph of the house and cotton gin reveals that the dwelling then featured a small porch with a balustrade, sawnwork detailing, and turned columns. A large two-story barn was also located on the farm.

The L-plan one-story frame house has a rear ell and rear additions. It has plain siding, two-over-two sash windows, interior brick chimneys, a replacement front door, and a wraparound front porch with replacement posts and screening. The dairy, in the field north of the house, is a one-room building of front-gable form, with one-to-five common-bond brick walls and six-over-six sash windows with segmental arches. At the rear is a frame shed addition.

The Hyman Mewborne House is representative of vernacular middle-class farmhouses built in this section of Lenoir County during the late nineteenth and early twentieth centuries. The brick dairy is a rare survival in this area. At least one other area farmer, Lemuel O. Moseley, whose farm is across U.S. Highway 58, operated a dairy in the late 1920s.

Mewborne-Bizzell House
built late nineteenth century
Mewborne's Crossroads

The Mewborne-Bizzell House was built for James M. Mewborne, who married a Palmer of LaGrange. The land on which it is located may have been part of Levi Mewborne's plantation before the Civil War. The one-story frame side-gable dwelling conforms to one of the most frequently occurring historic house types in the area. The house has exterior end chimneys, two rear ells, wide eave returns on the gable ends, a central entrance with transom and sidelights, and six-over-six sash windows. It was refurbished in recent years and has replacement porch posts and railing, vinyl siding, and a rear addition.

Behind the house is a two-story frame side-gable outbuilding of early-twentieth-century construction with exposed rafter ends and sash windows in the front and rear elevations. Its function is unknown.

Philips-Moseley House
built 1831
Mewborne's Crossroads vicinity

The 1831 Philips-Moseley House has architectural and historical significance as an illustration of the evolution of an antebellum coastal cottage. Although it appears to be a classic example of the coastal cottage house type, with its one-and-one-half-story main block, engaged front porch, and rear shed, the front porch was actually a later addition. The construction of the house was definitively placed in 1831 by a dated brick located in the east gable chimney. The house has hand-hewn sills, pit-sawn joists, and a pegged frame. The joints are marked with Roman numerals.

The house may originally have had a hall-parlor plan, but a partition wall creating a center hall was added early. The walls had wainscot and plaster finish, and the ceilings displayed wide flush sheathing. The interior had Greek Revival finish, evidenced by a mantel remnant and some mitred surrounds. The rear shed apparently had a recessed center porch area and small flanking rooms, typical of other early rear sheds in the area.

The exterior is covered with plain siding and has nine-over-six sash windows in the front elevation and narrow six-over-four sash windows flanking the gable-end chimneys. The chimneys are constructed of random common-bond brick with stepped shoulders. The engaged front porch is definitely an addition, because the original boxed cornice and wood-shingled roof are visible beneath the current porch roof. The porch was an early addition, for it contains the same hand-hewn floor sills and pit-sawn joists as the framework of the house. At the rear is a detached kitchen building, of much later construction, connected to the house by an enclosed passage.

The 1863 Koerner Military Survey Field Map shows "C. Philips" living at this location. Local residents remember this as the farm of Lemuel C. (Pomp) Moseley (1865-1940), a son of Wylie T. Moseley and his second wife, Martha. Pomp married Minnie Rice and became a wealthy cotton farmer. Pomp Moseley's daughters Lillian and Hattie inherited the house. It is owned by a grandson, George Henry, who lives in Wilson.

William Harper House (demolished)
built early nineteenth century
Mewborne's Crossroads

According to one source this two-story farmhouse of Federal architectural style was the home of Johnny Harper, who moved here from Falling Creek. It was demolished about 1995. According to local tradition the house originally stood beside a gristmill and pond on the Harper-Heath Farm a short distance to the east. The house was commonly known as the William Harper House. A graveyard containing two gravestones was found at the site said to be the original house location, but the stones were removed some years ago. One of these stones was for Jesse H. Vaus the "Elder," 1799-1854. It is possible that the Vaus family lived in the house at one time.

The two-story frame side-gable house had gable-end chimneys, a hipped front porch, and a rear ell with a shed porch that wrapped around the ell and the rear elevation of the main block. Aside from its form, the house retained little original Federal fabric on the exterior. The six-panel front door and three-pane transom were original, as were the nine-over-nine sash windows on the lower gable ends and the six-over-six sash windows on the upper gable ends and the upper front and rear elevations. The windows opening onto the front porch had four-over-four replacement sash. The original siding and the front and rear dentil cornice had been concealed or replaced by vinyl siding. The front porch posts were replacements. The rear ell had six-over-six sash that may have been original, but the plain ell porch posts appeared to be replacements.

The interior retained its original hall-parlor plan, with an enclosed stair with winders located between the hall and parlor. The second floor had a narrow center hall with flanking bedrooms. A few of the original six-flat-paneled doors remained, and the walls had flat-paneled wainscot with molded chair rails, with plaster above. Doors and windows had wide molded surrounds. The hall (east room) mantel had been removed, but original mantels remained in the parlor (west room) and in the east bedroom upstairs. These were handsome Federal-style mantels with Doric pilasters, plain architraves, and tall molded shelves. The ell had some early trim, indicating that it was either original or an early addition.

Behind the Harper House stood three early-twentieth-century outbuildings: a metal-covered packhouse, a frame tobacco barn, and a metal-covered shed that was a circa-1900 tenant house moved here and converted to a storage building. To the west, now located on the property of the adjacent Rountree-Askew-Moseley Farm, is a two-story side-gable frame barn, said to be antebellum in date, that was originally part of the Harper farm. This barn is now covered in metal.

Hartsfield-Taylor House
built 1812; overbuilt late nineteenth century, circa 1916
Kinston vicinity

The Hartsfield-Taylor House is an early Lenoir County homestead that was enlarged in two stages. The final enlargement, in about 1916, resulted in a two-story double-pile Classical Revival-style house with a spacious one-story front porch with a one-bay second-story balcony. The house is sited in a grove of oak trees well back from Tom White Road, which dead-ends at Stallings Airport. The house has a central entrance with transom and sidelights, large two-over-two sash windows, interior brick chimneys, vinyl siding, and a one-story kitchen ell with a back porch that was converted to a sun room and an attached deck.

The original house is believed to have been built in 1812, since family members report that that date is inscribed on a brick on the chimney stack of the large south chimney. According to family tradition, the original house was a two-story single-pile house that faced south. The only other evidence of this original house is the hand-hewn and pit-sawn floor joists in the basement area of one section, one Greek Revival-style mantel (now located in the dining room), and several Federal-style doors with six flat panels.

The interior consists of a large center hall with two rooms on each side on two floors. The staircase has a handsome closed string, paneled newel, and molded rail. The dining room mantel is of Greek Revival style, with Doric pilasters supporting a paneled frieze. The other mantels have bracketed colonnettes supporting wide shelves and appear to date from the late nineteenth or early twentieth century. Most of the doors have four flat panels. The interior fabric dates largely from about 1916, when the house reached its present size, with the exception of the Greek Revival mantel and Federal doors mentioned above. From 1979 to 1981 the house underwent a thorough renovation that replaced the plaster walls with sheetrock, replaced some of the wooden flooring, removed the partition wall between the living room and dining room, rebuilt the chimney between these two rooms, and installed chair rails and other replacement trim.

One outbuilding, a twentieth-century storage shed, stands to the rear. There is a family cemetery behind the shed, enclosed by a cast-iron fence. It contains approximately twenty gravestones, the oldest visible death date being 1875, when Dr. J. A. Hartsfield died. His wife, Rebecca Kornegay Hartsfield (1833-1896), is buried beside him. Other graves include that of Walter Green Taylor (1872-1935). The markers are marble headstones and granite monuments.

Addie Spencer Taylor, who grew up here in the 1920s, reports that, according to Taylor family tradition, a Mr. Hutchinn built this house in 1812. He never married and is buried in the family cemetery beneath a stone whose inscription is difficult to decipher. His niece is said to have inherited the property. She married Dr. Jacob A. Hartsfield, and they lived in the house during the mid-nineteenth century. They had one child, who died during the Civil War. The Pope family inherited the farm later in the nineteenth century, and about 1916 Walter Green Taylor (1872-1935) bought the farm. Addie Taylor says that the two first-floor rooms on the north side of the house had already been added to the original house at that time, and that her father, Walter, added the two upstairs north rooms, the attached kitchen, and the front porch. Two hundred acres were associated with the house at the time, but the dwelling has been separated from the farmland and is sited on a three-and-one-half-acre home tract. The house is now owned and occupied by Mr. and Mrs. W. Larry Taylor. Larry is the grandson of Walter Green Taylor.

The 1860 and 1870 censuses listed the household of Jacob A. Hartsfield (1822-1875) and his wife, Rebecca W. Kornegay (1833-1896). Hartsfield was a farmer and physician with real estate worth $4,000 and personal estate worth $14,800 in 1860. The only other member of his household, in addition to his wife, was a twenty-six-year-old white male named Reddin Pope. By 1870 Dr. Hartsfield, like all of his plantation neighbors, had lost his slaves, and his personal value was reduced to five hundred dollars. His household consisted of his wife and two young white male farm laborers.

Rountree-Askew-Moseley House and Farm
built late eighteenth century; enlarged 1800 and 1860
Kinston North vicinity

This house is the seat of an extensive farmstead and was constructed in sections, dating from the late eighteenth century. The oldest part of the house is the one-and-a-half-story section on the east end, which began as a two-room cottage with a central chimney (removed). This section is four bays wide and has the form of a coastal cottage with front engaged porch and rear engaged shed. Around 1800 a two-story three-bay-wide section was added on the west side of the cottage. A Flemish bond chimney with stepped weatherings is on the west gable end of this section. About 1860 the house was again enlarged, with a two-story rear ell with Greek Revival-style detailing added to the two-story section.

The exterior of the house is finished with plain weatherboarding, flush gable ends, and boxed front and rear molded cornices with patterned eave blocks. Windows are nine-over-six sash on the first floor of the front block and six-over-six sash on the second story of the west block. The openings have simple molded surrounds. The main entrance, in the west block, has a transom and sidelights. The front shed porch carries completely across the seven bays of the main elevation and is supported by distinctive vernacular sawnwork posts, apparently dating to the mid-nineteenth century. The east corner bay was enclosed to serve as a dining room in the 1960s.

The interior floor plan that resulted from the successive enlargements of the house above consists of small rooms in an additive sequence. The original one-and-a-half-story cottage has a hall-and-parlor plan with a rear shed room that was apparently used as the kitchen. This section has wide vertical-sheathed walls and six-flat-paneled doors, one six-raised-panel door in the loft, and a batten door in the rear shed. Access to the loft room is through an enclosed stair in the west corner of the cottage section. The stair is accessible from a door in the parlor of the two-story west addition.

The two-story west addition contains a parlor on the first floor and a bedroom on the second. The front entrance to the house was shifted to this addition, and the front door originally opened into a narrow hall, but the wall was removed and the front door now opens directly into the parlor. Directly behind this west addition is a two-story rear ell containing a bedroom on each level. The west addition contains its original Federal finish, consisting of flat-paneled wainscot with molded chair rails, plastered walls, ceiling sheathing, molded surrounds, and a handsome tripartite-style Federal mantel in the living room and a smaller Federal mantel of more modest design in the upstairs bedroom. The rear Greek Revival wing contains plastered walls and a stylish Greek Revival mantel in both rooms.

The dwelling was the seat of an extensive farm dating to the late eighteenth century, and many outbuildings survive—some being very rare examples of their type. These outbuildings include an antebellum cotton gin, an antebellum barn, a 1920s smokehouse, a 1920s dairy barn and silos, a 1920s milk house, 1930s handyman's quarters, a circa-1900 mule barn, tobacco barns, a circa-1890 cotton gin, a circa-1920 packhouse, and tenant houses. The antebellum cotton gin is the only documented one of its type in the county and one of only a handful surviving in the state. Lemuel Octavius Moseley purchased the farm in 1920. His daughter, Isabelle Fletcher Perry, and her family now own the property and live here.

Moore-Heath House (demolished)
built circa 1842-1848
Kinston North vicinity

Located at the edge of a field, this two-story house was one of the county's best examples of antebellum prosperity. Thought to have been constructed by Jesse Moore between 1842 and 1848, the house, with a hundred-acre farm, was purchased by Will Heath in the late nineteenth century. The handsome dwelling was heavily damaged by a fire around 1990 and has since been demolished.

The large Greek Revival-style dwelling was a double-pile hipped-roof example with a large central hall. The house was five bays wide and four bays deep, with a hipped-roof one-story front porch and a rear kitchen ell with a porch. All of the porches were supported by chamfered columns with vernacular capitals. Other architectural features typical of the style were interior chimneys, boxed eaves, corner pilasters, a frieze board beneath the cornice, six-over-six sash windows, and a double-leaf front door surrounded by a transom and sidelights.

The interior exhibited stylish Greek Revival detailing that was some of the most sophisticated in the county. Rare details included an arch located in the center hall that was supported by Doric pilasters. The open-string stairway (enclosed at a later date) featured a ramped handrail and decorative stair brackets. Other ornate elements included molded window and door surrounds with corner blocks, paneled window aprons, molded baseboards, two-panel doors, and mantels. The mantels were typical Greek Revival style with Doric pilasters supporting tall, plain architraves with molded shelves.

There were two outbuildings located behind the dwelling—a packhouse/barn and a rectangular building with a large interior chimney, windows and doors. It may have been a slave quarter.

Leon and Bela Sutton Farm
built circa 1905
Wheat Swamp vicinity

The Leon and Bela Sutton House is a large and well-preserved pyramidal cottage, a common house type in north Lenoir County in the early twentieth century. The farmhouse is somewhat larger than the typical pyramidal cottage in north Lenoir County and has a steep hipped roof with a central cross gable with a one-over-one sash window over the main entrance. It has two tall interior brick chimneys. The most significant feature is the hipped porch with Doric columns, which extends across the main facade, down the south elevation, and around the rear to the kitchen ell. The house has plain siding, one-over-one sash windows, and a center-bay entrance with transom and sidelights. The rear ell porch has been enclosed.

Behind the house are a smokehouse, a garage, a two-story front-gable packhouse, and a shed, all of traditional frame early-to-mid-twentieth-century construction.

Leon Sutton and his wife, Bela Suggs, had this house built about 1905. They owned a farm of approximately 1,000 acres at the site. They raised a family of eight children and lived there until their deaths. Leon survived his wife and died in the 1950s. His daughter Polly Sutton Rouse now owns the homeplace, which contains twelve acres, and lives there.

Moore-Foster House (demolished)
built circa 1840
Kinston North vicinity

Picturesquely located close to the old Kinston-Snow Hill Highway (NC Highway 58), this abandoned two-story dwelling was an excellent example of a transition Federal-Greek Revival-style farmhouse. Facing due south, the two-story frame house with a steep gable roof exhibited a front shed porch and rear shed rooms. The house retained its west-gable-end chimney of common-bond brick with stepped shoulders but had lost its east-end chimney. The house had plain siding, boxed molded cornices at front and rear, and flush gable eaves. It had its original nine-over-six sash windows beneath the front porch, nine-over-nine sash windows in the gable ends of the first story, and six-over-six sash on the second story. All openings had molded surrounds.

The interior originally had a hall-and-parlor plan, which was altered to a central-hall plan when a partition wall was added in recent years. An enclosed stair with winders was located between the hall and parlor and led to a small hallway with two flanking bedrooms. The upper stairwell had an original square newel with molded cap, simple balusters, and rounded handrail. The rear shed originally contained a center recessed porch, and this area had wide flush beaded sheathing. The only interior doors were Greek Revival style with two vertical panels.

The 1863 Koerner Military Survey Field Map shows an "A. Moore" living on this site. It is possible that this was the house of the Reverend Alfred Moore (1813-1870), who was a prosperous farmer with real estate valued at $12,500 and a personal estate of $18,000 in the 1860 census. His farm consisted of three hundred improved acres and three hundred unimproved (woodland) acres, where he had $1,500 worth of livestock, and his products included 1,500 bushels of Indian corn and 75 bushels of wheat.

The farm remained in the Moore family for many years and was inherited by Eliza Anne Mewborne.

E. Norman Dickerson Farm

built early twentieth century
Kinston North vicinity

Two tenant dwellings—one is a pyramidal cottage and the other a story-and-a-half side-gable house—typify tenant dwellings constructed in the county. They are located on the farm of E. Norman Dickerson, who moved to the county in 1895. Dickerson was a tobacconist from Oxford, in the heart of the "Old Tobacco Belt," and moved to Kinston in order to participate in the beginnings of large-scale tobacco cultivation in Lenoir County. He bought this large farm from either the Fields or the Heath family soon after he moved to Kinston, and these tenant dwellings and outbuildings apparently were built by him in the early twentieth century. Dickerson owned many farms in the county and never lived on this one. Many tobacco-related outbuildings survive, including a three-story packhouse.

Stallings Army Air Corps Training Center (Stallings Field)

built 1944-1960s
Kinston vicinity

Serv-Air hangar

Stallings Field, the Air Corps Training Center, is a complex of approximately thirteen buildings begun dur-

ing World War II and expanded in the 1950s. It was established in 1944 as an auxiliary base of the Marine Corps Air Station at Cherry Point (near the town of Havelock, on the Neuse River in adjacent Craven County). This complex, located adjacent to the runway now used by the regional airport, has been owned since 1962 by the North Carolina Forest Service.

The Serv-Air hangar was constructed in 1954 by the Serv-Air Corporation as an auxiliary hangar to handle the pilot training operations. It is a wide gabled steel-frame building that now houses the aircraft and offices of the Forest Service. It is completely sheathed in metal. The roof has seamed metal sheets; the walls are covered with corrugated metal. Each gable end can be completely opened by means of a row of hinged metal doors that are attached to an overhead track and can be folded into a freestanding metal frame located at each outside corner of the building. The low transverse walls have large metal casement windows and metal doors.

The interior of the hangar appears largely unaltered. The central section of the building is an open storage hangar, while the space along each side wall is partitioned into small offices and a coffee lounge. The building has a concrete-slab floor, and the steel frame is visible everywhere except in the office spaces, which have knotty pine paneling.

Adjacent to the runway are four barracks, a dining hall, two classroom buildings, a carpenter shop, a storage building, and an auto shop building. Several of the buildings date from 1944, and the remainder were constructed by the Serv-Air Corporation during the 1950s and by the Forest Service since 1962. The barracks, dining hall, and classroom buildings are long, low gabled frame buildings of nine or ten bays in length, with a door at each end and wooden sash windows. Both the exterior and interior of the dormitories, classrooms, and dining hall have been covered with replacement materials.

The history of Stallings Field Air Corps Training Center, popularly known as Stallings Field, began in the early 1940s, when Kinston and Lenoir County purchased 640 acres of land near the Dawson's Station community on which to build an airport. Local pilots and city employees cleared a small area as a landing site. On March 1, 1944, the Marine Corps opened an outlying field on this site as an auxiliary air base to Cherry Point Marine Air Station. Its main purpose was to serve as a backup facility for Cherry Point, but it was also used to train marine pilots. Kinston and Lenoir County leased the field to the government.

In 1951 the Stallings Field facility was leased to the Serv-Air Aviation Corporation, which was under contract to the United States Air Force to provide flight training for air force pilots. Serv-Air at its peak had 550 cadets, 685 employees, and 100 Air Force personnel and had a large impact on the economy of the Kinston-Lenoir County area. In 1953 the base was formally named Stallings Air Base in honor of Lieutenants Harry and Bruce Stallings, brothers from Kinston who were killed in 1945 while serving in the United States Army Air Corps. Before being phased out by the air force in 1957, Stallings Air Base trained some 4,000 Air Force pilots.

Stallings Air Base was vacant from 1957 until 1962, when a section was bought by the North Carolina Forest Service. Since then it has been used by the Forest Service as headquarters for forest fire fighting operations in eastern North Carolina. The Forest Service shares the greatly expanded runway with the Kinston-Lenoir County Regional Airport.

Some of the World War II-era buildings at Stallings Field have been demolished. The original hangar was a big, boxy metal and wooden building with a flat roof. It stood on the site of the main airport terminal and was demolished about 1975 when the terminal was constructed. The mess hall, post exchange, old headquarters building, and Kitty Hawk Club building have been demolished, and only a few of the existing buildings date from the war. The present complex is the result of alterations and new construction by the Serv-Air Corporation in the 1950s, the Forest Service since 1962, and the county of Lenoir and city of Kinston.

Dobbs School: Weil and Leonard Cottages
built 1929, 1930
Kinston vicinity

Dobbs School was established in 1929 as the Industrial Farm Colony for Women, on 488 acres of farmland seven miles northwest of Kinston. It was intended as a correctional school for young white women, an alternative to sending them to prison. In the first biennial report, published in 1932, Superintendent Marian F. Gallup described the campus as follows:

> There are two brick dormitory buildings, a cottage in which the farm director lives, a small house orig inally intended for an infirmary, a storehouse, dairy barn, mule barn and chicken houses and other sheds and shelters for stock. The capacity of the houses is sixty, without crowding. Eighty could be housed without serious crowding. The first building has four single rooms and five dormitories for four and five beds; it also has the office and small hospital quarters in it. The second building has all single rooms for girls.

Gallup went on to report that by March 1931 there were thirty-six inmates and three staff members housed in the A Building. The inmates worked on the farm, did sewing and mending, worked in the laundry, did canning, and performed unspecified "outside work." The farm as it had been developed by June 1932 consisted of a new fenced pasture, two new chicken houses, and a pigpen.

In 1944 the school became the State Training School for Negro Girls, and in 1945 the name was changed to Dobbs Farm. In 1967 the name changed again, to Dobbs School for Girls. In 1973 the name was shortened to Dobbs School. In 1985 the school shifted to become a boys-only school. The campus currently contains fifty-five acres.

All but three of the original campus buildings are gone. The two brick dormitories and one barn, probably the dairy barn, still stand, but the rest of the buildings mentioned in the biennial report are gone. In their place are substantial brick buildings constructed after World War II, which give the campus a look very different from the one it originally had. Dobbs School is a rural campus consisting of approximately fifteen brick buildings arranged in several rows facing a central driveway. The 1952 Administration Building is sited at the head of the driveway, and buildings constructed from 1929 to the present face the driveway.

Weil Cottage was named for the Weil family of Goldsboro. Gertrude Weil was on the school's board of directors during its early history. The two-story brick Colonial Revival-style dormitory is fourteen bays wide and three bays deep. It has a deep hip roof of slate. Its brick-veneer walls have a common-bond pattern with Flemish-bond accent courses. The central entrance is a double glazed door with transom set off by a concrete Doric surround, with pilasters supporting a paneled frieze and dentilled cap. Large nine-over-nine sash windows, those on the first story accented with blind stuccoed aprons, illuminate the building. The eaves of the central section of the building have a dentil cornice. The two end bays of the building are set off by monumental paired Doric pilasters that carry from the foundation to a wide frieze and molded eave at the roofline. The lower windows of these sections have jack arches with stuccoed keystones. On the rear are an original two-story projecting wing and a small one-story flat-roofed addition.

Leonard Cottage was named for Samuel E. Leonard, an important leader in the training school movement. It is a two-story brick Colonial Revival-style dormitory of scale and materials similar to Weil Cottage but of a different design. The dormitory is thirteen bays wide and approximately four bays deep. The three bays at each end of the facade project as gabled pavilions. The hipped roof has composition shingles. The main entrance has double glazed doors with a transom and a monumental Corinthian entrance stoop surmounted by a broken pediment with a turned finial. Windows are twelve-over-twelve wooden sash, with stuccoed lunettes over the first-story windows and jack arches with keystones over the second-story pavilion windows. The brick veneer is laid in a common-bond pattern with accenting Flemish-bond courses. The roof eaves have a classical frieze and molded cornice treatment. On the rear are small flat-roofed brick wings that may be an addition and an even smaller frame addition. At each end of Leonard Cottage are short flat-roofed two-story brick additions, of minimal classical design, that were probably added in the 1950s as recreational space.

Among training schools in North Carolina, Dobbs School was the second established for the rehabilitation of girls and young women. The first school was the Samarkand Manor School in Eagle Springs, in Moore County. It was established in 1918, primarily to address the problem of the "camp followers" who created problems at World War I military camps in the state. Dobbs School was established in 1927 to rehabilitate girls and young women who were in trouble with the law. In 1947 Dobbs School was converted to a training school for African American girls. Known as the State Training School for Negro Girls, this institution was established in 1944 in Rocky Mount and moved to the Dobbs School facility in 1947. It was the first training school for black girls in North Carolina.

Dobbs School was one of the early institutions devoted to the humane rehabilitation of young female offenders in the state. Like the original youth training school in North Carolina, the Stonewall Jackson Training School for white boys, established in 1909, and the three other schools for girls and boys, Dobbs School resulted from a revolution in the legal and prison systems brought about by the recognition that juvenile offenders should not be imprisoned with hardened adult criminals. Dobbs School has dual significance as the second training school for white girls and young women in the state and, beginning in 1947, as the first training school for African American girls. Leonard and Weil cottages at Dobbs School are architecturally significant for the high quality of their Colonial Revival design.

[One special source of the information in this entry is William R. Windley, "History of the Division of Youth Services 1909-1981," N.C. Division of Youth Services, Raleigh, 1981.]

Hodges-Mewborne House
built mid-nineteenth century
Kinston North vicinity

This dwelling is an extensively altered example of a coastal cottage, with an engaged front porch and rear shed rooms. It may have been built by Buck Hodges from Green County. John F. Mewborne bought it in 1947. The house is now owned by the KNC Corporation and is used as a temporary residence for plant officials.

Constructed in the mid-nineteenth century, the house retains a two-pane transom over the front door, gable-end brick chimneys with single stepped shoulders, and six-over-six sash windows. The dwelling has been extensively remodeled with such alterations as the replacement of the front porch posts with brick pillars and the raising of the rear roof to create a second story.

The interior consists of a central-hall plan, with two rooms flanking the hall on the first floor. The rear rooms are smaller than the front rooms. An open-string stair with chamfered newel post rises from the rear of the hall. The house retains its original wide floorboards and two mantels of vernacular Greek Revival design, one in the first-floor east room and one in the west bedroom.

There are no outbuildings remaining with the house, but across the road in woods with dense undergrowth is a small one-story side-gable building that is said to have been the detached kitchen.

Thomas Cunningham House
built circa 1900; remodeled 1938-1939
Kinston North vicinity

The Thomas Cunningham House, a one-and-a-half-story frame Craftsman structure with a hipped-roof rear extension incorporating a later carport, is a well-maintained early-twentieth-century farmhouse. The side-gable house is fronted by a one-and-one-half-story front-gable bungaloid porch supported by posts over brick piers with a connecting rail balustrade. There is a paired three-over-one window in the gable, and the front gable, like the sides, has exposed brackets. There are two log tobacco barns on the property, as well as two frame tobacco barns, a smokehouse, and a small hipped-roof frame structure (across from the carport) that may have been a washhouse. The house is presently occupied by Michael S. and Kaye Cunningham Morris. Kaye is the great-niece of previous owner Quincey Cunningham.

Clyde Cunningham Sr. House and Store
built 1938
Kinston vicinity

Constructed in a residential style most often seen in towns and planned neighborhoods of the early twentieth century, this two-story Dutch Colonial Revival-style house was erected for Clyde Cunningham Sr. in 1938 on the outskirts of Kinston. Clyde Cunningham married Hattie Aldridge of Greene County, and they had one child, Clyde Cunningham Jr. According to their son, the house replaced an earlier Cunningham family home on the property, which was moved to another site in the 1950s and later demolished. This finely detailed example of the Dutch Colonial Revival style is identified by its sloping gambrel roof and large second-story dormer, which rests above a central front gabled stoop. One of the two side porches has been fully enclosed, and the rear extension of the house, originally a porch, was later enclosed. Unlike its counterparts in town, the Cunningham House was the seat of an early-twentieth-century farm with domestic and agricultural outbuildings and cultivated fields. Remaining from the farm's productive pre–World War II days are a frame smokehouse, several tobacco barns, and a small gable-front frame store building, situated close to NC Highway 58, which the Cunninghams operated in the early to mid-twentieth century as part of their farm enterprise.

CONTENTNEA
NECK TOWNSHIP

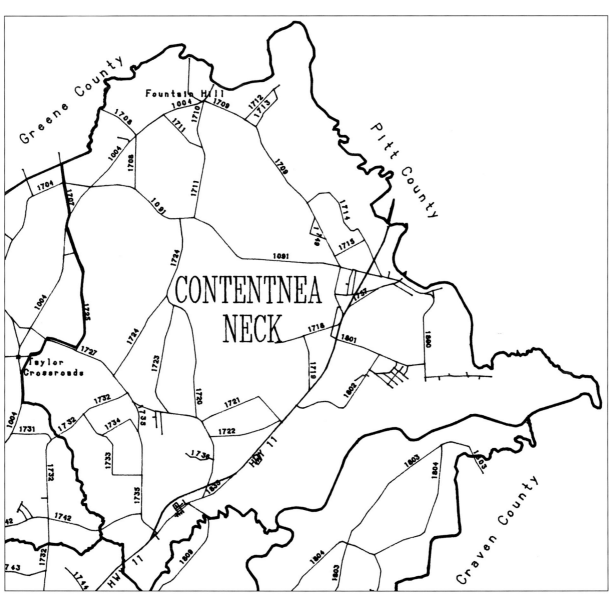

Redding Jackson House
built 1917-1918
Fountain Hill vicinity

This two-story farmhouse is an excellent example of the large, simply-detailed, Victorian-style dwellings found in the northern section of the county. The dwelling exhibits many original architectural details, such as a hipped roof, an entry transom and sidelights, and a wraparound front porch supported by three-piece square columns resting on brick posts. A rear kitchen/dining ell was originally flanked by porches, both of which have been enclosed.

The well-maintained house was the seat of a large tobacco farm and retains many related outbuildings and tenant houses, including three rare surviving log tobacco curing barns. Redding Jackson built this house for his family. According to tradition he hauled the lumber from New Bern to Grifton by boat, than to the house site by mule and wagon. The dwelling remains in the Jackson family.

Edwards Chapel United Methodist Church
built 1912
Fountain Hill

Surrounded by tall oaks, this small church was constructed in 1912 on the site of an antebellum church called Edwards Chapel on the 1863 Koerner Military Survey Field Map. This building—like many rural eastern North Carolina sanctuaries—features restrained architectural elements of the Gothic Revival style, such as lancet-arched windows with stained glass. Unlike many other churches in the county, this sanctuary has been altered very little, with only a mid-twentieth-century addition and entry vestibules having been added.

The 1863 Koerner Military Survey Field Map showed that the area was also the seat of the Edwards farm, and the crossing on nearby Contentnea Creek was called Edwards Bridge. Though the name of the community has been changed to Fountain Hill crossroads, many local residents still refer to the area as Edwards Crossroads and Edwards Bridge.

Hardee House
built 1850s
Fountain Hill vicinity

A good example of the one-story hipped-roof Greek Revival-style farmhouse that was popular in antebellum Lenoir County, this 1850s dwelling was originally located on the nearby Casey farm. The farm was bought by Henry Stokes in 1919, and in the early 1920s he moved the house to its present location for his daughter, who had recently married a member of the Hardee family.

The central-hall-plan house retains much of its original antebellum character with original interior woodwork including three post-and-lintel mantels, high ceilings, crossetted door and window surrounds, two-panel doors, and flat-paneled wainscoting in the hall. Other original elements include nine-over-nine sash windows and a transom and sidelights flanking the front entrance.

After the farmhouse was moved in the 1920s, the Hardee family constructed many outbuildings, including a packhouse, two equipment sheds, a stable, and a smokehouse. According to local tradition a member of the Hardee family was a painter and used one of the equipment sheds to store his paint equipment.

An antebellum or late-nineteenth-century outbuilding was also moved with the house. This small building is of heavy timber framing with mortise-and-tenon construction and with two side sheds and was last used as a corncrib and farm storage. A side-facade door and a four-over-four sash window and exterior flue indicate that the building might have been originally used as a servant's quarters or as a washhouse.

Elias Liverman Hazelton House
built circa 1871
Hugo vicinity

Located at the end of a long lane, this modest one-and-a-half-story farmhouse was built by Elias Liverman Hazelton around 1871. Hazelton (1845-?), a native of Pitt County, left school in 1863 to join the Confederate army and served in Company E, Sixty-seventh Regiment, from Lenoir County. After the war, he returned home and began work in a printing shop in Kinston. After marrying Bettie Coward of Greene County on April 4, 1871, Hazelton settled on this farm located about halfway between Grifton and Hookerton. Hazelton was apparently well educated and named the nearby crossroads Hugo after his favorite author, Victor Hugo. Hazelton was referred to by his friends and neighbors as the Squire of Hugo.

Hazelton's farmhouse is an example of a local vernacular house form that resembles the coastal cottage, with rear shed rooms incorporated under the gable roof, but lacks the engaged porch of the coastal cottage type. This "stripped coastal cottage" form was popular during the Civil War period. The hall-and-parlor-plan dwelling retains exterior end chimneys located on the front ends of the side gables. A narrow stair, leading to the loft, rises from the rear shed room. Two original mantels are intact and are examples of vernacular Greek Revival design.

The farm retains a smokehouse, tenant house, and circa-1875 one-and-a-half-story barn with heavy braced frame construction—a rare, surviving nineteenth-century outbuilding. Like many other farms in the county, this farmstead is now used for a large hog-raising operation.

Coward-Murphy Farm Outbuildings
built antebellum period
Hugo vicinity

This farm is of primary significance not for its dwelling but for its antebellum plank smokehouse, its original detached kitchen, and one of Lenoir County's only antebellum barns—rare survivals of these functional building types.

The original antebellum house, shown as the dwelling of "Jno Coward" on the 1863 Koerner Military Survey Field Map, was apparently replaced in the late nineteenth century by the present house, a one-and-a-half-story side-gable single-pile building. The interior central chimney serves the hall-and-parlor plan dwelling. A narrow, enclosed corner stairway leads to a finished loft. In the 1920s a new front house was constructed by George Hardee and connected to the first house with a breezeway. The new addition is Craftsman style with a central hall and two interior chimneys. The breezeway and space between the two buildings were later enclosed.

The antebellum smokehouse is a rare surviving example of plank construction. The logs are square hewn and wood shingles survive under the tin. The notching type cannot be determined because tin covers the exterior.

The original detached kitchen was renovated for use as a toolshed in the twentieth century. This small facing-gable building retains the original board-and-batten door with strap hinges and is of heavy-timber frame construction.

A very rare surviving antebellum barn is the most significant building on the farm. The two-story facing-gable building is of heavy-timber frame construction and originally rested on cypress stumps, some still in place. The three-room plan of the building is apparently original and includes a open corner stair to the second story. Three board-and-batten doors and a board-and-batten window shutter with strap hinges are original. Other windows are six-over-six and four-over-four sash. The rafters and collar beams have mortise-and-tenon construction. The second level retains a massive board-and-batten door complete with large (three-foot) strap hinges and a wooden latch. Wood shingles are intact under the standing-seam metal roof. This significant outbuilding is thought to have been used as a cotton gin at one time, although probably not originally.

Other outbuildings were constructed by later owners. Two intact circa 1925 log tobacco barns were constructed by George Hardee. R. Murphy constructed the garage, mule stable, frame tobacco barns, and shotgun tenant house in the 1940s and 1950s. The Coward-Murphy Farm thus contains intact examples of almost all types of agricultural outbuildings found in Lenoir County.

Harold Blount Sawyer House and M. D. Harris and Son Store
house built circa 1938; store built circa 1900
Hugo vicinity

The Sawyer House, a Craftsman bungalow, is the second house located on this site. The first was a two-story side-gable I-house built about 1900, which was moved to the back of the lot and converted into a packhouse. The original house was owned by the Harris family, who also operated a store/post-office, called M. D. Harris and Son, across the road.

This store closed during the Great Depression and was then moved to its present location beside the Sawyer House. The rare surviving turn-of-the-twentieth-century store/post office has one and a half stories and retains much architectural integrity. The front-gable building features gable returns, brick piers, and double front doors. According to local tradition the contents of the store were left completely intact after the closing, but most of the articles were carried off by thieves.

During the Great Depression Harold Blount Sawyer acquired the property and at that time had the I-house moved and proceeded to construct the present dwelling. The house is an excellent example of the Craftsman bungalow, exhibiting typical architectural elements of the style such as eave brackets, sidelights flanking the front door, engaged front porch supported by Craftsman posts, four-over-one sash windows, scrolled rafter tails, and engaged exterior end chimneys. An interior end chimney is found on the full-width rear ell. Numerous outbuildings survive, including a brick pumphouse, a smokehouse, a chicken shed, a garage, and a shotgun-style tenant house.

Phillips Log Kitchen
built mid-nineteenth century
Fountain Hill vicinity

This small outbuilding of plank construction—with narrow sawn logs—is actually an original detached kitchen that served a mid-nineteenth century dwelling and is the only documented plank example in the county. As on many Lenoir County farmsteads, the outbuilding outlived the original dwelling. This plank outbuilding survived when the farmhouse was dismantled about 1970. Constructed with full-dovetail notching, the building has sawn planks that fit closely together and required little chinking. Hewn-plank construction with full-dovetail notching is thought to have been a more common construction method than extant examples suggest, making this building a very important and rare surviving specimen. The original six-over-six sash windows are intact.

According to local tradition the original house also was of plank construction and was replaced with a frame house in the late nineteenth century. The present plank kitchen outbuilding served that frame house until being replaced with a frame ell circa 1900. At that time the plank kitchen house was moved a short distance and converted to a dwelling for the family's African American servant, Martha Brown. The original gable-end chimney was replaced by a drop flue at the same time.

According to one of the current owners, Martha Daughety, the original plank house and kitchen were constructed by the Phillips family, who possessed the original land grant. Though no house was located on this site on the 1863 Koerner Military Survey Field Map, an "E. Phillips" was located nearby.

Gilbert Town Community

developed in the early twentieth century
Hugo vicinity

Gilbert Town is an area along State Road 1091 between Hugo and Grifton that includes the dwellings of members of the Gilbert family. The land originally belonged to the Phillips family, and William Parker Gilbert acquired a farm there after marrying into the Phillips family. The majority of the houses along State Road 1091 were constructed in the 1910s in the Victorian style, using lumber sawn at the Gilbert Sawmill, located on the farm. A number of tenant houses stood here. A surviving one-room school served the area's African American community and was known as the Gilbert School. Another local school is no longer extant. A concrete-block store serviced the community in the mid-twentieth century.

Stephen Nathan Gilbert House

built 1908-1909
Hugo vicinity

Using lumber sawn at the nearby Gilbert Sawmill, this small but well-detailed one-story Victorian-style farmhouse was constructed in 1908-1909 by Stephen Nathan Gilbert for $1,000, of which $500 went for labor and $500 for supplies. Stephen Nathan was the son of William P. Gilbert, owner of the Gilbert Sawmill. The gable-and-wing dwelling is very similar to the Tom Abbott House, the residence of Stephen's sister and brother-in-law located nearby, but the central-hall plan is reversed. The house features a bay window on the front ell and sawnwork detailing on the front porch, both of which were very popular elements on farmhouses in the region in the early twentieth century.

The house is still the seat of a large farm, and many of the outbuildings remain intact, including a mule stable, packhouse, smokehouse, chicken shed, garage, tenant house, and many tobacco barns.

(former) Gilbert School

built circa 1905
Hugo vicinity

Constructed about 1905 to serve African American children in the Hugo community, this one-room schoolhouse is one of only a few historic black schools remaining in the county. Following school consolidation in the 1920s, a larger nearby school building was offered to the local African American community. The circa-1905 building was then decommissioned, having functioned as a school for only a couple of decades. The former Gilbert School has been moved several times and used for a variety of purposes by the local African American community, including as a Sunday school building for a local black congregation. Currently the building serves as a dwelling. The overall form and appearance of the small side-gable building are still those of a one-room schoolhouse. Such original elements as four-over-four sash windows and paneled doors add to the simple Victorian flavor of the building. Porches have been added to both the end and front facades. The gable-end entrance and the four-bay facade provide clues about the building's original educational use.

Tom Abbott House

built circa 1910
Hugo vicinity

One of several similar houses constructed between 1905 and 1915 in the community known as Gilbert Town, using lumber from the nearby Gilbert Sawmill, this one-story dwelling features modest Victorian-style elements. Constructed by Tom Abbott, the house is the mirror image of the nearby Stephen Nathan Gilbert House, built in 1908-1909, with a reversed floor plan.

All of the houses are based on a gable-front-and-wing floor plan and include separate rear ells. A bay window completes the front gable on the one-story, central-hall-plan Tom Abbott House. One chimney is located on the interior; the other is found on the exterior in a rear location. Turned posts support the wraparound front porch, which spans the entire front facade and is decorated with sawnwork detailing. Other typical Victorian-era details include pedimented gables, transom and sidelights around the front door, and corbeled caps on the chimneys.

Not only is the exterior of this abandoned house largely intact, but so is the interior. Four original mantels, paneling below the windows, transoms above the interior doors, tongue-and-groove wainscoting in the central hall, plastered walls, twelve-foot-high ceilings, and coat rails in three rooms are all intact.

The house was built for Tom J. Abbott and his wife, Lizzie, the daughter of William P. and Hannah Gilbert, whose farm is located across the road. Tom and his father-in-law, William P. Gilbert, ran the Gilbert Sawmill.

William Parker Gilbert Farm

built circa 1910
Hugo vicinity

Like a number of houses in the area, this Victorian front-gable-and-wing dwelling was constructed with lumber from William P. Gilbert's nearby sawmill. Unlike the neighboring dwellings of family members, William P. Gilbert Sr.'s house has two stories. The dwelling's features are typical of the Victorian style as rendered locally. They include a front projecting two-story bay window, pedimented gables, and a wraparound front porch with turned columns. The house retains a standing-seam metal roof, original mantels, and four-over-four sash windows. Outbuildings include a smokehouse, a large packhouse, a stable, and various tobacco barns.

William Parker Gilbert Sr. was a prominent citizen in the local community. He married Hannah Phillips, and after her death in 1884 he married Martha Sumrell. The Phillips family had owned the farm since the eighteenth century, and the original W. P. Gilbert dwelling (destroyed) was shown as "E. Phillips" on the 1863 Koerner Military Survey Field Map. The original dwelling, which stood at the end of a long drive across the road from the present W. P. Gilbert House, is shown in the 1906 *Kinston Free Press* Industrial Issue. Gilbert acquired the farm when he married into the Phillips family. Gilbert served as a county commissioner in 1906. The present Gilbert House apparently was built soon after 1906.

Along with his son-in-law, Tom J. Abbott, William P. Gilbert ran a sawmill that employed up to twenty-five people. This sawmill was located where the present Bill Gilbert house stands and supplied the lumber for a number of houses in the neighboring area. A photograph of the sawmill appears in the 1906 *Kinston Free Press* Industrial Issue. It is thought that W. P. Gilbert boarded schoolteachers for the nearby Gilbert School in his house as well.

Freeman House

built circa 1900
Hugo vicinity

This traditional one-story side-gable tenant house originally stood in a row of similar dwellings along the lane leading to the main house on the William Parker Gilbert Farm. The main house is gone, and the tenant houses were all moved a short distance to the main road. This house, the best-preserved example of the three or four remaining tenant houses, was moved to its current site in 1919 by the Freeman family and has been their residence since that time.

The three-bay building has a hall-and-parlor floor plan with an attached rear ell. A chimney is located on the gable end and another in the rear ell. The original four-over-four sash windows, flush gable returns, and standing-seam metal roof are intact. Remaining outbuildings include a smokehouse/woodshed, a shed, a tobacco barn, and two outhouses. Across the road is a tenant house of like design that has been abandoned.

Dunn-Cox House (demolished)

built early nineteenth century
Grifton vicinity

This two-story farmhouse was a very rare example of a modest dwelling with a one-room-over-one-room floor plan. The frame house was constructed in the early nine-teenth century and featured a front shed porch, supported by square columns, and rear shed rooms with a kitchen/dining ell. Moved from its original location, near Tick Bite in northeast Lenoir County, to the Grifton vicinity in the early twentieth century, the dwelling featured nine-over-six sash windows on the first floor and six-over-six sash on the upper floor. An asymmetrical entry led to one large room, and a corner stair led to the upper floor. This dwelling, being the only documented one-room-over-one-room Federal-era farmhouse in the county, is very significant to Lenoir's architectural history but was demolished in the 1980s. Portions of the interior woodwork and the stair survive and are stored in a packhouse on the farmstead.

Tom Worthington House

built late nineteenth century
Grifton vicinity

Sited on a small knoll overlooking the surrounding fields is the Tom Worthington House—a good example of a turn-of-the-century I-house with a two-story rear ell that forms a T-plan. The interior central paired chimneys and the interior end rear ell chimney are embellished with corbeled chimney caps. The two-story rear ell has been elongated with a one-story kitchen extension. An original breezeway was located on the first story of the rear ell but was later enclosed. Other architectural details include a transom and sidelights surrounding the front door, gable returns, six-over-six sash windows, and a three-quarter width front porch supported by six large square columns.

Will Worthington House

built 1870s
Grifton vicinity

The Will Worthington House is an excellent example of a modest Gothic Revival-influenced dwelling constructed in the late nineteenth century. The one-and-a-half-story house exhibits a double-pile central-hall plan and side kitchen/dining ell and is believed to have been built in the 1870s. The strongest identifying elements of the dwelling are the gabled dormers on the front facade—a large central dormer flanked by smaller dormers. The double-pile floor plan features rear rooms that are smaller than the front rooms—common in a number of postbellum rural farmhouses in the county. Two gable-end brick chimneys are located on the front half of the dwelling. The front porch extends along the entire facade of the house and kitchen ell and is supported by early-twentieth-century Doric columns. Other architectural details characteristic of the period include gable returns and four-over-four sash windows.

The original owner of this property is not known, but local tradition states that Will Worthington bought the farm from the Carr family in 1918. A packhouse, smokehouse, milk house, and modern shed are the only remaining outbuildings of a once-extensive farm complex that included numerous tobacco barns.

Wiggins-Phillips House

built circa 1860
Graingers vicinity

Constructed with an uncommon floor plan and chimney arrangement, this one-and-a-half-story farmhouse is a good example of the type built just before and after the Civil War in the county. Shown as the "A. Wiggins" farm on the 1863 Koerner Military Survey Field Map, this house has a traditional hall-and-parlor floor plan and features rear shed rooms that are incorporated into the overall roof gable in the manner of the coastal cottage, but it lacks an engaged porch. Many of the original details of the four-room-plan dwelling have been removed, such as the interior mantels and the exterior end chimneys, although the "ghosts" of two chimneys remain visible—one located on the front room and the other on a rear room of the opposite side of the house. Other typical architectural elements include an enclosed winder stair, flush gables, six-over-six sash windows, and a rear kitchen/dining ell with an enclosed breezeway. The house has belonged to the Phillips family in the twentieth century.

Rountree-Smith Farm

built 1880s
Grifton vicinity

During the 1880s Samuel H. Rountree (1825-?) had a dwelling built on this farm in the Bethel community and moved his family there from Kinston. The two-story dwelling is a good example of an I-house with a decorative front cross gable and a two-story rear ell. The original detached kitchen with an enclosed breezeway is located to the side of the house. A two-story wraparound porch is attached to the portion of the house that faces N.C. Highway 11. A three-quarter-width one-story porch is attached to the front facade, which apparently faced the original main road. All of the porches retain original turned posts and balustrades, an unusual occurrence even for a house of this era. There are four interior chimneys, all of them centrally located and decorated with corbeled caps. Other details include transoms over the doors, a standing-seam metal roof, and pedimented gables. Though the interior has been remodeled many times, two of the original mantels and the staircase newel post and railing remain intact.

The four-hundred-acre farmstead features many outbuildings, including a large hay barn, a packhouse with sheds, a brick smokehouse, a carbide house, a 1930s garage, a chicken coop, a stable, and various tobacco barns. The smokehouse—one of only a few documented brick smokehouses in the county—is constructed of bricks of two different colors laid in common bond. The carbide, or Delco, house is a rare surviving example in Lenoir County, where such outbuildings were once common on early-twentieth-century farms.

It is thought that Rountree sold the farm around the turn of the twentieth century. During the Great Depression the Smith family acquired the farm and has owned it since.

Johnny and Ninnie Bryant House
built circa 1900
Grifton vicinity

This frame house was constructed by an African American builder, Will Donald, for Johnny and Ninnie Bryant around the turn of the century. The Bryants were successful African American farmers in the Grifton community, and their farmhouse remains occupied by members of the Bryant family. The dwelling is an important architectural resource for the local community as a rare

surviving example of a successful turn-of-the-twentieth-century African American farm.

A good example of simple Victorian design, the two-story double-pile house has a hip roof and a projecting two-story bay window on the front facade. The chimney is interior and centrally located. The upper windows have six-over-six sash, the lower four-over-four sash. The dwelling has lost its original front porch and has been covered with asbestos siding simulating brickwork.

Harvey-Mewborne House
built 1810s-1820s
Taylors Crossroads vicinity

Thought to have been built in the 1810-1830 period, probably by Thomas Harvey Sr., this modest-size farmhouse is one of the best examples of the Federal style rendered in a story-and-a-half dwelling in the county. Thomas Harvey Sr. (1788-?) settled in Lenoir County apparently between 1800 and 1810, when he first appeared in census records. Listed as a farmer, Harvey by 1820 had established a family that continued to grow through the 1830s. His farm was eventually taken over by Thomas Harvey Jr. (1838-?). The property remained in the Harvey family until the early twentieth century, when it was acquired by the Mewborne family.

Somewhat similar in style to the Davis-Robinson House located in the Sandy Bottom community, the Harvey-Mewborne House has architectural features more elaborate than those usually seen on farmhouses of its size. The hall-and-parlor plan is typical, as well as the gable-end chimneys with single shoulders laid in Flemish bond—a pattern associated with early-nineteenth-century brick masonry. Separating the house from other period Tidewater cottages in the county are two dormer windows on what is thought to be the original front elevation. The dormers are decorated with denticulated moldings on the front gables and sides. Other striking Federal-style embellishments include tapered rake boards on the gable ends and bed molding along the boxed cornice. The single-pile house also features shed rooms off the rear and an early detached kitchen, possibly contemporary with the house. A breezeway connecting the kitchen to the house was later enclosed, as well as a porch on the rear shed addition. The configuration of the original front porch is unknown, and the existing porch is probably twentieth century in origin.

On the interior, placement of the enclosed stair entrance directly behind the front door is unusual and encourages speculation as to the dwelling's original orientation and front facade (though no other physical evidence supports a theory of reorientation). Consistent with the fashionably embellished exterior are interior treatments such as three-part mantels with dentil moldings, flat-paneled wainscot, six-panel doors, and simple two-part molded window and door surrounds. The second-story loft retains an original stair rail and newel post.

The once-large farming operation is denoted by numerous outbuildings including tobacco barns, modern sheds, and a tobacco packhouse. The dwelling's early-nineteenth-century smokehouse with hand-forged hardware was moved into Kinston to the site of Harmony Hall in the 1980s, courtesy of Ronald (Sam) Mewborne.

Odham-Rouse Store

built early 1920s
Grifton vicinity

A well-preserved example of the typical rural store in Lenoir County, this frame building has been in continuous operation in the area historically known as the Bethel community since its construction. The store was originally a small, square, one-room building and was enlarged, first with a rear extension and later with a side shed addition. To the rear of the store a residence was added as well. The hipped roof extends as a drive-through canopy over the fuel pumps on the front facade. The interior of the store is largely intact and retains the original hardwood floors. Supporting ancillary buildings include a shed, a pump house, and two outhouses. The store is located on the spot where a Bethel country store stood at the turn of the twentieth century.

Bethel Christian Church

built 1925
Grifton vicinity

This church building was constructed in 1925 after the former 1873 sanctuary was destroyed by fire in 1924. The congregation worshiped in the Rountree Masonic Lodge, located across the road, while the new sanctuary was under construction. The present church was dedicated on July 19, 1925, and substantially remodeled in 1956. Built with a nave-and-apse, or T-plan, configuration that is common for rural southern churches, this building retains pointed-arched windows and a standing-seam metal roof.

This congregation traces its history to the antebellum period, when it was a Union Baptist church. The original Bethel Union Baptist Church Meetinghouse was located directly across the highway from the present church building and in 1860 was the site of the Grand Council of the Union Baptist denomination of Christians. In 1870 the church reorganized as a Disciples of Christ Christian Church and continued to worship in the Bethel Meetinghouse until 1873, when a new sanctuary was constructed.

Bethel Christian Church produced the first dedicated missionary from the North Carolina Disciples of Christ—Almeda (Meta) Chestnutt (1863-1948). Meta Chestnutt attended the local Bethel Academy and Greenville Institute. After attending graduate school at the University of Nashville in Tennessee, she came back to teach at the Greenville Institute from 1886 to 1889, but she soon left for Silver City in the Chickasaw Nation of Oklahoma to teach Native Americans. During Meta Chestnutt's thirty-two years of administration in Oklahoma, the El Meta Bond College opened, and 2,500 people were trained under her supervision, including many future leaders in the new state. Chestnutt later served as a faculty member of Oklahoma Woman's College and in 1939 was recognized for her missionary work, becoming the first woman educator to appear before the Chickasaw legislature and to receive recognition from the Department of the Interior as highly influential in the fight for higher education for women.

[Source: Charles Crossfield Ware, *Hookerton History* (Wilson, N.C.: 1960), 8-11.]

(former) Bethel Academy and Masonic Lodge

built mid-nineteenth century
Grifton vicinity

This two-story gabled building is of significant importance to the history of education in Lenoir County. The building has been used for many purposes since its construction in the mid-nineteenth century. Originally the building was known as the Rountree Masonic Lodge, and later as the Bethel Masonic Lodge. It is thought that the building was used solely as a lodge until about 1880, when Squire Brooks and other prominent men in the Bethel Masonic Lodge began considering means to improve the educational opportunities of their children. After several months of planning they organized Bethel Academy and incorporated it under a board of trustees. Tuition rates were one dollar per month per pupil for the primary subjects and three dollars for advanced subjects. The first teacher was J. D. Murphy, a graduate of the University of North Carolina. For several years the school had only one teacher, and never more than two. The academy attracted students not only from the Bethel community but also from surrounding counties. Boarding students lived with families in the vicinity of the school. The building contained two stories: the upper was used as a Masonic hall, and the lower was one room with "high homemade desks" used as a classroom. The academy stood in a grove of large oak trees near the Disciples of Christ and Primitive Baptist Churches. The Bethel community also contained a blacksmith shop and a country store.

This arrangement of the building's dual uses continued for decades, even after the school became a public institution. At the time of the 1924 survey of public schools the building, still owned by the Masons, contained a single classroom on the lower floor with an enrollment of twenty-four pupils. In 1924 the Disciples of Christ sanctuary across the road burned, and during reconstruction church services were held in the lodge/school. After Lenoir County public schools were consolidated in the 1920s and Contentnea School was constructed nearby, the building continued in use as a

Masonic hall until the Masons relocated to a Masonic hall in nearby Grifton. In the 1930s the vacant building was renovated as a dwelling by Fred Rouse. During the renovation, the building was turned 180 degrees on axis and sited so that the side facade—now the main facade—faced the road.

The building retains much of its mid-nineteenth-century architectural character on the exterior, but the interior has been modernized. Original features include six-over-six sash windows (second level), gable returns, corner pilasters, and flush sheathing in the south gable—the most significant detail of the building's antebellum nature.

Coward-Barwick House

built 1870s
Tick Bite community

This one-and-one-half story side-gable double-pile dwelling was built by brothers-in-law Albert Galletin Coward and Moses Spivey during the Reconstruction era. Albert's daughter, Sarah May Coward (1869-1963), was approximately eleven years old when the house was built. Sarah married John Henry Barwick and moved to Kinston. In later years she and her husband bought her parents' farm and moved back to the family homeplace.

The well-maintained dwelling is one of the most elaborately detailed houses in the Tick Bite area of Lenoir County. The central-hall-plan house features gable returns and heavy corner pilasters—features carried over from the antebellum Greek Revival style. The chimneys are located on the interior and have corbeled caps. Other architectural details include a transom and sidelights surrounding the front door, six-over-six sash windows, and a wraparound front porch supported by large posts.

Samuel H. Coward House

built circa 1840
Tick Bite community

One of the best examples of the coastal cottage house in the Tick Bite community of Lenoir County, this dwelling was moved from its original site, nearby on the same tract of land; reoriented toward Contentnea Creek; and renovated, around fifteen years ago. Although a rear shed addition and front porch have been added, the house retains its distinctive broken roofline—a characteristic of coastal cottages. The front facade has an asymmetrical entry location, signifying the hall-and-parlor plan. Other exterior elements are six-over-six and four-over-four sash windows and a replacement exterior end chimney.

The house is believed to have been built by Samuel H. Coward in the early to mid-nineteenth century. The land on which the house sits is thought to have been transferred to Samuel from Ed Coward in 1840. Eugenia and Moses Spivey lived in the house from 1880 to circa 1900. A family cemetery is located on the original site of the house near Contentnea Creek.

S. Brown House

built circa 1850
Graingers vicinity

This small, finely finished story-and-a-half farmhouse is apparently the house shown on the 1863 Koerner Military Survey Field Map as the "S. Brown" farmhouse, but no other historical information is known. The vernacular house has a number of Greek Revival, mid-nineteenth-century construction details

Built with a central-hall plan, the house was enlarged with a side addition and rear kitchen/dining ell in the early twentieth century. Its steeply pitched roof is unusual for houses of the era. Intact exterior details include nine-over-nine sash windows, molded window and door surrounds, flush gables, and two exterior end chimneys. The major Greek Revival expressions on the exterior are the corner pilasters and eave treatment: paneled molded Doric cornerboards and a frieze band. Interior elements are five-panel doors, simple replacement mantel shelves, plaster walls, tongue-and-groove flooring, an open dog-leg staircase with original newel post, beaded-board finish in the staircase, and loft fireplaces.

Savannah Free Will Baptist Church

built 1919-1920
Graingers vicinity

Savannah Free Will Baptist Church originated as a bush shelter about 1870 in the general vicinity of the present church. The Reverend July Phillips served as the first pastor. Other pastors have included McRae Lanier, Henry Isler, Robert Grady, E. M. Hill, and the present pastor Dr. B. R. Anderson. The congregation eventually built a sanctuary, which was destroyed by a tornado in 1919. In 1919-1920 a modest Gothic Revival-style church replaced the earlier building. The present congregation is thought to be one of the largest rural African American congregations in eastern North Carolina.

Constructed of concrete block, the gable-front sanctuary was renovated with brick veneer and simulated brick buttresses in 1976. Architectural elements of the original church were retained in the renovation, including an entrance flanked by two crenellated towers and triangular-arched windows with stained glass. A new front facade with an entry vestibule was constructed during the renovation. Recently a modern detached addition has been built to the west of the church.

According to local tradition a two-story Masonic lodge, used by the local African American community, once sat on the church grounds but is not extant.

Bryant Cameron Langston House
built 1932-1936
Graingers vicinity

During the Great Depression a few houses were constructed in phases, and this Craftsman-style house is an example of that building procedure. Bryant Cameron Langston hired Fleet Pittman and John Sanderson to construct phase 1 of the house in 1932, then phase 2 was completed in 1934-1936. In phase 2, a new facade and side ell enclosed the original shotgun-style dwelling. Common Craftsman-style architectural details include an integral wraparound front porch supported by battered posts with brick bases and exposed roof joists. Bryant C. Langston's widow, Lena, still occupies this house.

Sharon United Methodist Church
built 1872; enlarged and remodeled 1922
Graingers vicinity

This church was constructed in 1872 as the Rose of Sharon Methodist Episcopal Church, South, Contentnea Township, on land donated by Bryant H. and Martha Langston. The sanctuary was moved on its site to accommodate a new road and extensively remodeled in 1922. The renovation included a new entry vestibule, classrooms, a pulpit, stained-glass windows, and exterior eave brackets. A marble cornerstone reads "Sharon Methodist Church 1872-1922."

The interior is well maintained and retains the 1922 renovated appearance. Architectural elements include vertical tongue-and-groove wainscoting, plastered walls, window surrounds, and five-panel doors. A large education side wing was added about 1957. Vinyl siding covers the exterior.

Canady Tenant House
built circa 1890
Graingers vicinity

Constructed by the Canady family, owners of neighboring LaFayette Plantation in the late nineteenth century, this house is a good example of a turn-of-the-century tenant dwelling. The one-story side-gable building retains its original floor plan, architectural features, and outbuildings. The originally detached kitchen was attached by a rear ell, and the side porch was later enclosed. Typical architectural details include six-over-six sash windows, one exterior end chimney (the other was removed), a three-quarter-width front porch, gable returns, and a boxed cornice. The outbuildings include a two-story packhouse, various tobacco barns, and a two-story smokehouse.

The present tenant recalled that a ninety-five-year old black man visited a few years ago and claimed to have been born in the house. The dwelling is the only one of the numerous Canady tenant houses presently occupied.

LaFayette (Whitfield-Dunn-Wiggins House)

built circa 1830
Graingers vicinity

An element in many local legends, this story-and-a-half house is Lenoir County's largest coastal cottage-form dwelling and one of the most significant antebellum buildings in the county. Local tradition has given the house the name LaFayette and associated it with the Lewis Whitfield family. Legend holds that the house was once used as a tavern and a Masonic hall. The house is also thought to have been purchased by John Patrick Dunn from the Whitfields, along with nearly five hundred acres of land.

Although Lenoir County's pre-1878 land records have been destroyed, available historical documents suggest that much of this tradition is true. After John Patrick Dunn's death sometime before 1863, his widow, Sarah, married H. S. Lee, whose name appears beside the house on the 1863 Koerner Military Survey Field Map. A letter written by Lee in 1867 and preserved in family records bears the address heading LaFayette, proving that the plantation was called by that name. Although Dunn is the earliest documented owner, it is possible that the house was built by the Whitfield family. Whitfield genealogy describes LaFayette as having stone pillars, solid porch columns, built-in porch seats, and eight-foot-tall doors, features that were found at this house. Careful analysis of the construction and architectural features indicates that it was built in the late Federal period, about 1830. When Lewis Whitfield died in 1849 his will conveyed "a part of Lands on Beaver Dam Branch called LaFayette" to his heirs. (Beaver Dam Branch lies just south of this house.) In the 1870s Laura Dunn Wiggins and her family lived at LaFayette. In 1890 B. W. Canady gained ownership. His daughter Lottie Canady inherited the house from her father.

The dwelling was used as a tenant house for a number of years before being abandoned in the mid-twentieth century. By 1979, when the house was purchased and renovations began, the dwelling had been vandalized and all but one of the mantels had been removed. The dwelling is five bays wide, and four bays deep and sits on a reconstructed stone and marl foundation, an early construction tradition rarely found this far inland. The steep gable

roof engages the front shed and rear shed rooms. Two large single-shouldered brick chimneys of common bond are located on each gable end and are supported by stone and marl foundations. A third chimney was originally located on the east rear shed room. Windows are nine-over-nine sash on the first floor and six-over-six sash on the second floor. A shed addition on the east rear facade was the only addition to the house, although that was replaced with the present similar-size addition. The center three front bays are open as a recessed porch, with large plain square post supports and evidence of a Chinese Chippendale balustrade that has been removed. The double front door has sidelights and a transom.

One of the most intriguing elements of the house is its floor plan. The front half of the first floor is divided by a center hall, with a transverse hall extending from the east side porch to the center hall (now used as a bathroom). The two halls, however, are not connected by a door. On either side of the center hall is a single large room. The two small shed rooms that flank the recessed porch open only into these rooms. The rear half of the house was divided into three rooms: a small room in the northwest corner, a large center room containing the stair (these two are now combined into one), and a room in the northeast corner with a built-in cupboard that apparently functioned as the original dining room. The original exterior shed room (now replaced) opened off this northeast room, also contained a built-in cupboard, and apparently served as the original kitchen.

The upper-floor plan is equally unusual. At the front and rear of this level, where the roof slopes to meet the first story, are large unfinished storage areas. The stair ascends from the rear of the first floor to a small hall in the center of the upper level, surrounded by three rooms: two on the east and one on the west. The west room originally extended nearly the length of the house, but was reduced in size during the renovation with a bathroom installation along the northern wall. Between the great room and the southeast chamber is a narrow unplastered hall (now a closet) that leads into the unfinished storage area at the front of the house.

The house is finished on both levels with plaster walls and ceilings and simple molded architraves around the openings. The only surviving original mantel, rendered in vernacular Federal design, is located in the east parlor. Its modest details include a dentil molding below the shelf and reeding on each pilaster. In each first-floor room, except for the southwest room, is a horizontal-sheathed wainscot with a simple molded chair rail. The southwest room contains a simple beaded chair rail and a plaster dado. The second-level rooms are finished in the same manner as the southwest room, with the exception of the great room, which has a flat-paneled wainscot. The first-floor doors are flat paneled, and the second-floor doors are batten.

A very unusual feature of the second floor is an interior transom, located in the center hall, which is a rectangular nine-pane casement window set directly above the door frame. Another unusual element of the second floor is the great room, originally the most finely finished room in the house, an honor generally reserved for the first-floor parlor. According to local tradition, the great room served as a Masonic hall, which would explain its fine finish. Another local tradition states that the house was originally used as a tavern, and the unusual features and floor plan tend to corroborate that tradition.

Outbuildings located nearby include tobacco barns, a packhouse, and tenant houses, but no domestic or agricultural outbuildings in the direct vicinity of the dwelling survive.

Charles Wilson Tilghman House (demolished)
built circa 1830
Graingers vicinity

Historic photographs of the Charles Wilson Tilghman house reveal a two-and-a-half-story, side-gable, double-pile, side-hall-plan dwelling that featured an asymmetrical facade and two exterior end chimneys (both on the south facade). This antebellum house form was common in New Bern, but the Tilghman House was one of the only known examples built in Lenoir County. Although the dwelling no longer exists, it is a significant part of the county's architectural heritage.

Architectural details expressed the Federal and Greek Revival styles, indicating that the house was constructed in the early nineteenth century and renovated in the mid-nineteenth century. Two of the most uncommon architectural details were a decorative transom over the front door and two nine-over-six sash windows in the third-story gable ends that featured arched heads with a keystone. This type of detailing was typical of elaborate Federal-era dwellings and very similar to that on the original circa-1812 portion of Cedar Dell.

The interior woodwork and mantels were Greek Revival in style, with window and door surrounds that featured crossettes and were probably added to the dwelling in a circa-1850s renovation. The original side-hall plan was not altered and exhibited an open stairway to the second and third floors with the original newel posts and balustrade. Documentary photographs taken circa 1945 show a two-story full-facade front porch (later replaced with a one-story full-facade porch) and a detached rear kitchen connected with a breezeway.

An outbuilding and some interior woodwork, including mantels, are all that remains of the Charles Wilson Tilghman House, demolished in 1991. The antebellum outbuilding was used as a cotton house, and some original features are intact, such as a board-and-batten shutter and hardware.

The house is identified on the 1863 Koerner Military Survey Map as the "Wilson Tillman" farm (and a William Tilman is listed in the 1820 census). This was most likely the farmstead of Wilson Tilghman, who operated a 720-acre farm in 1850 with a cash value of $8,000, of which 300 acres was improved. Tilghman, along with his six slaves (four males and two females), produced 800 bushels of Indian corn, 100 bushels of peas and beans, 10 bushels of Irish potatoes, 150 bushels of sweet potatoes, and 100 pounds of butter in 1850. The farm also produced twenty-five dollars worth of homemade manufactures and Tilghman owned four horses, five milk cows, four working oxen, fifteen cattle, and sixty swine in 1850. Wilson Tilghman, operating a water-powered mill, produced 3,500 pounds of cornmeal and 1,000 pounds of wheat flour, worth $3,000—in 1860. The mill was still in operation after the Civil War and produced $2,000 worth of flour in 1870.

Graingers (Station)
established mid-1890s

The small community of Graingers is traditionally known as Graingers Station, named for Jesse Grainger of Kinston, who owned the property when it became a depot stop on the Atlantic and North Carolina Railroad in the mid-1890s. During its years of prosperity the community contained a railroad depot, railroad section houses, a post office, several general mercantile establishments, an African American Masonic lodge, several churches, and a number of homes. Located at the center of the community are the D. W. Hamilton Store and house constructed circa 1896. Across the railroad tracks stands the only African American Masonic lodge remaining in rural Lenoir County. Though the circa-1881 Grainger Chapel Church of Christ was replaced in 1983, the original circa-1919 Grainger Baptist Church is intact.

The town prospered in the early twentieth century and was incorporated by 1930, with a population of 66. The population continued to grow, from 120 in 1940 to its largest size of 188 in 1960. Lenoir County suffered from a recession in the 1960s and experienced a population decline. By 1970 Graingers, like other small towns in the county, was no longer incorporated. The depot and all but one store were demolished in the late twentieth century.

Capstone Lodge
established circa 1905
Graingers

Capstone Lodge No. 131 in Graingers is one of a very few lodges remaining in rural Lenoir County and, more importantly, is the only surviving African American Masonic hall. The building is said to have originally served as a train depot, but it was donated to the Masonic chapter in 1905. The two-story front-gable form was popular for Masonic lodges throughout the region during the late nineteenth and early twentieth centuries. It may be that the second story was added when the building was converted to a lodge. Architectural details include two front entries, leaded stained-glass windows on the second story, flush gable returns, and the Masonic symbol on the front and rear gables.

D. W. Hamilton Store
built 1896
Graingers Community

In 1891 the Scotland Neck-to-Kinston branch line of the Wilmington and Weldon Railroad was completed from Greenville in neighboring Pitt County to Kinston. A depot was constructed on the line in northern Lenoir County four years later, about halfway between Kinston and Grifton. The depot, named Graingers after local farmer and community leader Jesse Grainger, a prominent agriculturalist who led the drive to introduce bright-leaf tobacco to Lenoir County in 1895, spurred the development of a crossroads inhabited by railroad workers and farmers.

Shortly after the depot was erected D. W. Hamilton (1861-?) constructed a small general store on the line, which was in operation by 1896. Prior to establishing his own business, Hamilton worked on his father's farm for a few years, then took employment as a clerk in Lizzie, Greene County, and in 1890 left for the frontier land of Texas and Mississippi. He returned to Lenoir County later the same year, then entered the mercantile business and soon became a prosperous businessman. In 1906 Hamilton owned several residences in Kinston and was a stockholder in the Orion Knitting Mill and the Bank of Kinston, besides operating his store and post office at Graingers. He also owned several lots in the new railroad community, including one adjacent to his store, where he had a house constructed about the same time the store was built.

As first constructed, the D. W. Hamilton and Son General Merchandise building was a typical country store, displaying a large false parapet front facade that concealed a gable roof. The original three-bay store featured a typical recessed double-leaf entry and a separate front door leading to a small hallway that functioned as the post office. Later, in the second quarter of the twentieth century, the store was enlarged with a side addition (featuring a separate recessed double-leaf entry) and a large hip-roof pass-through—added in the 1930s to cover fuel pumps. A circa 1906 photograph shows the original store with a board roof and a well to the side. The dirt road ran immediately in front of the store, much like today, but the mode of transportation was horse and buggy. Very little has been changed at the store since the early-twentieth-century additions, and such original interior features as shelving, counters, cash register, and operating ledgers remain in place. The store operated continuously from 1896 to 1997. It is presently owned by Roy Hamilton Jr., grandson of the original owner.

Graingers Railroad Section House
built 1890s
Graingers

After the Graingers railroad station was established in the 1890s, several bunkhouses—called section houses—were constructed for the railroad employees. This one-story-side-gable house is a rare surviving example and retains many distinguishing features, such as a five-bay facade and molded board-and-batten exterior. Evidence of the original central-bay portico is visible, as well as a later full-facade porch replacement. A central rear ell with flanking rear shed rooms is intact. Other architectural details on the exterior include gable returns and six-over-six sash windows. The interior of the hall-and-parlor-plan bunkhouse is intact and features such details as tongue-and-groove walls and ceilings, two flue mantels, and four-panel doors.

After the railroad abandoned the buildings, the Charles A. Broadway family purchased two of the bunkhouses and moved them off the railroad right-of-way. This house was moved only a short distance from its original location near the tracks.

Graingers Missionary Baptist Church
built 1919; enlarged 1938; reoriented and remodeled 1954
Graingers

Organized in the fall of 1916, the original Graingers Baptist Church met in a one-room frame building built about 1919 on land donated by Jane Clark. A Sunday school had been operated from the Graingers School since 1913. Charles Broadway Sr. later donated some adjacent property to the church. Around 1938 a two-story addition was constructed at the front of the church,—for Sunday school classrooms. The three-bay single-pile building resembled an I-house and even featured a two-story central-bay portico supported by square columns. This uncommon church form was turned 180 degrees in 1954 and remodeled with a sanctuary enlargement, an entry vestibule, and a new front porch. The rear two-story portion of the church was extended in 1956, creating the present-day form. Original stained-glass and two-over-two sash windows are intact. The interior was renovated in 1971, and the adjacent fellowship hall was constructed in 1973.

Blow-Hunt House
built early twentieth century
Graingers vicinity

A very good example of an early-twentieth-century I-house, this two-story side-gable dwelling has a front cross gable that creates a tri-gable roof. The full-facade front porch, supported by large square columns, features a cross gable over the entrance bay and a balustrade. The well-maintained building retains architectural elements that are common on this style farmhouse, including sidelights flanking the front door, six-over-one sash windows, a rear kitchen/dining ell, and a colored-glass window in the front cross gable.

Outbuildings include a smokehouse, garage, large barn, brick pump house, and farm equipment shed. Little historical information is available except that the Hunt family purchased the farm from the Blow family in the early 1930s.

M. F. Odom House
built circa 1900; enlarged and remodeled 1930s
Graingers vicinity

M. F. Odom enlarged and updated a circa-1900 traditional side-gable dwelling in the 1930s with a Craftsman-style renovation that included an engaged front porch and porte cochere. The dramatic porch supports are post-on-pier in design but have cypress trees for columns and marl bases. The foundation piers of the house are also of marl. This shell conglomerate, a traditional foundation material, was seldom used in the twentieth century. Other architectural features include sidelights flanking the front door, wainscoting, crown molding, an unaltered floor plan, a built-in china cabinet, and original mantels. "M. F. Odom 1936" appears in the concrete flooring of the smokehouse.

Charles A. Broadway House
built circa 1915
Graingers

Located in Graingers along the railroad tracks, the Broadway House is a good example of an American Foursquare-style house. The two-and-a-half-story hip-roof double-pile dwelling was constructed circa 1915 by Charles Albert Broadway Sr. The exterior of the house is intact and retains such elements as eight-over-one sash windows, a transom and sidelights with beveled glass flanking the front door, wide overhanging eaves, corner trim, a frieze band, and corbeled chimneys. A wraparound hip-roof front porch is supported by square columns. The hip-roof three-quarter-width rear porch has a shed room and an extension that originally covered a well/pump. The house is built on a central-hall plan except that the entrance portion of the hall was excluded, creating a more open floor plan.

The interior of the well-preserved farmhouse features elaborate architectural details such as pocket doors, five mantels (two brick), six-panel doors, eleven-foot ceilings with moldings, an open stairway with newel post and balustrade, and even the original light switches. An original stairway leads to a third-level attic.

A variety of outbuildings are located on the farm and include an equipment shed, a shop, a packhouse, a toolshed, a circa-1940s corn mill, tobacco barns, and numerous tenant houses. Also located on the farm are two railroad-related buildings, bunkhouses for railroad employees, which originally sat beside the railroad tracks. After Broadway purchased the abandoned board-and-batten buildings, he moved one behind his house and the other just a few feet away from the tracks to clear the railroad right-of-way.

Charles A. Broadway Sr. was a prominent member of the local community. He donated the land for Contentnea School, owned the nearby Graingers Store (not extant), and was the station master at the Graingers Railroad Station.

Contentnea School

built 1923-1924
Graingers community

Located in the once-prominent railroad community of Graingers, this two-story brick school, designed by acclaimed school architect Leslie Boney of Wilmington, was constructed in 1923-1924 and was the first of four newly consolidated rural schools to open in the county. The well-preserved Neoclassical Revival-style building is an excellent example of the consolidated schools of the 1920s and retains its original interior and exterior appearance.

Exterior detailing is typical of the style and includes a two-story pedimented entrance portico supported by fluted columns with Corinthian capitols. The double-door front entrance is flanked by sidelights and has an elliptical fanlight. Flanking wings feature one-story pedimented porticoes supported by Ionic columns that shelter arched entrances. Other signifying treatments include a thin concrete water table, original six-over-six sash windows, window lintels with keystones, and a corbeled cornice beneath a surrounding parapet.

In 1929 a two-story classroom wing was constructed on the south facade and attached with a two-story breezeway. Another wing, housing agricultural arts, was built in 1950 on the north facade and mirrors the size and form of the first addition. A separate cafeteria was erected to the rear of the school in 1950 and connected with covered walkways. The school was enlarged with more classrooms in 1956, and a gymnasium was built on the campus in 1957. Two other buildings, a teacherage and a shop building (originally the agriculture building), are contemporary with the school. Around 1925 a Craftsman-style dwelling was erected on the south side of the campus to serve as the teacherage and later became the principal's residence. It is now used as a private dwelling. The circa-1925 shop building, located to the rear of the school building, is a one-story hip-roof brick structure with an interior end chimney.

The 1929 wing now houses the main offices and has been recently renovated, while the rest of the building's interior is original and includes such details as hardwood floors, doors, chair rail, plaster walls, tongue-and-groove ceilings, and interior transoms. The auditorium retains paneled Neoclassical-style pilasters supporting a frieze band over the stage, tongue-and-groove wainscoting, and original seating. Classrooms retain original chalkboards and ceiling fans. The school's traditional corridor plan has not been altered, and the building even retains the original bathroom locations and plumbing fixtures.

Contentnea School was formed by the union of eleven rural schools—Graingers, Dunn, Bethel, Barwick, Airy Grove, Oak Dale, Hugo, Gilberts, Sand Hill, Sharon, and Contentnea. Charles Albert Broadway Sr., who lived on an adjacent farm, donated the original six acres of land for the school and assisted Lenoir County in becoming one of the first counties in North Carolina to complete consolidation of its white schools in the 1920s. When the school opened in October of 1924 there were twelve classrooms serving one hundred high school students, five hundred elementary school students, and nineteen teachers. The school has been used as an elementary school since the county consolidated its high schools in 1964-1965. The expanded 18.7-acre campus of Contentnea School served 574 students from preschool through fifth grade in 1984.

FALLING CREEK
TOWNSHIP

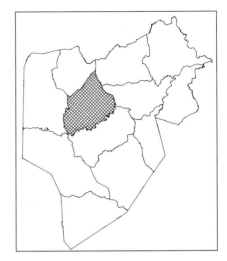

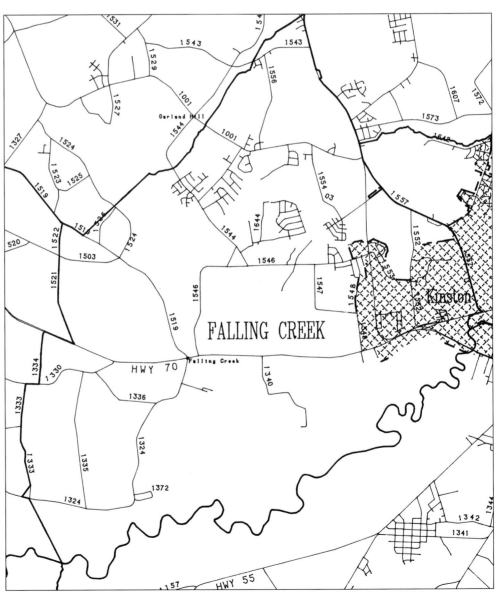

Munfred Brewer House
built circa 1860
LaGrange vicinity

This rather plain two-story dwelling was likely built by Munfred Brewer (1832-1904) in the late antebellum period or just after the Civil War, when he was beginning married life with Mary (1837-1907). By 1880 the Brewer family included not only Munfred and Mary but also five children ranging in age from nine to seventeen. A cemetery located on the farm offers not only genealogical information but also epitaphs extolling the lives of the Brewer family. Munfred Brewer's gravestone reads, "God gave, He took, He will restore; He doth all things well . . . ," which is as good an epitaph as any for a farm and household that survived the Civil War and the hardships afterward that broke many farming enterprises and spirits. Mary Brewer's gravestone reads, "A loved one from us has gone, A voice we love is still; A place is vacant in our home, which never can be filled." The house remained in the Brewer family until Rachel Brewer died in 1934.

In its unadorned simplicity the Brewer House speaks of the economically depressed era following the Civil War and may have been built during that period. The squat proportions of the three-bay two-story house are enhanced by the short four-over-four sash windows on the second story. One double-shoulder and one single-shoulder chimney define the gable ends. A full-width shed-roof porch supported by replacement turned posts shelters the single front entrance. Replacement asbestos-shingle siding now covers the exterior. A broad collection of outbuildings remains in place, ranging from an antebellum corncrib with hand-forged strap hinges to an early-twentieth-century smokehouse and, in the field behind the house, several tobacco-related buildings, including a packhouse with an ordering pit and flue-curing barns. An antebellum frame structure, possibly built as a dwelling, with a box cornice, exposed ceiling joists, and board-and-batten doors sits behind the main dwelling. This rich ensemble of buildings adds to the overall agricultural character of the Brewer farm.

Jake Dawson House
built second quarter of the nineteenth century
Falling Creek vicinity

Jake and Adelle Dawson bought this two-story antebellum farmhouse in 1910 from a Mr. Arthurs, who is said to have moved the house to its current site from the Institute community less than ten years before. Although this is not documented, other buildings are known to have been relocated from Institute after the school there closed in 1878 and many of the campus buildings were no longer needed. According to Martha Wade, Jake Dawson's granddaughter, the rear ell, originally a store at the front of the property, was attached to the house by her grandfather in the early twentieth century. The overall form of the single-pile center-hall-plan dwelling remains intact, though the house has been altered with replacement siding, and new windows. The exterior end single-shoulder chimneys appear to date from the turn of the twentieth century, when the house reportedly was relocated. Two elongated six-over-six windows flanking a double-door entrance, and three smaller six-over-six windows above, embody the typical fenestration pattern of late Federal and early Greek Revival design. Shed rooms, in standard fashion, project from the rear elevation.

Hodges-Efird House
built circa 1830
West Kinston

Located in the Efird Heights section of west Kinston, this one-and-a-half-story, hall-and-parlor-plan dwelling exemplifies the coastal cottage form. Identifying features are the engaged front porch with enclosed shed room and an engaged rear shed addition. James Arendell Hodges (1808-1859) probably constructed the house around 1830, and the farm stayed in the Hodges family until Benton Thaxter Efird moved in around the late 1920s. Bascom Lacue Efird Sr. (the present owner's father) purchased the farm during the Great Depression era. The Atlantic and North Carolina Railroad traversed the plantation in the 1850s. Although the house was the seat of a large farm throughout the nineteenth and early twentieth centuries, the farm and its cemetery have been engulfed by west Kinston suburban neighborhoods since the mid-twentieth century.

A kitchen with enclosed breezeway is attached to the side of the house. Original architectural features include nine-over-nine and six-over-six sash windows, two single-shoulder stepped brick chimneys with Flemish bond, and one Federal-style mantel. The mantel has a three-part design, with molded panels and shelf with a dentiled frieze. Of special significance are the three interior board-and-batten doors, which retain rare H and L hinges.

Outbuildings include a smokehouse, a tobacco barn, stables, an original barn, and a packhouse. The rare surviving antebellum "corn" barn is of heavy braced-frame construction and probably dates to the second quarter of the nineteenth century. What appears to be a large packhouse is actually a former African American Masonic lodge that was moved from Hill Farm Road nearby and renovated in the 1920s. A Hodges family cemetery is located close to the house and outbuildings.

Darden-Dawson House (Falling Creek Station)
built circa 1900
Falling Creek community

Falling Creek Station was located at this site on the Atlantic and North Carolina Railroad, (later known as the Atlantic and East Carolina Railroad). The station complex at one time included a store, a loading/unloading ramp, and a small office as well as the extant house and outbuildings. The house is known as the Darden-Dawson house, because the Dawsons bought the property from the Darden family in 1924. Maurice Rouse has owned the farm property since 1959, when the rerouting of the road necessitated the demolition of the store.

The dwelling, a typical one-story tri-gable form, featured a detached kitchen that was replaced with an addition about 1970. Thought to be older than the house, the kitchen building retains six-over-six sash windows, a central chimney, and a porch with a shed room. Architectural details of the house include four-over-four sash windows, eave returns, a transom over the front door, and an exterior rear chimney. Outbuildings include a 1920s maid's quarters, a packhouse, an outhouse, and numerous sheds.

Banks Chapel Missionary Baptist Church
built circa 1900
Falling Creek community

The Banks Chapel Missionary Baptist Church's simple design—a cross-gabled belfry over a clipped-gable narthex, lit from the sides by lancet double-hung stained-glass windows—is typical of vernacular turn-of-the-century rural eastern North Carolina churches. Besides gaining a later side-gable rear extension, the church has been altered by replacement siding and a new roof.

The church congregation was established in 1870 by a group of citizens including Jonas Evans, E. N. Patterson, and Robert Harper. Church services were held in a small house until the current building was built. Pastors of the church have included Squire Jones, E. N. Patterson, W. H. Bryant, Isaac Jordan, and the present minister Spencer Williams Jr. Deacons of the church have included E. L. Gray, Willie Kennedy, Thomas I. Patterson, Charlie Jones, and Charlie Bryant.

Rouse-Capps House
built circa 1850
Kinston vicinity

This two-story I-house, a good example of the transitional Federal/Greek Revival style of the mid-nineteenth century, has an unusual four-bay facade and a center-hall plan. The house was partially destroyed by fire in 1969 but was restored and enlarged in the early 1970s. The entire front portion of the house was restored, with the exception of the first-floor run of the three-story open stairway (now accessed from the rear ell). Chimneys laid in Flemish bond are located on each exterior end. Interior details include window surrounds with crossettes, a transom over the front entrance, six-panel doors, one board-and-batten door, and a door with rising butt hinges. Perhaps the most impressive features of the dwelling are the hand-carved vernacular Greek Revival-style mantels and the open three-story stair with simple Federal-style detailing. The mantels feature local interpretations of Corinthian-style capitals and flared columns, the only known examples in Lenoir County.

Noah James Rouse, an early owner of this house, later moved to Kinston, where he was a prominent lawyer, farmer, and member of the Gordon Street Christian Church. Rouse died in 1935. John Talbot Capps II moved to Kinston from Richmond, Virginia, to assist his father-

in-law in the operation of Hood's Drug Store in 1947. Around 1950 he purchased this farmhouse, adjoining the Caswell School in west Kinston. From 1953 to the early 1970s Capps owned and operated Parkview Drug Company and Parkview Book Store in Kinston. The house has been engulfed by suburban west Kinston but is protectively surrounded by large oak trees and is now known as Oakland. It is presently owned and occupied by James "Jimmy" H. Capps and family.

Warters-Parrott-Coleman Farm
established late nineteenth century
Falling Creek vicinity

A signature feature for travelers along U.S. Highway 70 between LaGrange and Kinston, this picturesque farmstead complete with a retinue of domestic and agricultural buildings was established prior to the Civil War, probably by the Warters family. Set in a grove of mature oak trees, the one-and-a-half-story frame dwelling in its present configuration reflects a housing form frequently built in the era following the Civil War and into the first decade of the twentieth century. The earliest section of the house is said to be in the elongated rear ell, thought to have been built in the antebellum period, most likely by a member of the locally prominent Warters family. James Marion Parrott (1824-1877) married Elizabeth Warters (1832-1903) and probably lived in a dwelling on this farm, which is believed to have been owned by Elizabeth's father prior to the Civil War. According to family tradition the property passed to Dr. James Marion Parrott III and subsequently to his daughter Elizabeth Parrot Coleman. Who constructed which portions of the house is hard to determine. Judging from birth and death dates and architectural evidence, however, the main one-and-a-half-story house appears to have been built either by James Marion Parrott shortly before his death in 1877 or by his widow, Elizabeth, within a decade following her husband's death. By the early 1930s the property had been converted to a farm manager's residence, and members of the Parrott family had moved into Kinston.

The well-kept main house remains mostly intact, and only the addition of a large shed-roof dormer on the front and the enclosure of the rear ell side porch have changed its overall original appearance. Equally significant on the farm is the profusion of outbuildings contributing to the agrarian appeal of the site. A pyramidal-roof dairy with board-and-batten siding, a frame weatherboarded smokehouse, and a clipped-gable garage define the rear yard and all date from the early twentieth century. To the rear and east of the house sits an array of agricultural buildings, including tobacco barns, a corncrib, equipment sheds, and a barn with a diminutive bell tower.

Herring-Wood-Hodges House (demolished)
built mid-nineteenth century; remodeled 1912; demolished late 1980s
Kinston vicinity

This antebellum farmhouse, extensively renovated about 1912 in the Colonial Revival style, was located near the present Frigidaire plant west of Kinston. Construction of the original two-story I-house is said to have begun prior to the Civil War, for William Herring (1810-1882) and his wife, Rebecca S. Herring (1814-1881), but not completed until after the conflict. The Herrings are buried in a cemetery adjacent to the site of the house. Following their deaths the farm and house were purchased by Dempsey Wood for himself and wife, Elmira. Eunice Wood (1880-1965), daughter of Dempsey and Elmira, married Robert Guy Hodges (1877-1945), and in 1906 they purchased the homeplace from her parents, who moved to Kinston. The Hodgeses initated a series of changes to the former vernacular Greek Revival-style farmhouse by first raising the low hip roof to a tall gable-end roof and extending the porch to include three sides of the dwelling. The most dramatic change was the addition of a monumental two-story pedimented portico on the front, supported by Doric columns. Graham Hodges (deceased), the youngest son of Robert and Eunice, inherited the house from his mother following her death in 1965.

After the substantial remodeling in 1912 the house constituted one of the most ambitious examples of the Neoclassical Revival style found in the rural areas of the county. In addition to the striking two-story portico, the dwelling had modillioned cornices and a rare surviving early-twentieth-century wood shingle roof.

Will Sutton House
built circa 1870
Falling Creek community

This one-story house is one of the county's best-preserved and most stylish Greek Revival-style cottages. Built circa 1870, it was one of the first houses constructed after the Civil War. Known as the "old Will Sutton" house, this small hip-roof dwelling was moved about a half mile from its original location in 1980 and restored by subsequent owners James and Joy Turnage. The center-hall-plan house is distinguished by bold Greek Revival features, including heavy corner pilasters and flush sheathing beneath the central-bay portico. One of the most finely detailed antebellum porticoes in the county, this example is supported by tapered fluted columns and pilasters. The sophisticated double entry is flanked by a transom and sidelights, which are embellished with a molded and pedimented surround capped by a fluted keystone. Joy Turnage "had fallen in love with the front porch," which exemplifies the Greek Revival style, of the previously deteriorated house and made sure that it was carefully restored. The six-over-six sash windows also exhibit pedimented surrounds. Though modernized, the interior retains such details as an original post-and-lintel mantel with molded shelf, door and window surrounds, paneled window aprons, and four-panel doors.

Dr. James M. Parrott House

built 1920s
Falling Creek community

In the 1920s Dr. James Marion Parrott had a summer cottage constructed at his family's farm, known as the Grove because of the large number of pecan trees. The land is believed to have been in the Parrott family since the original pre-Revolution land grant. The distinctive summer cottage, constructed of stuccoed concrete block, was built on the site of a previous farmstead, which retains the family cemetery and a tenant house.

Architectural detailing of the Craftsman-style house includes rafter tails, exposed brick lintels above the doors and windows, and three second-level dormers. The three-bay double-pile building has a unique floor plan that features an open ceiling in the living room with an open stairway and balcony leading to the second level. An engaged exterior end chimney is exposed on the interior and exterior. There is a small rear ell that houses the kitchen. Porches are located on three facades: a screened rear porch, a screened side porch with two sets of French doors, and an open side porch. Two concrete-block outbuildings, a stuccoed garage and a washhouse, have clipped gables.

Dr. James Marion Parrott (1874-1934) was a prominent individual in the early-twentieth-century history of Lenoir County. Parrott was educated at Kinston College, Wake Forest, Maryland, and Tulane. He began his medical practice in Kinston in 1896 and also took time to study in London (1897-1898). Parrott was a specialist in diseases peculiar to the South and in 1899 was selected by the United States Army to take charge of its First Division Hospital in Havana, Cuba, as a specialist in smallpox and yellow fever, during the Spanish-American War. In 1899 Parrott and his brother, Dr. William Thomas Parrott opened their offices at 109 East Gordon Street in Kinston—where the first typhoid serum was administered in North Carolina. Some of Dr. J. M. Parrott's important positions were president of the North Carolina State Medical Society, member and president of the State Board of Medical Examiners, trustee and president of the State Hospital for the Insane, state health officer (1931-34), and trustee and chairman of the Board of Trustees of Wake Forest College, where he

served for fifteen years.

Along with his brother, Parrott established one of the first hospitals in this section of the state in 1905. The hospital was the former home of James McDaniel and was located on Gordon Street in Kinston. The dwelling was given to the Parrotts for a hospital with the provision that a portion of the space be used for the treatment of the poor.

James Warters House

built 1840s
Falling Creek community

Located in a field near Falling Creek, this two-story dwelling has suffered considerable exterior alteration but remains a good example of a late Federal-style farmhouse. Constructed in the 1840s by James Warters, a fairly prosperous farmer who lived there until at least 1870, the I-house has a hall-and-parlor-plan, with an enclosed winder stair leading to the second level and another leading to the attic. The dwelling originally exhibited a central-bay portico with a second-level door on the front facade. Later the front porch/portico and a rear ell were removed. In the late 1920s the house was turned 180 degrees to face the road, and both original brick exterior end chimneys were removed (one was rebuilt). Beaded rake boards, flush gable ends, corner trim, and a boxed cornice are intact elements. Laura Warters McDaniel, wife of James Alexander McDaniel, was a daughter of James Warters.

The interior retains its original mid-nineteenth-century finish, although the dwelling has been used for storage for many years. Interior elements of the Federal period include window and door surrounds, a molded chair rail, nine-over-nine and nine-over-six sash windows, plaster walls, and rising butt hinges on the doors, once common in Lenoir County dwellings but now mostly replaced, so that very few remain in operation. The mantels have been removed, but one, stored nearby, is a good example of a two-part late Federal-style mantel with molded pilasters and a deeply molded shelf.

House
built first quarter of the twentieth century
Falling Creek vicinity

The picturesque siting and rural character of this two-story Victorian dwelling epitomize the modest Lenoir County farmhouse of the early twentieth century. Surrounded by a grove of shade trees, the largely intact house retains such typical architectural details as fully pedimented gables, six-over-six sash windows, and a central gable—a feature commonly found on houses of the period. Two exterior chimneys—one end and one rear—also help determine the age of the house. Modest interior detailing includes four simple Victorian mantels and a very narrow open stair in the central hall. Surrounding the house are a board-and-batten smokehouse and a tobacco packhouse, both early twentieth century in origin. The original owner of the house is unknown.

Bright Kennedy House
built circa 1850; listed in the National Register of Historic Places
Falling Creek community

Perhaps Lenoir County's most august example of antebellum prosperity was the Bright Kennedy House, which was converted for use as a packhouse about twenty years ago. The handsome two-story double-pile dwelling featured some of the finest Greek Revival and Italianate detailing in the county, though portions have been removed through the years. Jesse Kennedy (1781-1856) is thought to have constructed the house around 1850 for his son, Bright Kennedy (1820-1860s). The house was the seat of an extensive antebellum farm, as reflected by the thirty-eight slaves and eight slave houses that Bright owned in 1860.

The remaining exterior detailing on the large central-hall dwelling is mostly intact and includes Italianate eave brackets and dentilwork, pedimented and molded window surrounds, nine-over-nine sash windows on the first floor, six-over-six sash on the second floor, and four interior end chimneys. An elaborate foundation consists of brick latticework between piers. A historic photograph reveals that the front facade, which faces due east, exhibited a one-story full-width front porch. The double-door entry was flanked by a transom and sidelights and, along with the nine-over-nine sash windows, was embellished with ornate surrounds with hoods.

Most of the interior detailing has been removed, such as the large central-hall stairway (the balustrade was reused on the nearby Will Sutton House), all eight mantels, plasterwork, and the doors. Fortunately the intricate window surrounds, the beaded baseboards, and a secondary staircase that wraps around a built-in china cabinet are intact. The molded window surrounds feature crossettes and paneled aprons, and the front and rear hall windows retain original jib doors underneath the windows. The jib doors, a detail common on coastal houses, opened to improve ventilation and are the only known examples in Lenoir County.

Many twentieth-century agricultural outbuildings remain, as well as two original outbuildings that have been adapted for use as a garage and tenant house (their original uses are unknown).

The Kennedys were one of Lenoir County's largest

and most prominent antebellum landowning families. In 1912 two members of the family gave one of eastern North Carolina's most impressive plantations, Cedar Dell, to the trustees of the North Carolina Baptist orphanage to create the now well-known Kennedy Memorial Home.

James Alexander and Laura McDaniel House (Maxwood)
built 1914–1916
Falling Creek vicinity

Majestically sited at the end of a long tree-lined drive, this is the best preserved Colonial Revival-style dwelling in rural Lenoir County. The two-story house displays highly ornate architectural elements and has been meticulously preserved by the owners. The large double-pile dwelling was built for the McDaniels, who previously resided in Kinston, between 1914 and 1916.

James Alexander McDaniel (1867-1928) was a prominent Kinston businessman around the turn of the century and married Laura Evans Warters, daughter of James Warters of Falling Creek, in 1892. McDaniel developed Trianon, in Kinston, and built a house in the central square of that subdivision. After building a second house nearby, the McDaniels donated their first home to create the first hospital in the city (the now-demolished Robert Bruce McDaniel Hospital opened in 1906), and the grounds around the dwelling were converted to a city park. McDaniel, a merchant, also built an office on Queen Street, which later was converted to the Caswell Hotel, and was a director of Kinston Cotton Mills. He represented Lenoir County in the North Carolina legislature in 1907. The McDaniels' third residence, a handsome farmhouse known as Maxwood, was built on Laura McDaniel's family farm and supposedly designed by Laura herself.

The house follows the traditional center-hall plan and is distinguished by an eclectic blend of revival elements from the Federal, Italianate, and Greek Revival styles. Three gable dormers are adorned with arched six-over-six sash windows and molded surrounds with keystones. Other characteristics of the Colonial Revival style featured on the house include twelve-over-twelve sash windows, an elaborate elliptical fanlight with dentil molding,

and leaded-glass sidelights flanking the slightly recessed front entrance. The spacious dwelling also has a two-story rear ell, a side kitchen, a side porch with playful latticework posts, and a large two-story sunroom/sleeping porch.

Complementing the well-articulated exterior is a finely detailed interior with numerous identifying features, such as the exquisitely detailed foyer featuring a paneled wainscot, square fluted posts, and pilasters supporting a fully developed entablature and a two-run stair. Accurately reproduced Adamesque mantels, a built-in china cabinet with leaded glass, French doors, interior transoms, and bedroom lavatories are other significant original interior details. The original kitchen and bathroom fixtures, chandeliers, and most furnishings are completely intact.

In addition to the main house, a smokehouse and combination washhouse and generator shed survive. The generator machinery for the powerhouse remains intact. The entire ensemble, still owned by the family, has been well maintained and was painstakingly preserved by the late owner, Melissa Herring McDaniel of Wayne County. It constitutes represents one of Lenoir County's finest rural dwellings of the early twentieth century. Her daughter Laura Ellen Walker is the current owner.

Cedar Dell

built circa 1810-1820; remodeled 1880s; listed in the National Register of Historic Places
Falling Creek vicinity

Recognized as one of Lenoir County's most notable antebellum plantation houses, Cedar Dell exemplifies the height of Victorian design in its magnificent remodeled appearance from the 1880s. Originally constructed about 1820 as a two-story brick dwelling with a side-hall plan, much like a typical New Bern town house, Cedar Dell was enlarged into a Victorian mansion in the late nineteenth century.

On the exterior very little evidence of the dwelling's original Federal design remains, with the exception of a finely detailed modillioned cornice supported by a course of dentil molding. The Federal portion of the dwelling includes the three south bays of the five-bay main facade.

These three bays are protected by a well-executed one-story Eastlake-style porch with a low roof topped by a wrought-iron balustrade—a singular treatment in the county. Supporting the porch are chamfered wooden posts on flat-paneled pedestals set in a turned balustrade. Marking the Eastlake-inspired treatment are curved brackets at the top of each post, supporting pairs of rectangular panels pierced with geometric lower outer corners and intricate fascia composed of a pierced band above a row of two-dimensional pendants. The porch and adjacent bay window with like cornice treatments are stellar examples of Victorian exuberance.

A patterned slate roof carries to the sides of three false dormers on the front elevation and one on the rear. The dormers are lavishly ornamented with more Eastlake floral sawnwork set in king posts. Crowning the exterior Victorian remodeling are decorative interior end chimneys with elaborate paneled stacks.

The interior of Cedar Dell presents a center-hall plan two rooms deep. Southern rooms have some surviving Federal features, while those on the north contain excellent Victorian interiors. The main hall, a pleasing combination of both styles, is divided by a transverse hall screen of ornamental latticework, which springs from slender engaged reeded colonnettes. The stair rises from the north side of the hall in two flights to the second floor then continues in two additional flights to the attic. A magnificient massive Victorian square newel post with applied moldings, an incised rosette on each side, and a large turned knob on top anchors the stair on the first floor. The original ramped balustrade with rounded handrail, balusters square in section, and tapered posts continues from the first landing all the way to the attic.

Although all the Federal door surrounds in the two south rooms have been replaced with heavy casings with corner blocks and roundels, the original mantels and sections of the molded chair rail remain. The mantels are fine Adamesque-inspired designs with delicate sunbursts set in central tablets and in each corner block. The Victorian mantels are robust examples with incised scroll and floral motifs. The dining room in the northeast corner is the most elaborately finished room in Cedar Dell, complete with original nineteenth-century wallpaper above a wainscot which features a row of square flat panels containing roundels above a row of vertical rectangular flat panels. The room is dominated by an elaborately worked mantel. Brightly colored tiles in the opening, surrounded by pilasters and a frieze of incised rosettes and topped by a mirrored overmantel sporting spindled shelves for bric-a-brac, make this mantel a tour de force of Eastlake design.

A small but very significant complement of outbuildings and landscape features remains at Cedar Dell and includes some of the county's best-preserved antebellum domestic ancillary structures. Primary among the buildings is a brick kitchen, thought to be contemporary with the Federal-period main house, and the only such outbuilding surviving in the county. The diminutive, nearly square building is austere in its utilitarian appearance, with only a beaded rake board along its eaves to suggest any level of articulation. Like the kitchen, a small restored three-seat privy is located directly behind the house in what would have originally been the rear work yard for slaves and, later, domestic servants. Completing the antebellum outbuildings is a one-story frame gable-end structure with protruding ceiling joists and heavy brace-frame construction, moved from a nearby field closer to the house. This building is thought to have been a slave quarters, and such features as a sleeping loft add credence to its speculative history. A Victorian picket fence with Eastlake-style gates encloses the front lawn—the site of a fountain during its Victorian heyday.

Cedar Dell is said to have been built for Issac Croom Sr. around 1810. The earliest known occupant was Henry Herring, who deeded the house to his son, George W. Herring, in 1845. It is not certain how long before 1845 Henry Herring had owned the house, but the Herring family had lived in Lenoir County since the late eighteenth century. Croom is reported to have moved by the early 1830s to Alabama and is attributed with having Magnolia Grove, a palatial southern mansion, constructed about 1835 in Hale County, Alabama. Thomas Jefferson Kennedy purchased Cedar Dell from George W. Herring on April 28, 1855, and moved his family from a nearby farm, one mile northeast of the Falling Creek Railroad Station, into the house in 1856. His son, William LaFayette Kennedy, bought the house from his father on October 20, 1876.

W. L. Kennedy, who had enlisted in the Confederate army in the spring of 1862 at the age of sixteen, became one of the largest landowners in Lenoir County. He was director of two banks and the owner of Coahoma Mill. It was during his ownership of Cedar Dell that the Federal-style plantation house was transformed into a Victorian mansion. In 1912 Kennedy and his wife, Emily Hardee Kennedy, who had no children, deeded their house and approximately 1,200 acres of rich farmland to the trustees of Thomasville Baptist Orphanage. The deed provided Kennedy and his wife with a life estate in the house and property and prohibited use of the property for any purpose other than as an orphanage, to be called the Kennedy Memorial Home. From 1913 until the 1970s dormitories and other institutional buildings were constructed on the property, and it still functions as an orphanage.

Kennedy Memorial Home

established 1912; buildings erected between 1913 and 1970s
Falling Creek vicinity

Biggs House

Gymnasium

In 1912 Mr. and Mrs. William LaFayette Kennedy donated their home, the antebellum Cedar Dell mansion, which the Kennedys had remodeled and expanded after the Civil War, and 1,200 acres of surrounding land to the Thomasville Baptist Orphanage. They did so in the hope that a comparable orphanage could be established in Lenoir County. The resulting institution, Kennedy Memorial Home, was built between 1913 and 1935 (the primary initial buildings) along the original avenue leading from Secondary Road 1324 to the Cedar Dell mansion. Today the complex is marked by eight historic buildings, several modern structures, and the Cedar Dell mansion. The main entrance to the home has a metal-work arch bearing the name Kennedy Memorial Home. Stately brick dormitory buildings line the avenue leading directly to Cedar Dell, while ancillary buildings, including agricultural and recreational structures, are situated on a secondary path to the west. While the visual focus of the complex remains the antebellum brick mansion, the orderly grid pattern of roads and paths on the property, as well as the orientation and alignment of buildings, makes for a formal appearance, very institutional in design.

Visitors entering the grounds are met first by a comparatively new church building at the entrance. Immediately on the west sits the Biggs House, a brick two-story hipped-roof Neoclassical Revival children's dormitory built in 1914. It was named for its benefactor, Noah Biggs of Scotland Neck, North Carolina. The Biggs House is a physically imposing building, set back a short distance from the avenue and surrounded by trees. The house has a three-bay front facade, an attached hipped-roof front porch with a pedimented entry supported by turned posts over brick piers, and a projecting center pedimented bay. The six-over-six sash windows are segmentally arched, and the three openings in the projecting entrance bay—a transomed and sidelighted double-leaf entrance, a second-story window with a curvilinear cross stile reminiscent of Art Nouveau, and a fanlight window in the pedimented gable—give the house a grand appearance. The four corbeled interior end chimneys and corresponding projecting pedimented bays on each side of the house give a further impression of an estate dwelling rather than of an institutional dormitory.

Brokenhurst Hall, across the avenue from Biggs, is a brick one-and-a-half-story side-gable Craftsman bungalow with a one-story rear ell. Brokenhurst was built probably in the early to middle 1920s. The front and rear elevations each have a large gable dormer with a three-part window with eight-over-one sash. Except for in the later addition off the rear ell and the smaller Craftsman windows, the windows all have eight-over-one sash. Brokenhurst Hall also has a standing-seam metal roof, exposed rafter ends, and triangular knee braces—all typical features of the style.

South of Brokenhurst sits Pollock Hall, a brick two-story dormitory building with an attached hipped-roof bungalow-style porch, a side-gable porte cochere, and a one-story rear ell. Pollock Hall, built between 1920 and 1930, is more characteristic of an institutional dormitory than is Biggs or Brokenhurst, with its exterior quite plain apart from the porch, porte cochere, and hipped-roof dormer ventilator.

Parallel to the Kennedy Home's principal avenue is a service road where more original buildings remain. Near the north end of this road is the 1920s dairy grounds, which now consists of two small pyramidal-roof brick buildings connected by a frame addition. All of the connected dairy buildings are covered by standing-seam metal roofs and have exposed rafters. Across from this network of smaller buildings is a brick one-story front-gable outbuilding with a side shed extension, which may have been part of the dairy complex.

A large frame hipped-roof gymnasium, built around 1930, sits directly south of the dairy complex. A gymnasium was part and parcel of every school complex in the county. Prior to its demolition in the mid-1990s, this one was covered by an original standing-seam metal roof and had exposed rafters, three separate entrances, a small side shed extension, and an interior end brick flue. The building was lit by a series of six-over-six sash windows on each side.

A one-story brick hipped-roof building stands between the site of the old gym and a small frame Craftsman cottage at the end of the service road. The building, which apparently contained either classrooms or workshops, has a brick parapet in its center separating the older part, built between 1920 and 1930 from a section built probably between 1930 and 1940.

The Craftsman cottage located at the end of the service road is a one-story side-gable dwelling that still has its original twelve-over-one and six-over-one sash windows. It also has a small front gable dormer with a ten-light window over an engaged front porch, and an original rusticated concrete-block raised foundation. The porch has replacement wood posts and a plain-rail balustrade. The original frame one-bay pyramidal-roof garage/shed, with its hinged garage doors and two six-over-six sash windows, is still standing.

The Kennedys remained active patrons of the orphanage for the rest of their lives. One of the boys' cottages was named for Mrs. Kennedy's father, Pinkney Hardee, and paid for by Mrs. Kennedy with the diamonds her husband had given her during their marriage. The orphanage, which serves more than one hundred children, constructed other buildings after 1945 for residences and recreation, but nearly all the historic buildings on the campus are still in use.

Henry Loftin Herring Farm
built 1812; remodeled circa 1928
Kinston vicinity

The Henry Loftin Herring house, one of a group of significant coastal cottages in the county, has an 1812-dated chimney brick. The original portion of the house retains Federal-style details, including two exterior end brick chimneys and a high solid brick foundation with common bond—one of only a few such foundations remaining in the county. The chimneys are double shouldered and appear to have different construction dates. The 1812 date brick on the older one presumably gives the dwelling's construction date. Two fine Federal-style mantels survive on the interior. The parlor mantel has an ornate three-part design with all manner of carved embellishment.

Around 1928 the house was extensively remodeled in the Colonial Revival style. Exterior alterations included the addition of three gable dormers on the front facade and a large shed dormer on the rear facade. An elliptical-fanlight-shaped transom and sidelights surround the front door. A new kitchen and dining room ell was constructed to replace the original detached kitchen. Interior renovations included the modification of the original three-room floor plan—a hall-and-parlor type with an extra rear room. The floor plan was altered to a two-room plan by removal of the partition wall that divided the hall into two rooms (evidence of the wall's location appears on the ceiling). Paneled wainscoting was added to the living room and dining room, which are connected by French doors. Underneath the staircase, which is believed to have been rebuilt in 1928, is a built-in cabinet.

The farmstead, which the Herring family has owned for nearly two centuries, is listed as "W. Herring" on the 1863 Koerner Military Survey Field Map. This apparently refers to William Herring. More recent members of the family who resided there include William Isler Herring, Henry Loftin Herring, and Henry Bruton Herring. One of the best examples of a working farm in the county, the two-hundred-acre farmstead retains many outbuildings, including a cannery, a cotton gin, a large barn/mule stable, a tool-woodshed, a smokehouse, a garage, packhouses, tobacco barns, and various other sheds. Two of the outbuildings are rare surviving examples of their types. The cotton gin dates to the late nineteenth century and is one of only a handful documented in the county. The cannery—the only documented cannery in the county—operated on the farmstead in the 1920s. Fruits and vegetables, such as butter beans, were canned there under the Southern Seasoned Products label.

Jerry Sutton House (demolished)
built mid-nineteenth century; demolished circa 1970
Bucklesberry vicinity

Like many of Lenoir County's nineteenth-century plantation houses, this one-and-a-half-story coastal cottage was lost to demolition in the late twentieth century. A historic photograph shows the place around 1898 in a good state of repair, with members of the locally prominent Sutton family in a typical pose in the fenced front yard. The modest dwelling embodied one of the favored house forms of planters and farmers of the mid-nineteenth century, with an engaged front porch, exterior end chimneys, and a trabeated entrance of sidelights and transom. Simple wooden columns and a plain square-in-section balustrade complete the three-bay front facade set beneath a wood-shingle roof. The pattern of fenestration and commodious width of the house suggest a center-hall floor plan. An adjacent building in the background of the photograph is said to have been quarters for house slaves. The slaves reportedly stayed on the farm following the Civil War.

The farm is said to have had, in addition to the dwelling, a cotton gin and cotton press—a horse-powered mechanism used to bind cotton into bales for shipping. The press was made of local heart pine, and all the pieces were crafted by hand, including the twenty-one-foot screw. It was later transformed by Charles Andrew Sutton into an apple press for making cider.

The house was reportedly constructed for Jeremiah (Jerry) Sutton (1834-1900) during the 1850s, when he began to establish a family with his wife, Tabitha Hayes Sutton. The 1860 federal census shows Sutton and Tabitha, both twenty-eight years old, with a family of three boys and two girls. Sutton's mother-in-law, Charlotte Hayes, also lived in the home. The farm and house were inherited by John Clarence Sutton, Jerry's son, in the early twentieth century and remained in the family until the Great Depression of the 1930s, when they were sold to Dick Dawson and Leo Ferrell.

James Wood House
built 1850s; listed in the National Register of Historic Places, 1971
Falling Creek Vicinity

In 1836 James Wood (1815-1875) acquired a plantation from his father in the Falling Creek section of the county west of Kinston. Wood married first Elizabeth (Betsy) Sutton (1829-1849), who bore three children: Jesse, Dempsey, and Hattie Eliza. Sometime prior to mid-century, James started construction on a house for his growing family on the property. Progress on the dwelling proceeded slowly until halted by the outbreak of the Civil War. During the early 1850s James married Lucetta (1840-?) and by 1860 had two children by his second wife: Alamentia and James. By the start of the war the house must have been nearly complete, since the Wood family had been living there for some time. Soon after the war began James reportedly bought a home in Greensboro for a safe haven and relocated the women of the family there. He is said to have left his sons at the plantation to watch over the farm.

During Reconstruction, in a scenario probably fairly common in the economically depressed years after the war, the Wood House was congested, with James, his wife, Lucetta, and their three children living there, in addition to James's sons and their families. The crowded arrangement lasted apparently until 1882, when Dempsey Wood and his wife, Elmira (1845-1916), decided to move from the homeplace and purchase their own farm. They bought the former William Herring plantation, a five-hundred-acre farm about five miles east of Kinston on the old Kinston-to-New Bern road. James had died in 1875, but not until 1892 was his property formally divided between Dempsey and his younger brother, James. In 1905 the house was purchased by A. T. Rouse from James M. Wood (1858-?), the son who apparently inherited the dwelling. During the early twentieth century the house passed through several hands before being purchased by Mr. and Mrs. W. C. Emerson. It is now owned by James and Selma Carlin, who have restored it to its original splendor.

In its restored condition the Wood House constitutes a significant example of the mixture of the Greek Revival style with Italianate features—a common expression during the mid-nineteenth century illustrating the transition from the pure Greek Revival to the more elaborate Victorian eclecticism that became popular just before the Civil War. The two-story house has a low hip roof. The two-story centered hipped-roof porch with trabeated double-leaf entrances at each story and pilastered corners is a quintessential Greek motif. The house is further accented by a bracketed cornice with pendants, and the six-over-six windows with molded peaked arches and paneling—traits more closely associated with Italianate design. The paired exterior common-bond chimneys on either end display, in their comparative slimness, decorative panels, and double flues, an eclecticism reminiscent of earlier Jacobean chimneys. Inside, the center hall's stair features a heavy octagonal newel post joining a slightly curved handrail. Mantelpieces are unusual in their adaptations of older motifs. One plain Greek Revival mantel has a crossette corner panel, while another has tripartite cornices supported by unadorned attenuated pilasters. The walls are plastered, and the flooring is heart pine.

Although the Wood House has lost some of the flavor of an antebellum plantation seat by the absence of a period landscape and outbuildings, the remarkably intact character of the house, enhanced by the restoration, places the dwelling among Lenoir County's architecturally most significant buildings.

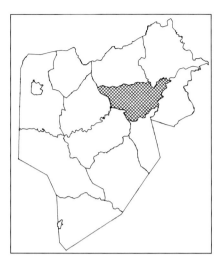

KINSTON
TOWNSHIP

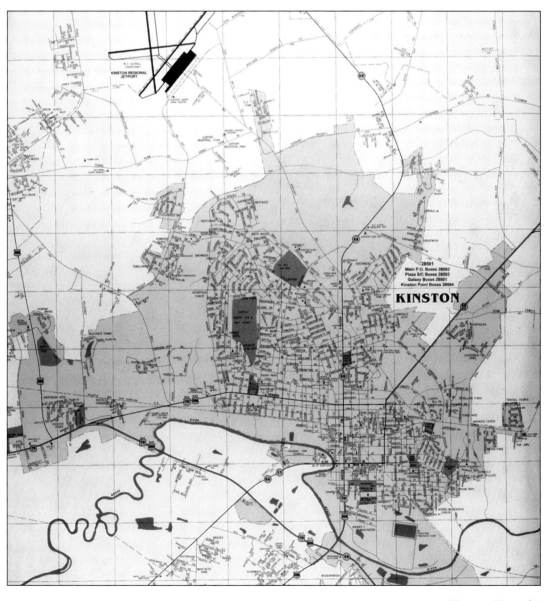

Tull-Worth-Holland Farm

house built circa 1825; (listed in the National Register of Historic Places 1992)
Kinston vicinity

The Tull-Worth-Holland Farm was established about 1825 by Henry Tull, whose plantation became one of the most prosperous in Lenoir County during the antebellum period. Both Henry and his son John greatly expanded their land holdings to cultivate corn and cotton and to produce turpentine and lumber. By 1860 the plantation had 148 slaves living in twenty-five dwellings, now demolished. In 1869 William H. Worth and two investors bought from John Tull 2,053 acres, which included this property, and Worth lived in this house for 19 years. A Quaker, Worth was active in the local Lousin Swamp Agricultural Club, the Grange, and the Farmer's Alliance, becoming its state business agent in 1889 and moving to Raleigh. The farm's most substantial agricultural buildings--the barn, stable and cotton gin--appear to date from Worth's tenure. In 1898 Worth sold 200 acres, including the homeplace, to J. W. C. Hill, the former overseer. Hill bought the property for his daughter Emily Hill Holland and her husband Jesse B. Holland. As they continued to farm the land with the help of tenants, tobacco became the primary crop. The 184-acre farm remains in the ownership of the descendants of J. W. C. Hill

The homeplace is a two-story frame, side-gable building, one-room-deep, with a hall-parlor plan. The house has some original beaded siding, original 9/9 and 9/6 sash windows, and front and rear entrance transoms. The interior retains a substantial amount of original Federal woodwork, including mantels, six-flat-panel doors, wainscots, molded surrounds and an enclosed stair. Other historic buildings on the farm include two late nineteenth century barns, a front-gabled cotton gin built about 1880, a circa 1890 cook's house, a Delco house, a circa 1925 playhouse, two turn-of-the-century tenant houses, and six early twentieth century tobacco barns.

Hill-Phillips House (demolished)

built 1840s; addition built circa 1910; demolished 1996
Kinston vicinity

The early history of this dwelling is not completely known, though it appears likely that Alexander Hill Jr., a farmer and descendant of a prominent family in Lenoir County, had the original one-and-a-half-story transitional Federal/Greek Revival cottage built. Probably dating to the 1840s, the original house was a good example of a small Federal-style farm dwelling with a hall-and-parlor floor plan, two exterior end chimneys, and transitional Greek Revival elements. It was later altered to a center-hall plan with a partition wall. The diminutive house displayed Federal and Greek Revival traits such as a three-part mantel, a chair rail, horizontal flush-sheathed wainscoting, six-over-six sash windows, and a board-and-batten door hung on hand-forged strap hinges. An enclosed winder stair led to the attic, where original shutters survived, with strap hinges and twisted iron hooks. The north chimney had been removed, but the original south chimney remained, encased between the old and newer sections, and was one of the largest chimneys in the county.

About 1910 the house was moved approximately seventy feet from its original site and reoriented in order for the Phillips family, owners of the property at that time, to construct a one-story gable-end addition to the side, converting the original house to a kitchen-dining function. The resulting combination—older house switched to rear kitchen, with newer section added in front—illustrated a common way of enlarging houses in the nineteenth and twentieth centuries.

When the front section was added, the original chimney and facade of the earlier house were preserved. Beaded weatherboarding and a six-foot-wide Flemish-bond chimney with paved shoulders remained as testaments to the original dwelling's character. Although the exterior of the original dwelling was re-sided, the original tapered and beaded rake board survived on the north gable end.

The one-story three-bay front addition echoed the steep roof pitch of the original dwelling and exhibited a center-hall plan, two exterior end brick chimneys, four-over-four window sash, simple mantels, and a small centrally located front gable. A small kitchen room was later added to the original dwelling's rear facade.

William Dove Tenant House
built circa 1930
Kinston vicinity

The weatherboarded William Dove Tenant House stands in the middle of a field just outside Kinston, its only outlying structures a frame outhouse and a clothesline. One of the many shotgun houses built in early-twentieth-century Kinston to house mill workers and tenant farmers alike, the Dove Tenant House, with its engaged gable-front porch and exposed rafters, takes its cue from the Craftsman movement, however humbly. Other characteristic elements of the shotgun house include the narrow elongated four-over-four sash windows and side recessed porch. The narrow form, with one room located behind the other, was also known as a railroad house. Its form, so suited to narrow urban lots, has no advantage in a rural setting such as this one. The house was moved to this site from Thompson Street, behind Sampson School.

Vincent R. Jackson House
built circa 1880-1890

Kinston vicinity

This well-preserved Victorian-era dwelling is a good

example of the type frequently built by middle-class farmers at the close of the nineteenth century and well into the twentieth. It likewise illustrates the application of traditional sawnwork ornament to farmhouses, which became a standard practice for period dwellings throughout the region. Architectural details remaining on this plain gable-and-wing house include four-over-four sash windows, gable end returns, and a handsome hip-roof front porch embellished with turned posts, a balustrade, and sawnwork brackets. A detached rear kitchen—a once common feature associated with period farmhouses but rarely surviving today—has two-over-two sash windows, pedimented gable ends, and an enclosed breezeway. Included with the outbuildings are a transverse barn, packhouse, and outhouse, as well as a rare surviving Art Deco-style fuel pump from the Imperial Company—another feature once standard on farms but rarely seen today. The house was built for Vincent R. Jackson and wife, Louise Stanford Jackson, during the 1880s. The farm and homeplace were inherited by Jesse W. Jackson and remained in the Jackson family until 1978, when they were purchased by James Tull Hill Jr. Today the homesite has been separated on a two-acre tract that is owned by Woodrow Heath.

Ben Faulkner House
built circa 1915

Graingers vicinity

Built for Ben Faulkner, a prominent landowner in the Graingers area, around 1915, this two-story hipped-roof frame house with a side-hall floor plan is an excellent example of the popular American foursquare house frequently constructed during the early twentieth century. Typical details include a hipped-roof dormer, a one-story wraparound front porch with a pedimented gable over the entrance supported by large round Tuscan columns, two-over-two sash windows, and a front door flanked by sidelights and a transom. The American foursquare house originated in the upper Midwest, predominately in Chicago's early-twentieth-century suburbs and in other large midwestern cities. Vernacular examples such as the Faulkner House were constructed widely, mainly because of exposure to the form in pattern books and popular magazines. Most examples were built between 1905 and

Agriculturally, the Faulkner farm is represented by a large number of early- to mid-twentieth-century outbuildings, including several tobacco packhouses, tobacco barns, farm equipment shed, greenhouses, a garage, a smokehouse, a pump house, and a traditional tenant house.

Enzel Sullivan House
built circa 1900
Kinston vicinity

Distinctive architectural features such as two rear ells, double front gables, and a slate roof distinguish this one-story farmhouse. More-traditional details include a transom and sidelights flanking the front entrance, one-over-one sash windows, two exterior rear chimneys, and a hip-roof front dormer. The front porch floor was removed during a recent renovation. The modest Victorian-style dwelling is known as the Enzel Sullivan House and was probably built around the turn of the century. Enzel Sullivan operated a country store on N.C. Highway 58 in 1946. The building used as a barn on the property was the original house, built by Benjamin Sullivan.

Quincy Faulkner House
built circa 1925
Graingers vicinity

Quincy Faulkner, born in 1862, constructed this well-detailed Craftsman bungalow around 1925. This one-

and-a-half-story dwelling displays many elements commonly associated with the style, including four-over-one sash windows, knee braces beneath eaves, shingles in gable ends, scrolled rafter tails, and sidelights flanking the front door. The door and sidelights feature beveled glass. A wraparound front porch and porte cochere are supported by heavy square posts on brick pedestals, and a balustrade surrounds the porch. Outbuildings include stables, a packhouse, and a smokehouse.

Ernest Quincy Faulkner Jr., who continues the family tradition of farming in Lenoir County, currently lives in this house, which he inherited from his aunts Ruth and Helen Faulkner. Both women were lifelong teachers in Lenoir County.

Horace Taylor House
built circa 1930
Kinston vicinity

Located adjacent to Kinston High School is the Horace Taylor House, built around 1930-1932 to replace an earlier dwelling on the farm. Horace Taylor's father, Simon Taylor, owned the farmland around this section of North Queen Street and where Lenoir Memorial Hospital was erected. Horace married Canary Cunningham, and they lived on Academy Heights Road in Kinston prior to building this house. Taylor was a farmer, and he and Canary had two children: Harold C. Taylor (deceased) and Edna T. Blake—one of the first people to be crowned Miss North Carolina. Designed in the Tudor Revival style, the one-and-a-half-story brick house remains virtually intact and displays exceptional elements, including a slate roof, decorative brick patterns and chimney stacks, and six gable dormers with slate facings. The well-preserved dwelling also has features commonly associated with the style: casement windows, a porte cochere, a board-and-batten front door with oversize strap hinges, and copper gutters.

The interior is completely intact and retains the original carpets, kitchen equipment, bathroom fixtures, wallpaper, and drapery hardware. Other interior features include original woodwork, six-panel doors, mantels, built-in ironing board, window and door surrounds, and an unfinished second story. The numerous tobacco-related outbuildings date to construction of an earlier dwelling on the site around 1900. This house was moved across the road. The outbuildings include a large packhouse, a well house, various tobacco barns, and a board-and-batten smokehouse.

Steve Fordham House (demolished)
built early twentieth century
Kinston vicinity

The Steve Fordham House was a good example of an early-twentieth-century traditional two-story single-pile farmhouse, known as an I-House. Square front porch columns with decorative vertical scoring enhanced the otherwise plain hip-roof dwelling. Other architectural details included two-over-two sash windows, two exterior rear chimneys, and a short hip-roof rear ell, as well as an elongated gable-roof rear ell. Associated farm structures included a garage that had been converted to a chicken coop and a well.

William Isler Herring House
built late nineteenth century
Kinston vicinity

This one-story gable-front-and-wing house is the original William Isler Herring House, which was built in the late nineteenth century and moved to the rear of the farm complex in 1938 for use as a tenant house when Thomas Jason Herring built a new residence.

Uncommonly fine architectural detailing defines the handsome dwelling, which features nine-over-nine sash windows, a transom and sidelights flanking both front and rear doors, gable returns, a frieze band, window and door surrounds, and molded corner pilasters. The Victorian nature of the house is evident in the design of the four elaborate mantels. An original detached kitchen was removed and converted to tenant housing.

Thomas Jason Herring's 1938 house is a traditional frame design with dormers and a front porch. An extensive collection of well-preserved outbuildings includes a smokehouse, an open-well shelter, a large packhouse, a garage, a playhouse, farm equipment sheds, a stable, an outhouse, two tenant houses, and various tobacco barns. A rare surviving hewn-log tobacco barn with square notching retains its original brick piers and a wrap-around shed.

Walter Dunn Jr. House (Jericho)
built circa 1820
Kinston vicinity

The Dunn and Loftin families have long been associated with the early history of Lenoir County, tracing ancestry to the colonial era. Walter Dunn Jr. (1788-1850), one of the county's most prosperous antebellum farmers, married Cynthia Loftin (1804-1887) in 1818. On land thought to have been in the Loftin family for years, Dunn built a finely executed Federal-style plantation house known as Jericho. Its name came from the nearby Jericho Branch, a small tributary of the Neuse River. Dunn quickly became a successful planter and by 1820 owned nine slaves; his slave count had risen to thirty by 1840, which ranked him among the largest slave owners in the county.

In addition to operating a prosperous farming enterprise, both Walter Dunn and wife, Cynthia, were active members of the Rountree Christian Church, established in 1827 in neighboring Pitt County. By August of 1828 a group of the Lenoir County members at Rountree began a branch known as Little Sister, about seven miles north of Kinston. The small congregation struggled for several years, ultimately becoming the base for the Gordon Street Christian Church in Kinston.

Walter Dunn Jr. continued to accumulate land and

slaves and by 1850 owned 860 improved and 1,720 unimproved acres, with a cash value of $10,240, supported by thirty-two slaves. That year Dunn owned 7 horses, 2 mules, 15 milk cows, 2 oxen, 13 other cattle, 30 sheep, and 150 swine. His slaves and working animals produced 3,500 bushels of Indian corn, 5 pounds of wool, 700 bushels of peas and beans, 15 bushels of Irish potatoes, 200 bushels of sweet potatoes, 100 pounds of butter, and 2 bales of cotton (400 pounds each). Dunn died in 1850, leaving his plantation in the hands of his wife and children.

After his death Cynthia, who never remarried, operated the farm, and by 1860 she owned eighteen slaves and six slave houses. Cynthia Dunn was an able planter and managed to pilot the farm successfully through the Civil War and Reconstruction. She remained devoted to her church and became a founding member of Gordon Street Christian Church. Her affairs were managed so well that during Reconstruction the Lenoir County Board of Commissioners asked her to become a member of its finance board—a tribute to her business acumen.

The early history of the Dunn House is somewhat shrouded in mystery. It is conceivable that a portion of the house was standing when Walter and Cynthia married in 1818, though no accounts survive to verify or refute that theory. The house stood until the 1920s in the form of two two-and-one-half-story single-pile sections connected at the corners simply by extensions of shed porches that formed, in essence, an open breezeway. The section which survives today was long thought to be the original house, executed in a hall-and-parlor plan with rear shed rooms and probably a full-length shed porch on the front (as evidenced by flush sheathing beneath the porch). Although the house was large, it was fairly typical for a planter of the early nineteenth century. Traditional thinking also suggests that sometime shortly after the main house was erected, probably within ten years, a detached two-and-one-half-story addition of nearly equal size was set on the southeast corner of the dwelling, creating an L-shaped configuration. Historic photographs reveal that this section had a side-hall plan, with an exterior end chimney and an entrance on the east facade. Perhaps one of the most unusual configurations ever constructed in the county, the side-hall portion was moved from the site in the early twentieth century and converted into a separate dwelling at a nearby location. It was subsequently destroyed. Without documentary evidence, including detailed accounts of the stylistic character of the destroyed side-hall section, it remains impossible to say which part of the Dunn House came first. Why the side-hall section was removed from the site is also unknown.

What is known is that the surviving two-and-one-half-story house, probably built for Walter and Cynthia Dunn around 1820, excepting the Victorian additions, remains as one of the county's best examples of the vernacular Federal style. A Victorian renovation added a rear kitchen ell, a wraparound front porch with a gable over the entrance, a front pedimented roof gable, and replacement windows in a two-over-two configuration. To the discriminating eye many of the Federal motifs are apparent, including two well-crafted, double-shoulder, Flemish-bond, exterior end chimneys, molded corner pilasters, molded cornice trim, window surrounds, and flush-sheathed walls on the front facade beneath the porch (now covered by substitute siding).

The original interior woodwork and other elements remain to illustrate the Federal influence that planters embraced during the prosperous era of the early nineteenth century. Mantels on the first floor are fashioned in three-part designs articulated with Federal motifs such as dentil courses and paneled pilasters. A chair rail and flat-paneled wainscoting survive in all rooms on both floors—a testament to the stylish intent of the design, as these elements generally do not carry to the secondary living spaces in similar period houses. Six-panel doors and plastered walls add to the integrity of the original character.

During the Victorian renovation the original hall-and-parlor plan with an enclosed winder stair located in the corner of the hall room was converted to a center-hall plan with an interior partition wall—the only significant alteration to the Federal interiors. The rear shed rooms retain chair rails and flush sheathing in the center section, thought to have been an original recessed porch. The second floor is divided into three rooms, with a partially enclosed corner stair leading to the attic. A well-crafted newel post embellished with carvings and the accompanying balustrade (which continues into the attic) are intact.

Although the house was the seat of an extensive plantation prior to the Civil War and a prosperous farmstead following the conflict, no antebellum or Reconstruction-era outbuildings survive. A tobacco packhouse of early-twentieth-century origin and a small toolshed are the only remaining support buildings.

Benjamin Parker House
built 1910
Kinston vicinity

By the late nineteenth century some African American families were able to amass land and, with lucrative professional occupations and farming enterprises, construct commodious, well-appointed houses in fashionable styles. Benjamin Parker (1877-1955), a successful carpenter, bricklayer, and farmer in the Harveytown section of northeast Kinston, constructed this large two-story double-pile farmhouse in 1910 in a vernacular Italianate style. The cornice, embellished with scrolled brackets, a hallmark of the Italianate style, differentiates this dwelling from the more modest type. The house is crowned by a low hip roof, and two interior chimneys served fireplaces in each of the four principal rooms in the center-hall plan. Other identifying details include sidelights flanking the front door and four-over-four sash windows. A small hipped-roof ell with a side porch and pantry extends from the rear elevation.

In addition to engaging in agriculture and the building trades, Parker was noted for having a molasses mill on his farm, which produced cane syrup.

SANDHILL TOWNSHIP

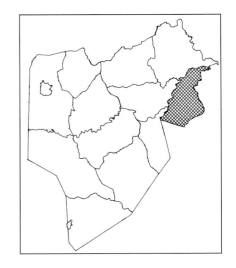

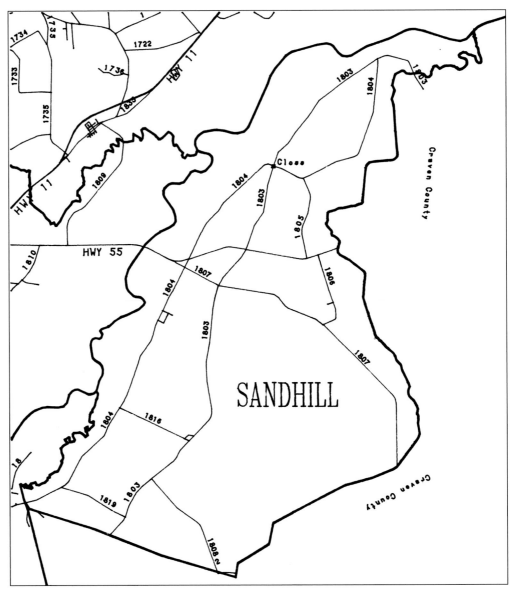

Jeff Alexander Daughety House

built early nineteenth century; moved and remodeled 1920s
Closs Crossroads vicinity

According to local tradition this two-story single-pile house is one of the oldest surviving dwellings in the northeastern section of the county. It is believed to have been built during the early nineteenth century. Although most of its early architectural details have been removed, the tall, narrow proportions, the asymmetrical fenestration on the front facade, and the hall-and-parlor plan are good indicators of the time of origin of the house. Remaining architectural details from the 1920s remodeling include an exterior end brick chimney, a standing-seam metal roof, and roof-mounted lightning rods.

The story surrounding the dwelling asserts that it has been relocated twice, the first time from across the road in "Richardson's Woods" to a location on the banks of the Neuse River. This early move (reportedly prior to the Civil War) occurred because the land where the house originally sat was found to be unsuitable for farming. The second location of the house is just east of the Daughety family cemetery and is shown on a 1902 United States Geological Survey map. Jeff Alexander Daughety inherited the house from Alex Daughety in 1908 and moved the dwelling to its present location in the 1920s. In this move the chimneys were removed, and only one was rebuilt. The rear ell was constructed, and the house was remodeled. The only remaining outbuilding is a smokehouse.

Felix Hill House

built 1914
Closs Crossroads vicinity

Local builder Daniel Daughety built this one-story gable-and-wing dwelling for the Felix Hill family in 1914. This stylish Victorian farmhouse has the original front porch, which wraps around the entire front facade and exhibits its original decorative sawnwork detailing and balustrade, a rare survivor for a house of this date. Many of the original architectural details are intact. They include one-over-one sash windows, a transom over the front door, a chair rail, mantels, and one overmantel with an inset mirror in the parlor. The only surviving outbuilding is a packhouse. The Hill family cemetery is located in a field to the rear of the dwelling.

Closs Crossroads

developed early twentieth century

Closs Crossroads is composed of two early-twentieth-century traditional one-story farmhouses, a country store, and numerous domestic and agriculture-related outbuildings. The circa 1900 dwelling, known as the Kilpatrick House, is an example of a common tri-gable frame dwelling with a rear ell. The modest Victorian-style farmhouse features a stained-glass window in the facade gable and decorative trim attached to the lower side of the gable returns. Known as a pattern board, this trim is an interesting local expression carried over from an earlier era into the postbellum period. This dwelling's outbuildings include a smokehouse, a hog farrowing barn, stables, a cotton gin, and a garage. Local tradition holds that this is the third dwelling constructed on the site, the previous house being a large two-story building.

The other dwelling located at the crossroads is a typical side-gable farmhouse constructed in 1915 by the Daughety family. Lemy Daughety operated a small store at the crossroads, as well as a farming operation. The small front-gable store building rests on a cast-concrete foundation and probably dates from the 1920s. A shed attached to the side of the store building was used as mule stalls. An icehouse used for the store is located on the farm.

The crossroads was named for the Reverend William Closs, a Methodist minister during the turn-of-the-century era. Until the early 1900s there was a post office named Closs located in the William Henry West store.

Sandhill Free Will Baptist Church
built circa 1888
West Crossroads vicinity

In May of 1888 the land for this African American church was purchased from the West family, and construction of the sanctuary followed soon after. The gable-front building exhibits elements of the Gothic Revival style, such as triangular-arched windows. The most distinctive feature of the building is the three facade towers with hipped roofs—typical architectural elements of African American churches. During a 1972 renovation the church was brick veneered, and a side wing was added.

Herman Dunn, a local resident, is the present record keeper and has been the gravedigger for the past sixty years. Dunn also made the cast-concrete vaults that make up most of the cemetery. The lids of the homemade vaults, most of which are painted white, bear names, birth and death dates, and sometimes epitaphs. The well-kept sanctuary and cemetery provide excellent examples of local African American building traditions and are significant in the religious heritage of Lenoir County.

Norman West House
built 1919
West Crossroads vicinity

Norman West built this one-story front-gable bungalow, in a popular farmhouse architectural style of the early twentieth century. The well-preserved dwelling retains many elements indicative of the style, including twelve-over-one sash windows and a large wraparound front porch supported by square wood columns resting on brick posts. The farmstead is surrounded by a host of early-twentieth-century outbuildings, including a smokehouse, a shed, a large barn, a brick pumphouse, tobacco barns, and a unique garage. The frame garage has a flat roof and a parapet, elements uncommon in rural Lenoir County.

Seth West Farm and Store and West Crossroads

house built circa 1876; store built early twentieth century; other structures built late nineteenth and early twentieth centuries

West Crossroads

Located on a high knoll overlooking the surrounding countryside, this two-story farmhouse was constructed by Seth West in 1876. A tradition holds that a family member saw the date inscribed on a framing member in the house. Seth West (1851-1907) was the son of W. H. West and Nancy Moye West of Sandhill Township. In 1874, he married Laura Anna West, the daughter of Jacob and Julia West, also of Sandhill Township. For twenty-two years Seth and Laura West lived on their farm, and Seth began to expand his agricultural interests to include the mercantile and lumber businesses. In 1897 the Wests moved to Dover in neighboring Craven County, where Seth continued in the lumber business and became president of the Dover Lumber Company.

When Seth West moved his family to Dover, he sold his farm and house to his wife's brother George West (1862-1937). A prominent landowner and farmer in the community, George had amassed a farm of over 1,500 acres by the time the *Kinston Free Press* printed its 1906 Industrial Issue. Perhaps his agricultural success was due to the "underlying strata of Marl from three to six feet below the surface" on his entire farm. George's production included corn, cotton, and tobacco. Besides farming, he operated a sawmill and cotton gin, as well as a gener-

al mercantile store. A leader in the community, he served as a member of the board of commissioners, a school committeeman, and a magistrate. He was married to Lottie A. Croom and had a family of ten children by 1906.

In 1907 George and Lottie had their last child, Willie Croom West, who eventually took over the farm from his father and continued in agricultural pursuits. He also maintained the family cotton ginning operation, country store, and sawmill.

The Seth West House is a common type of farm dwelling built throughout the region following the Civil War and Reconstruction, when many farmers began to increase their agricultural output and attain a degree of prosperity. Two stories high and arranged in an L shape, the frame house is sheltered by a low hip roof on the main block and an attached wraparound porch. Interior chimneys provide heat to all principal rooms, and a later shed addition runs the length of the back ell. The only change to the exterior has been the replacement of the porch balustrade and posts with modern wrought-iron supports. The interior retains the original floor plan and numerous mantels, which are rendered in vernacular Victorian style. The original detached kitchen was removed and located on a nearby farm.

This complex exemplifies the large turn-of-the-twentieth-century Lenoir County farmstead and continues to function as a working farm and sawmill. The farm retains a rich variety of tenant complexes and outbuildings located throughout the rural crossroads. Typical outbuildings associated with the main house are a packhouse, a large barn, a toolshed, a number of tobacco barns, and a smokehouse. Also sited at the big house, and not as common, are a cotton gin, sawmill, and store—once standard structures on prosperous farms. The small facing-gable store is quite intact and features gable returns, six-over-six sash windows, and a standing-seam metal roof.

Other members of the West family also built houses at the crossroads. Norman and Jake West both built dwellings there in 1919. The sawmill business continued to grow, and around 1952 Willie West relocated the sawmill a short distance to accommodate the thriving business. The sawmill has been operated by Willie's son, James Neil, since 1965.

Numerous dwellings, used by tenant farmers and sawmill workers, are located at the crossroads. Four of the tenant houses are typical one-story side-gable forms that retain their detached kitchen ells. Four others are of the one-story facing-gable type. The other tenant house is a one-story side-gable type with a unique roof profile that incorporates an engaged rear shed. The floor plan of choice was the two-room hall-and-parlor type.

Bethany United Methodist Church
built 1891
West Crossroads vicinity

Seth West and his wife donated the land for this modest church in the spring of 1891. Construction of the traditional front-gable sanctuary was completed that fall. The original frame building was a good example of a plain country church and featured such typical architectural elements as gable returns, a rear apse, and lancet-arched stained-glass windows. Between 1971 and 1977 a complete renovation of the building was undertaken by the congregation. This remodeling—like renovation at other churches in the county—included a side classroom wing, an entrance vestibule, brick veneer, and a steeple with chimes. The church cemetery surrounds the building on two sides. Seth West, who died in 1907, is buried here beneath a monument carved to resemble a tree trunk.

Rhem House
built early nineteenth century; overbuilt mid-nineteenth century
West Crossroads vicinity

The early history of this antebellum farmhouse is not known, although oral tradition asserts that it was constructed for the Rhem family, a once-active farming clan in the West Crossroads community. It survives as one of the only pre-Civil War houses in the Sandhill Township, where soils apparently were not as productive as in the fertile lands further south and northwest of the Neuse River. The overall appearance of the house today is that of a two-story center-hall-plan double-pile dwelling marked by four exterior end chimneys and a gable roof. Although this form of house was popular throughout the first half of the nineteenth century, it was not frequently built in Lenoir County. County farmers overwhelmingly favored the traditional two-story I-house and coastal cottage forms over the more spacious double-pile ones.

The dominant architectural features present a transitional Federal-to-Greek Revival character, with the exception of some earlier-nineteenth-century motifs, such as beaded ceiling beams in one of the principal downstairs rooms. The ceiling beams, coupled with obvious reorientation of chimney placements as well as differences between the two east-elevation chimneys (they are larger than the west chimneys and have corbelled bases), suggest that the house was originally a smaller dwelling. Possibly it was reoriented to face the adjacent road when the road was rerouted.

The Rhem House retains almost all of its original woodwork, mantels, doors, and windows. In recent years the dwelling has undergone restoration, preserving many original features such as six-over-six sash windows, molded window and door surrounds, and attic windows in the gable ends. Interior treatments are equally intact, with six original vernacular mantels composed of combinations of panels reminiscent of late Federal design, two replacement Neoclassical Revival-style mantels, an open staircase with newel post and balustrade, molded window and door surrounds, and four-panel doors. A mural was painted on the dining room wall that depicts the farm during its prosperous antebellum era.

Although at one time this dwelling was the seat of a large farming operation with numerous outbuildings, only two have survived—a packhouse and a commissary. The commissary is a rare surviving example. Such buildings were frequently constructed on farms throughout the county.

George Noble Farm
built 1946-1948
West Crossroads vicinity

In 1946-1948 George Noble moved his family's original farmhouse and built the present Craftsman-style dwelling on the same site. The original dwelling was a typical one-story side-gable house that had another dwelling connected to form a rear ell. This building now stands abandoned in an adjacent field. The present dwelling is a traditional one-story side-gable building with a front porch and porte cochere supported by post-and-pier columns. Other architectural features include a standing-seam metal roof, a solid brick foundation, a rear ell, and a well/pump on the rear porch.

The architectural significance of the George Noble Farm lies in the outbuildings, which include some of the most unusual and rare domestic and agricultural outbuildings in the northern part of Lenoir County. They include the smokehouse, dairy, stable/packhouses, equipment storage buildings, shower house, baby-chicken house, and tobacco barns. The dairy, on stilts, is one of only a few documented examples remaining in the county. The shower house is actually a 1930s homemade shower that was created with an ingenious use of cold and heated water drained from large second-level buckets. The water was adjusted to a comfortable temperature as a person stood on the cast-concrete floor.

The farm was the base of a large hog operation from the 1940s to the 1960s. Hogs were raised in a large shelter called the hog parlor. Located on the ground inside the parlor are small water spigots that were fed through underground pipes. The hogs could open the water spigots by nudging a trigger. The hog parlor also features a clever scale designed and constructed by George Noble. The farm originally raised tobacco, and two of the tobacco packhouses were adapted for use as hog farrowing houses.

Hickory Grove Church of Christ
built circa 1900
Sandhill vicinity

Constructed near the edge of a field, this church, affiliated with the Disciples of Christ denomination, is typical of churches found throughout the county. The front-gable sanctuary with modest Gothic Revival-style elements was built around the turn of the century and originally exhibited such common features as triangular-arched windows with four-over-four sash and gable returns. Like many of the county's church buildings, this sanctuary was remodeled in the 1970s with an entry vestibule, brick veneer, and a side wing. The steeple with a hip roof and triangular-arched vent is possibly original, as well as the colored-glass panes in the windows.

Jake Parrott Farm
built 1925-1926
West Crossroads vicinity

The one-story gable-front dwelling of Jake Parrott, constructed in the mid-1920s, is typical of dwellings in the area. The modest farmhouse retains many original elements, including three-over-one sash windows, two interior chimneys (flues), an integral front porch, and roof-mounted lightning rods.

A large complex of outbuildings, including two unusual corncribs—the only documented examples in the county—give the farm special significance. Typical out-buildings include a smokehouse, a farm equipment shed, an overflow, a milk house, and stables. The rectangular slatted corncribs were constructed circa 1925 and feature side gables and metal roofs. The most distinctive element of the cribs is the leaning exterior walls, which angle outward. The framing is exposed and covered only with interior slats, which allowed the corn to air-dry. The unique corncribs are supported by terra-cotta foundation piers that have been filled with concrete. The terra-cotta piers on the north crib are smaller in diameter and more intact than these on the south crib. Both cribs have two doors, opening on the south elevations.

The land was originally owned by Seth West but was purchased by the Borden family of Goldsboro before eventually being repurchased by Seth West's grandson, Jake Parrott. In 1925 the Borden family had the house and corn barns constructed but never actually lived on the farm. Local tradition asserts that the first flush toilet and septic tank in Lenoir County were constructed there. The farm was at one time a dairy and sold cream to the Hines Ice Cream Factory in Kinston. It retains many out-buildings used for the dairy operation, such as a milk house and stable for milking cows.

TRENT TOWNSHIP

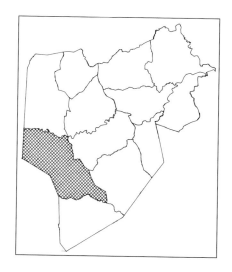

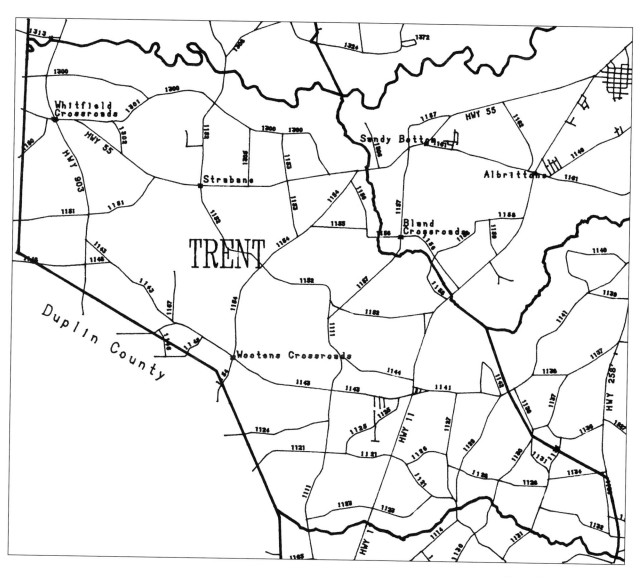

Davis Mill

mill and pond established mid nineteenth century; current buildings built 1947 and after
Strabane vicinity

A local landmark for more than 150 years on the main route from Kinston to Seven Springs in neighboring Wayne County, the Davis Mill continues to produce stone-ground cornmeal. The Lakeside Milling Company has operated the mill since 1981. Issler Davis purchased the land from the Jones family in 1850 and constructed a mill and millpond soon after. The mill buildings constructed at the site have been replaced numerous times, the most recently in 1947, after a 1940 fire destroyed a turn-of-the-twentieth-century mill house. The mill is thought to have served as a principal quartermaster depot for Confederate forces during the Civil War. In the early part of the twentieth century it became a favorite gathering place for the locals, providing recreational opportunities similar to those at Kelly's Mill on the outskirts of Kinston. An abandoned one-story frame bathhouse stands adjacent to the now-drained mill pond.

Remnants of the dam and slough are visible, but the site is most significant as a prominent collection of 1940s and 1950s industrial buildings, including the main mill house and an assemblage of cast-concrete storage silos—the largest examples of their type in the county. The 1947 mill building is an impressive two-story frame structure capped by a monitor roof with clerestory windows. A metal roof and multipaned sash windows articulate the utilitarian design. The building that housed the corn sheller machinery is situated just west of the mill house and is a plain structure clad in metal siding, with a covered pass-through for loading and unloading goods. The date of the sheller building is unknown, but architectural evidence suggests that it dates from earlier in the twentieth century. Constructed largely of cast concrete and concrete block, the other large-scale structure on the site is a six-unit silo and granary probably built during the 1950s when the milling enterprise was thriving. The structure is equipped with an elevator and conveyors—typical devices for storage units of this size.

Lewis P. Jones House

built circa 1920
Strabane vicinity

This handsome farm complex represents successful Lenoir County farms of the early twentieth century. Constructed by Lewis P. Jones circa 1920 as an addition to an antebellum farmhouse that was incorporated into the rear ell, the two-story double-pile dwelling exhibits modest Craftsman-era detailing. The large side-gabled main block features four-over-four sash, a wraparound porch with Craftsman wooden posts, and a gabled front dormer window. The present owner, Ella Ball, has resided in the house since 1950.

(former) Holy Innocents Parish School

built 1903-1904
Strabane vicinity

The only surviving original structure associated with the Holy Innocents Episcopal School at Strabane, this rare school building was constructed in 1903-1904 by the Holy Innocents Episcopal Church under the direction of the Reverend J. H. Griffith. Because it served the only known private, religious affiliated school operating in the county at that time, this building is a rare reminder of the church's influence in education in the county. Other religion-affiliated private schools that operated in the county were Lenoir Collegiate Institute (Methodist, 1850s) and

Tyndall College (Disciples of Christ, circa 1907-1929). In 1906 the Holy Innocents Parish School had around forty students, and Mary S. Winburn was the principal.

Holy Innocents Episcopal Church dates to 1871, when the land was purchased from a Universalist congregation, the parish was organized, and the church was admitted into the Episcopal Diocese of North Carolina. In 1882 a new building replaced the original but outgrown church. The present church replaced the 1882 building in 1957-1958.

Tradition holds that the church was named after an inspiring sermon delivered on a chilly winter Sunday. It concerned the innocence of the children who had braved the harsh weather to attend the service. A mother thought that Holy Innocents would be a most fitting name for the then-unnamed church.

Architectural detailing of the gable-front school building is similar to that on typical Lenoir County public schools, featuring six-over-six sash, flush gable returns, and small corner pilasters. After the school was discontinued, the building was converted to a community center (and later used for storage) and altered to a side-entrance plan. A circa 1906 photograph of the school reveals that the building originally featured a hip-roof front porch with a balustrade and turned columns, operable window shutters, and a multicolor paint scheme reflective of the Victorian era.

Wiley Joel Rouse House (the Sycamores)
built second quarter of the nineteenth century
Strabane Crossroads

Long referred to as the Sycamores because of the once-prominent alley of trees that lined the approach to the house, this one-and-a-half-story frame coastal cottage has been in the Rouse family since its construction in the early to middle nineteenth century. Regarded as one of the best-preserved examples of the form in the county, the house has an integrated front porch, or piazza, that places it in a class of dwellings built frequently in the section of eastern North Carolina between the Neuse and Cape Fear Rivers. Many stories have circulated about the date of construction for the house and place the date range from circa 1791 to later in the nineteenth century. Apparently John Rouse Jr., Wiley Joel's father, was living

on the property as early as the 1780s. Perhaps a portion of the current house was built over an earlier dwelling during the Greek Revival period by Wiley Rouse or his older brother Thomas Rouse, who is said to have received the homeplace through deed. The overall Greek Revival appearance of the house today is usually attributed to Wiley Rouse (1818-1883), who came into possession of the homestead sometime during the second quarter of the nineteenth century. The 1928-1929 *History of the Historic Community of Moss Hill* says that the Rouse House was built in 1825. (The original Rouse family home, built by Lang Rouse, is said to have stood in an "old field back of where Mr. L. P. Jones lives"). This significant nineteenth century house was constructed on land owned by the Rouse family for over two-hundred years.

Dominated by the colonnaded porch, which provided needed ventilation and a place for planters and their families to socialize and keep watch on daily activities on a plantation, the Rouse House is distinguished by a side detached one-room kitchen building, which is connected to the house by an extension of the front porch. This kitchen is an anomaly in Lenoir County as the only example of a period outbuilding with an exposed face common-bond brick chimney. Chimneys of this type were common among houses built in coastal towns such as New Bern but were less often incorporated into inland architecture. The only other example in the county is located on the rear ell of the Cobb-King-Humphrey House at Wyse Fork. Greek Revival style elements on the exterior include corner pilasters with molded capitals and bases, a dentil cornice above the front porch, and a stylized entry with dentils and punchwork set in a crossetted surround. With the possible exception of the Federal-inspired narrow open stair in the center hall, all significant interior treatments are in keeping with the Greek Revival style. The two- and six-panel doors have a variety of faux wood graining, as do portions of the wainscot. This treatment, done in a 1980s restoration of the house, replicates the original painting. The mantelpieces have simple pilaster-and-frieze designs typical of the period.

The modest 1850 production at the Sycamores was substantial compared to other Lenoir County planters. Wiley Rouse, then a thirty-one-year-old husband and father of four, had 75 tilled acres, 75 acres of woodland, and chief products of Indian corn (250 bushels), sweet potatoes (30 bushels), and swine (20). Thirty years later Rouse had expanded his farm to 240 acres of farmland and 168 acres of woodland and also, like many farmers after the Civil War, diversified his crops to include some production of cotton (5 bales), fruit (75 trees yielding 15 bushels), wheat, and additional livestock. Today the renovated house stands as a landmark in southeastern Lenoir County.

Union Baptist Church
built between 1926 and 1953
Strabane vicinity

Though construction on this handsome Neoclassical Revival church at Strabane Crossroads began in 1926, it was not officially completed until 1953. Church services were held in the basement from 1928 until 1951, when the sanctuary was finished, only to catch fire during the Christmas program. Again the congregation met in the basement while the sanctuary was repaired. Finally the present-day building was ready for services in April of 1953.

Architectural details of the restrained Neoclassical Revival design include common-bond brick construction (which is rare in the county), corner quoins, a water table, facade pilasters, arched windows and entrance transom, and a round window on the rear facade that provides light to the baptistry.

The Union Baptist Church traces its organization at Strabane to somewhere between 1800 and 1838. The congregation used the original church building until 1928.

Moss Hill School
built 1917, enlarged in 1950, 1955
Strabane vicinity

Erected in the era of public school consolidation during the early portion of the twentieth century, the Moss Hill School remains as one of the county's best-preserved historic schools still in use. The present two-story brick building was constructed in 1917 following the consolidation of the Moss Hill Academy with the school districts of Sandy Bottom, Blands, Byrds, and Moss Hill. Local leaders, including N. W. Davis, A. W. Rouse, and J. G. Whitfield spearheaded the drive for consolidation, and in 1926 the Moss Hill district was enlarged to encompass New Hope School, which increased the faculty to thirteen teachers. By 1924 the school was recognized as an accredited high school under the guidance of principal E. W. Glass. The facility was enlarged in 1950 with the addition of a two-story brick wing which created six classrooms, an industrial arts shop, a cafeteria, a home economics room, rest rooms, and storage closets. In 1955 a modern gymnasium was added to the campus.

The restrained design of the school reflects the talents of Wilmington architect Leslie Boney, who produced drawings for countless brick schools erected throughout eastern North Carolina during the 1910s, 1920s, and 1930s. Most recognizable on the seven-bay facade are the accent keystones set in soldier-course lintels above the six-over-six sash windows, and diamond motifs applied to the surrounding roof parapet. Protruding from the rear of the corridor-plan school is a one-story auditorium, which remains remarkably unaltered with its original theater seating and Colonial Revival-embellished stage.

In 1964, due to further consolidation of public schools in the county, Moss Hill changed to an elementary school containing grades one through eight. Additional unification of schools in 1967 removed grades seven and eight to Woodington Junior High School, and today Moss Hill offers kindergarten through sixth grade.

Mary Carr Davis House

built circa 1882
Moss Hill vicinity

This frame two-story Victorian farmhouse was built about 1882 for John Samuel Davis' widow, Mary Carr Davis, and her family. Mr. Davis died shortly before the new house was built, and the dwelling eventually passed to son John Carr Davis (1870-1943). John Carr Davis became a major cotton and tobacco farmer in the area, "owning 700 acres of land, with about 140 acres under cultivation" according to the Industrial Issue of the *Kinston Free Press*, and served as a county commissioner at the turn of the twentieth century. The house has remained in the Davis family.

A photograph of the dwelling taken circa 1895 reveals much about the original appearance of the typical Victorian-era farmhouse. The Davis home sported a neatly kept picket fence, which enclosed the front yard and provided an appropriate prop for the family to lean on during the photography session. The original two-story central porch, outfitted with turned posts and spindle balustrade, has the Victorian flavor of the otherwise typical I-house. Wood shingles on the roof and plastered neck bands on the exterior end chimneys complete the design.

Today the dwelling's chimneys remain in place (painted white), but the original shingled roof was replaced in the early twentieth century by standing seam-metal. The original central porch has survived and is still pierced in

the gable by a diamond louvered vent, as shown in the old photograph. However, the original two-tier porch with turned posts and balusters has been changed to a simple full-height portico without the second-story floor.

The small frame building visible in the 1895 photograph was probably the kitchen, which was removed and replaced by an attached one-story rear ell in the twentieth century. The later outbuildings on the property—a detached carport, a frame shed, and a cement-block storage shed—were built in the mid-twentieth century.

DeLeon Augustus Whitfield House

built circa 1900
Moss Hill vicinity

Though badly deteriorated, this two-story Victorian farmhouse was once the seat of a prominent farmstead in the Moss Hill community. The frame, side-gable house with a two-story rear ell is believed to have been built by DeLeon Augustus Whitfield (1870-1944) at the turn of the twentieth century. Until about twenty-five years ago the Whitfield family continued to live in the house. The original central front-gable two-tier porch, supported by turned and chamfered posts, is still standing, though much of the original balustrade is missing. Two common-bond brick chimneys still anchor the gable ends. Interior features such as plastered walls with beaded board wainscoting and simple wooden mantelpieces remain, though like the exterior they are in a state of deterioration. Signifying the once-successful farm are several surviving outbuildings, including stables, a smokehouse, and one of the county's few remaining examples of a stilted dairy, or milk house. The dwelling is only slightly visible from the road, as it sits beneath a thick growth of trees.

Davis-Robinson House

built first quarter of the nineteenth century
Sandy Bottom vicinity

Traditionally referred to as the Davis House, this exceptional example of the southern Tidewater cottage, complete with its sweeping engaged porch and diminutive dormer windows, was reportedly moved several miles from a site nearer the Neuse River. When the house was moved is unknown, but associations with the Davis family extend back to a land grant issued to Windel Davis Sr. in 1782, for a tract on which this house is thought to have been constructed. The dwelling was most likely built by one of Davis's sons, possibly James, or Jim Kit Davis. The field where the house apparently sat originally is still called the Jim Kit field, probably for Davis's son, and reportedly bricks can be found on the site. Family tradition relates that Jim Kit Davis left the house to his son, Egbert Davis, a major in the Confederate army. Egbert Davis married Elizabeth Lawson but had no children so he left the dwelling to his sister Eliza Davis, who married William Robinson, sometime during the late nineteenth century. The property remained in the Robinson family until the 1990s.

In the absence of factual accounts or documents such as land records, the date of construction can not be determined. Because of the overall Federal style of the house, a date of sometime during the late 1810s or 1820s is likely. If the dwelling was moved the considerable distance from its original site as claimed by tradition, then either the chimneys were moved with the house or the relocation occurred very early, since the exterior end chimneys look like original early-nineteenth-century designs (though now covered with stucco). The one-and-a-half-story cottage has several elements that rarely survive on period dwellings, such as the decorated dormer windows enframed by fluted pilasters carrying denticulated pediments, and original louvered shutters across the five-bay facade. Shutter hardware, including hand-forged strap hinges held by pintles and twisted hooks, remains in place, as it has for over 175 years. The porch columns and concrete-block foundation walls are modern replacements.

Although the interior has been altered somewhat from its original appearance with conversion from a hall-and-parlor plan to a center-hall one, striking Federal features remain. Most notable is the well-composed hall mantel with its three-part design supported by fluted pilasters and enlivened with bead-and-reel moldings and dentil courses on the entablature. A low paneled wainscot is also present in the hall as well as the parlor. Original shed rooms off the rear now house a bathroom and a portion of the kitchen/dining area. A small later kitchen ell was added to the rear.

The Davis-Robinson House remains as one of the county's most distinguished early-nineteenth-century coastal cottage-form dwellings and retains some of the most striking Federal-style treatments surviving in Lenoir County.

Leroy Quinn House

built circa 1900
Liddell vicinity

An important example of a style of Victorian era architecture that was rarely constructed in rural Lenoir County, this impressive two-story gable-and-wing-plan house was built by the Quinn family at the turn of the twentieth century. The long-vacant house, featuring a two-tier porch, retains grained baseboards, a molded stair newel post and balustrade, and door panels. Original robust paint schemes are found on the mantels and closet doors as well. The rear ell appears to predate the dwelling and could be an original small mid-nineteenth-century farmhouse that was incorporated into the house. A large ensemble of tobacco-related outbuildings has been retained.

Leroy Quinn occupied this house, which had been built by his father, for many years. In the mid-1990s it still remained in the Quinn family.

Daly's Chapel Free Will Baptist Church
built late nineteenth century
Liddell vicinity

Epitomizing the late-nineteenth-century simple country church forms found throughout North Carolina, this handsome building originally housed the congregation of Daly's Chapel Free Will Baptist Church. It is now used as a fellowship hall for the modern church facility. The building is one of the only unaltered nineteenth-century churches in Lenoir County. The one-story three-bay-by-three-bay building follows a traditional gable-front form with no steeple or belfry that was popular throughout the region. It features four-over-four sash windows and a double entry that are embellished with simple pedimented surrounds. Also of significance are architectural details such as the rear apse and the handsome corner pilasters with molded trim. The only alteration to the church is a small Craftsman-era addition to the north elevation. A large cemetery is located adjacent to the north and east sides.

Nunn-Quinn-Barwick House
built first quarter of the nineteenth century
Liddell vicinity

The early history of this vernacular Federal period frame coastal cottage is unknown. But the house's survival into the late twentieth century with its basic

integrity intact, particularly considering its use primarily as a barn, testifies to its sturdy construction and usefulness. Wright Nunn, a descendant of Swiss Protestants who had immigrated to New Bern in the eighteenth century, is listed in the 1850 United States census as a fifty-year-old farmer, who lived in this house with his wife, Nancy, and their six children. Whether Nunn constructed the house is undocumented, but by midcentury he was apparently the occupant. The house subsequently passed to the Quinn family and then to the Barwick family in 1925.

After being converted to agricultural use, the house suffered some alterations from its original appearance as a one-and-a-half-story coastal cottage with the archetypal engaged front porch, incorporated into a unified roof slope without any breaks. An original or early enclosed end bay on the engaged front porch has been removed, and the original detached kitchen was destroyed. Many original features survive, however—significant elements associated with early-nineteenth-century middling farmers and the dwellings they built. On the exterior, defining elements include beaded weatherboard siding, six-panel doors, and remnants of early hand-wrought hardware. The hall-and-parlor-plan interior is notable for features commonly linked to eighteenth- and early-nineteenth-century house construction, such as a large braced frame, a pegged structural system with half-dovetailed attic collar beams and skinned-pole rafters; a completely sheathed interior, and unfinished exposed hewn ceiling beams and a molded chair rail and baseboards. An original enclosed stair rises to the unfinished half story. Throughout the house period hardware—wrought nails, hand-forged strap hinges on pintles, and a rising butt hinge—remains.

This remarkable survivor ranks as one of the county's earliest dwellings and is in a class of house—that of the middling farmer—that rarely survives with so much physical integrity.

Liddell Cash Supply Store and Crossroads
established early twentieth century
Liddell community

The crossroads community of Liddell was established around 1910 in the extreme southwestern portion of Lenoir County, and named for the Liddell Gin Company, which had recently constructed two cotton gins in the vicinity. The flourishing community included a sawmill and many tobacco as well as cotton farms. In 1923 P. T. Smith constructed Liddell Cash Supply, a well-stocked general merchandise store that supplied the community with groceries, clothing, and farm supplies such as plows, fertilizer, and feed. After Smith's death a few years later, Leon P. Barwick purchased the store and constructed a modest dwelling adjacent, as well as a small fertilizer warehouse.

Liddell Cash Supply is larger than the typical Lenoir County rural crossroads store and retains its original storefront with recessed double entry, as well as all interior shelving, counters, and storage units.

Davis-Fordham-Grady House (Ira Davis House)
built circa 1825
Wootens Crossroads South

The timber frame one-and-a-half-story Federal-style coastal cottage, associated with the Davis, Fordham, and Grady families, has retained many of its original elements. Its first floor and formerly attached kitchen have considerable surviving interior finish. It is one of the few early-nineteenth-century coastal cottages, or piazza houses, left in Lenoir County retaining its original plastered porch ceiling, which still has its original pale blue wash, the popular color for that period.

Both house and kitchen rest on brick piers, and the standing-seam metal roofing that once covered the wooden shingles on both buildings has been removed. The small covered breezeway once linking kitchen to house is no longer standing, and neither is the east side of the house's former double-shoulder brick chimney. But many exterior elements are still in place, from the west end double-shouldered chimney, the boxed cornice, and weatherboard siding to the wooden louvered shutters and hardware such as door hinges and twisted iron shutter hooks. The front porch's flooring and original support posts have been removed, and the nine-over-six and six-over-six sash windows are either partly covered or missing panes.

The interior of the hall-and-parlor-plan house has paneled wainscoting, projecting baseboards, and six-panel doors. It also has a box stair with a plain-rail balustrade and square newel posts. Three Federal-style vernacular mantelpieces remain in the house, the most elaborate being a tripartite mantel with a center frieze tablet and cornice denticulation. Much of the original plasterwork, although in need of restoration, has survived on the first floor. The second floor has some plastering, but the walls and ceiling are mainly covered with tongue-and-groove sheathing. There are indications throughout the first floor of the house, particularly on the door to the box stair, of faux wood graining. Given the sky blue plastered porch ceiling, evidence of painting in the interior, paneled wainscoting, and molded door and window surrounds, it is clear that this farmhouse was built and owned by a family of above-average means.

Downstairs there is a heavy seven-panel door leading to the front porch room. The style of the door—three vertical panels at top and bottom, with a center horizontal panel between—and the wide plain door surround, indicates that this may have been added sometime after the house was built, possibly circa 1840-1850. Dr. Ira Davis and his family were living in this house by 1860. Dr. Davis is listed in 1860s and 1870s business directories as practicing in Kinston, which was the nearest town. According to local and family history, the small porch room was his office.

In an 1884 directory Dr. Davis is listed as practicing in Seven Springs (Wayne County), a longer distance away than Kinston but not an impracticable one. The possibility that the Davis family continued to reside in the coastal cottage becomes more remote by 1896, when Dr. Davis is listed as practicing in the northern Duplin County community of Serecta. Sometime between 1877 and the early 1890s the house passed from Ira Davis to Claude Fordham, the descendant of Fordhams who had settled in Craven and Jones Counties. Claude Fordham's father, Christopher (1824-1900), had attended the nearby antebellum Woodington Universalist Church. Claude Fordham presumably was in the area by the 1870s and may have moved into the Davis house as early as the 1880s. An iron gas fixture on the second floor, circa 1890, indicates that the Fordhams lit their house not just with candles or portable lamps.

Jim Grady bought the house in 1926 from the Fordham family. The house and kitchen were wired for electricity at about that time. In the earliest phase of lighting, gas carbonic lighting was used. In 1955 the Gradys moved to a new brick ranch house a short distance south. The old coastal cottage and kitchen have been used as storage ever since.

The kitchen, a frame one-story, three-bay side-gable structure, projects slightly forward of the house, an arrangement seen with other early-nineteenth-century farmhouses in the area, one example being the Wiley Joel Rouse House at Strabane Crossroads. Inside the kitchen the plasterwork, paneled doors, and wainscoting have finish comparable to that of the main house. The dining room is the first room off the breezeway, and the six-paneled entry door has a carpenter lock. The other two doors are also paneled, and nearly all of the windows have nine-over-six sash.

The two surviving outbuildings on the property are a frame tobacco barn and a large three-bay transverse barn, which were built at the turn of the twentieth century. The large barn, two stories high with two flanking shed extensions, was utilized as stables and storage. There are a frame outhouse behind the coastal cottage and, nearby, the sites of a frame smokehouse and buggy house. Nearly all the original vegetation around the farmhouse has been lost, except for a mature pecan tree by the west side of the house and a large pear tree between the outhouse and the smokehouse site.

Davis House
built early nineteenth century; moved 1920s
Wootens Crossroads vicinity

Moved in the 1920s to this site from the former Davis plantation, this is a significant but substantially altered one-and-a-half-story hall-and-parlor-plan building. The diminutively scaled structure, which appears to have been built as a dwelling, is a rare surviving example of a small antebellum Lenoir County farmhouse. Such architectural features as huge hewn sills, exposed ceiling beams, and board-and-batten doors with strap hinges indicate an early-nineteenth-century construction date. Unique qualities of the small dwelling are an asymmetrical facade and beaded flush sheathing that features feathered construction inside. The house has been used as a tenant house as well as a tobacco packhouse since its relocation.

Horace Barwick House
built late nineteenth century
Deep Run vicinity

The frame one-story side-gable house owned by Horace Barwick is a remarkably intact example of a post-Civil War Lenoir County farmhouse. It has an altered attached shed-roof porch sheltering a paired entrance flanked on each side by a twin four-over-four sash window. Paired front entrances, once a common feature of nineteenth-century houses in Lenoir County and other parts of eastern North Carolina, were often altered to a single entry in the twentieth century. The kitchen/dining ell is attached to the east side of the house instead of at the back, where there is a later extension.

A frame smokehouse just beyond the kitchen wing may be the only surviving original farm outbuilding; two early-twentieth-century outbuildings are a washhouse, and a packhouse across the road that was built in 1934.

Stroud-Chambers Log House (demolished)
built early to middle nineteenth century; demolished circa 1980
Wootens Crossroads vicinity

This small one-room hewn-plank house was representative of a type of construction that appeared as early as the eighteenth century in coastal North Carolina and persisted well into the mid-nineteenth century. Several examples were documented in Lenoir County during architectural surveys conducted in the 1970s, though only a few have survived. Displaying full-dovetail notching and thin planks, this building type was more common among middling farmers of the nineteenth century and often represented initial housing for homesteaders. This particular example, locally referred to as the Stroud-Chambers Log House, was notable for exceptionally fine corner timbering and a fully sheathed interior with board-and-batten doors. It is believed the dwelling was once heated by a mud-and-stick chimney and that the window openings originally had no sash but were simply covered by hinged battens.

Davis-Wooten House
built circa 1830
Wootens Crossroads vicinity

Referred to locally as the Betty Wooten House, so named for the daughter of the original owner (though census records give her name as Betsey), the two-and-one-half-story Federal-style plantation dwelling was built for John Davis, local planter and sheriff of Lenoir County. The house was likely built in the 1830s, as John Davis had already married Malissa Taylor and established a family of five by the time of the 1830 census. Davis was apparently quite prosperous, as evidenced by the twenty-six male and twenty-nine female slaves he owned in 1840. This would rank Davis as one of the leading slave owners in Lenoir County during the antebellum period, a planter certainly able to construct such a well-appointed and stylish dwelling.

The house was moved a short distance from an adjacent crossroads around 1975 and has undergone renovations over the last two decades. In its original form the two-and-one-half-story, five-bay dwelling sported one of the county's finest Federal designs, surviving more than 150 years with masterful woodwork and decorative painted surfaces. Attenuated proportions and slender brick end chimneys with steeply sloped shoulders marked the dwelling's original Federal style. On the exterior dentil cornices run the length of the front facade and side gables—treatments generally used only by prosperous and stylistically astute planters. A one-story side shed addition and a rear kitchen-dining ell complete the exterior appearance. Interior treatments include, in addition to the fancifully painted six-panel doors and paneled wainscot, some of the county's most intricately carved Federal mantels, composed of geometric shapes, sunbursts, reeded pilasters, and shelves supported by dentils and guilloche fret work.

During the modern renovations a replacement two-story porch and replacement brick exterior end chimneys were added. All of the original woodwork remains, but new paint schemes have been applied. The overall form and Federal style remain evident at the Davis-Wooten House, and the dwelling retains its place of significance as possessor of one of the county's most striking Federal-era interiors.

House
built first quarter of the twentieth century
Deep Run vicinity

The shotgun house, found throughout Lenoir County, became the tenant dwelling of choice in rural and small-town southern states during the late nineteenth and early twentieth centuries. This example, across the road from Deep Run Free Will Baptist Church, is one of the county's more intact versions and displays the traits commonly employed in the standard shotgun design. The modest gable-front dwelling has the typical linear plan, diminutive hip-roof front porch supported by chamfered posts, and interior chimney flue. Uncommon details are the sidelights flanking the front entrance and the stylish vertical four-over-four sash windows—a window type often seen in more ambitious bungalows of the period. The floor plan of the dwelling has not been altered, and the house retains the original recessed rear porch.

Deep Run Community
developed 1880s to 1950s

Deep Run was incorporated as a town in the mid-1930s, but its roots go as far back as 1884, when it was listed in *Branson's Business Directory* as having a post office. In 1884 farmers in this community were S. H. Davenport, Noah Hill and J. L. Stroud; by the 1890s Deep Run had a population of twenty people, a resident minister, and a general store operated by I. D. Sparrow. Dr. Henry Tull (1855-19?), who was instrumental in establishing Kinston's Orion Mills, had a cotton gin in Deep Run in 1910.

The town, still rural, has an assortment of late Victorian vernacular frame cottages, the former Deep Run School (built in the 1920s), and two small early-twentieth-century stores—a cement-block one-story commercial building with display bay windows, and a small three-bay frame structure with a double-leaf entrance and an attached hipped-roof canopy with exposed rafters.

Davenport-Heath House
built circa 1923-1924
Deep Run community

The Davenport-Heath House is a good, and very well preserved, example of a two-story American foursquare with Craftsman-style elements, a form rarely seen so intact in rural Lenoir County. John Davenport is said to have built this house in the early 1920s. It is possibly a mail order house from Sears, Roebuck and Company or Aladdin Homes. The house has retained its original pressed-tin roof and detailing, such as exposed rafters, paired porch posts, six-over-one sash windows, plastered walls, bathroom fixtures, and French doors. The entry vestibule is not original to the house, but the three mantelpieces with decorative enclosed copper fireboxes are.

House
built last quarter of the nineteenth century
Deep Run community

Illustrating the pervasiveness of certain traditional house forms is this modest one-story frame coastal cottage located across from Deep Run High School in the Deep Run community. This weatherboarded hall-and-parlor-plan house remains as one of the county's best examples of a coastal cottage built after the Civil War, when the form rapidly gave way to nationally popular forms such as rambling Victorian designs and early-twentieth-century bungalows. The house has a two-bay side extension incorporated by the engaged porch across the front facade. The attached rear kitchen ell has German siding, a popular early-twentieth-century molded weatherboard, and four-over-four sash windows; the rest of the house has six-over-six sash. A smokehouse and shed, both built after the house, attest to the property's original function as a working rural farmstead.

Copeland-Humphrey House
built circa 1825-1845
Deep Run vicinity

A large willow tree and a long dirt lane provide this attenuated one-and-a-half-story early-nineteenth-century coastal cottage with a picturesque quality. The hall-and-parlor-plan vernacular frame house faces south on a farm path just off a public road, rather than facing the road directly, suggesting that the house predates the road. Behind the dwelling sits a one-story early-twentieth-century rear kitchen ell connected by a now-enclosed breezeway. The early history of this important house is not known, although it is known locally as the Copeland House. A Humphrey family purchased the farm in the 1960s, and it remains in that family today.

One of several early-nineteenth-century coastal cottages remaining in the county, this house is distinguished by a steeply pitched roof, original chamfered porch posts, flush beaded horizontal weatherboard sheathing beneath the porch, and indications that there was once a balustrade. Two exterior end chimneys remain, one a single-shoulder stuccoed brick chimney, the other a double-shoulder common-bond brick chimney. Three mantels in the house have been removed, but the original vertically sheathed partition wall survives. The house is a common type of farm dwelling built frequently in Lenoir County in the early to middle nineteeenth century, but few examples survive today.

Johnny Hill House
built circa 1918
Deep Run vicinity

The Johnny Hill House (named for Johnny Emanuel Hill, the original owner) is a good example of a modest Victorian-style farmhouse. The one-story frame gable-and-wing dwelling has retained its architectural integrity. Decorative exterior features include Queen Anne gable windows, pedimented gables, paneled shutters, and an attached hipped-roof front porch with turned columns, a turned frieze, and turned balustrade.

The farm outbuildings, all thought to have been built at about the same time as the house, include a potato house, a washhouse, a smokehouse, stables, and a carbide house.

The site's original farmhouse, a small one-story frame side-gable dwelling in the field behind the farmhouse complex, is thought to have been built by Johnny Hill in the 1880s.

Davenport-Noble House and Store
built 1870s
Pink Hill vicinity

This small farmstead was a thriving middling enterprise from the era of Reconstruction through the mid-twentieth century. Grouped around a vernacular one-and-a-half-story frame coastal cottage built probably during the 1870s, the farmstead began to prosper following the Civil War and had a country store and numerous outbuildings by the twentieth century. The house and store are said to have been built by Stephen H. Davenport (1849-1919). Davenport married Cora Waller (1860-1909) in 1881, and it may have been as late as the early 1880s that the house was constructed. Stephen Davenport was a farmer, teacher, and local magistrate in the community of old Pink Hill. He and his wife are buried in the Davenport Cemetery on the farm. The Davenports' daughter, Denny (1883-1965), married John Thaddeus Noble in 1900 and they are said to have lived in the house, in which Denny was born and reared, during a portion of the early twentieth century. In 1914 the Nobles moved to a farm in the Southwood community and remained there the rest of their lives. They are buried in the Davenport Cemetery.

The house built for Stephen Davenport falls within a class of buildings constructed in the era following the Civil War, when architectural trends reflected a continuation of practices established in the antebellum period. One and a half stories in height with an engaged front porch and rear shed rooms, the house remains remarkably intact and illustrates building trends in the economically-depressed times after Reconstruction. Like its antebellum predecessors, the vernacular dwelling is distinguished by Greek Revival elements such as board-and-batten ceilings and chamfered posts on the porch, and overly modest post-and-lintel mantels and low paneled wainscoting on the interior. A rear detached kitchen building, connected to the house by an open breezeway, displays one of the county's best-preserved examples of this arrangement, used in the nineteenth century on both both large and modest dwellings.

Domestic and agricultural outbuildings, all of them from the late nineteenth or early twentieth century, include a log feed crib, a frame smokehouse, and an implement shed. A small country store, with its original paneled window shutters and four-panel front door, is situated on the road in front of the house and helps to complete this yeoman farmstead. Stephen Davenport reportedly operated the store on an "as-needed basis," opening it upon request. His granddaughter, Edith, recalled there was never any source of heat in the store. When asked how the family attended to customers in the winter, she replied, "we waited on them in a hurry." The store closed early in the twentieth century. In 1996 it was relocated to a site on N. C. Highway 11 at the edge of the Wilbur A. Tyndall Museum complex in Pink Hill. The restored building now houses an inventory of old store items.

House
built last quarter of the nineteenth century
Pink Hill vicinity

This long-unoccupied farmhouse, a one-story coastal cottage with a rear shed extension and detached frame kitchen, now stands behind a complex of modern bulk tobacco barns facing a dirt road. The original section and core of this house is a one-room log building with square corner notching and two board-and-batten doors. Since log construction was used prior to the Civil War and most certainly persisted afterward, it is conceivable that this one-room house was built in the late nineteenth century; other features, such as small four-over-four sash windows and beaded tongue-and-groove sheathing, are postwar elements. The exterior end chimneys have been removed. A small frame shed extension and a frame kitchen, connected to the east side of the house by a breezeway, were likely added in the early twentieth century. Under the standing-seam metal now covering the double-engaged roof are wooden shingles. Interior finish could best be described as vernacular. The simple wooden mantel with a console shelf may be a replacement, and the interior flush pine sheathing on the walls appears to have been applied after the Second World War. Regardless of its exact age and plain style, the house is a significant example of how long log construction persisted in rural areas of eastern North Carolina.

Tillman House
built first quarter of the nineteenth century
Jonestown vicinity

Little is known about the early history and ownership of this very significant hall-and-parlor-plan one-story house. Traditionally it has been associated with the Tillman family, though that family's connection to the earliest ownership is tenuous. Judging solely from architectural evidence, the dwelling appears to be one of a class of vernacular houses that often served as initial housing for homesteaders. Such features as handwrought nails, wide flush sheathing, and beaded siding, in addition to exposed ceiling beams on the interior, all point to a construction date no later than the 1810s. An accessible loft made for added sleeping space. A rear addition and common-bond brick chimney appear to be late-nineteenth century in origin and suggest the dwelling might have been moved to its current location at that time. Constructed in a era of the county's history from which few buildings remain, this diminutive house is extremely important in telling the story of yeoman farmers of the late eighteenth and early nineteenth centuries.

(former) Tyndall School
built between 1890 and 1915
Jonestown vicinity

In 1925, during the movement to consolidate many of the one- and two-room schoolhouses throughout the county into larger brick facilities, the Tyndall School was closed along with Piney Grove, Smith, Oak Grove, Trent, and Wooten, to form Deep Run School. The Tyndall School, a frame two-room building with a cross wing, like many schools of the period, was built with economy and utility as guiding design principles. Simple weatherboarding and multilight sash windows were standard elements. The cross wing on the rear allowed the school to be divided into sections, providing opportunity for a graded school to be conducted in the building. Very few school buildings from this era survive intact in Lenoir County making the Tyndall School a representative of a vanishing resource. The school was restored in 1996 principally by the Rex Noble family and is located on their farm.

NEUSE TOWNSHIP

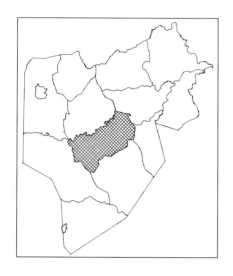

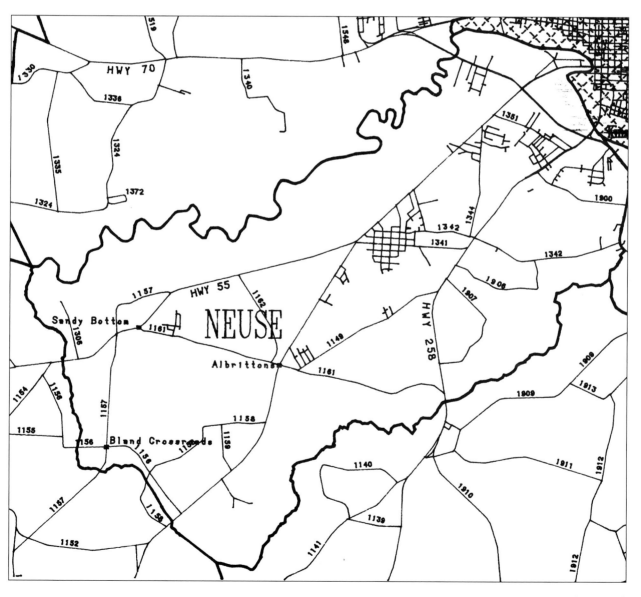

Alonzo Daughety House

built late nineteenth or early twentieth century
Rivermont vicinity

At the center of this small agricultural complex sits a modest turn-of-the-twentieth-century farmhouse associated with Alonzo Daughety, an African American farmer. Daughety and his family, including daughter Fannie (the current owner), lived in the house in the 1920s. The farmhouse is an excellent example of a story-and-a-jump form with a hall-parlor plan and side-gable roof. The frame dwelling has a three-bay front facade on the ground floor and two fixed-sash windows above. Raised high on brick piers, the house has one brick end chimney remaining, on the windowless side elevation, and a small, one-story ell projecting from the rear. In a very typical arrangement, the rear ell has a full-length porch, one bay of which is enclosed for a pantry. Attesting to the agricultural pursuits of the early owner are two outbuildings at the front of the house, a mule stable and a two-level packhouse with a side shed. Both buildings are marked by steep gable roofs and frame construction. They line the original farm path that terminated at the house, which rests on a rise in the surrounding fields.

Jesse Jackson House

built 1840s; listed in the National Register of Historic Places 1971
Jackson's Crossroads vicinity

On the bluffs of the Neuse River a short distance upstream from Kinston sits the Jesse Jackson House, one of the county's finest antebellum plantation dwellings, and one that preserves its historic connection to the river. According to family tradition, it was Jesse Jackson II (1817-1882), a planter reared on the banks of the Neuse in a nearby home, who purchased this house from neighbor Henry Jones about 1850. After the death of his first wife, Emma Davis Jackson (1820-1849), Jesse Jackson had sold his Lenoir County holdings and moved to Mississippi for a time. He returned to his native county within a year and purchased the Jones plantation, which included the house and approximately 1,000 acres, a typical size for a prosperous plantation in the 1850s.

Jesse Jackson II married a second time, the widow of William Howard Whitfield, Elizabeth Croom Whitfield. Jackson was an educated planter having attended Wake Forest College as a charter student. In addition to engaging in agricultural pursuits, he represented Lenoir County in the General Assembly during the 1845-1846 and 1847-1848 terms. Active in his community, Jackson was a founding member of the First Baptist Church in Kinston and a stalwart member of the local Masonic lodge. One of Jesse and Elizabeth's children, Jesse Jackson III (1854-1911), also attained prominence in the county. He married Eliza Ann Parrott in 1880, owned property in Kinston, and held stock in banks and railroads. He served two terms as Lenoir County treasurer. Both he and his wife are buried in the family cemetery located near the homeplace. Several generations of Jacksons owned the house and property in the twentieth century. Currently the property is owned by a direct descendent of Jesse Jackson II, Catherine Casteen Stewart, and her husband, Jim.

Since no documentary records exist for the property prior to the Jackson family ownership, it is hard to determine the date of construction. Presumably Henry Jones had the house built, probably in the 1840s based on the architectural evidence. The contemporary approach to the house is from a drive shaded by century-old walnut and elm trees flanked by mature pecans, though the original front elevation was approached from the river side. A millpond is situated to one side of the highway approach, adding a serene quality to the setting.

A historic photograph of the Jackson House aids in describing the two-story frame house of uncommonly well-appointed Greek Revival design. Remaining true to its historic appearance, the five-bay front facade facing the river is dominated by a well-preserved single-story portico of Grecian style—one of the few original porticoes surviving in the region. A transom and sidelights embellish the main entrance on the first floor, while only sidelights adorn the upper door. Dominating the rear elevation is a single-story shed porch with an enclosed end bay on the south and a square balustrade between square posts. Late in the nineteenth century the porch was connected to a single-story kitchen building further to the south. Completing the exterior are two gable end chimneys, the north one laid in a Flemish-bond coursing with concave weatherings—either an unusually late example of the technique or an indication that the dwelling was constructed earlier and later overbuilt. The south chimney is laid in a random common bond matching the perimeter foundation. A small enclosed cellar, entered through a bulkhead off the south gable end, provides evidence that the basement space was once used for domestic purposes.

Interior appointments in the center-hall-plan house reflect the conservative tastes common to the planter class in eastern North Carolina prior to the Civil War. Restrained elements of Greek Revival pattern book designs, like those fostered by architect Asher Benjamin (he published *Practical House Carpenter* in 1830) and his contemporaries, abound throughout the house. Principal among the pattern book-inspired features are the front door casing with a paneled cornice and paneled aprons beneath the sidelights, and a host of mantels all with similar Greek designs. The parlor mantel, for example, is composed of a pair of square pilasters supporting an entablature with two paneled end blocks and a horizontal fret below a simple molded cornice shelf—a typical, though robust design of the antebellum period. Complementing the overall Greek Revival style of interior treatments is the plain but masterfully-executed center-hall stair with square-in-section balusters and a molded handrail, which rises in two flights to the second floor and then in two additional flights to the attic. Heavily molded window surrounds with paneled aprons embellish the primary rooms on the first floor.

Since its acquisition by Jesse Jackson II, the house and varying amounts of the original 1,000 acres have remained in the Jackson family. The acreage has always stretched from the bluffs upon which the house sits all the way to the Neuse River, where the antebellum landing remains evident—a connection that allowed the Jackson plantation the access to markets and transportation routes necessary to sustain the farm and operate it profitably. Most of the farm's outbuildings date from the twentieth century, including several frame barns and equipment sheds. A holly tree behind the kitchen ell is said to have been planted in 1880. It, like the family cemetery enclosed by a wrought-iron fence, further connects the land to the people who have cherished the farm and house for nearly 150 years.

Hunter House
built mid-nineteenth century
Southwood vicinity

As with many dwellings that passed through numerous owners over the years and became rental housing generations ago, little is known about this important mid-nineteenth-century log dwelling covered in weatherboard. During the twentieth century it has been associated mostly with the Hunter family, who apparently moved it a short distance from its original location facing N. C. Highway 58 so that it now faces a secondary road. Allegedly, the dwelling once served as a school. The vernacular, one-and-a-half-story hall-parlor-plan log house falls into a class of buildings built by modest landowners throughout the nineteenth century because of their simple construction and use of readily available materials. The act of clearing land for agriculture produced logs ready for use in constructing homes. This example has a partly enclosed engaged front shed porch, supported by wood posts, and a rear shed addition, all under a single side-gable roof, the predominant roof configuration for houses in the area during the nineteenth century. The east gable roof was slightly cantilevered to protect what is thought to have been the dwelling's original mud-and-stick chimney, since replaced by a brick flue. The original enclosed stair, which branches off at the foot to the enclosed front shed room; beaded sheathing; and simple Greek Revival-style mantel have survived and suggest a mid-nineteenth-century construction date.

Webb Chapel United Methodist Church
built early twentieth century
Sandy Bottom vicinity

Webb Chapel United Methodist Church, an early-twentieth-century front-gable meeting house, has a cruciform plan that has been altered by later rear additions. The building was constructed of frame and likely covered with weatherboards, though it has been covered with yellow brick veneer in recent years. The church interior is lit by lancet-shaped stained-glass windows. Other buildings on the property are a modern administrative building and an open front-gable picnic shed. The shed has, at the other gable end, a chimney and grilling hearth, and there are two barbecue pits nearby. This type of recreational facility became a popular feature of early to mid-twentieth-century rural churches, as churches in comparatively isolated areas served as their communities' social hub. Today such sheds are seen less frequently.

Sandy Bottom Baptist Church
built late nineteenth or early twentieth century; enlarged 1950s and 1960s
Sandy Bottom vicinity

The Sandy Bottom Baptist Church was founded by local families in this rural community. The front-gable church with an enclosed projecting narthex follows a simple Victorian design popular in rural communities

throughout the South after the Civil War and well into the twentieth century. The sanctuary has three lancet-shaped windows along each side elevation, and one on each side of the narthex. Other than the small steeple (a mid-twentieth-century addition) and diamond louvered vent at the front, the building is very plain. Two additions to the rear, probably built in the 1950s or 1960s, enlarged the church facility for Sunday school rooms and a fellowship hall. Located adjacent to the church is a pyramidal structure with a barbecue pit, used during covered-dish suppers and church reunions.

Croom Meeting House
built first half of the nineteenth century
Sandy Bottom vicinity

The Croom Meeting House, which served as the home of the Sandy Bottom Primitive Baptist Meeting, has several associated stories about its early history. These concern its being moved at least twice and accepting slaves into the fold. Perplexity about its date of construction remains. Congregational records confirm that the meeting was established in 1803 by Lott Croom (1761-1830) as a division of a local congregation, and that by 1873 it was fully aligned with a Primitive Baptist association. The records also indicate that the newly formed congregation began meeting in the Brother Croom Meeting House, which suggests either that services took place in one of the Croom family homes or that a meeting house already existed by the date of the meeting's formal establishment.

Records indicate that, early in the history of the congregation, slaves were permitted to join, provided the church and the slaves' owners granted permission. A slave by the name of Benjamin was accepted into the church in 1807, and at least one other reference to the acceptance of slaves can be found in church documents. Slaves generally were allowed to attend worship with their owners and permitted to sit in pews located behind the pulpit, which stood in the center of the church.

Through the church's history, meetings were held either quarterly or yearly, depending upon the size of the congregation and other circumstances. By 1930 the dwindling membership changed the meetings to yearly events. Mary Moore Croom, the last surviving local member of the Sandy Bottom Primitive Baptist Church, died in 1950, bringing an end to the congregation as it had existed for nearly 150 years. Services took place occasionally between 1950 and 1954, when the last service was held in the meeting house. By the early 1960s the Croom family had assumed possession of the meeting house from the Primitive Baptist association, for annual family reunions.

The Croom Meeting House is recognized as the oldest remaining church building in Lenoir County, and one of the best-preserved pre-Civil War meeting houses in eastern North Carolina. Although its date of construction remains a mystery, oral traditions suggest that the church was moved about 1850 from its original site approximately one mile east on the north side of N. C Highway 55. The building was moved a second time in the 1970s when the Department of Transportation widened the highway, though it was moved only away from the road and not to a different location. The stark, undecorated one-story frame building represents the typical unadorned meeting houses constructed by Primitive Baptist congregations throughout the nineteenth century. The Primitive Baptist sect's disdain of ostentatious displays played a major role in shaping the appearance of meeting houses and often the dwellings of devout members. Following the typical gable-roof form with doors on both gable ends (one end door has been closed) and one door on a nongable elevation, this example is covered with plain weatherboards and has nine-over-nine sash windows protected by wooden batten shutters, likely a later addition.

A turn-of-the-twentieth-century remodeling on the interior, including a complete sheathing of all walls and ceiling with beaded tongue-and-grove boarding, has obscured what might have been evidence to support or refute the traditional construction date of about 1803. Numerous architectural elements that do survive suggest that the meeting house was built during the second quarter of the nineteenth century. Such features as the nine-over-nine sash windows, large wooden box locks, wide plank pine floors, and vertical board-and-batten doors were common elements on antebellum rural churches of many denominations. The benches as well as the pulpit are thought to be original to the church and likewise appear to be of antebellum origin.

The current configuration of the pulpit and benches reflects a post-Civil War arrangement, when the necessity to have slaves sit behind the preacher was no longer an issue. Sometime after the war the pulpit was moved from a central location in the meeting house to an end location in front of the door that was originally a slave entrance. A twentieth-century standing-seam metal roof now covers the building, but originally a wood shingle roof would have been applied.

The Croom Meeting House is significant for its associations with one of the county's early Primitive Baptist congregations and remains as a well-preserved early-nineteenth-century church building with an integrity of design not commonly found in modern times.

(former) Moss Hill School
built circa 1890
Sandy Bottom vicinity

The former Moss Hill School, a frame one-story, gable-and-wing building built to replace a school that burned in 1889, is now a private residence. The school, originally the Moss Hill Academy, was closed soon after 1924 when its students began attending a larger school, also called Moss Hill School. A 1924 survey of public schools found that the four-classroom school had 130 students enrolled. The building had a wraparound porch. Although some later windows have been added (including a bay window where the original chimney stood) and the porch posts have been replaced, the compact building on a brick pier foundation still resembles an early-twentieth-century school. The front gable with its diamond-shaped louvered ventilator is particularly characteristic.

Joseph R. Croom bought the property for three hundred dollars from the Board of Education when the school was abandoned. He willed the property to his daughter Bessie Croom Stroud, wife of Able Croom Stroud. She later left it to her nephew.

(former) Piney Grove School
built early twentieth century
Albritton Crossroads vicinity

By 1924 when the *Survey of the Public Schools of Lenoir County* was published by the state superintendent of public instruction, the Piney Grove School was one of fifteen one-teacher schools operating in the county. The purposes of the school survey were to identify the needs of each school district in the county and to present a plan of consolidation for the local board of education to follow. Piney Grove, which was built probably during the first decade of the twentieth century, was one of seven schools in the southern section of the county slated for decommission in order to create the Deep Run Consolidated School. The survey indicated that Piney Grove was a one-teacher school with six grades and an enrollment of forty-three. It was situated on two acres of land, with a good pump supplying well water and one toilet in bad condition. The building, as evident in a 1924 photograph reproduced for the report, had a two-room plan with a hip roof, which intersected with a centered front-gable porch housing two cloakrooms, one on either side of a recessed porch. Although other such schoolhouses existed in Lenoir County at the time, this form, with a hip roof and projecting entrance vestibule, was different from the more traditional plain, front-gable schoolhouse. A polychromatic paint scheme appeared on the building, with the weatherboard siding painted one color and the trim, including cornerboards, window and door surrounds, and a diamond louvered vent in the front gable, all painted a lighter color. The school was unpainted on the interior, had wood floors, and was heated by a wood-burning stove.

The consolidation plan came to fruition, and the new Deep Run School opened in the fall of 1926. James Herbert Albritton, a local farmer, had sold the original property to Lenoir County for the Piney Grove School, and when it was consolidated, he bought the property back from the board of education. Albritton converted the former school to a tenant house and used it as a dwelling until 1965. His granddaughter Ida Gay W. Dail moved it approximately a half mile south of its original location, where it now stands in a clearing behind a mid-twentieth-century ranch house, though it remains visible from the highway. When the school was converted to a tenant house, the front vestibule became an open porch.

(former) Will F. Harper Store
built 1930s
Albritton Crossroads vicinity

The former Harper Store is one of many early-twentieth-century Lenoir County rural stores now unoccupied and left to the ravages of time and the elements. The weatherboarded hipped-roof store still has its paneled double leaf entry and a mural reading "Drink Pepsi-Cola 12 oz. bottle 5 cents," dated 1937. This rare surviving element was once a common method of advertising.

SOUTHWEST TOWNSHIP

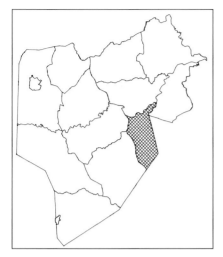

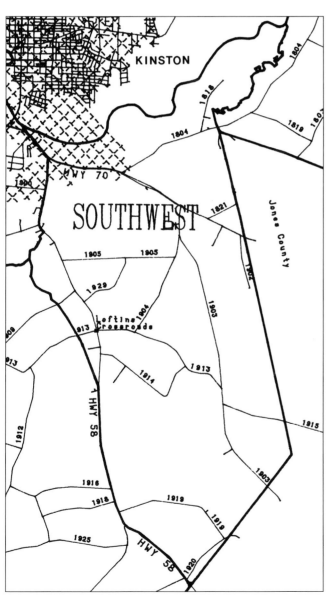

Miller-Stroud House

built early twentieth century
Kinston vicinity

The oldest section of this farmhouse which stands at the center of an extensive grouping of early-twentieth-century outbuildings, was constructed for the Miller family but purchased in 1921 by Thomas Walter Stroud. Stroud had married Penelope Williams on April 1, 1903, in the Woodington Township, where they lived until establishing their homestead at the former Miller home. Noted for their thriftiness and pride in farming the land they owned, the Strouds established a successful middle-class farmstead. The cross-gabled Victorian house purchased by the Strouds is typical for the period, with a central entrance and several extensions off the rear. A large screened porch covers the front facade, and an addition from 1929-1930 that Mr. Stroud built projects from the back elevation. Among the numerous outbuildings on the farm are a washhouse, a delco generator house, a two-story tobacco packhouse, a corncrib, mule stables, and two other barns/packhouses. The buildings are set beneath pecan and other deciduous trees.

Graham Place

built late eighteenth or early nineteenth century, altered mid-twentieth century
Kinston vicinity

The history, including the date of construction, for this early Tidewater cottage is largely unknown. Deed research indicates that the dwelling was traditionally referred to as the Graham Place. It was acquired by Thomas Walter Stroud in 1933 and remains in the Stroud family. Unique in Lenoir County for having such features as an engaged Flemish-bond chimney on one end elevation and a pent room on the other, this one-and-a-half-story dwelling also presents the county's only known example of a three-room plan or Quaker plan, so-called because of its association with Pennsylvania settlers in a document attributed to William Penn. The pent room—a feature frequently associated with eighteenth- and early-nineteenth-century domestic architecture—is a small shed-roof closet located on the west gable-end elevation adjacent to the large double-shouldered chimney. The engaged chimney on the opposite end protrudes only one brick width from the body of the house and features two interior corner fireplaces, which service the original enclosed end bay on the front porch and the adjacent parlor.

At some point the dwelling's three-room plan was converted to a center-hall arrangement with the addition of a partition wall, while the open portion of the engaged front porch was enclosed. A remnant of Federal-style wainscoting remains in the stair hall as the only significant surviving early woodwork. Other early treatments include nine-over-six sash windows and some beaded trim in the stairwell.

Two flanking rear ells were added to the house around 1900. In the 1950s when the dwelling was used as farm tenant housing, a number of renovations were performed, including covering the exterior with roll asphalt siding in the pattern of coursed brick, and some interior alterations. Although the dwelling no longer gives the appearance of an unaltered early frame farmhouse, its surviving chimneys, pent room, windows, remnant moldings, and overall form place it in a genre of house associated with the early occupation of inland coastal North Carolina.

Howard-Williams House

built circa 1890
Kinston vicinity

The construction of this two-story Victorian farmhouse is attributed to local builder C. C. Turner, believed to have built it circa 1890 for the prominent Disciples of Christ minister Curtis William Howard Sr. Howard was involved in education as well as holding pastorates at various regional Christian congregations, and in 1890 he became the Lenoir County superintendant of public instruction, an office he held for fifteen years. He also served for three years as coeditor of the *Kinston Free Press* with his longtime friend and classmate Josephus Daniels. After the Howard family owned the farm, it was purchased in 1917 by Brown Williams (1867-1950), who moved his family into the dwelling in 1920.

The side-gable I-house has three bays on the front facade and a hip-roof one-story wraparound porch. Setting this house apart from similar houses of the period are the interior rear chimneys—an uncommon placement seen in only a few examples in the county. Characteristically plain on the exterior, the house on the interior is notable for well-appointed Victorian features such as the center-hall staircase with turned newels and balusters and stylized mantelpieces with curvilinear friezes. Two nineteenth-century outbuildings remain on the property, a detached one-story one-room kitchen building (chimney removed) and a finely finished full-dovetail plank smokehouse with a board-and-batten door.

Kelly's Millpond and Mill

pond established early eighteenth century; mill house built early twentieth century
Kinston vicinity

It is said that as early as 1736 a grist mill operated on Strawberry Branch, a tributary of Southwest Creek a few miles from the county seat of Kinston. It is believed that by the time of the American Revolution the millpond and surrounding land were owned by Richard Caswell, North Carolina's first governor and a prominent landowner in Lenoir County. Like the Cobb-King-Humphrey House nearby, Kelly's Mill was strategically located and played an important part in the Battle of Wyse Fork during the waning months of the Civil War. During the latter part of the nineteenth century the mill house burned and was replaced by the current structure. The one-and-a-half-story frame building represents one of the best preserved mill houses in eastern North Carolina. Large exposed framing members on the interior support the weather-boarded building. Much of the original milling equipment for grinding flour, as well as the sawmill, remains in the building. The machinery attests to the multiple functions of the facility. With its pond with majestic cypress trees and Spanish moss, the site became a well-attended recreation spot in the early twentieth century and included a dance pavilion built over the water, bathhouses, barrel showers, diving boards, swimming platforms, and boating and fishing activities.

Jasper Gates House
built 1918
Southwood vicinity

The two-story American foursquare house was an extremely popular type of dwelling constructed across the United States during the 1910s and 1920s. This venerable house form was most popular in the midwestern states, though excellent examples remain throughout North Carolina in both small towns and rural areas. Part of the American foursquare's popularity resulted from the inclusion of several designs in period mail-order housing catalogues. The Gates House, built in 1918 for Jasper Gates (probably on land he either inherited or bought from his parents, Charles E. Gates and Ella Baker Gates) is thought to have been ordered from Sears, Roebuck and Company, one of the most largest manufactured housing companies, which sold the homes from 1908 until 1941. This three-bay frame house with its three-light hipped-roof dormer and attached hipped-roof front porch is very similar to two of Sears's 1918 catalogue houses, the Chelsea and the Hamilton. It was apparently ordered, then assembled, by Claude Douglas Brown at a cost of $2,365. In 1981 a one-story hipped-roof tenant house was appended to the side of the original dwelling.

Cobb-King-Humphrey House
built first quarter of the nineteenth century
Wyse Fork vicinity

Stories of houses' being used as hospitals during the Civil War abound in eastern North Carolina, but only a few can be documented. The Cobb-King-Humphrey House boasts the distinction not only of serving as a Federal field hospital during the war, but also of being right in the middle of the second-largest land battle fought in North Carolina during the conflict. The Battle of Wyse Fork was between the Confederate forces of Generals Robert F. Hoke and D. H. Hill, under the command of General Braxton Bragg, and the Federal divisions of Generals Palmer and Carter, under the command of General Jacob D. Cox. The battle, which took place March 8-10, 1865, resulted when the Confederates attempted to stop the Union forces from marching west from their supply base at New Bern to join General William T. Sherman's forces, converging on Goldsboro. After two days of skirmishing with Union forces the Confederates, realizing they were outnumbered, retreated toward Smithfield to join General Joseph E. Johnston's forces, to fight again, less than two weeks later at the Battle of Bentonville. As evidence of their occupation of the Cobb House, many of the Union soldiers wrote their names on the unpainted plaster in the dwelling's third-story garret. Many of these names remain today, a testament to the role the house played during the significant military engagement at Wyse Fork.

Situated on the main road from Kinston to New Bern just a short distance from Kelly's Millpond, the home was constructed early in the nineteenth century, probably for a Cobb family member. In addition to its Civil War notoriety, the house survives as one of Lenoir County's most significant intact Federal-style plantation houses. The two-and-a-half-story five-bay dwelling has an original rear two-and-a-half-story ell marked by an interior end exposed-face chimney—a treatment closely associated with residential architecture in New Bern from the same period. Commodious for its era, the house has two gable-end brick chimneys with freestanding stacks (one chimney was rebuilt in the twentieth century), and an early-twentieth-century replacement one-story full-width front porch. The well-appointed interior displays Federal elements slightly more sophisticated than those seen in similar period plantations. The center-hall stair, in typical fashion, has a simple square newel and balusters and ascends in a two-run layout with an intermediate landing. _____ in standard Federal three-part __ es grace each fireplace on the __ hile a retarditaire Georgian- __ cated on the rear ell's second

__ house, and interspersed with __ , sits a grouping of buildings __ King family's ownership of the __ ntieth century. Among the out- __ store building erected for the __ ally sat near the road in front of __ store built for Richard King, __ y 70; and a garage, smokehouse,

__ House

__ cendants, Robert Bond Vause (1830-1865) married __ an Adaline Jackson (1834-1909). He had this substantial two-story three-bay double-pile frame house constructed for his family in the early 1850s on property his wife likely inherited. Robert Vause enlisted in Confederate service in Company A, Fortieth Regiment North Carolina Troops, rising to the rank of second lieutenant. He was killed on February 18, 1865 at Fort Anderson in Brunswick County, North Carolina. Adaline then married Levi Russell (1834-1907). One of the Russell's sons, Henry W. Russell (1869-1954), inherited the homeplace and farm. He later purchased nearby Kelly's Millpond and turned it into a local recreational and entertainment establishment, as well as continuing to operate the gristmill.

Having the form of an antebellum plantation house, this dwelling consists of four rooms downstairs and four rooms upstairs and is divided on both floors by a wide center hall. This plan type persisted from the earliest occupation of North America by English settlers well into the twentieth century. Large interior chimneys pro-

vided fireplaces for each principal room, and two enclosed end bays on the hip-roof rear porch also embody typical, but rarely intact, treatments from this period. A hip-roof front porch shelters the plain sidelights and transom surrounding the front entry. An early-twentieth-century gable-roof brick smokehouse remains adjacent to the main house.

(former) Southwood School (demolished)
built 1926, demolished 1994
Southwood vicinity

"Modern" and "up to date" were the terms used to describe many of the substantial brick school buildings erected during the 1920s, one of North Carolina's most active eras of public school consolidation. When the Southwood School was built in 1926 to the design specifications of prominent architect Leslie Boney of Wilmington, the children of the community were treated to new technologies, including radiant heat from a central boiler, electricity for lights, and indoor running water and bathroom facilities. Such buildings constituted giant leaps in providing quality facilities for teaching the state's large rural population. Typical of Boney's Neoclassical Revival treatments were the low parapet walls concealing the shallow-pitch shed roof, brick corbeling on the cornice, and slightly projecting bays on either side of the centered entrance. The most recognizable Boney trait was the two-story central pedimented portico supported by fluted columns. The segmentally arched entrance bay led to a recessed double leaf entry door with sidelights and a partly covered fanlight transom. At the time of the school's demolition, former students reminisced about the early years of the school, when the five-cent hot dogs sold in the cafeteria were novelties in this rural farming region.

Elliot S. Russell House and Apiary

house built circa 1927; apiary built 1906
Southwood vicinity

At the center of this modest early-twentieth-century farmstead is the frame one-and-a-half-story hipped-roof vernacular farmhouse built for Elliot S. Russell by builder Benjamin Griswald. Erected in 1927 at a cost of $3,500, the Craftsman-inspired dwelling has an attached hipped-roof porch with replacement metal posts and four original hipped-roof dormer windows. Of particular note on the farm is an outbuilding that Henry William Russell, Elliot S. Russell's father, constructed in 1906 on the family farm at Wyse Fork. When the Russells moved to the Southwood community in the 1920s, they brought the hexagonal board-and-batten hipped-roof apiary, or bee house, with them. The apiary was used to store honey. This one-of-a-kind outbuilding in Lenoir County represents a local industry that apparently played an impor-

tant part on at least some farms during the early twentieth century. Period literature promoted such activities as possible sources of income for the enterprising farmer.

Elijah Loftin House

built circa 1880
Southwood vicinity

According to an entry in the 1906 Industrial Issue of the *Kinston Free Press*, Elijah P. Loftin was "One of the staunch old farmers of South West township . . . He is a man who loves his home, who centers his whole thought on his family and their interests, who is a horticulturalist of some note, doting on his grove of pecan, his yaupon tea orchard, his Japanese persimmons and chestnuts, and taking a pride in his pigeon cotes, chickens, cattle and swine." It is apparent from this description that Loftin's agricultural pursuits were varied and quite unusual for the time. His farm production in 1906 derived from a 1,500-acre property, of which 500 acres were cleared. His crops included corn, cotton, and tobacco—typical for an early-twentieth-century farmstead in Lenoir County. Loftin held the post of county surveyor for about twenty-five years in addition to operating his farm.

At the center of the Loftin farm is a finely detailed two-story Victorian house in a T-shaped configuration with a rambling floor plan, often seen in like dwellings. Family tradition suggests that the house was built circa 1880 to replace an earlier farmhouse, which burned in 1878. The weatherboarded dwelling has an entrance on the side of the front projecting ell, which is sheltered by a two-story porch with replacement bungalow supports. On the interior period mantels fashioned in simple but popular Victorian motifs grace each fireplace. The most striking interior feature is the hall staircase, which has heavily chamfered newel posts.

Surrounding the farmhouse is a good collection of early-to-mid-twentieth century domestic and agricultural outbuildings. Most of these buildings were probably commissioned by George Felix Loftin, E. P. Loftin's son, who took over the farm from his father. Remaining on the site near the house are a combination washhouse and carbide shed, a chicken brooder house, and an early-twentieth-century garage. Other buildings include a chicken coop, a barn originally used for cotton but converted to a tobacco packhouse, another barn, and a circa 1946 gambrel-roof dairy barn equipped with a hay hook and wagon portal. Today the farm is owned by George E. Loftin, George Felix Loftin's son, who resides in the house.

John Council Wooten House
built mid-nineteenth century
Loftin Crossroads vicinity

John Council Wooten (1825-1893), a First Lieutenant in the Confederate infantry, had this Greek Revival-style temple-form house constructed prior to his military service. The county's only surviving example of the style's quintessential form, the Wooten home follows the theme of an ancient Greek temple, complete with a columned pedimented portico and white-painted exterior. This rare surviving design also has a cantilevered balcony on the three-bay front facade. An abstracted sheaf-of-wheat balustrade encloses the balcony and is repeated on the interior side-hall stair. Other important interior elements include a square newel post with exaggerated chamfering on the corners, four-panel doors, and simple Greek Revival mantels with bold proportions in the standard post-and-lintel design.

A Victorian porch was added to the side of the house, which wraps around to the rear and connects to a late-nineteenth-century rear ell. Two large interior chimneys provided heat to rooms on both the first and second floors. John Council Wooten married Emmaline Kelly in 1845, and they had six children. The house remained in the Wooten family until 1911, when it was purchased by Lewis James Whaley. It remains in the Whaley family.

King's Chapel Church of Christ (Disciples of Christ)
built circa 1912, altered circa 1966
Southwood vicinity

King's Chapel Church of Christ was organized during the late nineteenth or early twentieth century and included many prominent members of the African American community. The early-twentieth-century church building retains its overall gable-front form as well as five lancet-shaped stained-glass windows on each side elevation—a typical design for small rural churches built throughout the county. The church was modernized in the 1960s, during the pastorate of the Reverend J. O. Williams Sr., with the addition of brick veneer. A marble cornerstone identifies the date of original construction as 1912.

House
built third quarter of the nineteenth century
Southwood vicinity

Exhibiting architecture that characterized most post-Civil War buildings in the region, this modest one-story, center-hall-plan cottage has Greek Revival elements carried over from the antebellum period. The hipped-roof, attached porch, and trabeated entry are treatments also found on prewar houses of the mid-nineteenth century. Original vernacular Greek Revival-inspired mantels provide other examples of retarditare elements. Although the date of construction for this dwelling is unknown, the architectural evidence points toward a post-Civil War origin.

Joseph Williams House and Farm
built circa 1914-1916
Southwood vicinity

Joseph Williams (1870-1961), a locally prominent landowner and farmer, as well as three-time Lenoir County Board of Commissioners member, built this substantial two-story Victorian farmhouse between 1914 and 1916. At one time the tract on which the house stands comprised 1,150 acres—a testament to Williams's success as a farmer. Representing the prosperous middle-class farmstead of the early twentieth century, the Williams Farm is centered around a simply detailed Victorian weatherboarded dwelling. The house has changed very little from its early appearance, judging from a 1942 photograph that pictures the dwelling with its original Doric columns supporting the front porch. Other defining features include two-over-two sash windows and interior chimneys with decorative corbeled caps. A one-story rear dining-kitchen ell has been enlarged by several later additions. Noteworthy is an extensive collection of original outbuildings arranged in a fashion typical of the period. Domestic outbuildings include a Delco generator house, a well house, and a washhouse with an attached woodshed. Situated farther from the house are the agricultural outbuildings, which include a stable, two packhouses, a large barn, and a small tenant house with a detached rear kitchen. Landscape features from the farm's formative years include a grape arbor just north of the house, and cedar and pine trees separating the house from cultivated fields.

Coleman-Wooten-Williams House
built mid-nineteenth century, renovated 1920s
Elm Grove vicinity

The construction history of this stylistically rather eclectic one-story-with-basement frame house is sketchy and not fully documented. According to local tradition a Coleman family had the dwelling constructed prior to the Civil War but moved to Alabama after the war and sold the property to the Wooten family. In 1910 David Williams, a prosperous farmer from the Woodington Township, purchased the farm and house and constructed a store at the Elm Grove crossroads. He is responsible for major renovations to the house, completed in the 1920s. Tradition also holds that an earlier house on the site had burned, and that the second house was constructed on the earlier dwelling's foundation. A partially plastered basement under one section of the house is said to have served as quarters for slaves in the antebellum period and consisted of four rooms, with three heated from interior chimneys. At what point the earlier house burned and the new house was constructed on its foundation is unclear, though much of the existing woodwork, such as four-panel doors and heavily molded mantelpieces, exhibits standard mid-nineteenth-century Greek Revival characteristics. A Gothic theme now dominates on the interior, with whimsical treatments including pointed arches in the form of a hall screen, a built-in corner cupboard with a sawtooth and dentil cornice molding, and a mantel with bracketed shelves and denticulated sunbursts. Whether these are original to the second house, which possibly dates to the mid-nineteenth century, is unclear.

Today the appearance of the exterior of the house is that of an early-twentieth-century Craftsman bungalow, fully expressed with a jerkinhead roof, hip-roof front porch, and false hip roof dormer. These characteristics apparently were applied in the 1920s by David Williams. The configuration of the house—a U shape, with a long front section and rear ells set perpendicular on either side—is one commonly seen on mid-nineteenth century houses, though rarely used in eastern North Carolina during that period. It was found more often in the region during the Victorian era. Whatever the chronology of building, the house beautifully illustrates how dwellings often change to accommodate the tastes of new owners and prevailing architectural fashions.

WOODINGTON TOWNSHIP

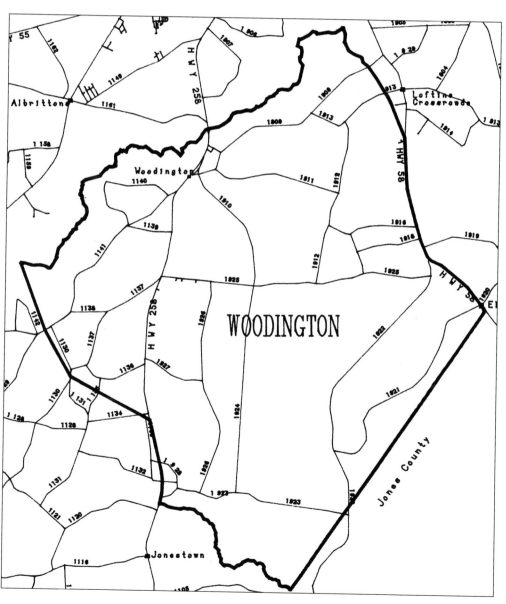

Egbert Waller Tenant House

built late nineteenth century
Woodington

This one-story side-gable five-bay-wide-house originally sat several hundred yards to the north on land that was part of the plantation known as Woodington, owned by Richard Caswell in the late eighteenth century. It reportedly has a mortise-and-tenon framework. The five-bay width hints at an antebellum construction date, but no visible fabric on either the exterior or interior dates prior to the late nineteenth century. The house has plain weatherboard, six-over-six sash, replacement doors, a replacement porch, a rear shed addition, and a tongue-and-groove interior with most partition walls removed. In the early twentieth century Egbert Waller, who ran Waller Brothers Gristmill nearby, moved the house to its present site and used it as a tenant house.

To the rear are a typical frame packhouse, a shed, and two tobacco barns of early-twentieth-century construction.

Egbert Waller Farm

built circa 1915
Woodington

About 1915 Egbert Waller, who ran the Waller Brothers Gristmill (demolished) in Woodington in the early twentieth century, enlarged his one-story house on this site to two stories and added a two-story rear ell. The imposing farmhouse with gable-end brick chimneys, occupying a prominent site at the main intersection of Woodington, represents the agricultural prosperity of the crossroads during the period. Successive generations of Wallers have remodeled the interior and replaced the porch with a Mount Vernon-style portico.

Three early-twentieth-century outbuildings remain: a smokehouse with a traditional overhanging front gable, a frame corncrib, and a two-room frame kitchen built about 1920. The kitchen was recently moved to a different site on the farm.

Millard Waller House and Sawmill

built 1920s
Woodington

This 1920s Craftsman bungalow, which faces the Deep Run Road, was the second residence of Millard Waller (1868-1926), co-owner with his brother Egbert of the Waller Brothers Gristmill in Woodington. Millard had this house built when he remarried after the death of his first wife. The house has a side-gable roof, which forms an engaged porch of arcaded brick in front and engaged shed rooms in the rear. Three gabled dormers project from the front slope of the roof. The large stylish brick house represents Millard Waller's old-age prosperity, and the end of the vernacular frame farmhouse tradition in Woodington.

To the rear are a typical packhouse and tobacco barns. Across the Deep Run Road stands Waller's Store and Sawmill, built in the 1920s. The sawmill was one of numerous gasoline-engine-powered sawmills that operated in Lenoir County in the early twentieth century. The front-gable frame building, now covered with metal, is unused and overgrown with vegetation.

Charlie Stroud House
built circa 1910
Woodington vicinity

Now rented, this farmhouse is a good example of the popularity of the I-house with decorative front cross gable in early-twentieth-century Lenoir County. Much of this farmhouse's original integrity has survived, including the rear kitchen-dining ell (partly two story) and the attached hipped-roof front porch supported by Tuscan posts. The house, surrounded by pecan trees, sits at a small remove from a state-maintained road.

According to documentation at the office of the Lenoir County register of deeds, Charlie Stroud, along with his five siblings, received a 177-acre tract in Woodington Township in 1904, a gift of their parents, William E. and Delia Stroud. The tract adjoined the properties of E. H. Waller, the Waller Brothers Gristmill, and M. H. Wooten. Charlie Stroud's brothers and sisters deeded him a ninety-three-acre portion of this tract in 1904, "Beginning at a stake on the Wilmington road and Rebecca A. Stroud's corner between William Stroud's house and the old Woodington church," bordered partly by Clark's Branch.

Piney Grove Church of Christ
built circa 1908
Woodington vicinity

The sturdy hexagonal brick narthex of this circa 1908 African American church deviates from the more traditional simple gable-front form and is more akin to small Anglican churches erected a century and a half earlier, predominantly in Tidewater Virginia. Upon closer inspection, however, the plain wood cross attached to the steeple, the louvered ventilators with decorative sawnwork, and the vernacular two-light lancet transom above the front entry speak more of rural Lenoir County. Little is known about the history of this frame church, which was later veneered with brick. The church has two rear additions that appear to have been built in the early 1940s. The Reverend Frank Graham was the first minister of the church, and his son, James, served as minister for sixty-four years.

Simpson Waller House
built 1918
Woodington vicinity

This two-story frame foursquare house is the only documented example of an Aladdin house in Lenoir County. Like the better-known Sears, Roebuck and Company, the Michigan-based Aladdin Homes supplied homeowners with prefabricated houses ready to be assembled. Simpson Waller, a young farmer, ordered this house from the Aladdin catalogue in 1918. Apart from a one-story side extension that Mr. Waller built for himself later when his son's family moved into the house, and replacement windows and siding, the house has remained relatively unaltered in its nearly eighty years of existence.

The design of the house—side-hall entry, slightly projecting front and side bays, attached hipped-roof porch supported by Tuscan posts, paired windows at the front, and a hipped roof topped by a hipped two-light dormer—is virtually identical to that of The Charleston house in Aladdin's 1919 catalogue. The Wallers have kept most of the fixtures that came with the house, including the trademark doorknobs and a brass genie knocker.

Jess Harper House
built 1902, enlarged 1928
Woodington

Jess Harper, whose ancestors had lived in the Woodington community for many years, built this house for himself on the main road in 1902 in the prevailing tradition, a one-story side-gable house with a center hall and two rooms. In the late 1920s he enlarged and remodeled the house into a bungalow in order to accommodate his eleven children. The resulting hybrid provides an interesting example of how some houses were enlarged in the 1920s. The remodeled house has a front-gable roof that engages a porch with battered posts set on brick piers. The original north chimney is gone; the south chimney has the initial H incorporated into the brickwork. The original core of the house retains tongue-and-groove sheathing and late Greek Revival-style mantels.

The farm has a one-story packhouse and a traditional smokehouse with a front-gable overhang. Jess Harper raised corn, tobacco, and cotton on his large farm until his death in 1935.

Grady-Harper House
built circa 1836
Woodington vicinity

According to a family Bible, Whitfield Grady (1789-1880) married Elizabeth Kornegay in 1818 in Duplin County, and in 1836 he moved his family to Lenoir County, to the Woodington area. Presumably Grady had this two-story gable-end Federal-style plantation house constructed for his wife and seven children after relocating to Lenoir County. Following the move the Grady family grew by another six children. The last child born to the Gradys, Susan (1845-?), ultimately gained title to the property. She married local farmer Jesse Harper. On November 12, 1897, Jesse deeded the house and its eighty-four-acre tract to his son, Blackledge (Susan Grady Harper's stepson). In 1936 the property was deeded to Blackledge's daughter, Lillian Eva Harper Kennedy.

Typical of many eastern North Carolina farmhouses of the early nineteenth century, the Grady-Harper House is not pretentious but is substantial and comfortable, the sort of practical building indigenous to the agricultural lifestyle of the area's population. The three-bay house with beaded weatherboard siding, arranged in a hall-and-parlor plan, is simply augmented with double-shouldered Flemish-bond chimneys, six-over-six sash windows, and an enclosed end bay on the full-width shed porch. An enclosed stair on the interior rises from the right side of the south room. Complementing the overall Federal design of the dwelling are first-floor mantelpieces composed of pilasters with panels surrounded by guilloche bands, a motif repeated and accompanied by incised geometric patterns in the mantel cornices. Walls are covered with plaster above a horizontal flat-paneled wainscot. The second floor is partially finished with unpainted flush sheathing and has a simple unadorned mantel in the south room. A striking feature on the second floor is a floor-to-ceiling stair newel, an element associated with early-nineteenth-century construction.

Adair Kennedy House

built circa 1933
Woodington vicinity

Owen Adair Kennedy and his brother, Cedric Arthur, married sisters, Mary and Lillian Eva Harper, respectively, in a double ceremony on January 6, 1932. Both brothers were farmers in the Woodington community and, after the wedding, established homesteads in the area. Cedric moved with his bride to a Harper family home associated with his wife, and Adair constructed this well-appointed Craftsman bungalow. The Kennedy House is a nicely preserved one-and-a-half-story version of the bungalow style, featuring an asymmetrical front facade with a three-light shed-roof dormer centered over the front-gable entrance. Significant elements in the design include the engaged front porch supported by battered wooden posts (paired at the entrance) over brick piers, and paired eight-over-one windows which flank the entrance. Other identifying features of the style include exposed rafter ends and triangular knee braces beneath the porch and gable-end eaves. Once typical on the Lenoir County landscape but now rapidly disappearing is the collection of domestic and agricultural buildings that supported the middle-class farm. Erected mainly during the 1930s, these outbuildings include a hipped-roof cover over an open well, a massive front-gable barn and equipment shed, a chicken house, and a quintessential smokehouse. This farmstead, still owned by the Kennedy family, remains as one of the county's best preserved Depression-era farms.

House

built circa 1890-1915
Vine Swamp vicinity

Located at the center of a modest-sized turn-of-the-twentieth-century farmstead is a small one-and-a-half-story Victorian farmhouse with a triple-A roof and three-quarter hip-roof front porch. Typically ornamented with turned porch posts, sawn brackets, and a turned balustrade, the dwelling represents one of the most popular house types in the county during this period. Reasonable prosperity, probably from agricultural output, is evident in interior treatments such as the tongue-and-groove sheathing on walls and ceilings and the two-over-two sash windows. A rear one-story ell with a side porch supported by chamfered posts completes the house.

The property has a small but interesting collection of outbuildings arranged behind the main house and down a farm path that stretches from the state road in front of the house to agricultural fields behind. Primary among these buildings is a diminutive one-story round-log building, which appears to have served either as the initial dwelling on the site or as a kitchen to an earlier house. Though log construction was commonly used in Lenoir County and the Neuse River basin prior to the Civil War, few examples survive. A date of construction for the log cabin is unknown, but features such as hand-forged strap hinges on the board-and-batten front door and vernacular Greek Revival woodwork in the composition of the mantel suggest a mid-nineteenth-century origin. Complementing the round-log walls are exposed log ceiling joists—another trait associated with prewar construction. A log smokehouse with nicely fashioned saddle corner notching and two log tobacco barns make this site one of the county's best collections of log-constructed buildings.

John Blackman Becton House

built first quarter of the nineteenth century; remodeled 1940s
Woodington vicinity

The Becton family emigrated from Massachusetts to Craven County in the early eighteenth century. A descendant, John Blackman Becton (1777-1838) established his plantation at Woodington Township in the early 1800s and built this two-story three-bay side-gable frame house. Before his death in 1838 Becton had established a prosperous small farmstead worked by sixteen slaves. One of his sons, Jarman (1833-1886), after serving in the Civil War married Eliza Jane Denny and settled on this farm. Eliza Jane Denny Becton was the sister of Dr. William W. Denny, who practiced medicine in nearby Pink Hill for almost half a century.

Originally built to a hall-and-parlor plan, the Becton homestead has undergone several remodelings through its history yet still retains an original common-bond brick end chimney, apparently the only early nineteenth-century chimney in Lenoir County with concave shoulders. A remodeling in the 1940s and a fire in the 1960s, which necessitated renovation, stripped some of the

dwelling's original features, but the overall appearance remains that of an early-nineteenth-century farmhouse. The Becton House is believed to have been built in 1808, following John Blackman Becton's 1806 marriage to Clarissa Wadsworth (1787-1818).

Vine Swamp School

built circa 1917
Vine Swamp vicinity

This modest early-twentieth-century one-story gable-end frame school was built about 1917 for African American children living in the Vine Swamp community. It probably functioned as a school facility until the 1950s, when many smaller black schools were closed and consolidated into larger buildings centrally located in communities. Beginning as a one-teacher school, Vine Swamp was later expanded to a three-teacher school offering first, second, and third grades to ninety to one hundred students. The schoolhouse is typical of rural schools built for the African American population during the 1910s and 1920s in eastern North Carolina. The ubiquitous design, featuring German siding, paired six-over-six windows, and exposed rafter ends, came to characterize a generation of school buildings that were codified by the evolving Rosenwald Fund, a program of grant assistance to southern rural black school districts established by Sears, Roebuck and Company president Julius Rosenwald. Although the Vine Swamp School has not been documented as receiving Rosenwald funds, the design is similar to designs published by the fund in 1920s booklets. Known faculty members at the school include Martha Ann Baker, one of the first teachers at the school; Baker's son, James E. Baker Sr., who taught from 1928 to 1930; and her granddaughter, Lynnetta B. Fields, who taught at the school in 1954.

The school is owned by Annie M. Loftin. Her son Garland Loftin lives on the property where the school is located. Currently used for storage, this school building represents one of only a few historic African American schoolhouses remaining in Lenoir County, making it an important survivor with great value in promoting the course black education charted in the early twentieth century.

Vine Swamp Church of Christ

built early twentieth century
Elm Grove vicinity

The Vine Swamp Church of Christ, a rural church built in the early twentieth century by its African American congregation, is a good example of a plain vernacular Gothic Revival church. The Vine Swamp Church's strongest elements—twin towers flanking a gable-front entry—are typical of African American vernacular churches. Exterior decoration includes rectilinear opalescent stained-glass windows, square louvered vents in the towers, and a later crucifix relief on the front. The formerly frame church was veneered with brick in the 1950s. There is a rear cross-wing cinderblock extension, built between 1950 and 1960.

According to longtime parishioners the church was founded by descendants of slaves who had met secretly to worship as early as the 1790s.

(former) Lynwood School

built circa 1914
Elm Grove Crossroads

Near Elm Grove crossroads sits the former Lynwood School, a gable-front frame schoolhouse built in 1914 in lower Lenoir County across from a pocosin that early students found difficult to resist. A former student recalled the "mossy banks" with "violets of many colors, bushy pink and regular running honeysuckle, ferns with curling bronze fronds, yellow jasmine and many bulbs including flycatchers." Regular visitors to this idyllic site—for more academic purposes—included E. E. Sams, the Lenoir County superintendent of schools, from Kinston. His visits were made first by horse and buggy and then, in the 1920s, by "a little black one-seater Ford with an oblong celluloid window in the back." In the late nineteenth century the crossroads community was known as Cadiz (or Cadez). The Branson's 1896 directory shows Cadiz with a population of twenty-five people and a general store run by D. F. Wooten. In 1905 the *North Carolina Yearbook* published by the Raleigh *News and Observer* listed another Cadiz merchant, A. J. Sutton, and Mamie Kinsey, a schoolteacher. In efforts to provide better educational opportunities for community children, residents Joseph Williams, David Williams, Jim Tom Spence, Ben Williams, and Joe Spence constructed the school for a cost of four hundred dollars.

When the school consolidation movement began, the Lynwood School, like most of the county's one-room schools, was decommissioned. It was converted to a residence and functioned as such for nearly half a century. Typical of rural schoolhouses, this example is a rectangular-shaped building with a single entrance on the front and a bank of windows along one elevation. This allowed teachers to orient desks toward the wall with the chalkboard, providing plenty of sunlight over the shoulders of students and also cutting down on the temptation to look out the windows.

The former school remained a residence until it was bought by James Williams and moved, along with its one-story frame detached kitchen outbuilding, to his nearby farm in 1979. The Williams family restored the school to its former appearance and has furnished it with desks, a wood stove, and 1920s schoolbooks.

Smith-Blizzard House

built early twentieth century
Deep Run vicinity

Now owned by Norman Blizzard, the front-gable one-and-a-half-story farmhouse built by the Smith family in the early twentieth century is a combination of vernacular nineteenth-century and early-twentieth-century Craftsman features. The hipped-roof wraparound front porch, for example, has the interesting stylistic juxtaposition of exposed rafters and turned-post supports. There are a paired front entrance with a paired six-over-six sash windows on each side and six-over-six gable windows. The farm complex is screened by mature pecan trees and a grape arbor behind the house.

Beyond the trees sit a 1930s two-story packhouse and a small frame kitchen (circa 1900) that was moved from a nearby farm. The kitchen's engaged porch is supported by chamfered posts and shelters a paired entry. The Smith cemetery is across a field. Decedents there begin with Jacob J. Smith (1853-1921), listed as a Kinston farmer in the 1890s Branson's directories, and end with his son, Isaiah Smith (1880-1953).

Miller-Nunn House (demolished)

built first quarter nineteenth century; second house built mid-nineteenth century; demolished early 1990s
Pleasant Hill vicinity

Prior to its demolition in the early 1990s this two-story early-nineteenth-century Federal-style house was recognized as one of the county's most interesting and significant plantation seats, long associated with descendants of the Swiss and German Palatines who settled at New Bern early in the eighteenth century. Thought to have been owned by the Miller (originally Mueller) and Nunn families throughout the nineteenth century, the property also has connections to the prominent Noble family active in the area from the eighteenth century. The date of construction is unknown, but architectural evidence points to around the 1820s for the main hall-and-parlor-plan dwelling. Except for the placement of the front door in the hall room, the house conformed to the proportions, scale, and layout of a side-hall-plan dwelling. The enclosed stair rose in the front corner of the parlor room, unheated and very narrow in width. Shed rooms, also unheated, carried across the rear elevation. Woodwork such as mantels, wainscoting, doors, and surrounds displayed subtle vernacular Federal motifs and profiles. The attenuated proportions of the house also constributed to the Federal feel of the design.

At some time, perhaps in the 1840s, a one-and-a-half-story Greek Revival style-building was erected adjacent to the main house, about ten feet from the dwelling's southeast front corner. A center-hall layout, exterior end common-bond chimneys, and an enclosed stair to a sleeping loft suggest that this building was used for dining, living, and sleeping quarters. Prominent Greek Revival-inspired woodwork on the exterior and interior lent an air of sophistication rarely seen on secondary buildings, generating speculation as to the original function of this addition. Louvered shutters on the building indicated a need for privacy, also suggesting living quarters. When the main house was demolished, this building was moved to neighboring Jones County.

PINK HILL
TOWNSHIP

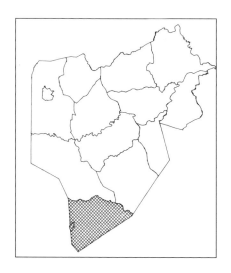

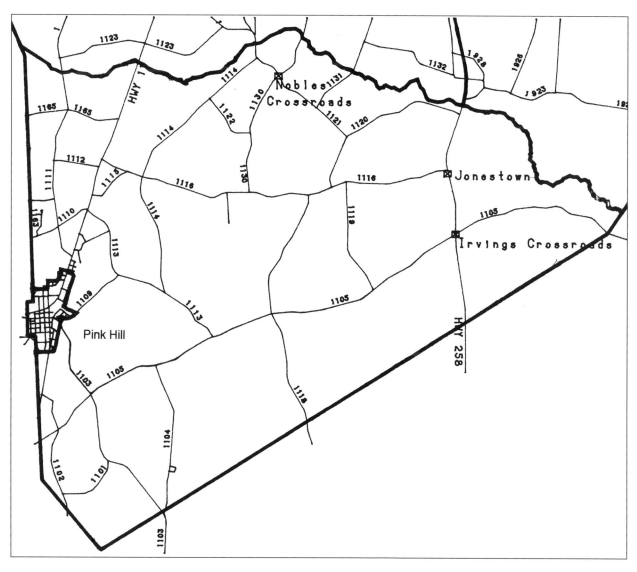

Steven Silas Turner House

built third quarter of the nineteenth century
Pink Hill vicinity

The decorative treatments associated with the coastal cottage house form in Lenoir County vary widely. This example, locally referred to as the Steven Silas Turner House, is a modified version of the coastal cottage that presents a combination of vernacular expressions of Greek Revival and simple Victorian-style details. Resembling such county landmarks as LaFayette plantation in the northern portion of the county and the Wiley Joel Rouse House at Strabane in southern Lenoir, the one-story frame Turner House has a recessed central entrance on the front and a single-bay engaged porch on the rear (now enclosed). Covered by a broad gable roof, the dwelling has one exterior end chimney surviving, though ghost marks clearly delineate placement of the other original chimney.

The most striking exterior features are the bold paneled corner pilasters and the fascia detailing—pendants at the corners of the house above a cornice with segments of applied molding—an idiosyncratic feature. Molding profiles suggest that Victorian influence was at work during the design and construction of the house, though the overall form and use of moldings reflect the Greek Revival idiom. The house was likely built in the post-Civil War period, but little is known about its early history.

Stroud Log House

built third quarter of the nineteenth century
Deep Run vicinity

This well-preserved round-log house has always sat on land owned by the locally prominent Stroud family, though traditions associate it with different members of the family. One story suggests that it was the home of Lutson Stroud (1842-1894), while another relates it to his older brother Amos (Boss) Stroud (1820-1902). Several factors suggest that the dwelling might not have been occupied by either of these men. The date of construction for the log house is undetermined, but architectural evidence indicates a date toward the latter nineteenth century, when both men would have already raised large families and attained a comfortable level of success in farming. If the house was built for a member of the Stroud family, it was likely a child of either Lutson or Amos. It might also have served as a tenant house on the Stroud farm.

The one-story one-room dwelling with habitable attic follows the form of a coastal cottage, with a sweeping engaged porch on the front and integrated shed rooms on the rear. Logs are saddle notched and exposed only on the front elevation beneath the porch; all other elevations are covered with standard weatherboards. A gable roof covers the entire house, and an extension on the west side suggests that the roof originally protected a mud-and-stick chimney. Two projecting members at ceiling height on the same end likely would have supported a cross member to hold the chimney in place. Plain four-over-four sash windows throughout and a simple board-and-batten door contribute to the vernacular and modest nature of the house.

Several important elements remain on the dwelling, adding to its overall importance as one of the few intact log houses remaining in Lenoir County. Vertical members set at each corner of the building are pegged into each log, apparently acting to tie all the logs together—an unusual feature not found on any of the other extant log buildings in the county. Porch posts are chamfered and mortised into the plate. The logs appear never to have been daubed with mortar, though tongue-and-groove sheathing covers all interior walls and ceilings. Access to the attic was by a ladder on the exterior of the dwelling (now removed). The house was moved from its original site in the 1930s to sit further from N.C. Highway 11, and it became a storage building.

(former) Quinn Store
built early twentieth century
Pink Hill vicinity

The Quinn Store, a combination store and residence, contains a traditional front-gable store with a traditional side-gable dwelling attached to the rear. The storefront had a canopied extension for gasoline pumps. A rear extension was later added to the side-gable house; it is now a tenant house. Owned and operated by Mack Quinn, the business became a focal point in the community, like many crossroads country stores throughout the county. Quinn and his family lived in the rear of the building and operated their store in the front. Quinn also ran a sawmill on the south side of the store.

Richard Noble House
built circa 1790
Originally located in Nobles Crossroads vicinity; moved north to U. S. Highway 258 in Woodington Township in 1996

This vernacular Georgian-influenced farmhouse remains as one of the oldest dwellings in Lenoir County and historically has been associated with the Noble family, one of the earliest families to settle in the southern portion of the county. Richard Noble II (1769-1854), a descendant of the Palatine colony (Swiss emigrants and German Protestant refugees) in New Bern, is credited with having the two-story side-gable dwelling constructed. In 1788 Noble purchased 317 acres in then-Dobbs County (Lenoir was formed from Dobbs in 1792) at the head of the Trent River, joining Cornelius Leary's and David George's lines. Whether this tract was the parcel upon which the Noble House was constructed is hard to determine, since few land records exists for Lenoir County prior to the 1870s. Based on the original location of the house and the tradition that Learys once owned much of the land in the area, the land purchase in Dobbs County could be the house site. Certainly Richard Noble was active in southern Lenoir County during the late eighteenth century, giving credence to a construction date of about 1790.

Richard Noble II appears in the census of 1800. By that time he had married Mary Ann (Polly) Kinsey (1771-1856) and had a family of one daughter and four sons. He remained the head of household until the 1850 census, when his son, Richard Noble III, and his family were apparently living in the house with Richard II and Polly, who by then were in their early eighties. By 1856 both Richard Noble II and his wife had passed away and were buried in the family cemetery, located a short distance from the house on the family farm.

The presumed date of construction for the Noble House is based primarily on the architectural information evident on the dwelling and the land purchase and marriage of Richard Noble to Mary Kinsey. These point to a construction date around the last decade of the eighteenth century. An overall Georgian scheme for this relatively plain farmhouse also supports the traditional date for the dwelling, as does the hall-and-parlor floor plan. By no means can the Noble House be considered a high-style dwelling, but rather it reflects what probably would have been the common expression of the time—a modest vernacular interpretation of prevailing English precedents. Even in its advanced state of deterioration the house has simple but fine craftsmanship and durability, qualities that guided many builders during the early history of the state. The overall plainness of the house is interrupted on the exterior primarily by the wonderfully crafted original single-shoulder Flemish-bond brick chimneys and beaded clapboard siding. One remarkable surviving feature is the wooden battens on the second-floor windows and rear shed rooms, which apparently functioned as closures for the openings. This type of window treatment was relatively common during the eighteenth and early nineteenth centuries, predominately in rural areas, where the scarcity and high cost of glass often prohibited its use on the entire house. The battens were fastened with hand-forged iron strap hinges.

The shed-roof front porch is supported by original tapered and chamfered posts bearing evidence of a balustrade now gone. Like the window battens, this type of porch post was often used on early dwellings but rarely survives. Little alteration has occurred on the interior, and such original treatments as vertical-board sheathing throughout complement the modest Georgian features.

Three finely rendered mantelpieces with simple pilasters and molded shelves have arched firebox openings, a hallmark of Georgian design. An enclosed stair to the second floor and hardware such as the hand-forged strap hinges and twisted I-hooks are common features of period farmhouses. A one-story side kitchen wing was connected to the house and appears to date from the early nineteenth century, yet another remarkable surviving feature of this extremely important house. In the mid-1990s, the house was moved by Mr. Johnny Grady from its original site to a new location on U. S. Highway 258 about four miles to the northeast.

Until the early 1990s the farm retained a cotton gin located a short distance from the house. The presence of a gin indicated the success of the farming operations there. The cotton gin probably dated from the second half of the nineteenth century and appeared to be a typical agricultural outbuilding, raised above the ground on large posts, which allowed wagons to deliver and pick up cotton underneath. A stable is the only remaining outbuilding on the site. It is a typical frame gable-roof structure covered with weatherboards, likely of the same period.

Richard K. Noble Farm
built late nineteenth century
Jonestown vicinity

Richard Kinsey Noble was born in the Pink Hill Township in 1853 and emerged after the Civil War as one of the area's most prosperous farmers and active citizens. He was the son of Richard and Catherine Noble. Like his father, who had also served as a sheriff's deputy, Richard acted as a justice of the peace. A strong commitment to education led him to serve on the county board of education, as well as as a county commissioner. Noble's farming interest enabled him to amass one of the largest landholdings of the late nineteenth century in the Pink Hill area. In 1906, when he was featured in the Industrial Issue of the *Kinston Free Press*, Noble owned 1,400 acres of land and cultivated 250 acres. His farm produced primarily cotton, and his gin had a capacity of twelve bales a day, a considerable amount for the period. He was married to Zobedia Davis, daughter of Lends and Nancy Davis, also of the Pink Hill Township. Their children

included Garland, Rexford, Vera, Vierna, Vendetta, and Verdie Noble. Verdie became a schoolteacher and ended up with the homeplace.

At the center of Noble's political and farming enterprises was his residence, today one of the county's most intact and best-maintained Victorian farmhouses. Although the actual date of construction is unknown, the house was likely built in the 1880s, when Richard Noble would have been old enough and well-established in his farming operations to erect such a spacious house. Built in a two-story gable-front configuration with a two-story wraparound porch, this house follows a form more typically constructed in towns. (Turning a dwelling's narrow side to the street fits smaller town lots more adequately.) The porch provides the most dramatic feature of the house with its original chamfered posts, turned balustrade, and latticework frieze. Common weatherboards cover the exterior, and standing-seam metal shelters the roof. The front facade has only two bays, and the offset door leads to a side hall, defining the layout of the interior. One large interior chimney provides heat to the two principal rooms on each floor. A large ell appended to the northeast elevation is said to have been Noble's original house on the site, which he later overbuilt into the present dwelling. Trailing off the back of this side appendage is a standard rear kitchen/dining room ell with a side porch.

Situated beneath a grove of mature oaks, seen in their youth in the 1906 photograph of the house in the *Kinston Free Press*, the house has a rural, unspoiled setting which adds to the farm's late-nineteenth-century character. A grouping of period outbuildings includes a small frame potato house, a brick well house, an earlier kitchen building, a smokehouse, and a washhouse.

Areatus Stroud House
built circa 1918
Pink Hill vicinity

Although this two-story farmhouse is a good example of a Victorian-period I-house, the decorative two-story attached hip-roof front porch sets it apart from the more typical one-story versions. The first-floor porch balustrade has been replaced; however, the second floor has part of its original turned railing, and both stories have turned wood posts with sawnwork brackets. Both porch ceilings are painted a light blue, a common feature in farmhouses on which owners wanted to replicate the bright blue skies of eastern North Carolina. Other exterior details, such as the gable-end single-shoulder chimneys, the gable returns, and the shuttered two-over-two sash windows, suggest that this was a comfortably prosperous farmstead. A grove of mature pecan and magnolia trees around the house and several frame outbuildings further indicate the prosperity of the agricultural operations.

The house was built by Areatus Stroud about 1918 on land acquired through a land grant to the Stroud family in the eighteenth century. Currently owned by Marion Stroud, Areatus's grandson, the house has been renovated.

Leary-Stroud House
built circa 1790
Pink Hill vicinity

This two-story three-bay frame farm dwelling is one of the small number of houses surviving from either the late eighteenth or the early nineteenth century. Located in the southern section of the county not far from the headwaters of the Trent River, the land where this house sits is said to have originally belonged to the Leary family. According to family tradition Isaac Stroud (1795-1871) was the first Stroud to live in the house. He married Elizabeth Boyette (1800-1869) in 1818. Three successive generations of male Strouds are said to have owned the property and included Isaac's son Jonas, his son Areatus, and in the twentieth century Areatus's son Quentin. The house was moved a short distance back from the road in 1947 to make way for the construction of a new house on the farm. Jerry Stroud now owns the farm.

Without sufficient documentary evidence, assigning a date of construction to the house is difficult, since so few properties of its era and style survive in Lenoir County to use as comparisons. Architecturally the Leary-Stroud House would suggest a date sometime during either the decade preceding or following the turn of the nineteenth century. But the area in which the dwelling was built was considered backcountry during that period—a perfect place for retarditaire building practices. In other words, the house could date from as late as the 1810s, whereby Isaac Stroud could have had it built for himself and his wife. Another possibility is that the house was already standing when Isaac purchased the farm, having been built for a Leary family member. Regardless of its exact date of construction, the house is one of the county's best examples of a simple vernacular Georgian-style dwelling of the backwoods.

Like its period counterpart the Richard Noble House (located within the same region of the county), the Leary-Stroud House embodies building practices common in rural sections of the county at the time. The house can best be characterized as an expression of vernacular interpretations of simple Georgian ideals that had been used by builders for nearly a half century. Rendered in a plain three-bay hall-and-parlor plan, the house, in a photograph taken in the 1890s, had a full-width shed porch on the front, two gable-end chimneys, and apparently unglazed windows on the second floor. The window openings appeared to be covered with batten shutters. A decorative slat balustrade and simple wooden posts articulated the front porch and were likely not original to the house, though they could have been early additions. Raised-panel shutters were visible on the first floor, adding a level of sophistication to an otherwise modest exterior.

Within a decade the Stroud family posed for a second portrait in front of the dwelling, and a few changes had occurred. Window openings on the second floor were fitted with six-over-six sash, the porch balustrade and posts were replaced with smaller square-in-section members, and what appears to be a fresh wood-shingle roof covered the house and porch. Today the exterior look is completed by beaded siding (surviving mainly on the front elevation), a Victorian two-story full-width porch on the front, and two-story shed rooms across the rear. When the house was moved in 1947, it lost its original chimneys. A kitchen that sat on the right side of the house has also been lost.

Nearly unblemished on the interior, the house offers an exceptional look at some of the best-preserved domestic spaces in the county. The overriding design element is the raised panel, a common device used in wainscoting, doors, and mantels. This simple but bold feature signifies the dwelling's origins in the Georgian era. A light wash on the first-floor woodwork appears to be the original finish applied to the fully sheathed interior. Located at the rear of the partition wall is an enclosed stair that leads to the second floor, which mimics the plan of the first. Woodwork on the upper floor compares favorably with that of the first floor, including simple mantels, composed of mitred surrounds and two raised panels set in the frieze, and board-and-batten doors. The sheathed second floor is striking with its weathered but unfinished pine surfaces. A molded chair rail is set above horizontal sheathing, adding a decorative feature not often seen in such rural properties.

A section of balustrade, perhaps from the original porch or somewhere on the interior, survives and is stored on the second story of the Victorian porch. This balustrade, which terminates at one end with a finely carved newel post, is a striking element rendered with typical Georgian profiles and pegged construction. This thoroughly Georgian treatment lends credence to the earlier date of construction, as well as suggesting that the Leary-Stroud House might have been a more elaborate dwelling than its current appearance suggests. Today, this important house hides beneath its Victorian changes, a dwelling of outstanding value to understanding the tastes and capabilities of Lenoir County's backcountry citizens during the county's formative years.

(former) Pleasant Hill Masonic Lodge
built early twentieth century
Jonestown vicinity

The former Pleasant Hill Masonic Lodge, a two-story tri-gable frame building, is now a storage structure with a large shed addition able to accommodate a flatbed truck. In spite of its altered integrity, the building's lodge character is still evident in its substantial size, six-over-six sash windows, gable returns, cornerboards, altered front two-paneled door, and brick pier foundation.

Pleasant Hill Lodge No. 304 was organized in 1870 and met in the farmhouse of J. H. Kinsey nearby in Jones County until 1874, when a lodge building was built near Nobles Mill in Lenoir County, some five miles from the Kinsey house. In 1903 the second lodge building was constructed about three miles from Jonestown and four miles from the old Nobles Mill lodge building. The lodge measures twenty-six by forty feet and cost $351.76. The lodge grew and prospered throughout the twentieth century, and continued to use this building until the 1960s, when membership outgrew the space. A new lodge was constructed about 1974 between Deep Run and Pink Hill and continues in use. It is one of the very few Lenoir County Masonic lodges to survive into the late twentieth century. The first two buildings in which the lodge met have been demolished, thus the third lodge building has special significance to the members.

Jackson Hill House
built circa 1886
Pink Hill vicinity

The enduring quality of the one-and-a-half-story, three-bay coastal cottage house type is evident in this well-preserved late-nineteenth-century example associated with Jackson Hill, a local farmer. Representing one of the traditional types of Lenoir County farmhouse built by middling farmers throughout the nineteenth century, the Hill House displays elements commonly found on coastal cottages. An engaged front porch and rear shed room additions, incorporated under one side-gable roof, create the signature profile. The house also has a small side addition on the east elevation. A single-shoulder end chimney with a corbeled base helps date the house after the Civil War. Nestled beneath a canopy of mature trees, the house retains only two outbuildings, a frame smokehouse and tobacco barn built in the early twentieth century.

(former) Pine Forest School
built early twentieth century
Pink Hill vicinity

Although this one-story frame school building was converted to use as a dwelling during the 1920s school consolidation movement, it maintains its original appearance to an astonishing degree. When compared to a photograph in the 1924 *Survey of the Public Schools of Lenoir County*, the former Pine Forest School appears virtually intact.

It was built as a one-teacher two-room school for white children in the Pink Hill community. The configuration of the building—a gable-and-wing form—is typical of schools constructed in Lenoir County prior to the consolidation movement. The school remains on its original site, which amounted to an acre and a half when the school was operated by the board of education. When the building was surveyed in 1924, water came by pump from a well, and one toilet was in place. Although the layout of the interior is not known, the school was apparently divided into two rooms, with two cloakrooms located in the building. In typical fashion the school had what were described as "home-made desks" and was heated by a single stove. The school covered seven grades and had an enrollment of forty-three students.

Retaining such original exterior details as its hip-roof porch, narrow six-over-six sash windows, projecting eaves, and diamond louvered ventilators, the building embodies a type rapidly disappearing from the countryside. The former school remains an important vestige of the opportunities available to rural families attempting to educate their children.

Joe Jones House
built circa 1900
Jonestown vicinity

This ornate Queen Anne-style two-story farmhouse was built for Joe Jones around the turn of the twentieth century but suffered a disastrous fire in the 1970s and is in ruins today. The single-pile house has a two-story front porch. The first level is a replacement Neoclassical-style porch, but the upper front-gabled balcony is original and has turned posts with decorative brackets and wide molded eave returns. A one-story rear wing has a side porch with identical trim. The interior center-hall plan has a wealth of fancy millwork, with a closed-string stair with ornate turned balusters, diagonal-sheathed wainscot, surrounds with corner blocks with rondels, and a parlor mantel with mirrored overmantel. Behind the house are three gable-front outbuildings, a smokehouse and two sheds. These appear to be approximately the same age as the house.

Joe Jones and his brother Ed ran the Jonestown Store and Post Office in the early twentieth century. They were the sons of Woodrow Jones, founder of the store. Joe Jones' daughter, Winona Adams (deceased), inherited the house.

Sally Taylor House
built fourth quarter of the nineteenth century
Pleasant Hill vicinity

Illustrating the utilitarian nature of simple log construction dating from after the Civil War, this one-room log house is one of the best-preserved one-room log dwellings surviving in the county. It was enlarged later with a frame side addition. The projecting gable roof on the fireplace-end wall suggests that the cabin might have originally had a mud-and-stick chimney, since removed. Well-crafted saddle notching holds the round logs tightly in place. Since no residue remains on the logs, it appears that the walls were never daubed. Spaces between the logs were covered on the interior by wood sheathing. One window, now boarded up, has a four-over-four sash. Both the front and back doors are plain board-and-batten types.

Little is known about the early years of the log house, though family tradition asserts this was that it was the home of a Sally Taylor. The number of surviving log buildings suggests that this was not a significant type of construction. However, other well preserved examples from the era do remain in the county, indicating that a number of struggling farmers or tenants built such houses after the Civil War. The Taylor House is one of the best-preserved examples remaining in the county.

(former) Taylor School
built first decade of the twentieth century
Pleasant Hill vicinity

Unlike the neighboring Pine Forest School, the Taylor School, when changed to a dwelling following the consolidation of one- and two-room schools in the 1920s, lost some of its original character as a simple one-room schoolhouse. Based on a photograph included in the *Kinston Free Press* Industrial Issue of 1906, the "New Taylor School House" was at that time a recently constructed building, covered by a crisp wood-shingle roof and having a single-door entrance on the gable end. In a typical arrangement, a bank of large windows was located along one of the side elevations (usually on the east), likely opposite the wall holding the blackboard. Most such school buildings had the windows on the east wall. Desks were generally arranged to face the blackboard, allowing natural light to flow over the shoulder of students.

By 1924, when the *Survey of the Public Schools of Lenoir County* was published by the state superintendent of public instruction, the Taylor School had deteriorated slightly. Set on a two-acre site, the building was valued at only two hundred dollars and contained one classroom, a cloakroom, and a stove. The enrollment for the year was twenty-five. The building had problems such as "window panes out; steps need repairing; windows not properly placed; ventilation and lighting very poor; floors not oiled; general arrangement of classrooms bad." This commentary could have been applied to many of the frame one- and two-room schools in the county at the time of consolidation. Following its conversion to a house, the building gained a side addition and some of the windows were made smaller. The overall form of the school remains intact.

Elkanah K. Davis House
built fourth quarter of the nineteenth century
Pink Hill vicinity

Elkanah K. Davis as born in 1857 in the Pink Hill Township to Senerse and Nancy Davis. By the early twentieth century Elkanah Davis had established a family and was living in this commodious two-story gable-and-wing Victorian house. In 1906 when the *Kinston Free Press* printed an industrial issue of the newspaper, Davis was listed as "owning 436 acres of choice farm land, with about 125 acres under cultivation. He raises fine crops of cotton, corn, tobacco and home supplies." He had married Laura Jones, and they had five children.

Also pictured in the newspaper was the Davises' rural two-bay side-hall-plan dwelling in its original unaltered appearance. The photograph of the Davis House shows an attached hipped-roof three-quarter wraparound porch on the first and second stories. A rear kitchen ell was visible, and the house did not have the surrounding mature pecan and oak trees that it has today. The roof of the wraparound porch is all that remains of the original porch. The second-story sidelighted entrance no longer leads to a floored second-story porch. The gable ends are pierced in the peaks by small circular windows set in diamond-shaped surrounds. The interior is well preserved, with standard Victorian accoutrements such as the plain dogleg stair in the entry hall, with a chamfered newel post, and beaded board tongue-and-groove sheathing. There are wide baseboards, five-paneled doors, and peaked-arch lintels above the windows. The mantelpieces consist of turned pilasters with simple consoles as mantel shelf supports. The Davises, like many families, lost their farmhouse during the Great Depression. It was bought at auction by Amos and Bertie Howard in the early 1930s and has remained in the Howard family.

Old Pink Hill Crossroads

developed from the 1840s to 1900
Pink Hill vicinity

In the 1840s when a post office was established on the plantation of Anthony Davis (1819-1894), the community of old Pink Hill was formed at the junction of State Road 1105 and State Road 1118. The community revolved around the enterprises of Davis, who in the late 1850s saw the need to have a doctor in the community and persuaded Dr. William W. Denny of Guilford County to move to Pink Hill and set up a practice. The house that Denny lived in for many years remains in the community. Anthony Davis is said to have built it for the doctor, although the dwelling might have been constructed after Davis's death. At one time the community had a grocery, a shoe store, another mercantile establishment, a hardware store, a spirits and wine shop, and a forge and cooperage.

Davis built a church for Pink Hill, which was used by

an African American congregation following the Civil War. The Bay Chapel Church, and Dr. W. W. Denny's one-story frame hipped-roof house are still intact, as are two 1890s farmhouses. The current cinderblock replacement Bay Chapel Church stands a short distance from its front-gable frame predecessor, built at the end of the nineteenth century. Although the windows have been boarded up and the once-prominent gable returns have been removed, the original weatherboarding and cornerboards remain on the earlier building. Lewis P. Tyndall's late-nineteenth-century gable-front frame general store was moved back from its original crossroads location and is now used for storage. Finally, there is an early-twentieth-century log smokehouse on the grounds of a 1900 frame tenant house.

According to local legend, the settlement was named after the wildflowers that grew on the hill on which Anthony Davis built his house. In 1900 when the Kinston and Carolina Railroad from Kinston to Beulaville and Chinquapin, in adjacent Duplin County, passed through three miles west of the Pink Hill community, families and businesses began to migrate to the nearby tracks, abandoning the old settlement. In just seven years a town, also named Pink Hill, was incorporated at the new location.

Anthony Davis House

built mid-nineteenth century
Pink Hill vicinity

Anthony Davis (1819-1894) was a progressive leader in southern Lenoir County and is credited with founding the community of Old Pink Hill, the original settlement located about three miles east of the current town of Pink Hill. Davis established a farm in this rural community which was the nucleus of a setttlement in the mid-nineteenth century. In addition to leading the development of Pink Hill, Davis was active in politics, serving as a county commissioner and state legislator. He donated two acres of land and cash to be applied to the construction of a new building for Christian Chapel Free Will Baptist Church in January 1894, the year he died.

Paralleling Davis's diverse community activity was the eclecticism of the Greek Revival-style coastal cottage that he had constructed, probably during the late 1840s or 1850s. The low sweeping roof of the one-story frame cottage extends into an engaged porch on the five-bay front facade. The fenestration pattern of door-door-window-door-window might not be original to the dwelling; however, the heavily paneled porch posts with Greek Revival moldings at each base and capital appear to be antebellum. The porch extends on the west elevation by a gable-end hip roof, which connects to a small kitchen building. A latticework frieze is applied to the porch and probably dates to the Victorian era. On the rear a single shed extends the full width of the house and side kitchen. One original exterior chimney remains between the west gable end and the attached kitchen, but the original kitchen chimney has been removed. The overall proportions, form, and decorative elements place the Davis House squarely in the genre of mid-nineteenth-century Greek Revival farmhouses.

The house sits majestically on a small rise surrounded by old oaks and cedars, prominent trees on antebellum farms. During the Great Depression of the 1930s a descendant of Anthony Davis sold the farm in order to save his own property from foreclosure. The Barnetts, a local African American family, purchased the farm and still own it. Many outbuildings remain, but all are associated with the tobacco culture and date from the early to middle twentieth century. The only other feature that remains from Davis's occupation is the family cemetery, located at the back of the farm. Two monumental obelisks mark the cemetery and attest to the prominent place that this family once held in the Old Pink Hill community.

Davis House
built second quarter of the nineteenth century; remodeled turn of the twentieth century, circa 1927
Pink Hill vicinity

Located in the center of the old Pink Hill community, this two-story frame I-house was likely built by a member of the Davis family, perhaps the father of John Ivey Davis (1855-1927) or, as one family tradition asserts, John Ivey himself. Although the house appears to have a Victorian origin, tradition relates that it could have been constructed as early as the 1830s. No known records exist to confirm that theory. The house and farm passed to John Ashley Davis (1892-1978) who undertook a

major remodeling in the 1920s. Referred to as "Ash," Davis was instrumental in bringing electricity to rural Lenoir County. He served as a member of the board of directors of Tri-County Electric Membership Cooperative for thirty years. He designed and built a brick home said to have been one of the first fully electrified homes in the area.

Situated on a prominent rise in old Pink Hill, the dwelling has a two-story attached front porch supported on both levels by chamfered posts with sawnwork C-scroll brackets; the plain-rail balustrade between the posts has been taken down. A gable-end chimney laid in a common bond buttresses each side elevation. There is a twentieth-century rear extension connecting the house to its original detached kitchen, which has a rear engaged front-gable porch supported by two Tuscan posts. Outbuildings include a large modern farm equipment shed built around an early-nineteenth-century cottage, and a packhouse. There is also an old fire alarm bell on the property, brought to the farm from Kinston by Ash Davis.

Aretus Jones House
built mid-nineteenth century
Pink Hill vicinity

By the late antebellum period the merging of classical styles, including the Federal and the Greek Revival, with the emerging Romantic Revivals, such as the Italianate and Victorian styles, allowed builders to craft some wonderfully eclectic and idiosyncratic houses. This two-story frame center-hall-plan dwelling now changed to a hall-and-parlor plan illustrates that confluence of styles with its interesting array of architectural features on the typical I-house form. The overall vertical proportions resemble those of an early nineteenth-century Federal-style house, though all other decorative motifs suggest a date of construction in the mid-nineteenth century. The house is thought to have been built for Aretus Jones Jr. (1810-1874). The Jones family lived in the area prior to the Civil War, though little else is known about the early history of the house.

The current first-floor four-bay fenestration pattern might represent a later change, three bays having been a more common treatment. The seven-panel door surviving on the secondary entrance, however, as well as the paneled frieze on the full-width shed porch, accord with the intriguing interior decorative schemes. In the parlor on the first floor the mantel, which resembles a three-part Federal design, is enlivened with inset diamond and rectangle motifs across the frieze—applications linking the design to the more stylish Victorian themes that began to sift slowly into local building practices by the mid-nineteenth century. Other less expressionistic woodwork includes typical Greek Revival corner blocks on some door surrounds and simple flush sheathing for walls. Standard flat and ovolo moldings reflect Greek Revival pattern book profiles.

TOWN OF PINK HILL

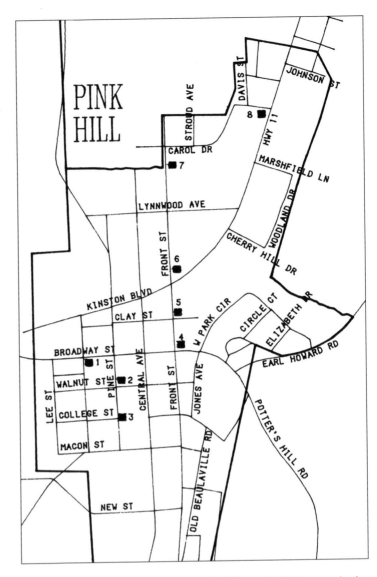

In 1900 when the Kinston and Carolina Railroad from Kinston to Beulaville and Chinquapin in Duplin County was constructed three miles west of the old Pink Hill community clustered around the Anthony Davis plantation, families gradually began to desert the settlement and move closer to the tracks. A town, also known as Pink Hill, grew up around the railroad, right on the Duplin County border. In 1907 the new Pink Hill was incorporated with Jesse J. Smith named mayor and George Turner, O. A. Garden, and T. A. Turner appointed commissioners.[1] One of the earliest settlers of the new town was Lewis Parker Tyndall, who had run a store at old Pink Hill. About 1900 he moved to the new town and built a large frame I-house at 201 Clay Street. Still retaining its comfortable two-story front porch with gingerbread trim, it is a landmark of the settlement period. Tyndall helped to establish a business district along Broadway Street by constructing a large one-story brick store, known as the Lewis Parker Tyndall and Sons Store (now Jones Furniture Company), at the northwest corner of Broadway and Front Streets. Another storekeeper who moved to town to take advantage of the railroad connection was Isaac Howard. In 1912 Howard left the country and built a house like the Tyndall House, an I-house with a two-story porch, on Broadway Street. Directly in front of his dwelling he built a store, which he ran until 1935. This one-story gable-front building and the Howard House still stand. Other early residents of the town built modestly stylish one and two-story frame houses of Victorian style along Clay Street, Broadway Street, and Jones Avenue. Builders finished these town houses with hipped roofs, decorative front gables, and porches trimmed with gingerbread.

Pink Hill was a progressive community in the 1920s. West Broadway Street developed during the decade with the construction of the Pink Hill Presbyterian Church, a small stylish Colonial Revival-style sanctuary, and frame Craftsman-style houses on spacious lots. In the late 1930s and 1940s two-story brick Colonial Revival-style houses and a picturesque Tudor Revival brick house with turreted entrance were built there as well.[2] A second major church, a handsome brick Colonial Revival-style sanctuary, was built in 1929 on Walnut Street for the Pink Hill United Methodist Church, which had been organized in 1916. (This building was demolished to make way for a larger sanctuary.)

One of the first brick consolidated schools in Lenoir County was built in town in the early 1920s to replace a brick schoolhouse that had been built in 1911. In 1924 the two-story school had 386 pupils enrolled in eleven grades. This building was demolished in 1928, and the larger one-story school, designed by well-known school architect Leslie Boney of Wilmington, was built on the same Pine Street site.[3] The long Classical Revival-style school with large windows and a flat roof with decorative brick parapet, served as an elementary school until the late 1990s and then was demolished.

In the late twentieth century Pink Hill is a bustling agricultural market town with a population of about six hundred. Stores catering to the farm trade are scattered along both sides of Broadway Street, the main street, to the east and west of Central Avenue. These mostly one-story brick buildings date from the early to middle twentieth century. The small town has a grid plan bisected by Highway 11, which heads north to Kinston, and Highway 241, which heads south to Wilmington. The railroad line was removed about 1929.

Notes

1. Sharpe, *New Geography of North Carolina*, 3:1394; Wilbur A. Tyndall, Pink Hill historian, notes in Pink Hill survey file, State Historic Preservation Office; Powell, *Annals of Progress*, 4.

2. The Pink Hill survey files, compiled by Robbie Jones during his 1993-1994 survey of Lenoir County provided much of this specific information.

3. *Heritage of Lenoir County*, 123-124.

1. Pink Hill Presbyterian Church

built circa 1925
200 block of West Broadway Street

The Pink Hill Presbyterian Church is a diminutive building of Colonial Revival style. The front-gable form, three bays wide and five bays deep, has frame construction. A pedimented entrance porch with a barrel-vaulted arch is supported by slender posts. The double-door entrance has pilasters and a pedimented overdoor. Large nine-over-nine sash illuminate the sanctuary. A turreted bell tower with louvered ventilators surmounts the roof. The exterior of the church has been covered in vinyl.

2. Pink Hill United Methodist Church (demolished)

built circa 1929, demolished 1995
Walnut Street

The Pink Hill United Methodist congregation, organized in 1916, built this two-story brick Colonial Revival church in 1929 with the assistance of a grant from the Duke Foundation. This building was one of the best examples of the Colonial Revival ecclesiastical style in Lenoir County, from the front facade's clipped-gable roof and large oculus window to the interplay of segmentally arched and round-arched double-hung windows along the sides of the church, all decorated with brick and cement voussoirs and keystones. The five segmentally arched eight-over-eight windows on the first floor lit the former administration area of the building; the five round-arched double-hung windows above them, in addition to the oculus windows at the church's front and rear facades, lit the actual worship area. The octagonal wooden steeple had corner pilasters and arched louvered ventilators. Directly below the steeple was the church's enclosed front entrance, a simple projecting brick front-gable narthex with paneled double-leaf entrance doors surmounted by a fanlight transom.

The church, which had seen almost fifty years of service to the congregation, was replaced in the late 1960s-early 1970s by a more modern structure on the next lot. The older Colonial Revival church was used as an auxiliary building for the congregation as recently as 1980. The church was demolished in 1995.

3. Pink Hill Elementary School (demolished)

built 1927-1928; enlarged 1950s, 1980s; demolished 1997
East side of Pine Street

The Pink Hill Elementary School was one of only a few first-generation consolidated schools that survived in Lenoir County as late as 1997. The one-story brick building was designed by noted school architect Leslie Boney of Wilmington. The classical-style building had three projecting bays that broke up the long facade with bands of tall six-over-six sash windows. The central bay contained a recessed double-door entrance with transom and sidelights, protected by a bracketed stoop. Decorative brick cornices and roof parapets enlivened the building, as did the diamond-shaped motifs in the parapets. Windows were surmounted by flat arches with accent blocks. The school retained a great deal of architectural integrity, since the additions that had enabled it to continue to serve the community were not attached to the building but merely connected by walkways.

The roots of this school go back to 1910, when George Turner advocated building a public school in Pink Hill. He realized his goal one year later. The first school was a two-story building with an auditorium on the second floor. It was demolished between 1927 and 1928, and the new eight-room school was built. Shortly afterward a seven-room addition was constructed. Two rooms were added to the school in the 1940s. The school served the elementary grades in recent years and was demolished in 1997.

4. Isaac Howard House and Store
built 1912
201 Broadway Street

Isaac Howard (1861–1935), who was raised on a farm outside Pink Hill, moved into town and built this house in 1912. The two-story, side-gable frame house has the traditional form of a farmhouse. It is well preserved, with plain siding, four-over-four sash windows, exterior end chimneys, and a rear kitchen ell. A double front porch shelters identical center-bay entrances with transoms and sidelights at each story.

Howard ran a general store directly in front of his house from about 1912 until his death in 1935. The front-gable frame building was moved beside the house and converted to a packhouse in later years. The store is extremely well preserved, with plain siding, four-over-four sash windows, and a double-door entrance sheltered by a wooden awning. At his father's death James Earl Howard, born in 1905, inherited the house. The present owner purchased it in 1990.

5. Lewis Parker Tyndall House
built early twentieth century
201 Clay Street

The Tyndall House is one of the finest surviving examples of early Pink Hill architecture. Lewis Parker Tyndall was a storekeeper in the original settlement of Pink Hill, located three miles to the east. In the early twentieth century he moved to the present location of the community, bringing Dr. William W. Denny with him. He built a traditional farmhouse, two stories high with side gables and exterior end chimneys, and adorned it with a very decorative double front porch, with turned posts with sawnwork brackets, enclosed by a turned balustrade. Each level of the facade has a central door with transom and sidelights. The house retains its plain siding with cornerboards, two-over-two sash windows, and pedimented gables.

Tyndall, one of the town's first merchants, built a large one-story brick store about 1900 at the northwest corner of Broadway and Front Streets. Now Jones Furniture Company, the store still stands.

6. Ernest Roscoe Maxwell House
built circa 1925
North East junction N. C. Highway 11 and Front Street

Ernest Roscoe Maxwell, Pink Hill's mail carrier in the 1920s, built this Craftsman-style house—the first brick house in Pink Hill. The one-story side-gable house is two rooms deep, with such stylish Craftsman details as clipped end gables and a small Palladian window in each gable end. The six-over-one sash are set singly and in double and triple bands. The front-gabled entrance porch has replacement posts. A two-story garage apartment, reportedly E. R. Maxwell's lodging earlier in the 1920s, sits behind the house. At one time the property had a two-stall stable with a tack room and a shed.

7. James Tindal House
built circa 1840, remodeled 1970s
409 North Front Street

James Tindal (1814-1894), a farmer and carpenter, built this house for his family about 1840 on land purchased from Richard Noble. The house contained a hall-parlor plan with a center chimney. The house and farm were about five miles northeast of the current Pink Hill community. Tindal used heart pine from a nearby grove. Around 1900, James's son, Andrew J. Tyndall (1849-1927), added two rear rooms and replaced the original chimney with two exterior end chimneys.

About 1915 James's grandson, Andrew Herman Tyndall (1891-1945), built a new house nearby, and the old homeplace became first a tenant house, then a pack-house. In the 1970s James's great-grandson, Wilbur Tyndall, moved the house to its current location and renovated it. He discovered that the flooring in the rear addition was marked "Andrew J. Tyndall, Lynchburg," indicating that the lumber had been sent to Andrew Tyndall via the nearby railroad station at Lynchburg. The tongue-and-groove floors, walls, board-and-batten ceilings, and doors are original to the house; the windows and chimneys have been replaced. The roof was rebuilt with an overhang not found on the original house. In 1900 the original detached log kitchen was replaced by a frame kitchen. The second kitchen, not moved with the house, still stands near its original site.

8. Wilbur A. Tyndall Tractor Museum
established 1974
West side of N. C. Highway 11 .4 mile north of the junction with N. C. Highway 241

Wilbur Tyndall, a man fascinated with the history of his native Pink Hill region, established a museum of early to mid-twentieth-century tractors, cars, and farming equipment in 1974. Tyndall converted a mid-twentieth-century car repair shop, a front-gable concrete-block building, for his museum by adding an open shed around all four sides as a display area. The vehicles and implements are lined up in this space, as well as inside the building and in an adjacent vehicle shed. Tyndall has loaned parts of his collection to the Screen Gems Studios in nearby Wilmington as props for movies.

A short distance southeast of the museum is an unusual burial structure that is unrelated to the museum. This grave house, a small hipped-roof building sheathed with tin, contains the graves of Ivy Smith (d. 1922) and his two wives, Sarah (d. 1916) and Viette (d. 1938). Viette, Smith's second wife, is said to have had recurring dreams of her husband outside in the rain, so she had the shelter built. Window openings in the structure allow the graves to show. Grave houses, once a fairly common method of protecting graves in North Carolina, are now quite rare.

GLOSSARY OF ARCHITECTURAL TERMS

ADAMESQUE *See* Federal Style.

ARCADE A range of arches supported on piers or columns, attached to or detached from a wall.

ARCHITRAVE The lowest part of an entablature, sometimes used by itself as a casing for a window or door.

ART DECO A style of decorative arts and architecture popular in the 1920s and 1930s, characterized by the use of geometric, angular forms; also referred to as Moderne or Art Moderne.

ART MODERNE *See* Art Deco.

ART NOUVEAU STYLE A style of decoration, popular during the late nineteenth and early twentieth centuries, based on flowing, sinuous forms frequently derived from the structure of various parts of plants.

ATRIUM A skylit central court in a contemporary building or house.

BALCONY A platform enclosed with a low parapet, railing, or balustrade and projecting from a wall, usually in front of a window or other opening.

BALUSTER A short pillar or colonnette, often turned with classical moldings and having a base, shaft, and cap; balusters support the handrail and enclose the side of a staircase.

BALUSTRADE A row of balusters surmounted by a railing that forms a low enclosure, often found on porches, terraces, balconies, roofs, staircases, and altars.

BARGEBOARD A board, often molded, carved or otherwise ornamented, that runs at a sloping angle the length of the gable end of a building and covers the junction between the wall and end rafter pair; also known as vergeboard or vargeboard.

BAS-RELIEF A decorative feature that is slightly raised or embossed above a uniform surface.

BATTERED Having a slight incline from perpendicular, particularly a porch support on a bungalow porch.

BATTLEMENT *See* crenellation.

BAY An opening or division along a face of a structure. For example, a wall with a door and two windows is three bays wide. A bay can also be a projection of a room or facade having windows.

BEADED WEATHERBOARD A weatherboard finished with an incised and rounded edge.

BEAUX ARTS Style of classical architecture, popularly associated with the Ecole des Beaux-Arts in Paris, that prevailed in France in the late nineteenth century and that was adopted in the United States and elsewhere circa 1900; eclectic use and adaptation of French architectural features combined so as to give a massive, elaborate, and often ostentatious effect.

BELFRY A bell tower, or the room where bells are placed.

BELT COURSE, BELTING *See* string course.

BOND The pattern in which bricks are laid.

BOX PEW A church pew screened or enclosed by a high back and sides.

BRACKET A divide, either ornamental, structural, or both, set under a projecting element, such as the eaves of a house.

BROKEN PEDIMENT A pediment over a doorway or window having its raking cornice interrupted at the crown or apex.

BUNGALOW STYLE An early-twentieth-century architectural style that grew out of the Arts and Crafts movement of the late nineteenth century. Its basic characteristics are long, low profiles; overhanging, bracketed eaves; wide engaged porches with square, squat brick piers supporting wood posts; and informal interior arrangements.

BUTTRESS A vertical mass of masonry projecting from or built against a wall to give additional strength at the point of maximum stress. Sometimes wooden buttresses are added to frame Gothic Revival-style buildings as decorative, but not supporting, features.

BYZANTINE REVIVAL The revival of a style of architecture developed chiefly in the fifth and sixth centuries in the Byzantine empire, characterized by arches, domes, mosaics, relief carving, and decorative masonry.

CANOPY An ornamental, rooflike projection or covering.

CANTILEVER A bracket or horizontal beam, whose length is greater than its breadth, that projects out beyond a wall to support a balcony, pediment, or entablature.

CAPE COD COTTAGE A one-and-one-half-story house whose rear roof slopes to cover rear shed rooms. This house type is traditional to Cape Cod, Massachusetts.

CAPITAL The topmost member, usually decorated or molded, of a column or pilaster.

CASEMENT A window hinged or pivoted on one of its sides to open and shut.

CHAMFER A bevel or oblique surface formed by cutting off a square edge.

CHEVRON A V-shaped decoration generally used as a continuous frieze or molding. This treatment is typical of the Art Deco style.

CLASSICAL Embodying or based on the principles and forms of Greek and Roman architecture.

CLIPPED GABLE A gable the peak of which is truncated for decorative effect; often the roof overhangs the missing peak.

COLONIAL REVIVAL STYLE Late-nineteenth and early-twentieth-century style that combines features of classical and American Colonial architecture.

COLONNETTE A small-scale column, generally employed as a decorative element on mantels, overmantels, and porticos.

COMMON BOND A method of laying brick wherein one course of headers is laid for every three, five, or seven courses of stretchers.

CORBEL The projection of masonry courses in a stepped series so that each course of bricks or stones extends further forward than the one below. Corbeling appears in parapets, chimney shoulders, chimney caps, and masonry cornices.

CORINTHIAN ORDER The slenderest and most ornate of the classical Greek orders of architecture, characterized by a slim fluted column with bell-shaped capital decorated with stylized acanthus leaves; variations of this order were used extensively by the Romans.

CORNERBOARD A vertical board nailed on an external corner of a frame building as a method of finishing and joining the ends of the weatherboards.

CORNICE The uppermost part of an entablature, usually used to crown the wall of a building, portico, or ornamental doorway. The term is loosely applied to almost any horizontal molding forming a main decorative feature, especially to a molding at the junction of walls and ceiling in a room.

CRAFTSMAN STYLE *See* Bungalow style.

CRENELLATION Alternating indentations and raised sections of a parapet, creating a toothlike profile sometimes known as a battlement. Crenellation is a detail found most commonly in the Gothic Revival style.

CRESTING Ornamental ironwork, often highly decorative, used to embellish the ridge of a gable roof or the curb, or upper cornice, of a mansard roof.

CROSSETTE A lateral projection of the head of a molded architrave or surround of a door, window, mantel, or paneled overmantel; also known as an "ear" or "dog-ear."

CRUCIFORM PLAN A plan shaped like a cross.

DENTICULATED Having dentils.

DENTILS Small, closely spaced blocks, often toothlike, used as an ornamental element of a classical cornice.

DORIC ORDER A classical order most readily distinguished by its simple, unornamented capitals and tablets with vertical grooving, called triglyphs, set at regular intervals in the frieze.

DORMER WINDOW An upright window, set in a sloping roof, with vertical sides and front, usually with a gable, shed, or hip roof.

DOUBLE-SHOULDERED CHIMNEY An exterior chimney with sides that angle inward to form shoulders twice as the chimney ascends from the base to the cap.

EASTLAKE STYLE A forerunner of the Stick style with rich ornamentation and heavy brackets, named after the English architect Charles Lock Eastlake (1833-1906), a pioneer of the Tudor Revival.

EAVES The projecting edges of a roof, usually above a cornice, designed to shed water beyond the faces of the walls of a building.

ECLECTIC OR ECLECTICISM A method of design in architecture in which elements from a variety of stylistic sources are selected and combined in new and original ways.

ELL A secondary wing or extension of a building, often a rear addition, positioned at right angles to the principal mass.

ENGAGED PORCH A porch the roof of which is continuous structurally with that of the main section of the building.

ENGLISH BOND A method of laying brick wherein one course is laid with stretchers and the next with headers, thus bonding a double thickness of brick together to form a high-strength bond.

ENTABLATURE The horizontal part of a classical order of architecture, usually positioned above columns or pilasters. It consists of three parts: the lowest molded portion is the architrave; the middle band is the frieze; and the uppermost element is the cornice.

EXTERIOR END CHIMNEY A chimney located outside the walls, usually against the gable end of a building.

FACADE The face or front of a building.

FANLIGHT A semicircular window, usually above a door or window, with radiating muntins suggesting a fan.

FEDERAL STYLE The style of architecture popular in America from the Revolution through the early nineteenth century (in North Carolina from about 1800 to 1840). The style reflects the influence of the Adam Style popularized by Scots architects Robert and James Adam which emphasized delicate variations of classical Roman architecture.

FENESTRATION The arrangement of windows on a building.

FINIAL An ornament, usually turned on a lathe, placed on the apex of an architectural feature such as a gable, turret, or pediment.

FLEMISH BOND A method of laying brick wherein headers and stretchers alternate in each course and, vertically, headers are placed over stretchers to form a bond and give a distinctive cross pattern.

FLEURON A floral motif, especially one used as a terminal point or in a decorative series on an object.

FLUSH SHEATHING A wall treatment consisting of closely fitted horizontal boards with joints that are carefully formed to be hidden and flush, giving a very uniform, flat siding appearance.

FLUTING Shallow, concave grooves running vertically on the shaft of a column, pilaster, or other surface.

FRIEZE The middle portion of a classical entablature, located above the architrave and below the cornice. The term is also used to describe the flat, horizontal board located above the weatherboards of most houses.

GABLE The triangular portion of a wall formed or defined by the two sides of a double-sloping roof; often referred to as an A roof.

GAMBREL ROOF A roof with two pitches rising into a ridge, the upper slope being flatter than the lower one.

GEORGIAN STYLE The prevailing style of the eighteenth century in Great Britain and the North American colonies, so named after Kings George I, George II, and George III. It is derived from classical, Renaissance, and Baroque forms.

GOTHIC REVIVAL STYLE The nineteenth-century revival of the forms and ornament of medieval/Gothic European architecture, characterized by the use of pointed arches, buttresses, pinnacles, and other Gothic details in a decorative fashion. The style was popular for church architecture.

GREEK REVIVAL STYLE The mid-nineteenth-century revival of the forms and ornamentation of the architecture of ancient Greece.

HALF-TIMBERING In medieval times, a structural system consisting of a timber-framed building, the interstices filled with masonry and usually stuccoed. The term also describes the later practice of applying boards to the face of a wall in imitation of half-timbered construction.

HEADER The end of a brick, sometimes glazed.

HIP ROOF A roof that slopes back equally from each side of a building. A hip roof can have a pyramidal form or have a slight ridge.

HOOD MOLDING A projecting molding on the face of a wall, usually over a door or window, designed to throw off water; also called a label molding.

IN ANTIS PORTICO A roofed space that is recessed beneath the main roof of a building, with detached or attached columns and a pediment.

INTERNATIONAL STYLE The general form of architecture developed in the 1920s and 1930s by European architects; characterized by simple geometric forms, large untextured often white surfaces, large areas of glass, and the general use of steel or reinforced-concrete construction.

IONIC ORDER A classical order distinguished by a capital with spiral scrolls, called volutes, and generally dentil courses. This order is more elaborate than the Doric but less so than the Corinthian.

ITALIANATE STYLE A revival of elements of Italian Renaissance architecture popular during the middle and late nineteenth century; characterized by the presence of broad projecting or overhanging cornices supported by ornate sawn brackets. Other features include the use of arched windows and heavy hood molds.

JACOBEAN STYLE The style of architecture in England in the first half of the seventeenth century. It continued the Elizabethan style, with a gradual introduction of Italian models in architecture.

JALOUSIE WINDOW A window made of glass slats, or louvers of a similar nature.

KEYSTONE The central wedge-shaped stone at the crown of an arch or in the center of a lintel.

KNEE BRACE A nonstructural diagonal member used as exterior ornamentation and extending from the facade to the eave of a building. This element characterizes the Craftsman style of American architecture.

LANCET WINDOW A narrow, sharply pointed, arched window.

LATTICEWORK Work consisting of crossed wooden strips arranged to form a diagonal pattern of open spaces between the strips.

LINTEL A beam of wood or stone that spans an opening; in masonry construction it frequently supports the masonry above the opening.

LOUVER A series of horizontal (unless otherwise noted) slats, generally sloping or adjustable, designed to block sun, rain, or vision and to permit passage of air.

LOZENGE A diamond-shaped decorative motif; usually one of a series.

L-PLAN A building plan in an L-shape form.

LUNETTE A half-moon window, or the wall space beneath an arch or vault.

MEDIEVAL STYLE The style based on Romanesque and Gothic architecture in Europe, characterized by round-arched or pointed-arch openings and decorative trim. These elements were popular in North Carolina from about 1850 to 1900.

MEZZANINE The lowest balcony or forward part of such a balcony in a theater; also a low story between two other stories of greater height in a building.

MINIMAL TRADITIONAL STYLE A style popular for houses in the 1940s and 1950s, characterized by gabled forms with simplified classical or medieval decoration.

MISSION REVIVAL STYLE Early-twentieth-century revival of the architecture of colonial Spanish settlements featuring stuccoed masonry walls, clay tile roofs, balconies, and arched openings; sometimes called Spanish Colonial Revival style.

MODILLION A horizontal bracket, often in the form of a plain block, ornamenting or sometimes supporting the underside of a cornice.

MOORISH REVIVAL STYLE A variation on the Spanish Colonial Revival style characterized by domes, arcades of ogee and lancet-shaped arches, and multicolored trim.

MULLION A vertical member separating and often supporting windows, doors, or panels set in a series.

MUNTIN A strip of wood separating the panes of a window sash.

NARTHEX The vestibule of a church.

NAVE The main part of the interior of a church.

NEOCLASSICAL REVIVAL STYLE The revival of design features from ancient Greek and Roman precedents. It generally refers to the renewed interest in classicism around the turn of the 20th century.

NEWEL POST The principal post used to terminate the railing or balustrade of a flight of stairs.

NICHE An ornamental recess in a wall or other surface, usually semicircular in plan and arched.

OBELISK A tapering, four-sided monument.

OCULUS A round window.

OGEE A curve made up of a convex and a concave part.

ORIEL WINDOW A bay window, especially one projecting from an upper story.

OVERMANTEL A framed mirror or panel surmounting a fireplace.

PALLADIAN WINDOW A three-part window design

featuring a central arched opening flanked by lower square-headed openings, separated from the central part by columns, pilasters, piers, or narrow vertical panels.

PALMETTE A conventionalized shape in the form of palmately spread leaves or sections, used as ornamentation.

PANEL A portion of flat surface set off by molding or some other decorative device.

PARAPET A low wall along a roof or terrace, used for decoration or protection.

PEBBLEDASH An exterior wall finish popular in the Craftsman style and made by pressing small pebbles into wet mortar.

PEDIMENT A crowning element of porticos, pavilions, doorways, and other architectural features, usually of low triangular form, with a cornice extending across its base and carried up the raking sides; sometimes broken in the center as if to accommodate an ornament; sometimes of segmental, elliptical, or serpentine form.

PENDANT An ornament suspended from a roof, vault, or ceiling.

PERGOLA An arbor, usually constructed of a double row of supports with an open framework between.

PIER A short piece of masonry, square or rectangular in section, used to support the frame of a building; also a pillar or post from which a gate or door hangs.

PILASTER A shallow pier or rectangular column projecting only slightly from a wall. Pilasters are usually decorated like columns with a base, shaft, and capital.

PLINTH BLOCK A block at the base of a door frame, chimneypiece, etc., against which the skirting is butted.

PORTE COCHERE A projecting porch that provides protection for vehicles and people entering a building; a common feature of the early-twentieth-century Colonial Revival and Bungalow styles.

PORTICO A roofed space, open or partly enclosed, often with columns and a pediment, that forms the entrance and centerpiece of the facade of a building.

PRAIRIE STYLE Style of architecture developed from the Prairie School, a group of early-twentieth-century architects of the Chicago area who designed houses and buildings with emphasis on horizontal lines corresponding to the flatness of the midwestern prairie of the United States.

PRESSED METAL Thin sheets of metal molded into decorative designs and used to cover interior walls and ceilings, also used on exteriors, especially in early-twentieth-century commercial structures.

QUEEN ANNE STYLE A late-nineteenth-century revival of early eighteenth-century English architecture, characterized by irregularity of plan and massing and a variety of textures.

QUOINS Ornamental blocks of wood, stone, brick, or stucco placed at the corners of a building and projecting slightly from the front of the facade.

RAFTERS Structural timbers rising from the plate at the top of a wall to the ridge of the roof and supporting the roof covering.

RAISED PANEL A portion of a flat surface, as of a door or wainscoting, that is distinctly set off from the surrounding area by a molding or other device and is raised above the surrounding area.

RANCH HOUSE A one-story house type with a low-pitched roof, built mainly in the American suburbs after World War II; also called a rambler.

REEDED Shaped to resemble a series of adjacent, parallel convex strips.

REHABILITATION The process of returning a property to a state of utility, through repair or alteration, that makes possible an efficient contemporary use. In rehabilitation, those portions of the property important in illustrating historic, architectural, and cultural values are preserved or restored.

RENAISSANCE REVIVAL A mid-nineteenth-century architectural style adapting the classical forms of fifteenth and sixteenth-century Italian architecture, characterized by blocklike massing with refined classicized decorative detail around regularly organized windows.

RESTORATION The process of accurately recovering the form and details of a property as it appeared at a particular period of time by removing later work and replacing missing original work.

RETURNS Horizontal portions of a cornice that extend part of the way across the gable end of a structure at eave level.

ROMANESQUE REVIVAL The revival in the second half of the nineteenth century of massive Romanesque forms, characterized by the round arch.

RONDEL A small disk of glass used as an ornament in a stained-glass window.

RUSTICATION Rough-surfaced stonework or imitation stonework.

SASH The frame, usually of wood, that holds the pane(s) of glass in a window; may be movable or fixed; may slide in a vertical plane or may pivot.

SAWTOOTH DESIGN A pattern resembling the teeth in a saw, frequently applied to brickwork in which a course of brick is laid diagonally to the face of a wall so that the ends project like saw teeth; also applied to a roof with a series of sloping skylights that in profile present a sawtooth pattern.

SCROLLWORK Decorative work in which scroll forms figure prominently.

SEGMENTAL ARCH An arch formed on a segment of a circle or an ellipse.

SHEATHED Having a covering or lining fastened to the structural framing members over which another finish layer is sometimes placed.

SHED ROOF A roof having a single slope.

SHOTGUN A front-gable house having all the rooms opening one into another in a line from front to back; usually one room wide.

SHOULDER The sloping shelf or ledge created on the side of a masonry chimney where the width of the chimney changes.

SIDELIGHT A framed area of fixed glass of one or more panes positioned beside a door or window opening.

SILL A heavy horizontal timber positioned at the bottom of the frame of a wood structure, which rests on top of the foundation; also, the horizontal bottom member of a door or window frame.

SINGLE-SHOULDERED CHIMNEY An exterior chimney with sides that angle inward to form a single shoulder as the chimney ascends from the base to the cap.

SPANDREL Paneling used to fill the triangular shape below a stair stringer or between a post and lintel.

SPANISH COLONIAL REVIVAL STYLE See Mission Revival Style.

SPINDLE FRIEZE A row of lathe-turned spindles included as the uppermost decorative feature of a gallery or porch below the cornice; also known as an openwork frieze.

SPIRE A tapering roof surmounting a steeple.

STOOP A small porch; a small raised platform, approached by steps and sometimes having a roof and seats at the entrance of a building.

STRETCHER The long face of a brick laid horizontally.

STRING COURSE A projecting course of bricks or other material forming a narrow horizontal strip across the wall of a building, usually to delineate the line between stories; also referred to as a belt course.

STUCCO A mixture of cement, lime, and sand used for coating the exterior of a wall; also, to coat a wall with stucco.

SUNBURST A flat, usually elliptical, ornament with a design in relief of rays emanating from a center.

SURROUND The border or casing of a window or door opening, sometimes molded.

TERRA-COTTA A ceramic material used either structurally or decoratively in architecture. Such tiles molded decoratively and often glazed were used for facings for buildings or as inset ornament. Tobacco farmers experimented with terra-cotta blocks for building curing barns in the 1920s and 1930s.

TONGUE AND GROOVE JOINT An edge joint of two planks or boards consisting of a continuous raised fillet or tongue on the edge of one member that fits into a corresponding rectangular channel or groove cut into the edge of the other member.

TRABEATED Built with posts and lintels; hence, a term used to describe a standard Greek Revival entrance door having a transom and sidelights.

TRACERY Ornamental work consisting of divided ribs, bars, or the like, as in the upper part of a Gothic window, in panels, and in screens.

TRANSOM A narrow horizontal window unit above a door.

TRANSVERSE Lying in a cross direction; a cross section.

TRUSS ROOF A roof made of a pair of common rafters tied together by a collar beam or a pair of principal rafters anchored by tie and collar beams.

TUDOR REVIVAL A style popular in the early twentieth century, characterized by motifs associated with medieval English architecture, such as steep gables, diamond-paned windows, and picturesque chimneys.

TURNED Fashioned on a lathe, as a baluster, newel, or porch post.

TURRET A small slender tower derived from medieval castle construction, usually at the corner of a building and often containing a circular stair. The Queen Anne style employs the turret as one of its primary characteristics.

TUSCAN ORDER A classical order similar to the Doric but simpler; usually more massive than the Roman Doric, less massive than the Greek Doric, and more adaptable to varied types of structures than either of those.

TYMPANUM The space enclosed between an arch and a horizontal lintel; also the triangular surface bounded by the sloping and horizontal cornices of a pediment.

VENEER A thin layer of wood or other material used for facing or inlay.

VERGEBOARD See Bargeboard.

VERNACULAR In architecture, as in language, the nonacademic local expressions of a particular region. For example, a vernacular Greek Revival structure may exhibit forms and details derived from the principles of formal classical architecture but executed by local builders in an individual way that reflects local or regional needs, tastes, climatic conditions, technology, and craftsmanship.

VESTIBULE An entrance hall, usually shallow, acting as a link between the outer door and the interior rooms of a building.

VICTORIAN The general term used to describe the wide variety of eclectic revival styles that were introduced in British and American architecture and decorative arts during the reign of Queen Victoria (1837-1901).

VOUSSOIR A wedge-shaped masonry unit in an arch or vault whose converging sides are cut as radii of one of the centers of the arch or vault.

WAINSCOT A decorative or protective facing applied to the lower portion of an interior wall or partition.

WEATHERBOARDING Wood siding consisting of overlapping horizontal boards usually thicker at one edge than the other.

WRAPAROUND PORCH A porch that extends around more than one elevation of a building; a popular feature of the turn-of-the-twentieth-century Queen Anne style.

Brick Bond Patterns

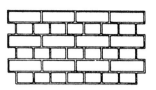

English Bond

Stretcher   Header

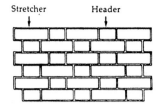

Flemish Bond

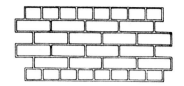

Common Bond

Chimneys

Plain

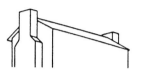

Exterior End

Interior End

Central

Corbeled

Internal Flanking
Hallway

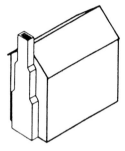

Double Shoulder
(Paved Shoulder)

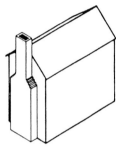

Single Shoulder
(Stepped Shoulder)

Classical Orders

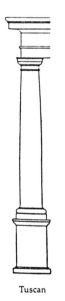

Tuscan

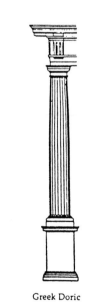

Greek Doric

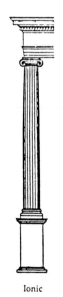

Ionic

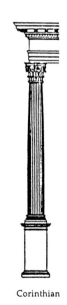

Corinthian

Composite

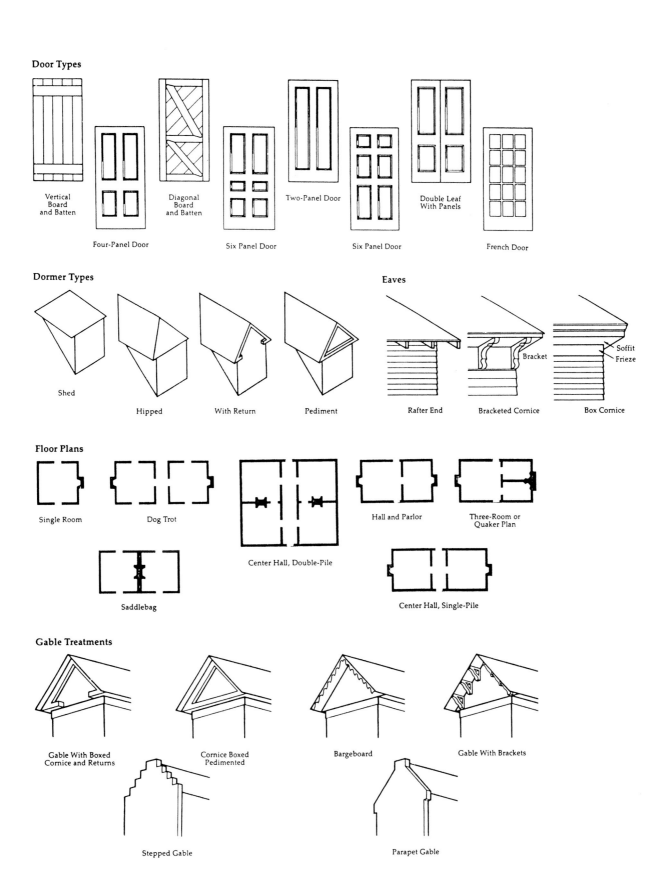

Door Types

Vertical Board and Batten

Four-Panel Door

Diagonal Board and Batten

Six Panel Door

Two-Panel Door

Six Panel Door

Double Leaf With Panels

French Door

Dormer Types

Shed

Hipped

With Return

Pediment

Eaves

Rafter End

Bracketed Cornice

Bracket

Box Cornice

Soffit

Frieze

Floor Plans

Single Room

Dog Trot

Center Hall, Double-Pile

Hall and Parlor

Three-Room or Quaker Plan

Saddlebag

Center Hall, Single-Pile

Gable Treatments

Gable With Boxed Cornice and Returns

Cornice Boxed Pedimented

Bargeboard

Gable With Brackets

Stepped Gable

Parapet Gable

Log Corner Timbering

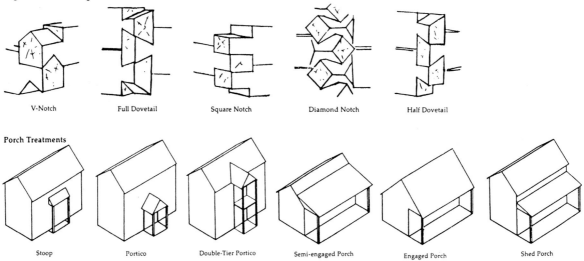

V-Notch   Full Dovetail   Square Notch   Diamond Notch   Half Dovetail

Porch Treatments

Stoop   Portico   Double-Tier Portico   Semi-engaged Porch   Engaged Porch   Shed Porch

Roof Types

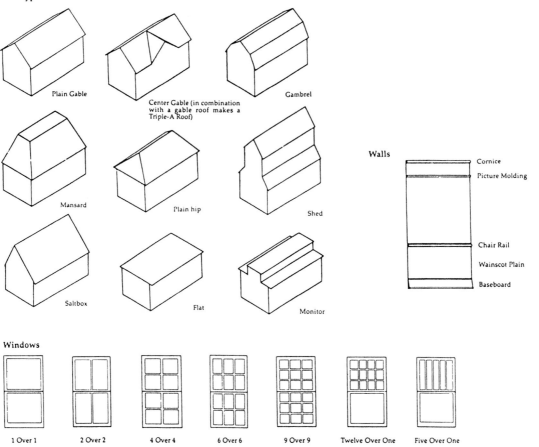

Plain Gable

Center Gable (in combination with a gable roof makes a Triple-A Roof)

Gambrel

Mansard   Plain hip   Shed

Saltbox   Flat   Monitor

Walls

Cornice
Picture Molding
Chair Rail
Wainscot Plain
Baseboard

Windows

1 Over 1   2 Over 2   4 Over 4   6 Over 6   9 Over 9   Twelve Over One   Five Over One

450

BIBLIOGRAPHY

Books, Articles and Reports

Anderson, Mavis. *A Lincoln City Celebration.* Kinston: Black Artists' Guild, Inc., 1985.

Archbell, Lillie V. "Kinston in the Sixties," "Historic Buildings in and near Kinston," "Editor's Column,"*Carolina and the Southern Cross*, 1 (November 1913, February 1914): 1-3, 8-10,12.

Austin, T.E. "Tobacco Marketing Warehouses and Their Location in the Urban Landscape of the Eastern Flue-Cured Belt of North Carolina." Master's thesis, East Carolina University, 1977.

Biennial Report of the Superintendent of Public Instruction for North Carolina of 1924-1926. Raleigh: State Superintendent of Public Instruction, 1926.

Bishir, Catherine W. *North Carolina Architecture.* Chapel Hill: University of North Carolina Press, 1990.

Black, Allison. "Historic and Architectural Resources of Kinston, North Carolina." Research report, State Historic Preservation Office, North Carolina Division of Archives and History, Raleigh, 1989.

Branson's North Carolina Business Directory, Raleigh: Levi Branson, 1869

Branson's North Carolina Business Directory, Raleigh: Levi Branson, 1872.

Branson's North Carolina Business Directory, Raleigh: Levi Branson, 1877-78.

Branson's North Carolina Business Directory, Raleigh: Levi Branson, 1884.

Branson's North Carolina Business Directory, Raleigh: Levi Branson, 1890.

Branson's North Carolina Business Directory, Raleigh: Levi Branson, 1896.

Catalogue of the Officers and Students of Lenoir Collegiate Institute, Male and Female, 1857-1858. Kinston: American Advocate Office, 1858.

Clark, Walter, ed. *The State Records of North Carolina.* 16 volumes (11-26). Raleigh: State of North Carolina, 1895-1906.

Compendium of the Tenth Census of the United States. Pt. 1, Washington, D.C.: Government Printing Office, 1883.

Corbitt, David Leroy. *The Formation of the North Carolina Counties, 1663-1943.* Raleigh: State Department of Archives and History, 1950.

Cross, Jerry. "The Peebles House in Kinston: A Research Report for the Structure Restored as Harmony Hall." Research Branch, North Carolina Division of Archives and History, Raleigh, 1990.

Crow, Jeffrey J., Paul D. Escott, and Flora J. Hatley. *A History of African Americans in North Carolina.* Raleigh: Division of Archives and History, 1992.

Doughton, Virginia Pou. "Bright Spot in LaGrange," *The State* (September 1980), 10-12.

_____. "The Davis School in Winston," *The State* (July 1981), 22-24.

Dreyer, Martha A. "Kinston's Architecture 1762-1930: An Inventory and History." Research report, City of Kinston and North Carolina Division of Archives and History, Kinston, 1981.

Eighth Census of the United States, 1860. Washington, D.C.: Government Printing Office, 1864.

Eleventh Census of the United States, 1890: Report of the Statistics of Agriculture. Washington, D.C.: Government Printing Office, 1895.

Evans, Eli N. *The Provincials: A Personal History of Jews in the South.* New York: Atheneum, 1973.

Fourteenth Census of the United States. Vol. 6. Washington, D.C.: Government Printing Office, 1920.

Gatewood, Willard B., Jr. *Eugene Clyde Brooks: Educator and Public Servant.* Durham, N.C.: Duke University Press, 1960.

General Catalogue of Wake Forest College, North Carolina. Raleigh: C. E. Taylor, 1892.

Hanchett, Thomas W. "The Rosenwald Schools and Black Education in North Carolina." *The North Carolina Historical Review* 65 (October 1988): 387-444.

"Harmony Hall Dedication." Kinston: Lenoir County Historical Association, May 17-18, 1984.

Herring, Nannie Braxton. "History of LaGrange," manuscript, circa 1919, 1955. Original in the LaGrange Town Hall.

The Heritage of Lenoir County, North Carolina. Kinston: Lenoir County Historical Association, 1981.

Illustrated City of Kinston, Lenoir County, North Carolina. Kinston: Kinston Chamber of Commerce [?], 1914.

"Industry in Kinston," *The State,* August 14, 1943, 20-26.

Johnson, Guion Griffis. *Ante-bellum North Carolina: A Social History.* Chapel Hill: University of North Carolina Press, 1937.

Johnson, Talmage C. and Charles R. Holloman. *The Story of Kinston and Lenoir County.* Raleigh: Edwards and Broughton Company, 1954.

Jones, Robbie D. "The Historic and Architectural Resources of Lenoir County, North Carolina ca. 1790-1945." Research report, State Historic Preservation Office, North Carolina Division of Archives and History, Raleigh, 1995.

Jurney, R.C. and W. A. Davis, *Soil Survey of Lenoir County, N.C.* North Carolina Department of Agriculture, 1927.

Kinston and Lenoir County, North Carolina. Kinston[?]: Kinston Chamber of Commerce, 1917.

Kinston City Directory. Charlotte: The Interstate Directory Company, 1902.

Kinston City Directory. Richmond: Hill Directory Company, 1908-1909.

Kinston City Directory. Richmond: Hill Directory Company, 1916-1917.

Kinston City Directory. Richmond: Hill Directory Company, 1920.

Kinston City Directory. Charleston, S.C.: Baldwin's Directory Company with *Kinston Daily Free Press,* 1928.

Kinston City Directory. Charleston, S.C.: Baldwin's Directory Company with *Kinston Daily Free Press,* 1936.

Kinston City Directory. Charleston, S.C.: Baldwin's Directory Company with *Kinston Daily Free Press,* 1946.

"Kinston Has Everything." *State,* August 18, 1951: 6-7, 19-21.

Kohler, Mike. *Two Hundred Years of Progress* Kinston: Kinston-Lenoir County Bicentennial Commission and the Lenoir County Board of Commissioners, 1976.

Lane, Harriet C. "Historic Buildings in and near Kinston," *Carolina and the Southern Cross* 1 (November 1913): 12.

Latham, John (ed.) *Historical & Descriptive Review of the State of North Carolina.* vol. 2. Charleston, S.C.: Empire Publishing Company, 1885.

Lefler, Hugh Talmage and Albert Ray Newsome, *North Carolina: The History of a Southern State.* Chapel Hill: University of North Carolina Press, 1963.

Little, M. Ruth. "Historic Structures Survey and Evaluation Report, North Carolina Global Transpark, Study Areas 1 and 2." Research report, State Historic Preservation Office, North Carolina Division of Archives and History, Raleigh, 1993.

Lounsbury, Carl R. *An Illustrated Glossary of Early Southern Architecture and Landscape.* New York: Oxford University Press, 1994.

Magill, Eliza Walters. *Fool John and Other Stories.* N.p., 1975.

Martin, Jennifer. "The Historic and Architectural Resources of Duplin County." Research report, State Historic Preservation Office, North Carolina Division of Archives and History, Raleigh, 1992.

Newsome, A.R. "Twelve North Carolina Counties in 1810-1811," Pt. 2, *North Carolina Historical Review* 6 (April 1929), 171-189.

Ninth Census of the United States, 1870. Washington, D.C.: Government Printing Office, 1880.

North Carolina Yearbook, 1905. Raleigh, N.C.: News and Observer, 1905.

North Carolina Yearbook, 1910. Raleigh, N.C.: News and Observer, 1910.

Nowitzky, George I. *Norfolk, Marine Metropolis of Virginia, and the Sound and River Cities of North Carolina.* Raleigh: the author, 1888.

Pate, R. Bruce. *A Moment In Time: The History of Lenoir Collegiate Institute.* Durham, North Carolina: Carolina Academic Press, 1981.

Pezzoni, J. Daniel. "The Historic and Architectural Resources of Onslow County." Research Report, State Historic Preservation Office, North Carolina Division of Archives and History, Raleigh, 1989.

Powell, William S. *Annals of Progress: The Story of Lenoir County and Kinston, North Carolina.* Raleigh: North Carolina Department of Archives and History, 1963.

Powell, William S., ed. *Dictionary of North Carolina Biography.* Vol. 1. Chapel Hill: University of North Carolina Press, 1979.

Programme and Directory of the Fiftieth Anniversary and Jubilee and the Fifty-Sixth Session of the North Carolina Conference, November 23-30, 1919. Kinston: Saint Augustus A.M.E. Zion Church, 1919.

Report on the Productions of Agriculture, 1880. Washington, D.C.: Government Printing Office, 1880.

The Rock. Kinston, N. C.: Black Artists' Guild, Inc., 1986.

Sandbeck, Peter. *The Historic Architecture of New Bern and Craven County.* New Bern, N.C.: Tryon Palace Commission, 1988.

Seventh Census of the United States, 1850. Washington, D.C.: Government Printing Office, 1853.

Sharpe, Bill. *A New Geography of North Carolina.* 4 vols. Raleigh: Sharpe Publishing Company, Inc., 1954-1965.

Smith, Penne. Abstract for thesis on A. Mitchell Wooten, University of Delaware, 1997.

Survey of the Public Schools of Lenoir County. Raleigh: State Superintendent of Public Instruction, 1924.

Szylvian, Kristin, "Public Housing Comes to Wilmington, North Carolina," *North Carolina Humanities*, 3, No. 1 (Spring-Summer 1995), 52-58.

Tenth Census of the United States, 1880. Vol. 6, *Cotton Production.* Washington, D.C.: Government Printing Office, 1884.

Thirteenth Census of the United States. Vol. 6. Washington, D.C.: Government Printing Office, 1910.

Tilley, Nannie Mae. *The Bright-Tobacco Industry 1860-1929.* Chapel Hill: University of North Carolina Press, 1948.

Twelfth Census Reports, United States Census Office. Vol. 5, *Agriculture Statistics.* Washington, D.C.: Government Printing Office, 1900.

Tyndall, Clifford. "Lenoir County During the Civil War." Master's Thesis, East Carolina University, 1981.

W., G. B., and Mrs. F. H. "Kinston in the Sixties." *Carolina and the Southern Cross* 1 (November 1913): 1-3.

Ware, Charles C. *A History of Atlantic Christian College.* Wilson, N.C.: Atlantic Christian College, 1956.

_____. *Hookerton History.* Wilson, N.C., 1980.

Whitfield, Emma Morehead. *Whitfield, Bryan, Smith and Related Families.* Vol. 1: *Whitfield.* Westminster, Md.: privately published, 1948.

Zuber, Richard L. *North Carolina During Reconstruction.* Raleigh: State Department of Archives and History, 1969.

Archival Sources

East Carolina University Manuscript Collection, East Carolina University, Greenville, N.C. James Lewis Jones Manuscript. William Blount Rodman Collection. Smith-Grady Family Papers.

Heritage Place, Lenoir Community College, Kinston. Photographic Collection.

Kinston Housing Authority, Kinston.

North Carolina Collection, University of North Carolina, Chapel Hill. Sanborn Fire Insurance Maps of Kinston, 1885, 1891, 1896, 1901, 1908, 1914, 1919, 1925, 1930, 1955.

Southern Historical Collection, University of North Carolina, Chapel Hill. Elizabeth Washington Grist Knox Papers.

State Archives, North Carolina Division of Archives and Historoy, Raleigh. Delia Hyatt Collection, Private Collections. Koerner Military Survey Field map of Lenoir County, 1863. Lenoir County Deeds. Lenoir County Wills. United States Census Records, 1800-1920 (microfilm), National Archives, Washington, D.C.

State Historic Preservation Office, North Carolina Division of Archives and History, Raleigh. National Register of Historic Places nomination forms. Research reports. Survey files of historic properties.

Wooten, A. Mitchell Private Papers, Collection Verna Wooten Ewell, Kinston.

Newspapers

Kinston Daily Free Press

Kinston Daily News

Kinston Free Press

Kinston Journal

Lenoir County News

News Argus, Goldsboro

News and Observer, Raleigh

Interviews

Barrus, Alban K. Jr., interview by Penne Smith, Kinston, November 1994.

Best, Ezekiel K., Jr., interview by Penne Smith, Kinston, 1996.

Brewer, Billy, interview by Jim Stewart, Kinston, May 1997.

Cowper, Virginia, interview by Penne Smith, Kinston, November 1994.

Crawford, P. H., interview by Penne Smith, Kinston, 1997

Dawson, Ted, interview by Penne Smith, Kinston, 1995.

Dillahunt, Joseph, interview by Penne Smith, Kinston, December 1994.

Dyer, William M. Jr., interview by Ruth Little, Kinston, May 7, 1993.

Ewell, Verna Wooten, interview by Penne Smith, Kinston, November 1994.

Harvey, William, interview by Penne Smith, Kinston, November 1994.

Lewis, Marianna LaRoque, interview by Penne Smith, Kinston, December 1, 1995.

Little, Virginia White, interview by Ruth Little, Raleigh, 1995.

Moye, Clarence, interview by Penne Smith, Kinston, December 1994.

Oettinger, Leonard Jr., interview by Penne Smith, Kinston, November 1994.

Perry, Isabelle Fletcher, interview by Ruth Little, Lenoir County, September 1997.

Pressly, Marianna Rochelle, interview by Penne Smith, Kinston, November 23, 1994.

Pulley, Rose, interview by Penne Smith, Kinston, November 18, 1994.

Scarborough, Benjamin Franklin III, interview by Ruth Little, Lenoir County, June 16 and 18, 1993.

Sharp, Mamie Wooten, interview by Ruth Little, Lenoir County, May 4, 1993.

Tyndall, Wilbur and Cliff, interview by Penne Smith, Pink Hill, 1995.

Walker, Louvenia, interview by Claire Cannon Foster, Kinston, 1993.

Wilson, the Reverend Cozelle Mills, interview by Ruth Little and Penne Smith, Kinston, November 15, 1994.

INDEX

Note: Numbers in bold face refer to illustrations

Hardee, George, 347, 348
Hardee, Pinckney, 62, 64
Hardison, Charles C., 210
Hardison, Daniel, 330
Hardison, Felix, 330
Hardison, Felix, House, **330**
Hardison, John G., 330
Hardison, Margaret, 330
Hardison, Martha, 330
Hardison, Proctor, 330
Hardy (family), 310
Hardy and Newsome, 285
Hardy Brothers Store, 74, **75, 315**
Hardy Building, 265
Hardy Oil Company, 74, 315
Hardy, Herman, 290, 291
Hardy, Hugh Emery (Emory), 269, 312
Hardy, Hugh Emery, Tenant House, **269**
Hardy, Hugh Holton, 269, 312
Hardy, Dr. Ira, 265
Hardy, Jesse H., 311
Hardy, Langhorne, 270
Hardy, Lemuel, III, 310
Hardy, Logan D., Sr., 313
Hardy, Logan Donald, 313
Hardy, Logan Donald, House, 38, 313
Hardy, Logan Donald, Sr., 315
Hardy, Logan Donald, Tenant House, **313**
Hardy, Louisa Truitt Daniel, 310
Hardy, Mary Ann, 328
Hardy, Parrott Mewborn, 28, 310
Hardy, Richard Henry, 299
Hardy, Richard Henry, House, **299**
Hardy, S. P. *See* Hardy, Stephen Parker
Hardy, Stephen Parker, 306, 314
Hardy, W. P., 296
Hardy-Newsome Bean Harvester Factory. *See* Hardy-Newsome Manufactory
Hardy-Newsome Manufactory, **290**-291
Hargett, Joseph C., 95, 97, 142
Harmony Hall. *See* Bright-Pearce-Peebles House
Harper (family), 423
Harper Hotel, 284, **294**
Harper's Grocery, 250, **252**
Harper, Blackledge, 422
Harper, Claudia, 250
Harper, George Green, 252
Harper, Jess, 422
Harper, Jess, House, **422**
Harper, Jesse, farm, 81
Harper, Johnny, 337
Harper, Lillian Eva. *See* Kennedy, Lillian Eva Harper
Harper, Martha Eleanor, 328
Harper, Mary. *See* Kennedy, Mary Harper
Harper, Mrs., 294
Harper, Robert, 367
Harper, Susan Grady, 422
Harper, Will F., Store, **410**
Harper, William, House, **337**
Harper-Heath Farm, 337
Harrell, S. M., 138, 226, 229

Harris (family), 348
Harris, M. D., and Store, **348**
Harrison, J. P., House. *See* Harrison, Dr. Joseph P., House
Harrison, Dr. Joseph P., 145, **152,** 177
Harrison, Dr. Joseph P., House, 150-151, **152**
Harrison, Dr. Joseph P., Office, **177**
Harrow (plantation), 15, 18, 19
Hartge, Charles, 187
Hartsfield House, **334**
Hartsfield, G., 334
Hartsfield, Jacob A., 338
Hartsfield, Dr. Jacob A., 338
Hartsfield, Rebecca Kornegay, 338
Hartsfield-Taylor House, **338**
Harvey (family), 239, 353
Harvey Circle, 238, 239
Harvey Gardens, 238
Harvey Motor Company, 194
Harvey School, 233, **237**-247, 250
Harvey's Department Store, 239
Harvey, A., and Company, 93, 173
Harvey, Amos, 64
Harvey, Charles Felix, Sr., 226, 231, 239
Harvey, L., and Son Oil Company, 239
Harvey, L., and Sons, 144, 236, 239
Harvey, Lemuel, 87, 88, 173, 182, 226, 231, 239
Harvey, Lemuel, School, 238-239
Harvey, Thomas, Jr., 353
Harvey, Thomas, Sr., 46, 353
Harvey-Mewborne House, 46, **48, 353**
Hatch, John, 82
Hawkins, Jesse, 142
Hayes, Charlotte, 375
Hazelton, Elias Liverman, 76, 347
Hazelton, Elias Liverman, House, **347**
Heath (family), 341
Heath, Henry, 323
Heath, J. C., 260, 263
Heath, Thomas, 323
Heath, Thomas A., 329
Heath, Will, 339
Heath, Woodrow, 379
Hebron Christian Church, 336
Heights, Vernon, 232
Henderson, Les, 150
Henry, George, 337
Herring (family), 46, 202, 273, 373, 375
Herring House, **273**
Herring, Bryan, 273
Herring, C. L., 319
Herring, Edward Matchet, 46, 273
Herring, Elizabeth, 273
Herring, George W., 45, 373
Herring, Henry, 45, 373
Herring, Henry Bruton, 375
Herring, Henry Loftin, 375
Herring, Henry Loftin, House and Farm, 374-375, **374**
Herring, J. G., 64
Herring, John, 273
Herring, Joshua, 270, 273, 301
Herring, Nannie Braxton, 290, 299

Quality Map of

KINSTON and LENOIR CO., N.C.

INTERSTATE HIGHWAYS	95
U.S. HIGHWAYS	70
STATE HIGHWAYS	11
SHOPPING CENTERS	▲
FIRE STATIONS	◒
TOWNSHIP LINES	— —

© 1998
QUALITY MAPS, INC.
P.O. BOX 194
HUNTERSVILLE, NC
28070

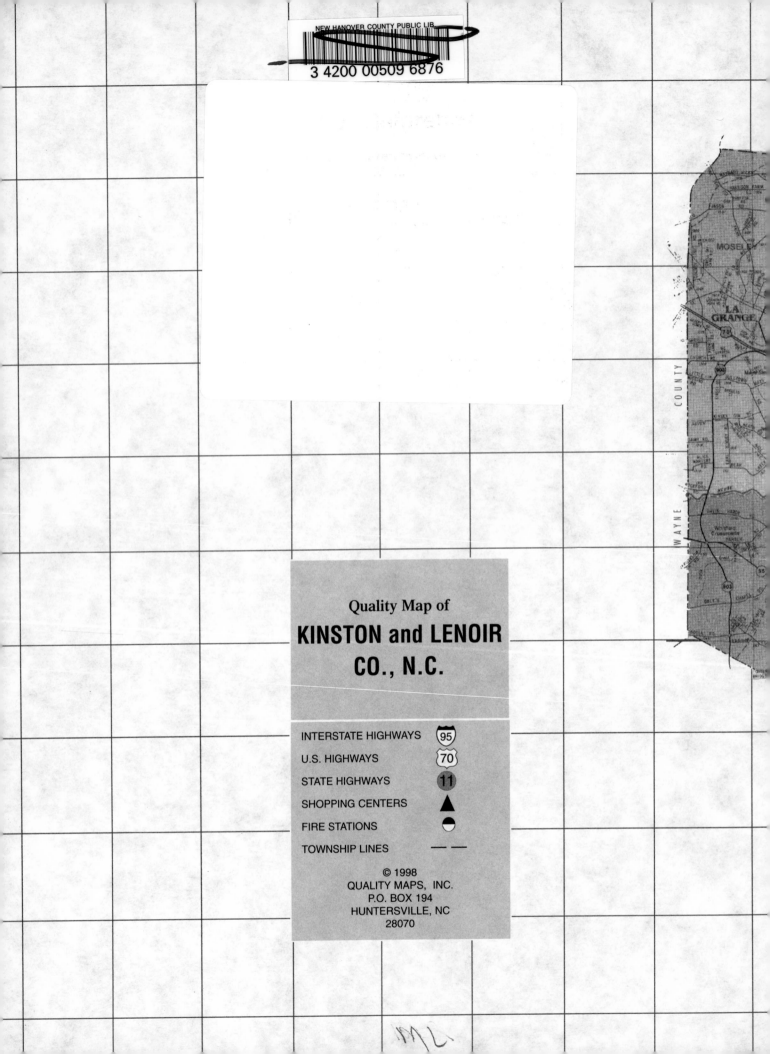